I0763117

C.K.

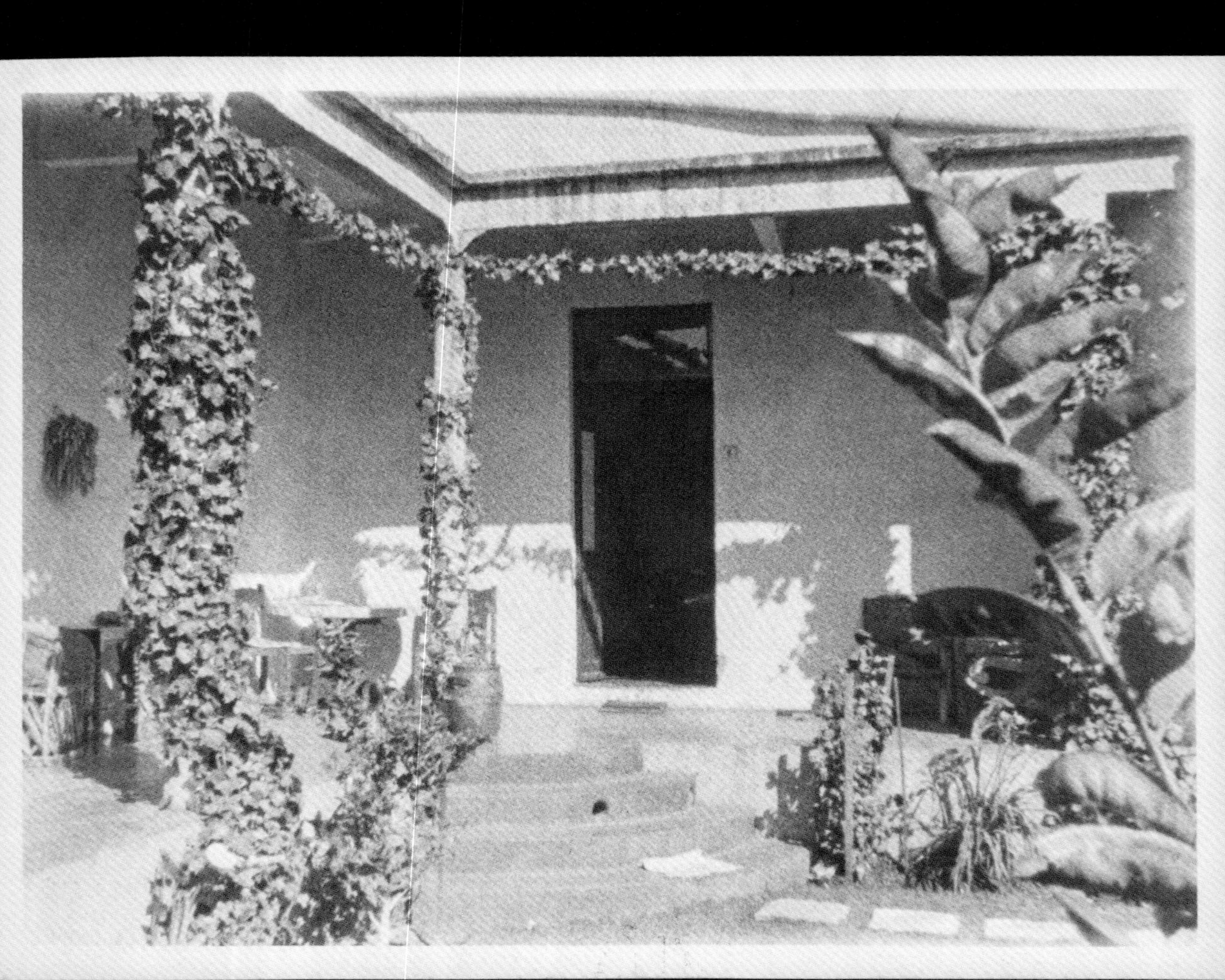

Mara Romeo Kahlo, Mara de Anda, and Frida Hentschel

CASA KAHLO

Frida Kahlo's Private Home and Sanctuary

Rizzoli Electa

Contents

Preface

In 1930, my great grandmother and great grandfather Matilde and Guillermo Kahlo—Frida Kahlo's parents—bought a house that would eventually become known as Casa Kahlo in Coyoacán, a neighborhood right outside of Mexico City. Our family had lived in the area for some time already at that point. Casa Azul, the house where Frida and her sisters grew up, was just a few blocks away, and it was where Frida lived with her husband the artist Diego Rivera. Our family has always been incredibly tight-knit, and living close to one another has always been a priority.

The story of Casa Kahlo, except to true insiders, has not been told. Casa Azul was very much a "public" house—it was where Frida received artists, writers, and revolutionaries. She and her husband were like local ambassadors to the creative cognoscenti of the time. But Casa Kahlo was her spiritual home: it was where the people who anchored her—her beloved parents, sister and *sobrinos*—lived. It was her private sanctuary, away from her volatile marriage. At Casa Kahlo, she maintained a small studio in the basement and eventually taught legions of loyal students in its garden. Casa Kahlo was also where she brought close friends—it was where she felt truly at home. Family meals were cherished, with everyone gathered around the table with a view of the lush garden teeming with grapefruit trees, flowers, and animals. This closeness with her family girded Frida, and indeed all of the family took solace in knowing they had such a strong network of support and love. This house has provided shelter for the Kahlos for nearly a century and it is one of the greatest symbols of our bond and devotion to each other.

In this book, we finally are able to tell the full story of the Kahlo family, and indeed a more complete story of Frida, for the first time. A few years ago I made the decision to turn the house into a museum and invite the public in to see everything we have saved and safe-guarded: art, clothing, letters, jewelry, books, recipes, and much more. The process of writing this book, with my daughters Mara and Frida, has provided a richer, and more profound, perspective on what my family has done and contributed. To look back is not always easy, but the process gives more than it takes. We hope that the reader finds inspiration in Frida's story, and her love of family, of Mexico, of life.

—Mara Romeo Kahlo

Frida, ca. 1938. Photo by Rosa Covarrubias

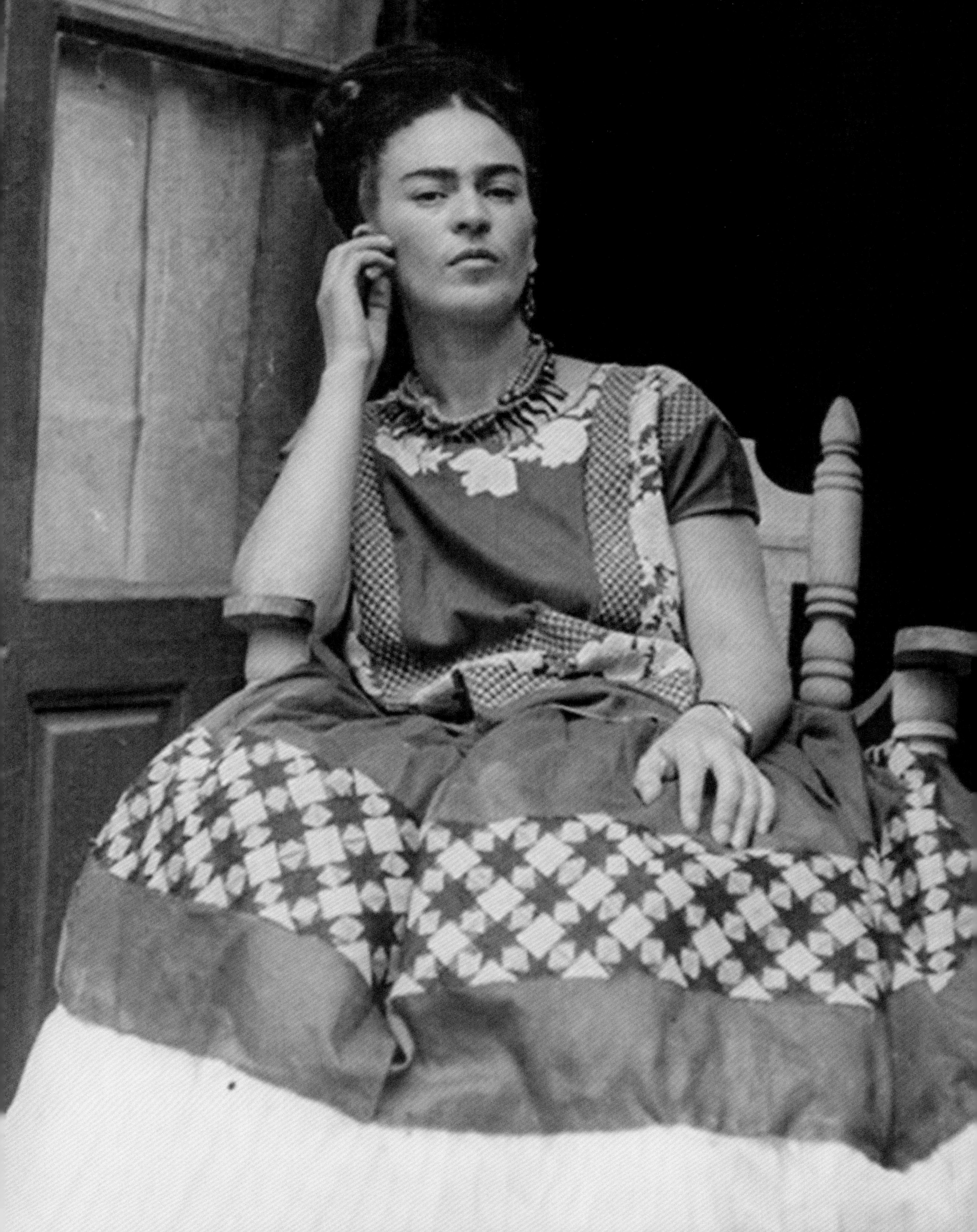

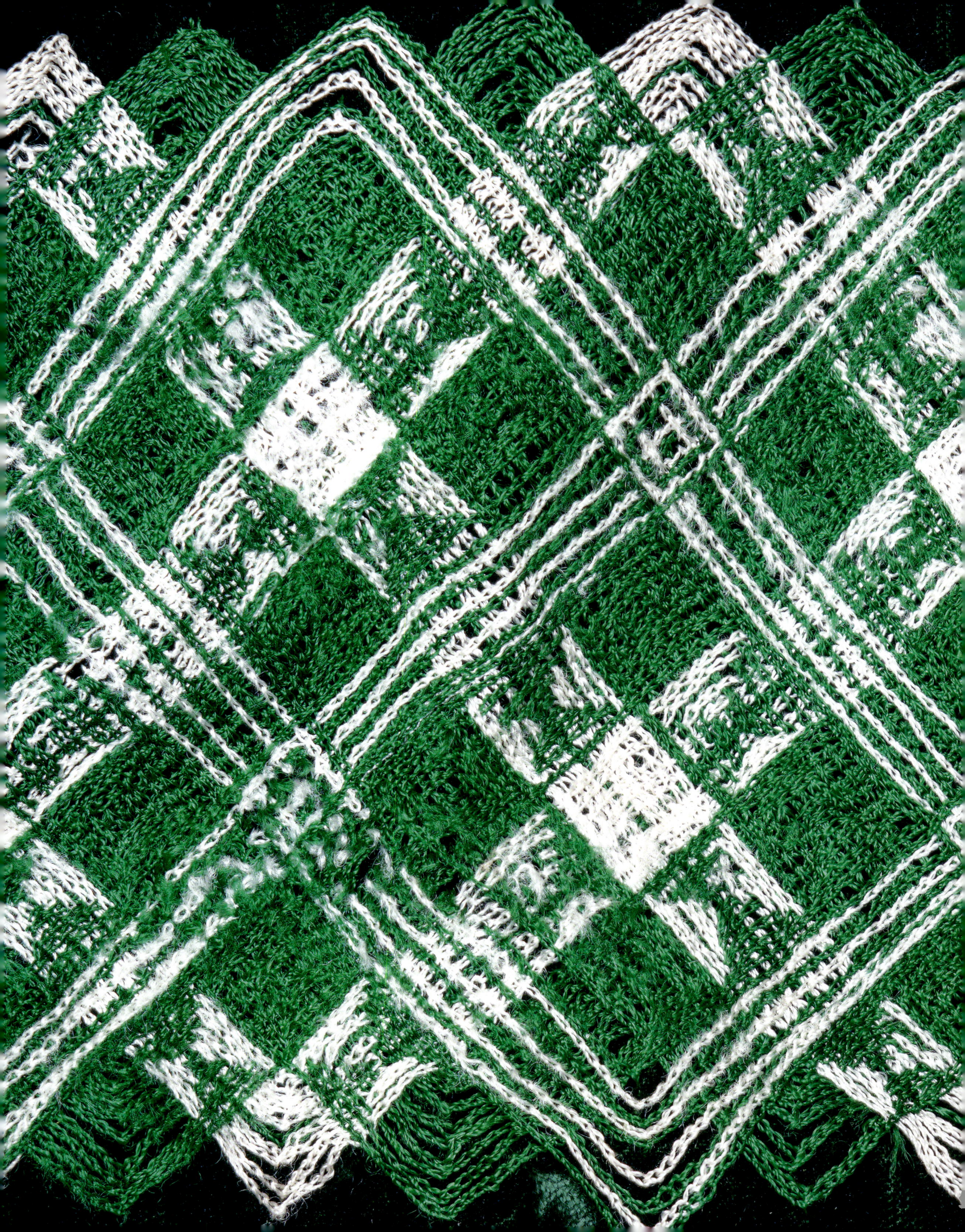

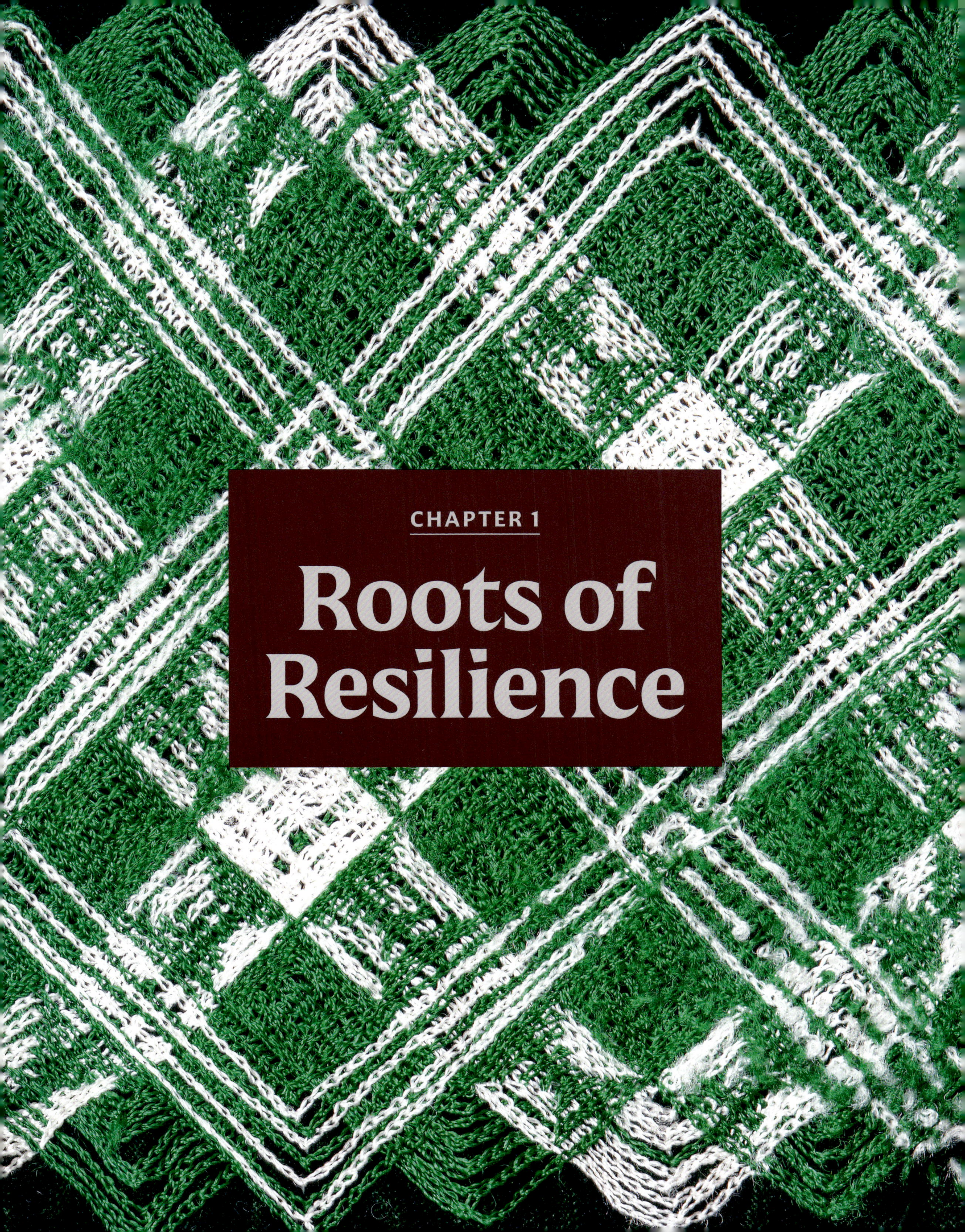

CHAPTER 1

Roots of Resilience

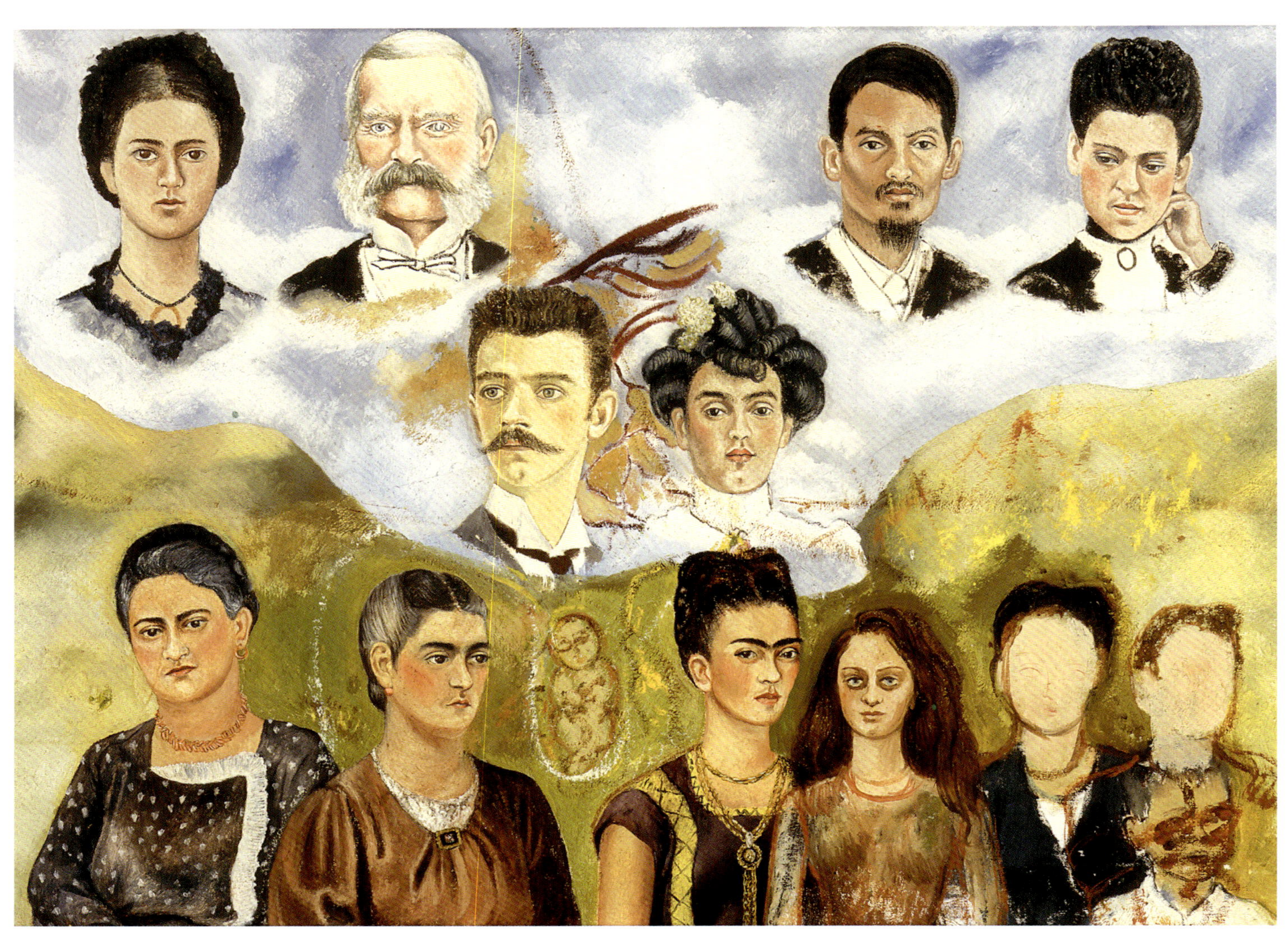

Frida Kahlo, *Portrait of Frida's Family*, 1950–54. Oil on Masonite, 16 x 23.25 in. (41 x 59 cm)

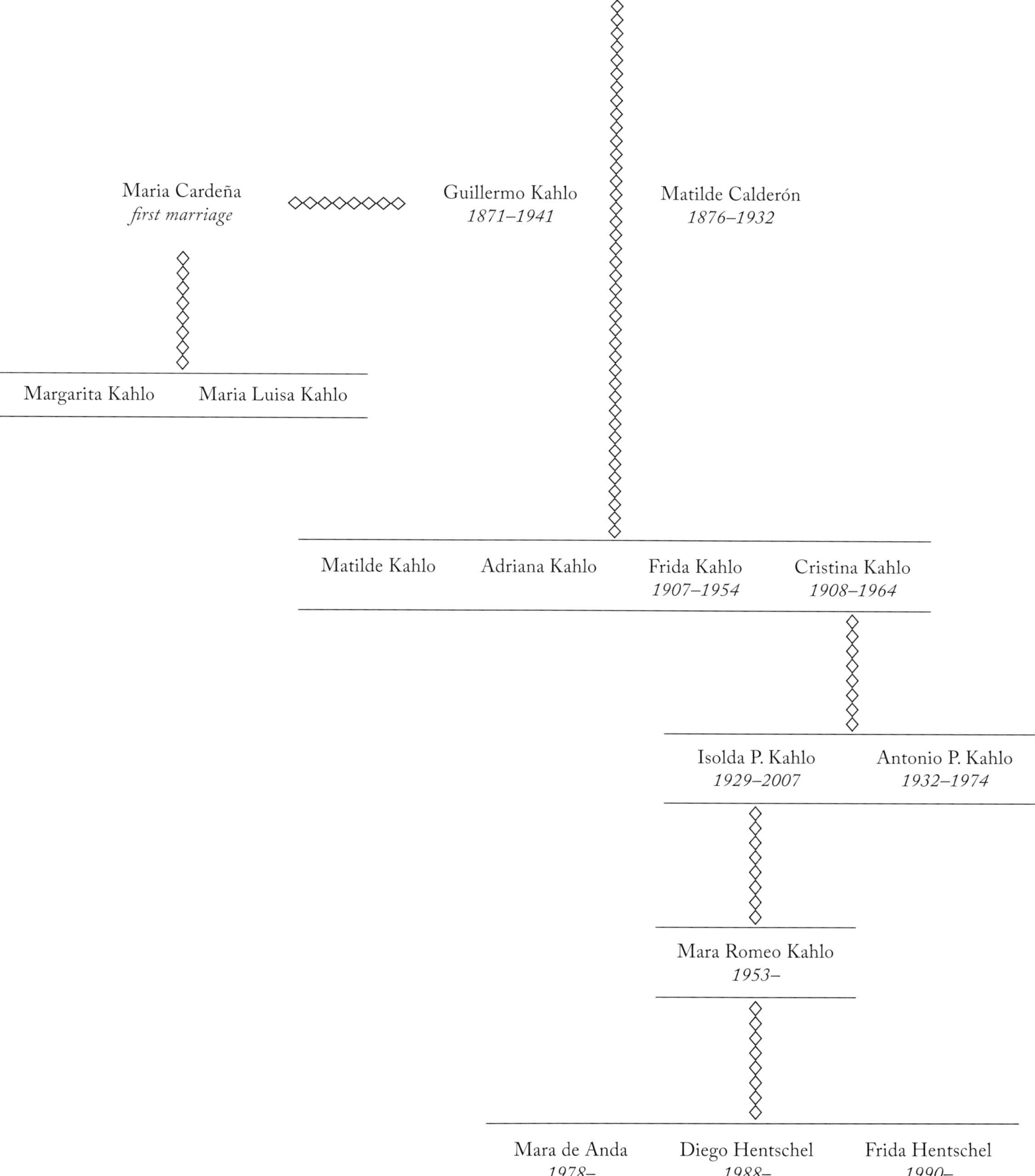
Maria Cardeña
first marriage
Guillermo Kahlo
1871–1941
Matilde Calderón
1876–1932
Margarita Kahlo
Maria Luisa Kahlo
Matilde Kahlo
Adriana Kahlo
Frida Kahlo
1907–1954
Cristina Kahlo
1908–1964
Isolda P. Kahlo
1929–2007
Antonio P. Kahlo
1932–1974
Mara Romeo Kahlo
1953–
Mara de Anda
1978–
Diego Hentschel
1988–
Frida Hentschel
1990–

Frida Hentschel Frida Kahlo's father, Guillermo Kahlo, arrived alone in Mexico in 1890, when he was just 18 years old. He came from Pforzheim, Germany, a town with a well-established jewelry and watchmaking industry. At that time, the Mexican government under President Porfirio Diaz's liberal policies encouraged immigration to further industry, and Guillermo immigrated under this pretense. In our family story, however, he left his hometown because he didn't get along with his stepmother. Whatever the reason, the story of our family begins with his decision at a young age to come to Mexico. When he arrived in Veracruz, he changed his last name from Kühlo to Kahlo on the very wise advice of an immigration official. The Mexican pronunciation of his original last name would no doubt have prompted teasing or worse: "Kühlo" is pronounced exactly as the word "culo" in Spanish, which means ass. He found employment in a jewelry shop, La Perla, a German-owned business. He later worked as an accountant in another German-owned business (Cristalería Hermanos Loeb), where he met Matilde, his future wife. A few years after his arrival, he felt at home in Mexico and requested citizenship, which was granted in 1894, at which time he also changed his name from Wilhelm to Guillermo. He always felt welcomed in Mexico and loved the warmth of our culture. He learned Spanish very easily, but he still wanted his children to understand their roots and taught them German.

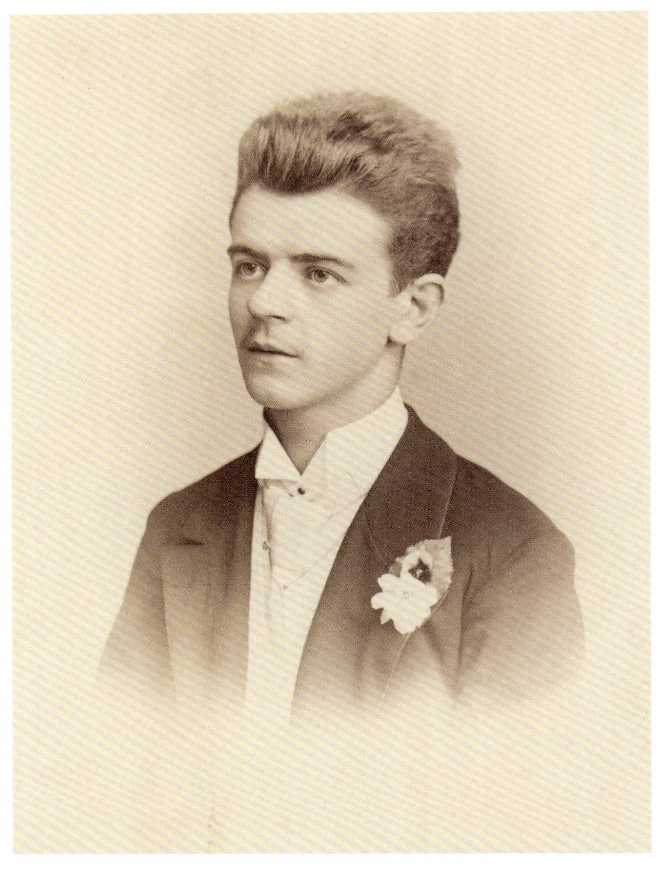

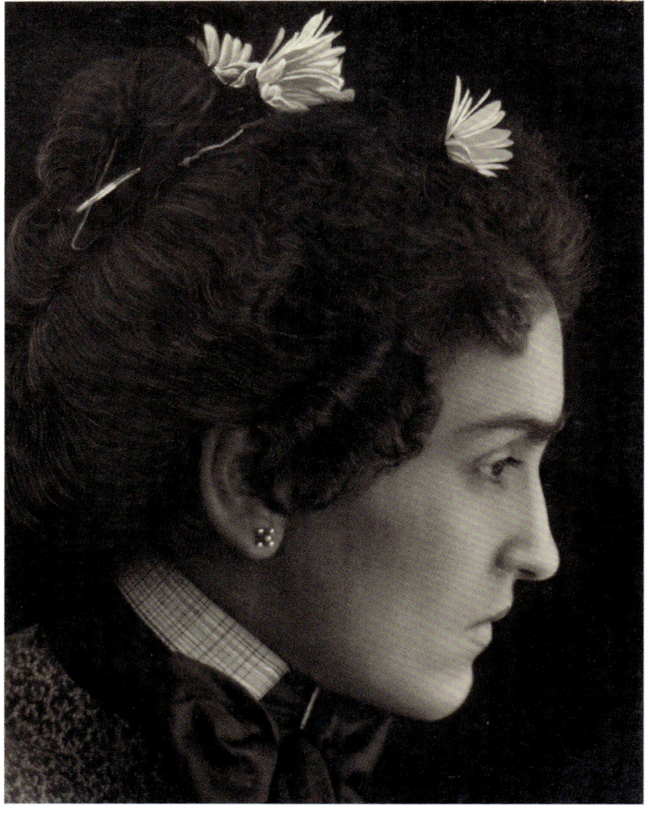

TOP Guillermo Kahlo, Frida's father, Mexico, ca. 1891. Photo by Wolfenstein Studio

BOTTOM Matilde Calderón, Frida's mother, Mexico, ca. 1898

OPPOSITE Matilde and Guillermo's wedding portrait, Mexico City, February 21, 1898

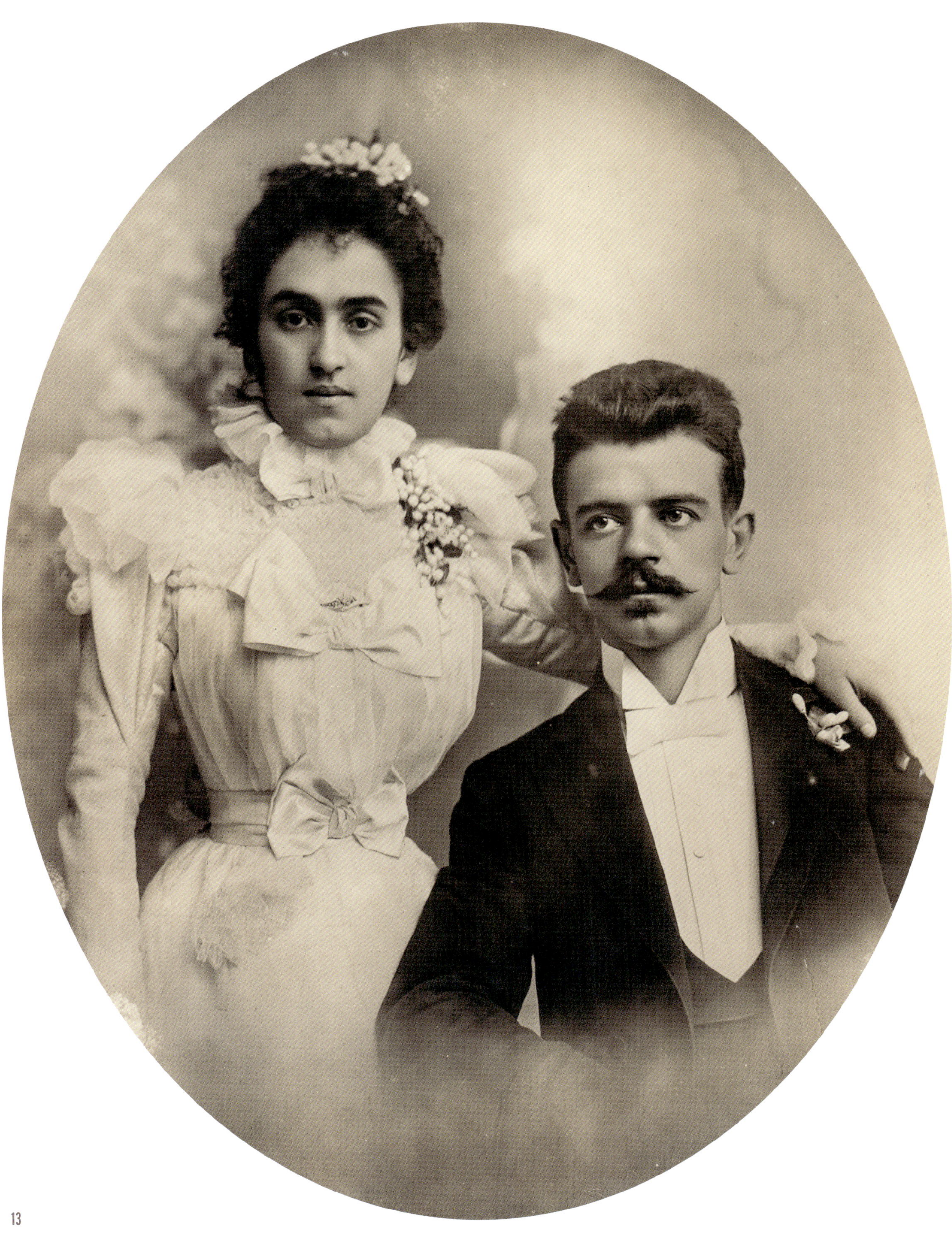

A mi chula

Mati.

Novbre 23/98.

Guillermo.

Eventually, given his sensitive and artistic nature, Guillermo abandoned his accounting job and became a full-time photographer. We understand that it was Matilde's father who first taught Guillermo photography. He later established his photography business and had his first institutional client: Casa Boker. Soon after, President Porfirio Diaz's administration hired Guillermo to photograph federal buildings, monuments, and churches, and he was granted the title of "First Official Photographer of the National Cultural Patrimony of Mexico." Guillermo was very proud of this title and his work beautifully documented the country at the time. His work was published regularly in esteemed magazines. Frida admired his hard work and loved spending time with him, and often accompanied him on many of his excursions.

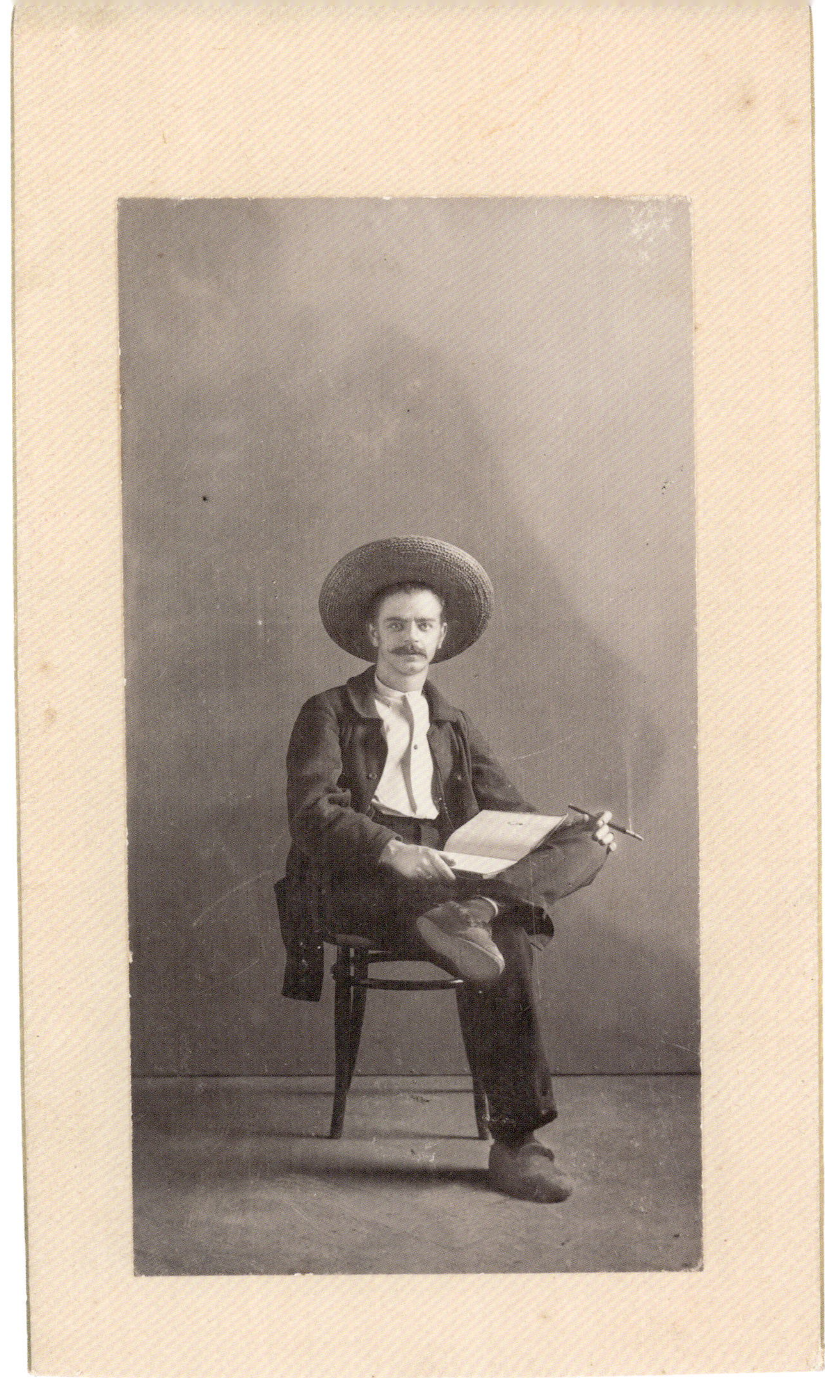

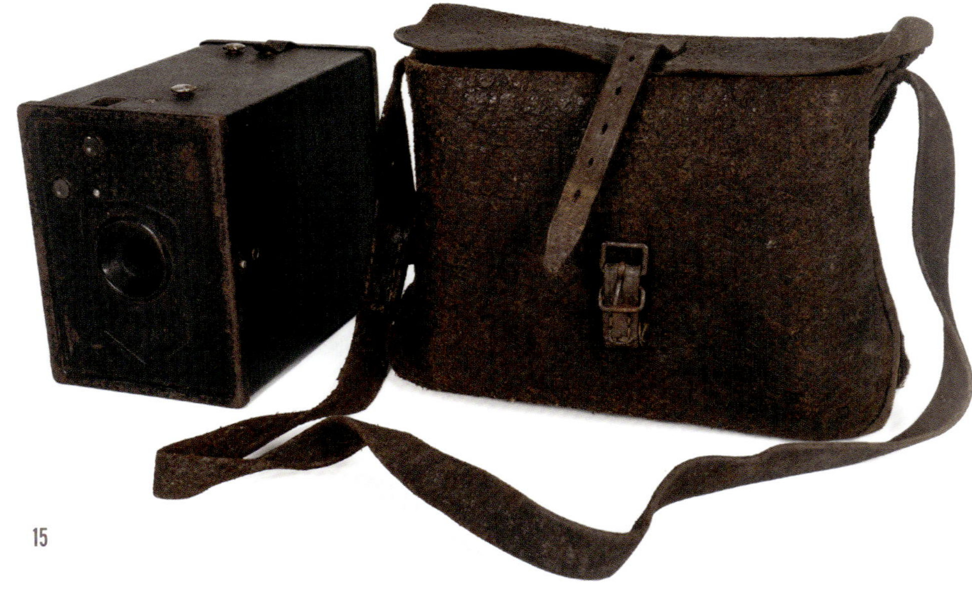

OPPOSITE AND ABOVE Guillermo Kahlo, *Self-portrait*, Mexico, November 23, 1898, with dedication on the back

LEFT Guillermo's portable Agfa camera with case

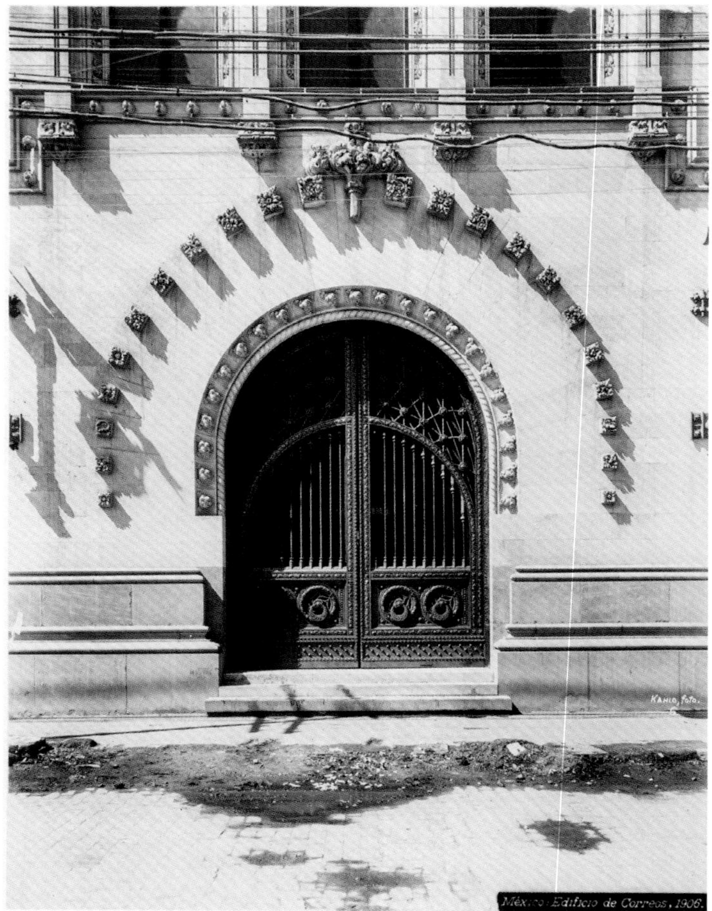

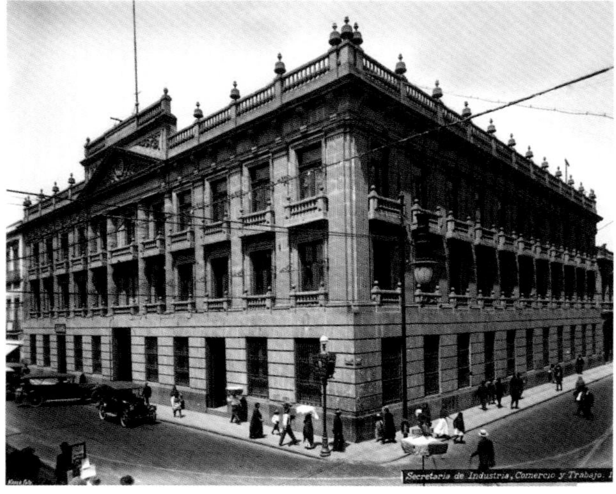

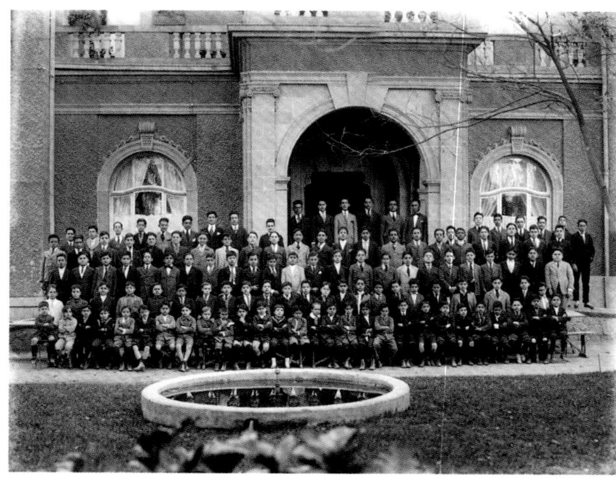

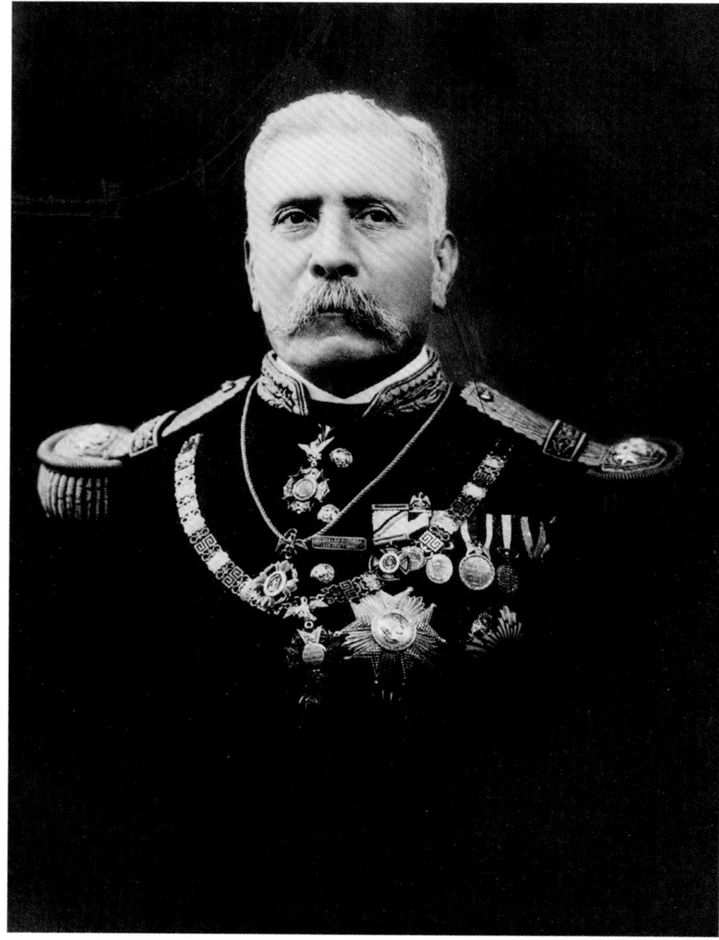

ABOVE, LEFT TO RIGHT All photos by Guillermo Kahlo: Post Office, Mexico City, 1906. Ministry of Industry, Commerce, and Labor, Mexico City, 1922. Students in front of The English School, Paseo de la Reforma 80, Mexico City, ca.1905. Mexican President Porfirio Díaz, ca. 1905. All photos are original prints from 11 x 14–inch glass negatives from a collection of over 200 plates in the family's archives. Guillermo specialized in the architectural documentation of Mexico's commercial, religious, industrial, and public buildings and was appointed the first official photographer of Mexico in 1904. He made a significant contribution to the historical record of the nation's heritage.

OPPOSITE An article about Guillermo, 1970s

ZOOM RETROSPECTIVO

Emiliano Rivera

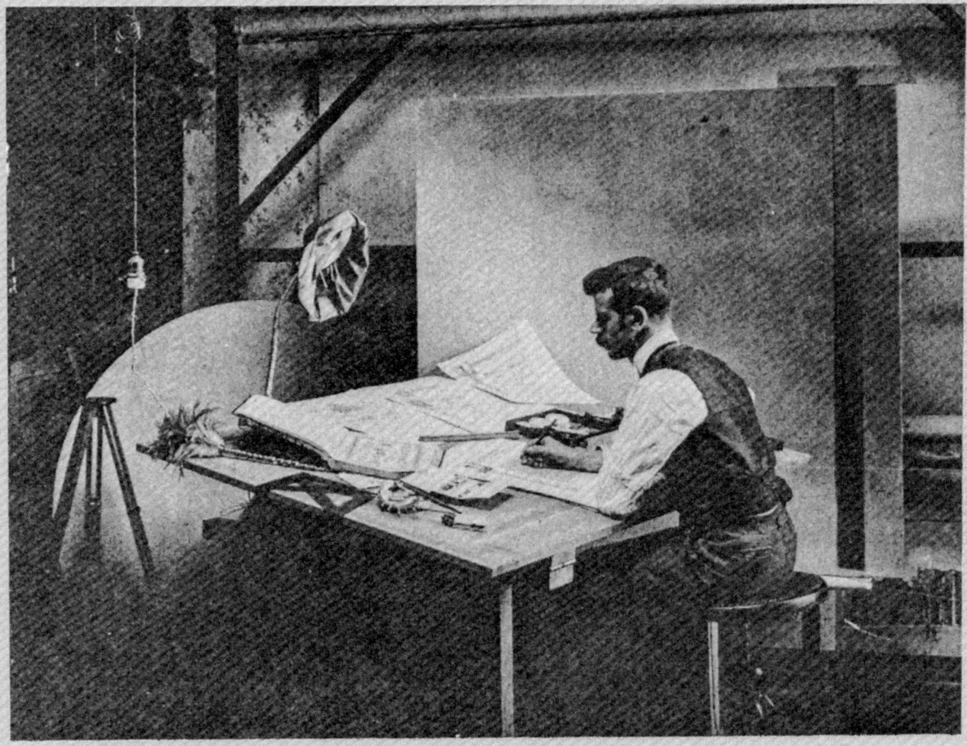

Autorretrato de Guillermo Kahlo

FOTOGRAFOS MEXICANOS

Guillermo Kahlo

En México, en la segunda mitad del siglo XIX, el fotógrafo no era en sentido estricto un profesional. Apenas la capa social aristocratizante que se consolidaba durante el régimen porfirista impulsó el retrato y las condiciones propicias para la profesionalización de la fotografía. En esta época se sitúa la aparición de dos relevantes fotógrafos: Fernando Ferrari Pérez, ingeniero y además fotógrafo aficionado de gran calidad, laureado en París por sus trabajos, fundador del Museo del Chopo; y Guillermo Kahlo.

Guillermo Kahlo había nacido en Baden-Baden, Alemania en 1872. Desde muy temprana edad su interés por la fotografía se había despertado al contacto con los aparatos fotográficos que su padre, Enrique Kahlo, vendía en su ciudad natal.

Guillermo llegó a México en 1891 en compañía de los hermanos Diener quienes fundaron la joyería La Perla. Al instalarse en la ciudad de México entró Guillermo como contador de la Cristalería Loeb, más tarde estuvo en la Casa Bocker que abandonó para dedicarse profesionalmente -quizá uno de los primeros- a la fotografía; para ello había encargado a Alemania su equipo.

A los dos años de haber llegado había ya contraído matrimonio; de este enlace nacieron sus hijas Margarita y María Luisa. Sin embargo su esposa murió tempranamente y Guillermo contrajo segundas nupcias con Matilde Calderón, fruto de esta unión fueron: Frida (la pintora), Matilde, Adriana y Cristina.

Guillermo Kahlo era despreocupado y no sentía mayor apego al dinero, así lo demuestra la anécdota[1] que achaca el despilfarro de sus dos herencias en fuegos artificiales que prendía en Coyoacán, en donde estableció su residencia en las calles de Londres, en la casa que actualmente es el Museo Frida Kahlo. Pero los problemas económicos que su carácter le causaron se vieron subsanados después de que el gobierno de Díaz le pidió que retratara a personalidades políticas y posteriormente que ejerciera su especialización en fotografía arquitectónica. Por orden de José Ives Limantour, Ministro de Hacienda, viajó por la República para fotografiar edificios civiles y religiosos de la época virreinal así como las principales construcciones reali-

1.- véase: Zabludovsky, Gina. ¿Ha existido la fotografía artística mexicana? en *Artes visuales* No. 1, 1973.

la casa ya designada. Que la referida niña es
nieta por línea paterna de los finados Jacobo
Enrique Kahlo y Señora Enriqueta Kaufmann y por
línea materna del finado Ciudadano Antonio Calderón
y de la exponente. Fueron testigos de este acto los
Ciudadanos Ricardo Gutiérrez y Cárlos Romero González
mayores de edad, originarios de México y residentes
en esta Villa el primero soltero el segundo casado
siendo éste pariente de la niña presentada. Leída que
les fue la presente acta á la compareciente y testigos la ratificaron en todas sus partes y firmaron.

Luis Rivas C.

Ysabel G. Vda. de Calderón

Ricardo Gutierrez

Romero González

278 En la Villa de Coyoacan á las 9 nueve de la ma-
Doscientos seten- ñana del día 5 cinco de Agosto de 1907 mil
ta y ocho novecientos siete, ante mi Luis Rivas
Mares Camilo Arechiga Juez del estado Civil en esta
Natural. Municipalidad, compareció la Señora
Amelia Mares de 19 diecinueve años, sol-
tera, sin profesion, de este origen y vecindad
domiciliada en el Barrio de los Reyes, casa
sin numero: y presentó vivo un niño
que nació en la citada casa, el día 18
dieciocho de Julio proximo pasado
á las 11 once de la noche: y le puso por
nombre Camilo Mares. La compareciente manifestó, que el niño que
presenta, es hijo natural suyo. Fueron testigos de este acto, los Ciudadanos
Pablo Flores y Luis García, mayores de
edad, casados, empleados, de esta vecindad, el primero de este origen y el segundo
de Huamantla, Tlaxcala. Leída que
fue la presente á la compareciente y
testigos la ratificaron y firmaron los
que supieron con el Juez que

Matilde and Guillermo had a boy, Wilhelm, in 1905, who died. One year after his death, Frida was born. Beyond the similarities and interests Frida and Guillermo shared, he poured a lot of love into Frida. After the loss of a child, her birth was likely all the more important and meaningful.

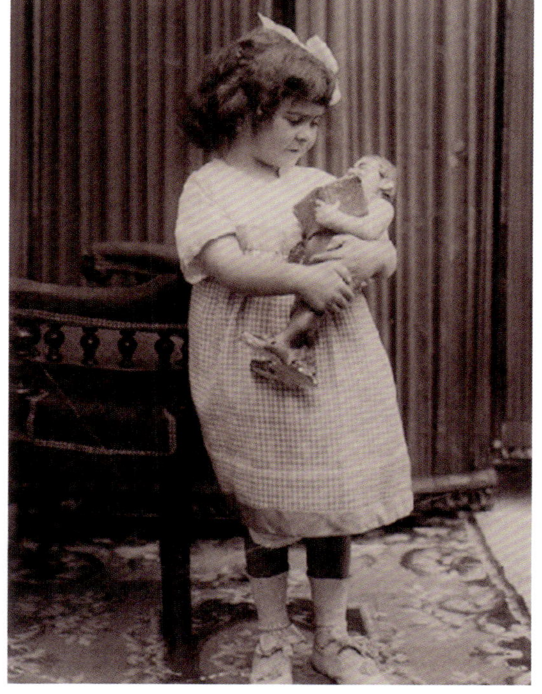

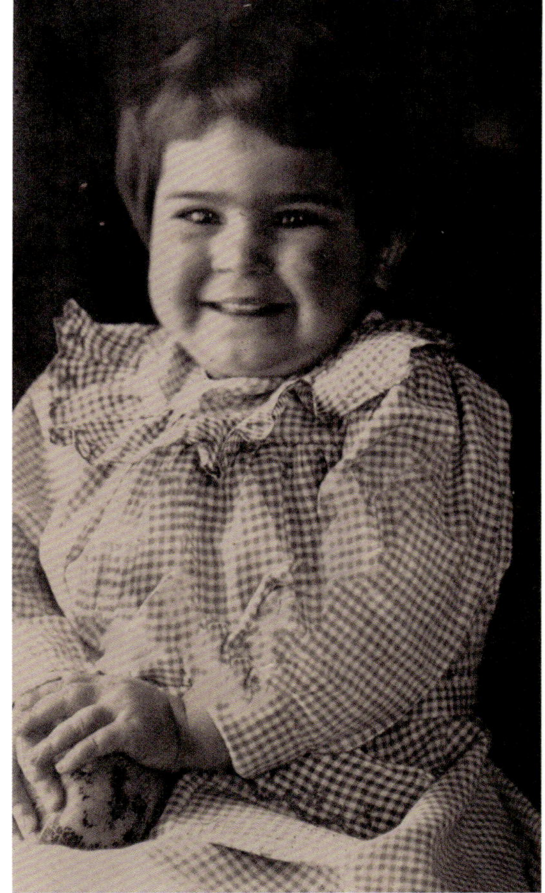

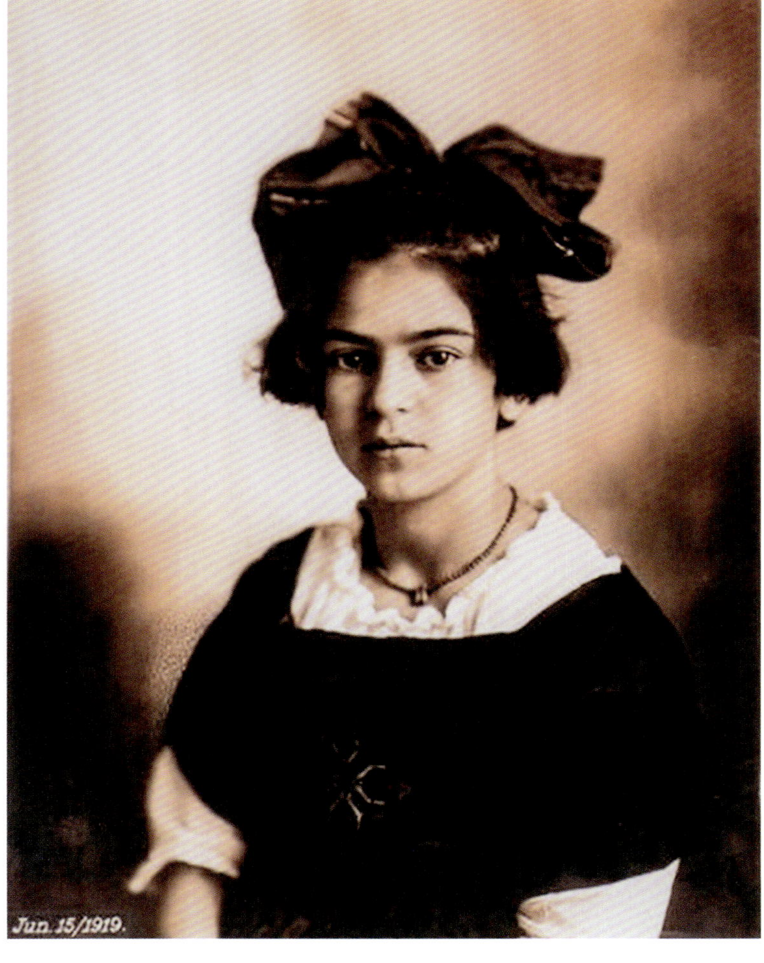

OPPOSITE Frida's birth certificate, Mexico City, 1907

ABOVE Frida, age 3 from 1910; age 5 from 1912; and age 11 from 1918. Photos by Guillermo Kahlo, whose photos provided a comprehensive and intimate record of the family's early history in Coyoacán.

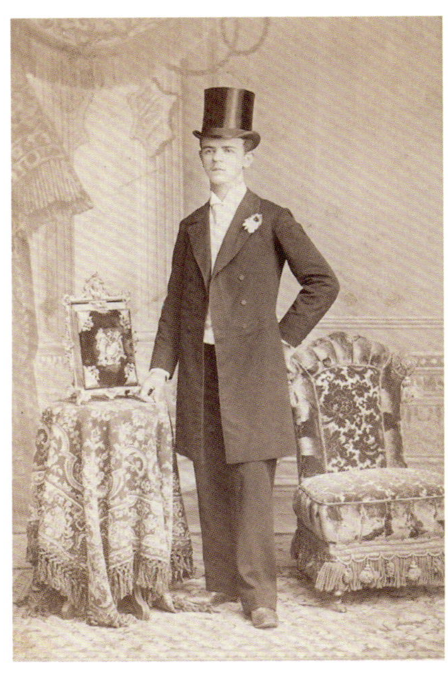

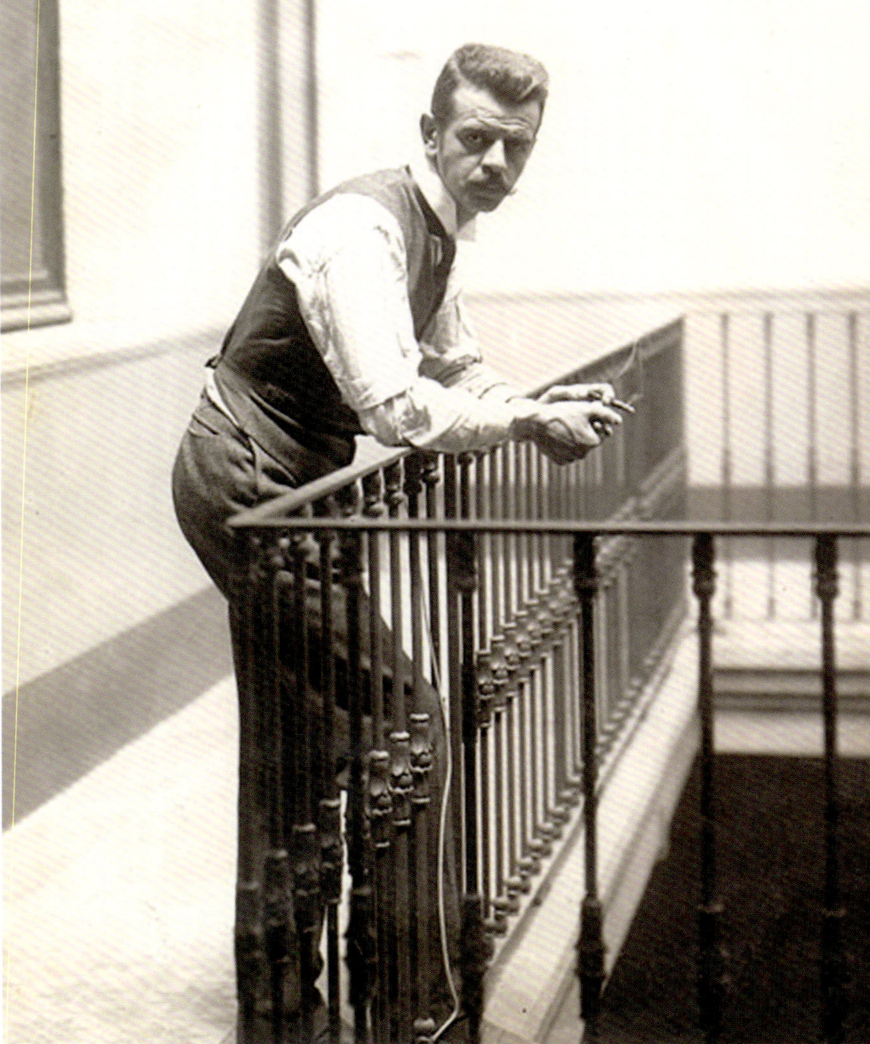

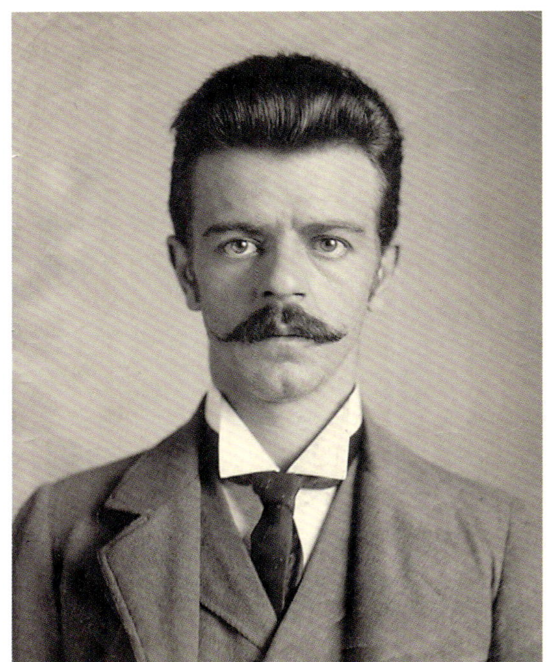

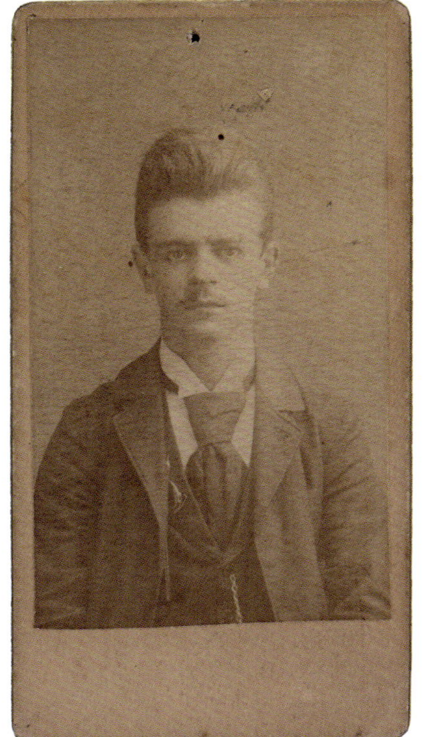

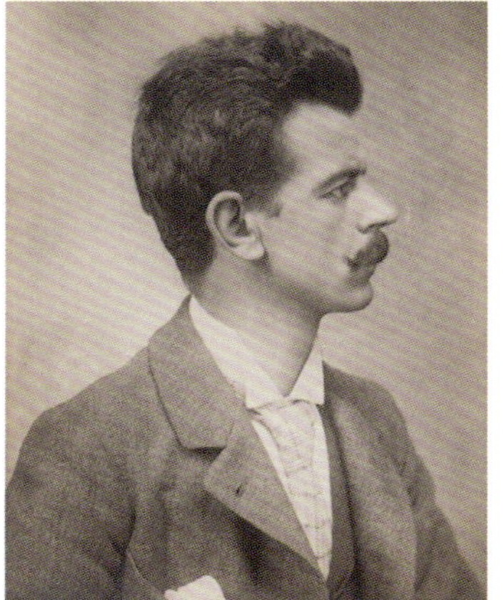

A series of portraits and self-portraits of and by Guillermo.

TOP Guillermo Kahlo, Mexico City, July 1892; photo by Nicolás Winther. Guillermo Kahlo, *Self-portrait leaning against a rail*, ca. 1907

BOTTOM Guillermo Kahlo, *Self-portrait*, Mexico City, ca. 1904. Guillermo Kahlo, Mexico City, ca. 1893. Guillermo Kahlo, *Self-portrait*, Mexico City, 1910. Guillermo's artistic sensibilities are reflected in his self-portraits, where he explored personal identity and the expressive potential of photography beyond documentary work.

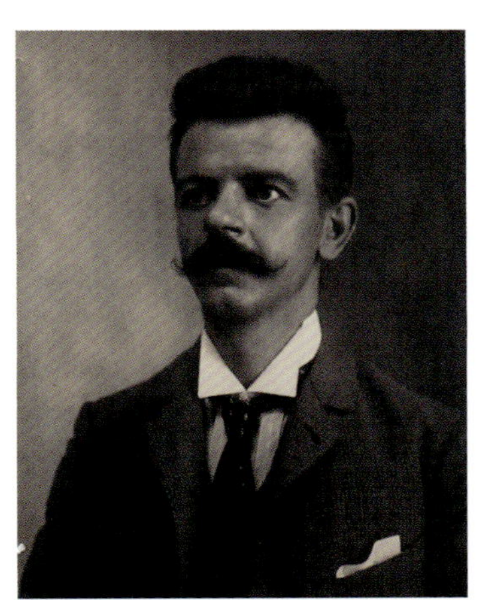

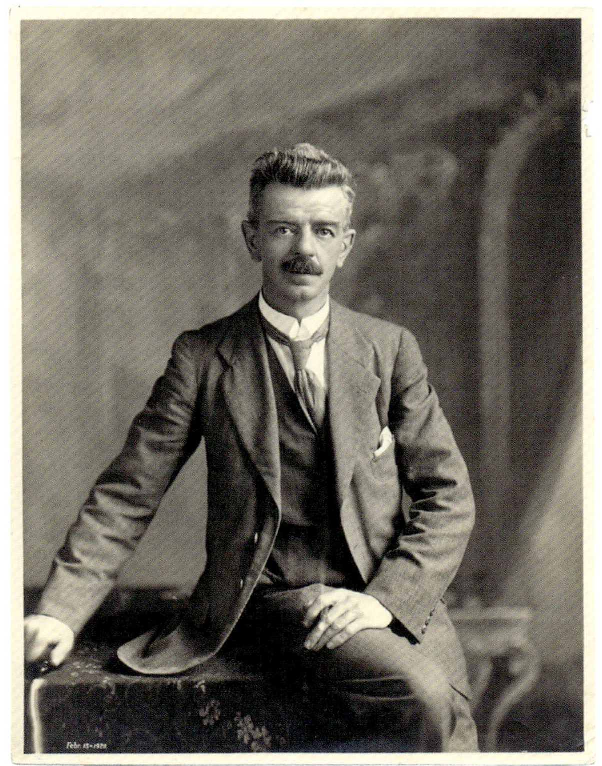

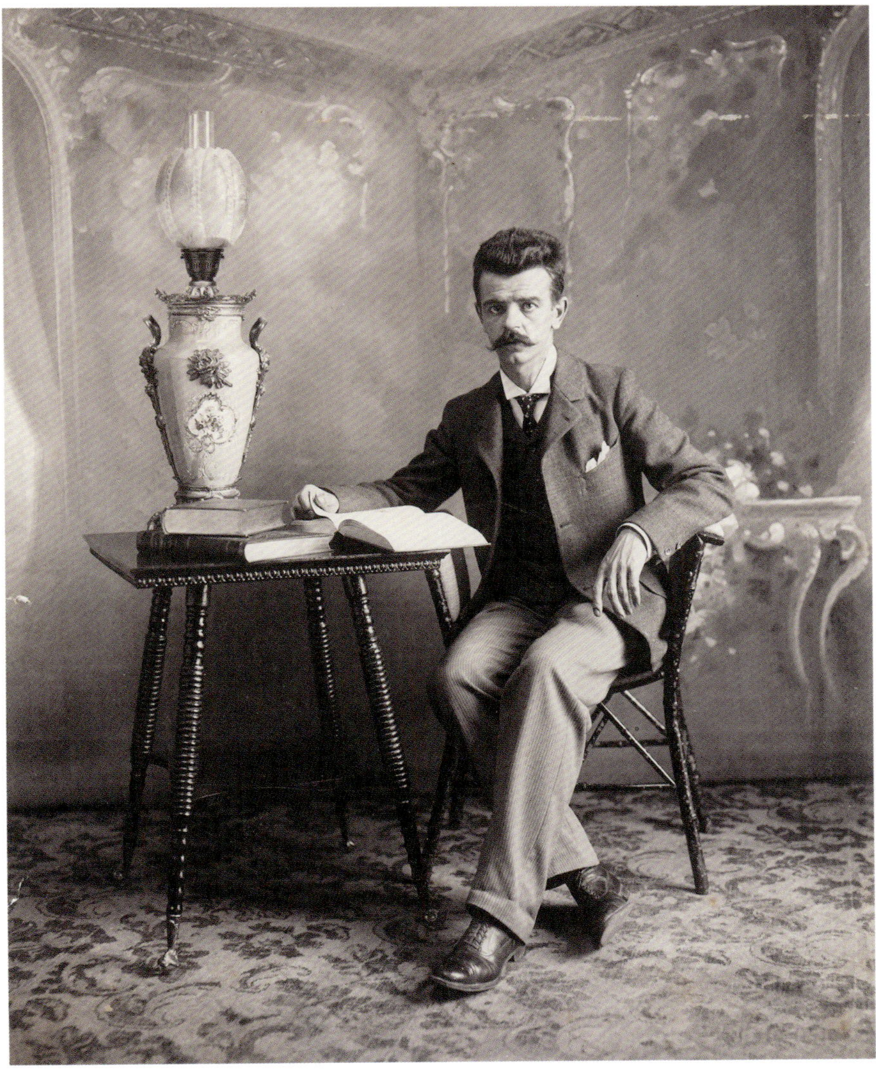

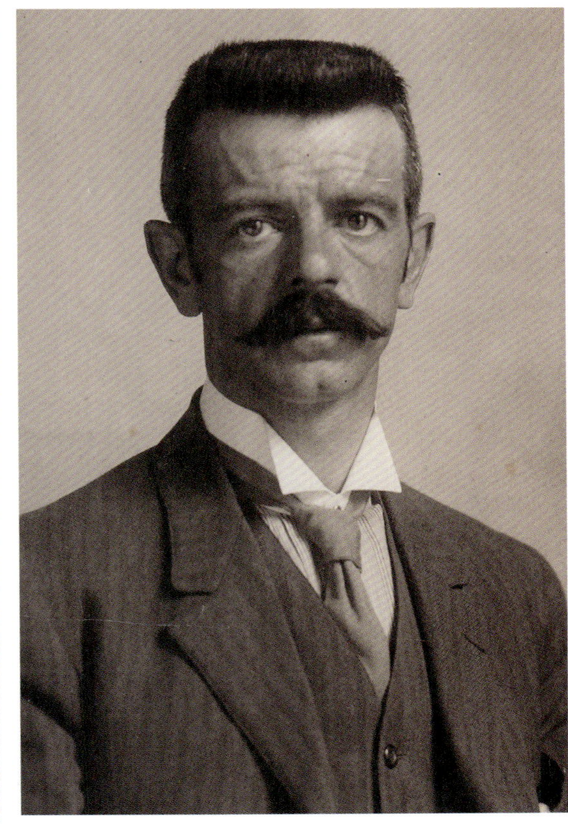

TOP Guillermo Kahlo, *Self-portrait*, Mexico City, ca. 1907. Guillermo Kahlo, *Self-portrait*, February 15, 1920

BOTTOM Guillermo Kahlo, *Self-portrait*, Mexico City, ca. 1903. Guillermo Kahlo, *Self-portrait*, Mexico City, ca. 1912

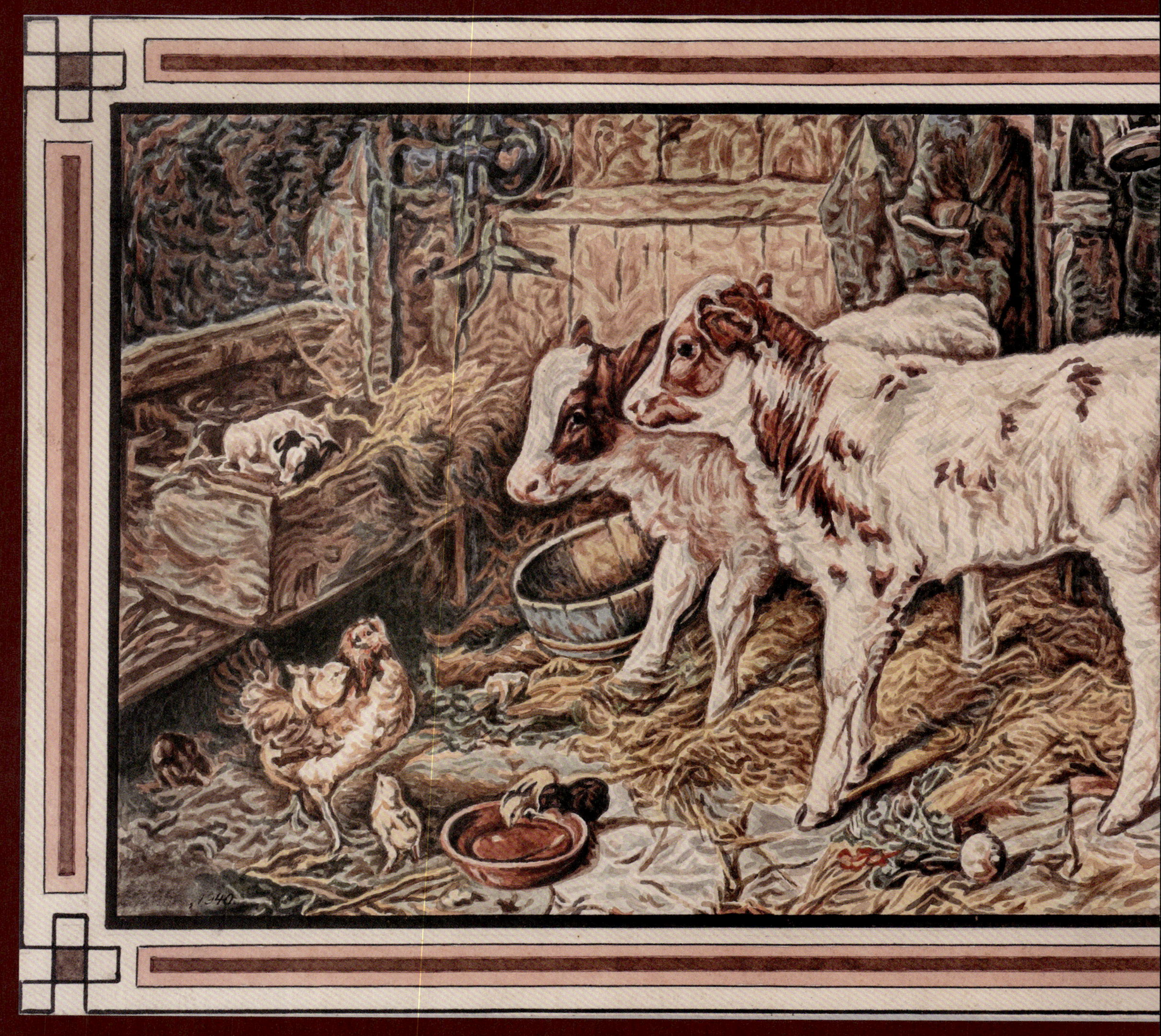

ABOVE Guillermo Kahlo, *Barn*, October 1940. Watercolor on paper, 12 x 18.5 in. (30.5 x 47 cm)
OPPOSITE, TOP Guillermo Kahlo, *Embroiderer*, October 1938. Watercolor on paper, 15.5 x 13 in. (39.5 x 33 cm)
OPPOSITE, BOTTOM Guillermo Kahlo, *Still Life*, March 1939. Watercolor on paper, 12 x 18.5 in. (30.5 x 47 cm)

Beyond his photo work, Guillermo was also a painter who specialized in still lifes with meticulous detail.

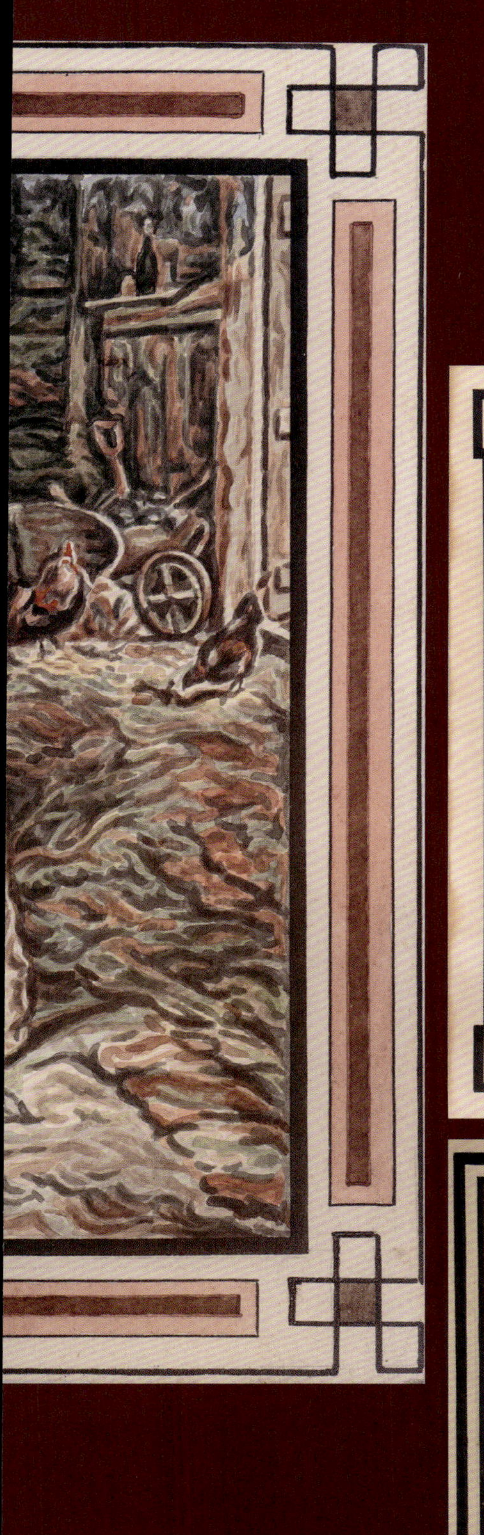

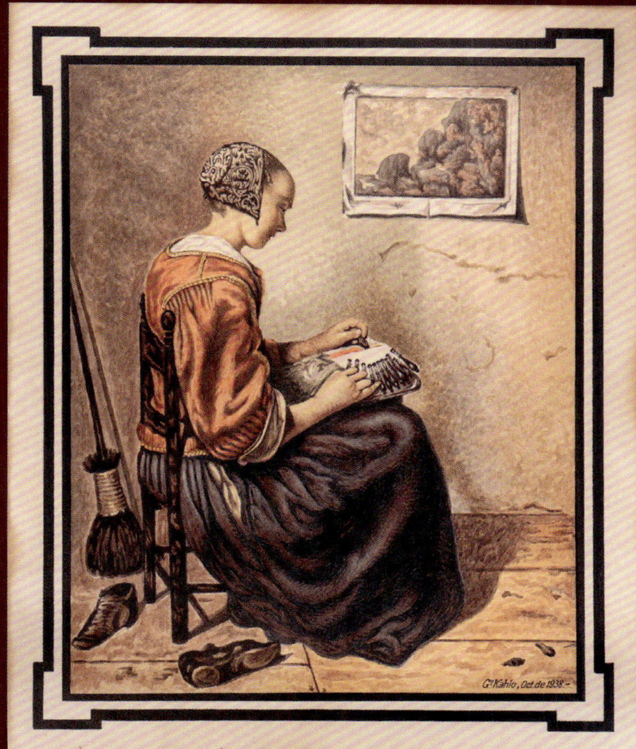
Gº Kahlo, Oct. de 1938.-

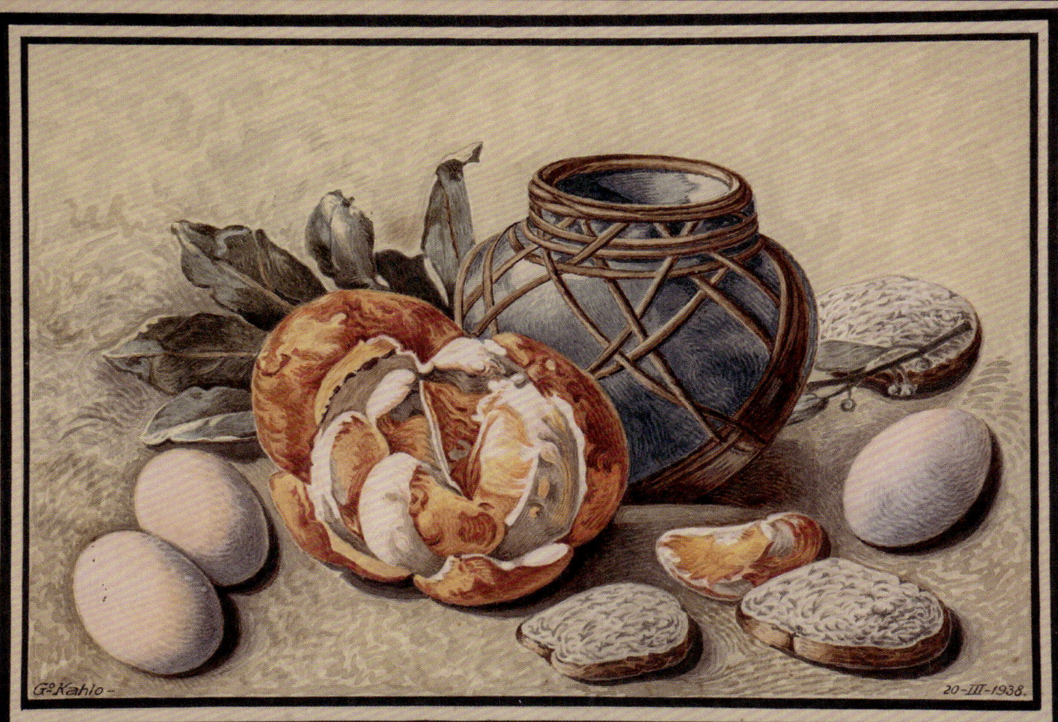
Gº Kahlo-
20-III-1938.

Mara Romeo Kahlo Guillermo, my great grandfather and Frida's father, was an attentive parent and a talented artist, in both photography and painting. He was also a perfectionist. Few people know about his work, but his influence was profound on Frida as an artist. She learned how to see with an artist's eye from her father, and he represented to her resilience and hard work. In addition to going with him to his various job sites, she helped him develop negatives, as well as retouch and color the images with short strokes; these gestures would reappear later in her paintings. Frida's artistic inclinations were present from a very early age and her father nurtured them. He would show her his techniques and "tricks of the trade" with care and discipline, and with this, they grew closer. They shared challenges as well: he was epileptic and Frida had polio as a child, which resulted in her right leg being thinner and shorter. Living with chronic illness requires strength, acceptance, and self-love and this bonded them further. Frida found in Guillermo a role model who strove for greatness, no matter the circumstances.

The excursions Guillermo and Frida went on brought them to many little towns around central Mexico. Each of them loved the local markets, which were rich with vibrant colors and aromas from the food, herbs, and spices. Frida would talk to the Indigenous and local people and learn about the properties of the various spices and herbs. They shared many meals on these trips—mole, quesadillas, *sopes*, and other foods. Frida's love for Mexican popular art also grew during these formative experiences.

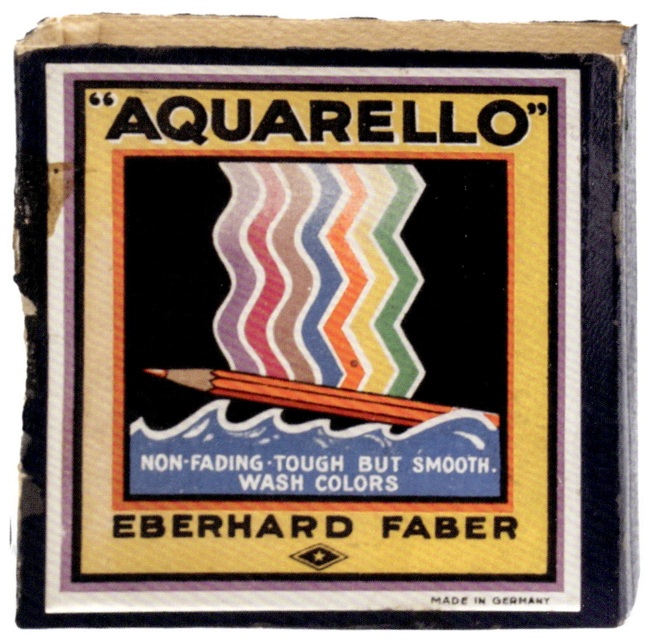

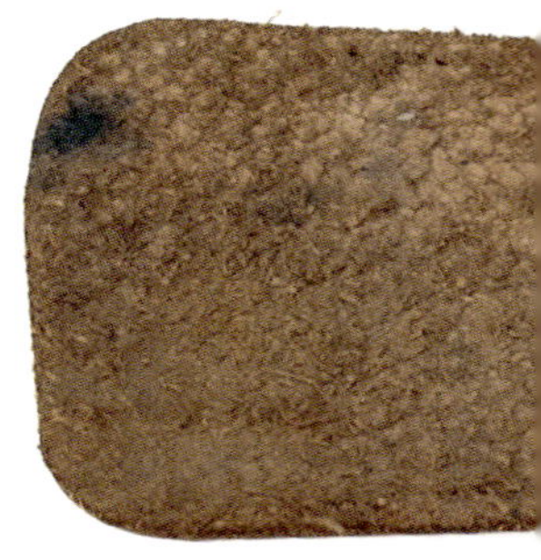

Guillermo's art supplies: German Aquarello colors, leather pencil case, and calligraphy set

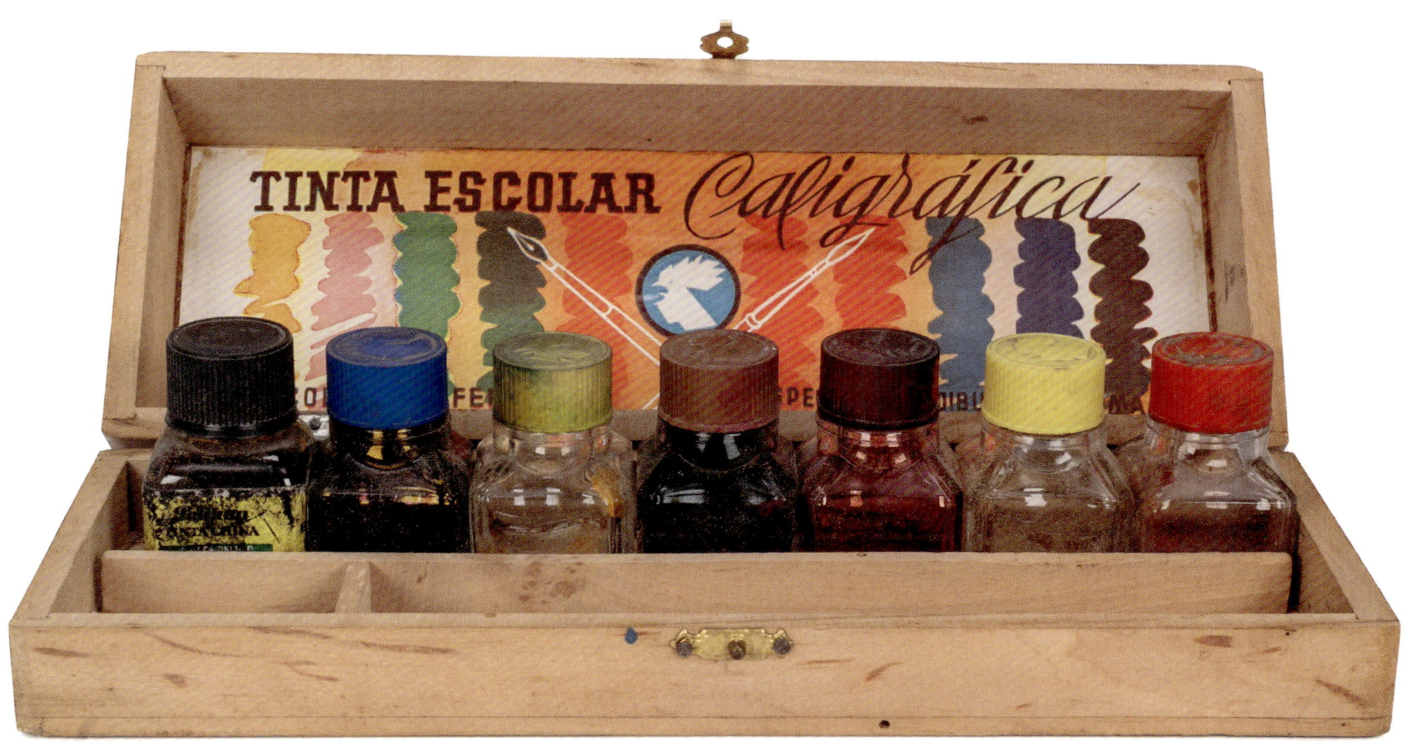
TINTA ESCOLAR Caligráfica

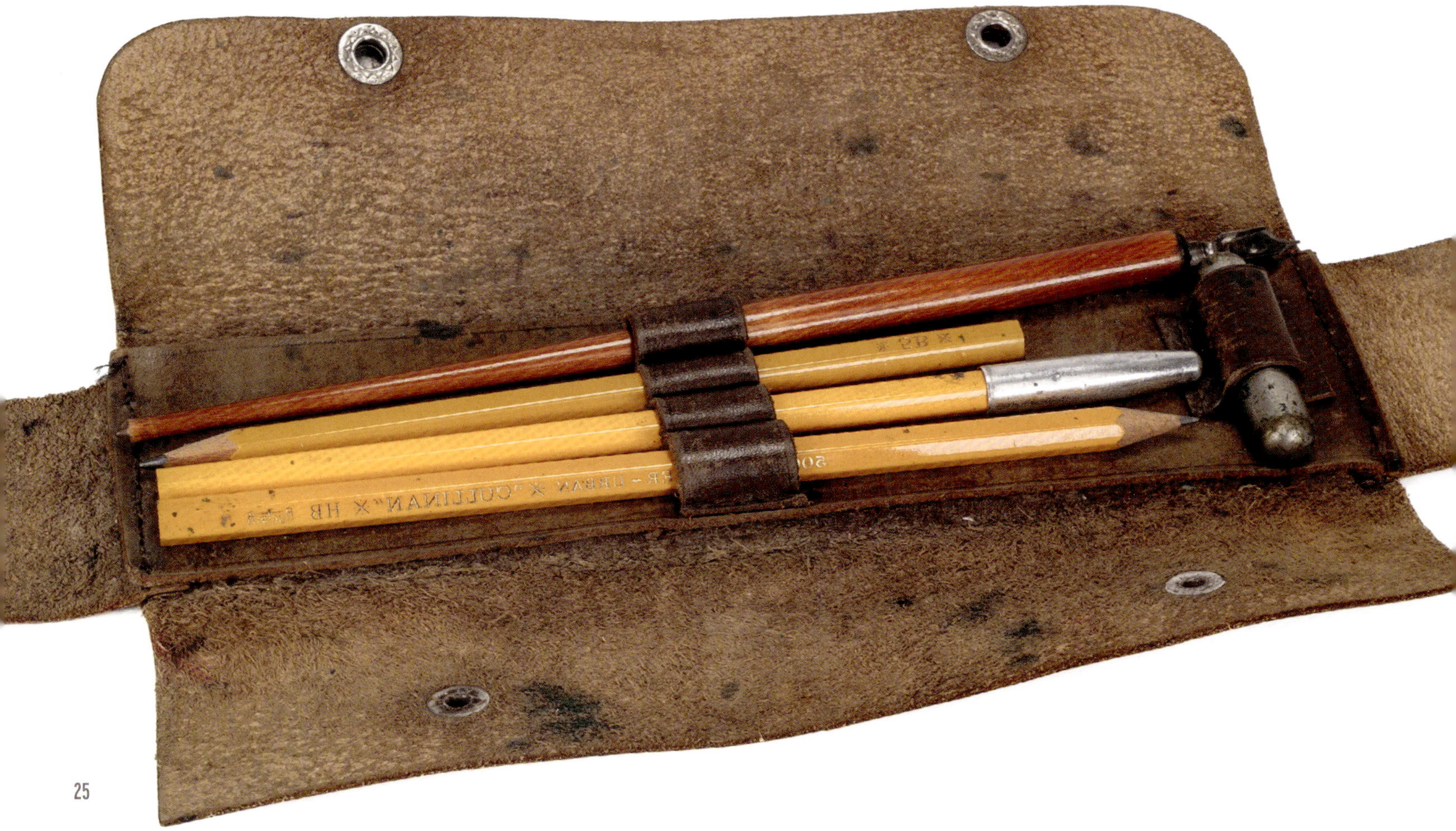

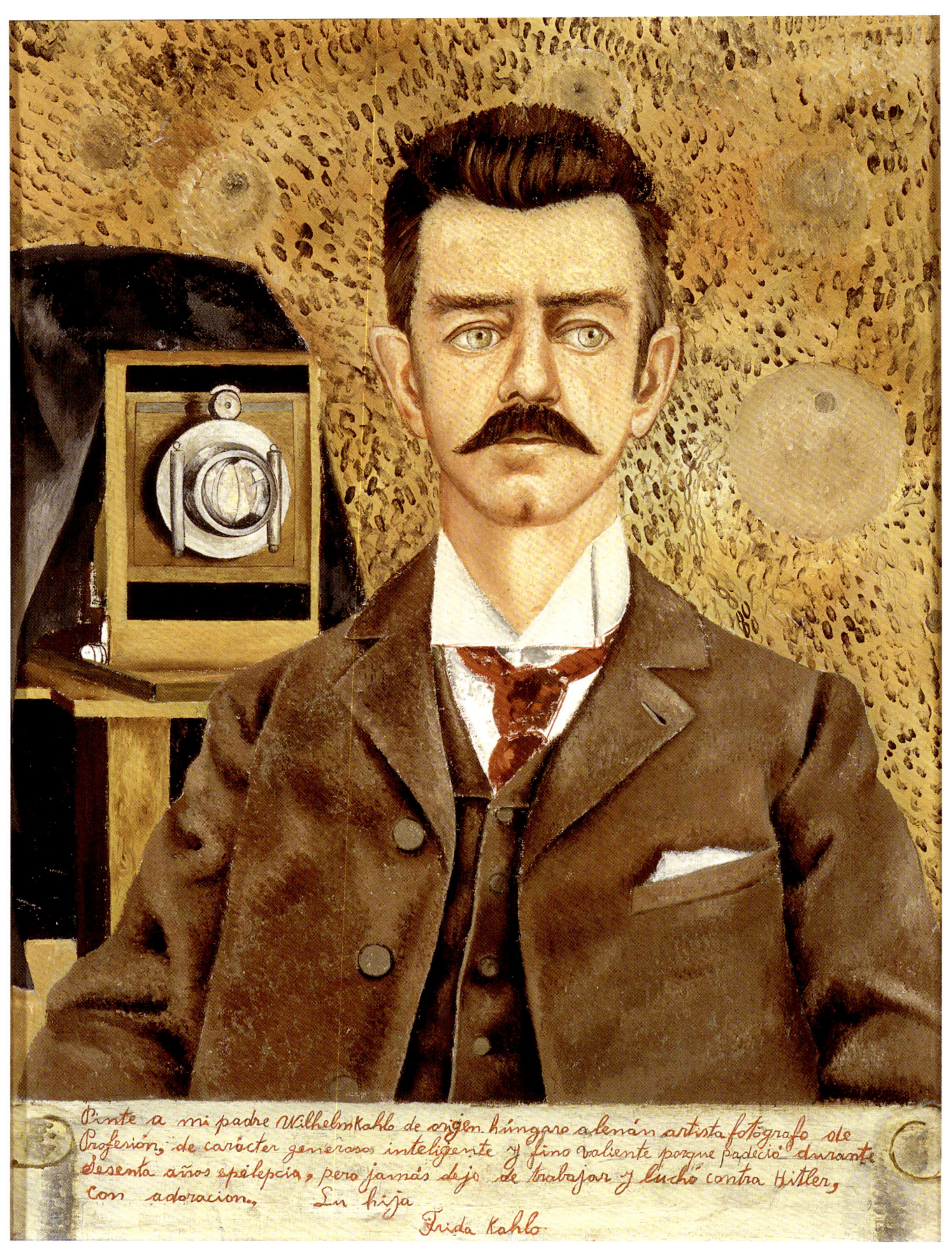

Frida Kahlo, *Portrait of My Father Wilhelm Kahlo*, 1952. Oil on canvas, 24 x 18.5 in. (61 x 47 cm)

Mara de Anda Guillermo was known for being meticulous in all that he did. Sometimes when a clock stopped working in the house, he would dedicate hours to its repair. Coming from Pforzheim, which is known for its jewelry and watchmaking, his skills were advanced. But if something didn't go well, and with his temper, he would throw it to the floor, stomp on it, and start from scratch. My grandmother Isolda told this story over and over again as a testament to his perfectionism and his *mecha corta* (short fuse). Frida often went with Guillermo to his studio on Londres Street in Coyoacán, the Mexico City neighborhood where the Kahlo family lived. She learned much from him.

Mara Romeo Kahlo Guillermo loved to make things with his hands—his many artistic pursuits are a testament to that. And his creativity extended to creating a puppet theater at home—he made marionettes and performed stories for his daughters.

One story he performed was about a boy who wanted to leave home and experience the world. In this story, the boy set out on his journey with some bread and cheese. After walking for a long time, he stopped to eat and encountered an old woman. He shared his food with her, and she was so grateful she gave him three golden apples and told him if he cut each one open, he would be granted a wish. His journey continued for days.

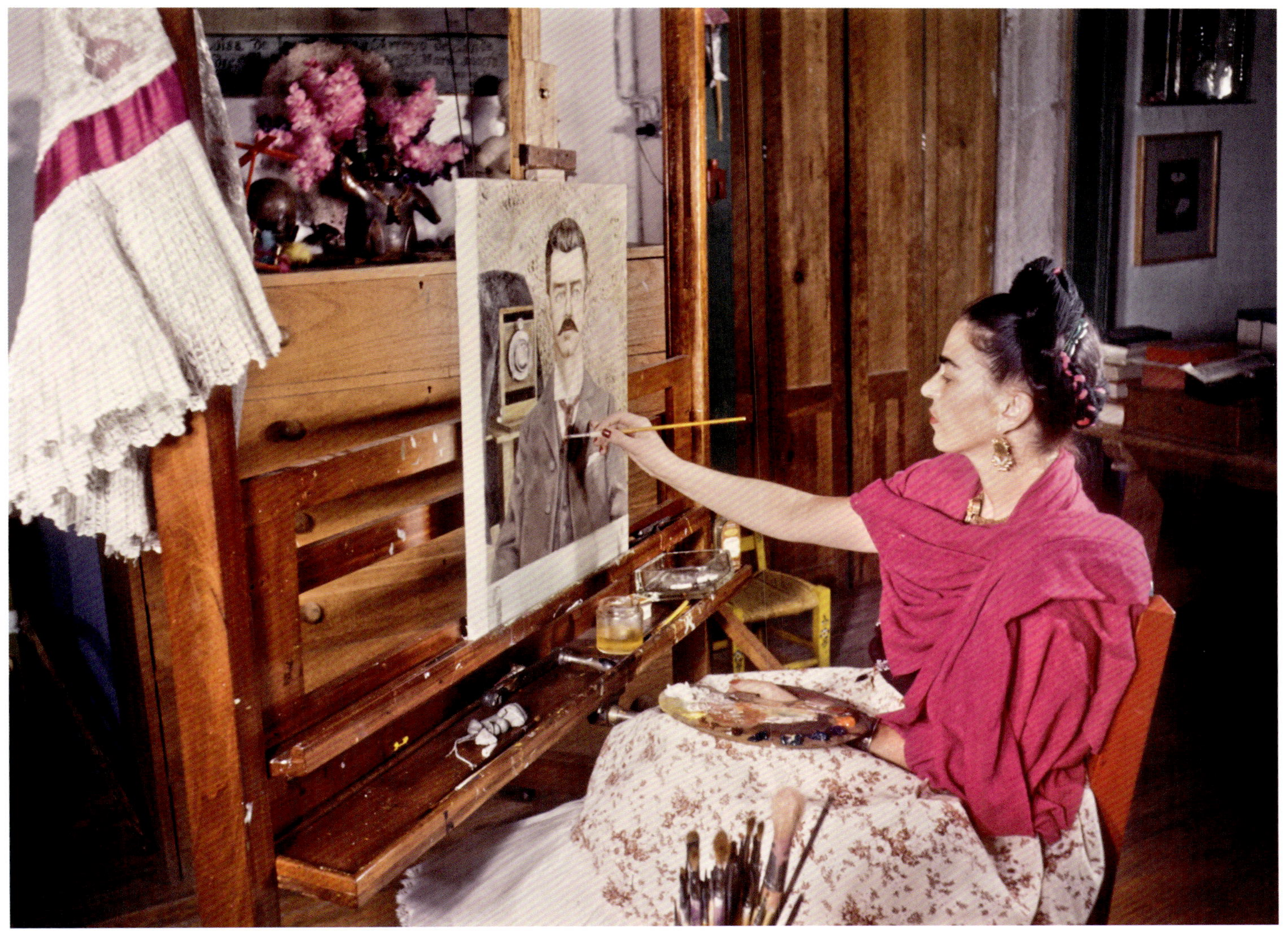

Frida painting her father's portrait in her studio in Casa Azul, Coyoacán, 1951. Photo by Giséle Freund

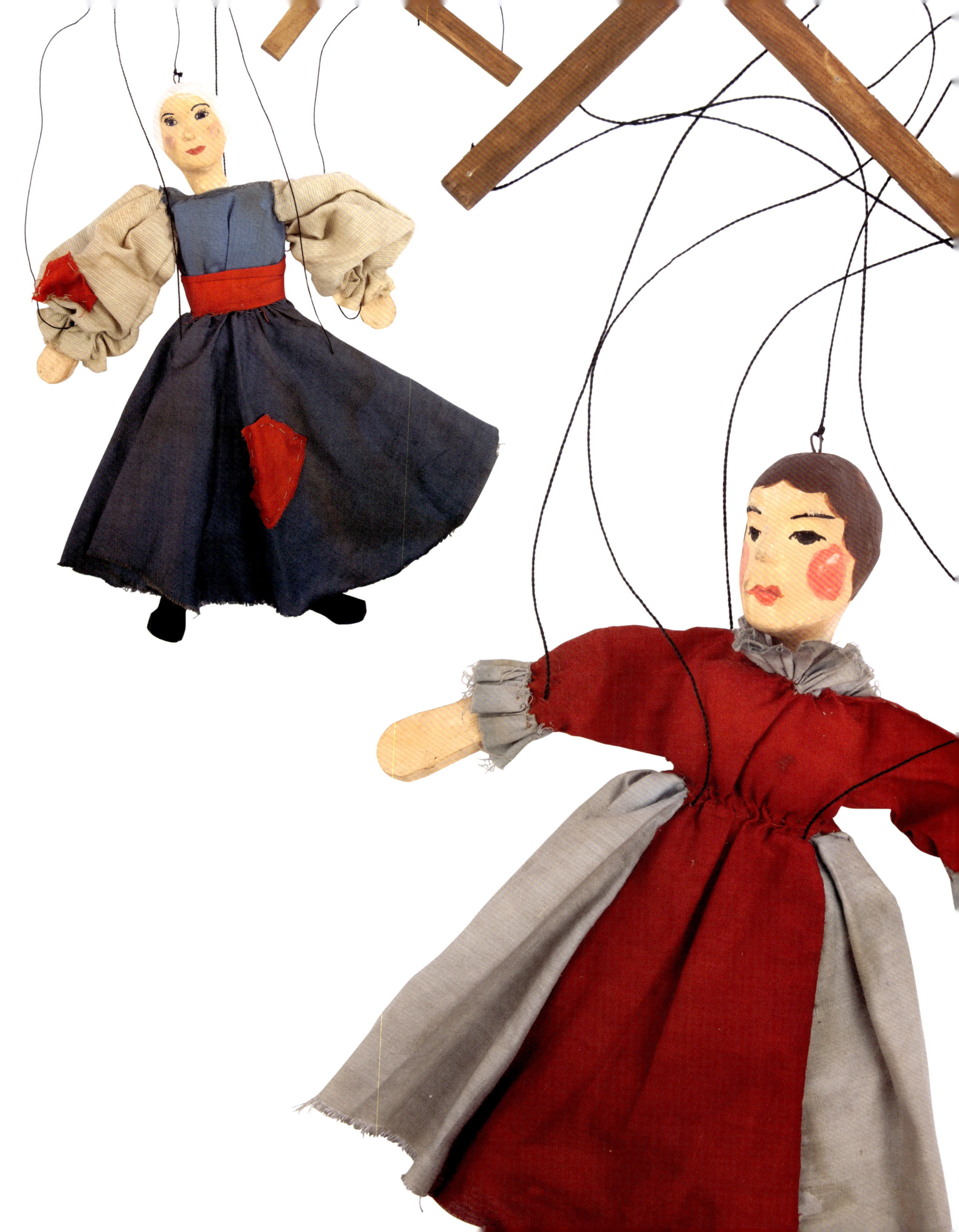

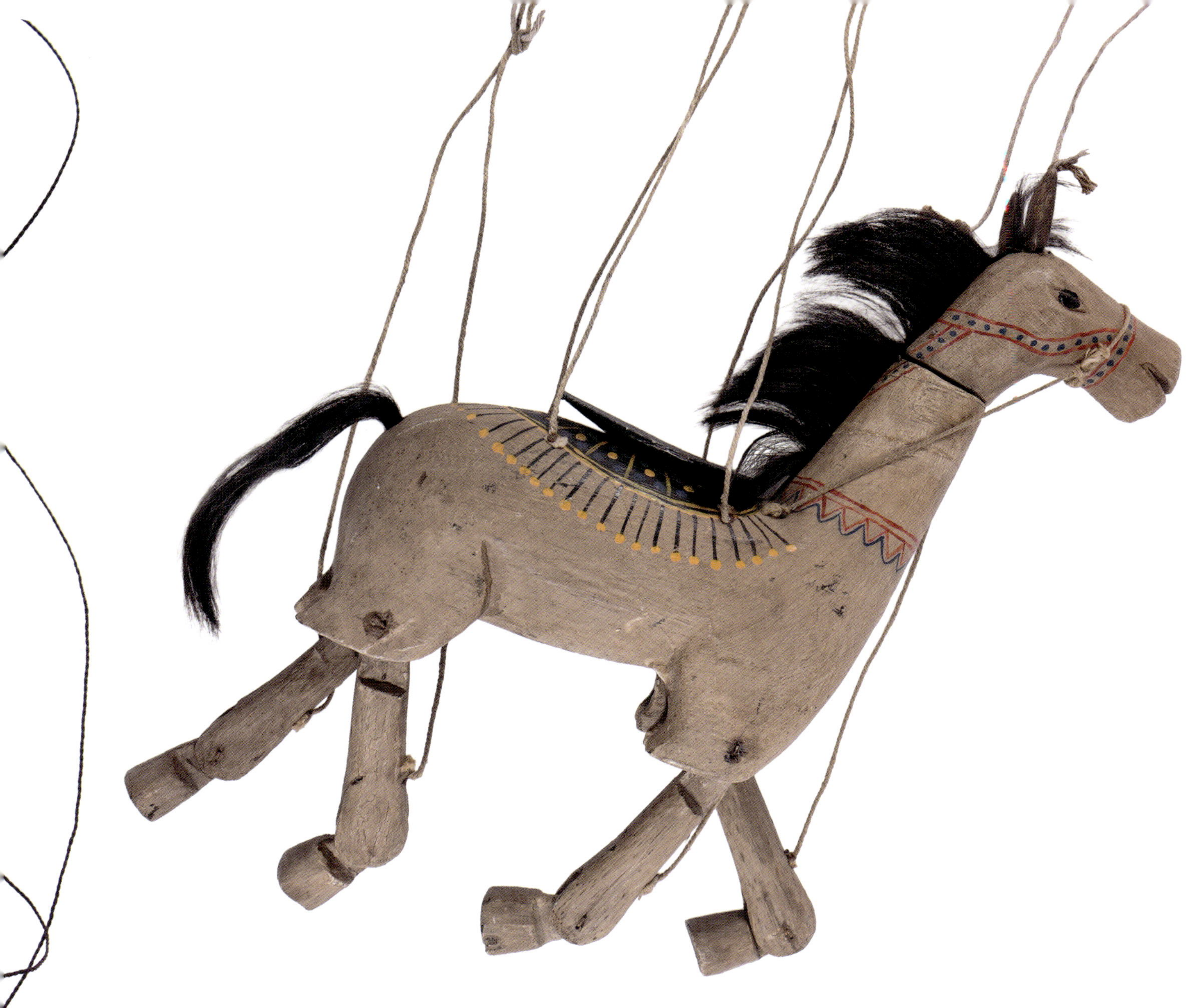

One morning he sighed, "I'm so tired, I would sell my soul to the devil to make it to the next town," and suddenly a big cloud of smoke appears and Lucifer, the devil, presents himself. And the boy enters into a pact with the devil. Ten years go by, and the devil comes back and demands his soul. But he is not ready to go with him, so he cuts into one of the apples and asks for a giant fig tree that whoever eats from cannot stop until the boy says so. The devil comes in and cannot resist the figs and once he starts, he cannot stop. The devil begs to get down from the tree and the boy asks him for another ten years. Ten years pass and the boy hears someone knocking on the door and realizes it is the devil coming to take his soul. He goes to the basement and gets another apple, cuts it and says whoever touches the nails he has will be stung until I say so. The boy, who's now a family man, asks the devil to pass him a nail to finish hanging the last photo of him in the house. And the devil gets stung endlessly by the many nails. The boy said I can have them stop stinging you, but I want another fifteen years. The devil leaves and fifteen years pass. He hears a knock, and he realizes it is the devil yet again. He cuts the last apple and says I wish that when someone takes this cane, the cane will hit them. The devil enters and the boy, who's now an old man, asks the devil for his cane so he could go with him. The cane starts hitting the devil and the boy says, "If you want it to stop hitting you, it means I will never go with you," and the devil leaves forever in a cloud of smoke.

Guillermo's handmade marionettes, ca. 1900, made of wood and mixed media. Guillermo would use these and other handmade puppets to tell stories to Frida and her sisters.

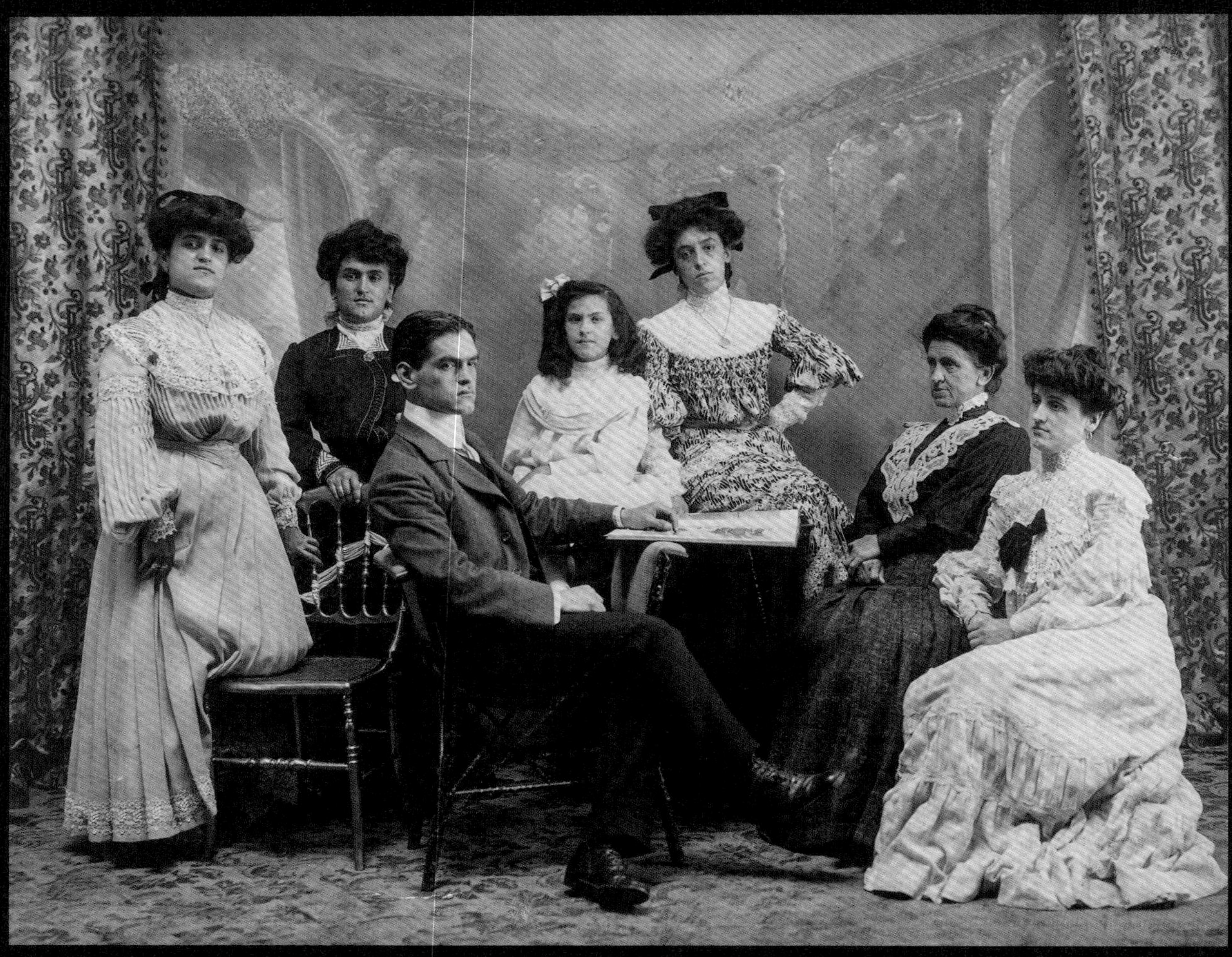

Frida's maternal lineage, the Calderón y González family, Mexico City, ca. 1895. From left to right: Isabel, Matilde, José Antonio, unidentified child, Isabel González y González (Frida's grandmother), Ana (Frida's aunt), and Guadalupe (Frida's aunt)

Frida's mother Matilde Calderón had 10 siblings, of which only 5 made it to adulthood.

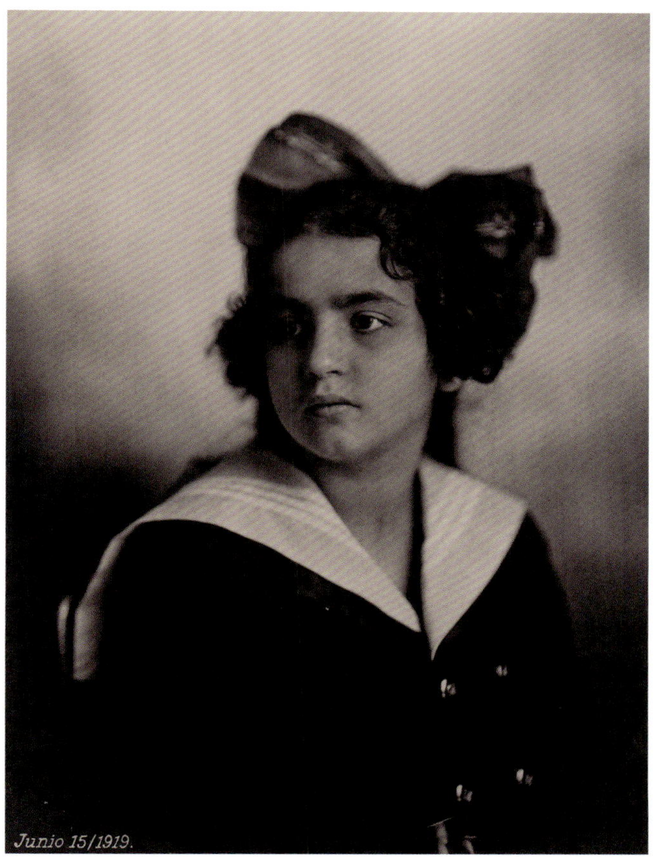

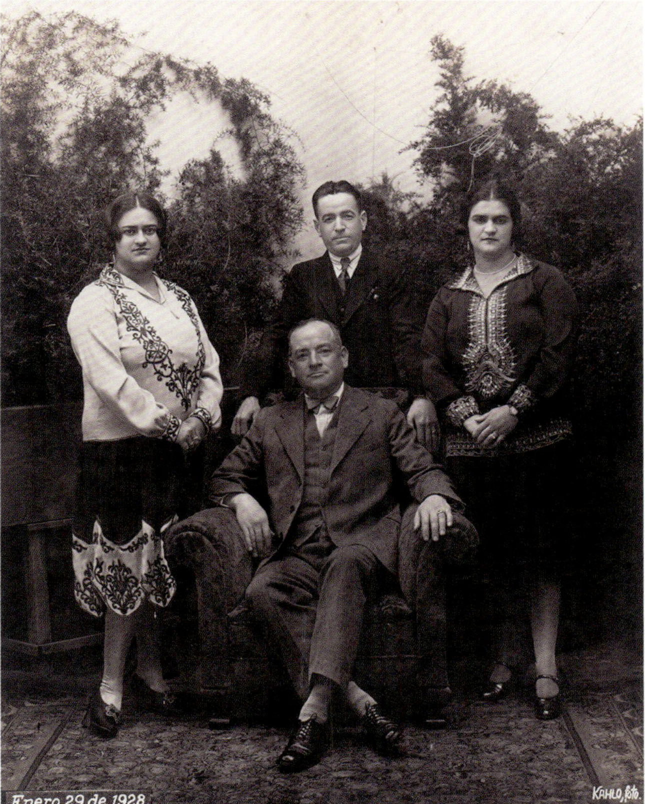

Mara de Anda Frida's mother, Matilde, came from a large Catholic family. Originally there were 15 brothers and sisters, but only five lived to adulthood. They were a very tight family. Frida and her sister Cristina loved to say that Matilde was from Oaxaca, a myth that has persisted. Matilde was in fact born in Mexico City, and her parents were from Hidalgo and Michoacán, neighboring states of the city. Matilde reinforced in her young daughters the importance of relying on family and leading by example. This trait has remained throughout generations.

Guillermo and Matilde had four daughters together: Matilde (1899), Adriana (1902), Frida (1907), and my great-grandmother Cristina (1908). Their only son, Wilhelm, died the same year he was born, in 1905. The four daughters were strong-willed and sometimes unconventional in their decisions. Matilde Kahlo left her marriage and remarried a divorced man (Francisco Hernández). Adriana married a widower (Alberto Veraza) and became a loving stepmother to Carlos Veraza. Cristina married Antonio Pinedo Chambon but separated from her husband early on. Frida, as many know, married the artist Diego Rivera twice. They had a deeply passionate—and unusual—relationship that has been chronicled for decades.

Both Guillermo and Matilde encouraged their daughters to accept and have respect for everyone. And they taught this by example. Frida's parents did not share religion nor the same culture, yet they had a very loving and respectful relationship. They taught their daughters to treat everyone equally, from Indigenous people, immigrants, and workers to artists and politicians. Everyone was to feel welcome in their home. Frida became more vocal about these principles as the years passed. With her school friends, she shared the desire to break with societal rules that would differentiate between socio-economic classes.

TOP Cristina, Frida's sister, Coyoacán, Mexico City, June 15, 1919. Photo by Guillermo Kahlo

BOTTOM Standing, left to right: Matilde Kahlo (Frida's sister), Francisco Hernandez (Matilde's husband), Adriana Kahlo (Frida's sister). Seated: Alberto "El Güerito" Veraza (Adriana's husband), Coyoacán, January 29, 1928. Photo by Guillermo Kahlo

Mara Romeo Kahlo Matilde was very religious coming from a family of devout Catholics; Guillermo was an atheist. It must have required a lot of understanding on both parts to come from such different perspectives on religion—and also a lot of love. They were married in a Catholic church, and Matilde raised her four daughters as Catholics, but their father's atheism also influenced them. The eldest sisters, Matilde and Adriana, became devout Catholics, and although Frida and Cristina made their first communion—which they did together—the younger sisters drifted away from the church. And later in life, Frida believed more in the power of nature than in a Catholic God. Nevertheless, in difficult times, like when she had surgery, she would ask God for help. Growing up in a household with a devout mother, you must take some of it to heart. The family believed in the teachings of the Catholic church as a solid foundation for helping people and your community, though this didn't necessarily extend to practicing religion in a formal way.

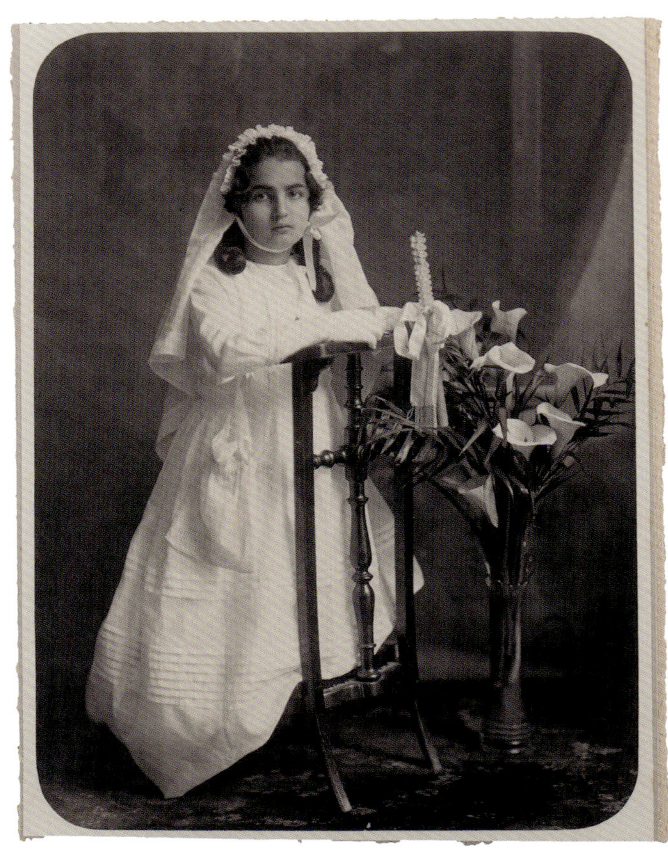

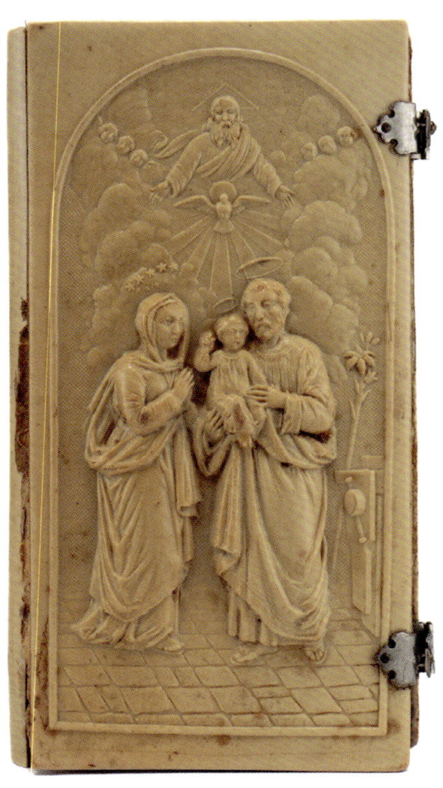

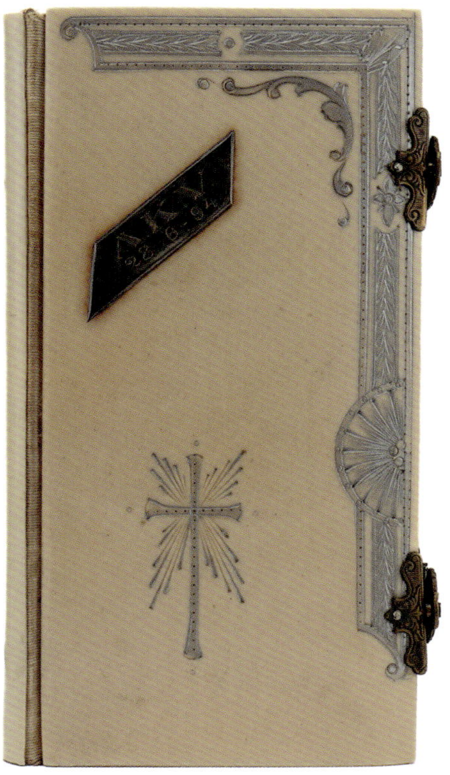

TOP Cristina at her first communion, ca. 1920. Photo by Guillermo Kahlo. Despite their father being an atheist, Cristina and Frida made their first communion together, following their mother's wishes.

BOTTOM Communion booklets for Cristina and Frida, 1920

OPPOSITE Frida at her first communion, ca. 1920. Photo by Guillermo Kahlo

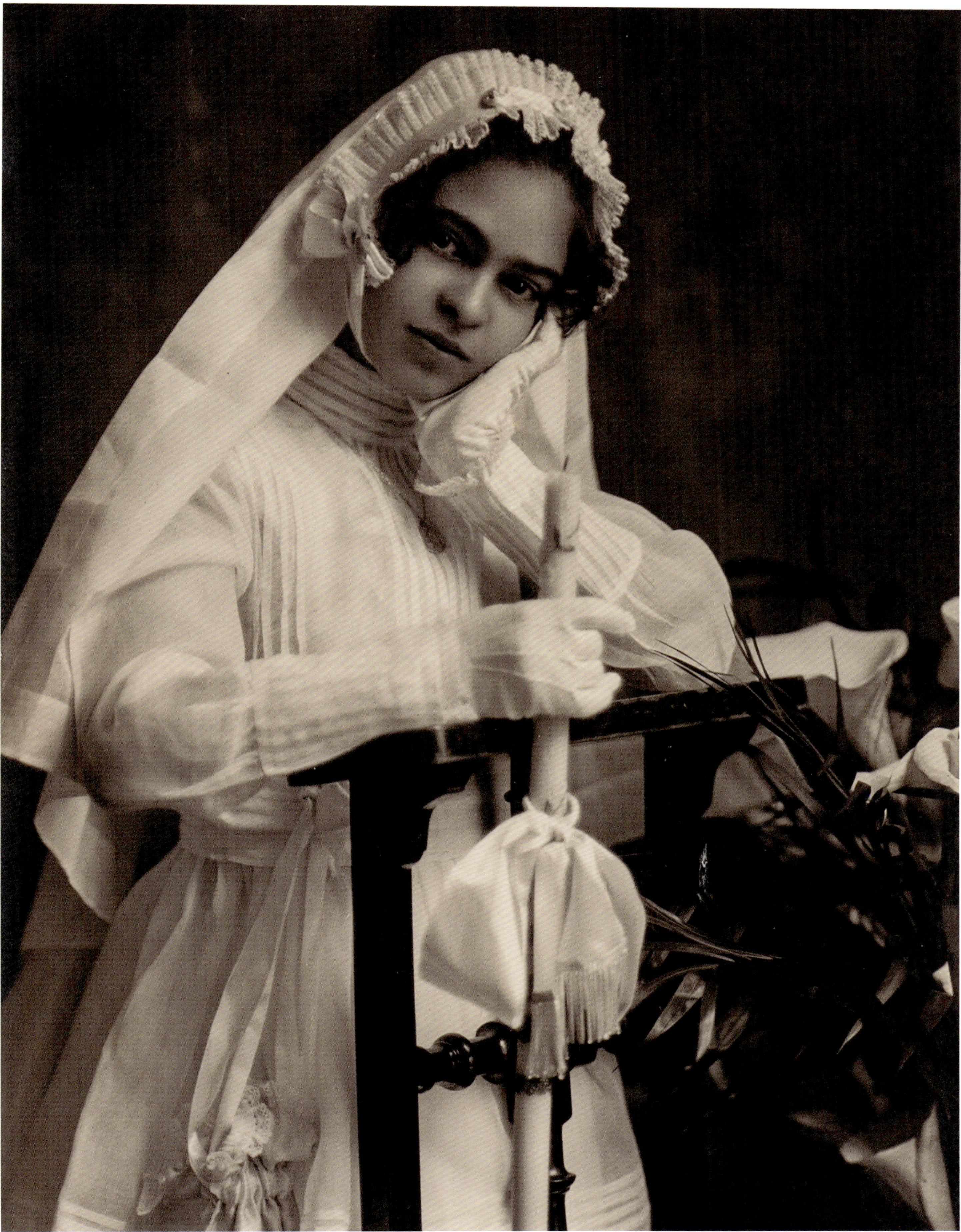

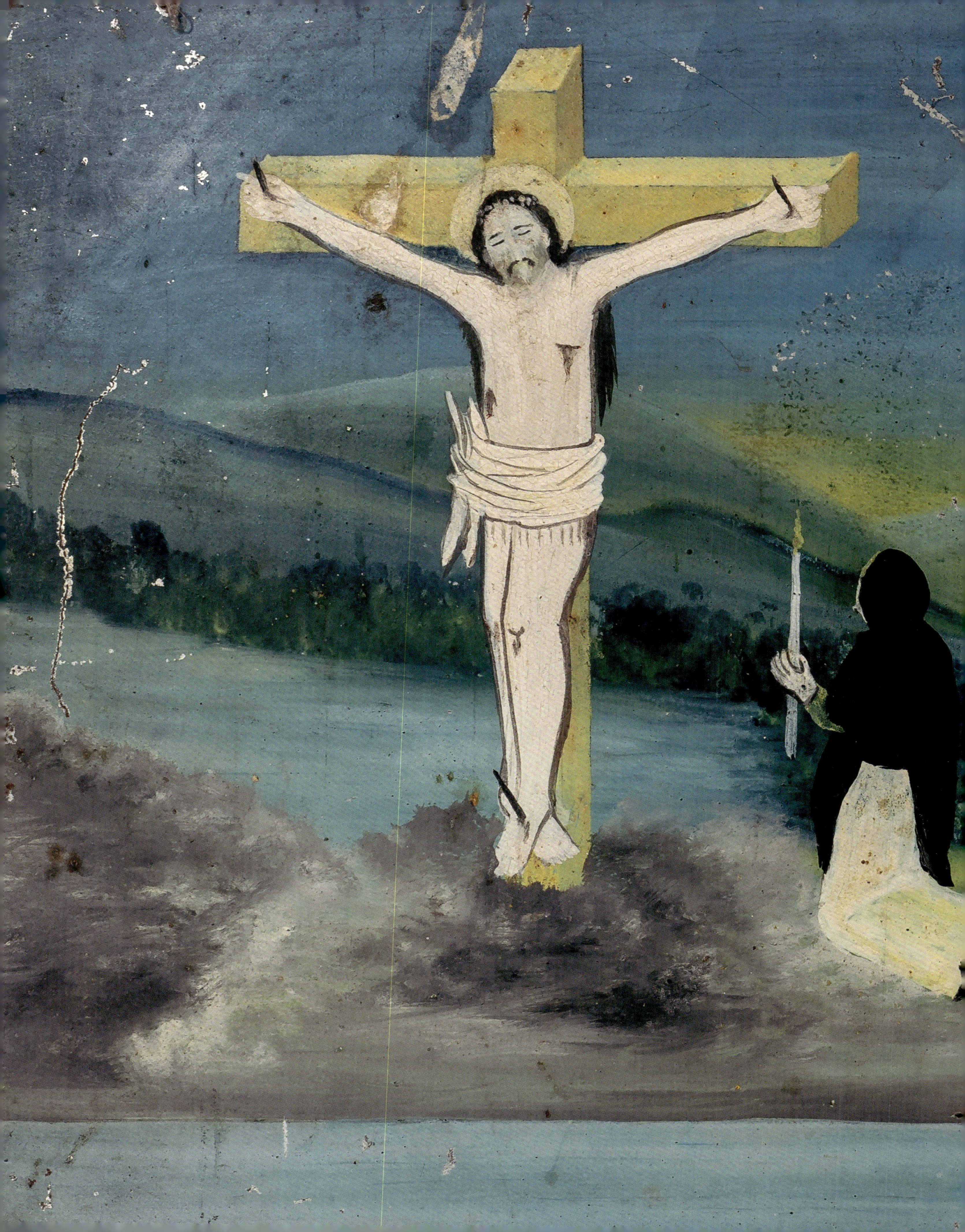

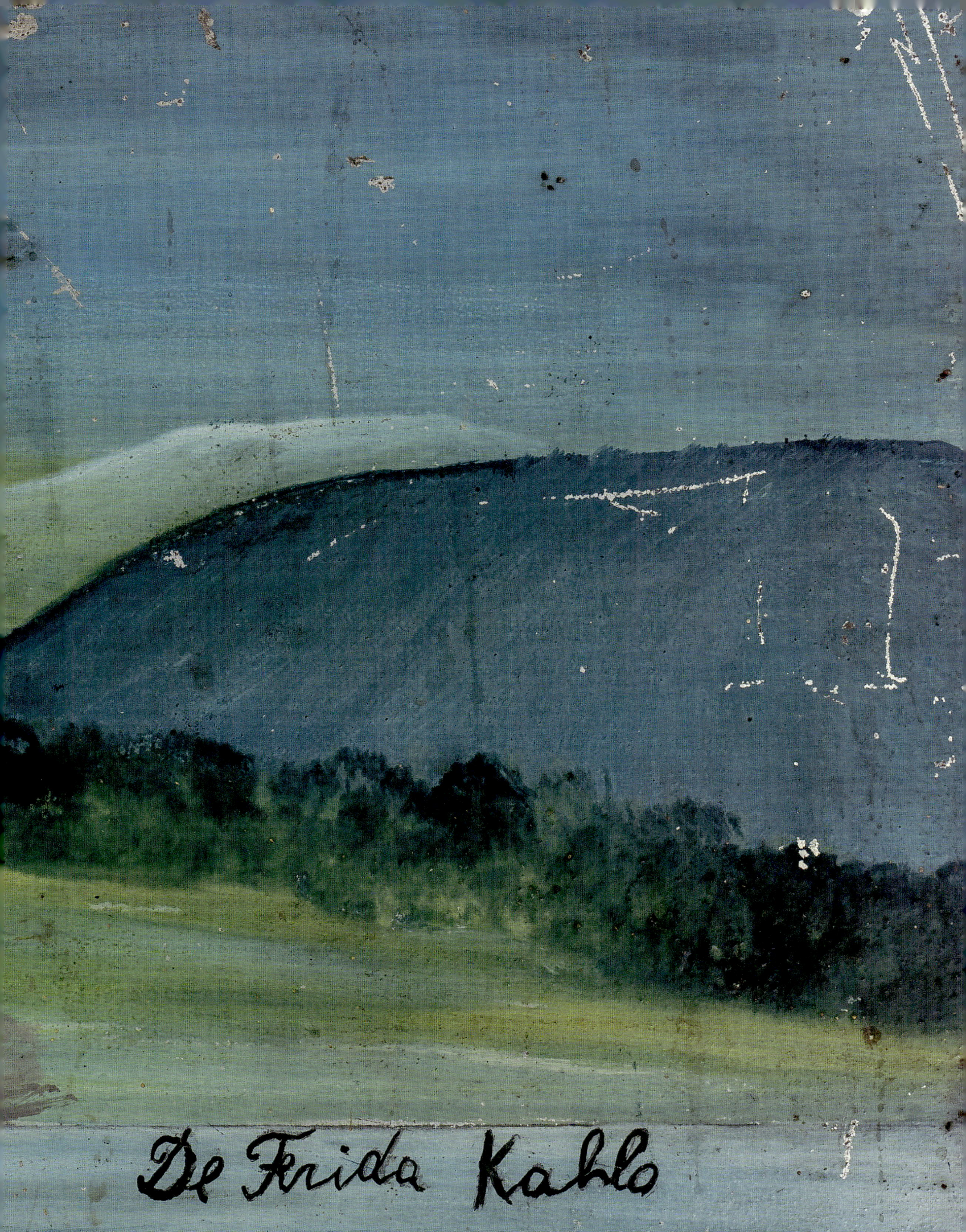
De Frida Kahlo

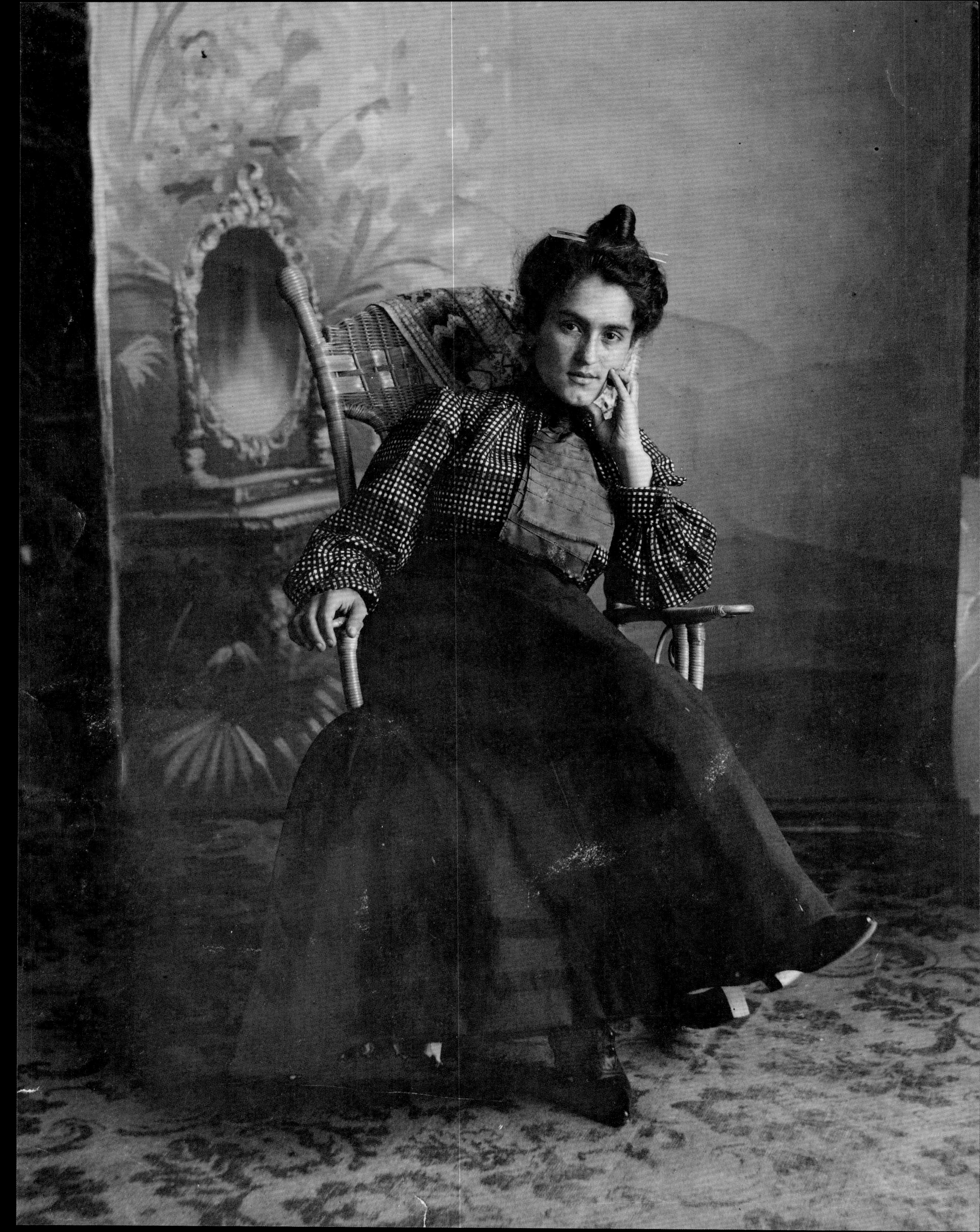

Although Frida was closer to Guillermo because of their similar interests and personality traits, she was very attentive and very caring toward her mother. In 1932, when her mother became ill, she made the journey by train from the United States to Mexico to be with her. She also painted an ex-voto asking for her recovery.

Mara de Anda Frida was in Detroit with Diego when her sisters sent a telegram telling her to come back, since Matilde was very ill. It took her five days to get to Mexico City, as there had been massive floods at the border. She traveled with a friend, Lucienne Bloch, who was an assistant to Diego while he was commissioned to paint murals in different cities throughout the US. Frida arrived home just in time to say goodbye to her mother. It seemed like Matilde was waiting for Frida before passing on. It was a devasting and unexpected loss for the entire family, including my grandmother Isolda, Frida's niece.

Frida Hentschel Matilde taught her daughters to be self-sufficient, strong, and to care deeply for family, community, and animals. When Frida started working in 1922, it was unusual for women in Mexico to hold jobs, but she had her as a role model, who was working in the early 1890s when she met Guillermo. And early on Frida and her sisters understood the power and freedom that providing for yourself gives you. She raised four strong women, who were unapologetically themselves, and never fully relied on men for their financial security.

Mara Romeo Kahlo When they were young, Matilde would take Frida and Cristina to the market in Coyoacán, and they loved to hide from her. Frida and Cristina were always "partners in crime." Their mother would get angry because she often couldn't find her daughters and would spend a lot of time looking for them. They loved the market because there were many animals for sale, and they were always trying to get her to buy more, even though they already had many animals at Casa Azul—the house they grew up in and the house Frida and Diego eventually shared together—including ducks, chickens, rabbits, dogs, cats, and birds. Matilde would get frustrated telling them "No, no, no, I don't want any more animals." And she would often lament to herself that bringing her youngest daughters to the market was fraught because they always ran away, delaying her, and always ended up bringing more and more animals to their house. But surely, she secretly loved this dynamic, because it happened quite often.

When it was apricot season, Matilde always purchased the stone fruits to make marmalade. Frida and Cristina would help their mother in the kitchen, and after they dried the apricot seeds, they would paint them in different colors and use them to play a game like jacks, called *matatenas*. When I was very little, my grandmother Cristina and I repeated the same routine, and would spend hours playing.

PREVIOUS SPREAD Frida Kahlo, *Ex-Voto*, 1932. Oil on plate, 10 x 14 in. (25.2 x 36 cm). As she grew up, Frida moved away from religious dogma. But when she had to undergo surgery, she would ask God for protection. This ex-voto also reflects this ambivalent relationship she had with the religious teachings she had as a child and her beliefs later in adulthood. She made this ex-voto in 1932 when her mother was very sick.

OPPOSITE Matilde Calderón, Frida's mother, Mexico City, ca. 1900. Photo by Guillermo Kahlo

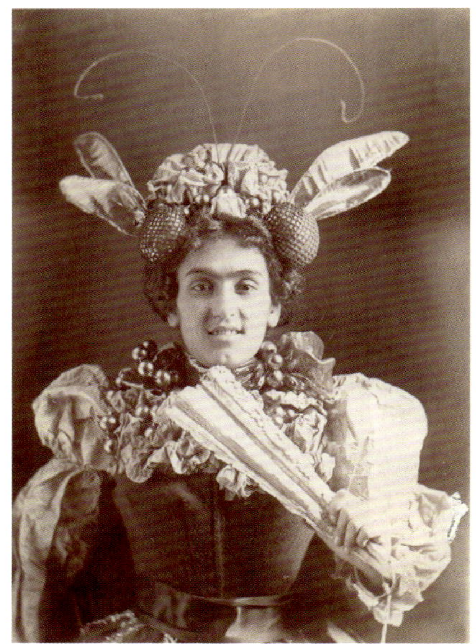

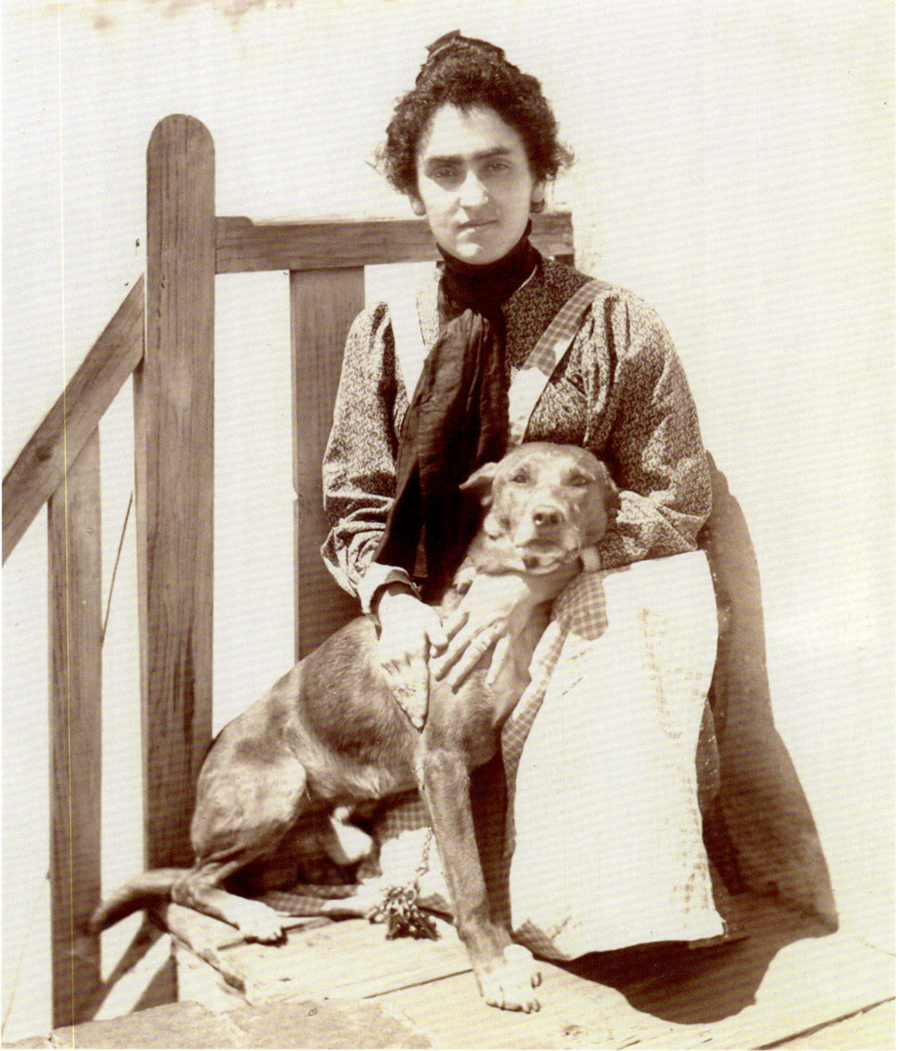

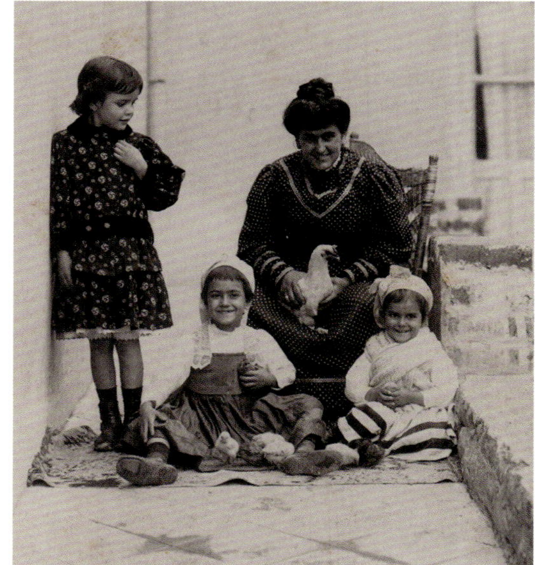

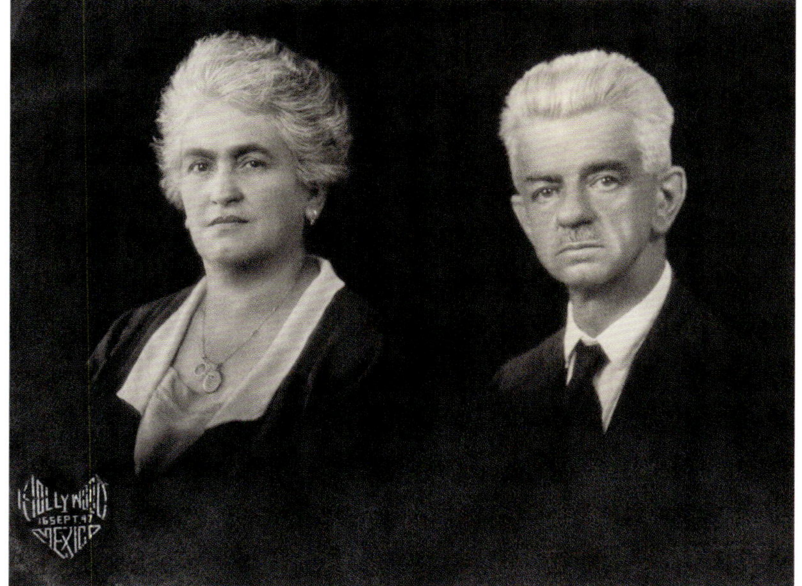

CLOCKWISE FROM TOP LEFT Matilde Calderón in party dress, ca. 1910, and with her dog, ca. 1898. Photos by Guillermo Kahlo. Matilde Calderón and Guillermo Kahlo, Frida's parents, June 20, 1932. Photo by Hollywood Studio. Margarita Kahlo Cardeña (Frida's sister from her father's first marriage), Matilde Calderón (seated), and Frida's sisters Matilde and Adriana Kahlo, Casa Azul, Coyoacán, ca. 1906. Photo by Guillermo Kahlo

Matilde was a strong influence on her daughters; she cared for animals, family, and traditions, and always fostered independence in her daughters.

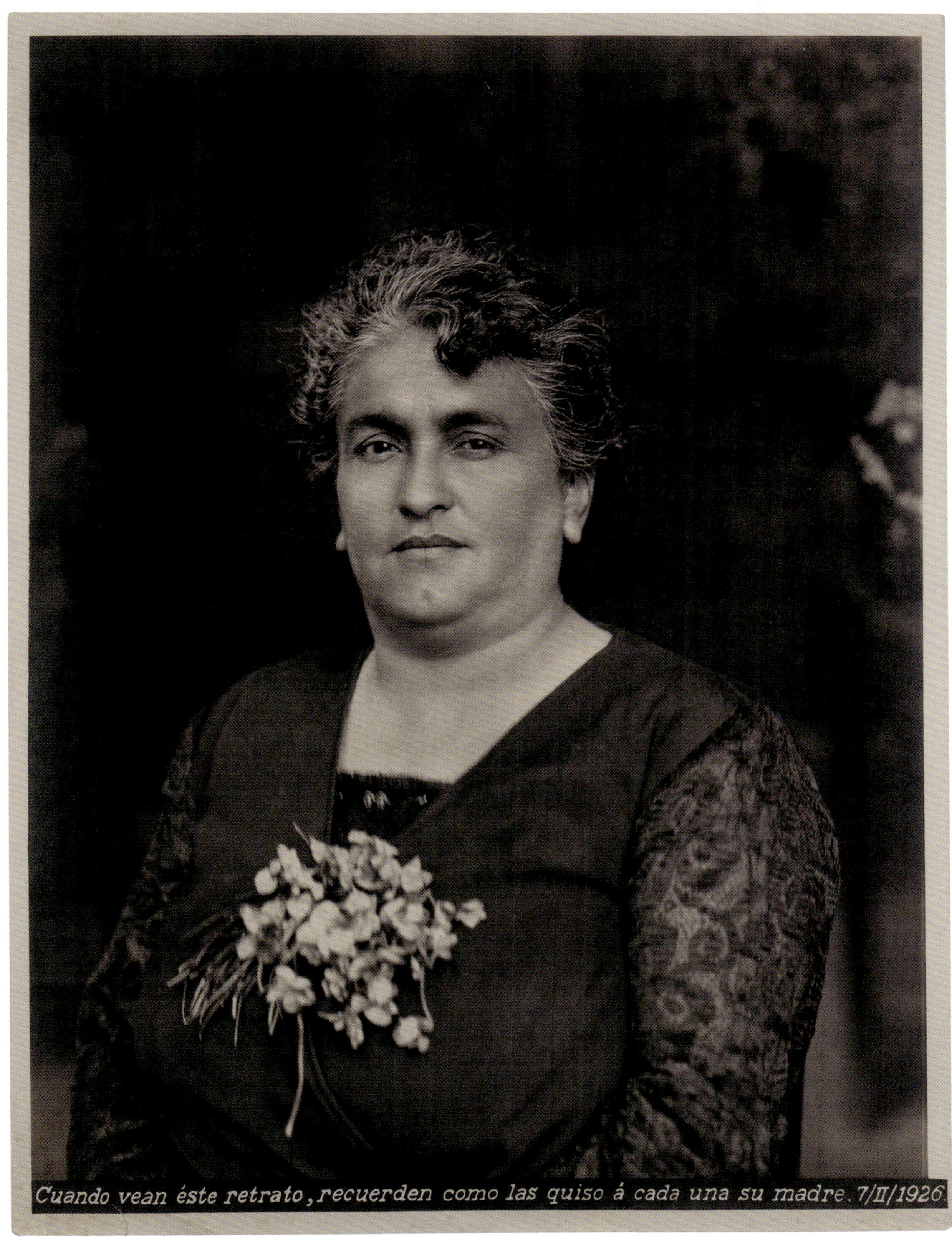

Matilde Calderón, February 7, 1926. Photo by Guillermo Kahlo.
Inscribed at the bottom with, "When you see this portrait, remember how your mother loved each of you."

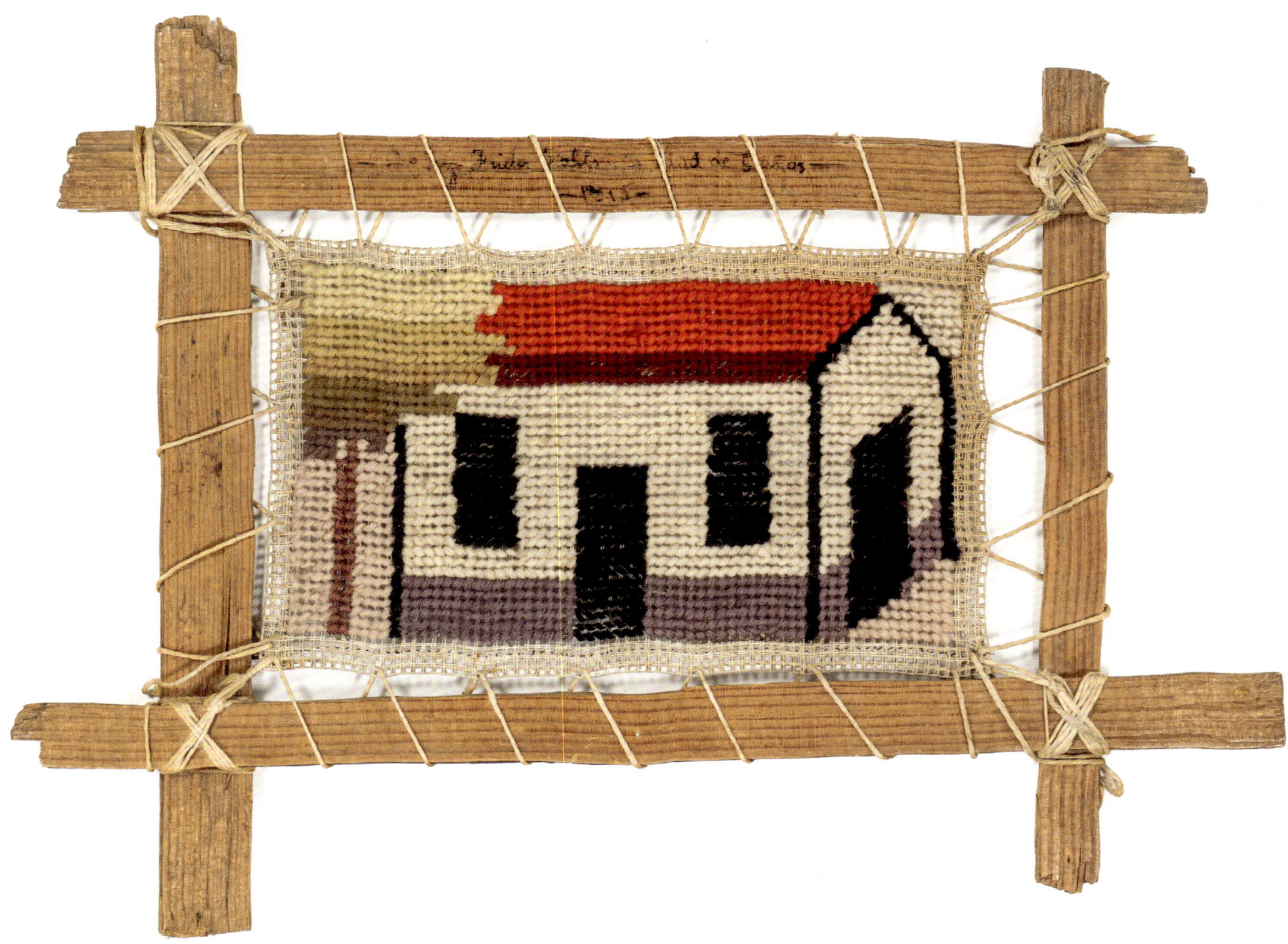

When the Mexican Revolution began, Guillermo's main client—the government—collapsed. Work become scarce and this impacted his health. Around 1922, Frida started working to help support her family in the spirit of solidarity. She worked counting inventory in a woodshop, as a cashier/bookkeeper, and eventually she was able to work in more creative environments. By early 1925, Frida began working in the engraving and print workshop of Fernando Fernández, who provided her the first opportunity to learn various graphic techniques. Recognizing her talent and potential as a graphic artist, Fernández encouraged Frida to practice drawing. During this time, Frida developed a keen eye for detail and portraiture by copying the engravings of Swedish painter Anders Zorn, whom Fernández admired.

ABOVE Frida Kahlo, Embroidery of a house, 1912. Wood, fabric, and thread; 11.5 x 14.25 (29.5 x 36.5 cm). Frida showed her artistic ability from a very young age. Inscribed on the top of the wood frame is, "Frida Kahlo made this at the age of 5." Frida's mother taught cross stitch, a skill that has been preserved by four generations.

OPPOSITE, TOP Frida Kahlo, *Santa Sofia Cathedral, Istanbul*, 1925. Pencil on paper, 4 x 5 in. (10 x 13 cm)

OPPOSITE, BOTTOM Frida Kahlo, *Structured World*, 1925. Pencil on paper, 4 x 5 in. (10 x 13 cm)

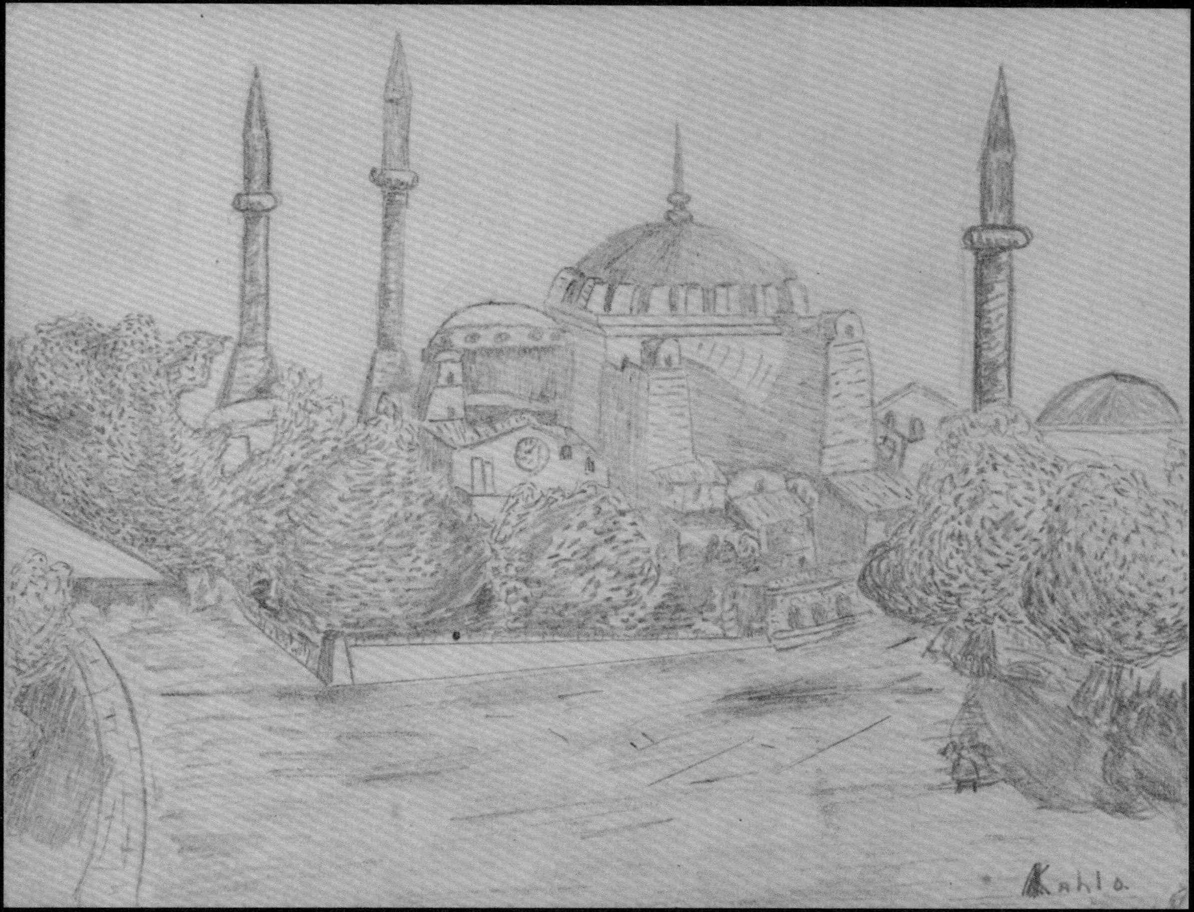

Kahlo.

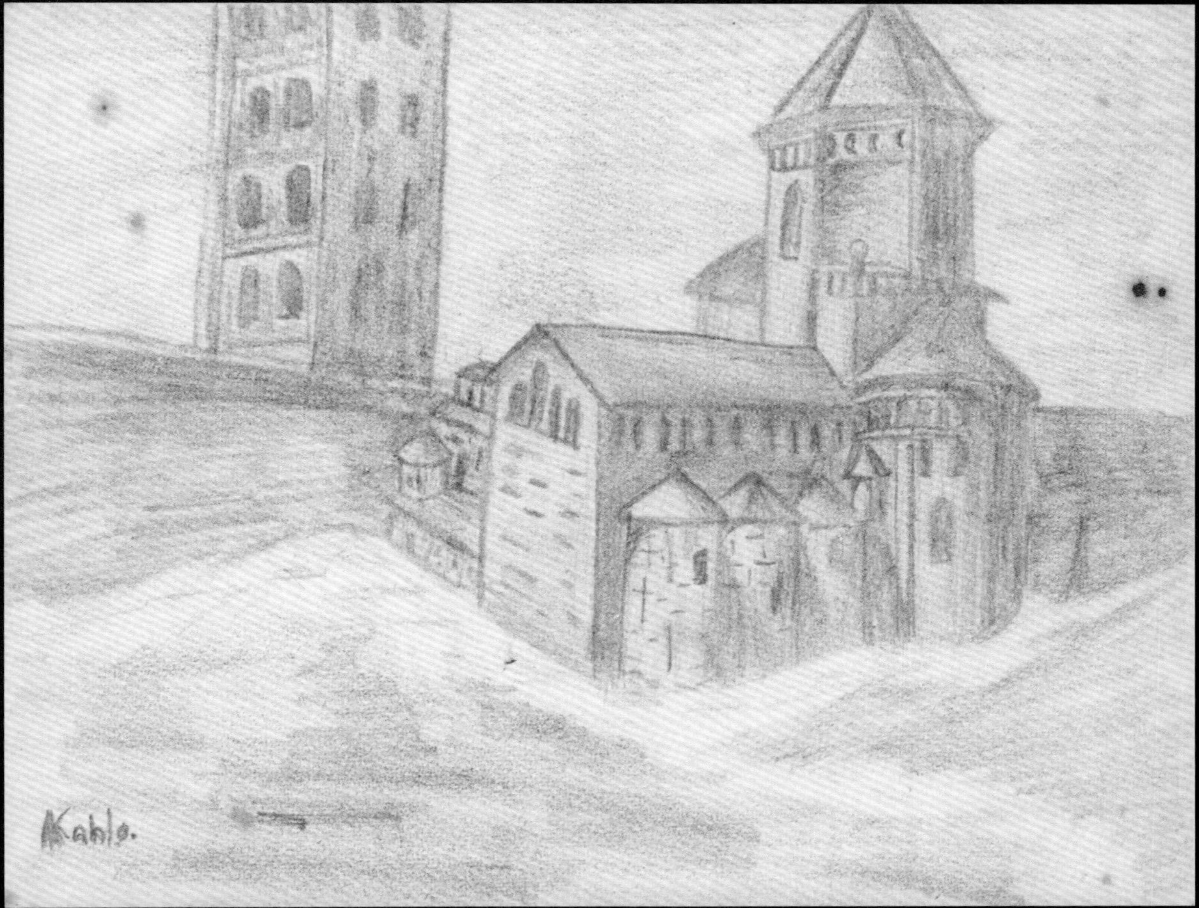

Kahlo.

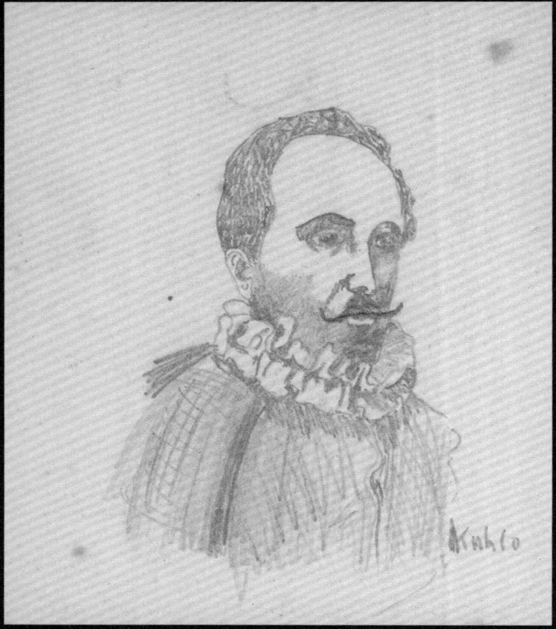

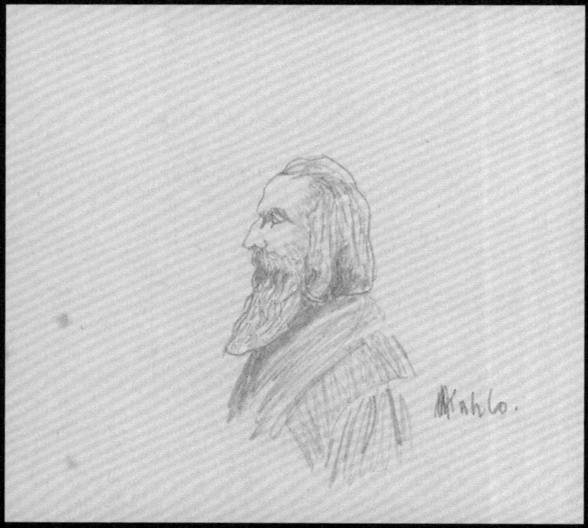

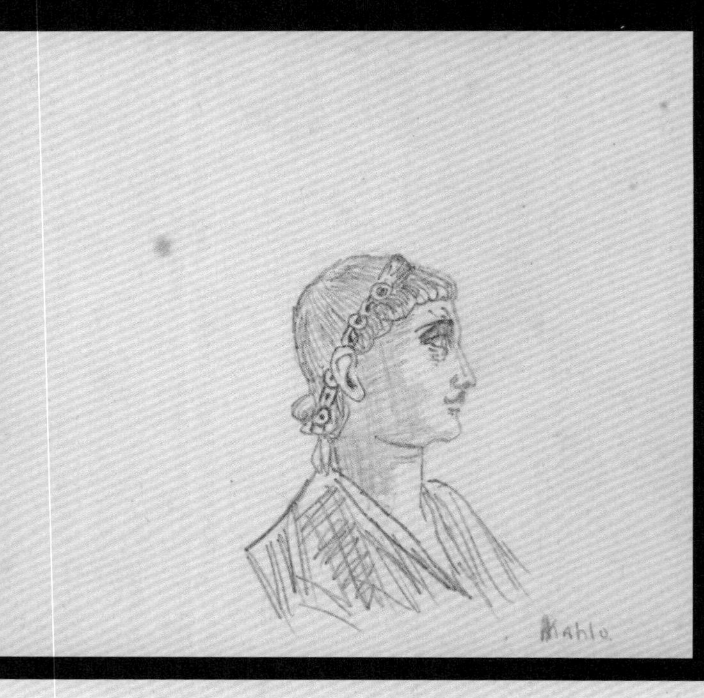

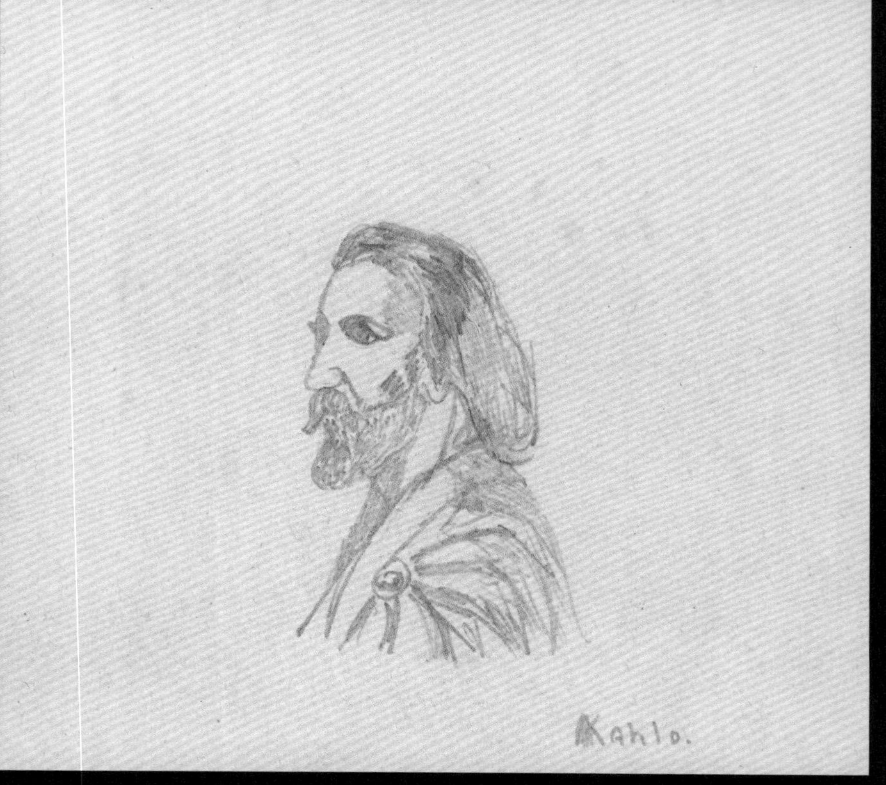

ABOVE Frida Kahlo, anonymous portraits, 1924. Pencil on paper, 3.5 x 3.25 in. each (9 x 8 cm) (shown at different scales)

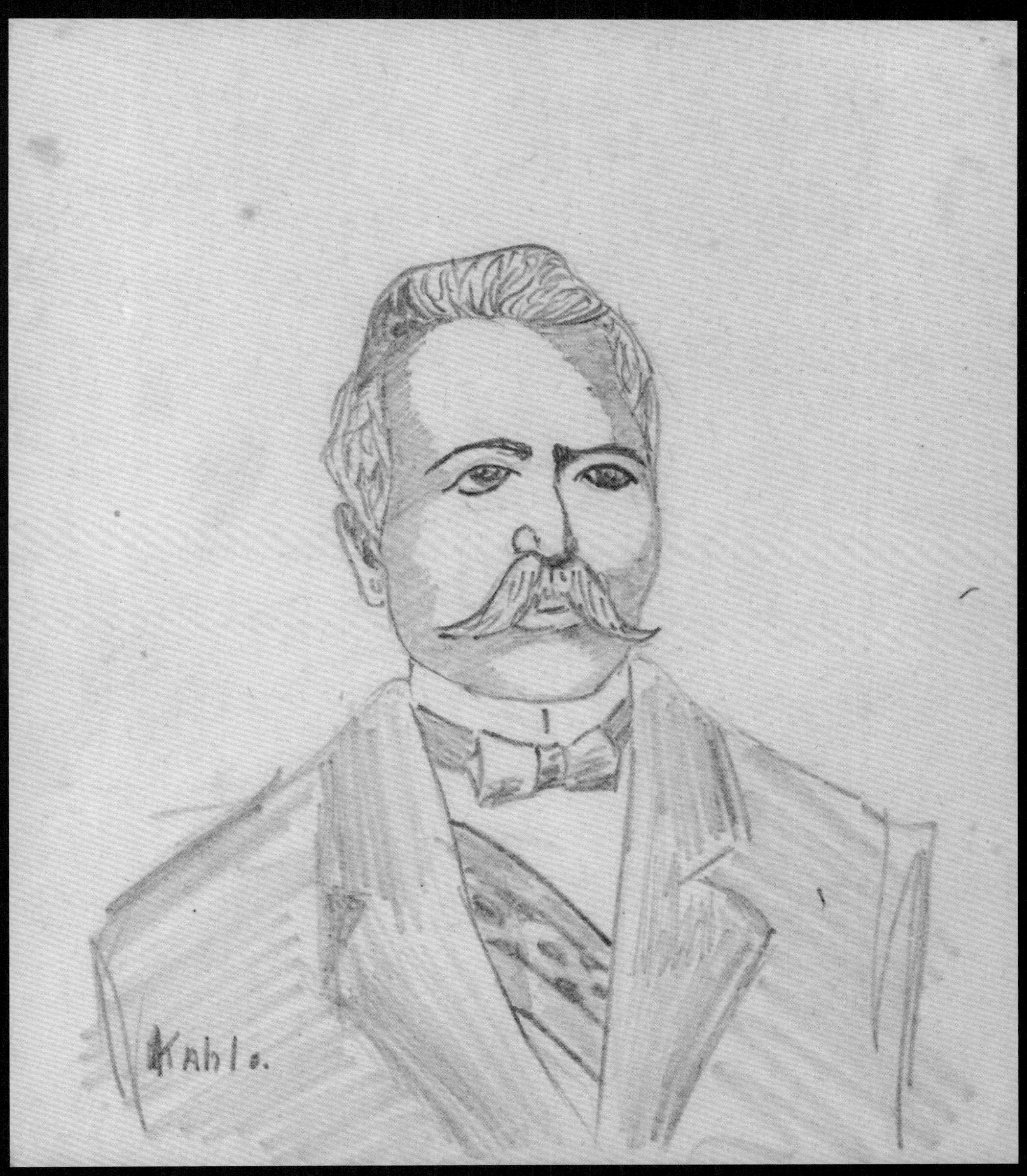

Frida Kahlo, *Porfirio Diaz*, 1925. Pencil on paper, 3.5 x 3.25 in. (9 x 8 cm)

During 1924–25, Frida worked in an engraving and printing workshop where she learned about several graphic techniques. These pencil portraits and the landscapes on the previous page were made during her formative years.

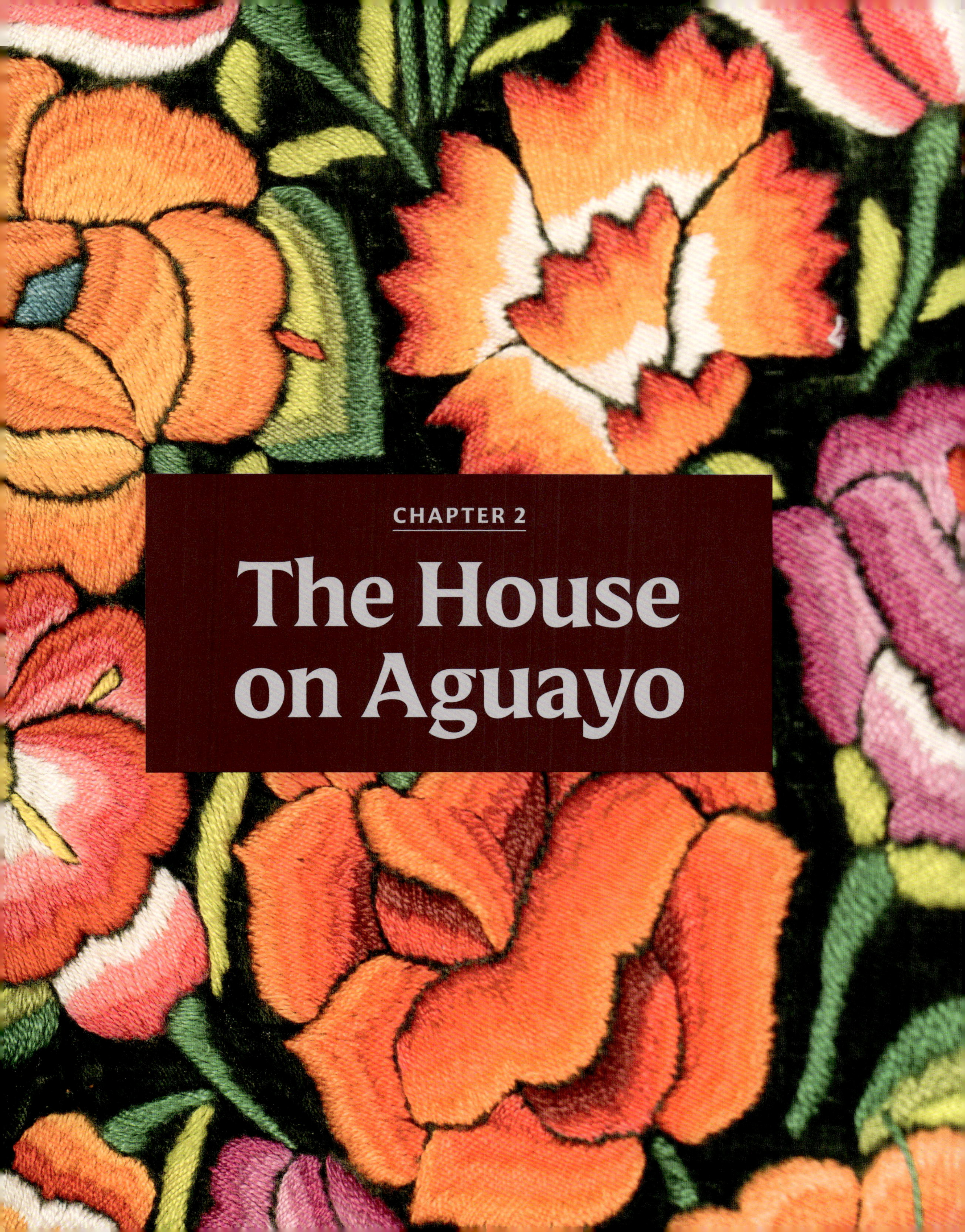

CHAPTER 2

The House on Aguayo

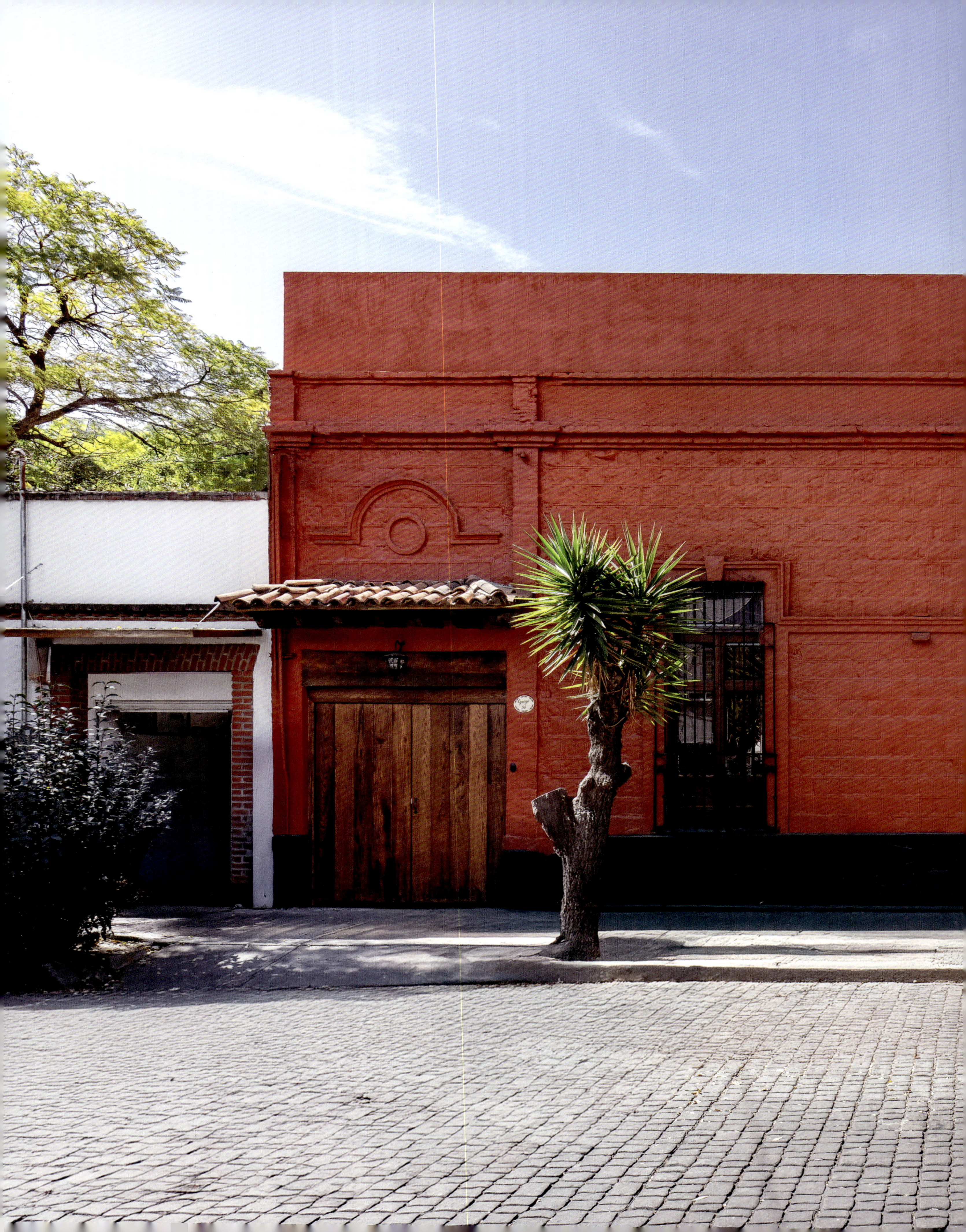

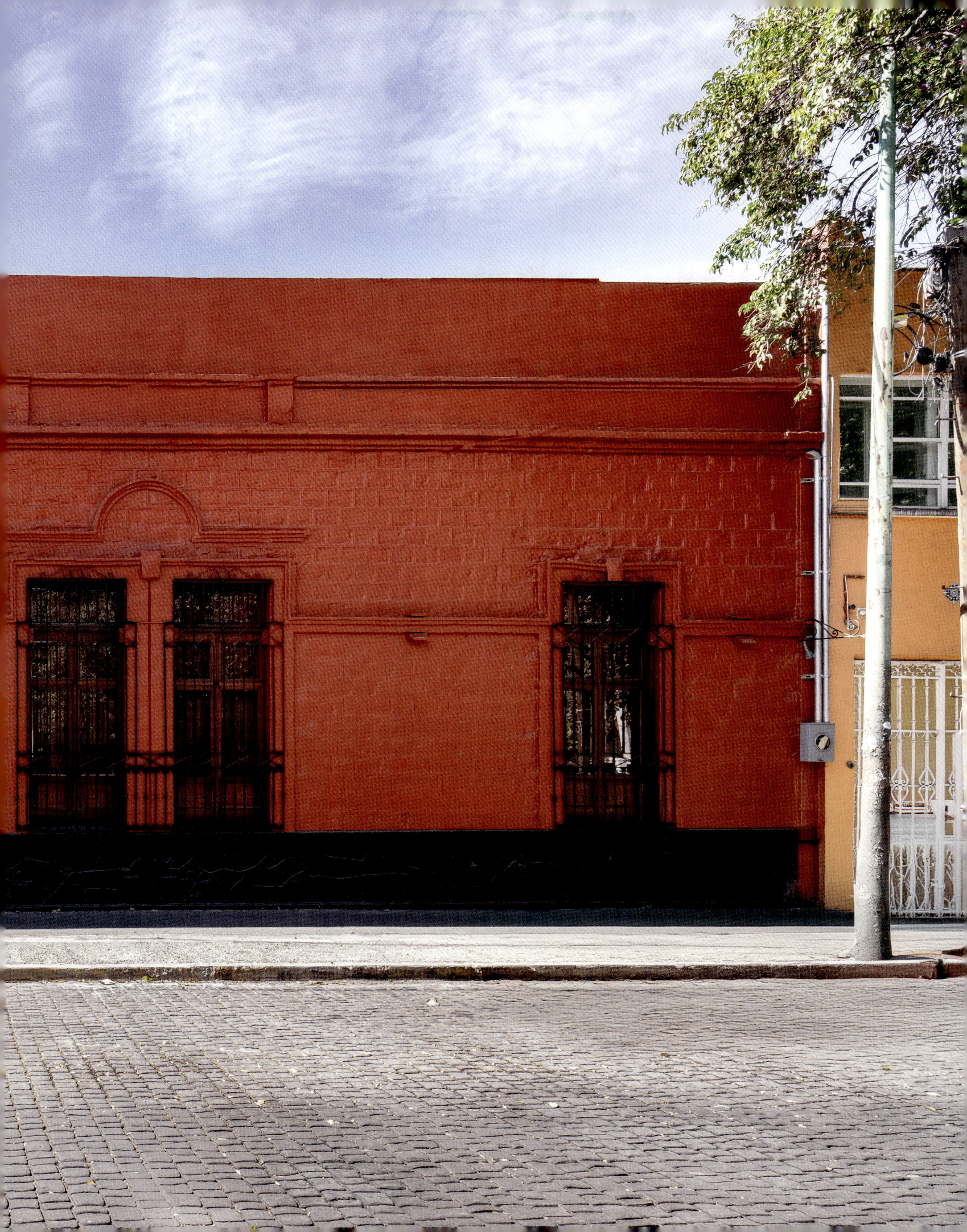

Mara Romeo Kahlo My great-grandmother, Matilde Calderón, bought the house at Aguayo 22 in Coyoacán in 1930—Casa Kahlo. While Frida was away in San Francisco, she sent her parents money to help renovate it. In 1931 they were able to move. Shortly before Matilde's death in September 1932, she sold it to her four daughters: Matilde, Adriana, Frida, and Cristina. Just a few years later, Frida bought it from her sisters, and eventually transferred ownership solely to Cristina, who needed her own place to live. Frida also lived in Casa Kahlo for a few years in the late 1940s, from around 1947 to 1950. The house has been at the center of the Kahlo family for nearly a century. It has been witness to our family stories. It has welcomed plenty of visitors, some of whom would eventually become like family. My grandmother Cristina sheltered Spanish and Cuban refugees here. Many of them became lifelong friends, and others, literally, family—Isolda, Frida's niece and Cristina's daughter, married a Spanish refugee (Julio Romeo del Valle). This house was the place where the charity Cristina founded called La Ayuda distributed food and other supplies to mothers in need. The kitchen was the focal point, as it is for many families. And it's the room in which Frida left a lasting homage to this beloved place with a mural, filled with beautiful trees and birds which were ever-present in the courtyard. Kahlos have been sharing their lives with each other in this place for 5 generations. It was a safe space in every sense of the word for the entire family, and very much for Frida. While her identity as a great painter and the wife of a well-known artist dominated Casa Azul, Frida the daughter, the sister, and the aunt is what shone through at Casa Kahlo. There you could find her singing while playing her guitar, or making bawdy jokes, or crying with her sisters. This house is a witness to who we really are as a family.

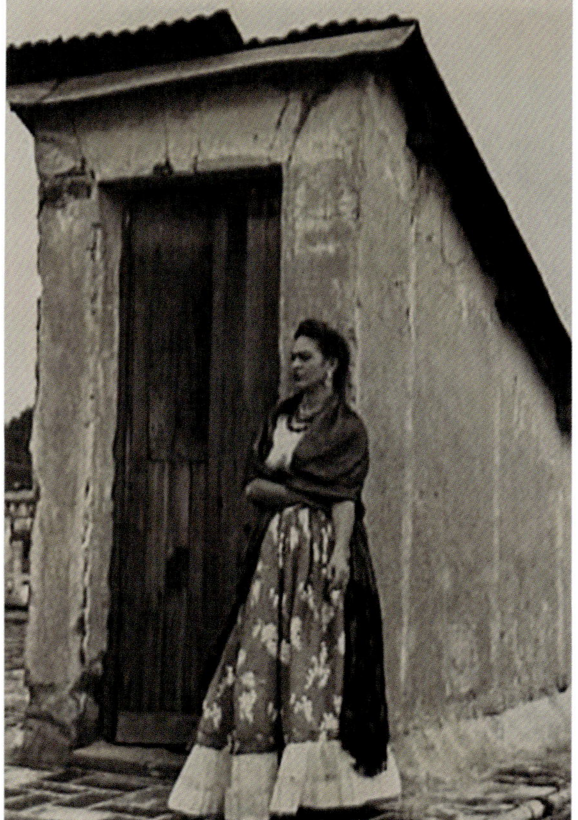

PREVIOUS SPREAD The facade of Casa Kahlo today, originally Aguayo 22 but in later years renumbered as Aguayo 54, Coyoacán, Mexico City. Despite having gone through many transformations over the last 100 years, the facade is largely unchanged since the Kahlo family purchased it. The house has served as the Kahlo family's home and sanctuary for generations.

TOP Cristina and Matilde Kahlo, Frida's sisters, in the corridor of Casa Kahlo, Coyoacán, ca. 1953

BOTTOM Frida on the roof of Casa Kahlo, Coyoacán, 1930. Photo by Lola Álvarez Bravo

OPPOSITE The entry corridor to Casa Kahlo, Coyoacán, today

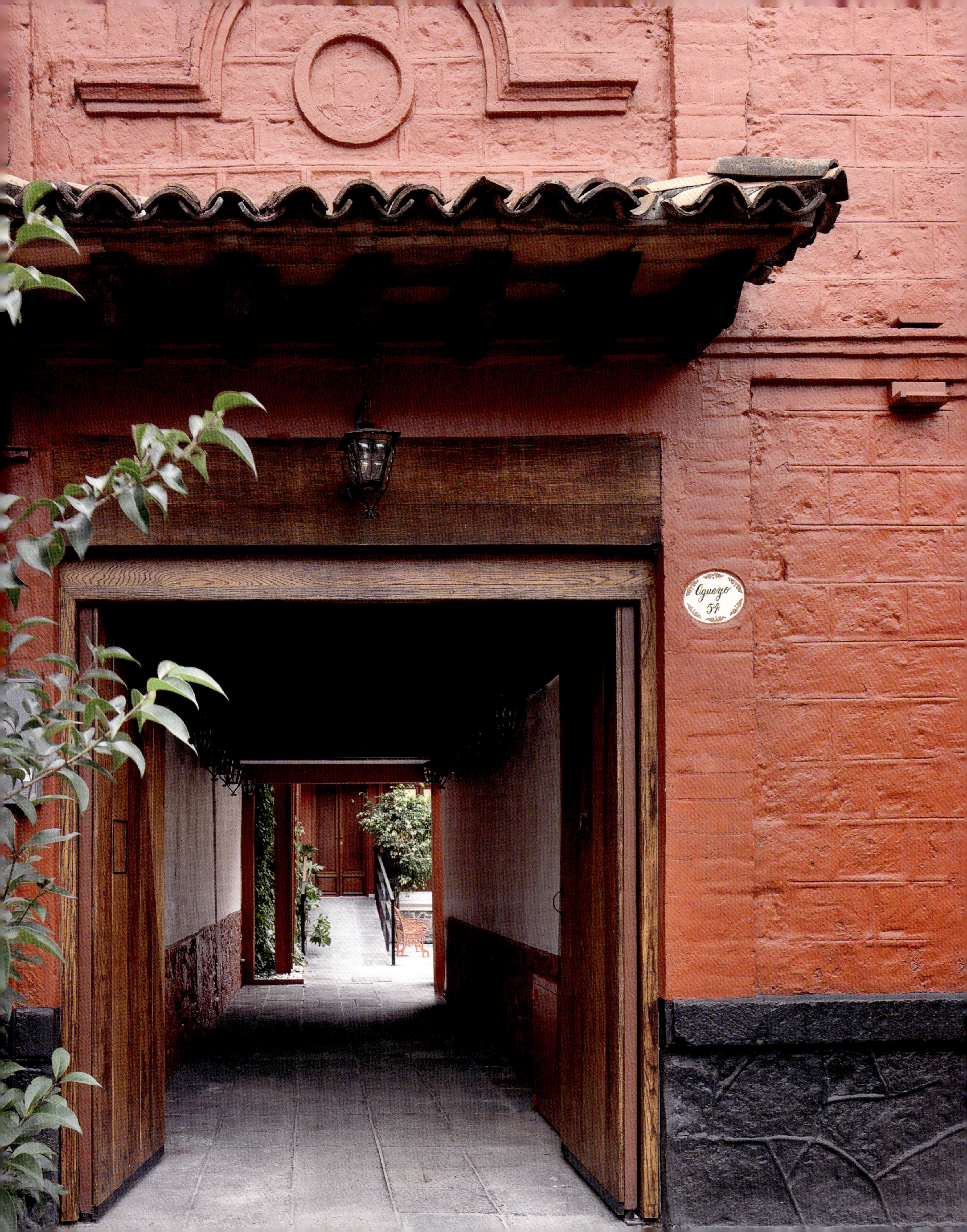
Aguayo
54

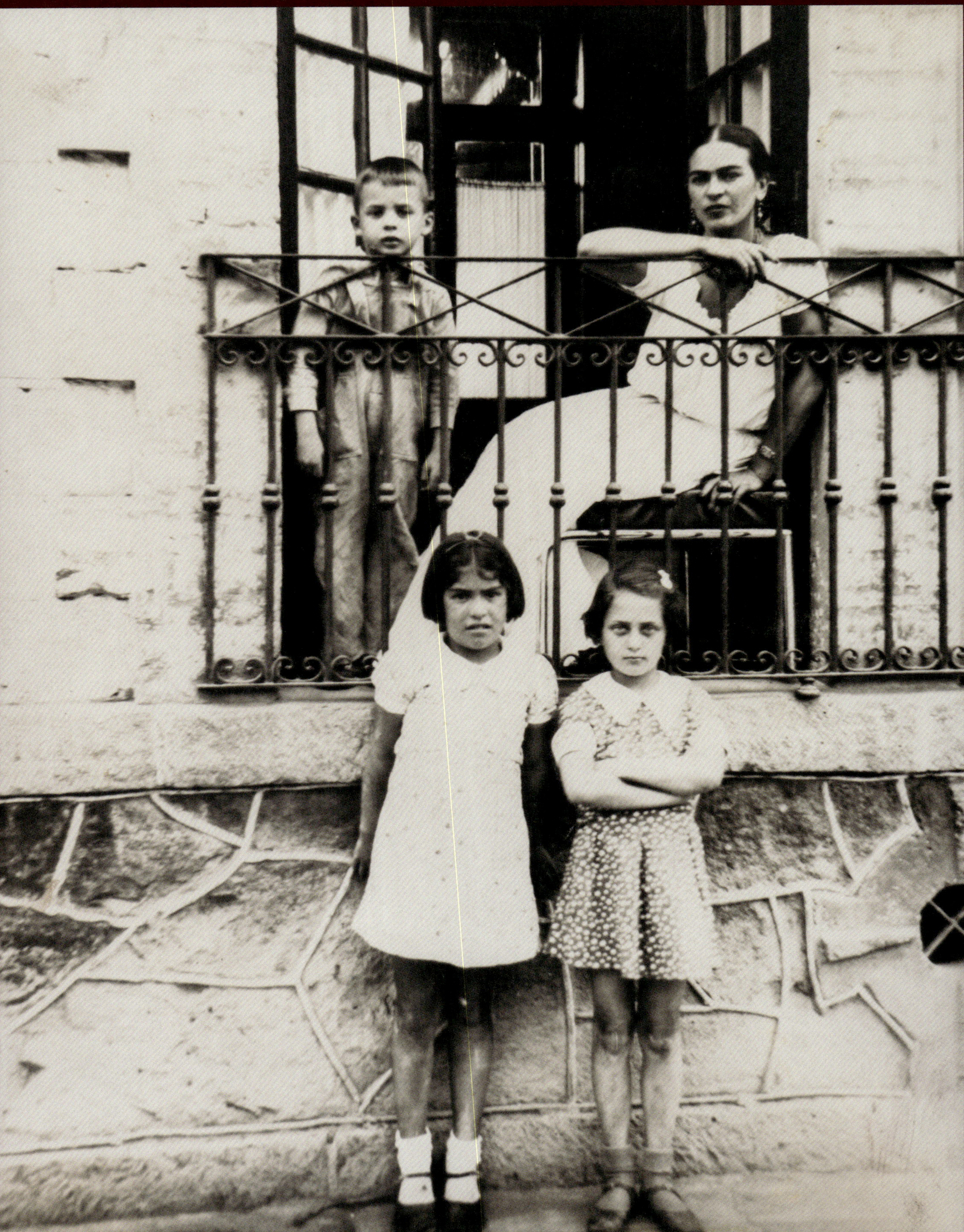

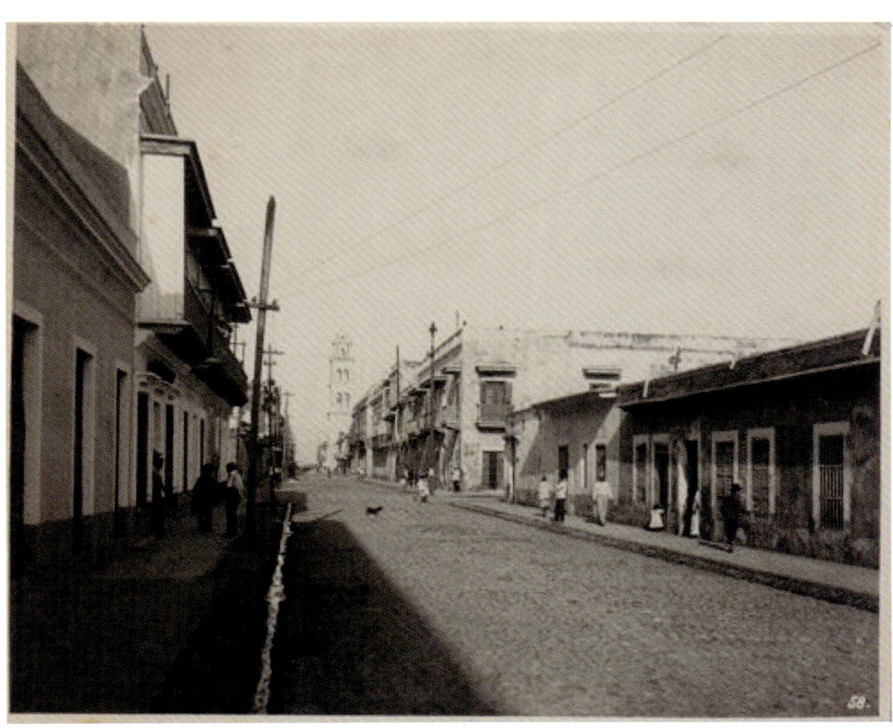

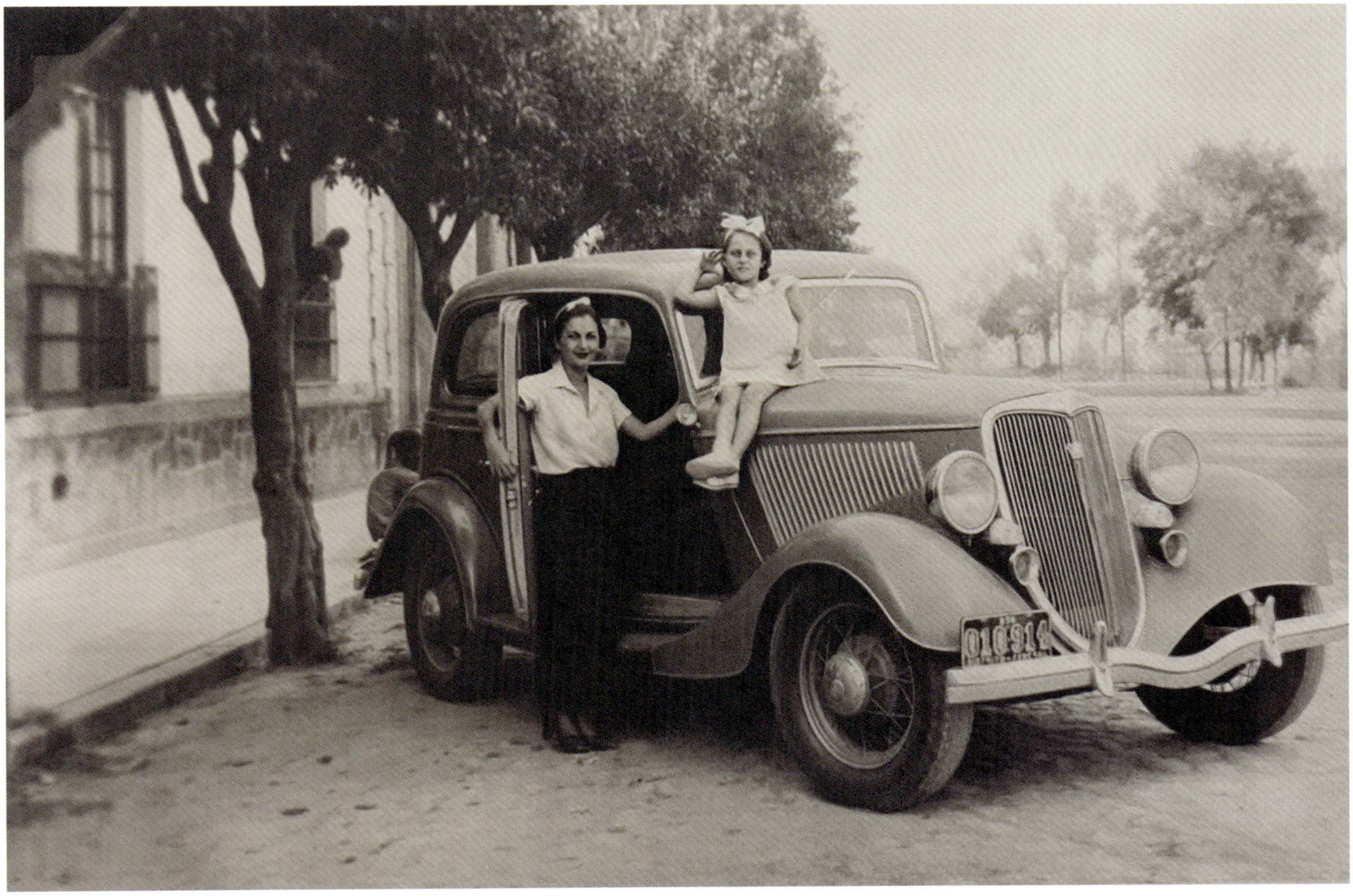

OPPOSITE Antonio Kahlo (Frida's nephew), Frida, Guadalupe Calderón (Frida's cousin) and Isolda Kahlo (Frida's niece) on the balcony at Casa Kahlo, Coyoacán, ca. 1936. Photo by Guillermo Kahlo

TOP A street in Coyoacán, ca. 1934

BOTTOM Cristina and her daughter Isolda outside Casa Kahlo, Coyoacán, ca. 1934

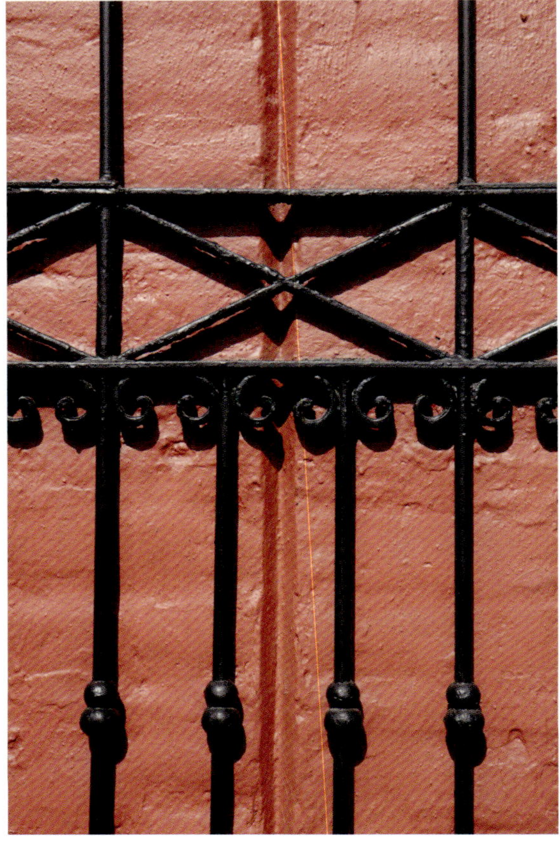

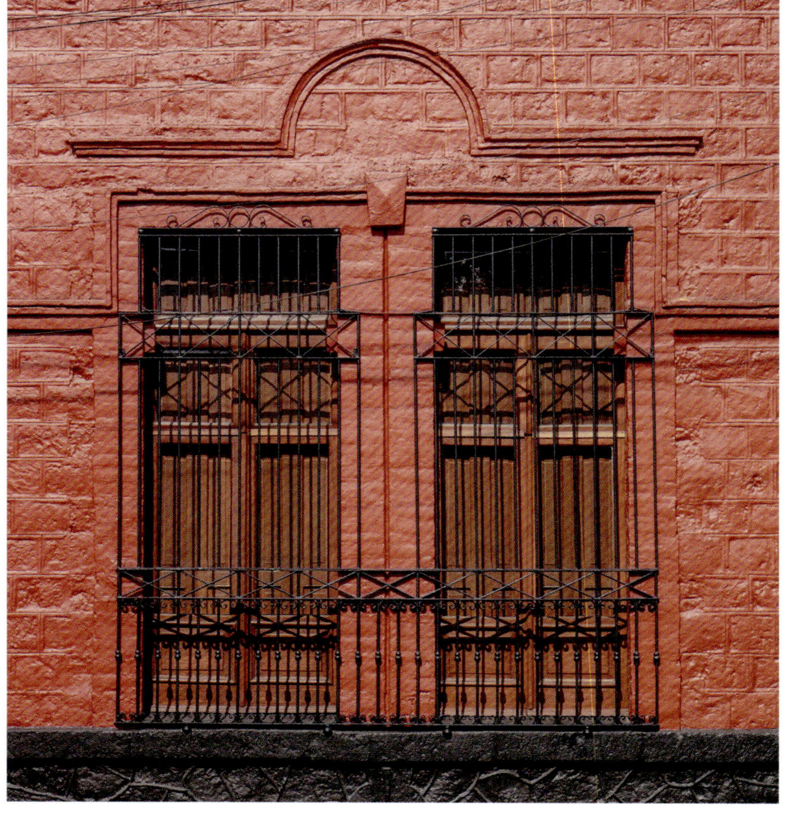

ABOVE AND OPPOSITE Details of Casa Kahlo, Coyoacán, today

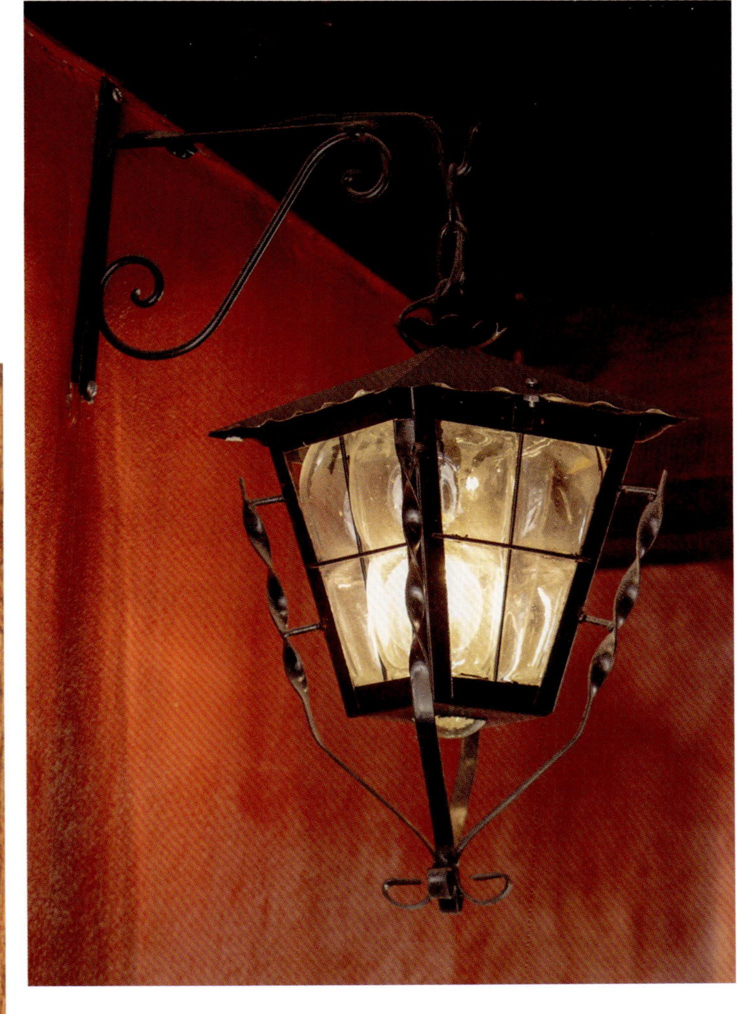

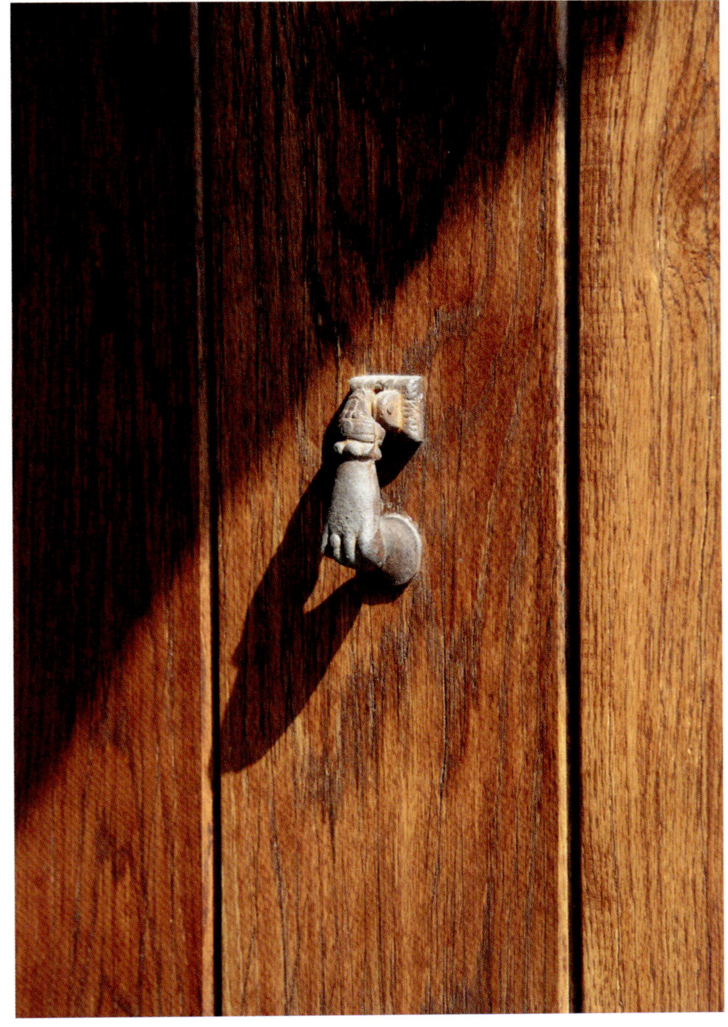

FOLLOWING SPREADS Views of the courtyard, Casa Kahlo, Coyoacán, today

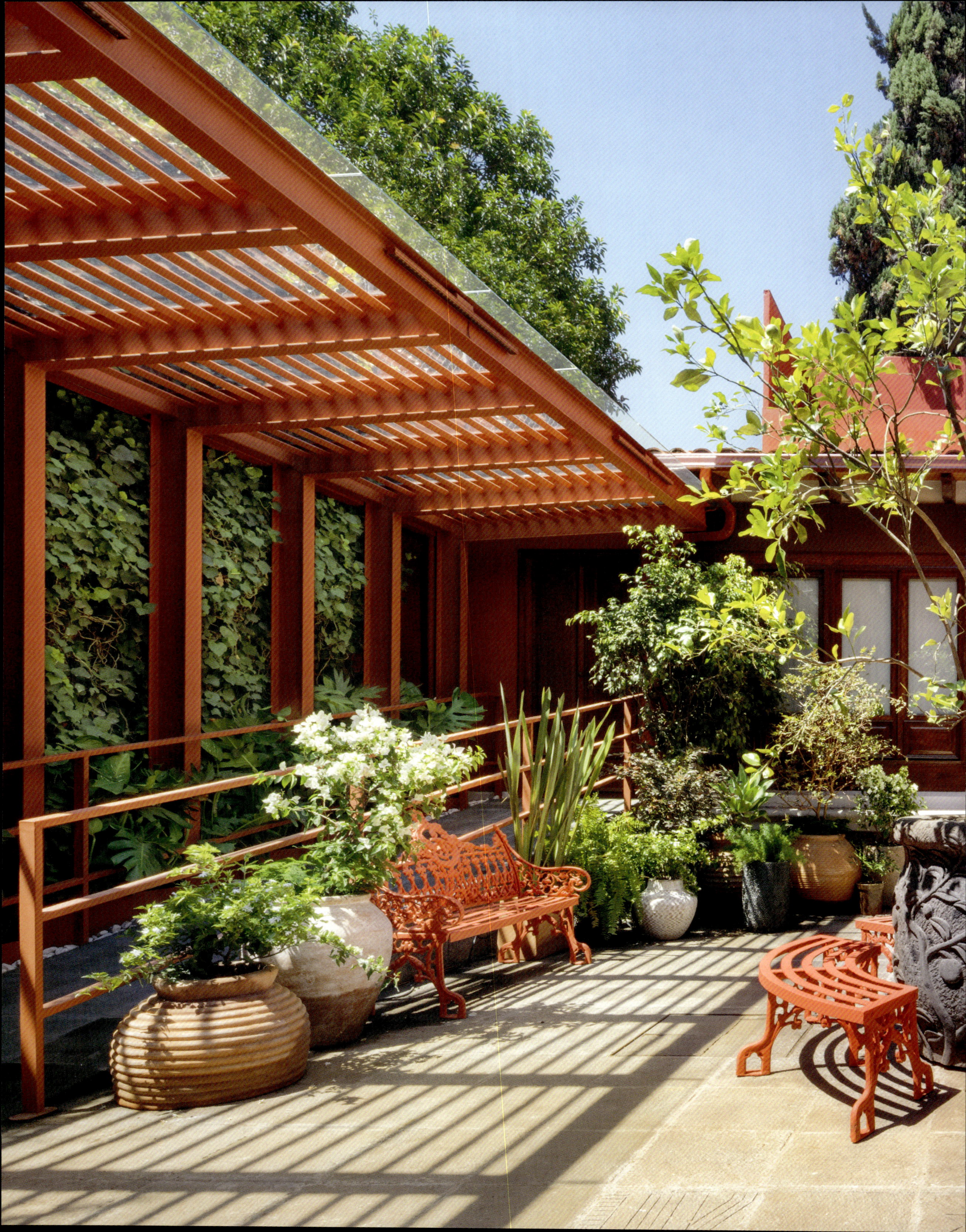

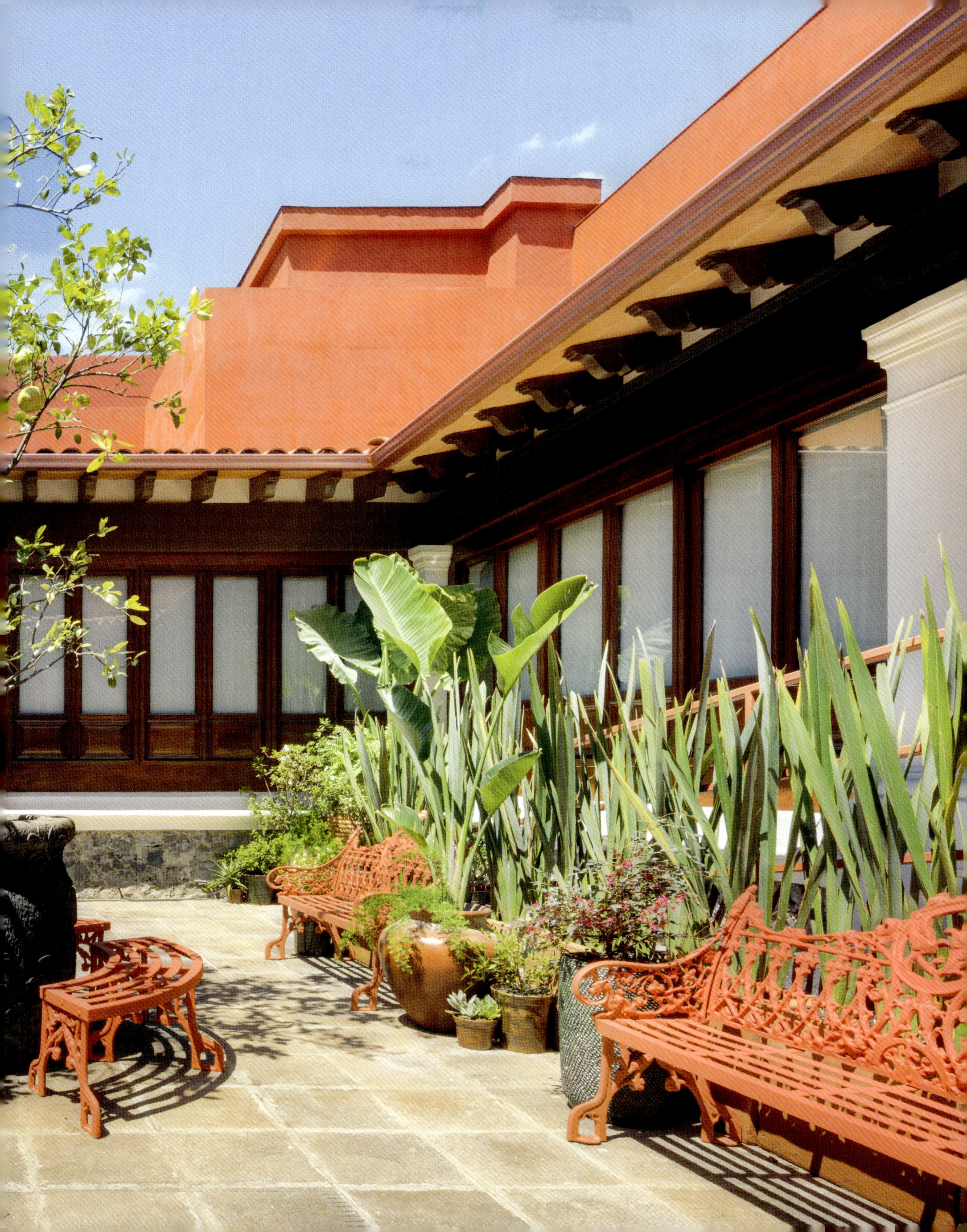

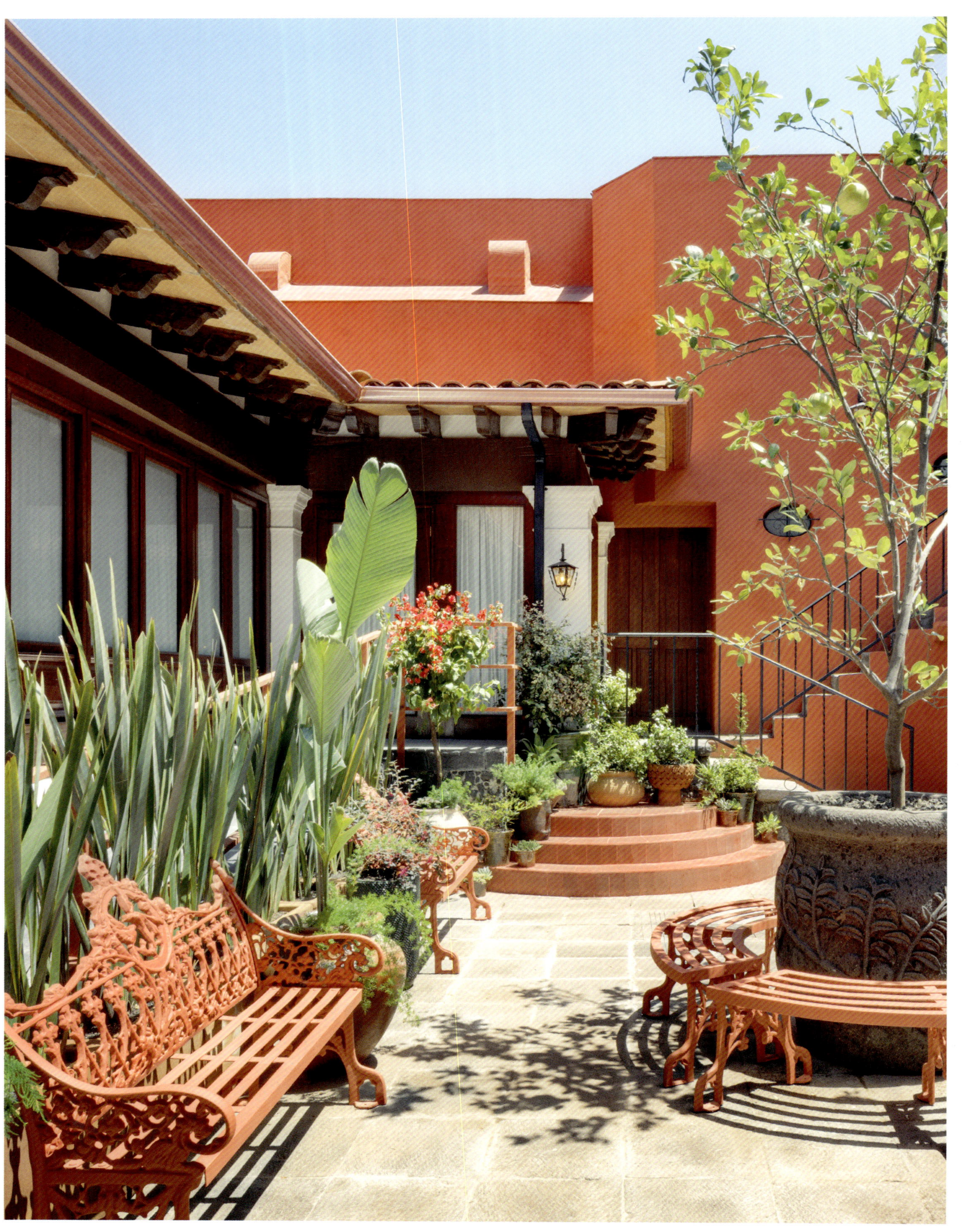

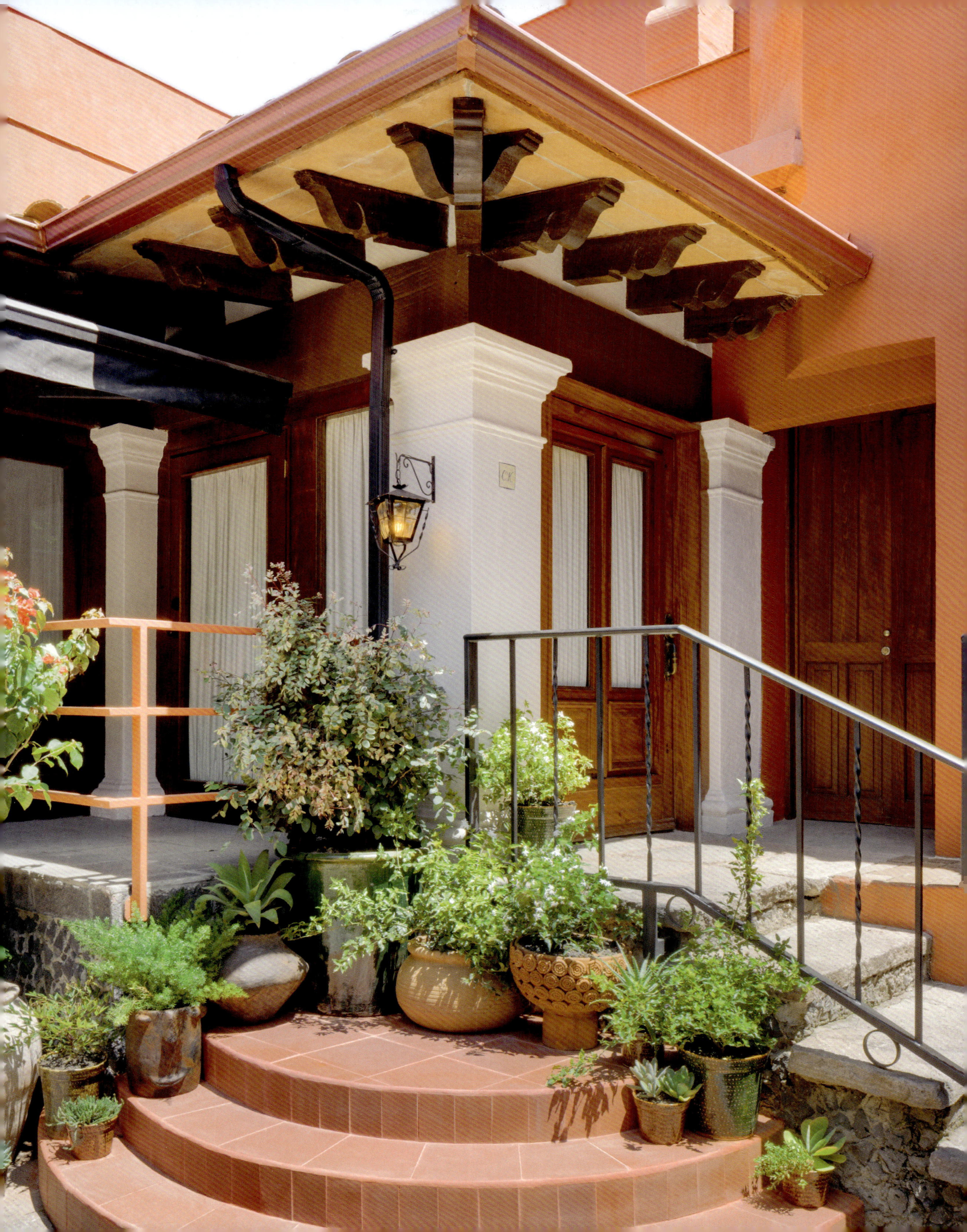

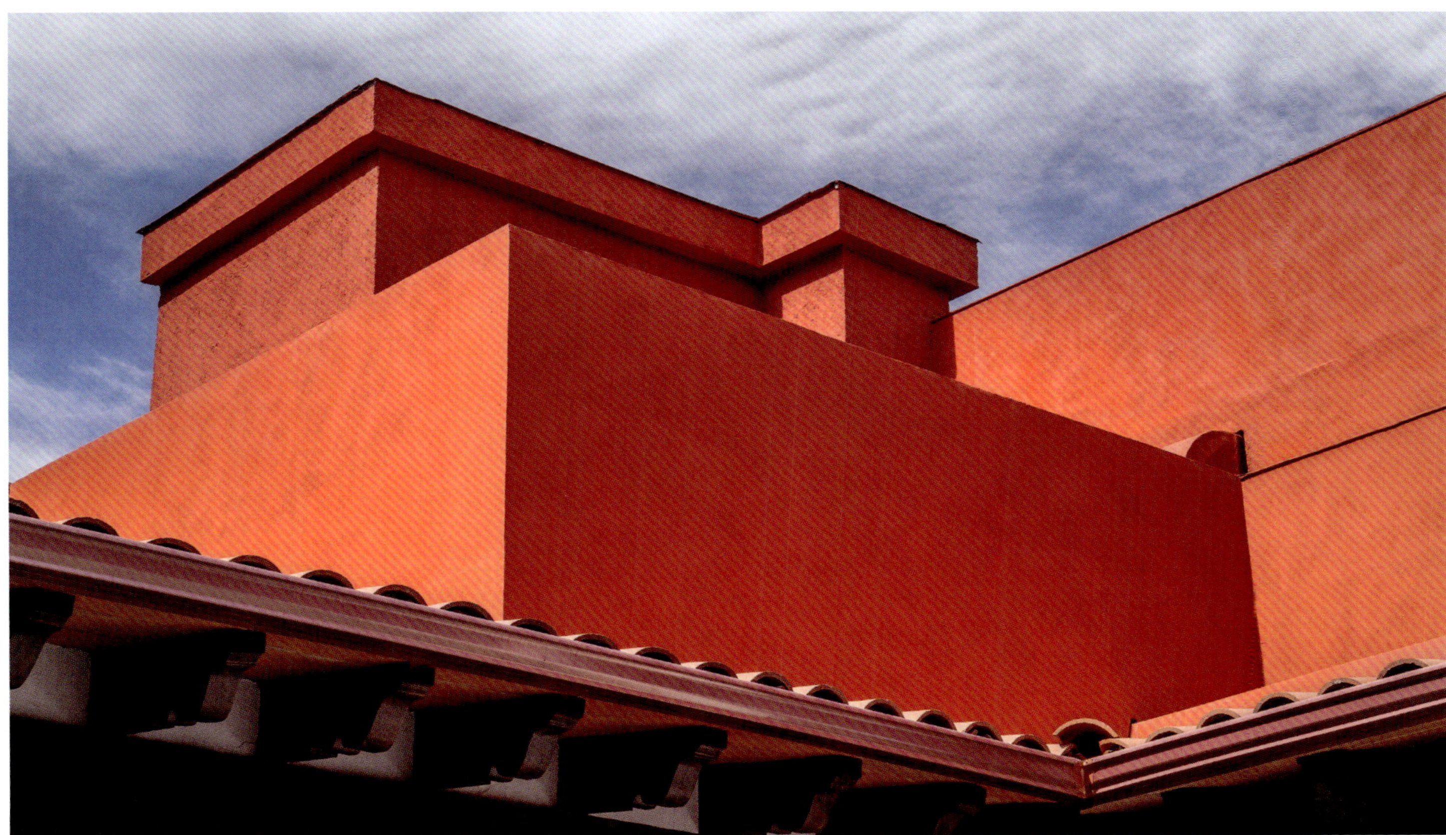

Frida Hentschel Frida and Diego Rivera married in 1929 and lived with the Kahlo clan in what was then the family house, Casa Azul. Not long after, the newlyweds moved to Reforma, in Mexico City's center. They only stayed there for a couple of months; family lore has it that Frida missed her family too much and insisted they be closer to home. Diego was commissioned to paint several murals in various cities in the United States—they traveled to San Francisco, New York, and Detroit. When they returned to Mexico in 1932, she moved back into Casa Azul. Prior to the couple returning home, Frida's parents Matilde and Guillermo decided they did not want to share a house anymore, so they bought Casa Kahlo.

At the time, Cristina and her children were also living in Casa Azul but they eventually moved to Casa Kahlo in the late 1930s, when my grandmother Isolda became a "señorita" (colloquial for "coming of age"). Around 1936, Frida bought Casa Kahlo for a symbolic sum and then resold it to Cristina for the same amount in 1940. Every weekend, the sisters (and their father, Guillermo, while he was alive) gathered for family get-togethers. These gatherings lasted for hours, and always with copious amounts of food. And even though Casa Kahlo was just a few blocks from Casa Azul, it was the house at Aguayo 22 that they chose.

When Frida lived here, she was already a registered teacher at the school for Painting and Sculpture, known as La Esmeralda, in Coyoacán. As a result, many artists and students came to the house, and they became friends with Cristina and her daughter Isolda. The house on Aguayo was seen as the Kahlo family home base. Everyone who lived or spent time here put something into the house, so there are many embedded memories. Matilde and Guillermo remodeled the house before moving in, then later Cristina renovated it, and then later still my grandmother Isolda and my mother Mara changed it yet again. You can still feel the spirit of everyone who lived here. Guillermo stayed in the house for a time after his wife died, but then moved in with his daughter Adriana until his death in 1941.

Casa Azul was frozen in time when Frida died. Casa Kahlo has a very different energy, since successive generations of the family have lived here and kept growing its legacy. This house feels alive.

OPPOSITE AND ABOVE Details of roofline and interior courtyard, Casa Kahlo, Coyoacán, today

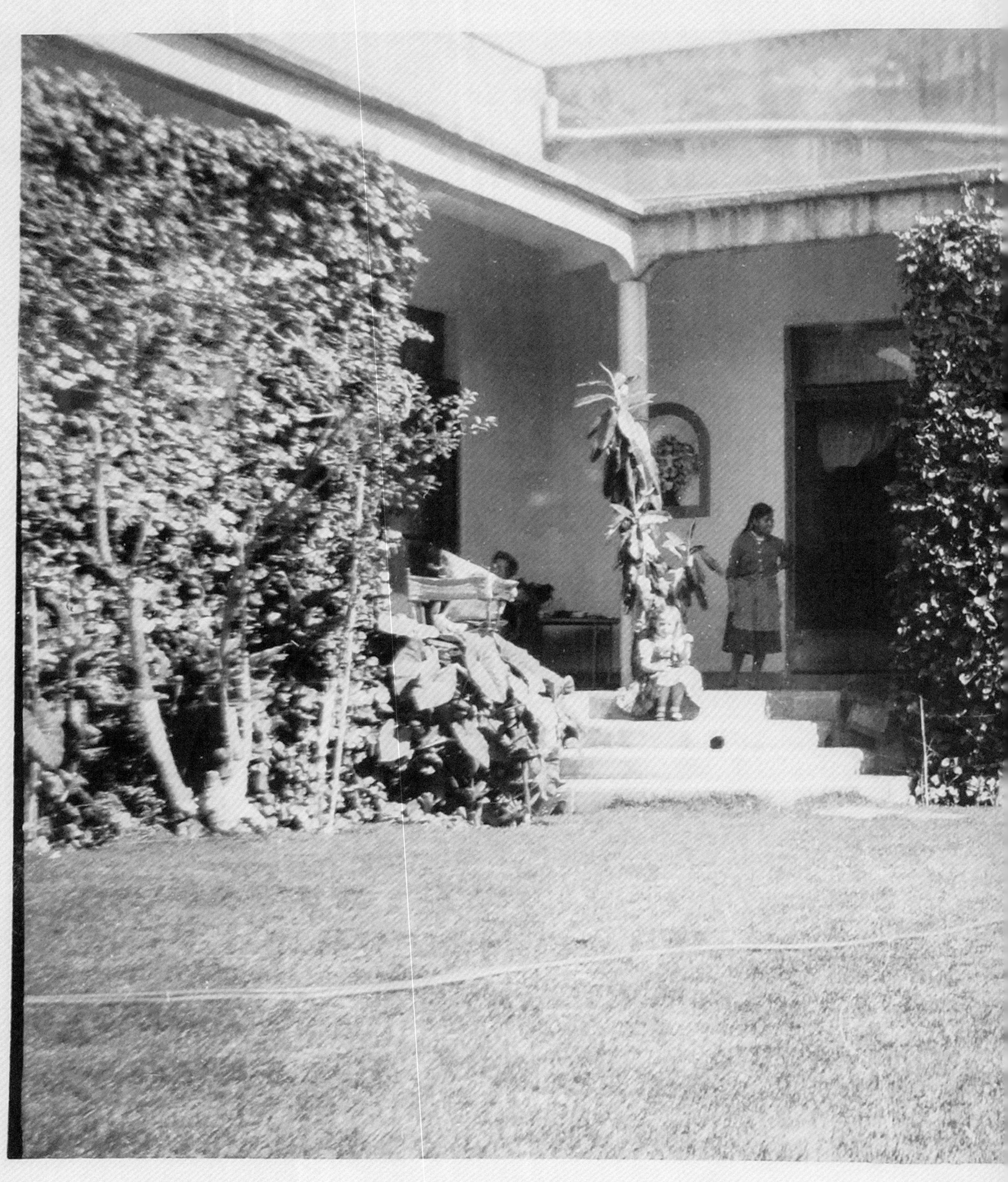

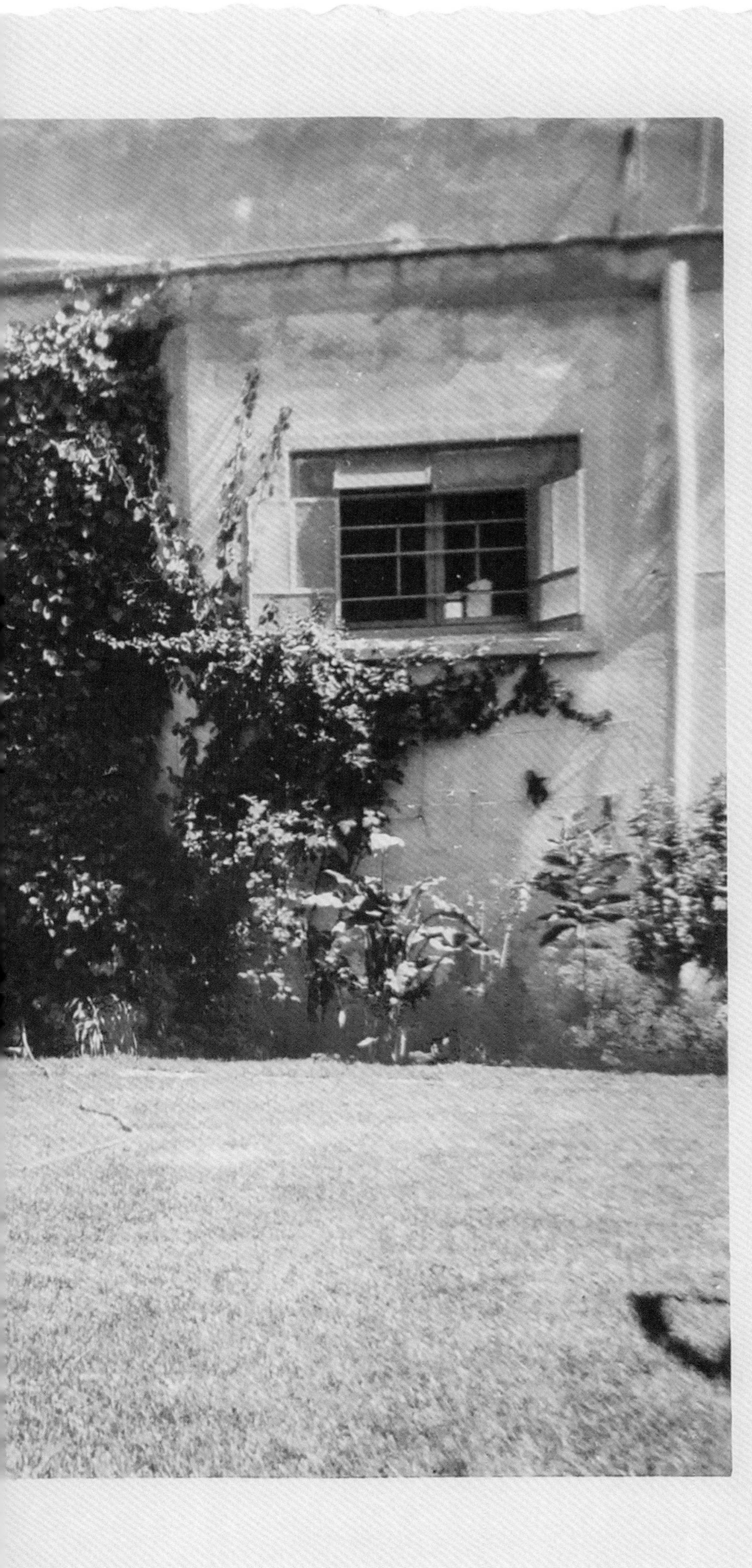

Mara de Anda When Cristina, Frida's sister, moved into the house she added a bathroom and a loft to one of the bedrooms (which used to be Guillermo's studio). And when my grandmother, Isolda, lived there, she made some additional changes: she closed in the terrace and moved the entrance stairs, and she added an outside kitchen. Eventually she added a bedroom outside and another over the garage, which she rented out for extra income.

When my mother Mara and my siblings lived there, the Kahlo Family Estate offices were located there, and my mother created a separate entrance to access them. She also added a new wing with two bedrooms. Every inhabitant of the house left their mark. This house has sustained every generation who has lived here. We have always felt safe here.

Mara Romeo Kahlo, Frida's grandniece and co-author of this volume, sitting on the stairs in the courtyard at Casa Kahlo, Coyoacán, ca. 1957. After Frida's parents' death, Casa Kahlo went to her sister Cristina. She lived and raised her children Antonio and Isolda there until her death in 1964.

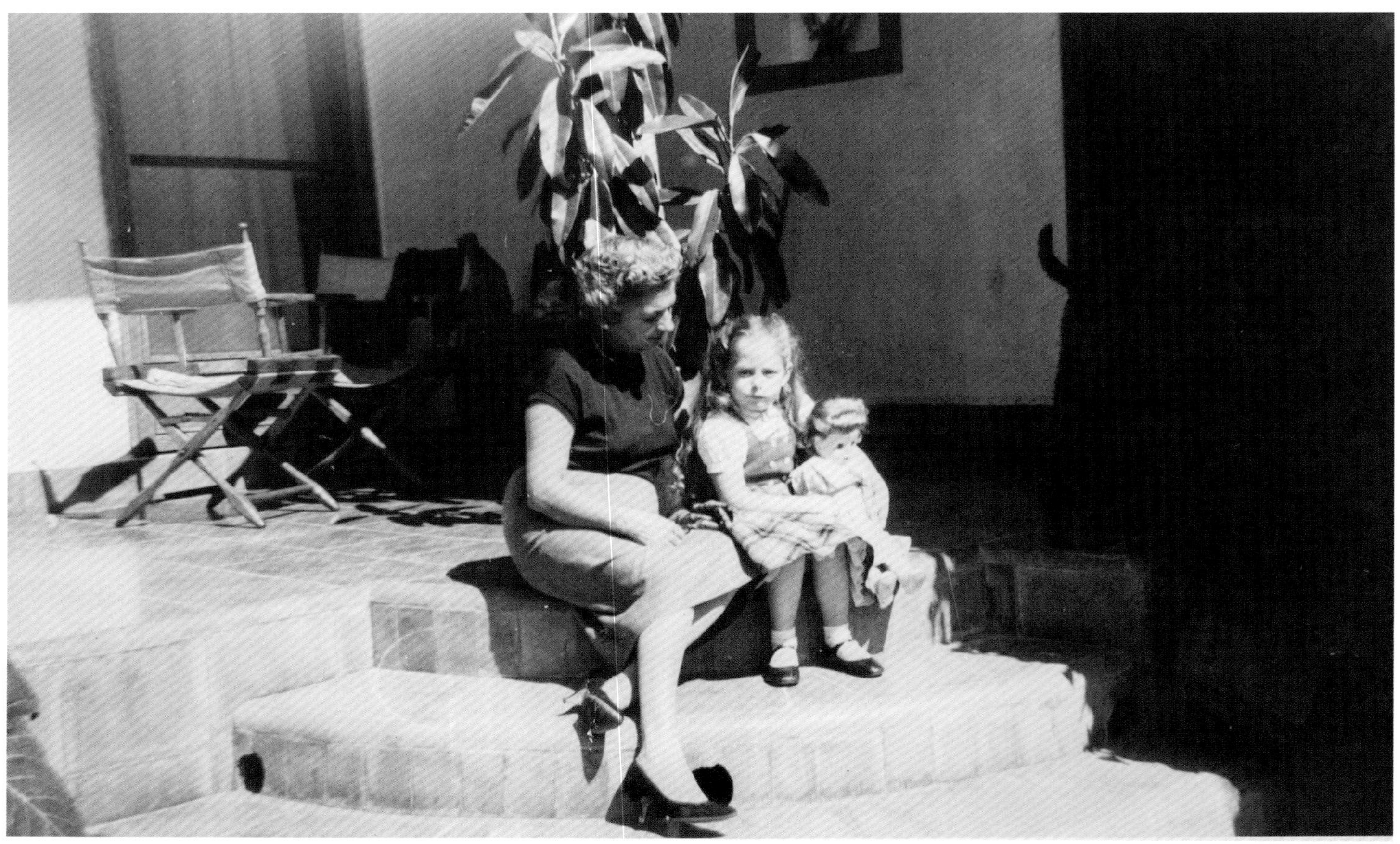

Frida Hentschel Our mom Mara, Frida's grandniece, took her first steps in the house's garden. When Cristina passed away, my grandmother Isolda, who inherited the house, moved in along with my mother, who was then 11. When Isolda passed away in 2007 at the age of 75, my mother, my brother Diego, and I moved in. We lived there until 2015, and my mother lived on her own at Casa Kahlo until February 2023. While my grandmother Isolda was a hoarder, my mom is the archivist. She meticulously kept records of all the personal effects and ephemera—mountains of material so rich with history. At the point when she had inventoried over 2,000 items, she decided it was time to share it with the world. It was a momentous decision but one that made sense—it was time to open the house to the public. As Frida's heirs, we feel compelled to tell the stories and reveal the secrets that this house has kept for almost a century.

Mara Romeo Kahlo When Porfirio Díaz, the president of Mexico, was forced out of office, setting off the Mexican Revolution, my great-grandfather Guillermo lost his biggest client. A pioneer of industrial photography in Mexico, he slowly ran out of money. He was also paying for Frida's many operations which put additional financial strain on the family. He was forced to mortgage Casa Azul. When Frida married Diego, he paid off the mortgage and put the house under Frida's name as a wedding gift. Eventually, in 1930, Matilde bought Casa Kahlo. The exact details are unknown, but part of the mortgage, savings, and inheritance from Matilde's family allowed them to buy the house on Aguayo. It was a very rudimentary house, which needed further investment for improvements, which Frida helped with and that took over a year.

ABOVE Cristina and her granddaughter (and Frida's grandniece) Mara Romeo Kahlo, at Casa Kahlo, Coyoacán, ca. 1957. Mara visited her grandmother's house almost daily—and in fact took her first steps in the yard of Casa Kahlo. Animals, especially dogs, were always present in the family home.

OPPOSITE Cristina and Mara at Casa Kahlo, Coyoacán, ca. 1959

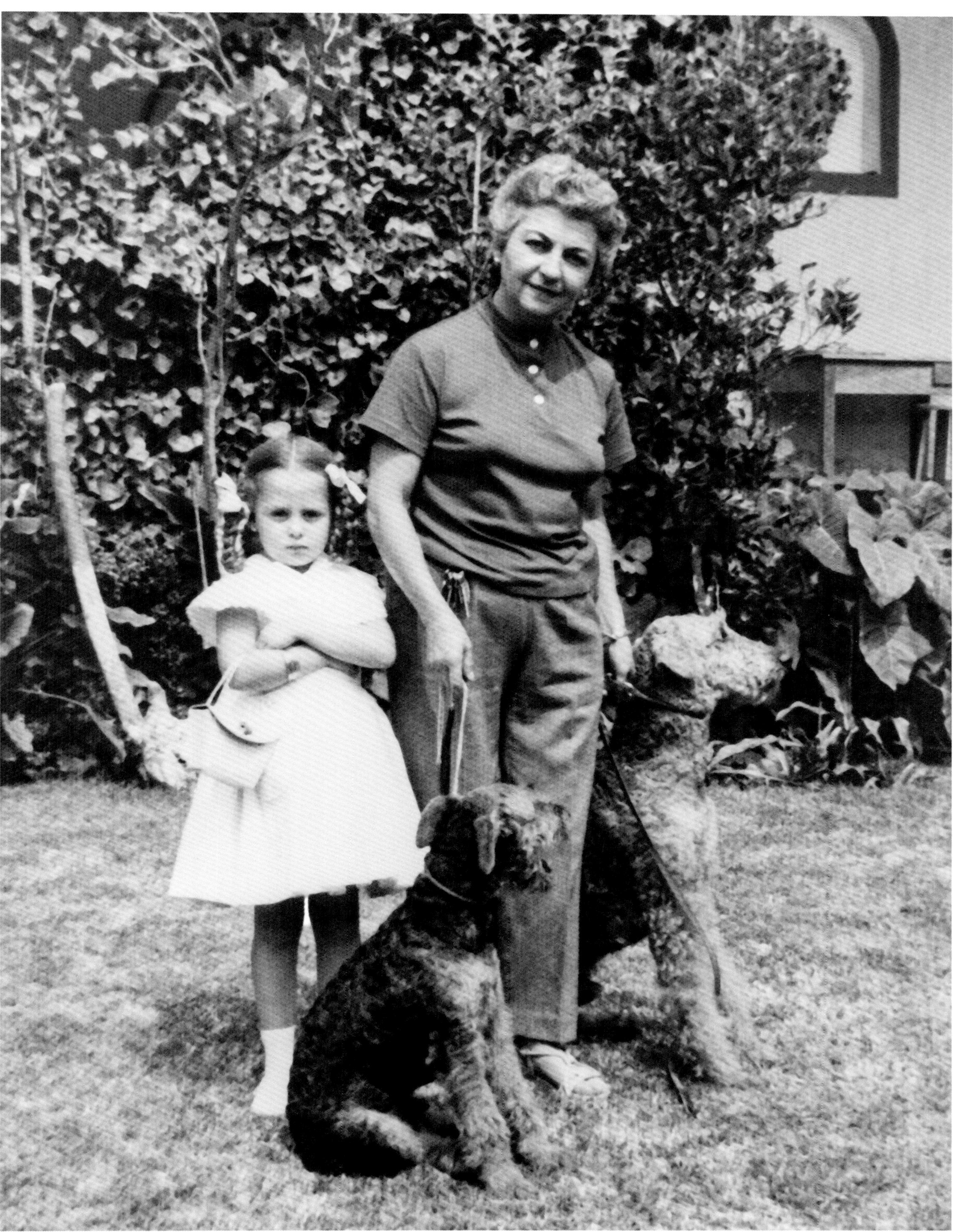

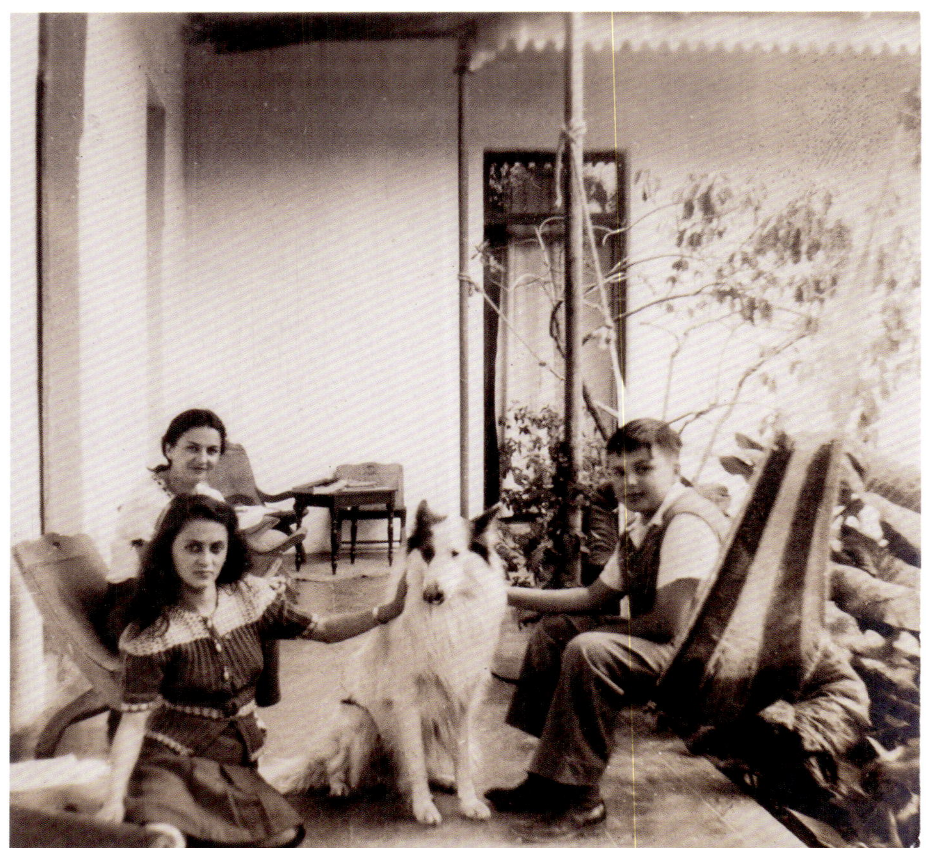

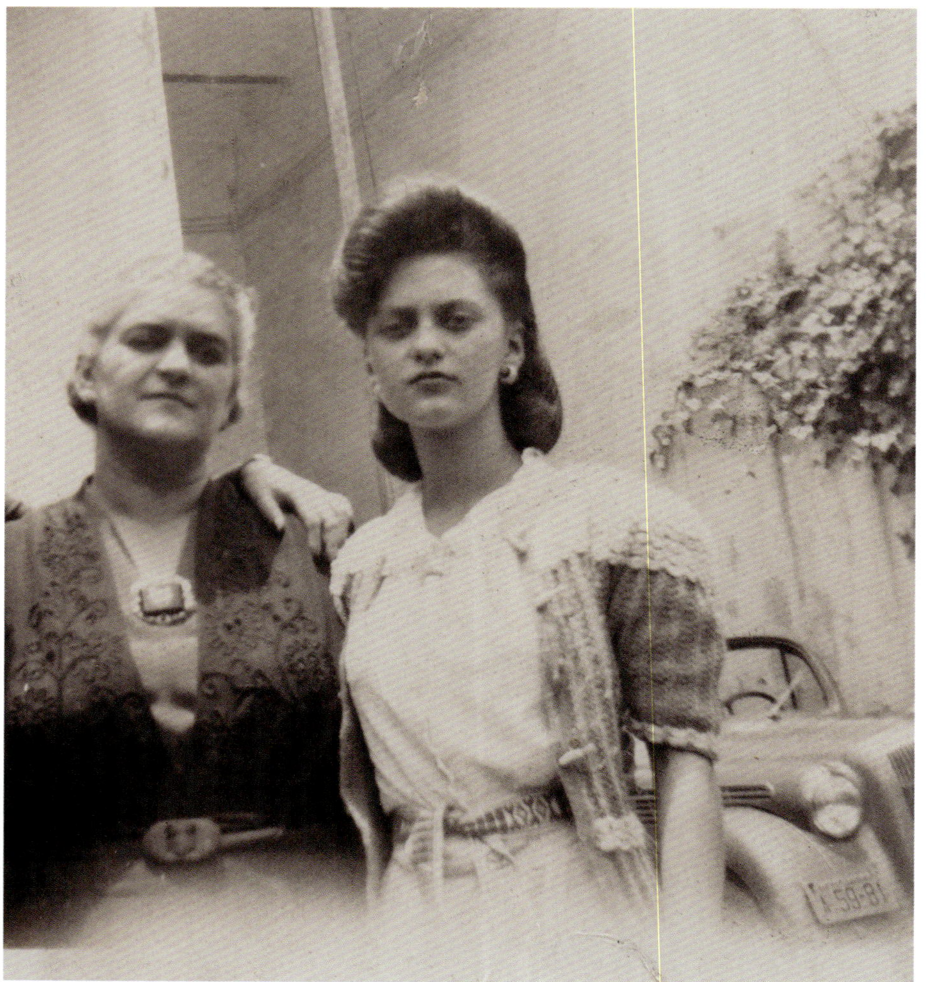

Living in the house at Aguayo, I felt like the spirits protected me. In Mexico there are so many robberies, but unbelievably we never experienced them at Casa Kahlo. On several occasions the door to the house was left open the entire night by mistake, but nobody entered the house. I really felt that Frida and my grandmother Cristina were there—you could almost feel and see them.

TOP Cristina, Isolda, and Antonio at Casa Kahlo, Coyoacán, ca. 1945

BOTTOM Adriana, Frida's sister, and Isolda at Casa Kahlo, Coyoacán, ca. 1948

OPPOSITE Frida on the porch at Casa Kahlo, Coyoacán, ca. 1948. After one of her most difficult surgeries, Frida convalesced at Casa Kahlo, under the care of her sisters. And in the late 1940s, Frida lived at Casa Kahlo for several years.

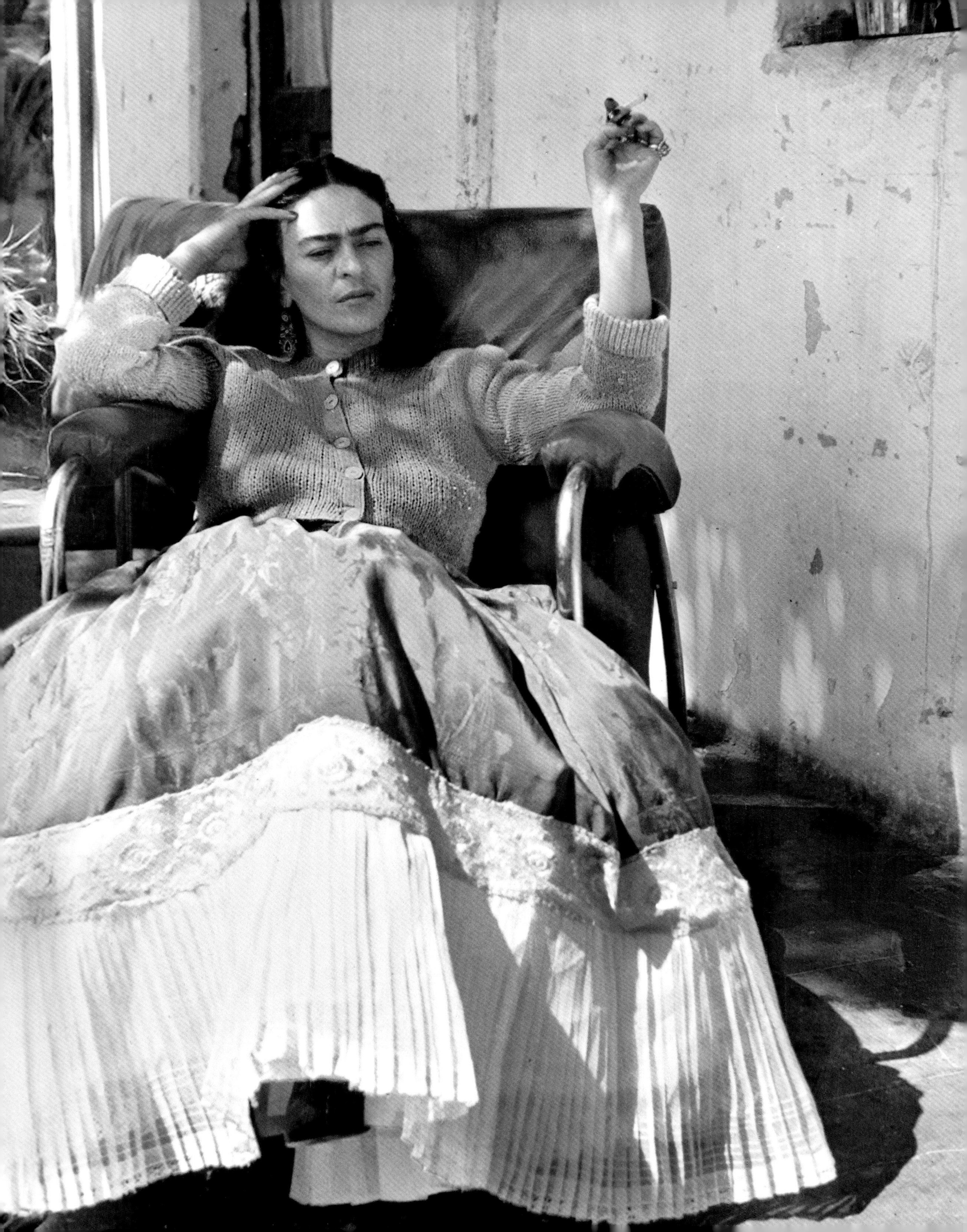

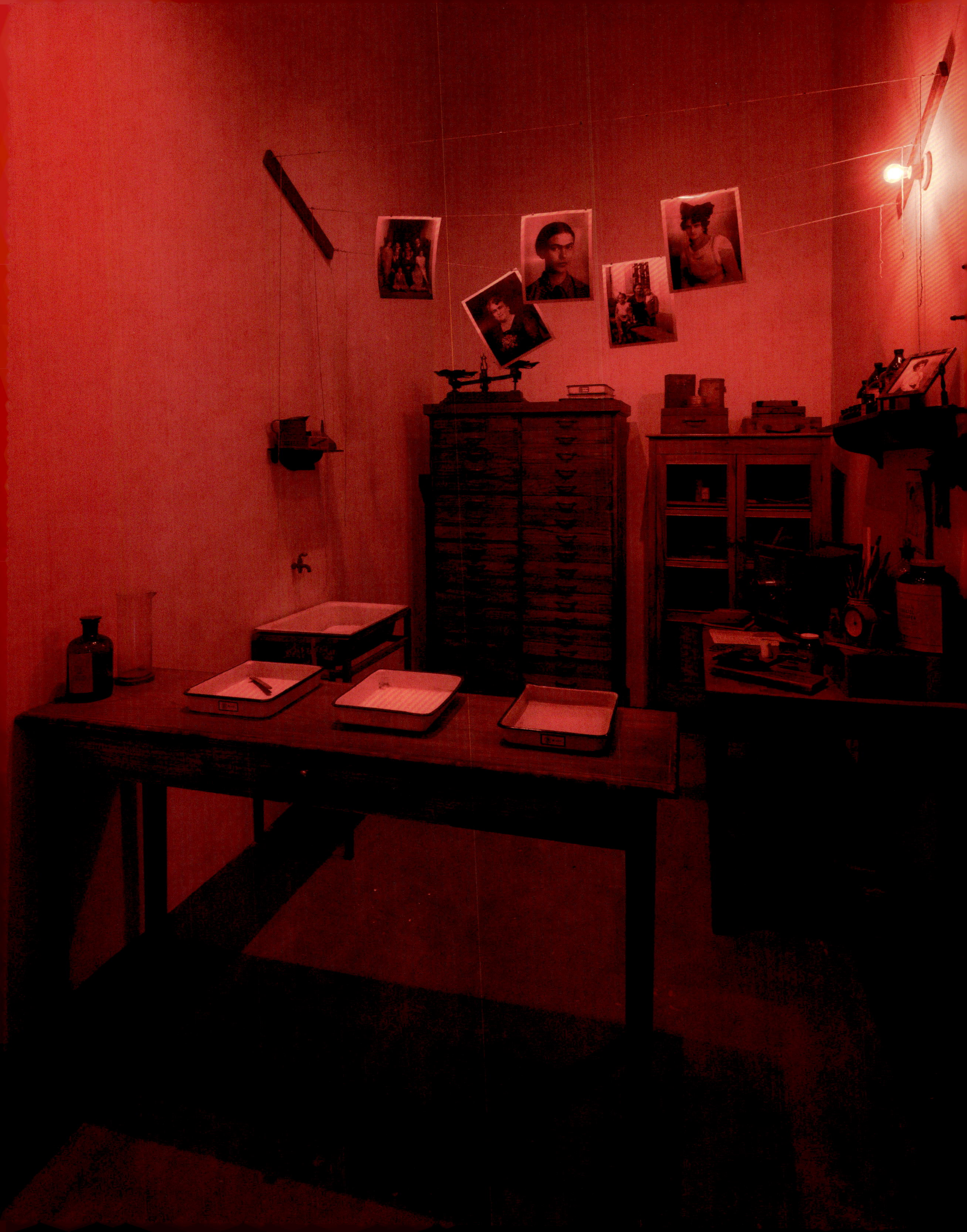

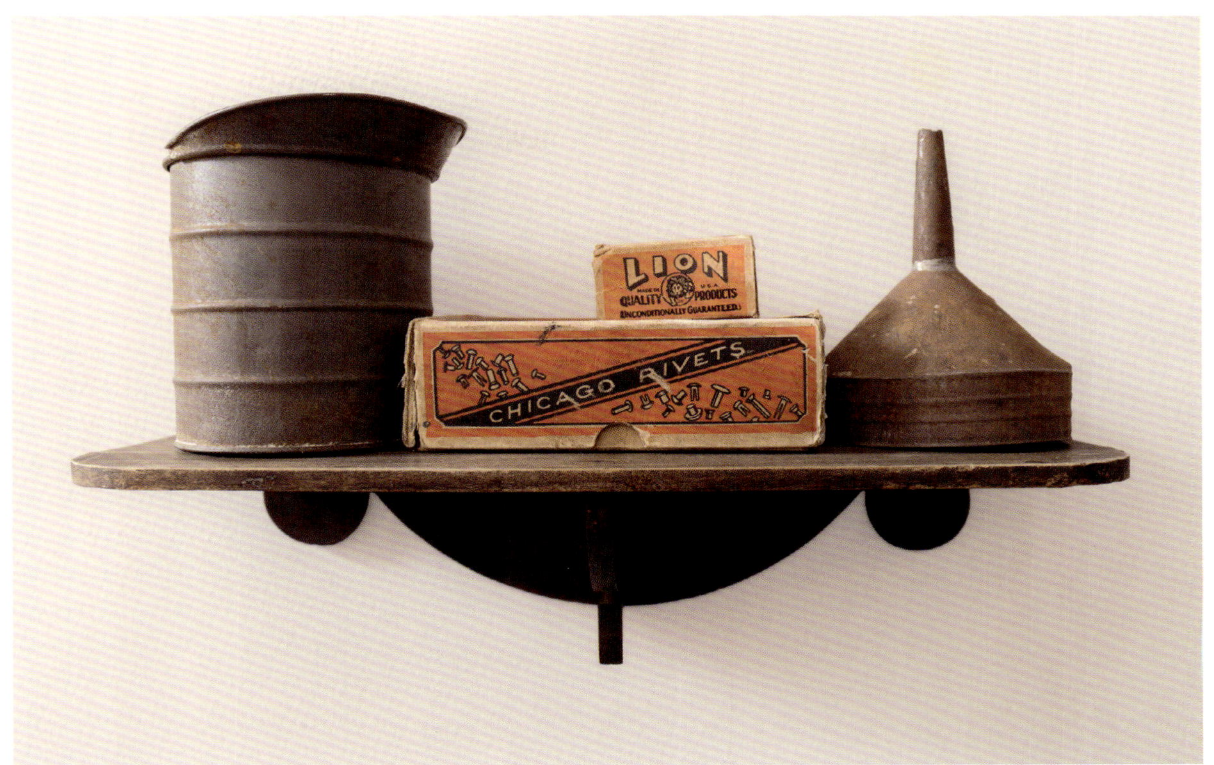

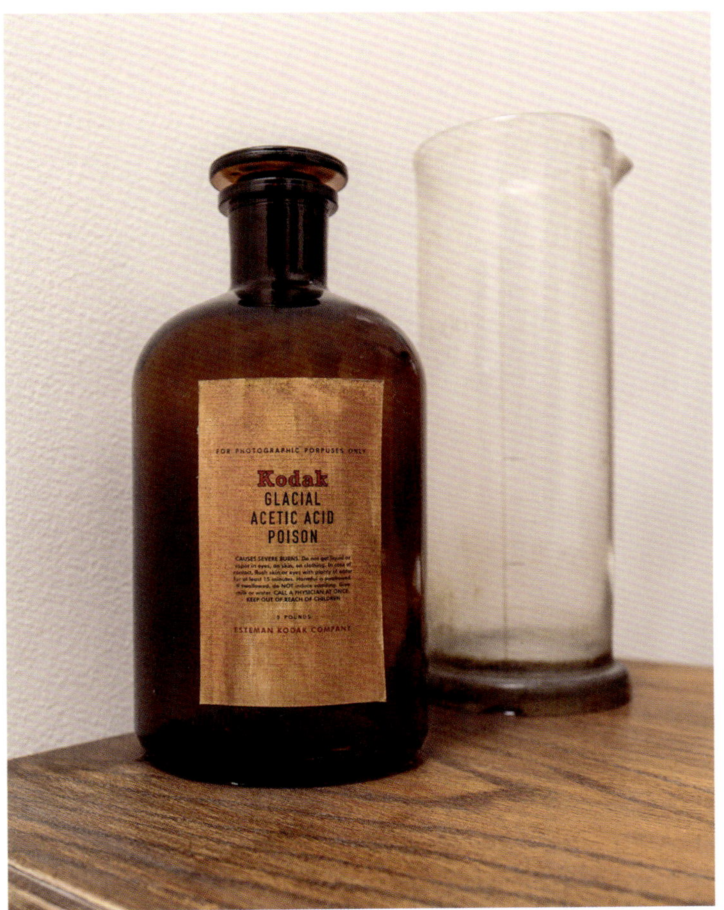

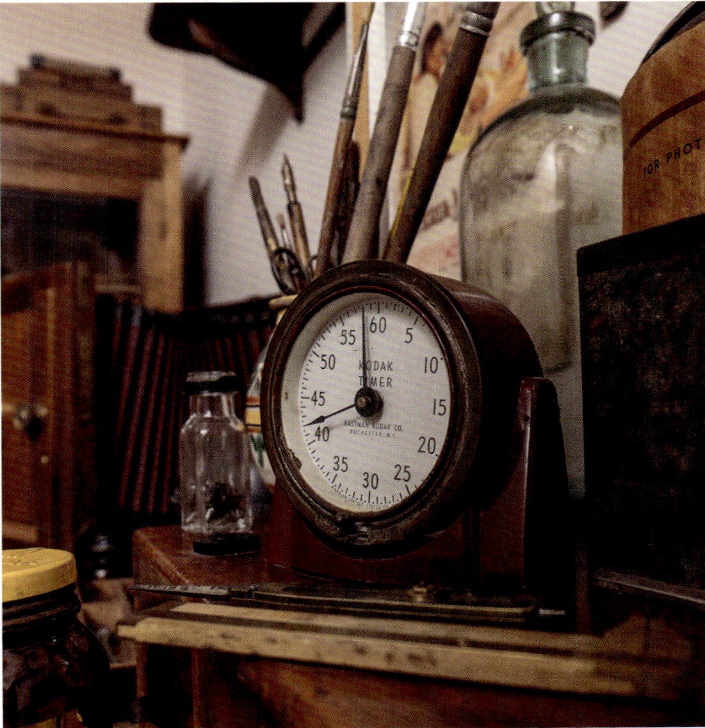

Guillermo's dark room and details of his photography equipment and supplies at Casa Kahlo, Coyoacán. After a time of financial hardships, Guillermo moved his photography studio into his home.

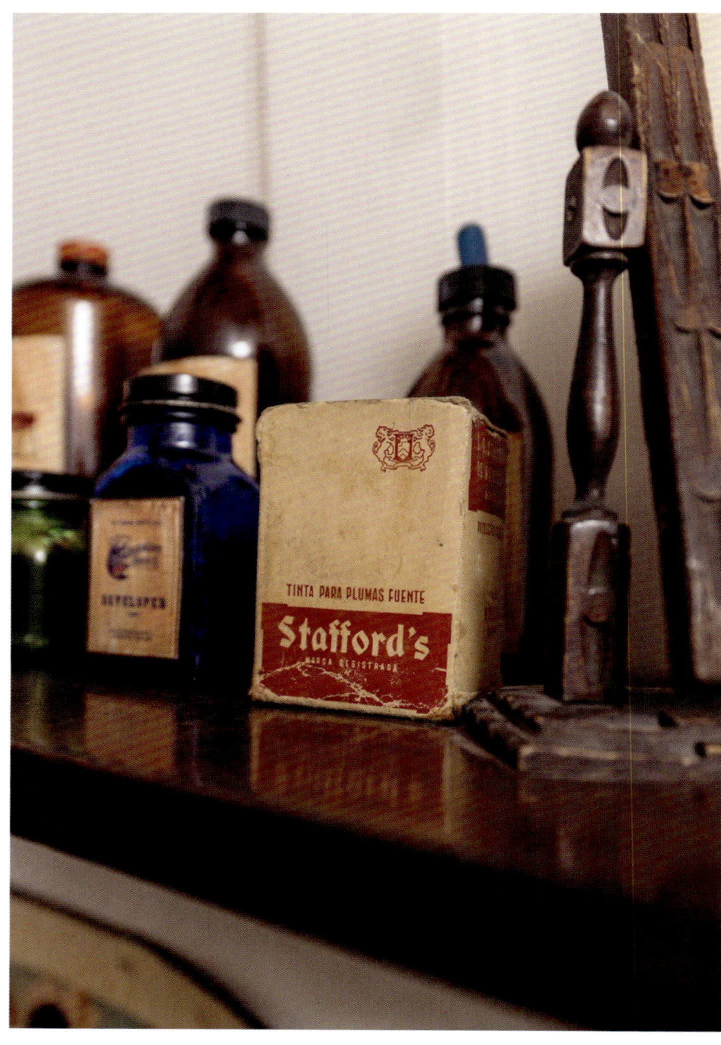

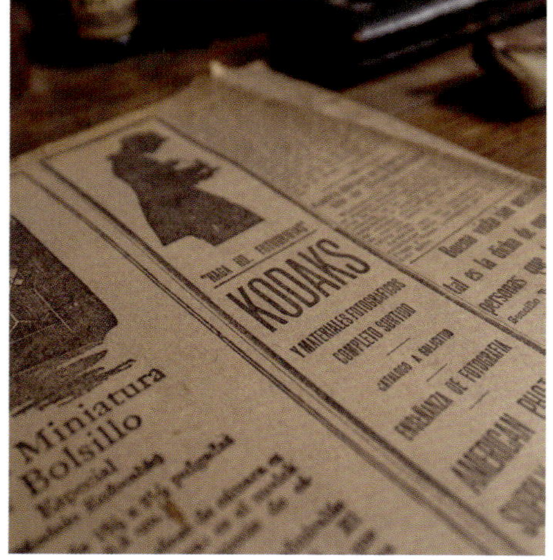

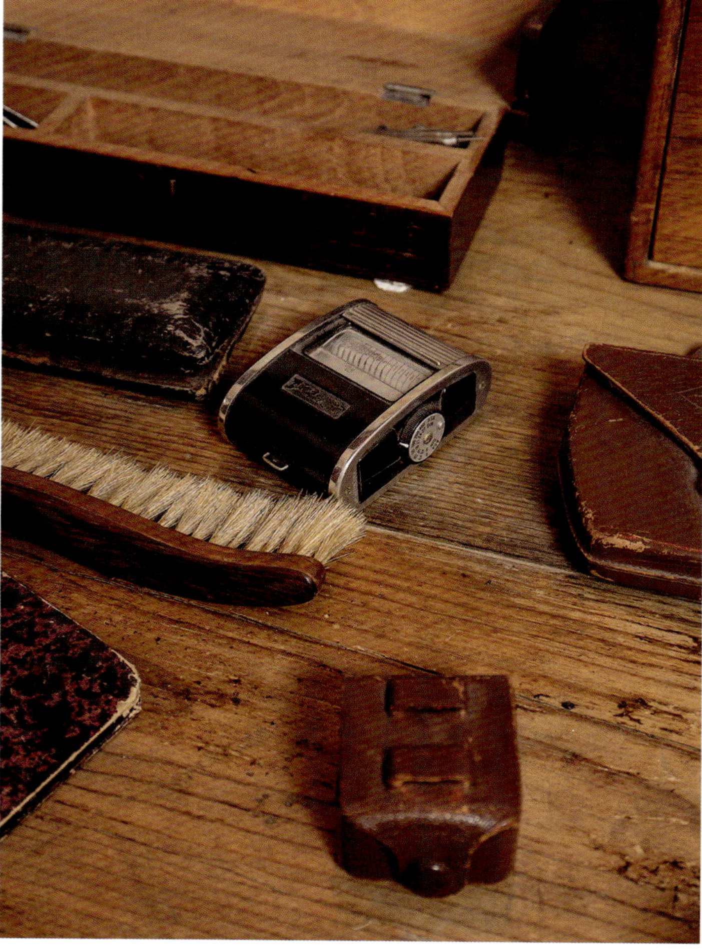

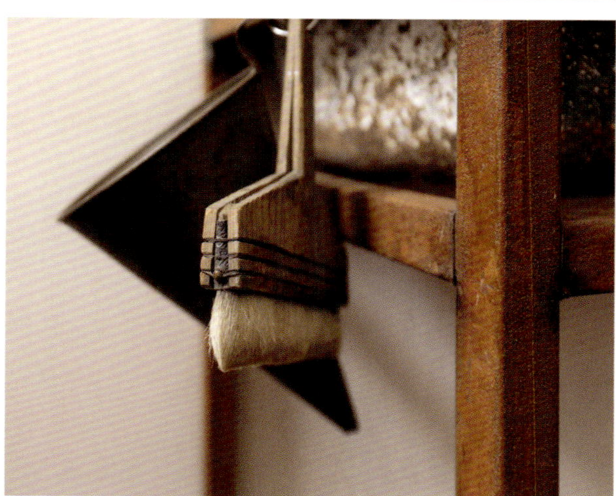

Guillermo's original photography equipment and supplies and desk with self-timer. He would spend hours working in his studio.

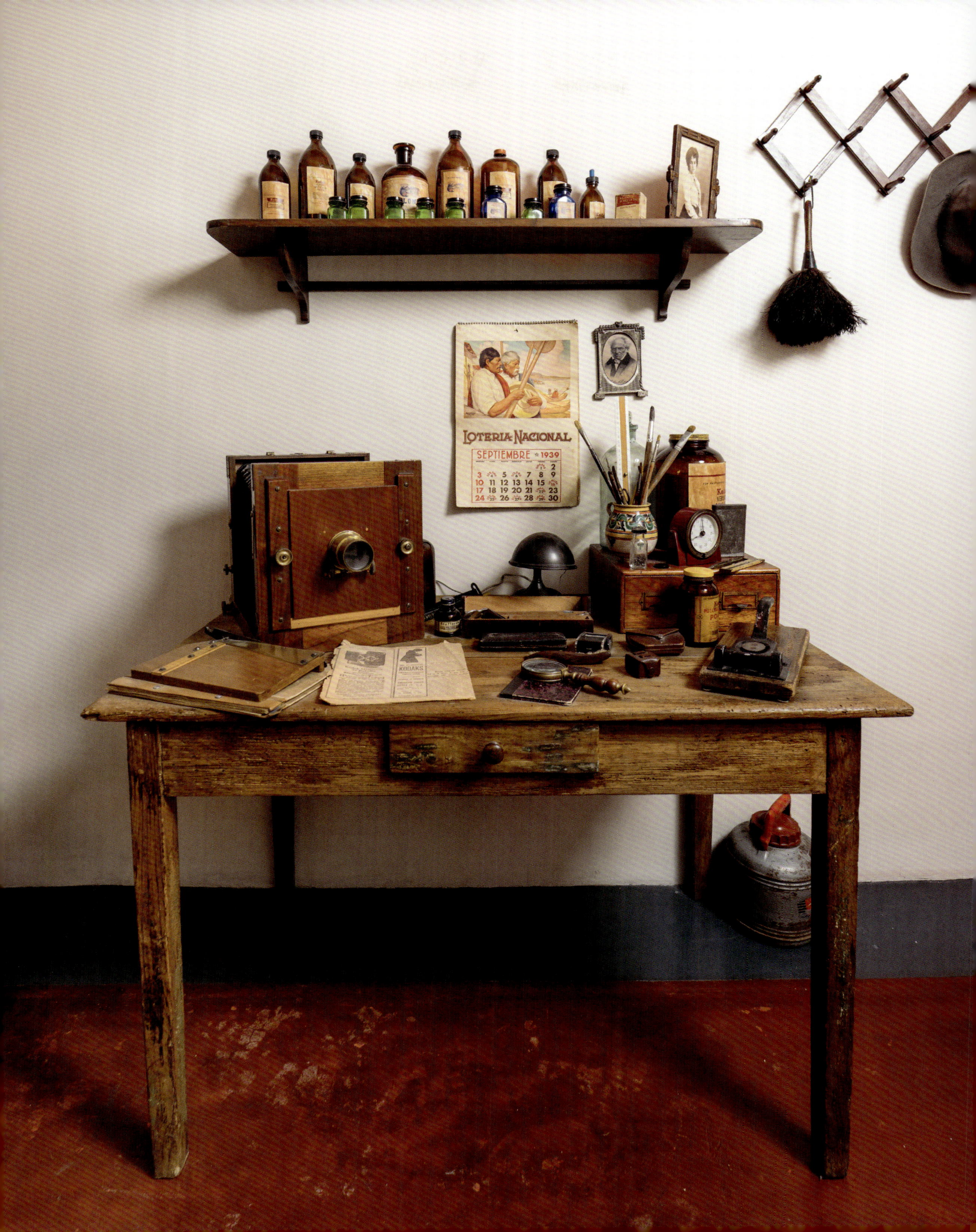
LOTERIA NACIONAL
SEPTIEMBRE 1939
KODAKS

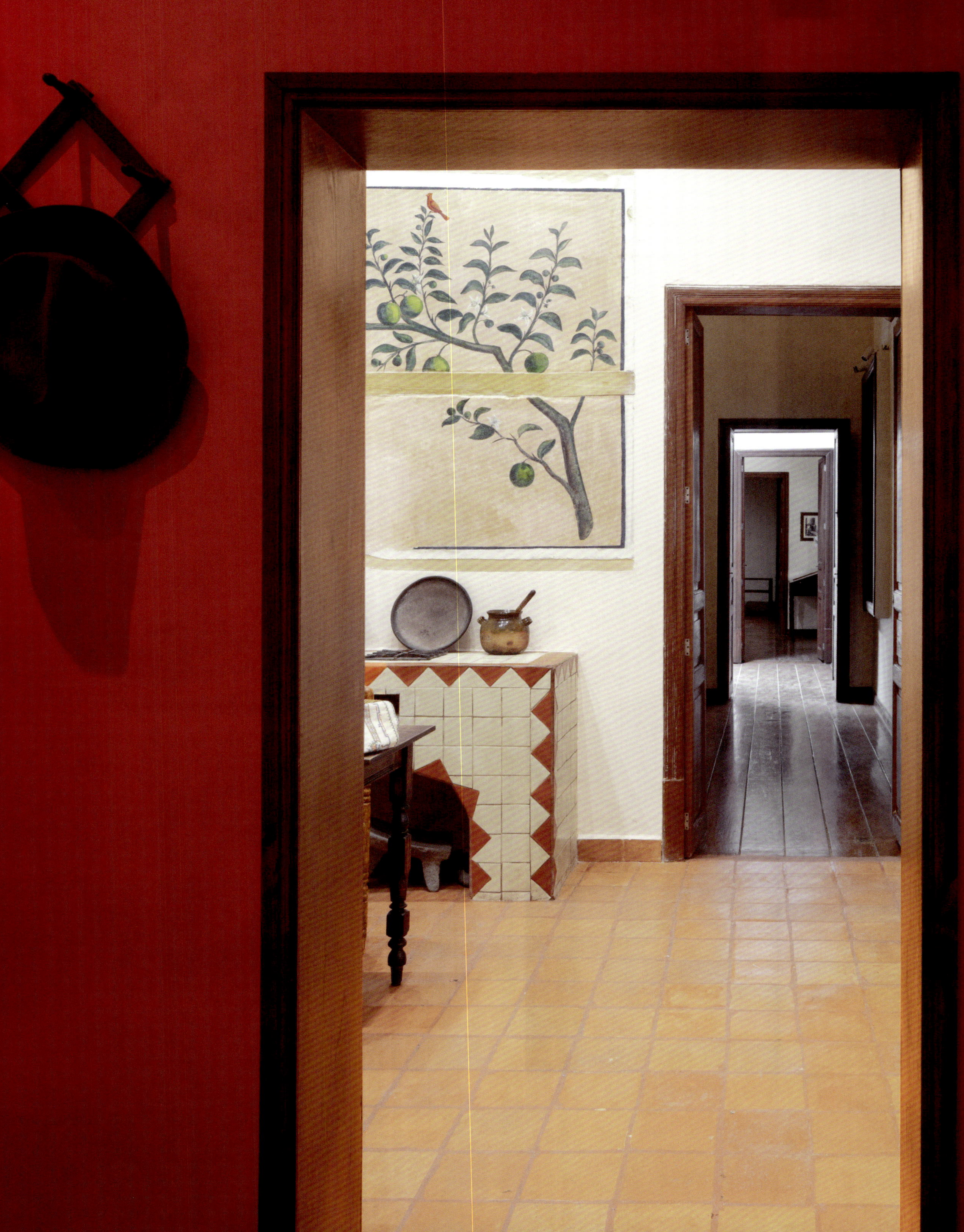

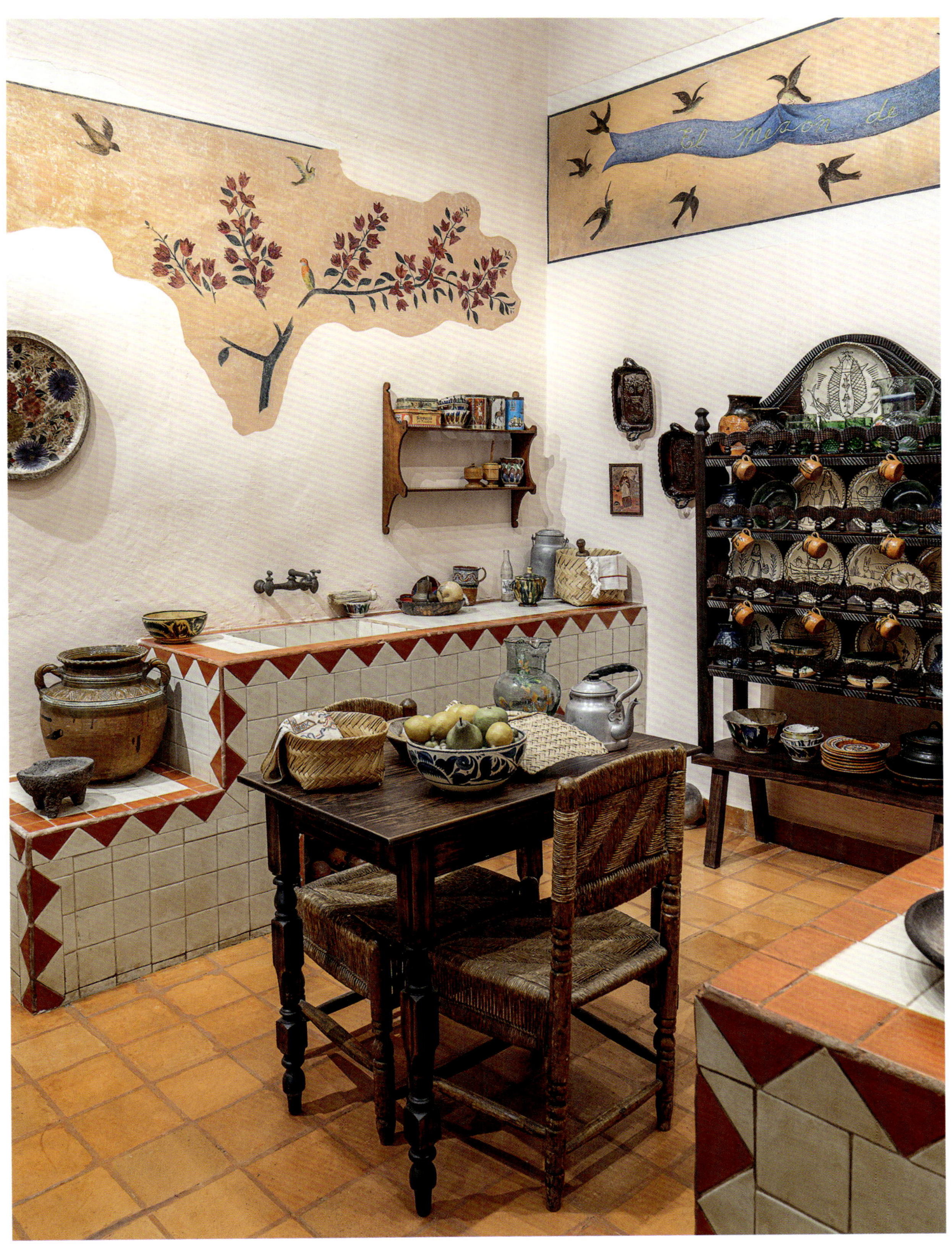

OPPOSITE The view into the kitchen from Guillermo's dark room in Casa Kahlo, Coyoacán

ABOVE The kitchen at Casa Kahlo, Coyoacán

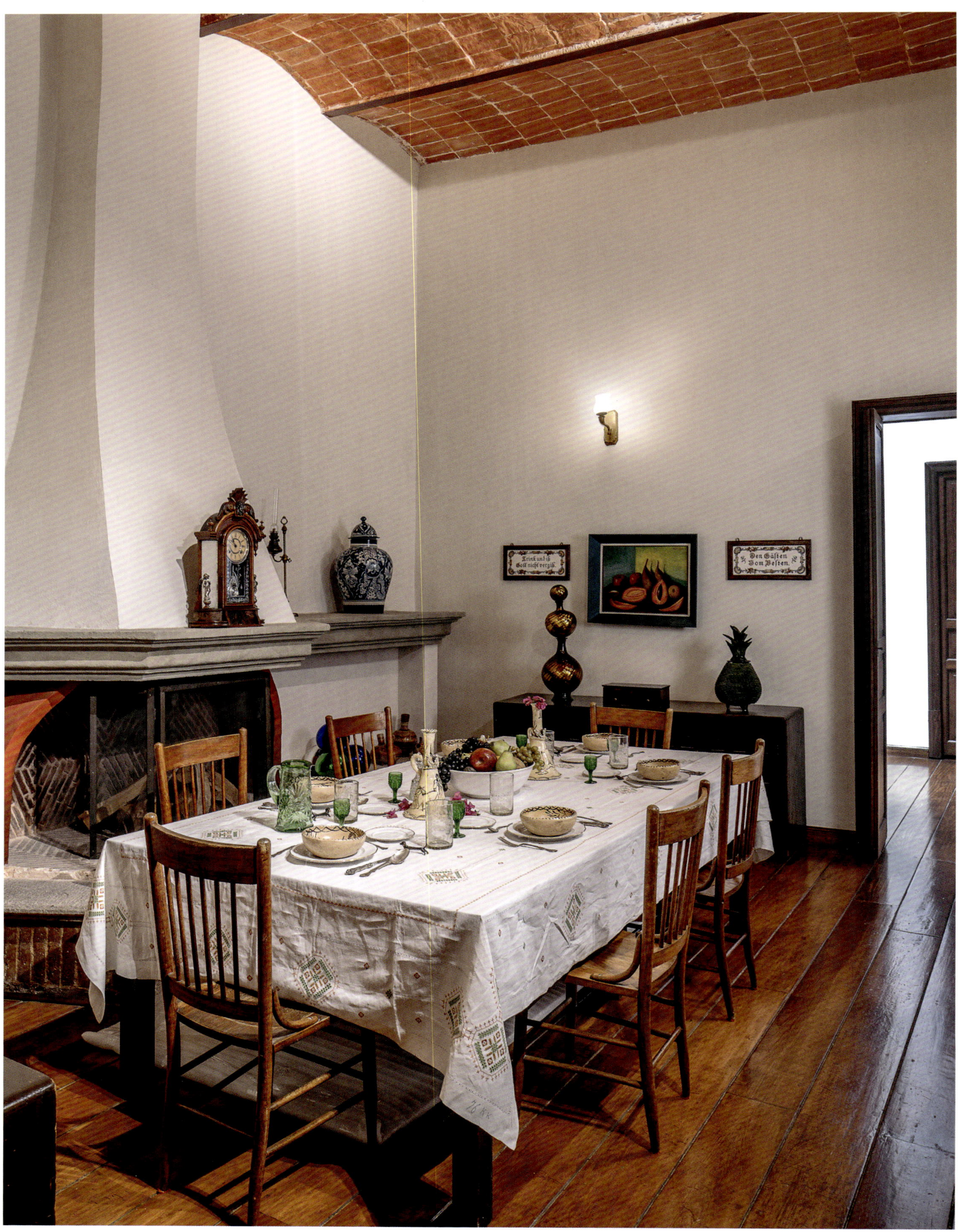
Trink und iß
Gott nicht vergiß.
Den Gästen
Vom Besten.

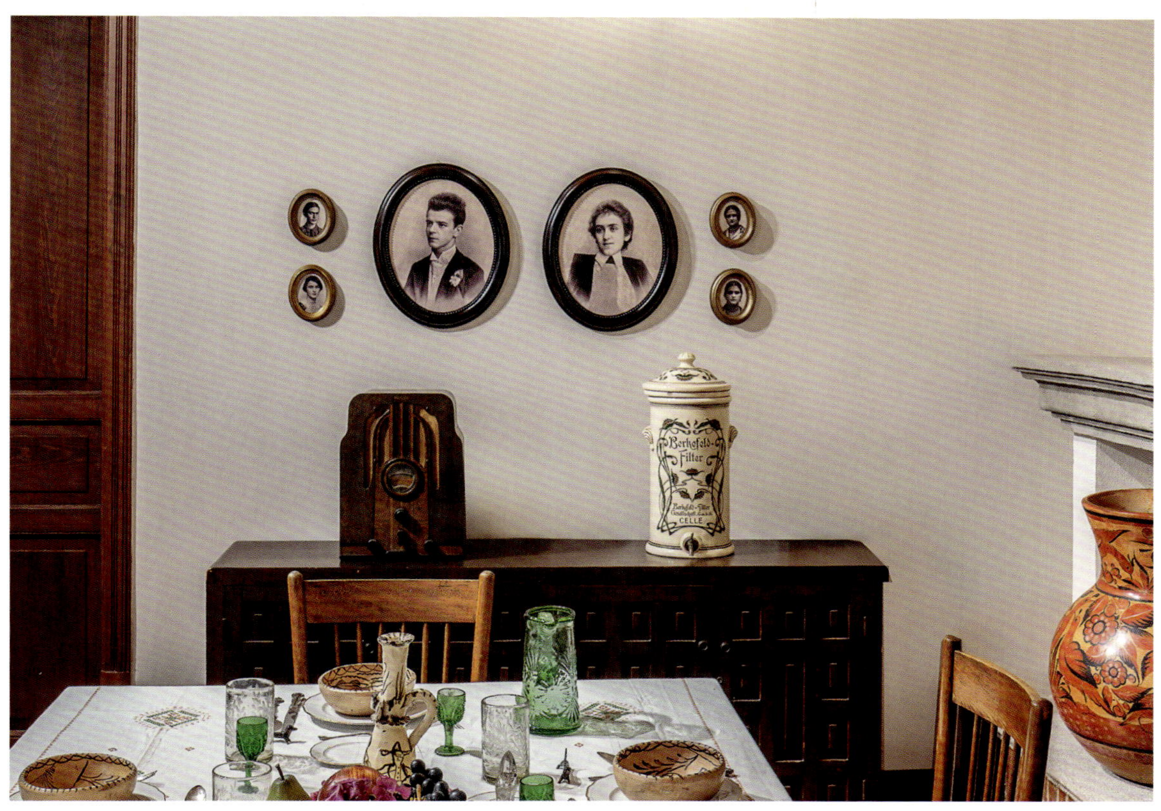

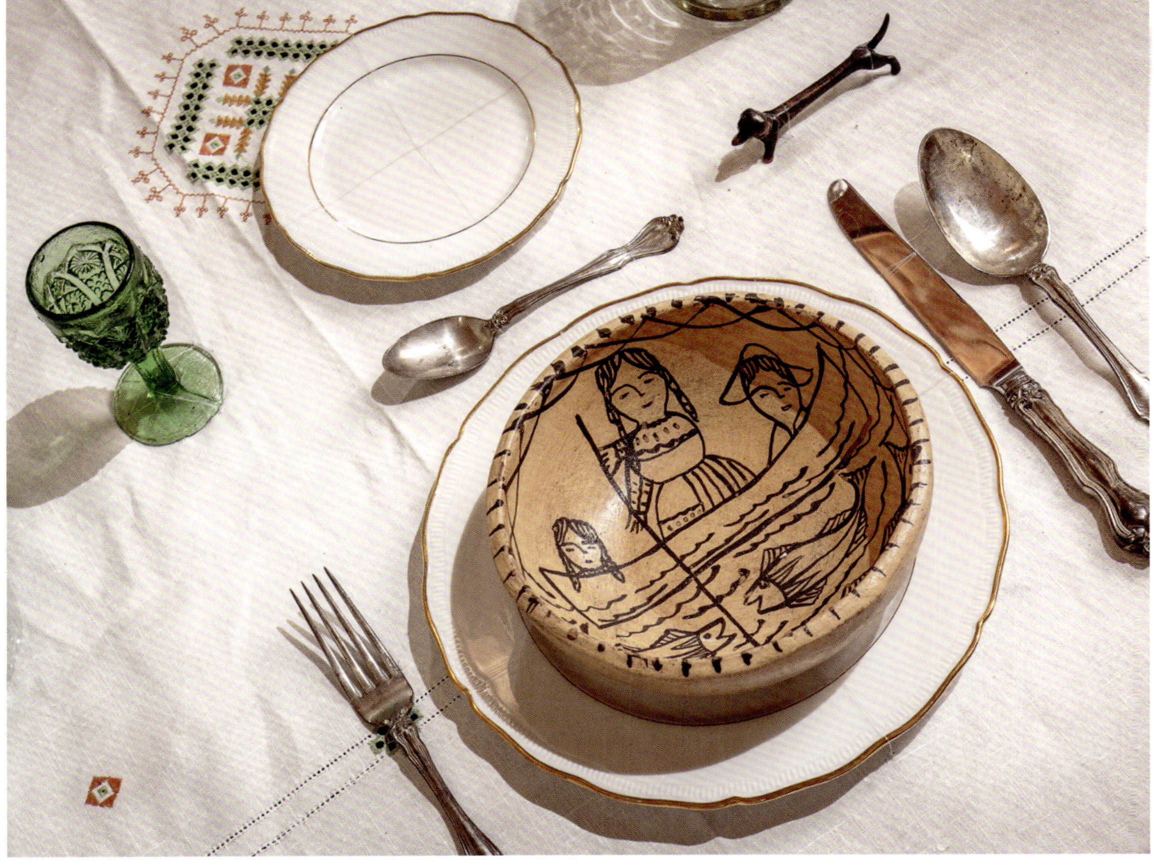

OPPOSITE, ABOVE, AND FOLLOWING SPREAD The dining room at Casa Kahlo, Coyoacán

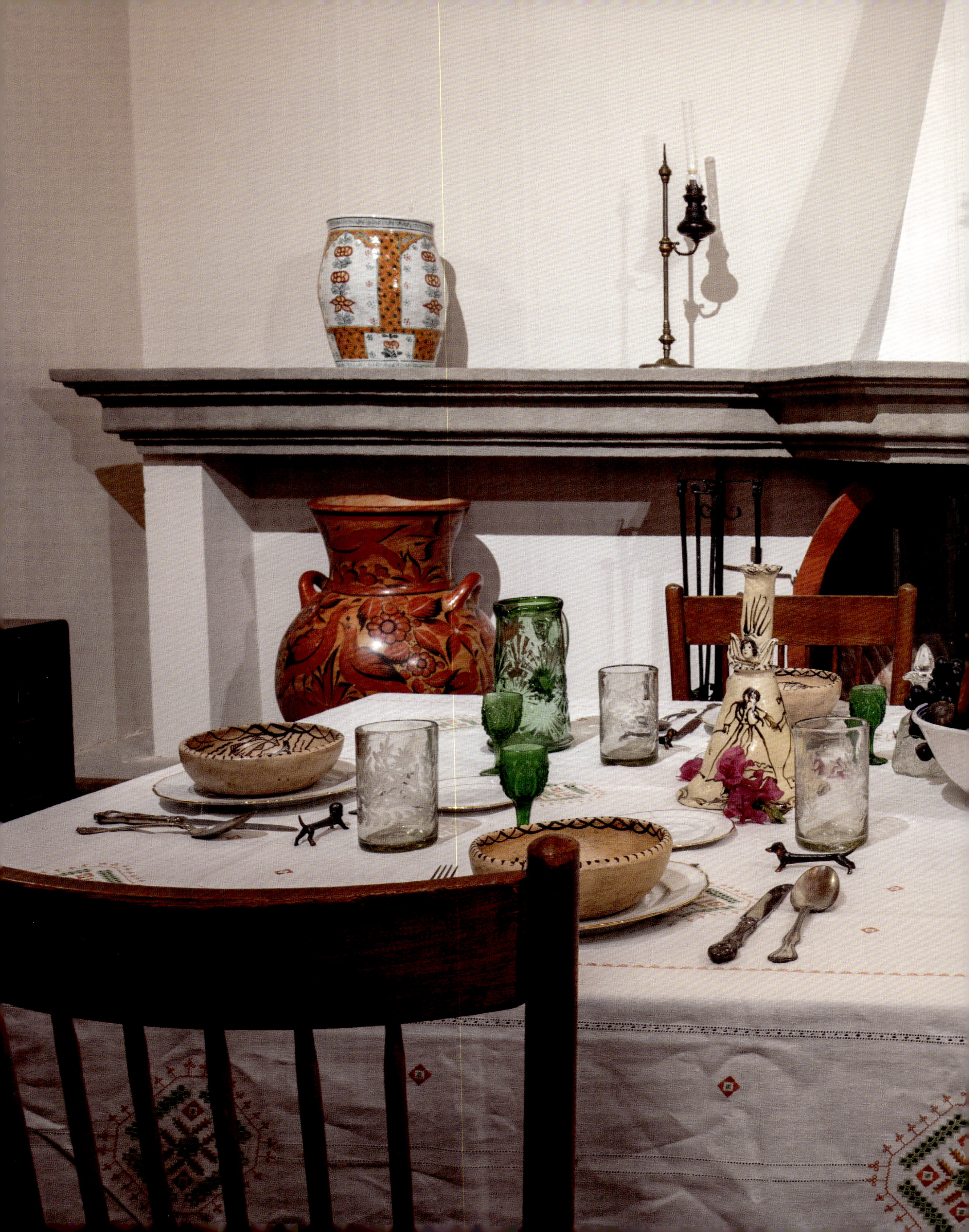

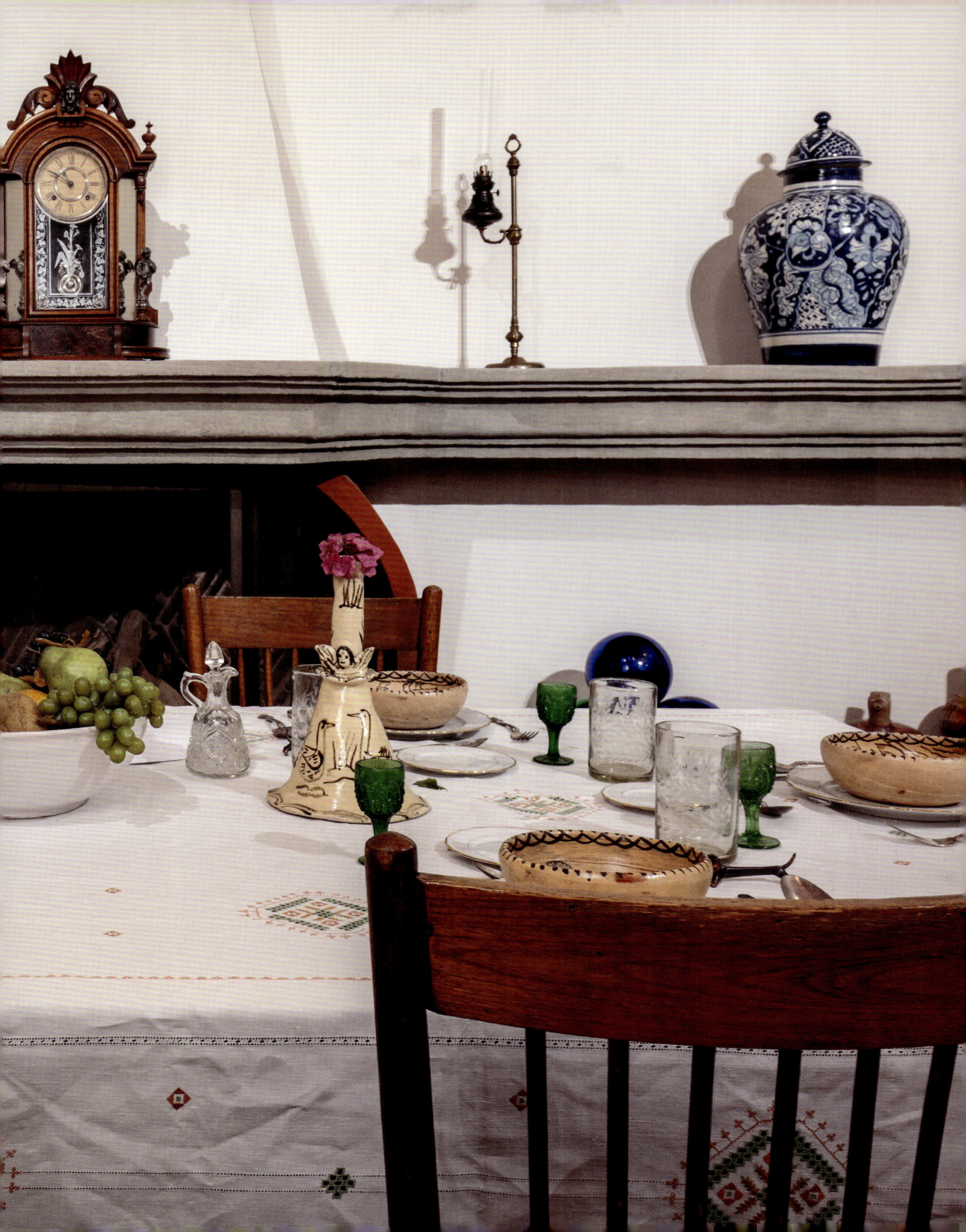

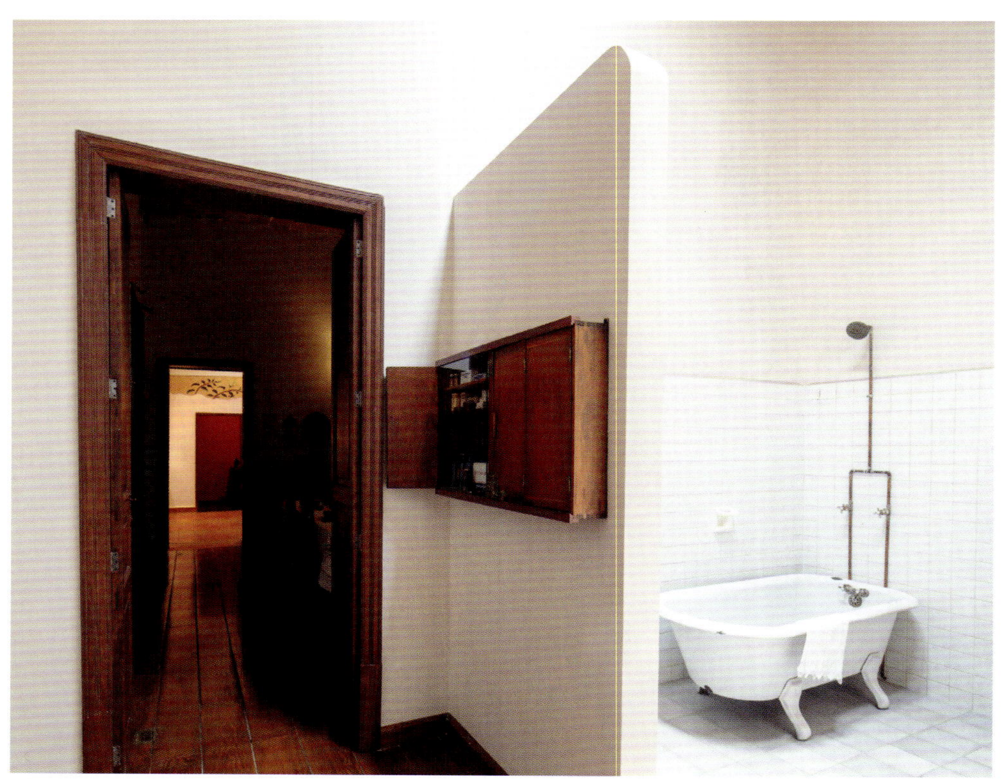

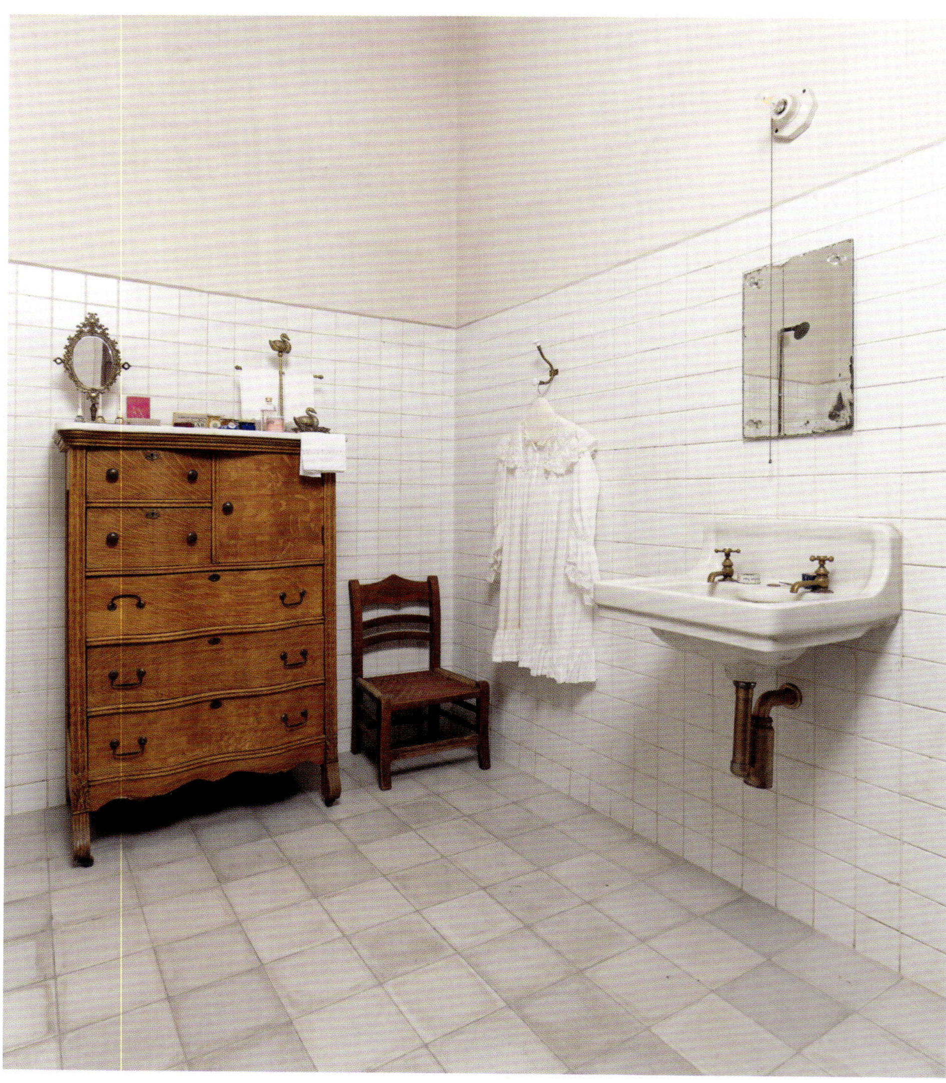

ABOVE AND OPPOSITE The bathroom at Casa Kahlo, Coyoacán

FOLLOWING SPREAD Detail of bathroom medicine cabinet, Casa Kahlo, Coyoacán

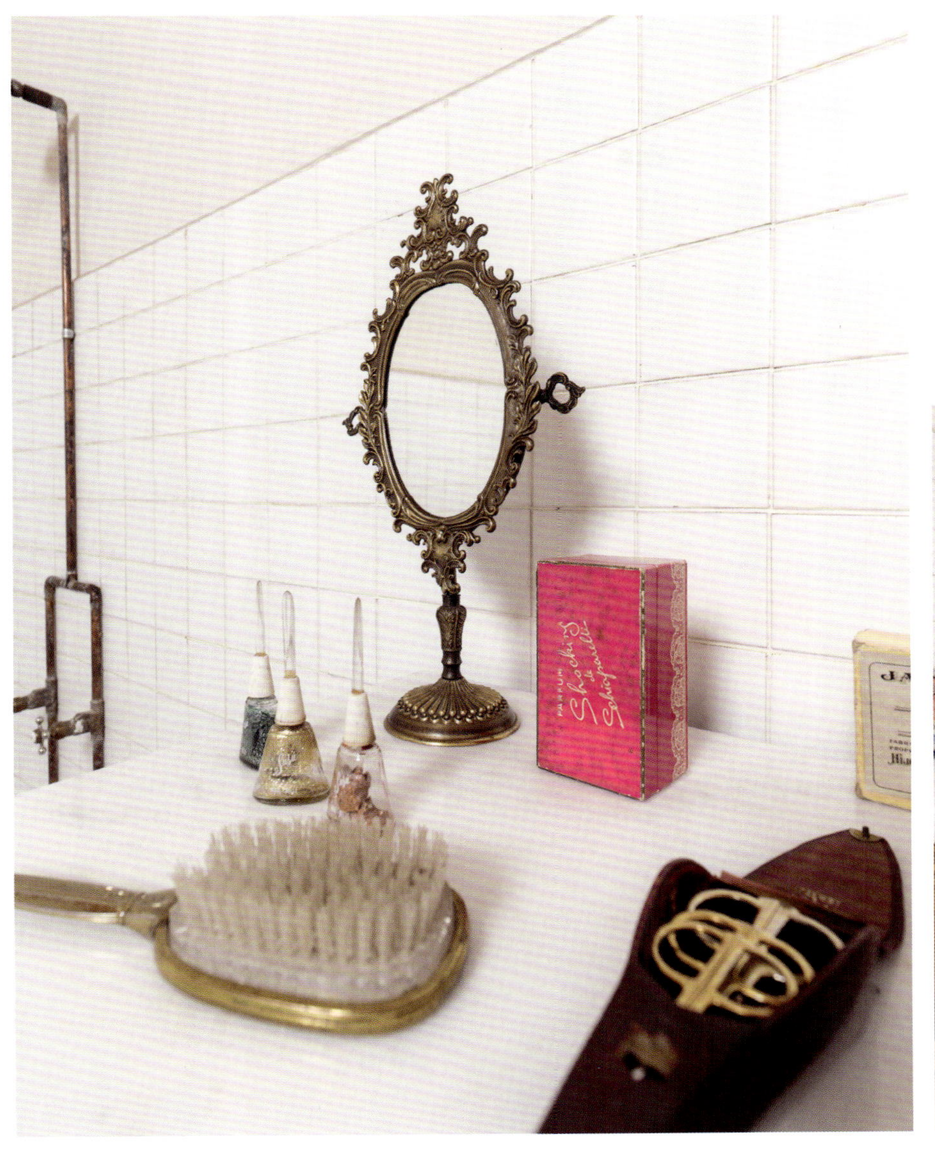
PARFUM
Shocking de Schiaparelli

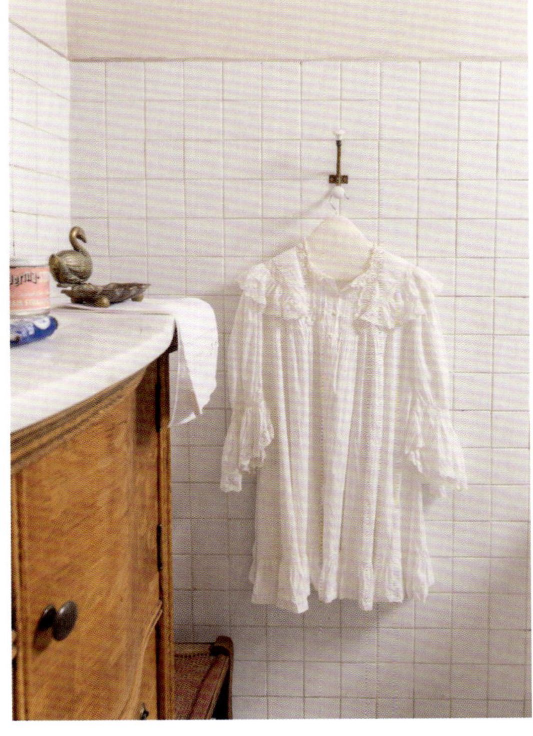

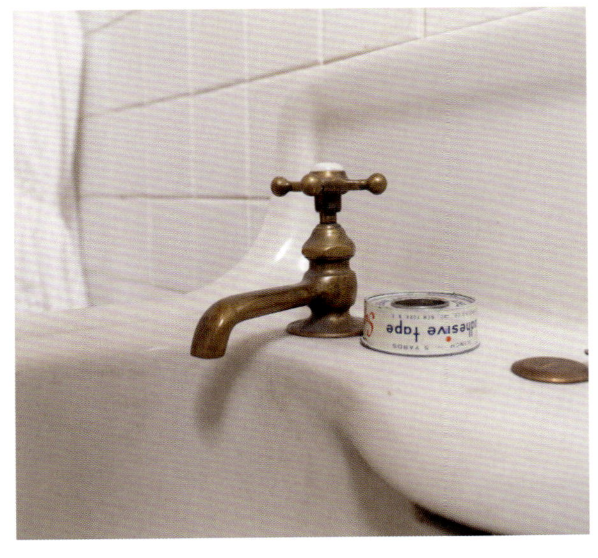

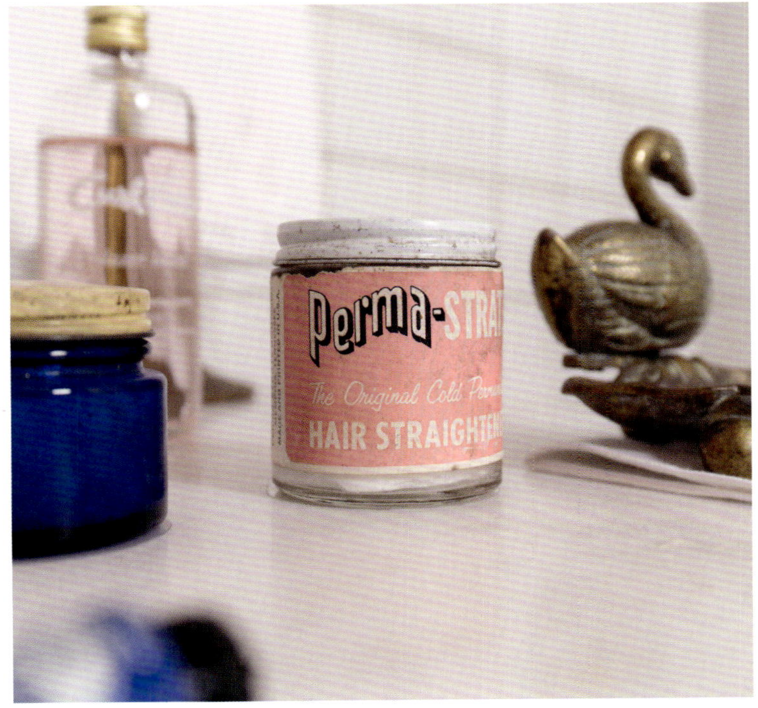

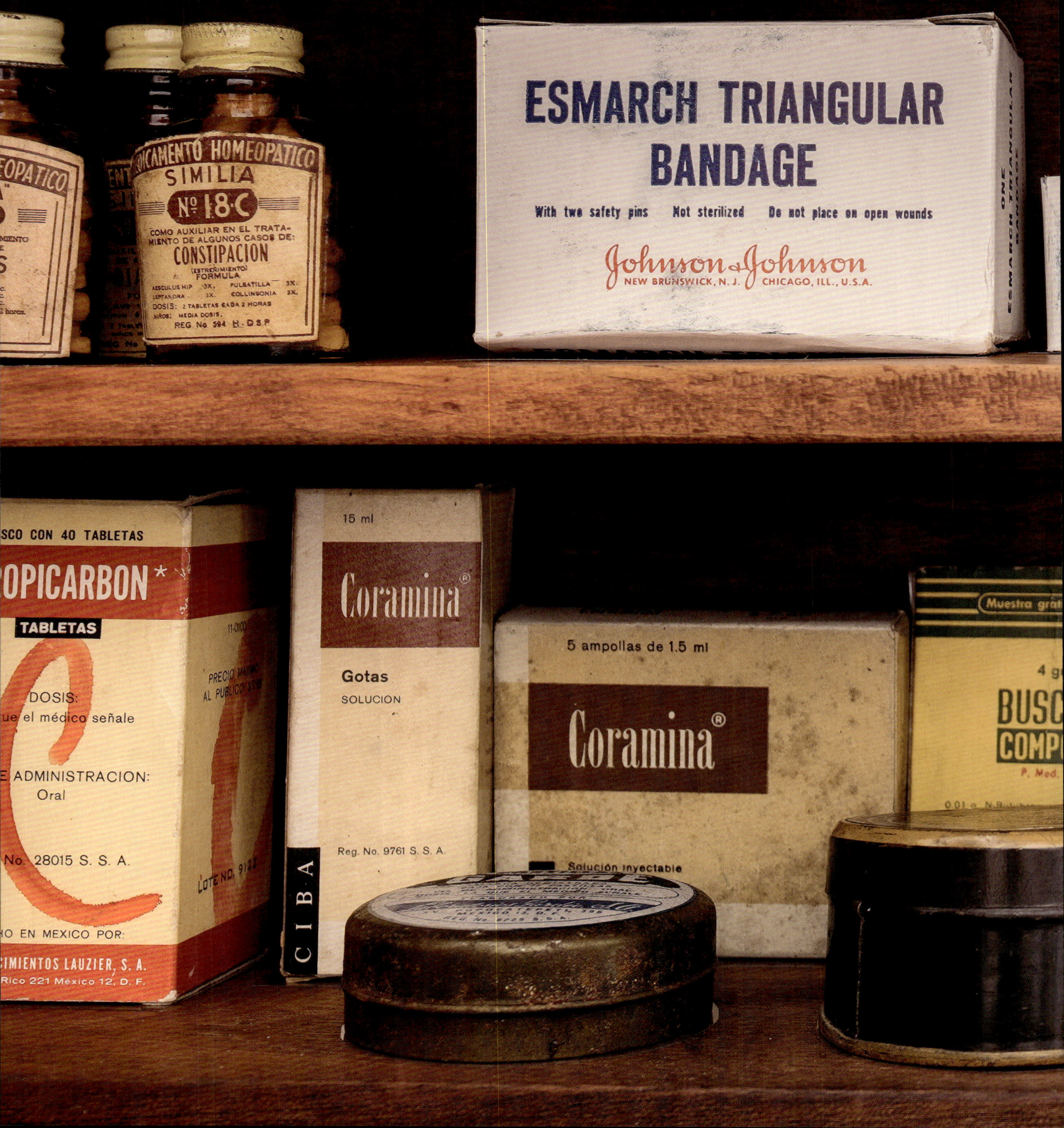

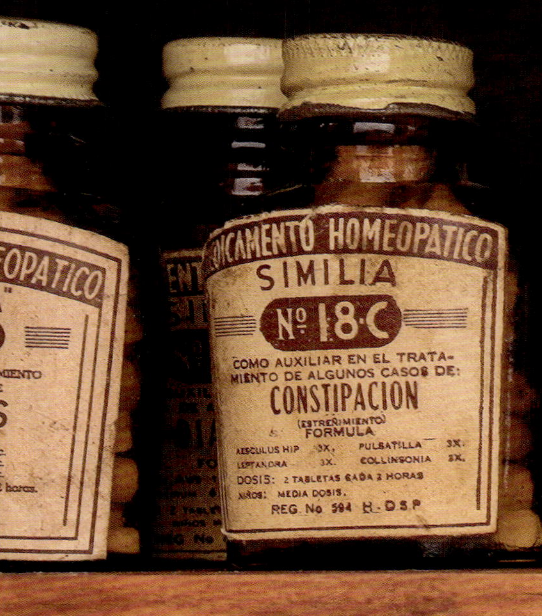

MEDICAMENTO HOMEOPATICO
SIMILIA
Nº 18-C
COMO AUXILIAR EN EL TRATAMIENTO DE ALGUNOS CASOS DE:
CONSTIPACION
(ESTREÑIMIENTO)
FORMULA
DOSIS: 2 TABLETAS CADA 2 HORAS
NIÑOS: MEDIA DOSIS.
REG. No 594 H. D.S.P.
ESMARCH TRIANGULAR
BANDAGE
With two safety pins
Not sterilized
Do not place on open wounds
Johnson & Johnson
NEW BRUNSWICK, N. J.
CHICAGO, ILL., U.S.A.
SCO CON 40 TABLETAS
OPICARBON *
TABLETAS
DOSIS:
ue el médico señale
E ADMINISTRACION:
Oral
No. 28015 S. S. A.
HO EN MEXICO POR:
CIMIENTOS LAUZIER, S. A.
Rico 221 México 12, D. F.
15 ml
Coramina®
Gotas
SOLUCION
Reg. No. 9761 S. S. A.
CIBA
5 ampollas de 1.5 ml
Coramina®
Solución inyectable
Muestra grat
BUSC
COMP

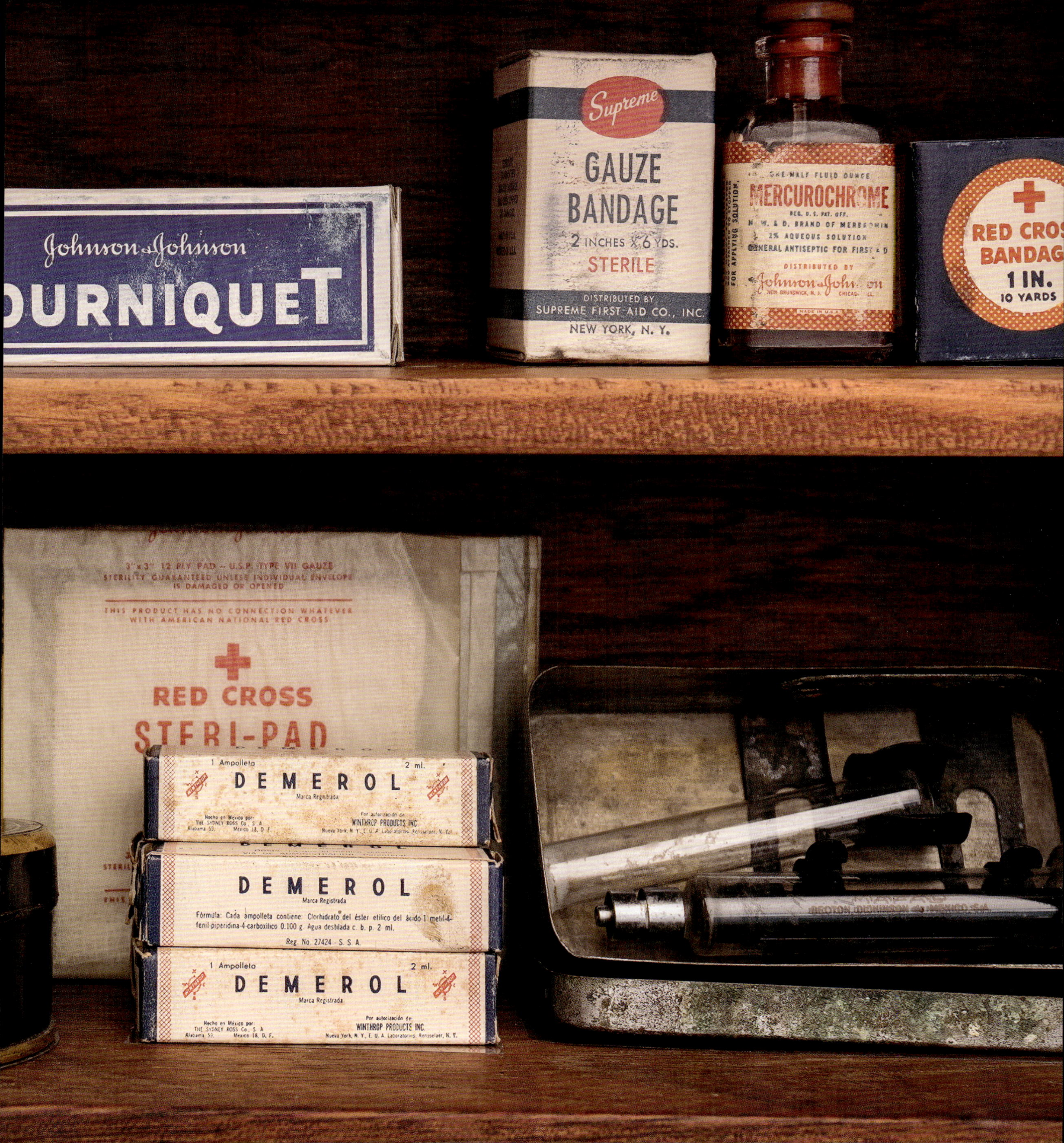

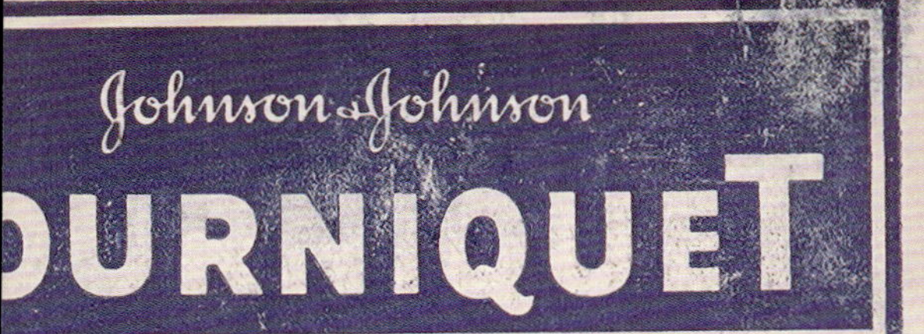
Johnson & Johnson
OURNIQUET

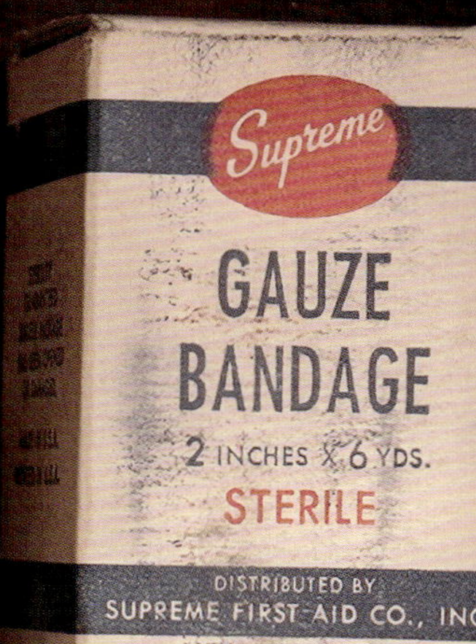
Supreme
GAUZE
BANDAGE
2 INCHES X 6 YDS.
STERILE
DISTRIBUTED BY
SUPREME FIRST-AID CO., INC.
NEW YORK, N. Y.

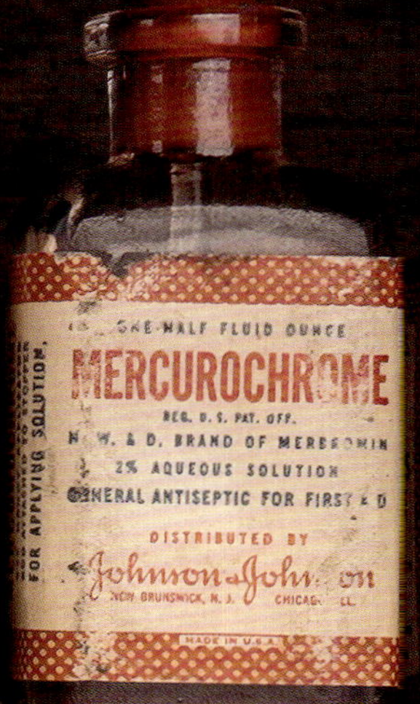
MERCUROCHROME
2% AQUEOUS SOLUTION
DISTRIBUTED BY

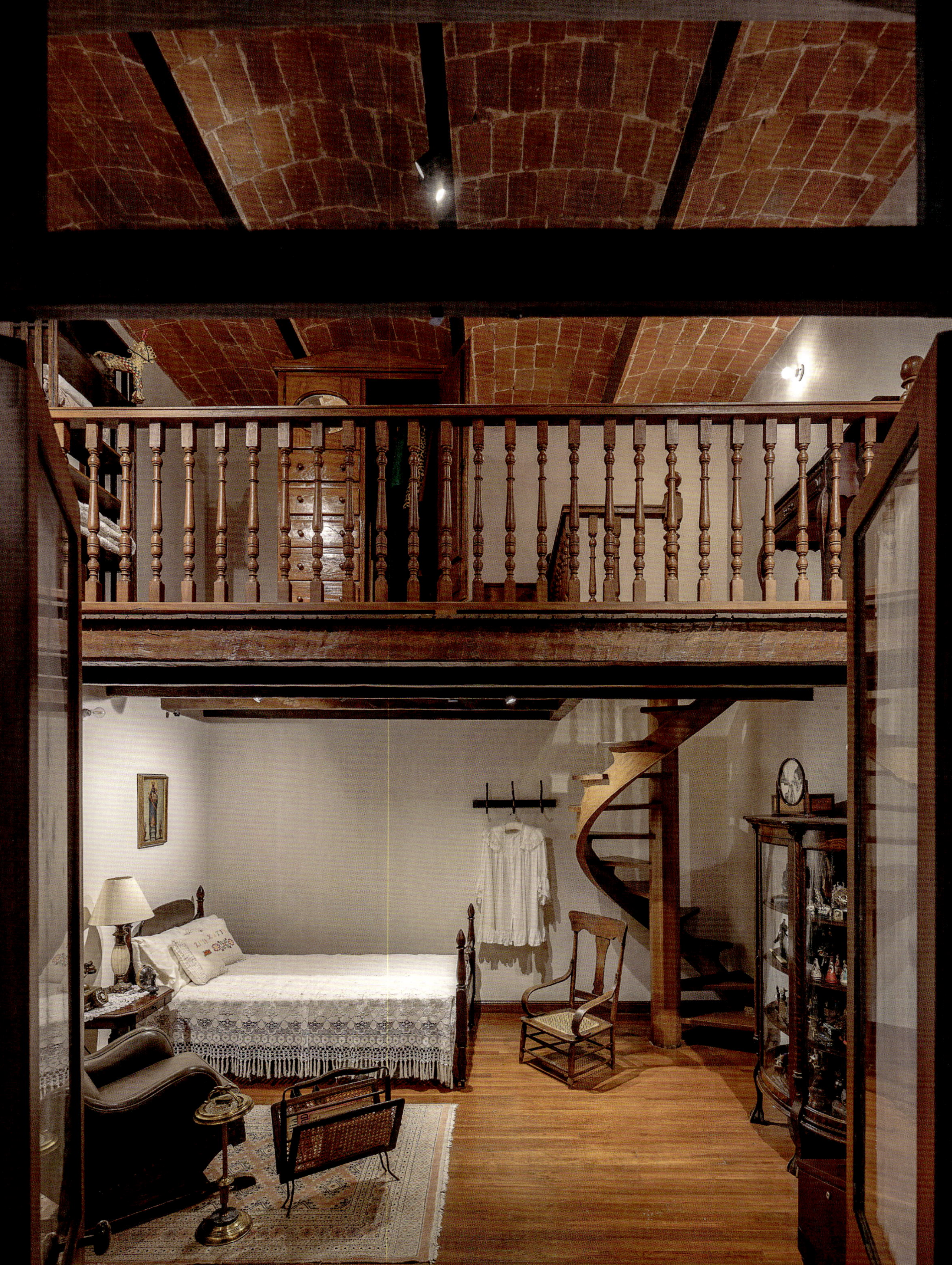

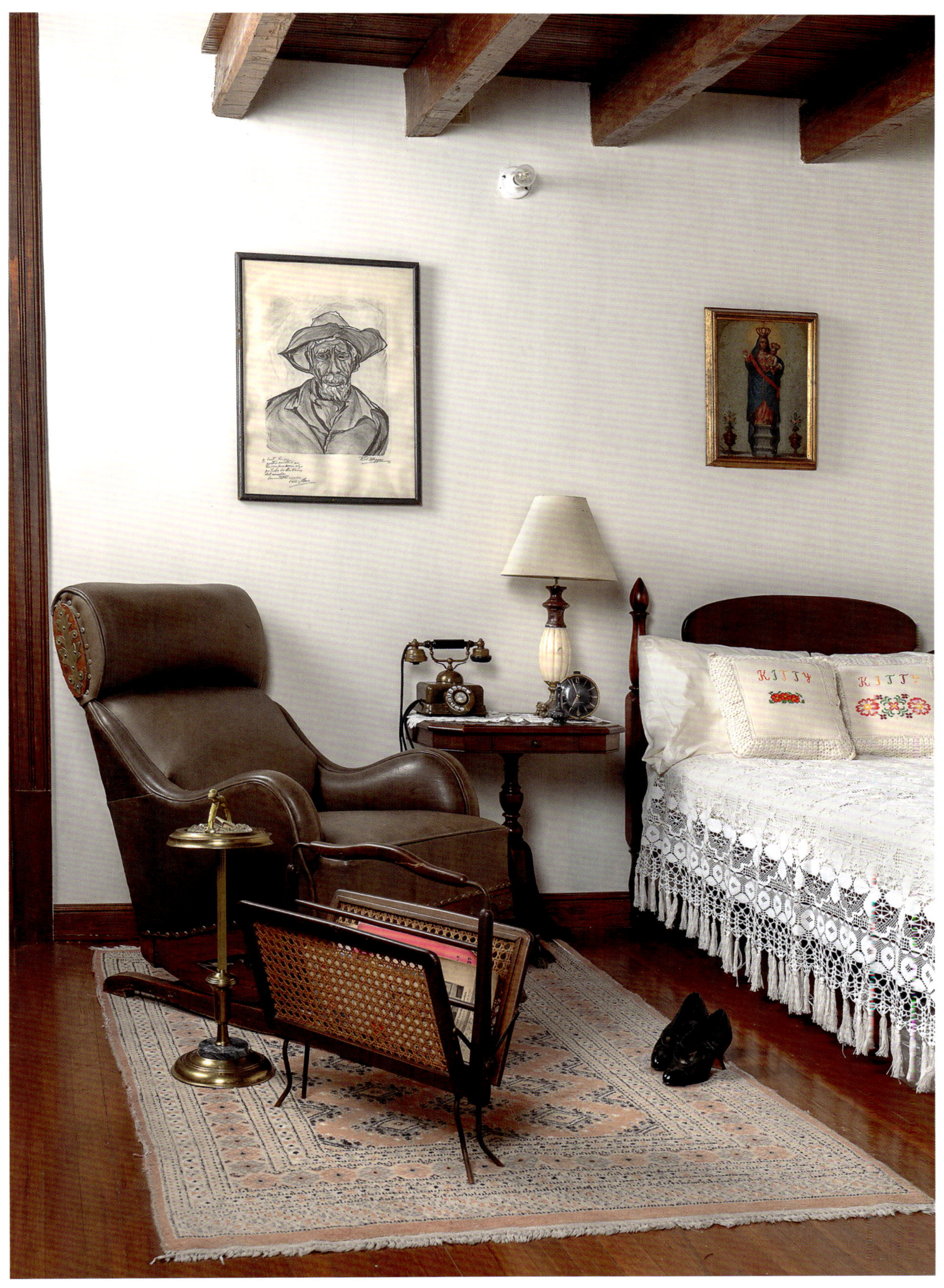

OPPOSITE AND ABOVE Cristina's bedroom at Casa Kahlo, Coyoacán

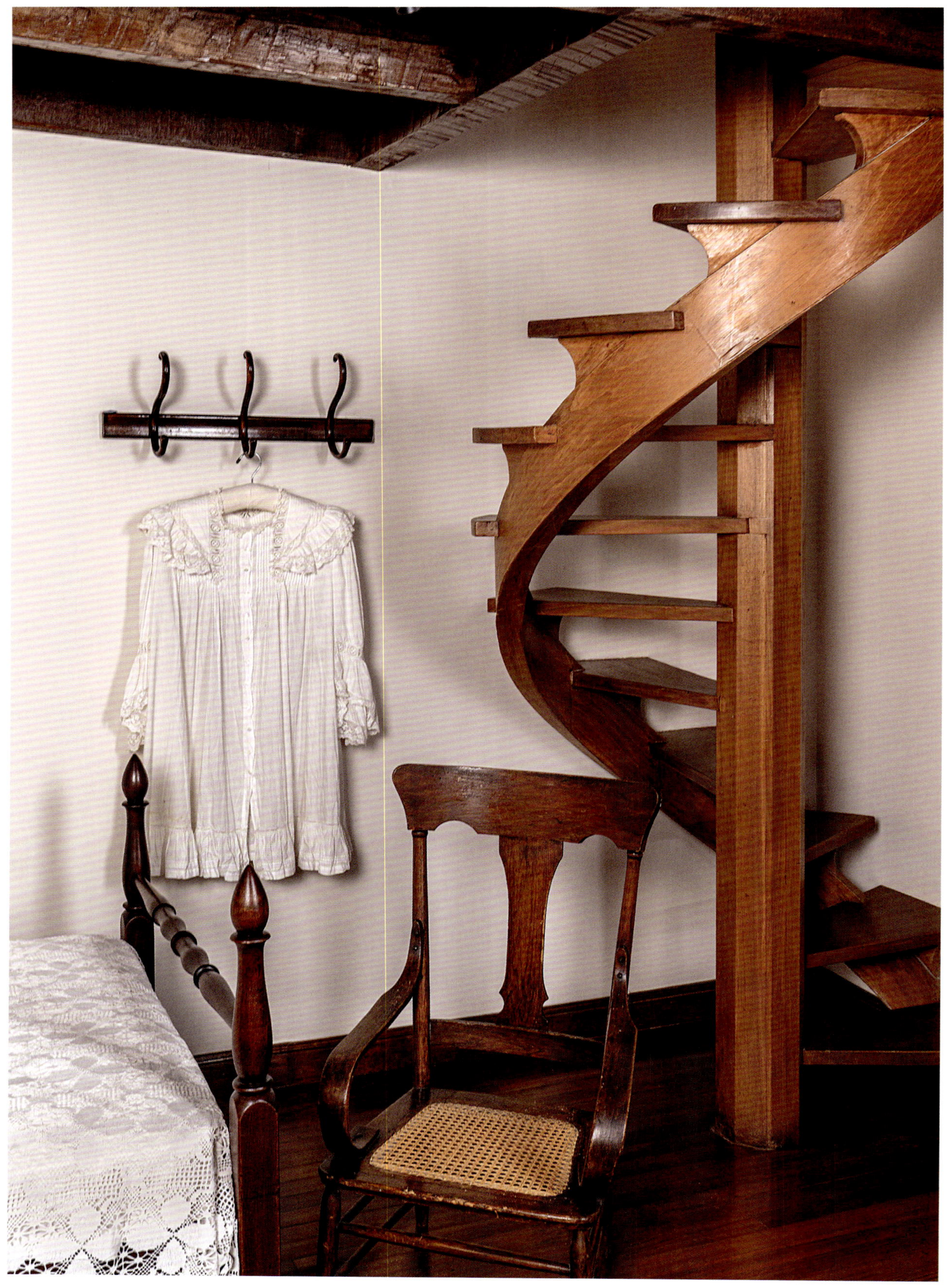

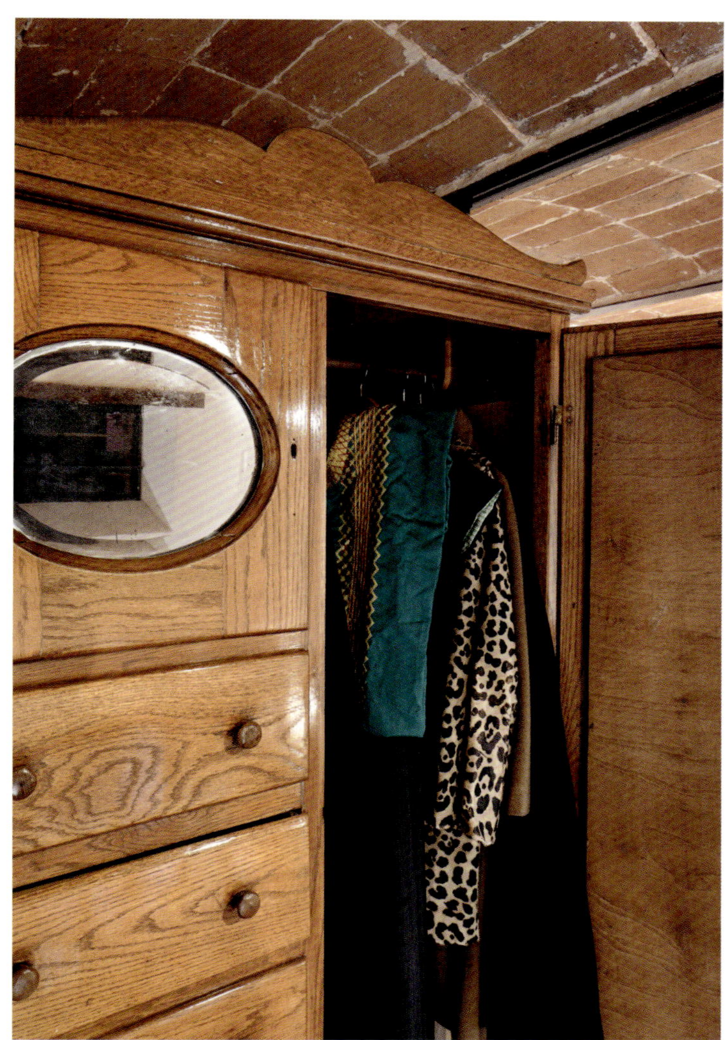

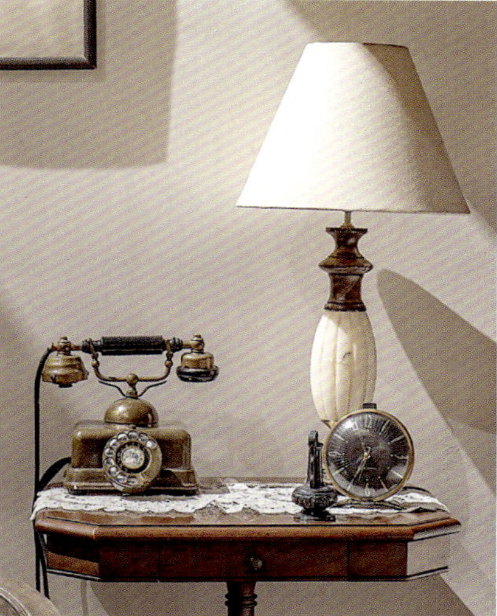

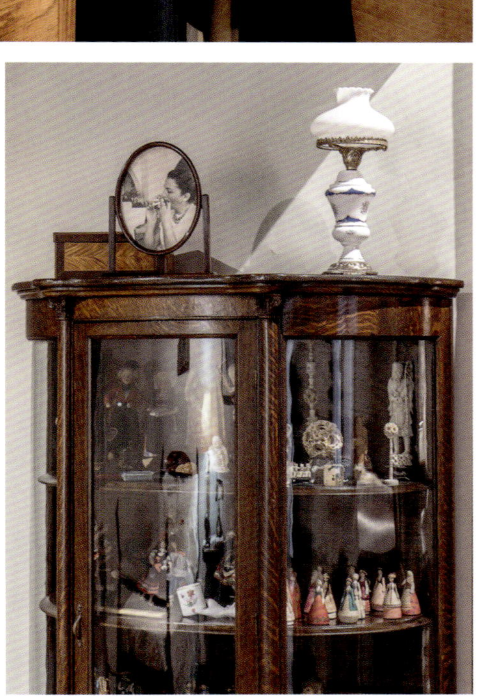

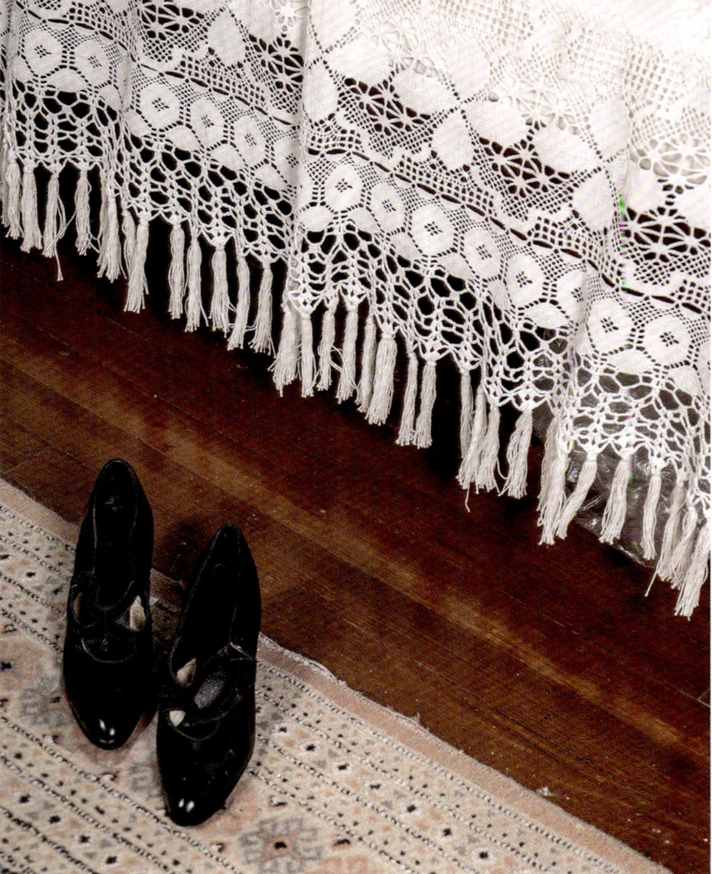

OPPOSITE AND ABOVE Details of Cristina's bedroom, Casa Kahlo, Coyoacán

Mara de Anda One of the most interesting parts of the house on Aguayo is the basement. Frida spent a lot of time here hiding from Diego. Whenever she fought with him, she came to the house to have time alone. Her sisters protected her and never let on where she was. The basement was her private world, where she wrote and painted. It is said that she brought her lovers here. We know that she was emotionally connected to other men, such as Leon Trotsky and the artist Josep Bartolí (also known as José Bartolí). This was a place she could have private time with them away from Diego. Frida really enjoyed the attention of men. I think she was mostly attracted to their intellect and their capacity to appreciate her for her own intellectual gifts, her extraordinary creativity, and her unique way of seeing the world. Based on her letters and the stories that were passed down through generations, we know this was the case with Bartolí, the photographer Nickolas Muray, and the artist Isamu Noguchi. They were all brilliant, sensitive, caring, and unique. Just like Frida.

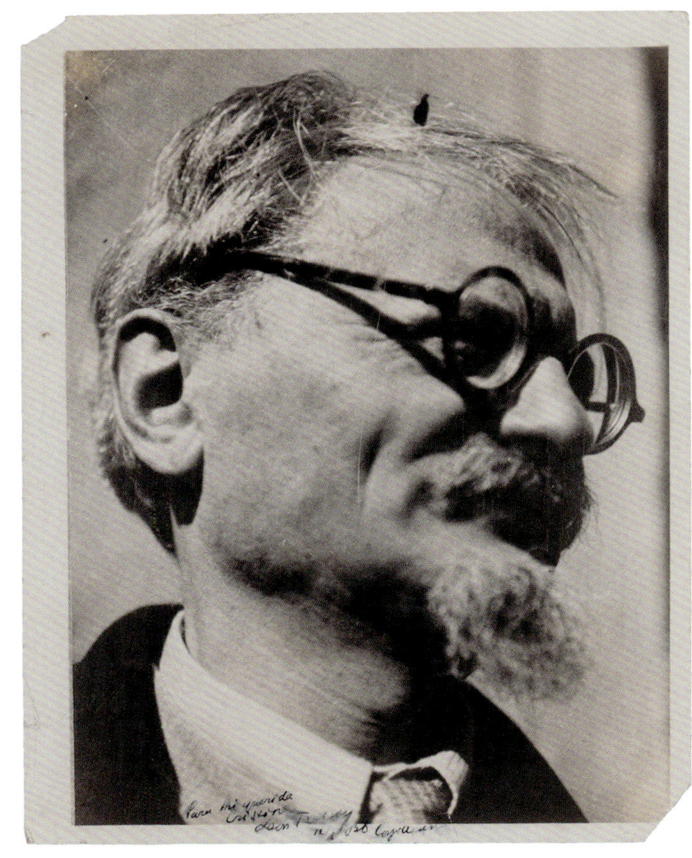

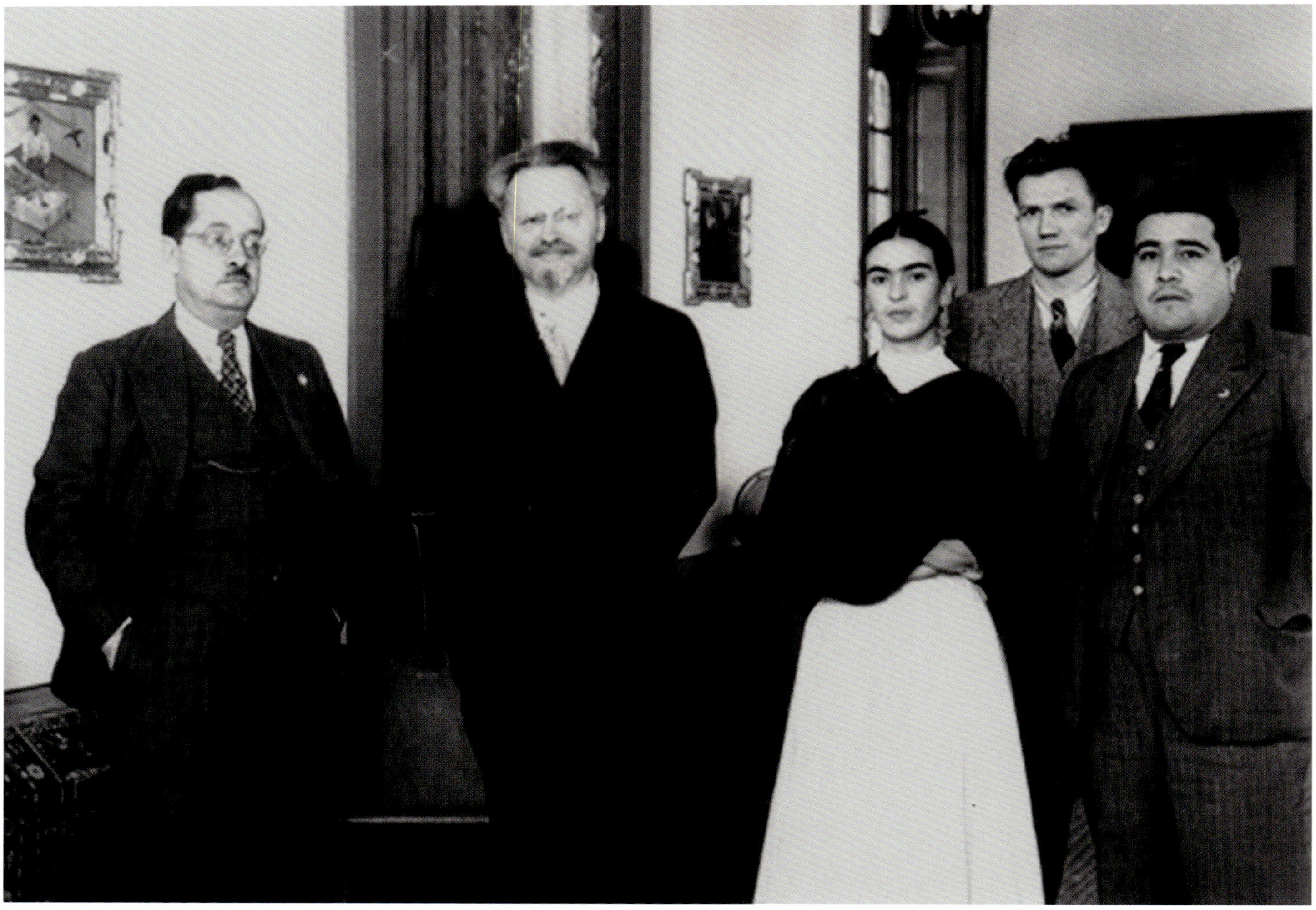

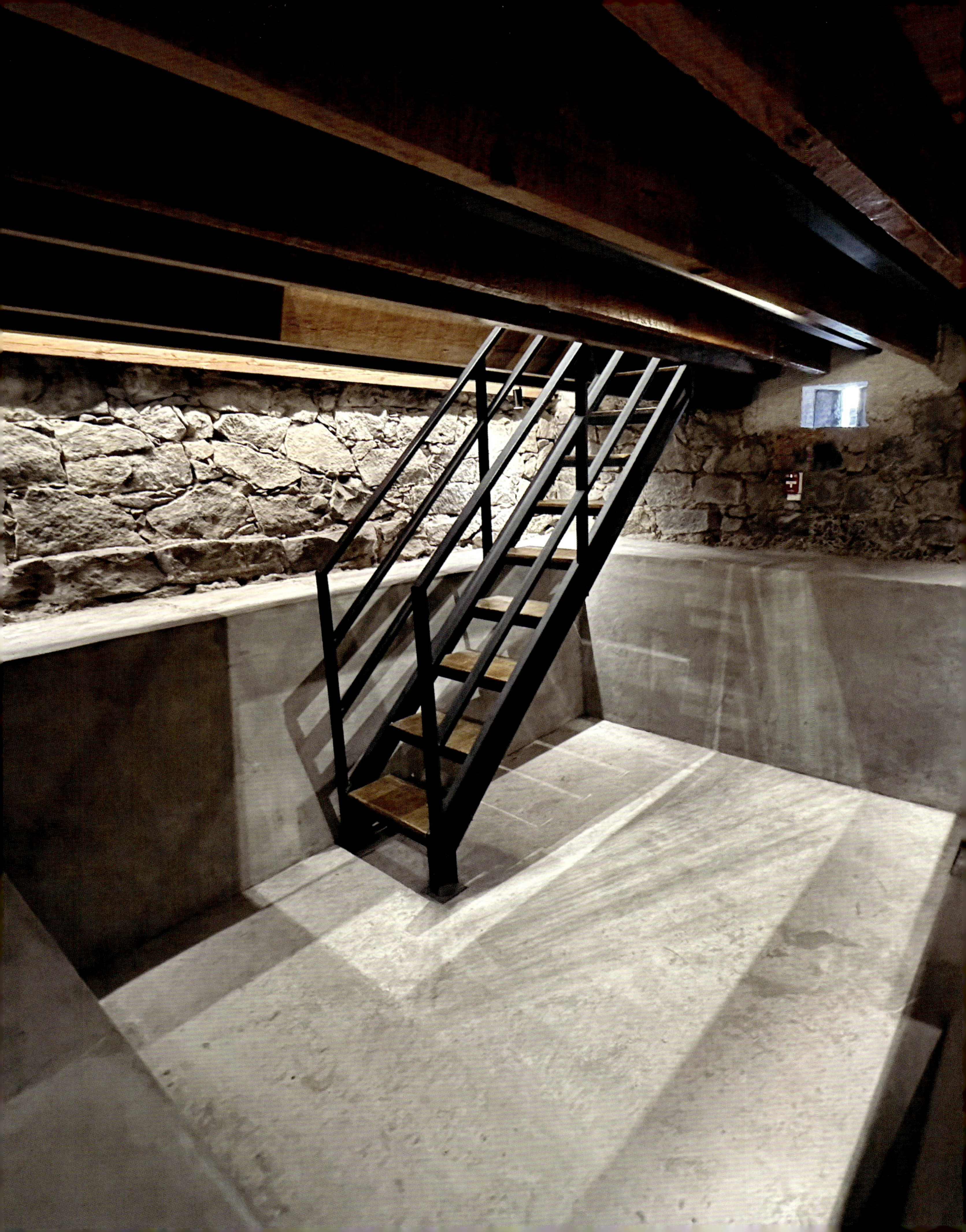

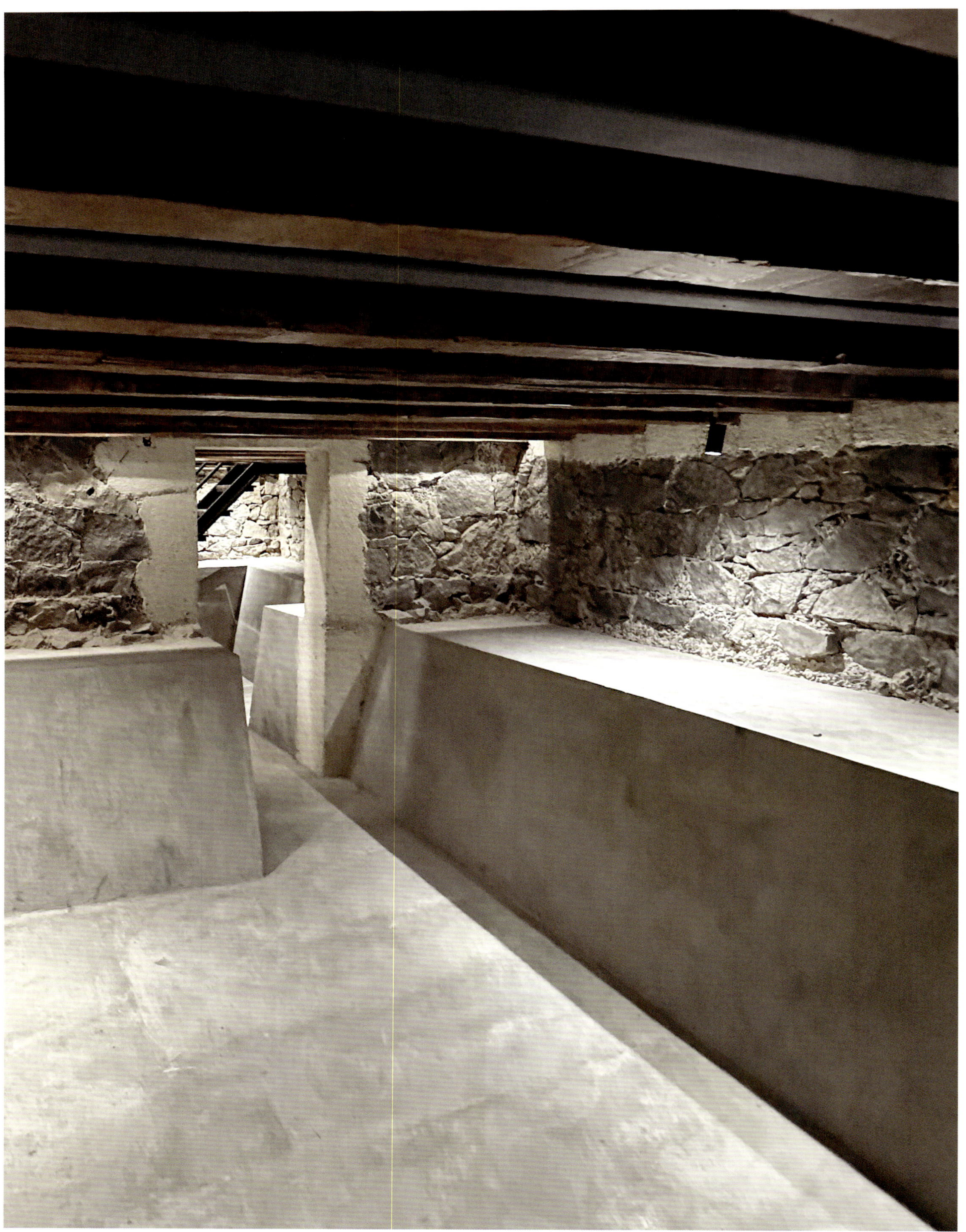

Frida Hentschel Frida loved Diego very much and married him twice. She was very attracted to his talent as an artist, his intelligence, and his politics. But her emotional connection and closeness to Diego faded over time. He was paying attention to other women and, as a famous painter, he was very busy. He was emotionally unavailable to her, and she longed deeply for that kind of connection, especially when her health started to deteriorate. She found some solace in being close to her family, as well as from the male companions and friends she would receive as visitors to Casa Kahlo. Their letters to her were often sent to this house. This second life filled a void in her.

Mara Romeo Kahlo Josep Bartolí was a Spanish painter and writer who fought in the Spanish Civil War. He was a friend of my grandmother Cristina who invited in refugees from the war. Frida met Bartolí in 1946, during a troubled time in her relationship with Diego. Distanced from him and having just returned from New York where she had surgery, Bartolí encouraged her to move to Casa Kahlo to be with her sister Cristina. And she did. According to Cristina, Bartolí was very smart and handsome. Not only had he fought in the war, but he escaped to France, only to be arrested and transported to Dachau concentration camp. Although he had suffered a lot, my grandmother remembered he was a lovely person to be around. That's why Cristina introduced him to Frida.

Around this time Frida adopted the name "Mara" for some of the correspondence with her lovers, including Bartolí. And she also signed some of her paintings Mara. The name Mara comes from a Tarzan movie. Johnny Weissmuller, the famous actor who was known for playing Tarzan, lived in Acapulco, Mexico. He made the movie *Tarzan and the Mermaids*, starring Mexican actress Linda Christian. Her character, a mermaid, was named Mara. Frida actually met Linda before the filming began at the newly opened Estudio Churubusco in Coyoacán. Linda sought out Diego because she wanted him to paint her portrait. She shared details of her movie character and the peculiarity of this mermaid who grew legs every full moon, walking out of the sea to procreate. Frida was fascinated by this character and identified with the name of Mara. I love this story so much because it's the origin of my name.

Mara de Anda Spaces are witnesses and keepers of memories, holding the energy of the people and events that took place there. This house has held the stories of generations. It still holds the energy of its inhabitants, its pets, its gardens. This house holds so much love, so much family, so much Mexico. This house has sheltered us, and allowed us to live—and relive—our stories and memories. It has allowed us to build our lives time and again, to grow our family, and to protect our legacy.

PAGE 84, TOP Leon Trotsky, Mexico City, ca. 1938

PAGE 84, BOTTOM Left to right: Antonio Villalobos, Leon Trotsky, Frida, Jean van Heijenoort, and José Escudero Andrade, Coyoacán, ca. 1937

PAGE 85 AND OPPOSITE The basement in Casa Kahlo, Coyoacán, today. The basement became a refuge and sanctuary for Frida, and around 1938, during Leon Trotsky's political exile in Mexico, it was also his occasional hiding place.

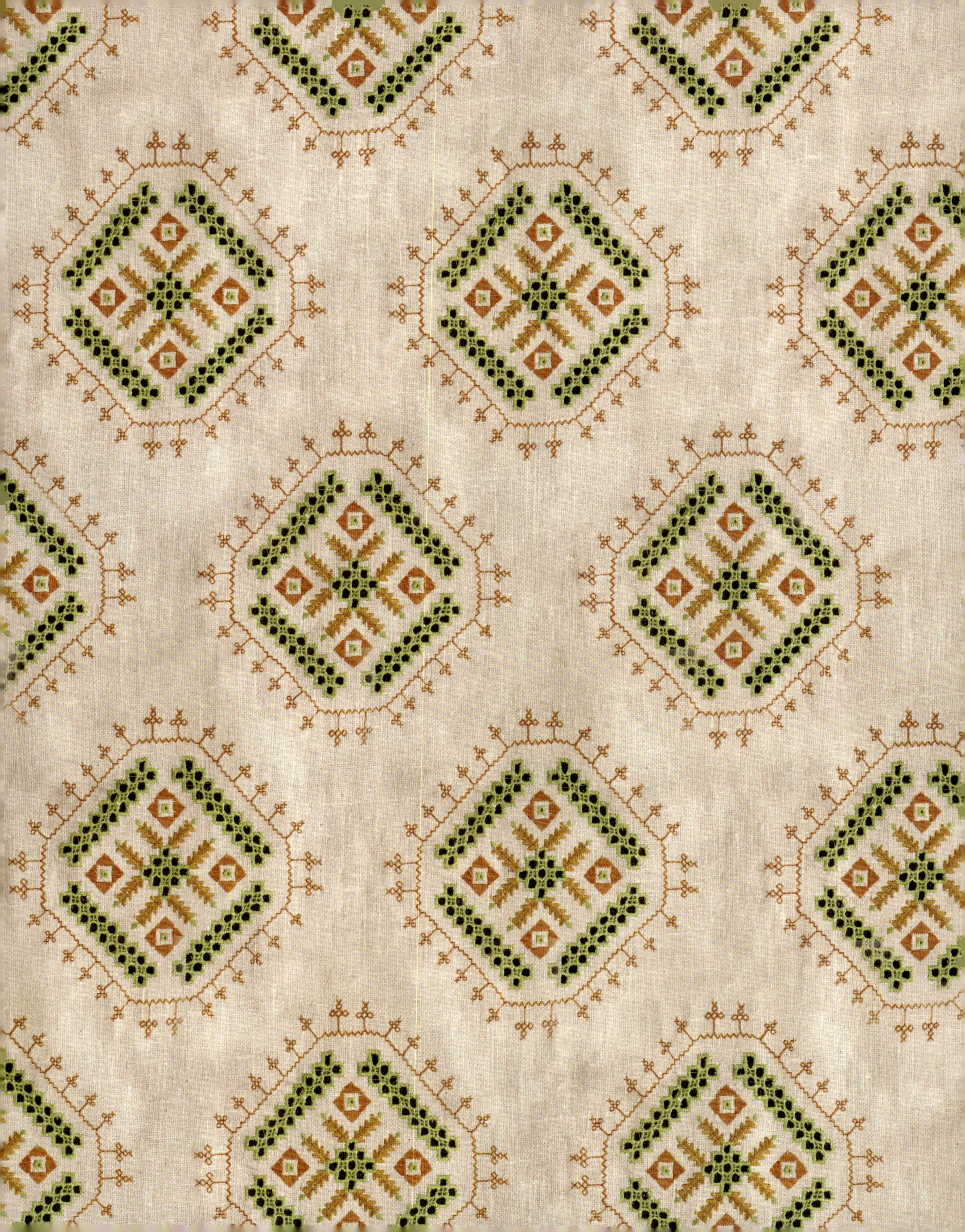

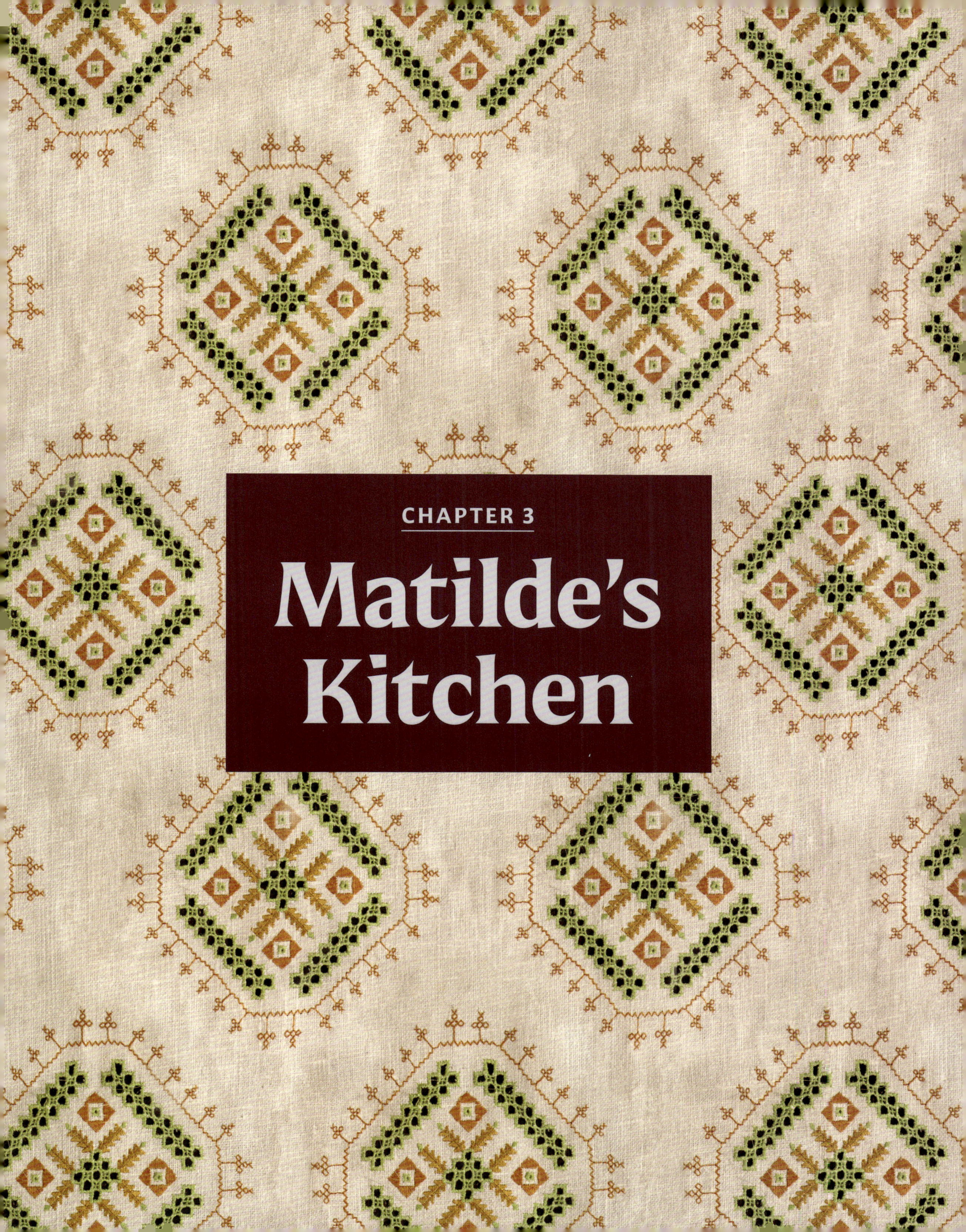

CHAPTER 3

Matilde's Kitchen

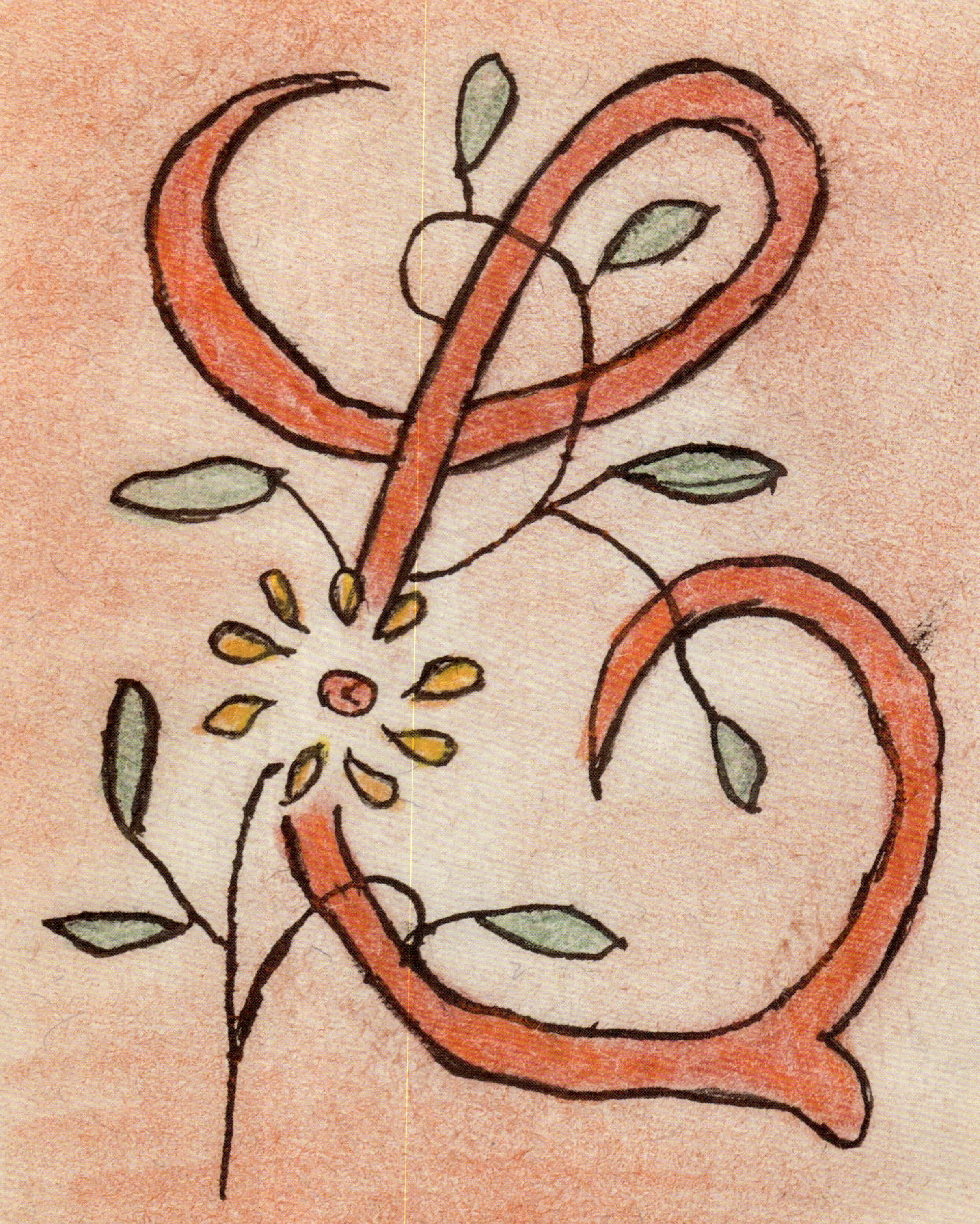

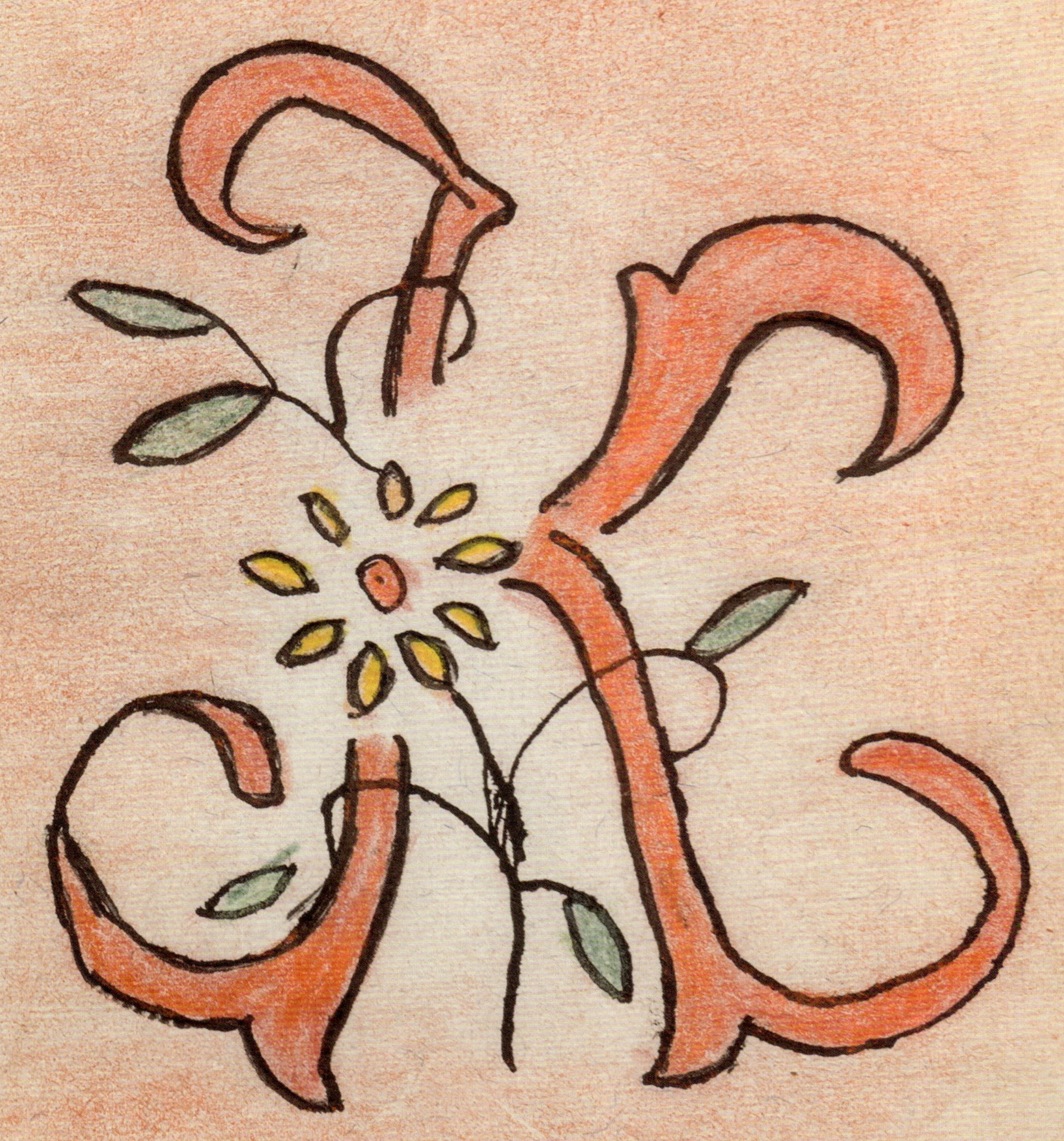

Frida Hentschel Mexico is a rich country in so many ways, and we Mexicans are crazy about it. We love our ancient roots and the knowledge and traditions that come from Indigenous communities. In school, we studied the history of the conquerors, but at home, we turned to the wisdom of our ancestors. We cherished ancient remedies and the traditions from our grandmother and from the ancestors that preceded her. Our family acknowledges our deep roots culturally and from *la tierra madre*.

Food traditions are one of the many aspects of our culture passed down through generations. The purest form of our love is expressed through food. In the Kahlo family, we have kept recipes and cookbooks from so many of Frida's relatives: from her grandmother Isabel, her mother Matilde and her sisters, and from Frida's own sisters and niece Isolda (my grandmother), creating a vast familial culinary record of delicious Mexican food.

The kitchen was the heart of Casa Kahlo. It's where everyone congregated—it's always been like that. It's the place where good stories, good meals, and good feelings come together.

Mara Romeo Kahlo My great aunt Frida loved to eat everything Mexican: tamales, *charales* (tiny fish), *chapulines* (grasshoppers), quesadillas, *elotes* and *esquites*, *sopes*, tostadas—the list goes on and on. Cristina, my grandmother, and her other sisters were great cooks. Frida didn't cook since it required long hours of standing, but she loved sitting down in the kitchen while the preparations took place. She always enjoyed *la chorcha* (a lively party). So many recipes from Frida's mother and the sisters have been preserved. They made many different dishes, and there are cookbooks and collections of handwritten recipes. It was Matilde who taught her daughters how to cook. She loved fresh vegetables and spices and would go to the market almost daily. And there were always flowers on the table—the beauty of the food, the flowers, and the décor created a magical atmosphere.

Mara Romeo Kahlo My great-grandfather Guillermo was German, and his native tongue continued to be spoken in our family for generations. All the Kahlo girls spoke German. There was and remains a large German presence in Mexico thanks to the Mexican president Porfirio Díaz from the early twentieth century, and the German school in Mexico City is still the top choice for many families.

In keeping with the tradition in my family, I was sent to the German school to study. My Tía Adriana's house was just three blocks away, so every Tuesday and Thursday,

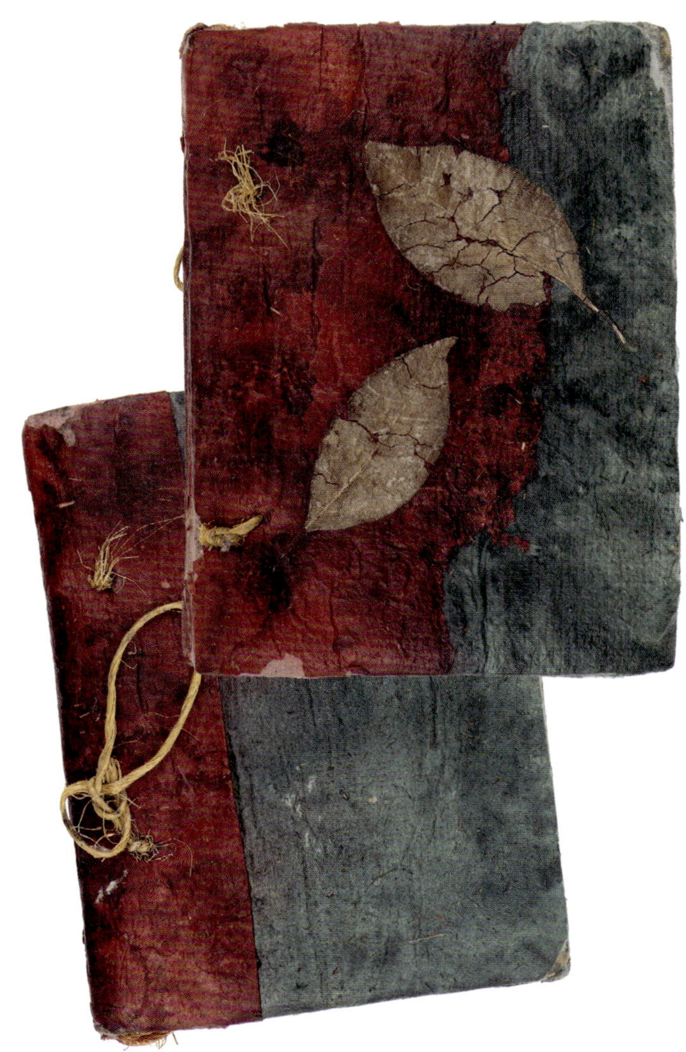

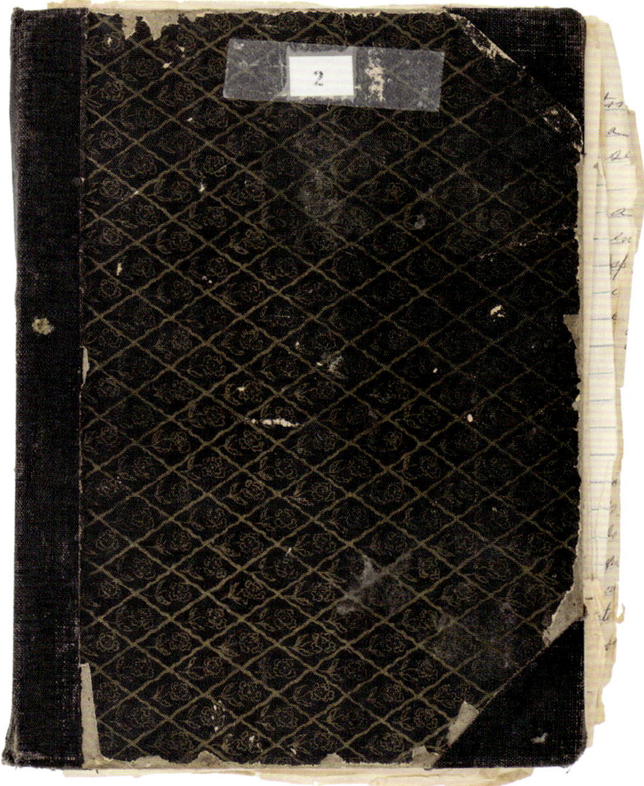

PREVIOUS SPREAD Pages from Frida's sister Cristina's cookbook

RIGHT AND OPPOSITE Kahlo family cookbooks and recipes. The family's collection of recipes dates back five generations. Cookbooks and individual recipes come from Frida's grandmother, her mother, aunts, and sisters, and were eventually passed down to Isolda, Frida's niece.

INDICE:

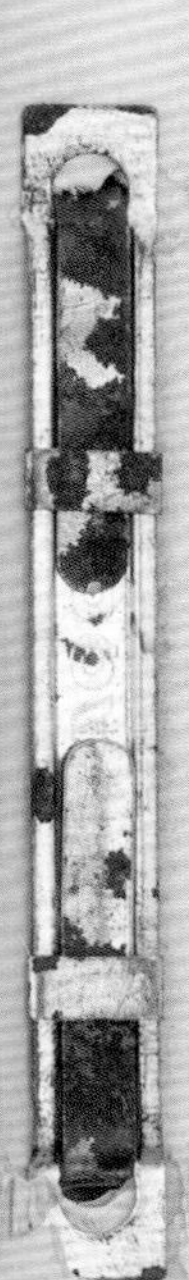

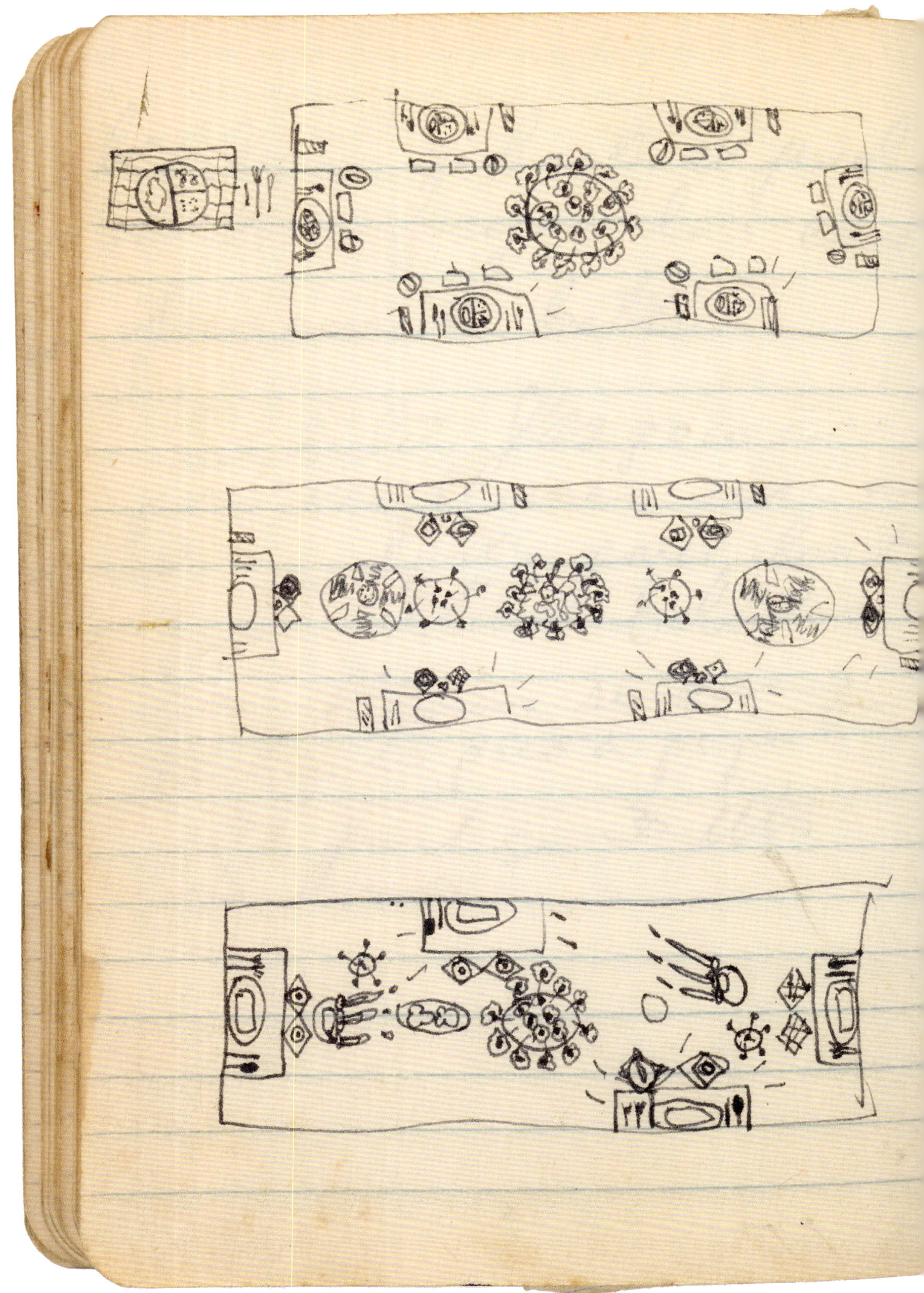

I went with my friend to eat lunch there—she was a great cook. My aunt always made my favorite dish—pea puree (peas with milk and butter). It was so delicious and so simple but she added a special *sazón* to make it her own. She was also known for making meringues with a creamy sauce. I still remember how they tasted to this day.

Adriana and my grandmother Cristina both kept chickens. My grandmother kept them for the eggs—she often used those eggs to feed the refugees she had taken in, as well as feeding them *frijolitos con nata* (beans with cream). Every Saturday, after they finished the distribution of food to the community through the charity Cristina had founded called La Ayuda, Adriana would cook. I remember her cutting off the chickens' heads and them still walking around. As a child this was a wild, and frightening, sight to behold!

Tía Frida loved everything made with corn. Adriana would make her *pasteles de elote* (corn cakes made with butter, milk, and a bit of cheese). We still have her handwritten recipe. Many of these recipes were simply jotted down on loose sheets of paper, which were carefully preserved over the years. One of the cookbooks we have is *La Cocinera Poblana*—it was a gift Frida gave her niece when she married. Part of the inscription read: "Isolda *maravillosa*, Here you have 'buten' recipes . . . that belonged to your grandmother." Instead of writing *muchos* she wrote *buten*, the Low German word for "outside." At some point in the family history, a child must have confused the word for *muchos* and it stuck. You see the word used throughout the letters and notes that we have saved.

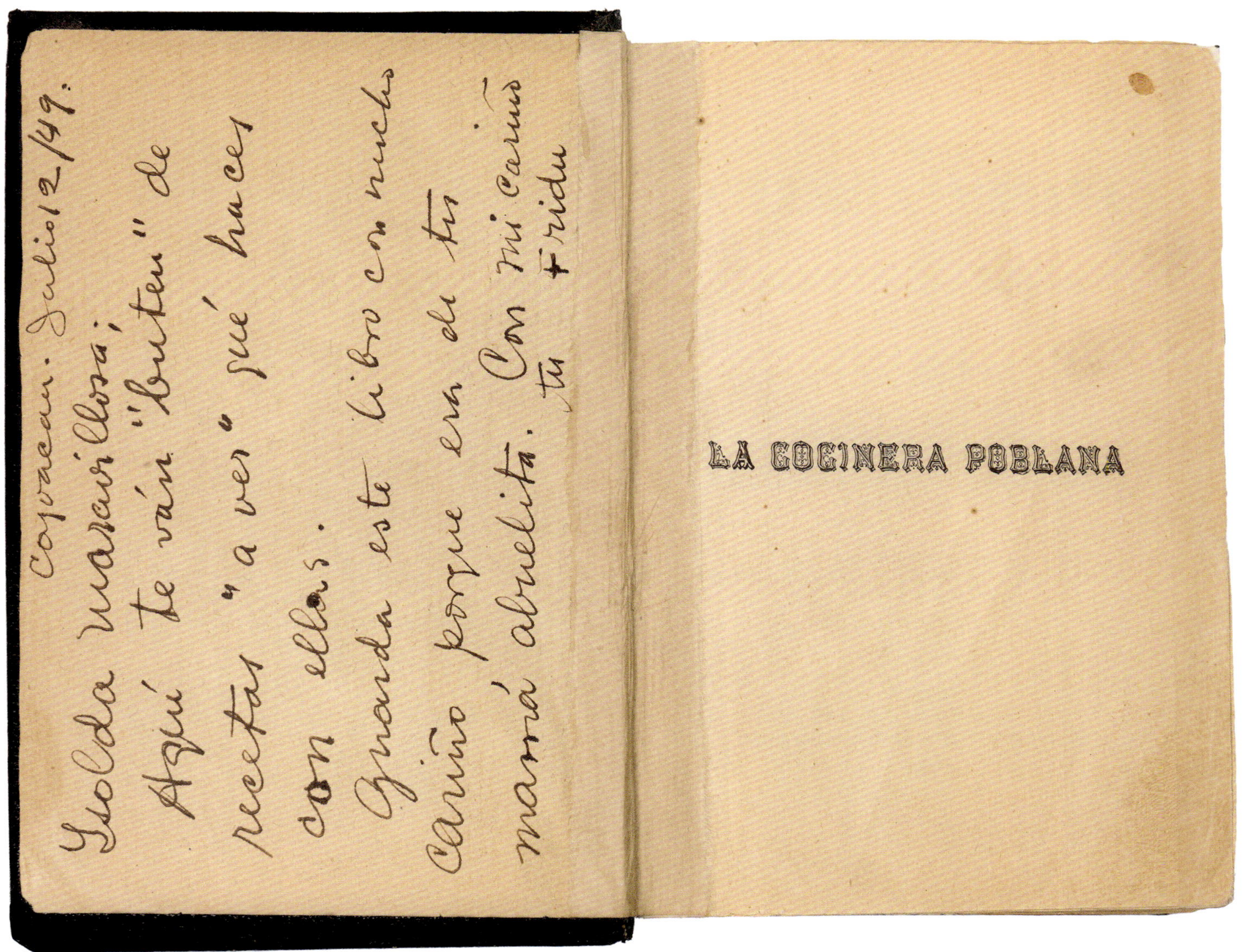

OPPOSITE Table seating arrangements by Isolda, Frida's niece, ca. 1950. The extensive record from the family's archive reflects the history and the Kahlo women's dedication to preserving and sharing their culinary traditions.

ABOVE *La Cocinera Poblana* cookbook, dedicated to Isolda by Frida, July 12, 1949. Frida gave this cookbook to Isolda with the inscription, "Isolda *maravillosa*, here you have 'buten' recipes, let's see what you make out of them. Hold on to this book with a lot of love, since it belonged to your grandmother. With my love, your Frida." *Buten* was a word the Kahlo family used throughout their letters to mean *muchos* (many).

de mantequilla y una
cucharadita de azúcar
se forran muy bien con
la pasta, que se hará
cerniendo la harina y
haciendo con ella una
fuente, en el centro se
pone un huevo y el resto
del azúcar se mezcla
todo con la espátula,
agregándole el resto de
la mantequilla, cuando
se forme una pasta que
ya no se pegue en las
las manos se pone en
la mesa para que se
extienda con el rodillo

dejándola de medio
centímetro de grueso.
Con esto se revisten las
manzanas se barnizan
con las yemas de huevo
y se meten al horno hasta
que se doren se colocan en
un platón en cuyo fondo
se halla espolvoreado
la nuez picada y el azú-
car glassé se sirven
calientes.

Manzanas al horno
(Puebla)

6 manzanas finas
2 cucharadas de mantequill

8

se cortan se barnisan con huvo y se reb
elcan en la almendra picada y se meten
al horno 10 minutos

Polborones de abellana
cantidades

arina tostada 1/4 k sin tostar 1/4 abellana 1/4
tostada asucar pulberisada 1/4 2 yemas 4
manteca 200 gr un poco de royal o carbona
to un pliego de papel parafinado 200 gr
asucar pulberisada

M de H

se dora la arina en el horno mobien
do constantemente con la espatula de
madera hasta tomar color de oro se deja
enfriar perfectamente se une con la
otra arina y el royal se bate la man
teca con la espatula y se agregan las
yemas, y el asucar con la arina y la
abellana tostada y molida se une esto
al batido y una bes incorporado se basia
á la tabla empastando con la raspa
se palotea se cortan los polborones se pon
en la charola se meten al horno caliente
cuando an enfriado

Empanadas
cantidades

harina 300 gr mantequilla 125 gr sal 5
rollal 20 gr leche 1/8 de litro huebos enteros 8

M de Haserlas

Se cierne la arina con el rollal se
forma una presa y en el sentro se,
ponen los huebos y la leche se trarabaja

9

con los dedos incorporando la arina y
despues la mantequilla con la raspa se
empasta y se deja reposar 5 minutos se
palotea y se cortan se rellenan al gusto
camote y piña cocada o pescado se doblan
se barnisan con huebo y se meten al horno

Mostachones de piñon
cantidades

azucar granulada 300 gra piñon mondado
125 gra se muelen los piñones juntamente
con 1/4 de kilo de azucar luego ~~luego~~ la
azucar que sobra se hase fondan cuando
está a punto de bola se le mescla el piñon se
sigue batiendo hasta mesclar y formar
una pasta, se engrasan los moldes espolbore
ados de azucar se hasen unas bolitas y se
moldean, si la pasta está palida se le
agrega unas gotas de carmin una bes ya
oreadas se ponen sobre papapel parafinado

Galletas de jeringa

arina 1/2 k azucar pulberisada 150 gr royal
mantequilla 300 gr yemas 6 bainillina
asucar pulberisada para ensima

M de Haserlo

se acrema la mantequilla se le pone la
azucar pulberisada despues las yemas
una a una en seguida el sabor que se
a elejido la arina sernida con el royal
se pone esta pasta en jeringa y se corta
n los pasteles se meten al horno caliente
y cuando esten dorados se bañan con
asucar pulberisada

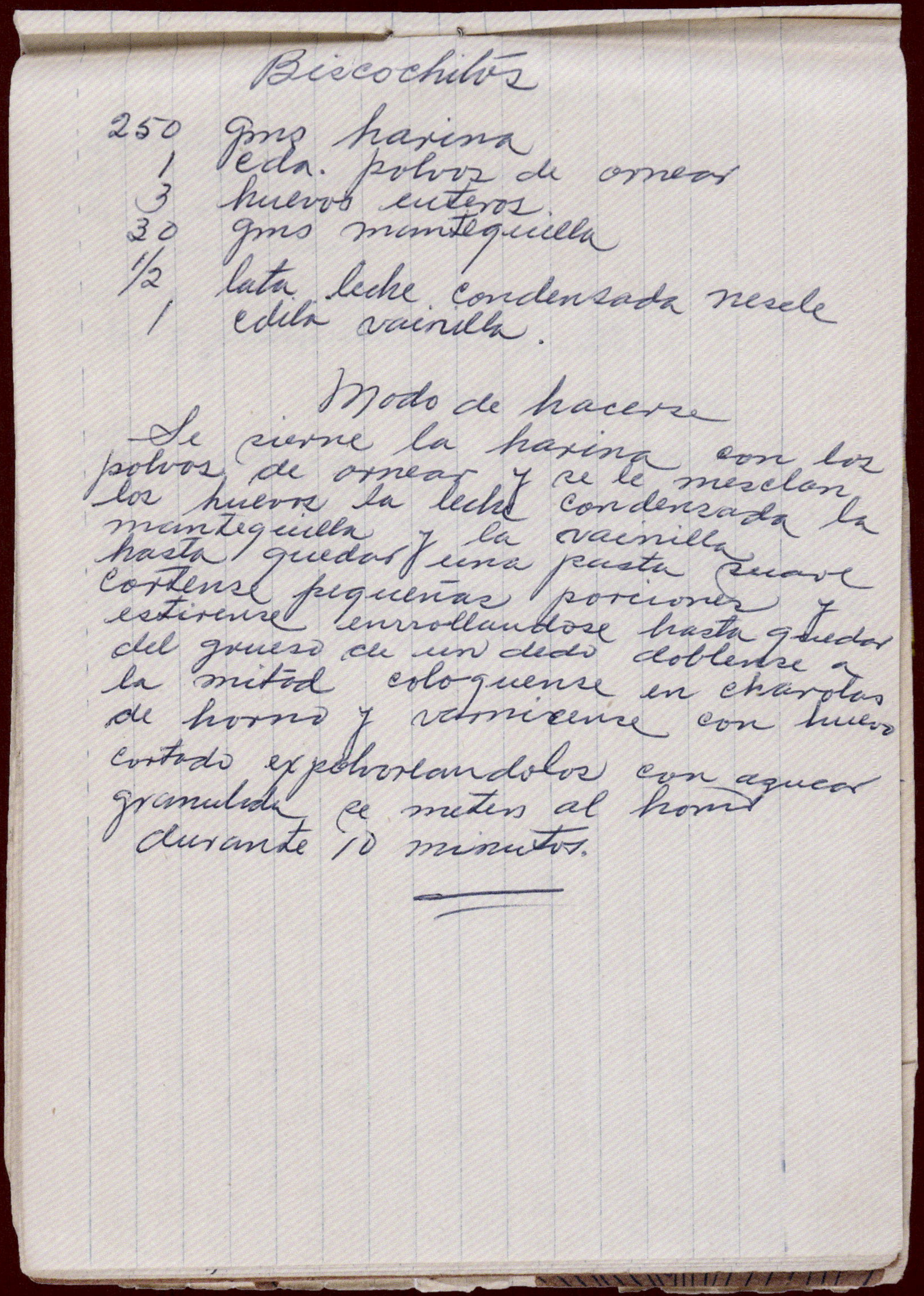

Biscochitos

250 gms harina
1 cda. polvos de hornear
3 huevos enteros
30 gms mantequilla
1/2 lata leche condensada nesele
1 cdita vainilla.

Modo de hacerse

Se cierne la harina con los polvos de hornear y se le mesclan los huevos la leche condensada la mantequilla y la vainilla hasta quedar y una pasta suave cortense pequeñas porciones y estirense enrrollandose hasta quedar del grueso de un dedo doblense a la mitad cologuense en charolas de horno y barnicense con huevo cortado expolvorlandolos con azucar granulada se meten al horno durante 10 minutos.

OPPOSITE Handwritten recipes for (top) baked apples from Puebla, and (bottom) hazelnut wedding cookies, empanadas, and pine nut meringue cake

ABOVE Handwritten recipe for *biscochitos* (little pound cakes)

Receta de panquecitos de azúcar o de sal muy buenos.

---

2 tazas de Harina flor
2 cucharaditas de royal
1 " de sal o
1 tacita de café de azúcar
3 huevos
1/2 taza de leche.
3 cucharadas de sopa de mantequilla.

Se cierne la harina con el royal y la sal o azúcar
Se baten los 3 huevos y se le revuelve la leche y la harina ya preparada se engrasan los moldes, y se llenan a la mitad para que esponjen y se meten al horno —

Zwiebel und Petersilie wird fein gehackt. Goldgelb geröstet, über die geschnitten Semmel gegeben, vermischt das passierte Eipulver wird mit Milch und Salz vermischt über den Knödel gegossen u. nach kurzem stehen vorsichtig mit Mehl vermischt, durchgeformt und 10 Min. in Salzwasser gekocht.

Mehlspeise:
1/4 Mehl
8 dkg Crememagarine
Prise Salz Vanille
84 gr. Mehl, 13 Dotter, 13 g. Eier, 25 dkg Zucker,
1/4 l Himbeersaft.

Milch mit Salz und Vanille zum kochen gebracht, das passierte Mehl eingerührt, geröstet bis sich die Masse vom Kessel löst,

Nockerln: 8 kg gem. Mehl - Salz,
8 l Milch, 40 dkg Eipulver, 75 dkg Margarinechen

Mehlspeise: 24 Eier
72 dkg Kristallzucker
20 dkg zerlassene Crememagarine, Zitronenschaale, 1 Esslöffel Rum.
Fülle: 2/8 l Wasser, 50 dkg Kristall, 75 dkg Crememagarine, Kaffeextract.
50 dkg Marmelade zum bestreichen
120 dkg Fondant, Kaffeextract.
Herst: Erst warm dann kalt geschlagen, Masse mit Mehl und zerlassene Magarine vermischt, befettet und in bestaubten Kuchenformen gebacken, nach erkalten durchgeschnitten und mit folgender Creme zusammengesetzt: Wasser u. Zucker zu Faden gekocht

gestaubt, mit Knochensuppe aufgegossen, gut verkocht und abgeschmeckt.

Hecht: portioniert
mit Salz, Paprika gewürzt, bemehlt und Öl bestrichen am Rostgebraten.
50 dkg Öl
Salz, Paprika.
40 dkg Crememagarine, geh. Petersilie, Salz, Pfeffer, Senf, 1 Zitrone, Worcestersauce.

Sauce: 16 Dotter, 2 Öl
Kuli: 25 Öl, 30 dkg Mehl.
Einlage:
30 dkg Schoten, Tomaten, Salz, Pfeffer, Senf, Worcestersauce, etwas Zucker.

Kartoffel:

getunkten Haselnüssen belegt

21. XII. 53

1. Menü am 18. Jänner 1941
Fridattensuppe
Rindsroulade
Kartoffellaibchen
Obersalat

Suppe: Rindsknochen, W.Z.G. 3 l Milch, 30 dkg Öl
Salz, etwas Zucker, 1/2 kg Mehl, 15 dkg Eipulver.

Roulade: 14,60 hinteres Rindfleisch
Schweinefleischreste, 8 Semmeln, 15 dkg Öl, fein. Zwiebel.
Salz, Pfeffer, Majoran, etwas Öl.
Herst: Das Fleisch wird zu große Schnitzel geschnitten geklopft, mit Salz, Pfeffer geröstet, mit der faschierten

German recipes Guillermo left for his daughters, featuring dishes from his homeland.

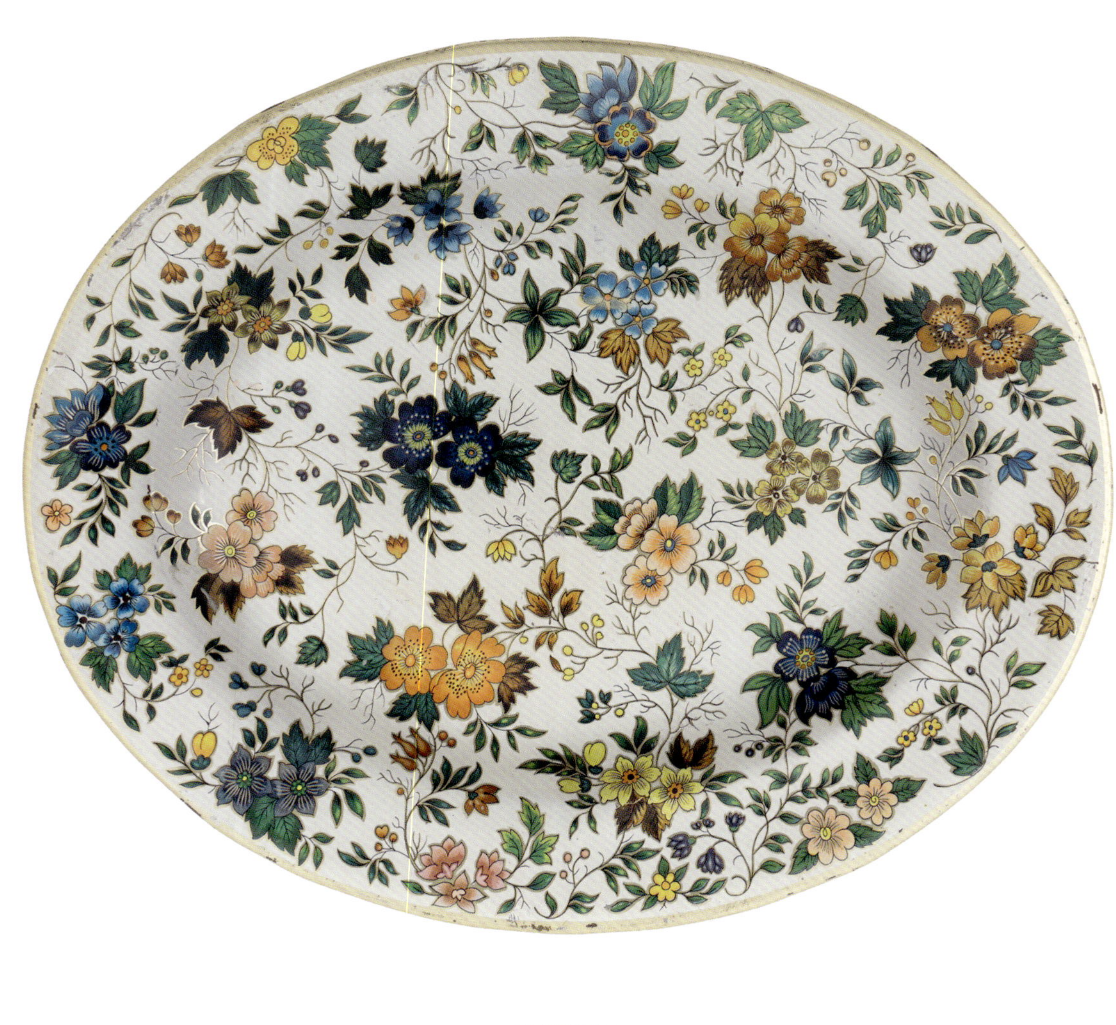

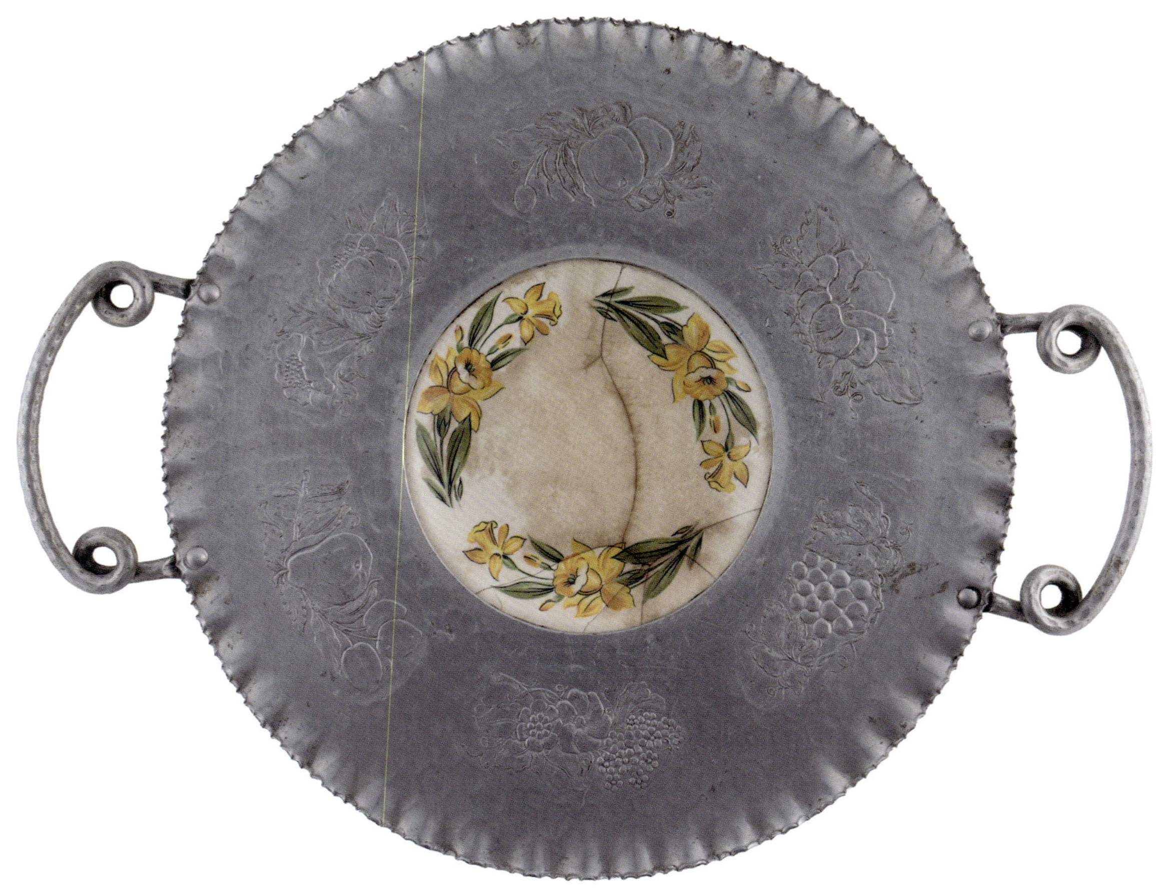

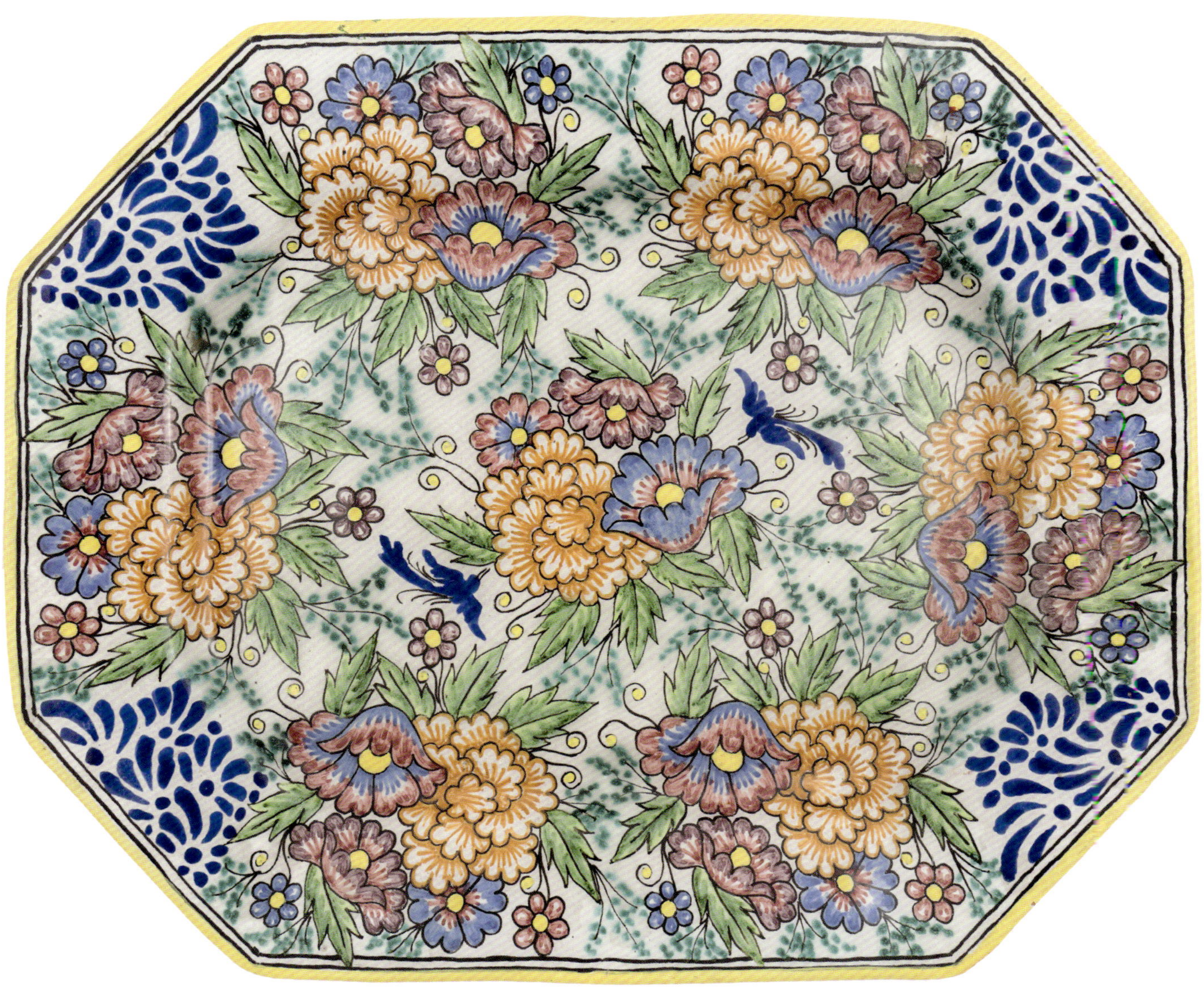

ABOVE AND OPPOSITE Plates and platters from Casa Kahlo, Coyoacán

Mara de Anda In our family, home remedies and the healing power of nature have been passed down through the generations. Matilde, Frida's mother, believed in natural remedies, which she shared with her daughters. When Frida contracted polio, Matilde went to the market where they sold healing herbs, and often bought walnut tree wood, which she boiled and then used the water to soak washcloths that she used on Frida's leg to reduce inflammation. She made teas from the flowers of the lemon and grapefruit trees. This tea seemed to calm Guillermo and relieve his anxiety and nervousness. Cristina, Frida's sister, later made this same tea for Isolda hoping it would work in similar ways. Our family also made a tea from corn silk that was used to clean and purify the kidneys. My grandfather and Isolda's then husband, Julio, who was a doctor, had kidney stones, and Isolda and Cristina insisted he drink the tea for a couple of days before having a medical procedure. After a week, and contrary to his expectations, he painfully expelled the stones.

Mara Romeo Kahlo At the house there was a grapefruit tree planted outside the kitchen terrace and we always had a good view of it. It was huge and colorful; it smelled delicious when the flowers were in bloom and it produced the biggest grapefruits. The garden was always green, filled with flowers and plants: bougainvilleas, magnolias, roses. The greenery attracted birds and lizards—the garden at Aguayo was teeming with life. And Frida immortalized the flora and fauna of the garden on the walls of the kitchen.

During my childhood, I visited my grandmother Cristina often. I remember sitting in the kitchen and looking at the murals while having breakfast or dinner. This is such an indelible memory. The murals were painted on three walls. When sitting at the kitchen table, I saw a grapefruit tree, a canary, a cardinal, and a blue bird—I used to play and talk to them in my head. It evoked in me a deep connection to nature.

On one wall, Frida had painted a big undulating garland—like you see in so many of her paintings—carried by sparrows. On the garland she painted these words: "El mesón de los Gurriones," (the Sparrows Tavern). But this inscription has a double meaning. The family joked that the house was secretly "El mesón de los Gorrones": a *gorrón* is a person who overstays their welcome, something like a freeloader, but not as overtly offensive. It was the perfect slogan for our kitchen! Visitors to the house were always welcome to stay for a meal. If there was not enough food for everyone, they would somehow stretch what they had so everyone could have a seat at the table. At the very end of the painted garland, there is another inscription: "Idea de Cristi y Toño Kahlo" (Cristi and Toño's idea), referring to Frida's sister Cristina and her son Toño (short for Antonio).

On the other side of the mural, there was a bougainvillea and a tree with white flowers, a magnolia. Like most gardens in Mexico, we have always had bougainvillea at Casa Kahlo. On the branch there is a green and yellow parakeet. You enter the kitchen and are immersed in this colorful room, filled with all kinds of life.

Mara de Anda When my grandmother Isolda remodeled the kitchen around 1963, somewhat unbelievably, she painted over two of the three walls and installed cabinets. Paradoxically this helped preserve the mural for all these years. She used to say, "the everyday erases much of the extraordinary" (*lo cotidiano borra mucho de lo extraordinario*). For Isolda, the mural was one of the things her eccentric aunt left behind, not the work of the world-famous artist that she is now.

Mara Romeo Kahlo When I decided to convert our house into a museum, I hired an art restorer. I hadn't seen the murals in sixty years, but I was sure they were there. It was an emotional rollercoaster, not knowing if the restoration would be successful. I was excited. But days passed and the restoration team was not finding anything. In my mind, I traveled back in time and imagined myself as an eight-year-old sitting at the table. I directed them to where I remembered the canary was painted on the wall. And hours later, they called me saying they had found the first sign of a tree underneath the layers of paint. I was beside

OPPOSITE Detail of kitchen mural painted by Frida at Casa Kahlo, Coyoacán. From her earliest memories at her grandmother's house, Mara Romeo Kahlo remembered the kitchen walls covered with murals. A recent restoration brought them back to life.

FOLLOWING SPREAD Kitchen with the mural painted by Frida on the three walls at Casa Kahlo, Coyoacán

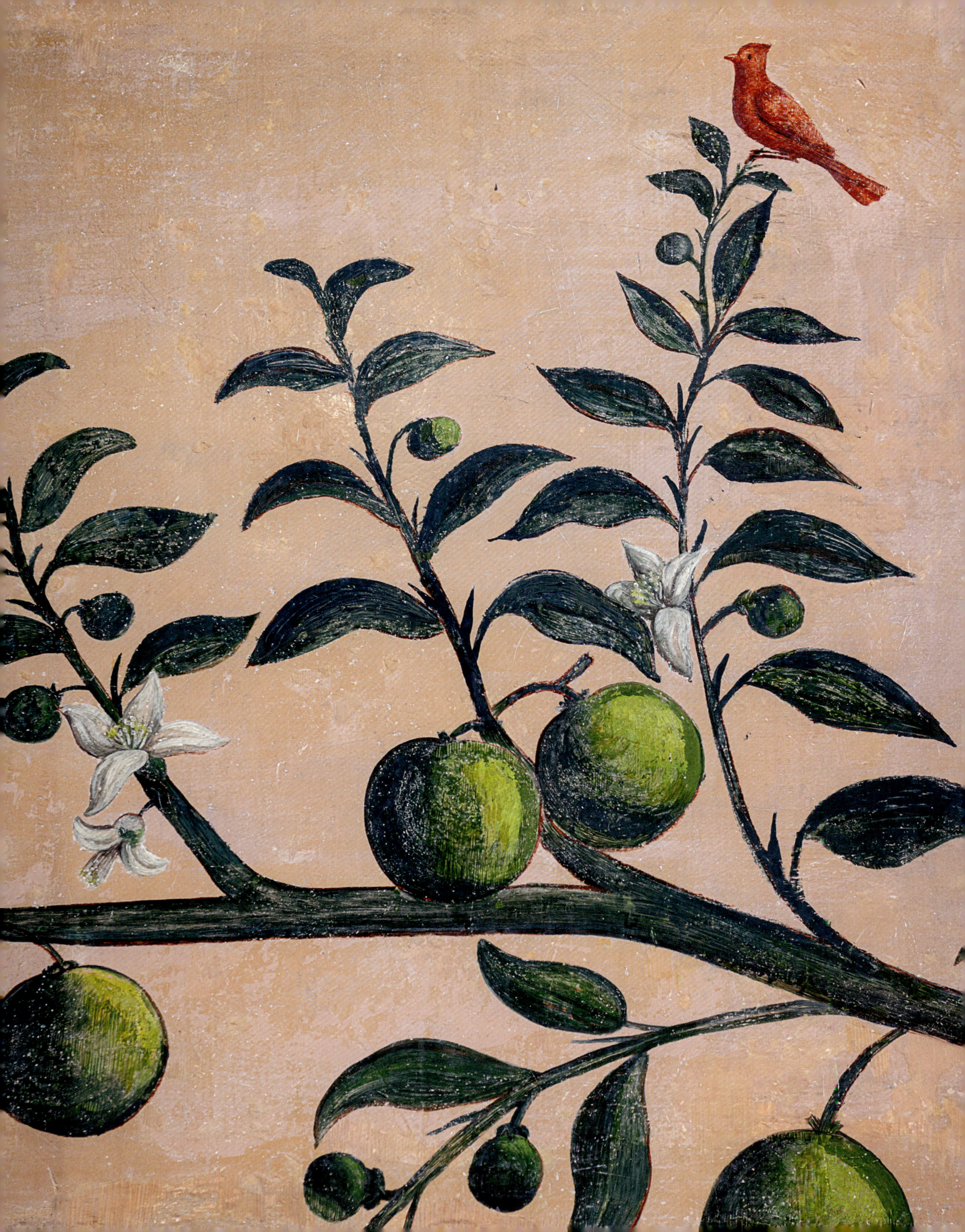

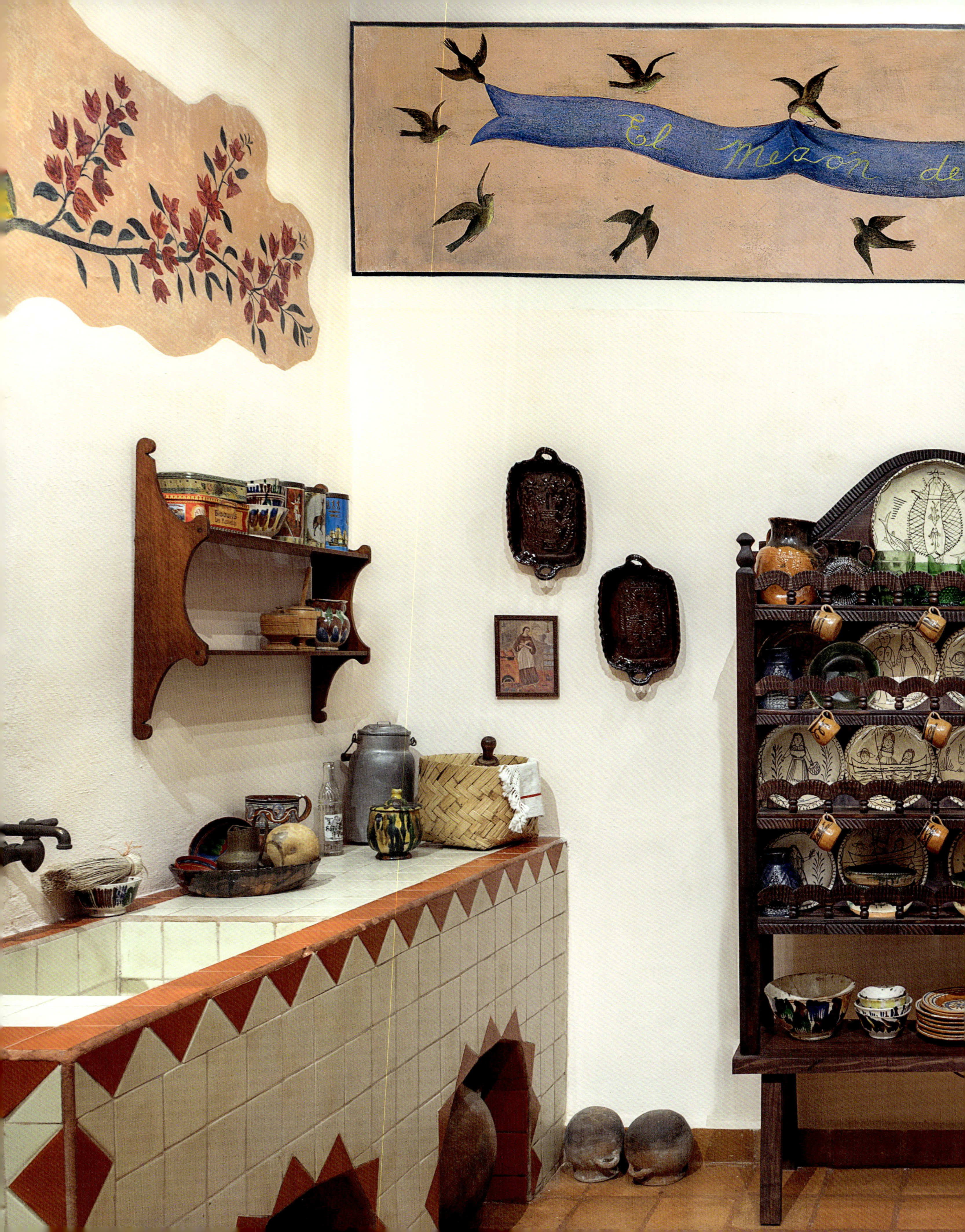
El Mesón de

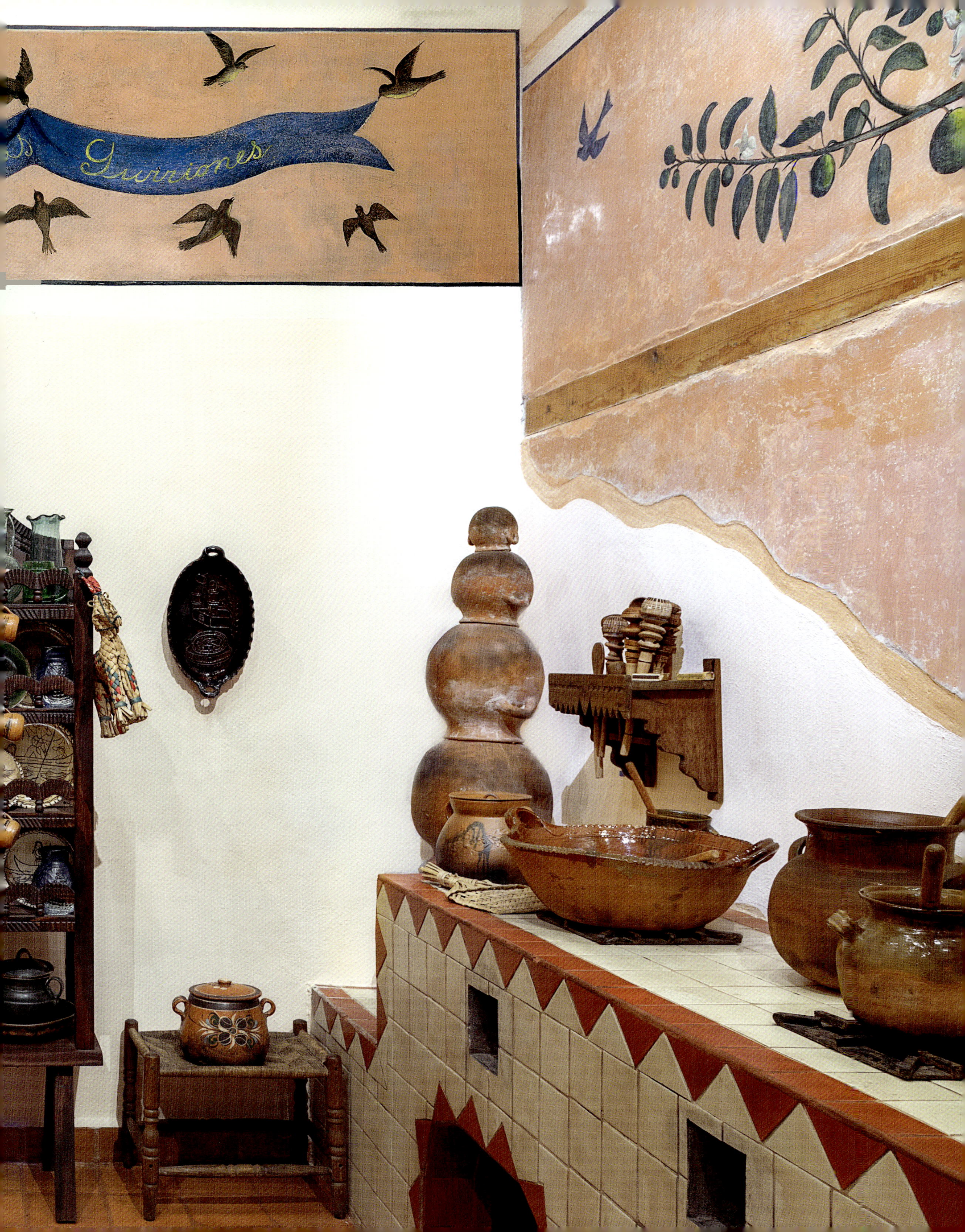
s Gurriones

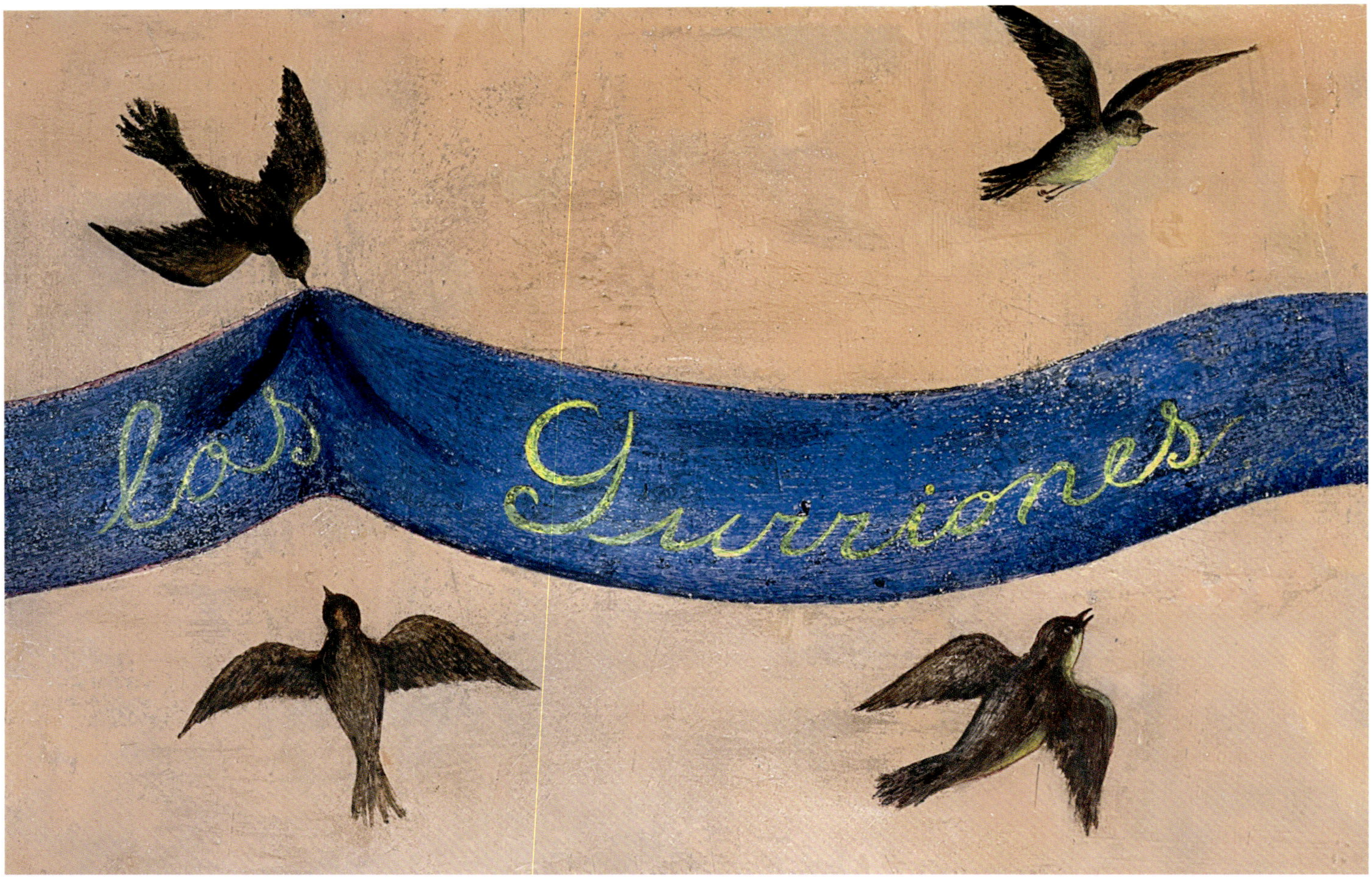

myself. Seeing that mural emerge from the walls after decades of not seeing it has been healing in many ways—it reconnected me to my grandmother, to Frida, and to all the Kahlo sisters again. I felt as if my whole family, my entire lineage, was celebrating together.

The restoration of the mural is one of the many visual embodiments of our family history as we restore and protect our roots. The grapefruit tree placed so prominently is a metaphor for this.

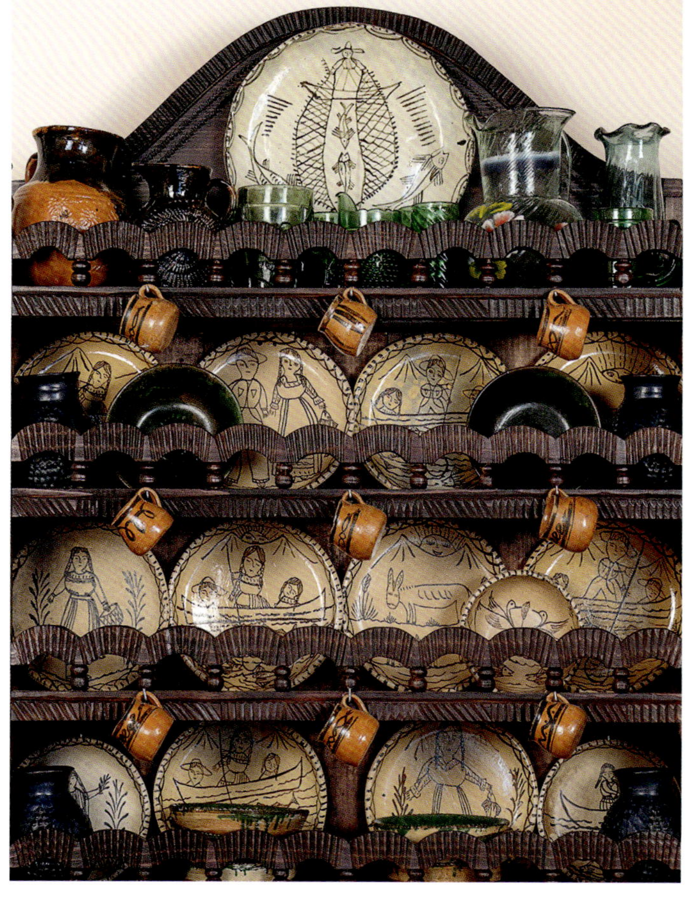

ABOVE Detail of center kitchen mural, with an inscription that reads "El mesón de los Gorriones" (the Sparrow Tavern) at Casa Kahlo, Coyoacán

RIGHT Detail of the wooden hutch in the kitchen with plates, cups, and vases, Casa Kahlo, Coyoacán

OPPOSITE Detail of kitchen mural inspired by the lush garden at Casa Kahlo, Coyoacán, which featured bougainvillea, magnolias, a grapefruit tree, and birds

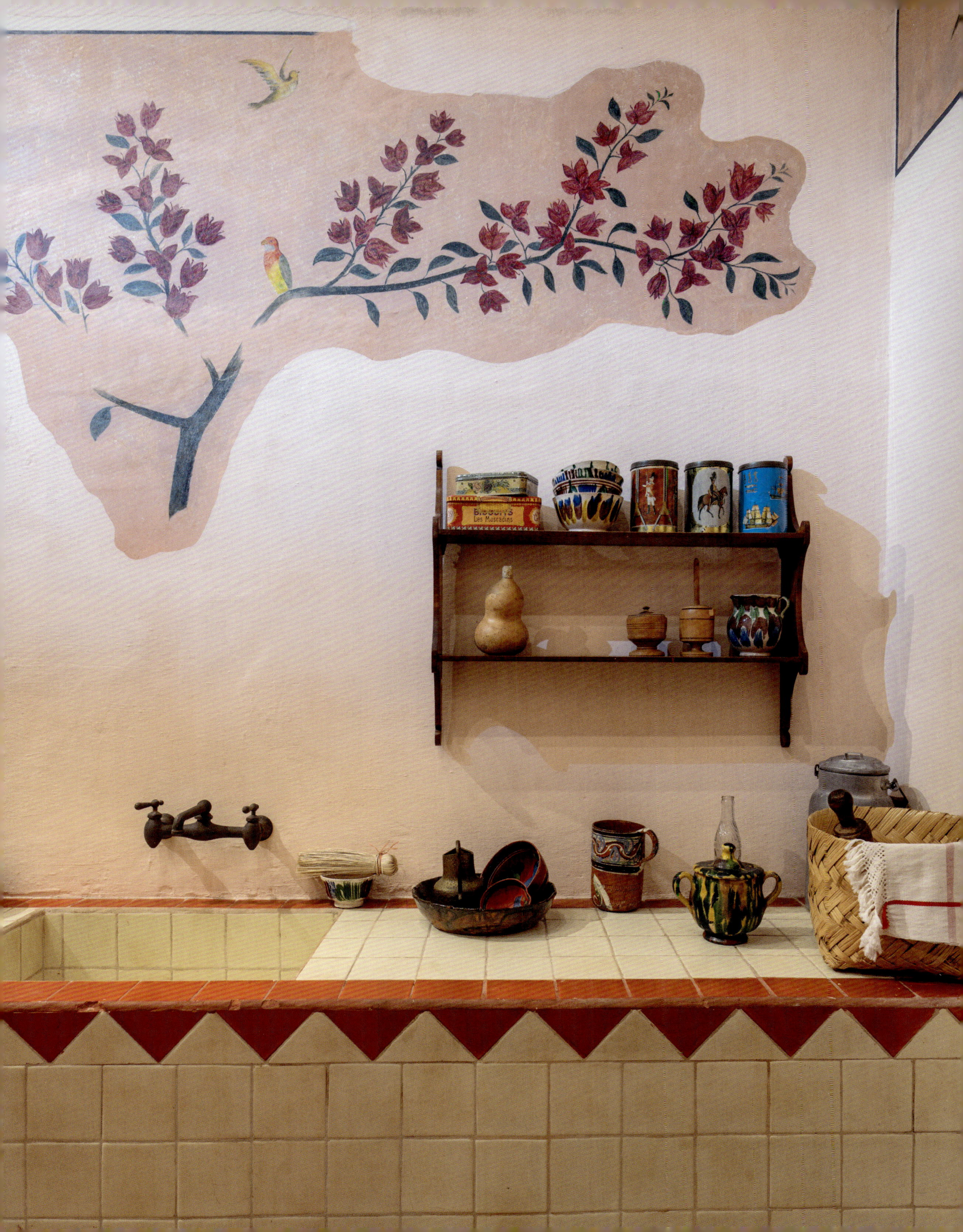
BISCUITS
Les Muscadins

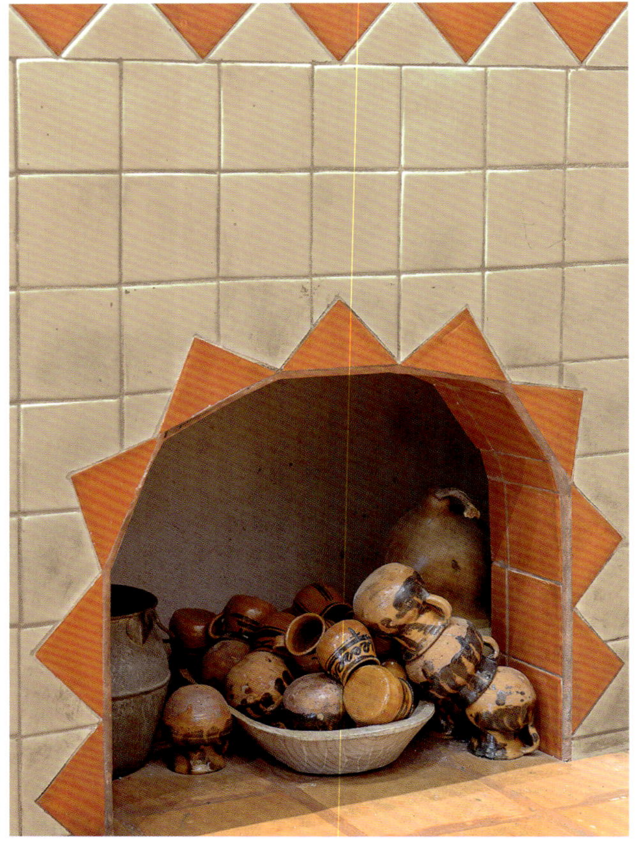

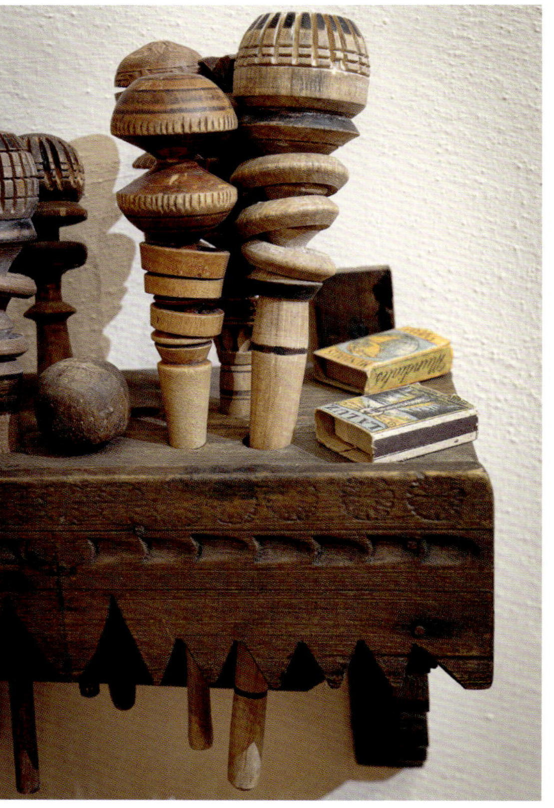

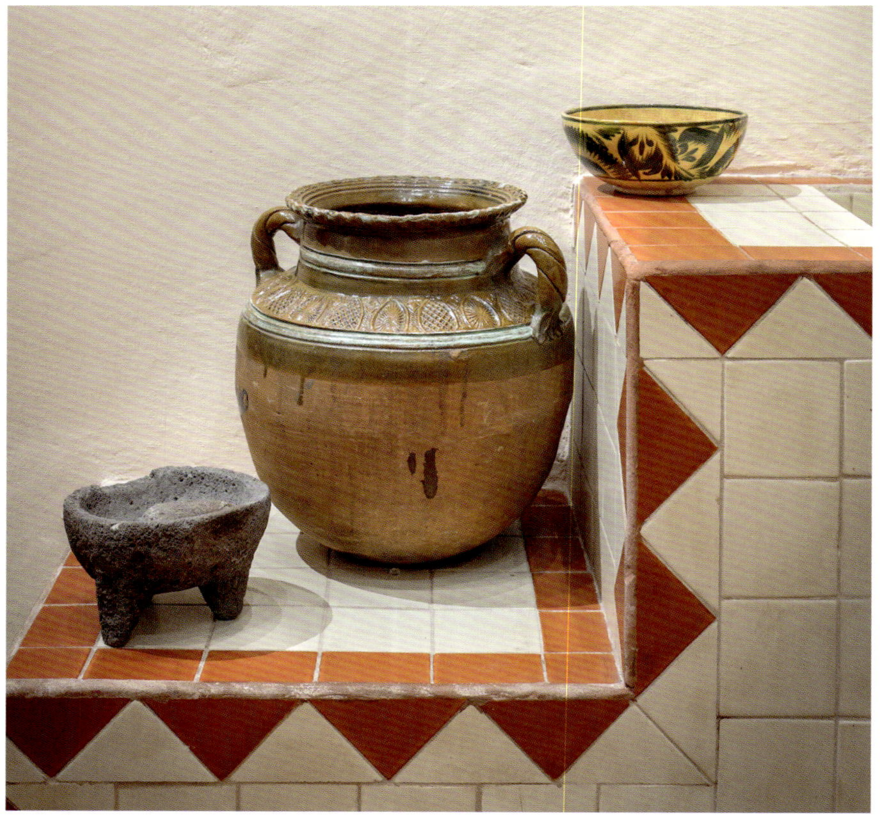

Details of kitchen, Casa Kahlo, Coyoacán

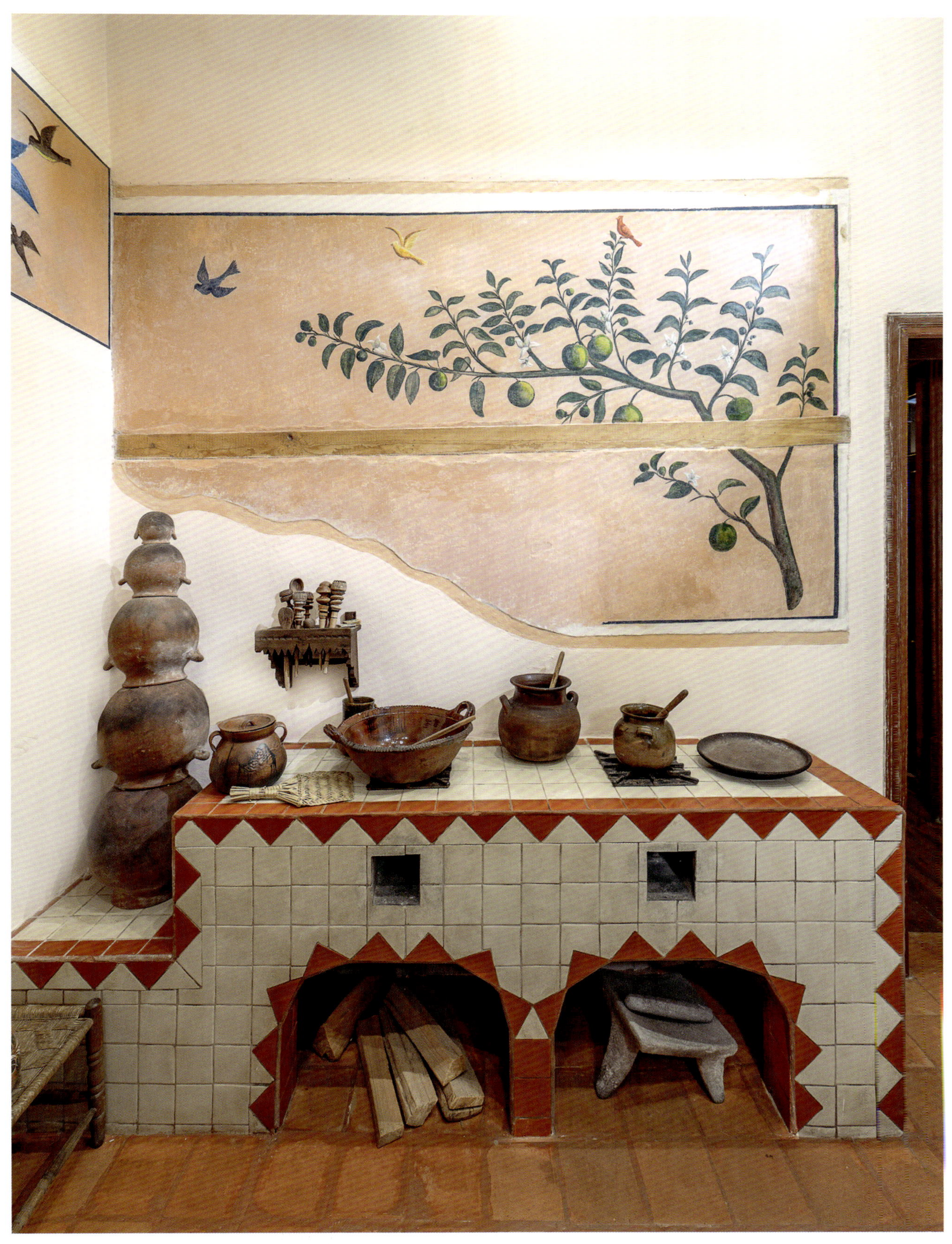

At Casa Kahlo, birds were (and remain) frequent visitors. Frida's mural in part pays tribute to the variety of birds that were ubiquitous at the house during her lifetime.

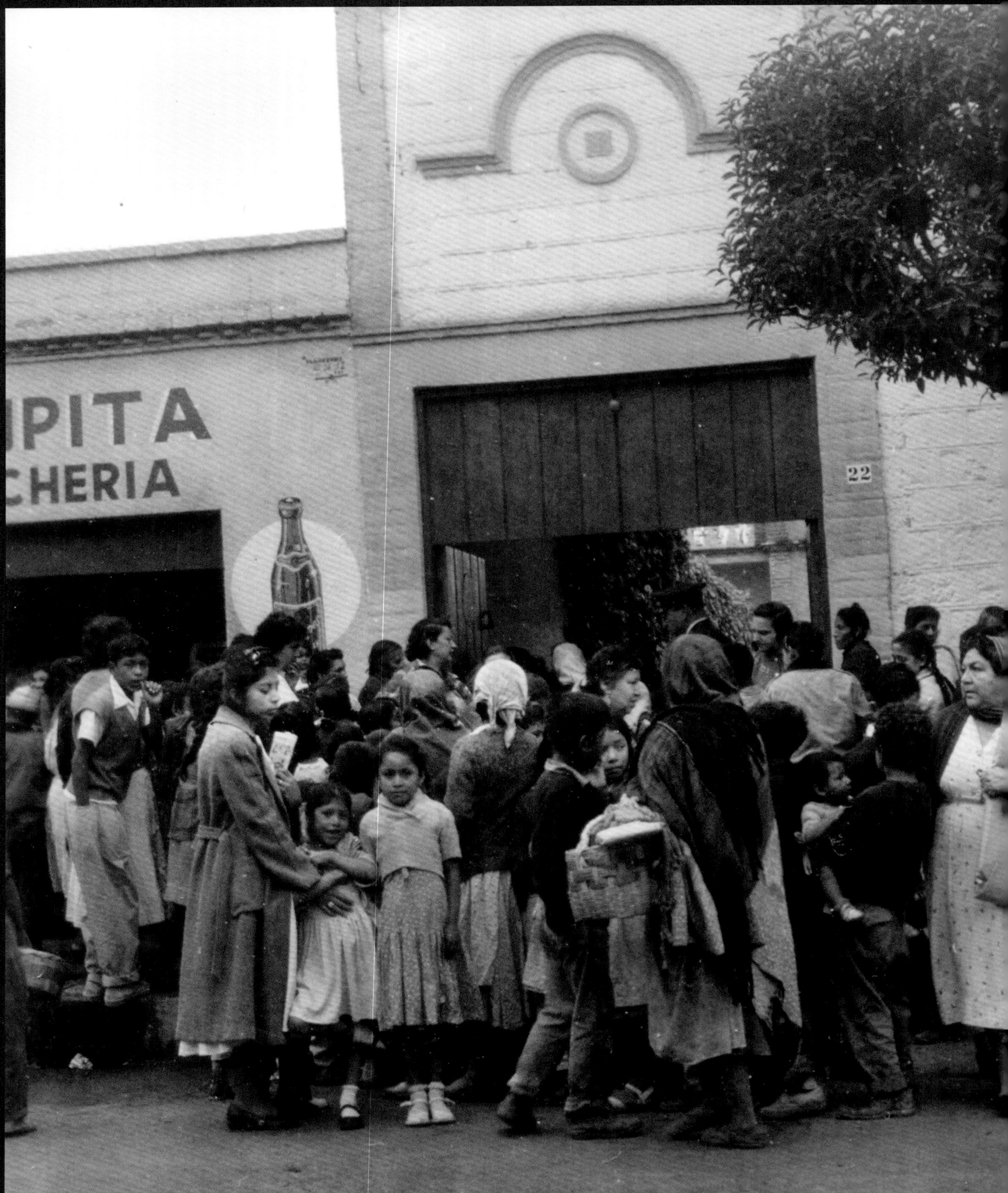
UPITA
CHERIA
22

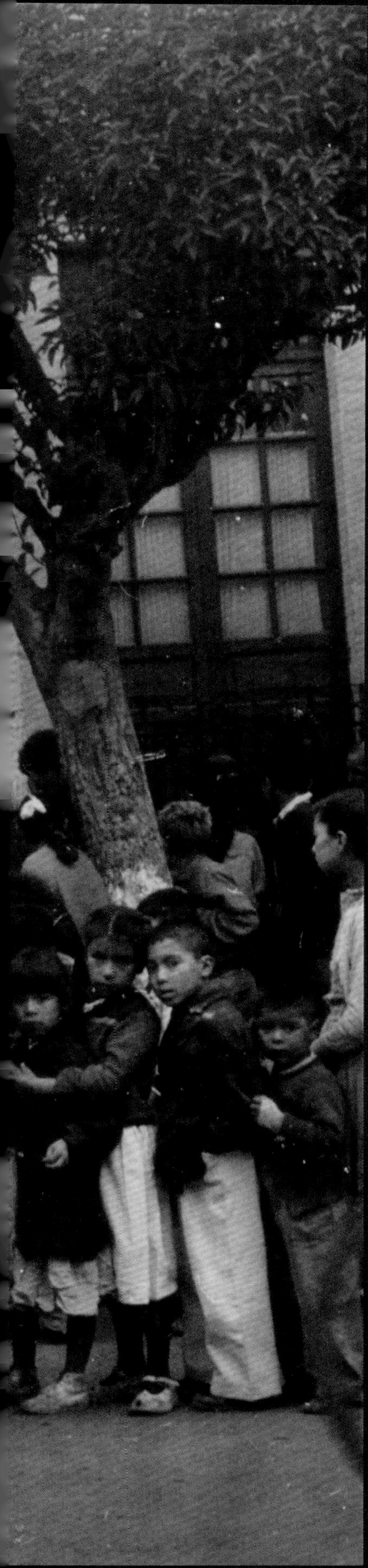

Frida Hentschel Generosity has been a constant thread in the family ethos. Frida and her sisters learned the tradition of helping others from their mother Matilde. Matilde helped soldiers during the Mexican Revolution, no matter which side they were on, and also cared for injured animals that ended up taking shelter at the house and never leaving. During the holidays, the entire family got involved in helping the needy. During Día de los Reyes Magos (Day of the Three Kings), the family would dress up and give out gifts throughout Coyoacán. Frida and Cristina dressed up, and so did the other members of the family: Cristina dressed up as the Virgin Mary on a donkey, accompanied by Adriana's husband Güerito Veraza dressed as Saint Joseph. Frida dressed up as Baltazar, one of Three Kings, who was believed to have the ability to read children's minds. Baltazar would know if they had been naughty or nice, which allowed him to prepare the most special gift for the child. Frida loved this character.

Mara Romeo Kahlo The idea for La Ayuda came from my grand-mother, Cristina. She was always aware of the income disparity in Mexico, but it was during one moment while she was having dinner at a fancy restaurant where it was driven home: when the check came, she realized it could have paid for a week's worth of food for one household. She promised herself never to set foot in expensive restaurants again and started helping mothers in need. Inspired by her own story and financial difficulties over the years, she began providing assistance to a handful of single mothers

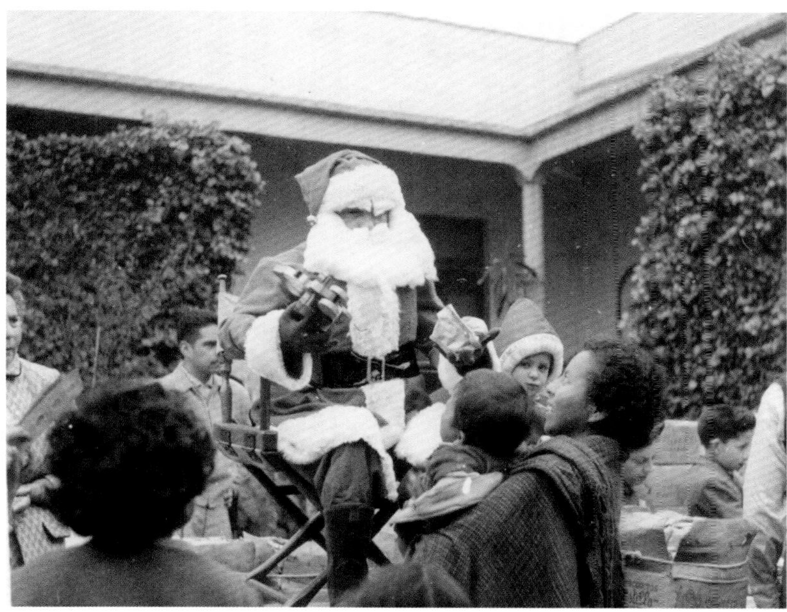

LEFT La Ayuda, the charity organization founded by Cristina in which many of the Kahlo sisters were involved, was administered from Casa Kahlo, Coyoacán. The organization provided weekly packages of food staples. Recipients of the aid would gather outside while they waited for their basket of goods, ca. 1954.

ABOVE Santa Claus and his little helper, Mara Romeo Kahlo, giving holiday gifts to beneficiaries' kids during Christmas, ca. 1957.

and eventually she endeavored to make this work more official. She founded La Ayuda, which was sponsored by various businesses and a bank. She opened the gates of Casa Kahlo in 1952 to give more than 500 *canastas básicas* (basic food baskets) and cleaning staples. Each *canasta* contained a kilo of rice, sugar, beans, oil, soap, and 2 kilos of masa for tortillas that would last one week. All of the Kahlo sisters helped with the effort every Saturday for many years. Separated from her husband without financial assistance, my grandmother worked very hard to give her two children, Isolda (my mother) and Antonio (my uncle), a good life. She understood deeply that so many people in her community were in need, particularly single mothers raising children.

Frida Hentschel I remember my grandmother Isolda telling me that they would walk through Coyoacán, and when they saw little boys and girls alone in the street, they would ask about their mothers. They started with the community around Coyoacán, and people started to show up for help. As the word spread, people from different neighborhoods started to come to Casa Kahlo.

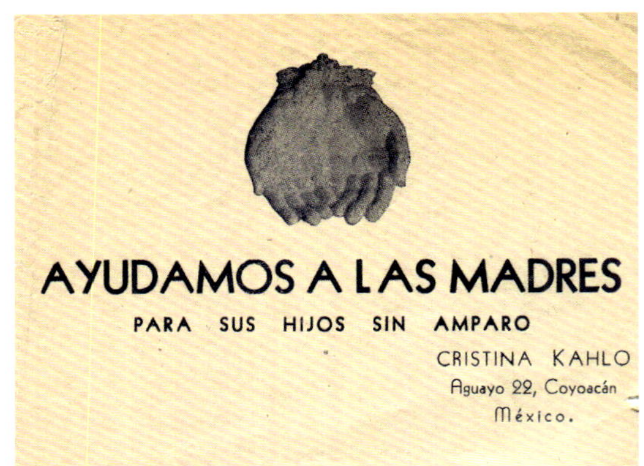

AYUDAMOS A LAS MADRES
PARA SUS HIJOS SIN AMPARO
CRISTINA KAHLO
Aguayo 22, Coyoacán
México.

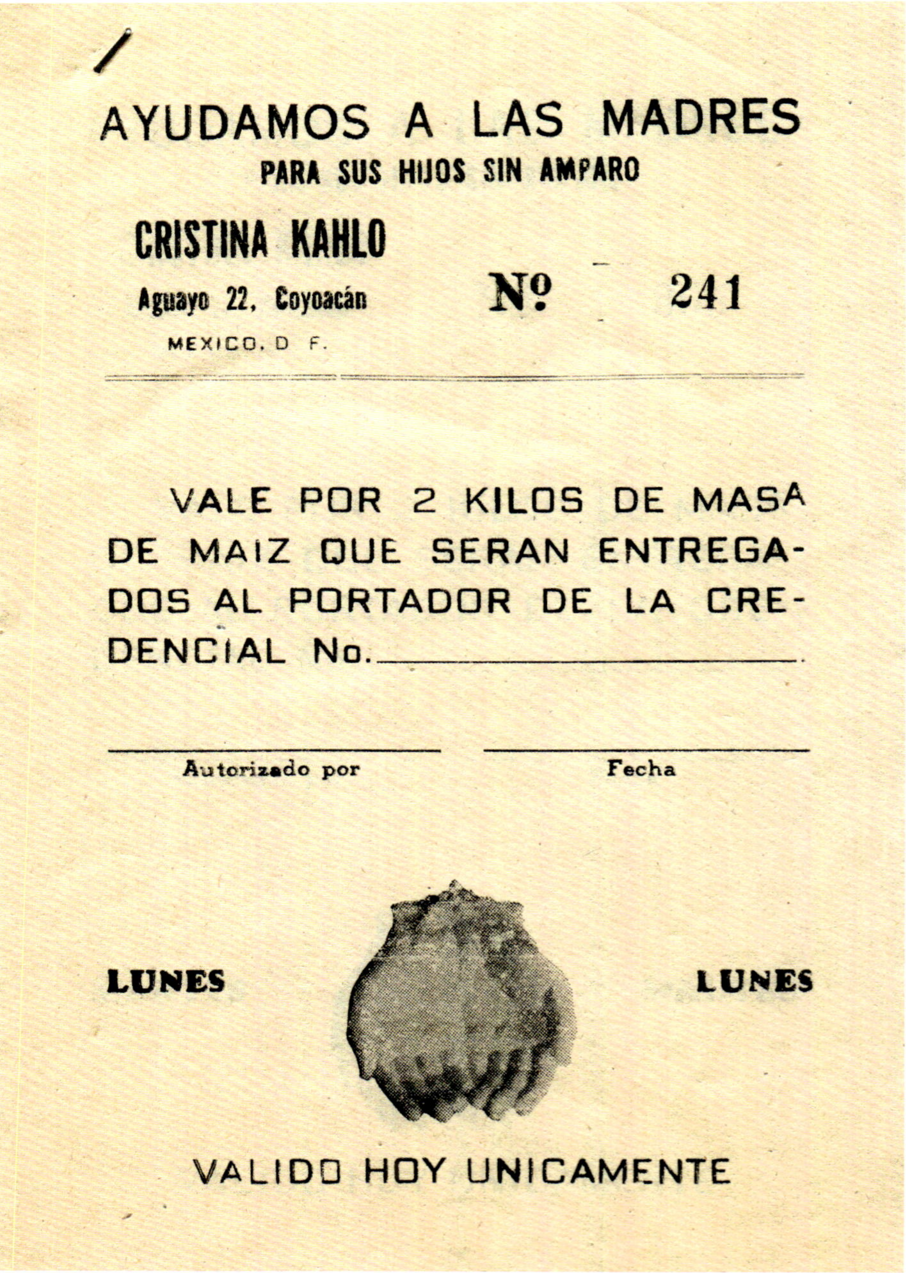

AYUDAMOS A LAS MADRES
PARA SUS HIJOS SIN AMPARO
CRISTINA KAHLO
Aguayo 22, Coyoacán
MEXICO, D. F.
Nº 241

VALE POR 2 KILOS DE MASA DE MAIZ QUE SERAN ENTREGADOS AL PORTADOR DE LA CREDENCIAL No.__________

Autorizado por

Fecha

LUNES LUNES

VALIDO HOY UNICAMENTE

La Ayuda credential and food voucher, ca. 1954. Every beneficiary of aid was registered and provided credentials to present at the weekly distribution of food.

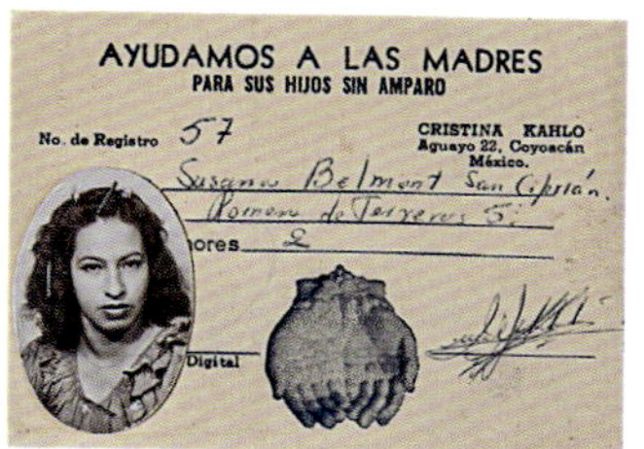

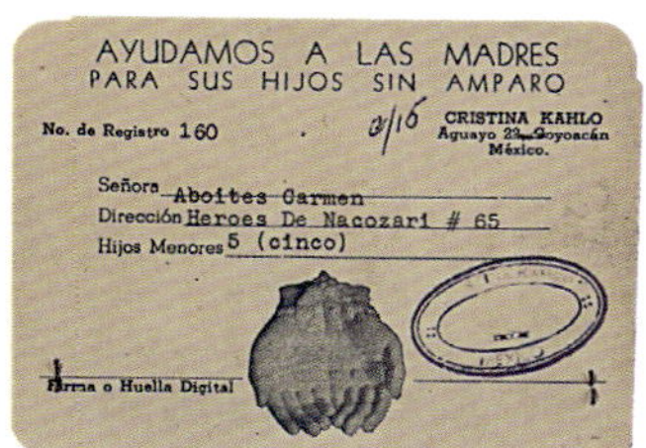

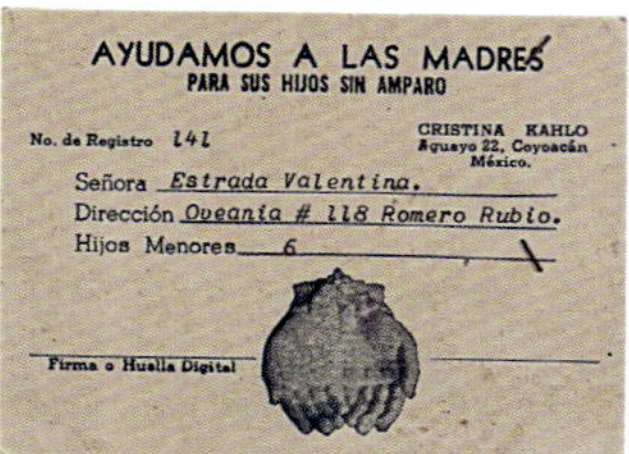

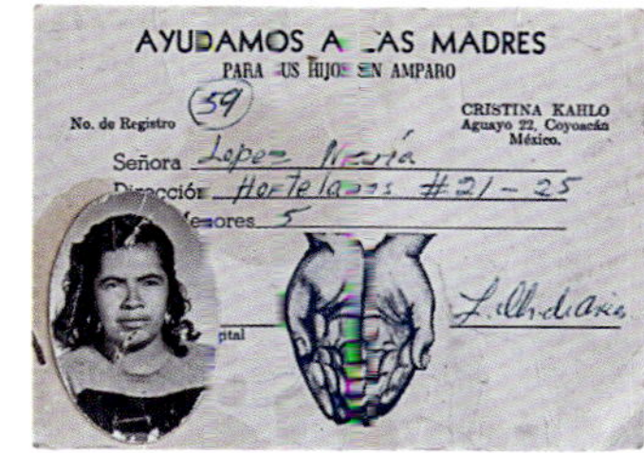

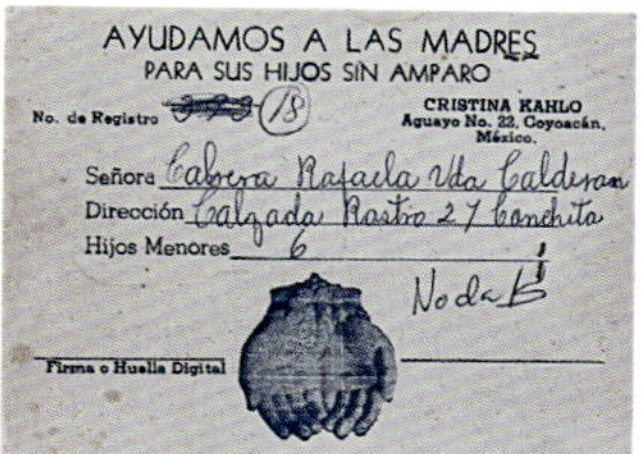

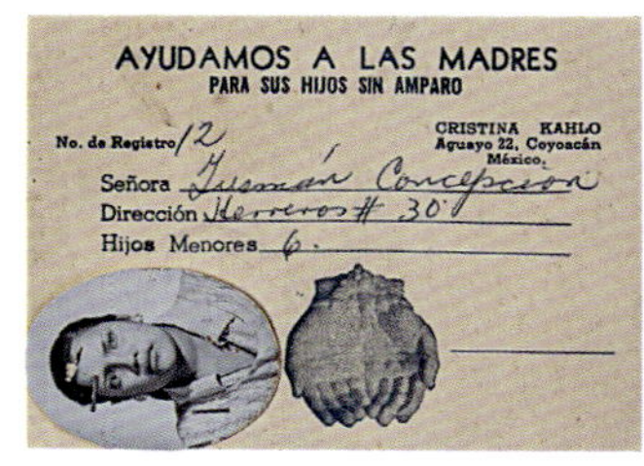

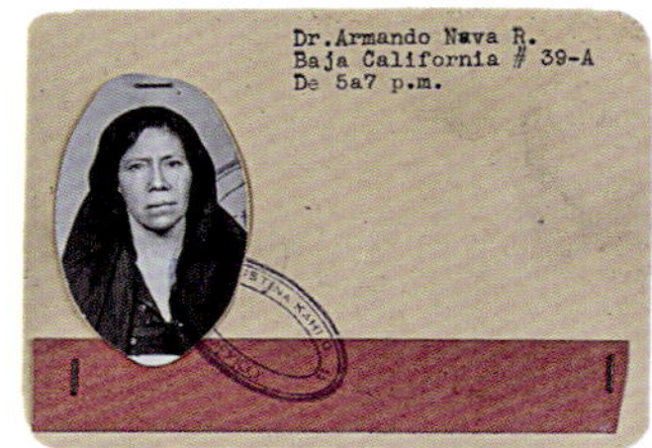

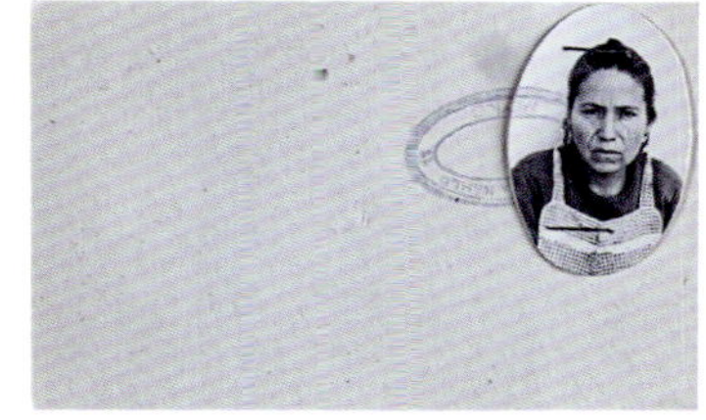

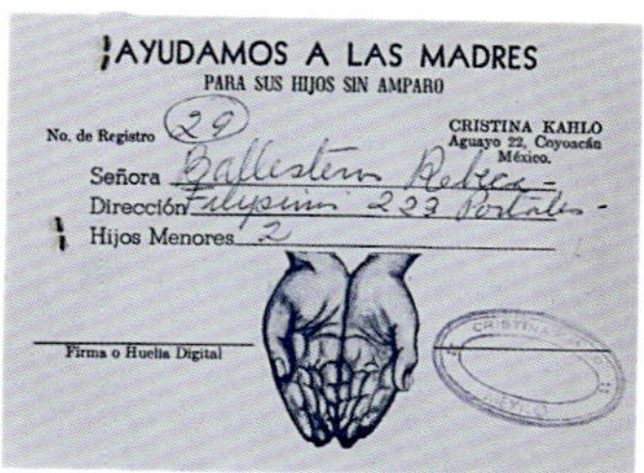

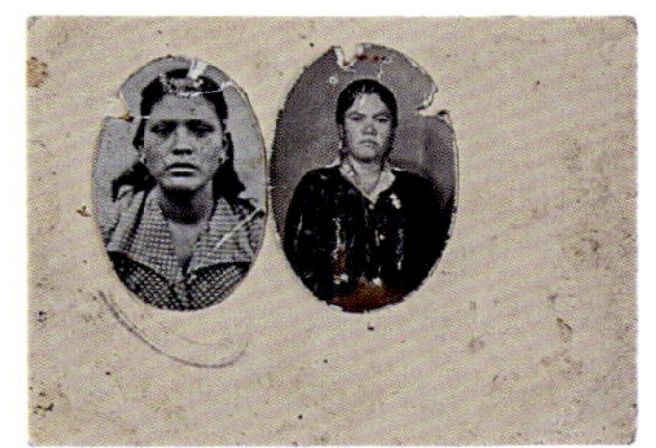

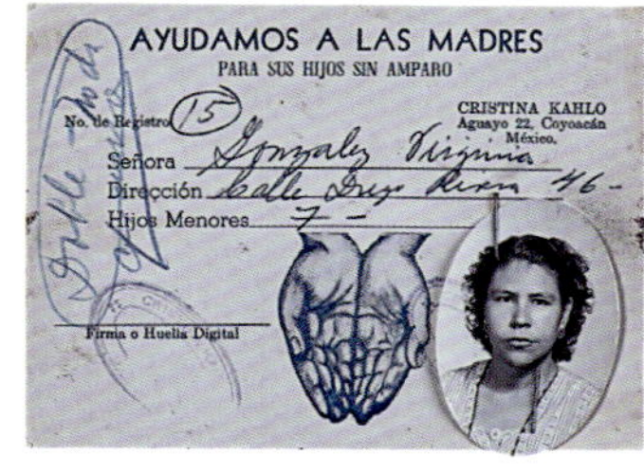

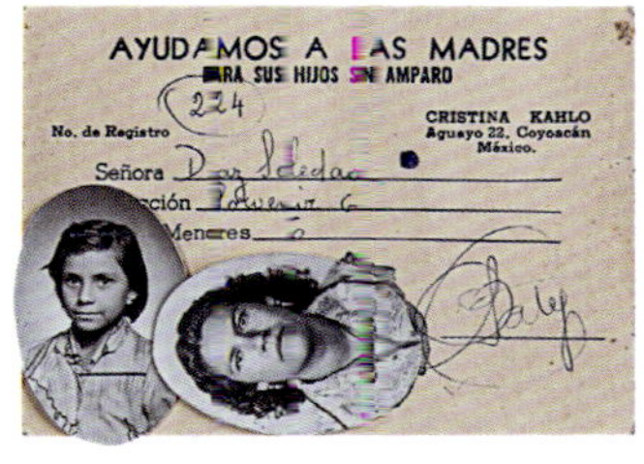

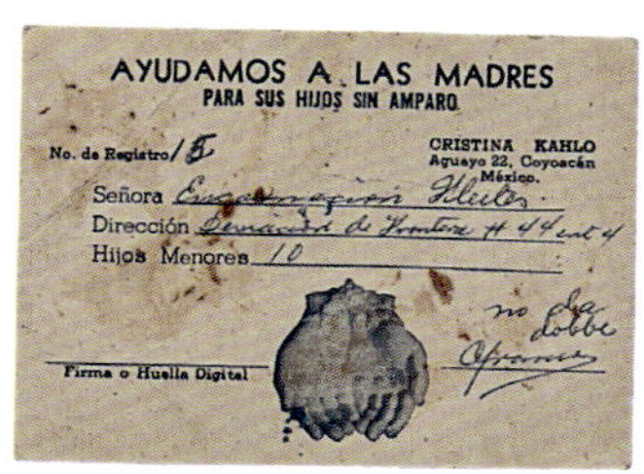

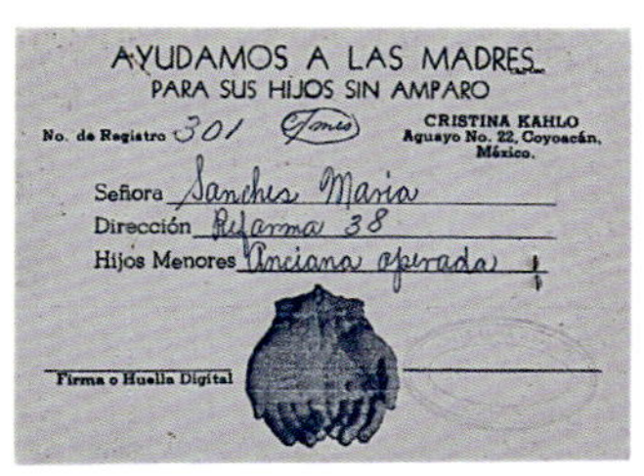

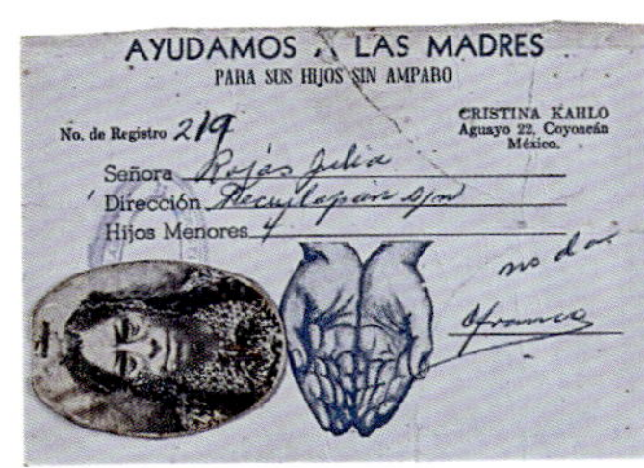

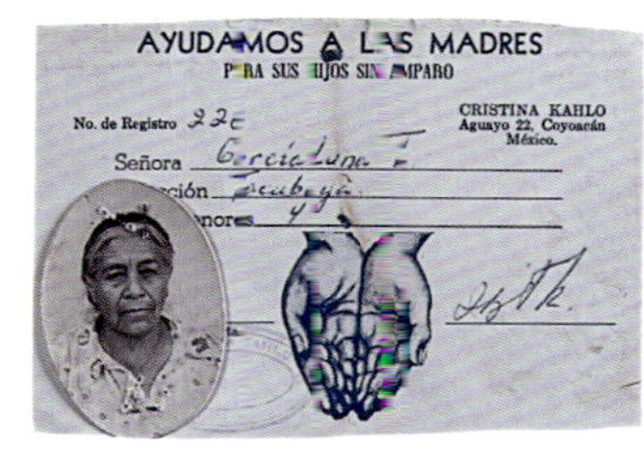

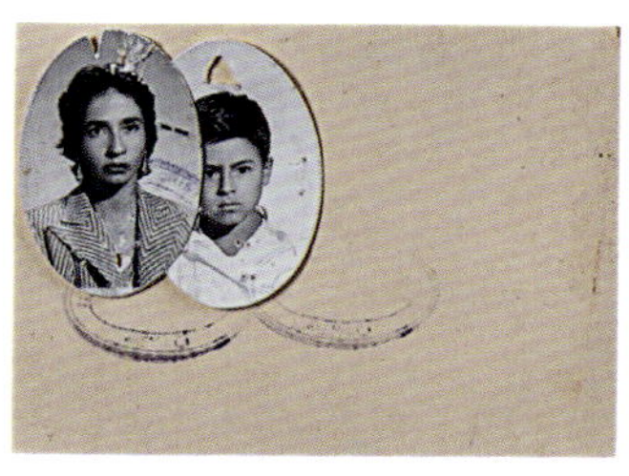

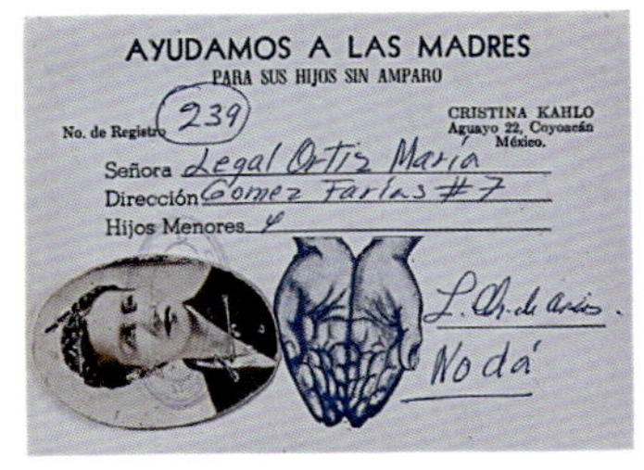

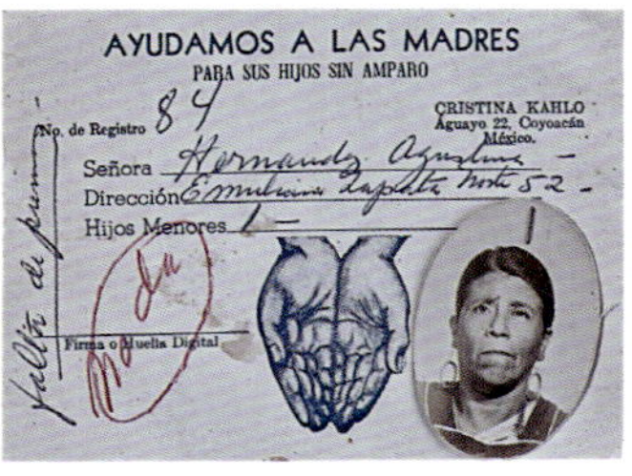

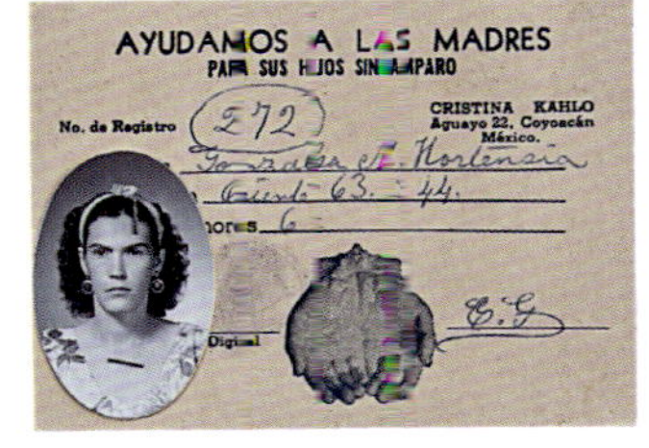

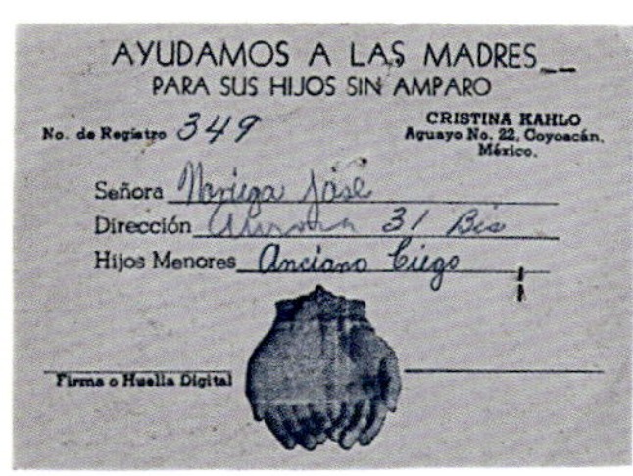

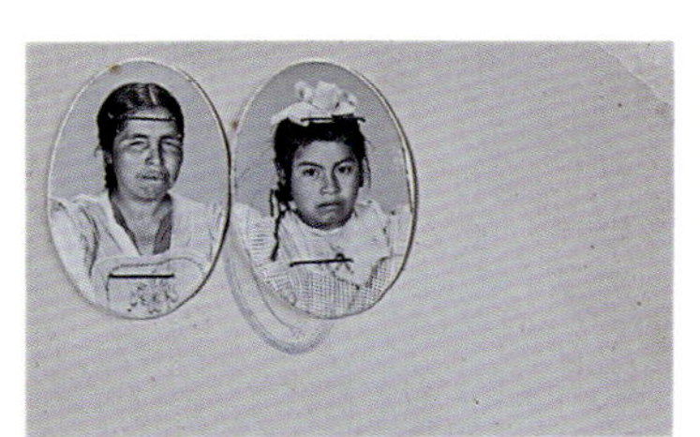

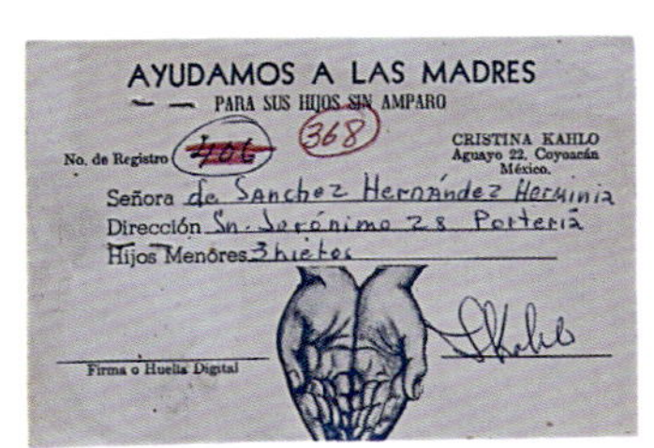

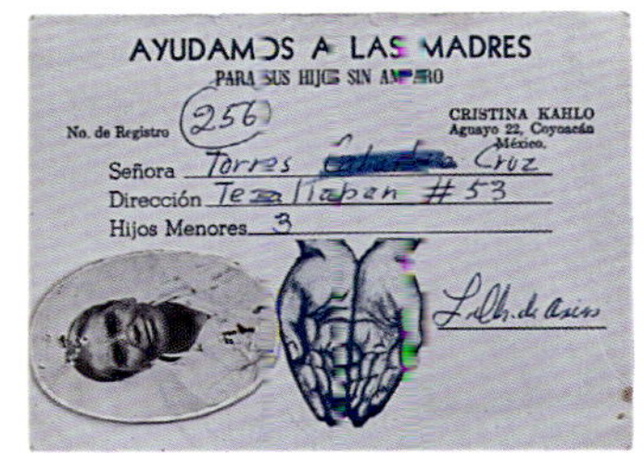

ABOVE Twenty-four La Ayuda credentials featuring photos and signatures of the recipients.

FOLLOWING SPREAD Stills from a film documenting one of the distributions of food by La Ayuda at Casa Kahlo, Coyoacán, ca. 1954

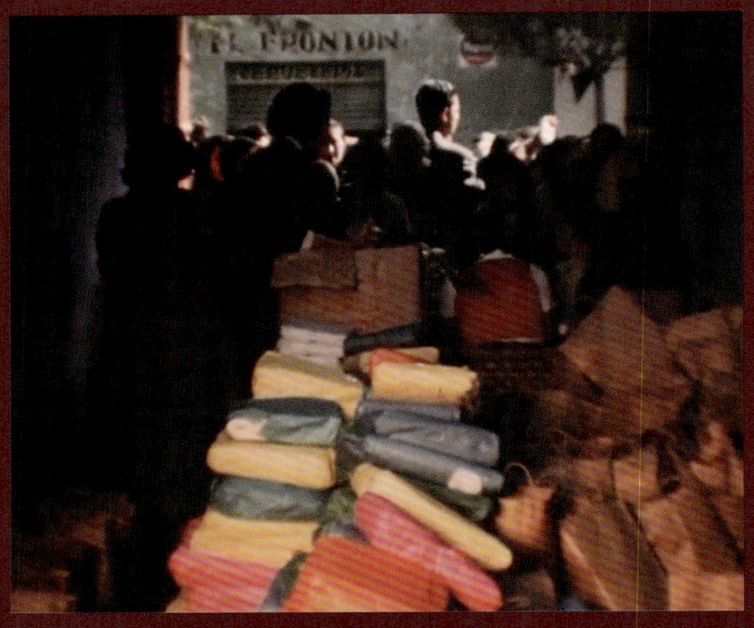
EL FRONTON
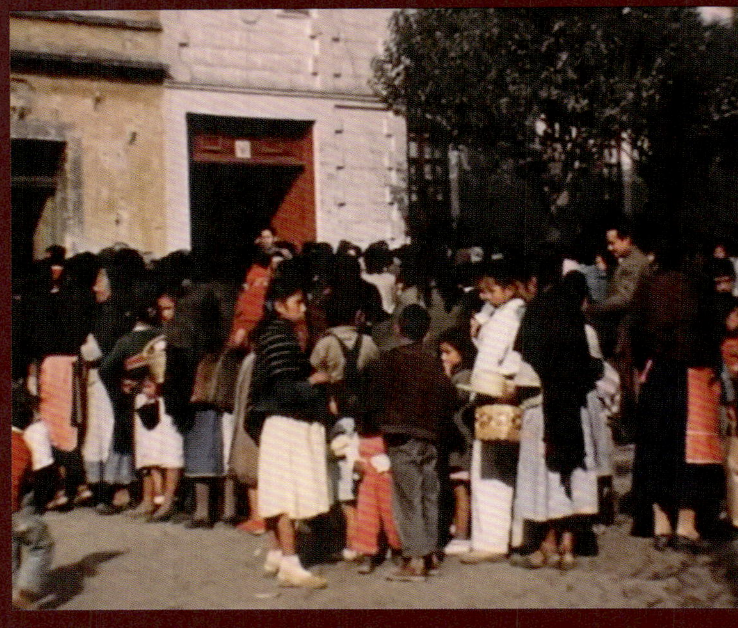
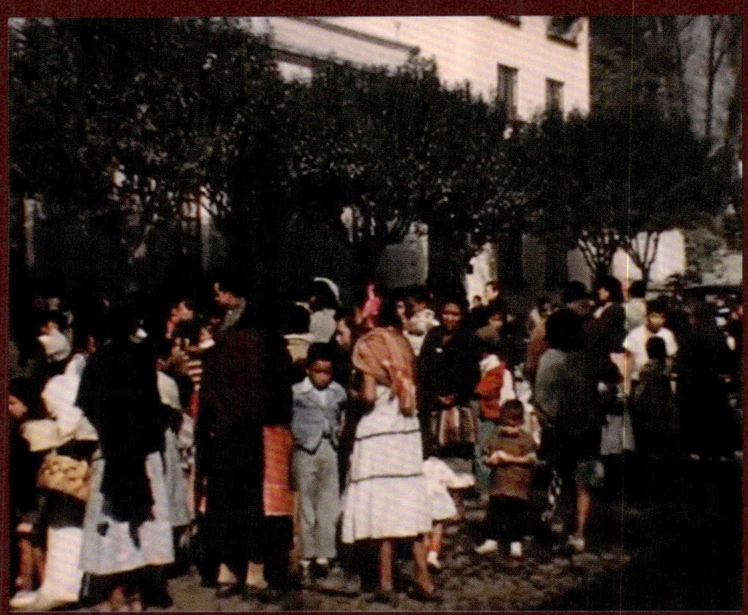
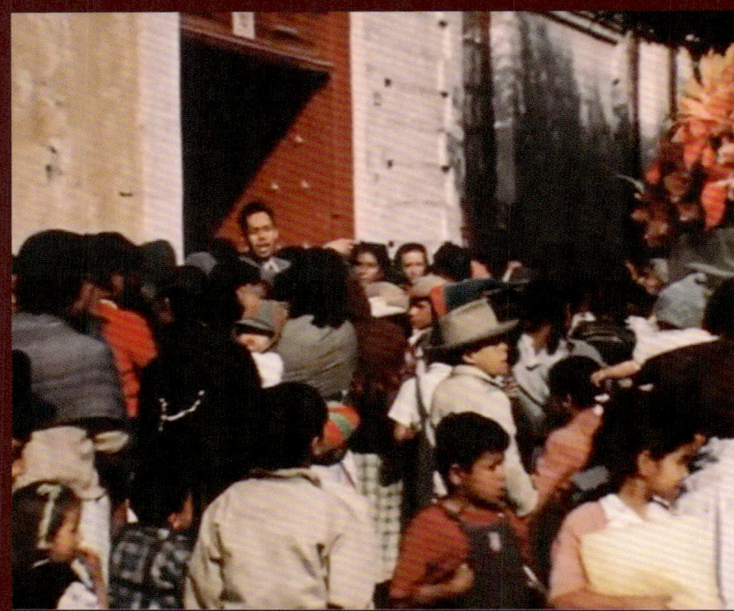
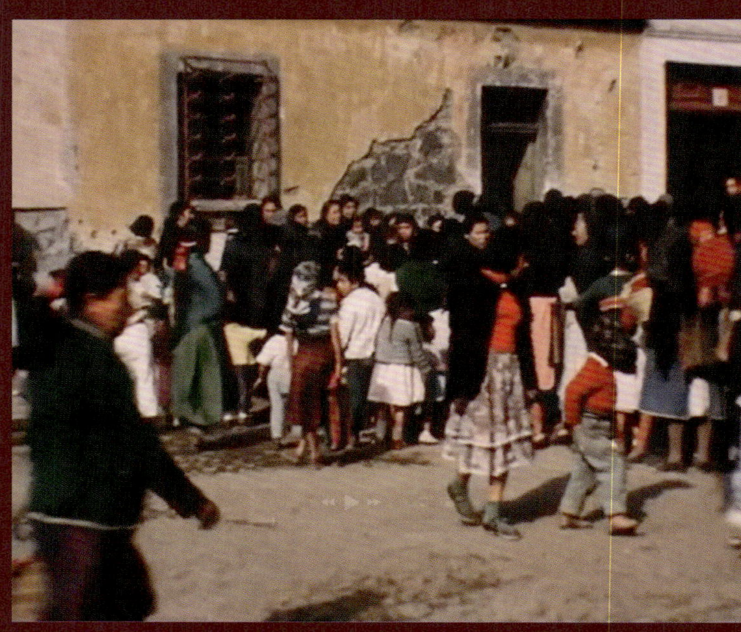
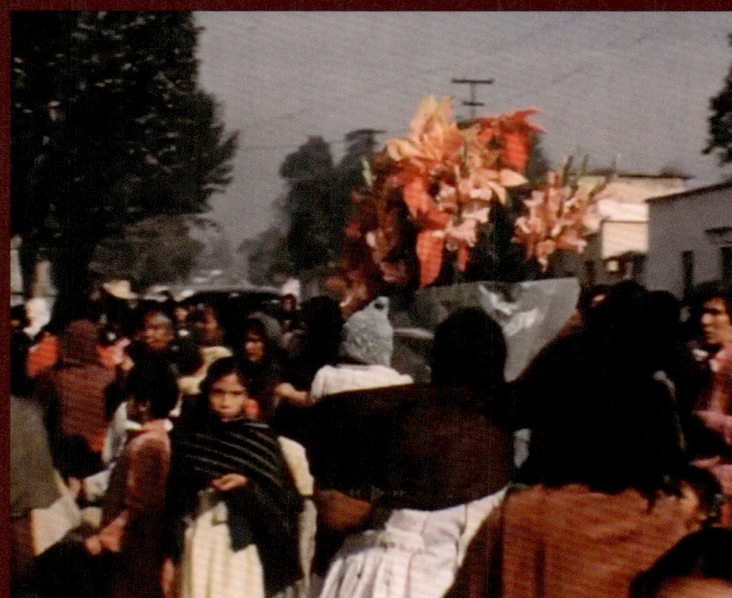

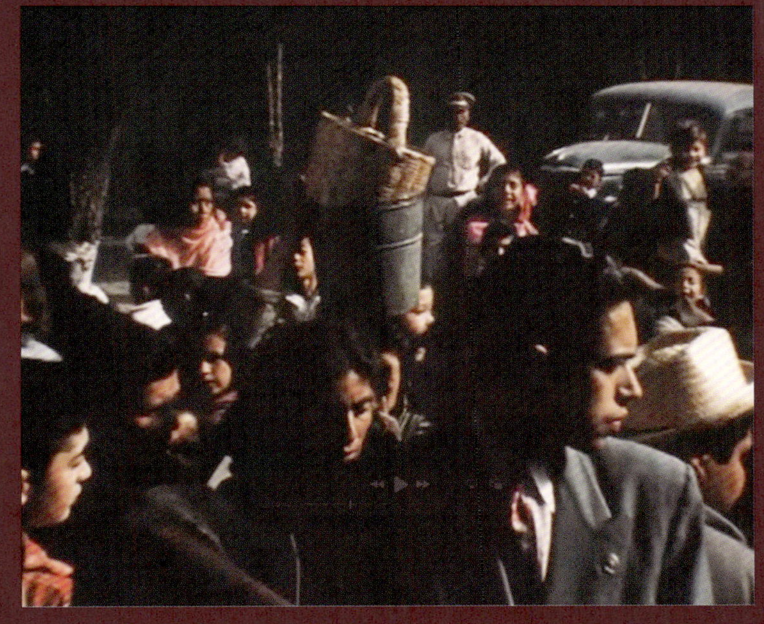
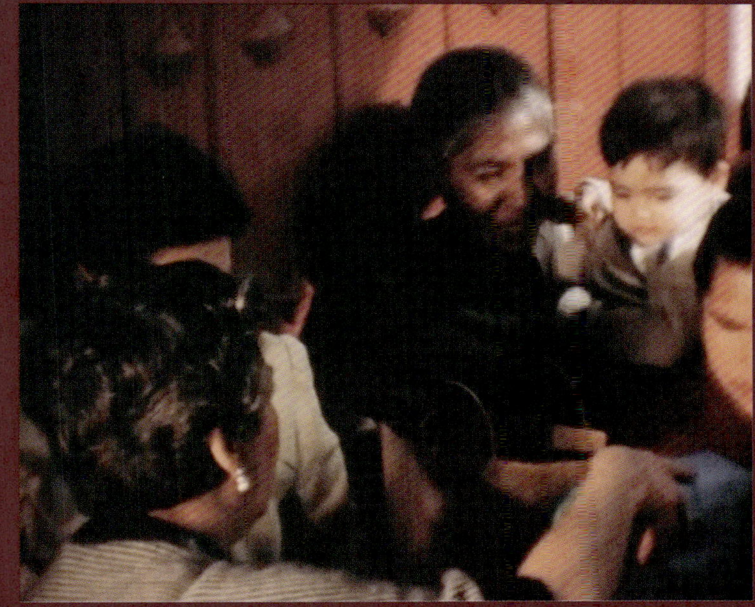
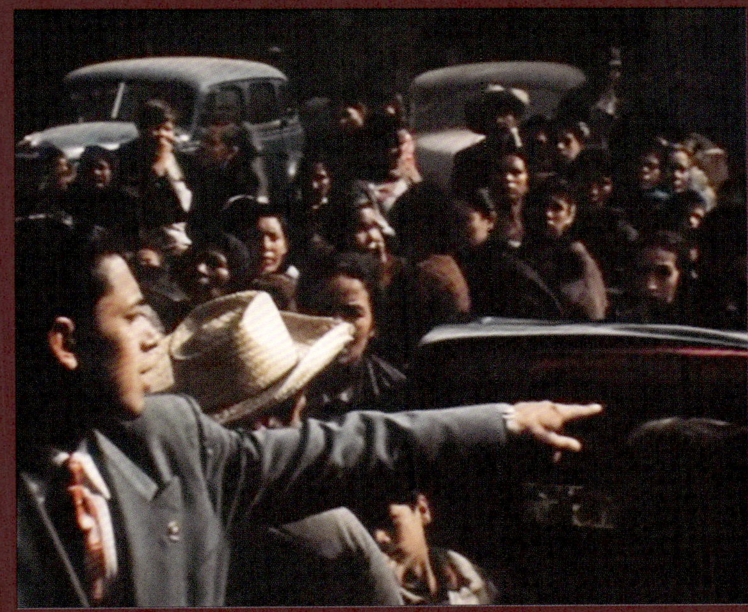
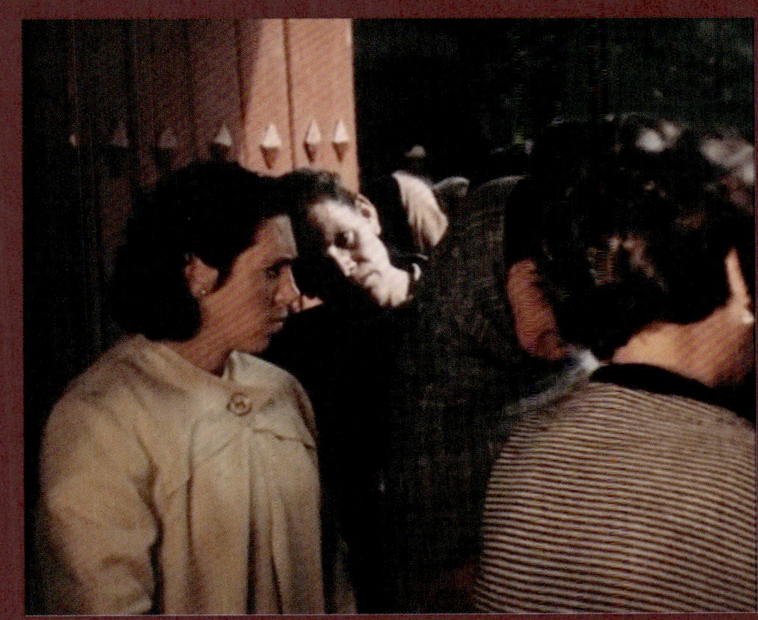
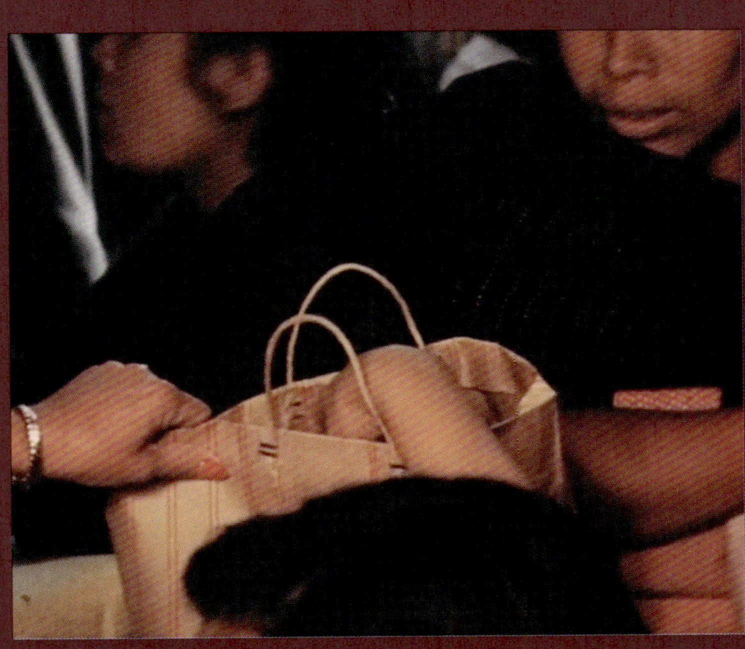
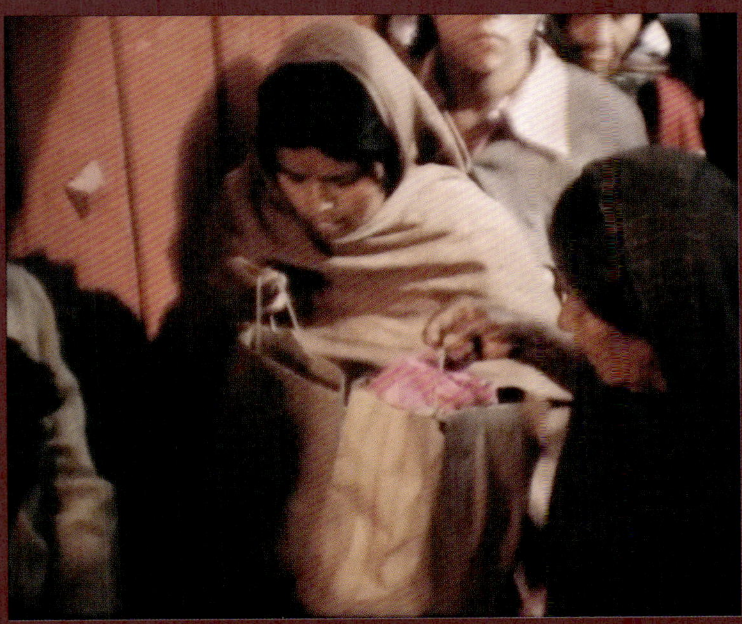

...iendo todo lo que...
El cuarto cuesta 12 d...
bastante horrenda con...
del mundo entero. Te...
siento y me traen fr...
Wolfe, a Julio y Ma...
en la calle y se iba
viaje fue cansadísimo
por fin salí de e...
ano estan mas cham...
[illegible]ata y todos? Ext...
yo que pienso en...
12 semana Sab...

CHAPTER 4

Sisterly Bonds

10 de M

Chaparrita de
"Mamá" de
Recibe de tu
el cariño q

CRIST

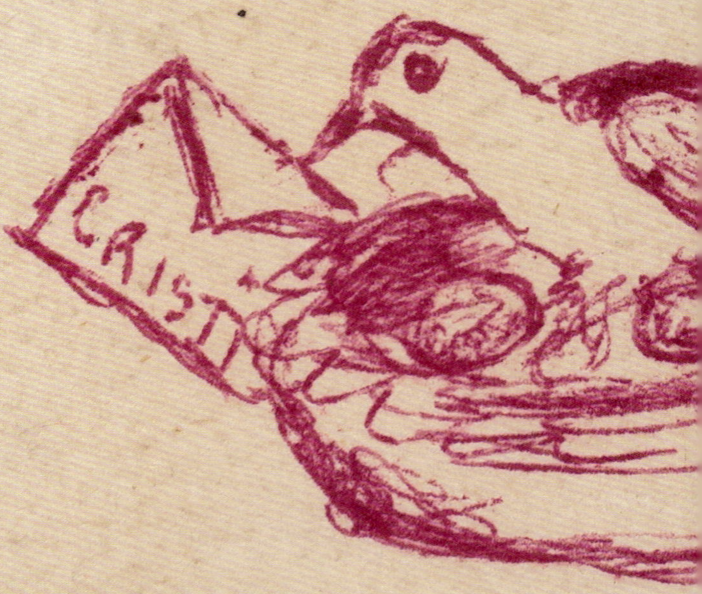

de 1948.

mi vida,

i corazón!

ija Frida

el amor.

Mara Romeo Kahlo The four sisters—Matilde, Adriana, Frida, and Cristina—were very close. The age difference between the elder sisters and Frida and Cristina had no impact on their relationship. They had an indestructible bond. Matilde and Adriana Kahlo were 8 and 4 years older than Frida, respectively. Frida and Cristina were "Irish twins," only eleven months apart. There are so many stories that shine light on their sisterhood.

When Matilde was a teenager she had a boyfriend, and she ran away from home to be with him. It was the young Frida who helped her sister escape through the balcony. Their mother was *muy enojada* with her daughter and, for some years, made it clear that the family should distance themselves from Matilde. But, as she always did, Frida defied the rules, and she maintained her relationship with her. Frida knew where her sister lived but hid the address from the family for many years. When Frida had her life-altering bus accident in 1925, it was her sister Matilde who went every day to the hospital to take care of her.

Frida was never able to carry children of her own and suffered miscarriages. Frida's older sister Adriana also endured miscarriages, and she was able to provide Frida with true empathy; this was deeply comforting to Frida.

My grandmother Cristina and Frida were "partners in crime" and each other's safety net. When Cristina separated from her husband, Frida took her sister and her children into her house. She hired Cristina to help with everything. She became Frida's secretary, chauffeur, nurse, and companion. When Frida went through several operations, Cristina was by her side. When Cristina traveled to be with Frida when she went to the United States, Adriana took care of Cristina's daughter Isolda, my mother, and Matilde took care of her son Antonio (Toño).

Frida Hentschel The sisters also embraced Matilde and Adriana's spouses. Paco Hernández, Matilde's husband, was a successful businessman and would help the family financially when needed. He did this out of love and without a hidden agenda, and the family was very grateful for his kindness. Alberto Veraza, nicknamed El Güerito

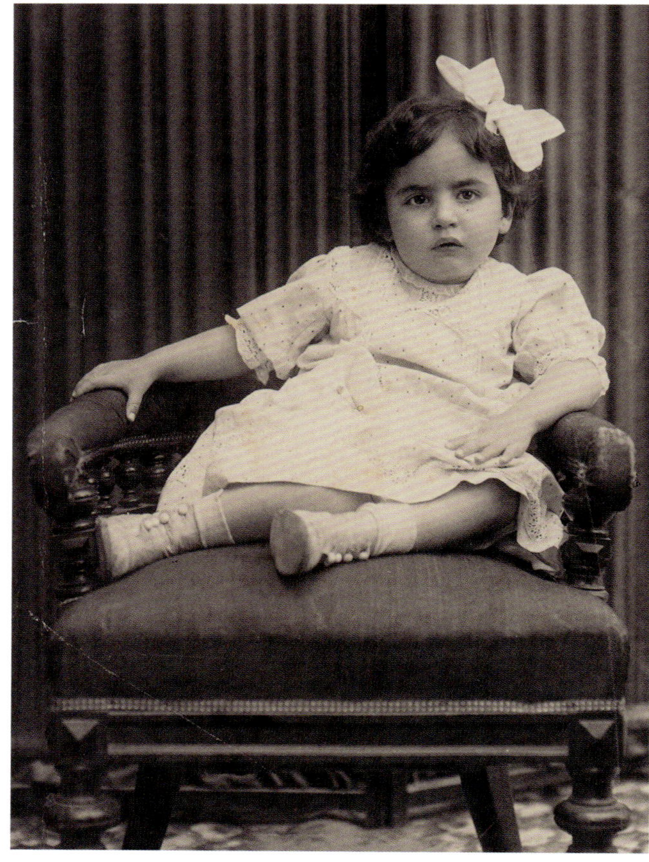

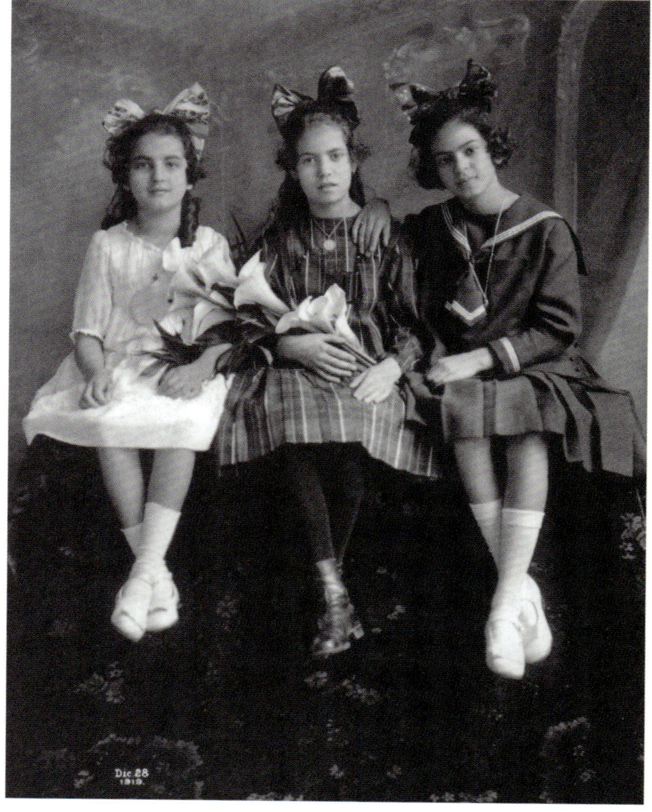

PREVIOUS SPREAD Mother's Day note from Frida to her sister Cristina, May 10, 1948. Later in her life, Frida would refer to Cristina as her "mother."

TOP Cristina at age 2, in 1910. Photo by Guillermo Kahlo

BOTTOM Cristina, unidentified child, and Frida, Coyoacán, December 28, 1919. Photo by Guillermo Kahlo

OPPOSITE Frida with her sisters Matilde, Adriana, and Cristina, Coyoacán, ca. 1914. Photo by Guillermo Kahlo

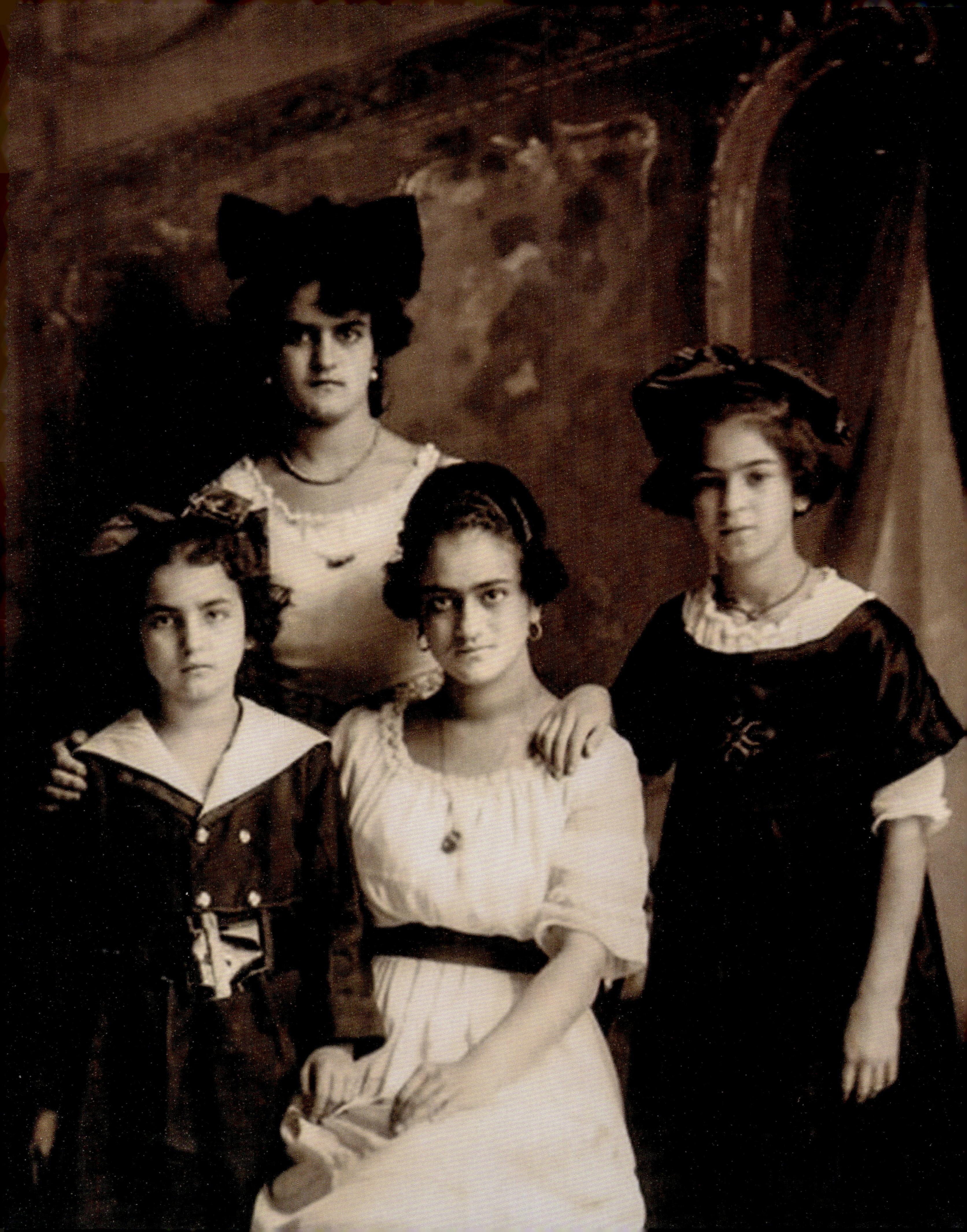

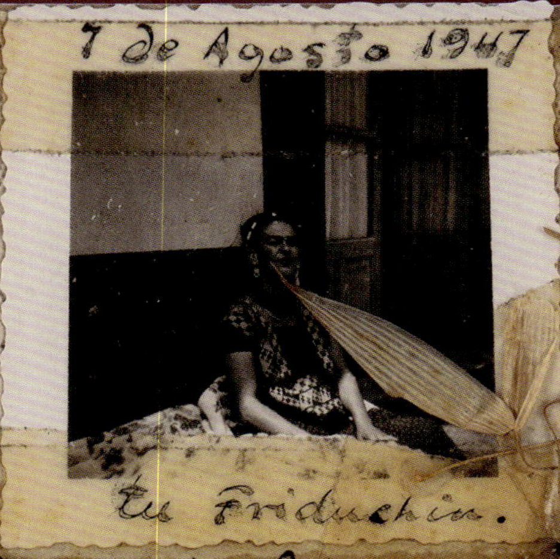

7 de Agosto 1947

tu Friduchín.

Querito lindo;

Perdona éste pequeño recuerdo, porque la "brujez" me abruma, pero te lleva todo mi cariño que siempre, hasta el dia que me muera, será el mismo para ti, a pesar de que tú ya no me quieres como ántes.

¿Porqué? ¿QUIEN SABE?

Tu

Friduchín.

("the blondie"), Adriana's husband, was amusing and was deeply loved by everyone. El Güerito, who was a widower, had a son named Carlos. Carlitos was also welcomed as family. We still have letters and dedicated photos from Frida to el Güerito and to Paco and her sisters.

Mara Romeo Kahlo While Frida was away—either accompanying her husband Diego during his travels to the US, recovering in the hospital, or recovering at home from one of her surgeries—her sisters always helped her keep the houses clean and orderly. They tended to their animals at Casa Azul or in their San Angel house. Her sisters kept her household running like clockwork—paying bills, hiring help, painting the house, etc. And since it was often Cristina, not Diego, who accompanied Frida for her surgeries or exhibitions, her sisters Adriana and Matilde took care of Diego while Frida traveled. They would bathe him, iron his clothes, cook for him.

Mara de Anda Can you imagine bathing your sister's husband! It was unusual but clearly they did it for Frida, because of their close relationship. They sewed his clothes, too. In a letter to Frida, they wrote, "Today, we went to see Diego because we delivered the shirts that I sewed for him and gave him a bath, so don't worry, he's doing well." This was all done for Frida—they would do anything to support her.

Frida Hentschel They all cared for Diego, as an extension of their love for Frida. Cristina in fact risked her life twice for her brother-in-law. When Leon Trotsky, the exiled Russian revolutionary, was staying at Casa Azul, there was an assassination attempt on his life. There were generals with guns everywhere, and they were looking for Diego. Cristina told Diego to jump into the back of her car. One of the generals asked to inspect the car and asked her to get out. She firmly held her ground, told them she was on her way to pick up her kids from school, and instructed them to let her go. The general saw Cristina's calm and composed attitude, and didn't doubt her. If the general would've continued with the search in her car, both would have likely been killed. The other harrowing incident was when Diego had a serious fight with fellow muralist David Alfaro Siqueiros.

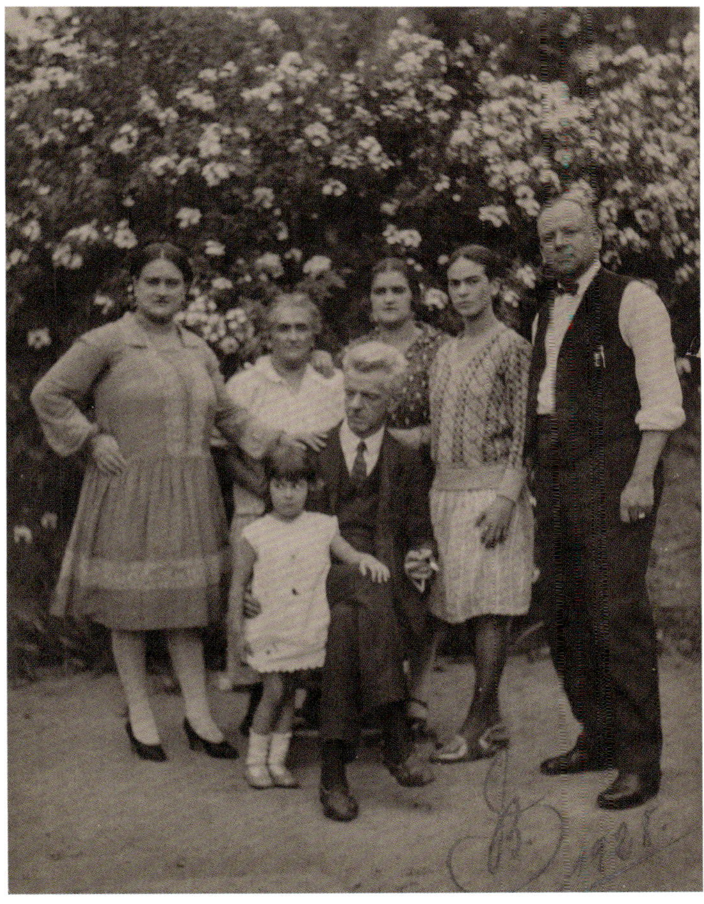

Brandishing guns which they were pointing at each other, Cristina intervened. Both Siqueiros and Diego had very strong political views and were very passionate. Sometimes they agreed, but when they didn't, fights escalated very quickly.

Mara Romeo Kahlo The letters the sisters wrote to each other are amazing—they wrote almost daily. In them, Frida wanted to know everything—which movie they went to, where they went to dinner, what kind of tacos they ate. They relayed to each other the most minute and mundane details of their lives. In nearly every letter she wrote, Frida expressed her longing for Mexico and family.

OPPOSITE Letter with photo from Frida to her brother-in-law Alberto ("El Güerito") Veraza, August 7, 1947

TOP, PICTURED LEFT TO RIGHT Matilde Kahlo, Matilde Calderón, unidentified child, Guillermo (seated), Adriana (behind Guillermo), Frida, Adriana's husband Alberto Veraza, Coyoacán, 1928.

Viernes 24 de Mayo 1946.

Cristi lindísima -

Cómo te extraño! Ya estoy desde ayer en el dicho Hospital. Ya ví al Dr Wilson pero todavía no sé nada definitivo porque a penas me hizo el primer exámen. Quiere tenerme en cama una semana. Yo te iré escribiendo todo lo que me digan y me hagan. El cuarto cuesta 12 dólares diarios. La comida bastante horrenda como en todos los hospitales del mundo entero. Pero los amigos me consienten y me traen fruta y todo. Ya ví a Ella Wolfe, a Julien y Muriel, me encontré a Olga en la calle y se iba antier para Mexico. El viaje fué cansadísimo y horrible pero ya, por fín salí de esa mierda. Cómo están mis chamacos y Al-guerito Malita y todos? Extraño muchísimo a Trejo y yo me quiero ir para mi casa. En esta semana sabré definitivamente qué piensa el Dr Wilson y si puede hacer algo o nó. Nueva York está muy chocante. Kurtz se ha portado maravillosamente conmigo y me ha atendido como si fuera mi pariente. Ya ves que aquí la gente es realmente amable. Linda yo creo que les dí a todos mal

la dirección del Hospital. Avísales que
la correcta es:

321 East 42nd Street
Hospital for Special Surgery
New York City. N.Y.

Pero me pueden escribir siempre a
la casa de Julien y de allí me
traen las cartas y es quizá mejor
pues es más seguro.
Dile a Ali Malita Carito Luisita mi
tía Bela el güerito, a todos, que a ti
te voy a escribir todo lo que vaya
sabiendo de nuevo para que tú se los
chismosees pues me dá mucho tra
bajo escribir tanta carta. Estoy en
una cama más dura que las
piedras del pedregal.
¿Como estás tú y los niños? Bert
y Ella te mandan muchísimos besos.
Escribeme por favor todo lo que ha
pasado allá. ¿Se ha portado bien
María? Ella me ha dado una
ligera ayudada pero ya la conoces
de bodocona y egoista.
Te extraño como ni siquiera tienes una
ligera idea. Te adora tu
Frida

Besa mucho a mi Isol y al Mijuis – Cuídame mucho a mi Diegüito.

27 de Mayo - Lunes. 1946

Cristi de mi vida,

Acaba de llegar tu cartita, la primera que recibo de Mexico y me dió hartisimo gusto, pero mucha aflicción por la niña ¿que te dijo exactamente el Dr.? ¿Que viste al Dr. Max Luft? Si ves que no dá resultado llevala con Faril pues ya van tres veces que se disloca ese piecito y no sea que después tenga otras consecuencias.

Yo estoy hasta ahorita bien, pues nada mas me han tenido en observación. Además del Dr. Wilson me han visto especialistas en nervios y otros que Wilson mismo trajo. Yo creo que lo más seguro es que me quiten el lopsiodol pero me asegura Wilson que no va a ser lo mismo que las otras funciones pues en lugar de ponerme [illegible] dentro me quitarán, y descansaré muchisimo. De los huesos de la espina y que todavía no me dá un diagnóstico exacto, pero todo cuanto me diga te lo iré escribiendo no te aflijas pues realmente estoy muy

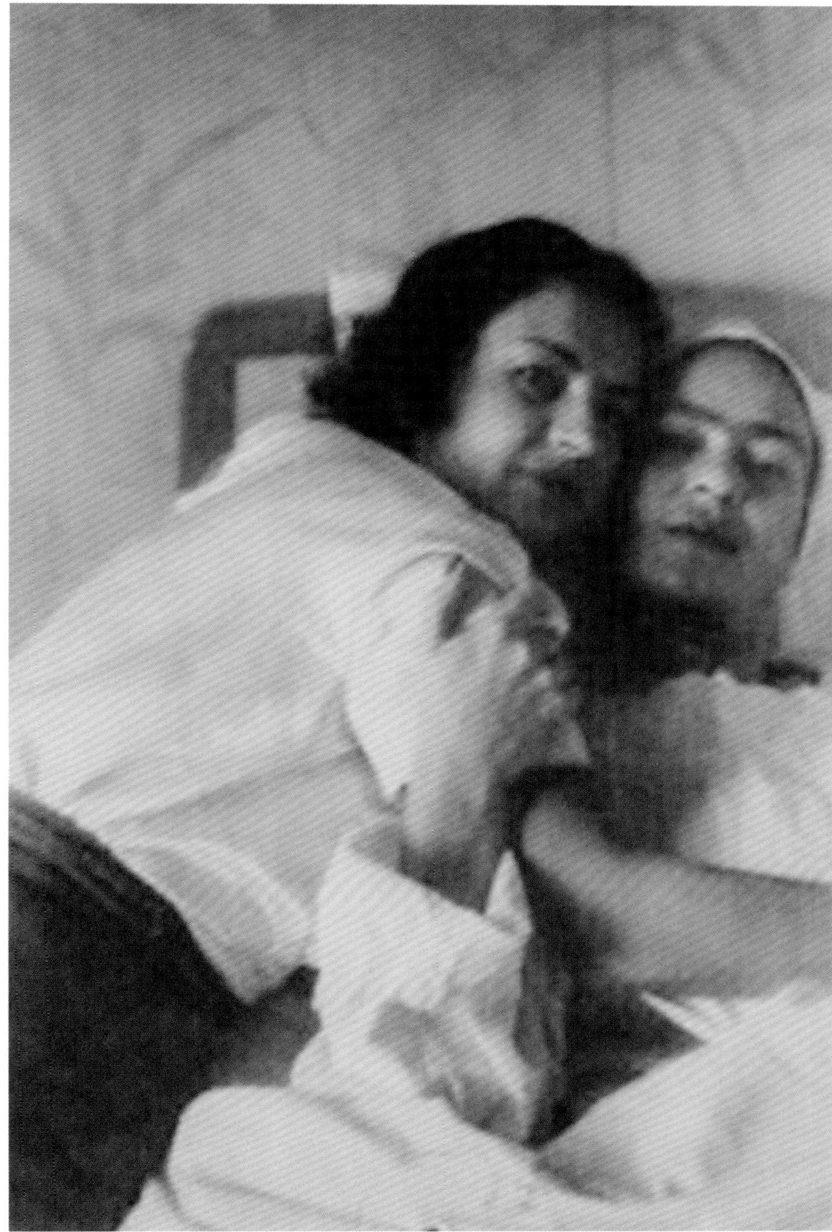

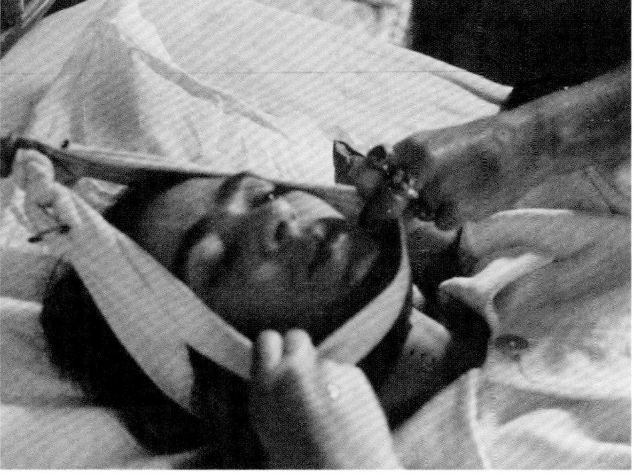

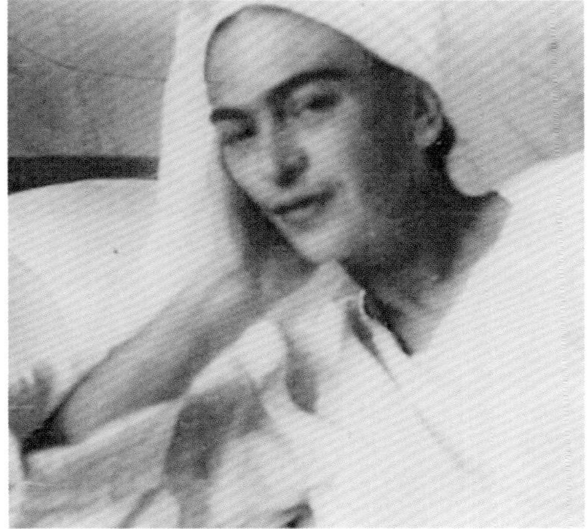

PREVIOUS SPREAD AND OPPOSITE Letters from Frida to Cristina, May 24, 1946, and May 27, 1946, respectively. Frida wrote to Cristina often when she was away. These letters were written when Frida was in New York City (she includes her address at the hospital on 42nd Street) for a medical evaluation. In her letter of May 24th, she writes about various mundanities—how hard the hospital bed is, the terrible hospital food, visits from friends—all while she awaits news from her doctor. In the May 27th letter, Frida relays that the doctor wants to perform surgery on her, one that would be very complex and painful. She asks Cristina to travel to New York to be by her side.

TOP LEFT AND BOTTOM RIGHT Frida convalescing with Cristina in a New York hospital in June 1946.

TOP RIGHT Frida in her bed at Casa Azul after one of her surgeries, ca. 1949.

Cristina was always by her sister's side. When Frida underwent surgeries and during her recoveries, she always asked for her sister. Cristina provided unconditional support. In 1946, Cristina joined Frida in New York for 3 months while she was there receiving medical care.

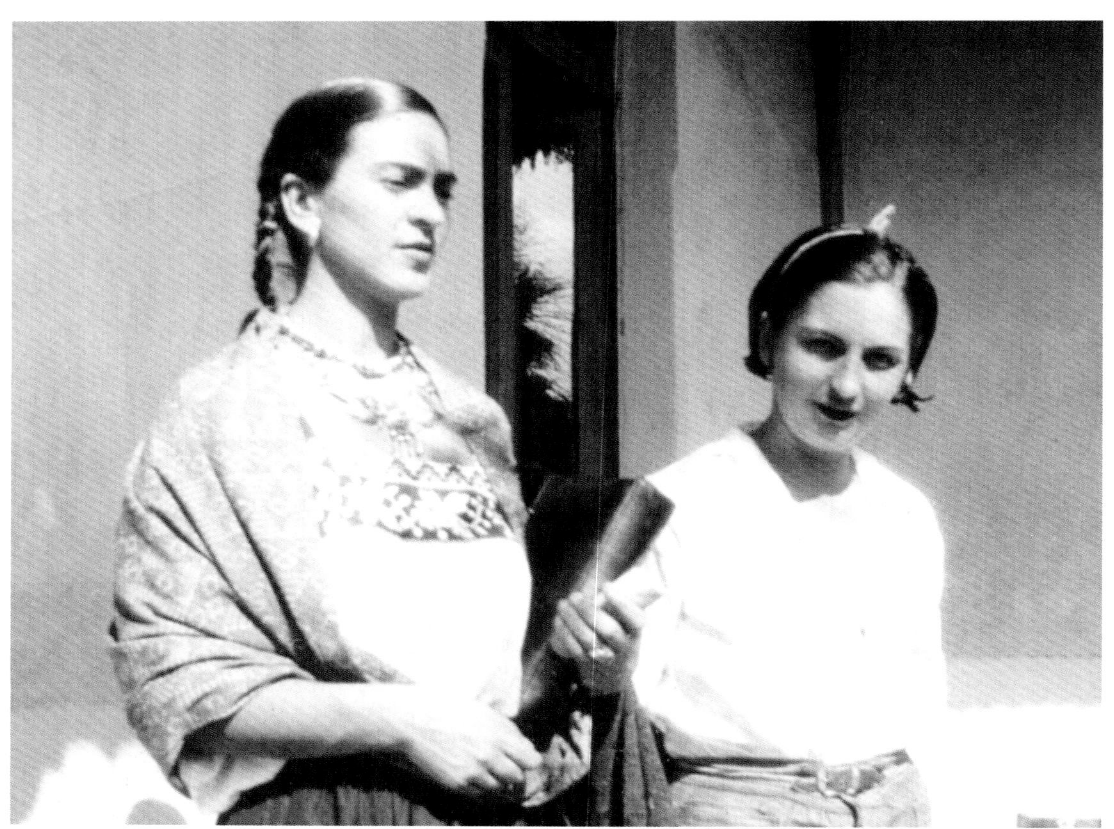

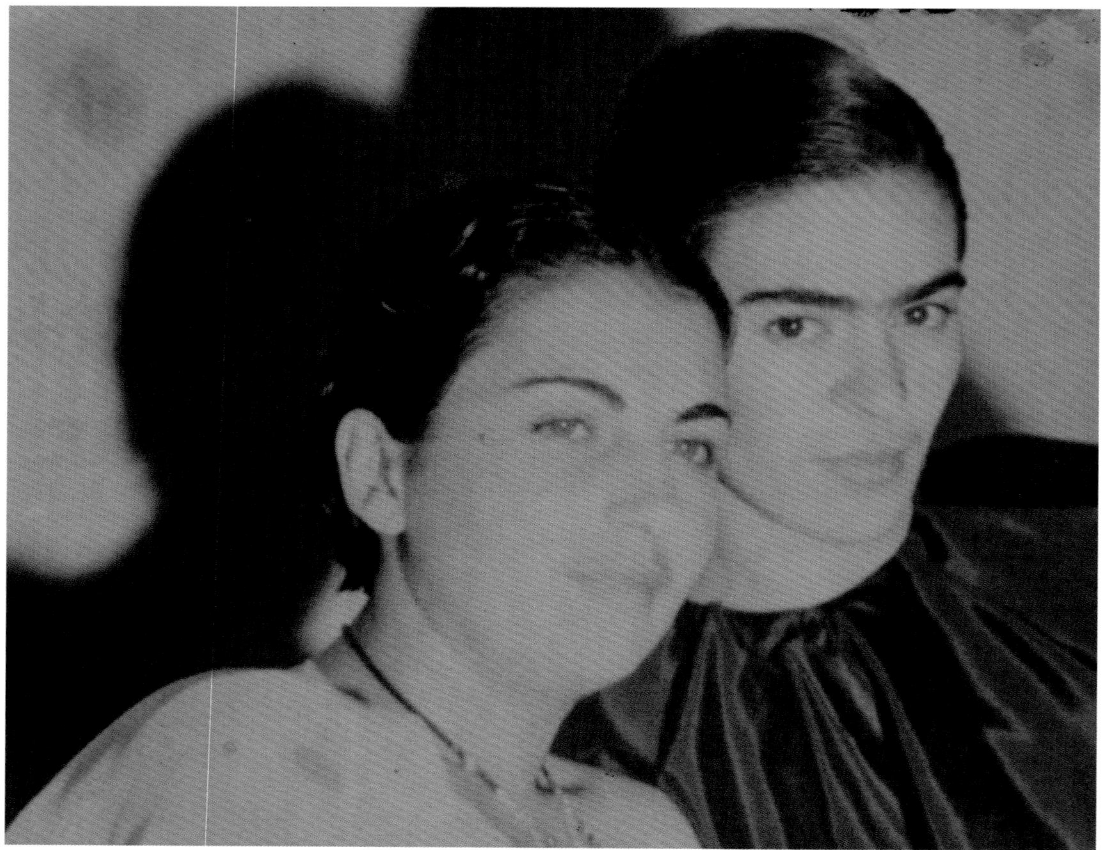

Frida and Cristina, ca. 1930 (top), and ca. 1934 (bottom); latter photo by Guillermo Kahlo.
Frida and Cristina's relationship was unbreakable. They were best friends, partners-in-crime, and caretakers for each other.

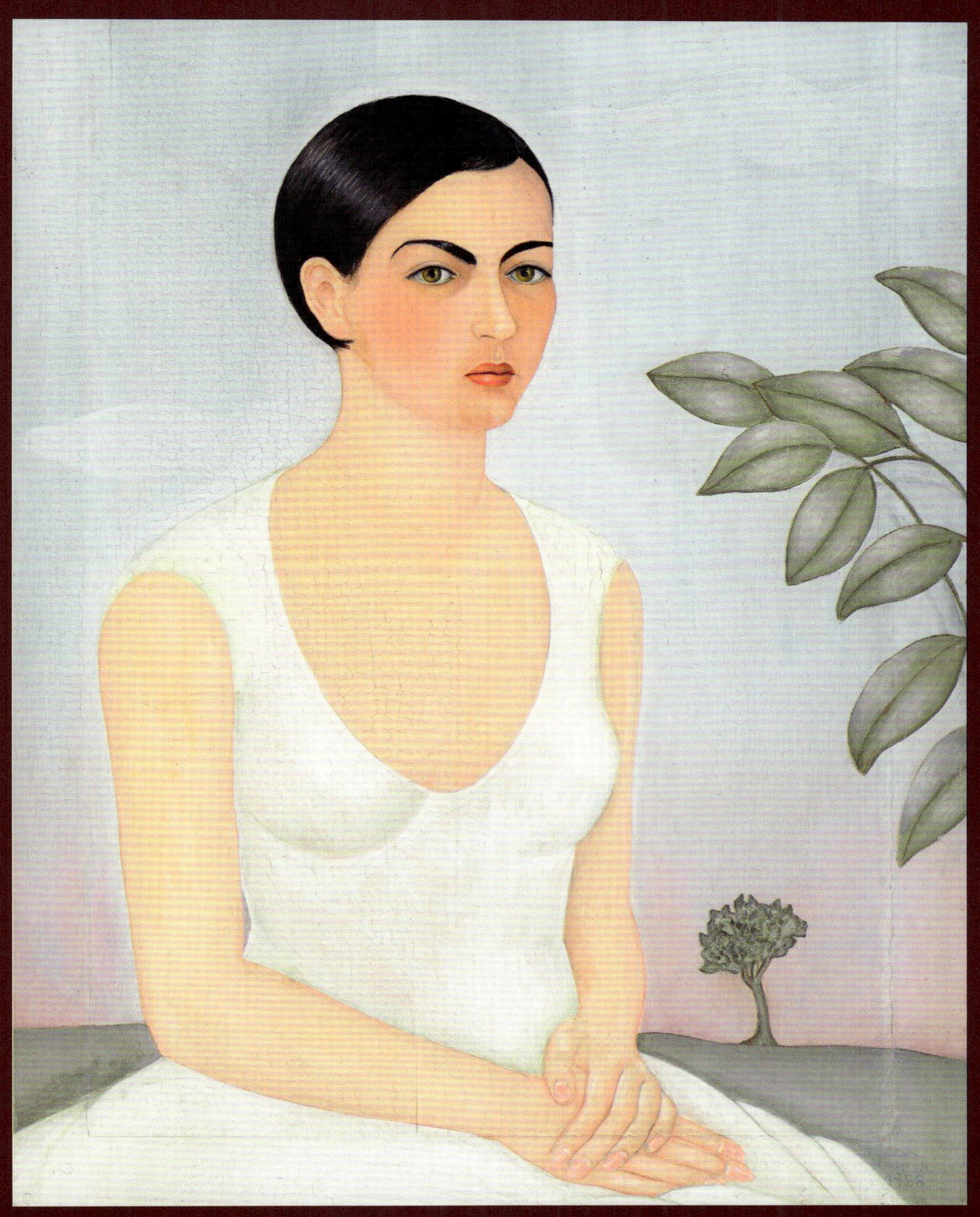

Frida Kahlo, *Portrait of Cristina, My Sister*, 1928. Oil on wood, 39 x 32[illegible] in. ([illegible]9 x 81.5 cm)

Mara Romeo Kahlo Their copious letter-writing extended beyond the nuclear family to their relatives. Matilde Calderón, Frida's mother, shared the same close-knit relationship with her own sisters and brother. The Calderón aunts and cousins were also very close.

Frida Hentschel Cristina and Frida were particularly close, and their personalities were very similar. They went to primary school together (they were in the same grade) and they made their first communion together. They made all kinds of mischief together. They both had the opportunity to learn German through the German Embassy, which offered language classes to the children of German families.

As they got older, they relied on each other more and more. When Frida had her first solo exhibition at Julien Levy Gallery in New York in 1938, Cristina traveled with her by ship. And when Frida had to undergo a major surgery in 1946 in New York, she wrote to Isolda saying, "Sorry I have to take your mother away from you, but without her I don't dare take any risks." It was Cristina by her side through everything that life had in store for her. And that's how Frida always expressed her love for her sister: "You are the other half of my life." In her later years, Frida even started calling Cristina "Mama" and "Mami linda" because Cristina would take care of her just like a mother would.

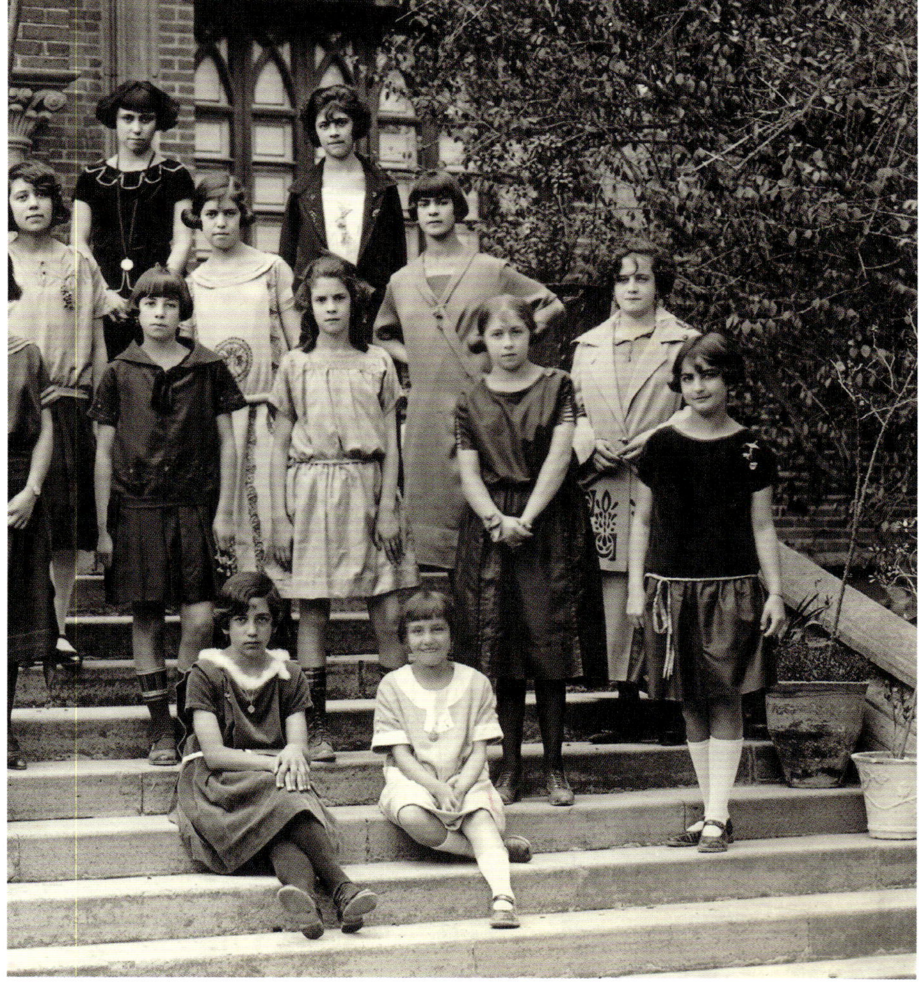

TOP Frida at age 4 (far right) and Cristina at age 3 (seated center right), ca. 1911. Frida and Cristina, only 11 months apart, went to school together.

BOTTOM Group school portrait at Casa de Jacobo Caldés, Coyoacán, ca. 1920. (Frida is pictured on the far right of the second row and Cristina is on the far right of the first row.) Photo by Guillermo Kahlo

OPPOSITE Frida and Cristina leaning against a car, ca. 1937, Mexico, during one of the many excursions Frida and Diego Rivera took to neighboring towns to draw inspiration.

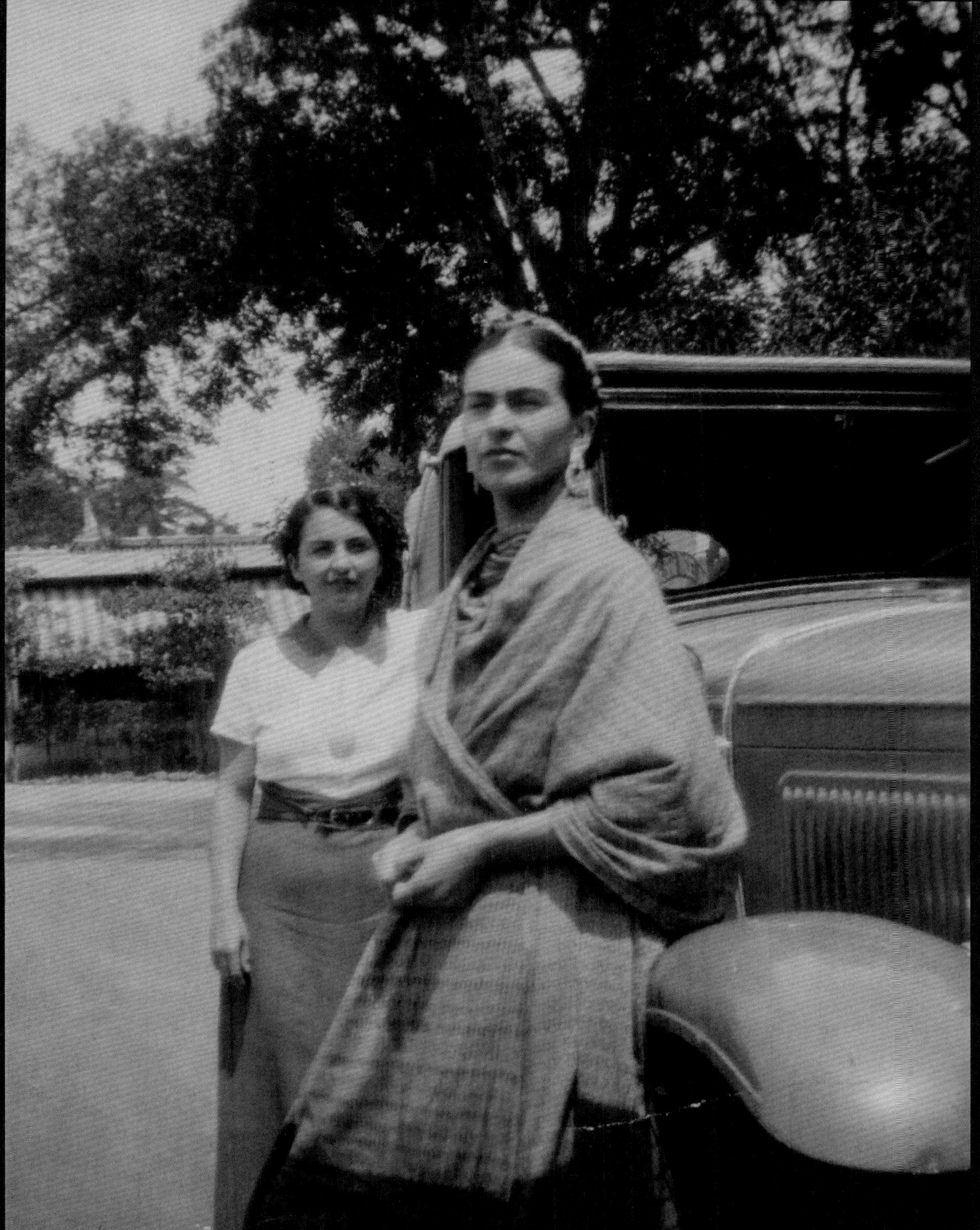

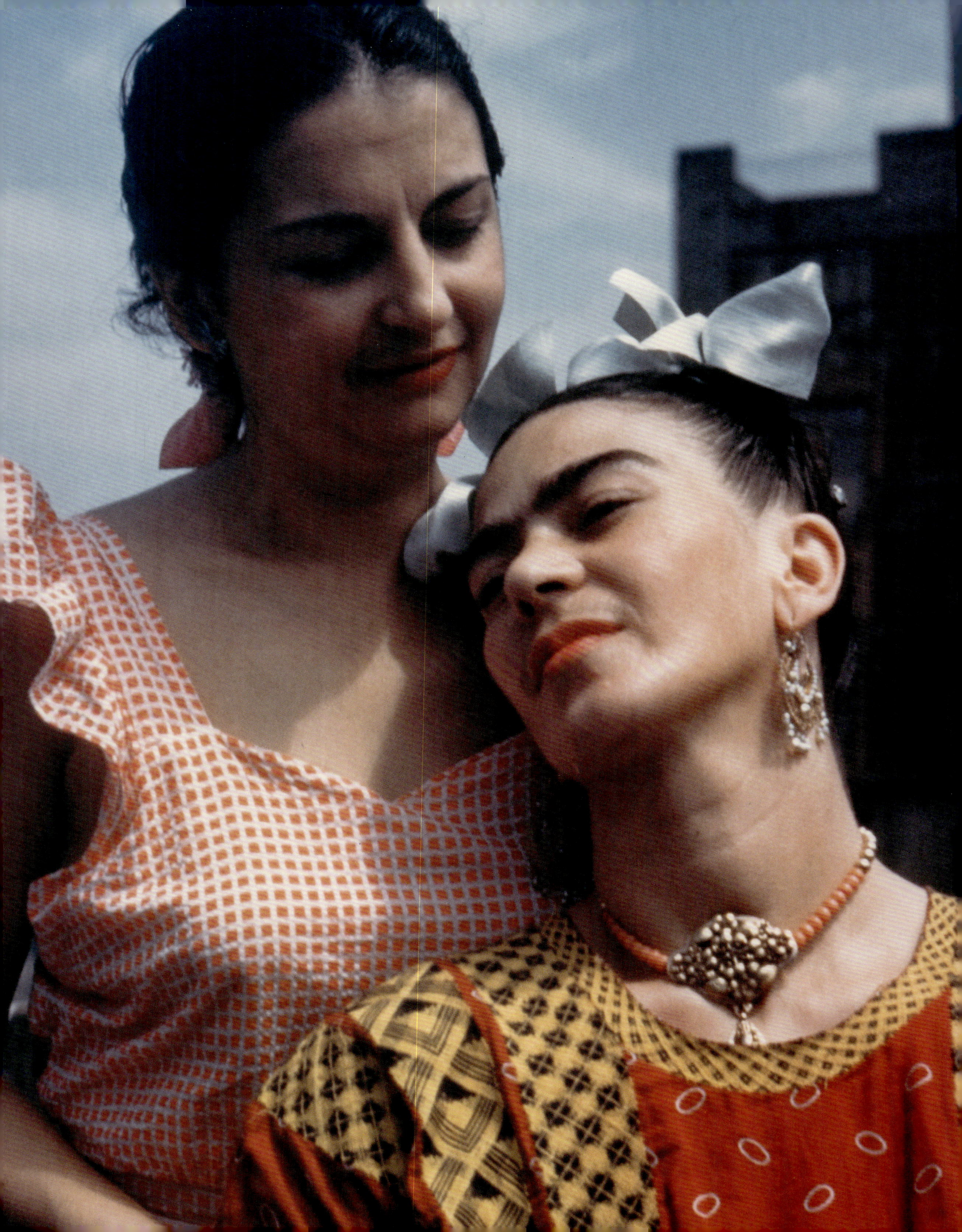

Agosto de 1950.

Para mi Cristi. Hospital Inglés.

Chaparrita de mi vida,
Mi Mámushka idolatrada!
Aquí tienes a tu Frida,
Por el dolor, maltratada!

NICK LAS MURAY
18 EAST 48th STREET
NEW YORK CITY

Pero con tu gran ternura,
tan cuidada y consentida,
Es la más feliz criatura
de ésta tierra, desdichada.

Ya pronto andará "jugando"
tu hija que tanto te ama,
Ya nó la verás tristiando...
acostadita en su cama!
Tu Fridu, empezó a vivir!!!
Chaparrita de mi vida;
Se acabó nuestro sufrir.
Yo te vivo AGRADECIDA!

Frida

OPPOSITE Cristina and Frida, New York, ca. July 1946. Photo by Nickolas Muray

ABOVE Letter from Frida to Cristina, August 1950, on the back of a photo by Nikolas Muray. Frida had surgery at the Hospital Inglés in Mexico in 1950. She opens the letter, "For my Cristi: *Chaparrita* of my life, my idolized *mamushka*, here you have your Frida," and closes with "I am forever GRATEFUL to you."

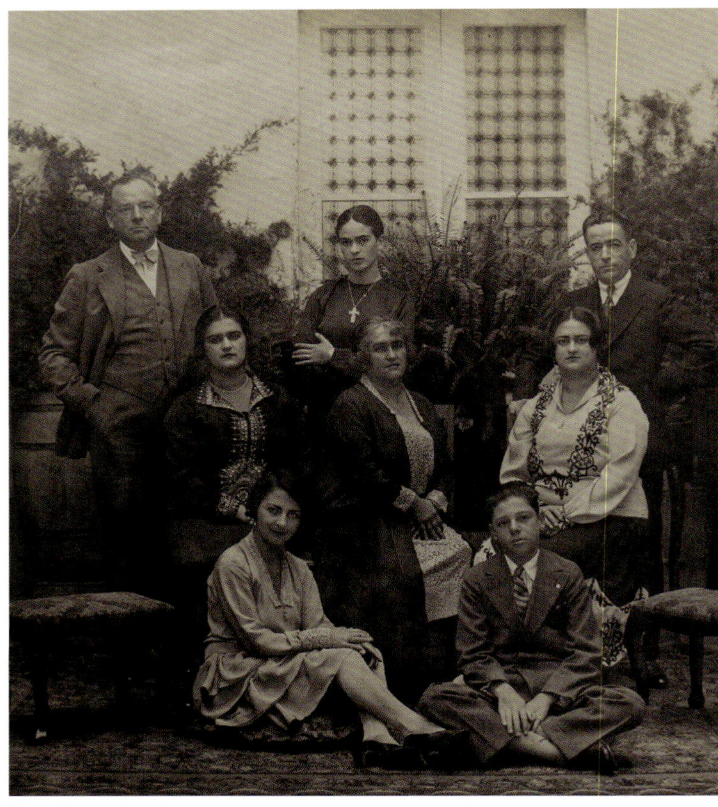

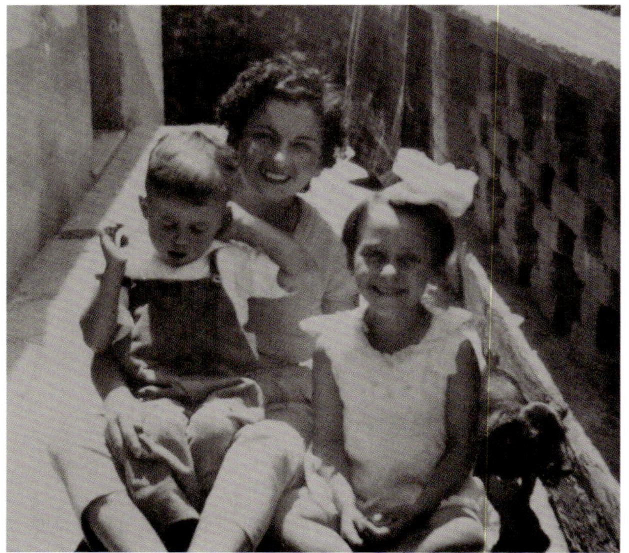

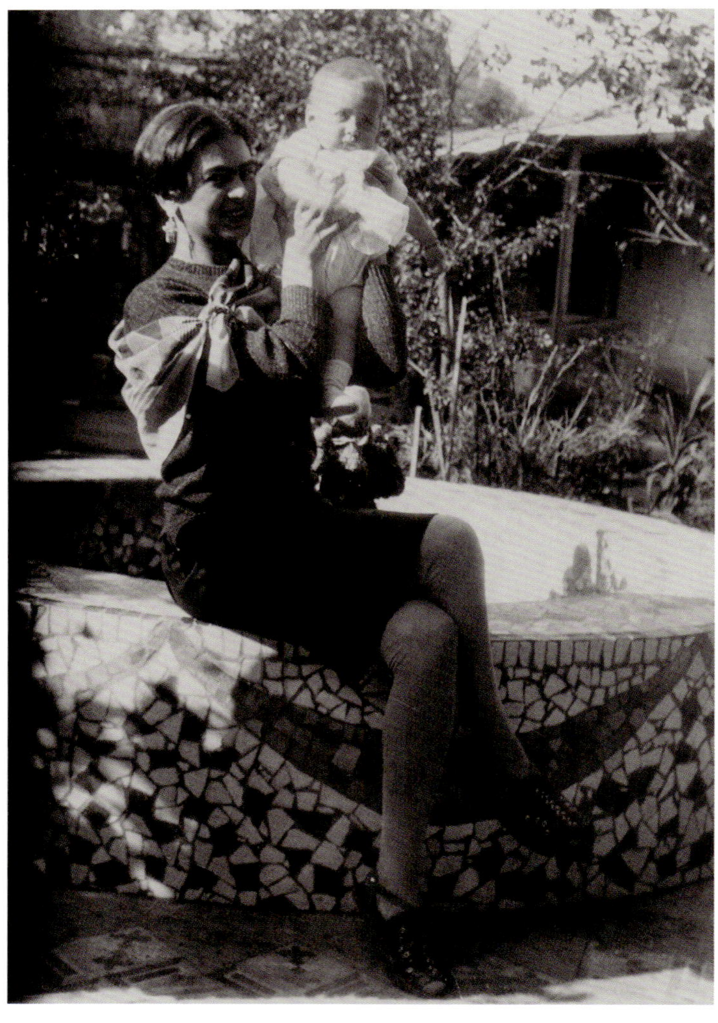

TOP The Kahlo y Calderón family portrait, Casa Azul, Coyoacán, January 29, 1928. Photo by Guillermo Kahlo. Pictured standing, left to right: Alberto Veraza (Frida's brother-in-law), Frida, and Francisco Hernández; seated, left to right: Adriana (Frida's sister), Matilde Calderón (Frida's mother), Matilde Kahlo (Frida's sister); seated on the ground, left to right: Cristina and Carlos Veraza

BOTTOM RIGHT Frida with Isolda at a year old, 1930

BOTTOM LEFT Cristina with her two children (Frida's nephew and niece), Antonio and Isolda, on the patio of Casa Azul, Coyoacán, ca. 1932

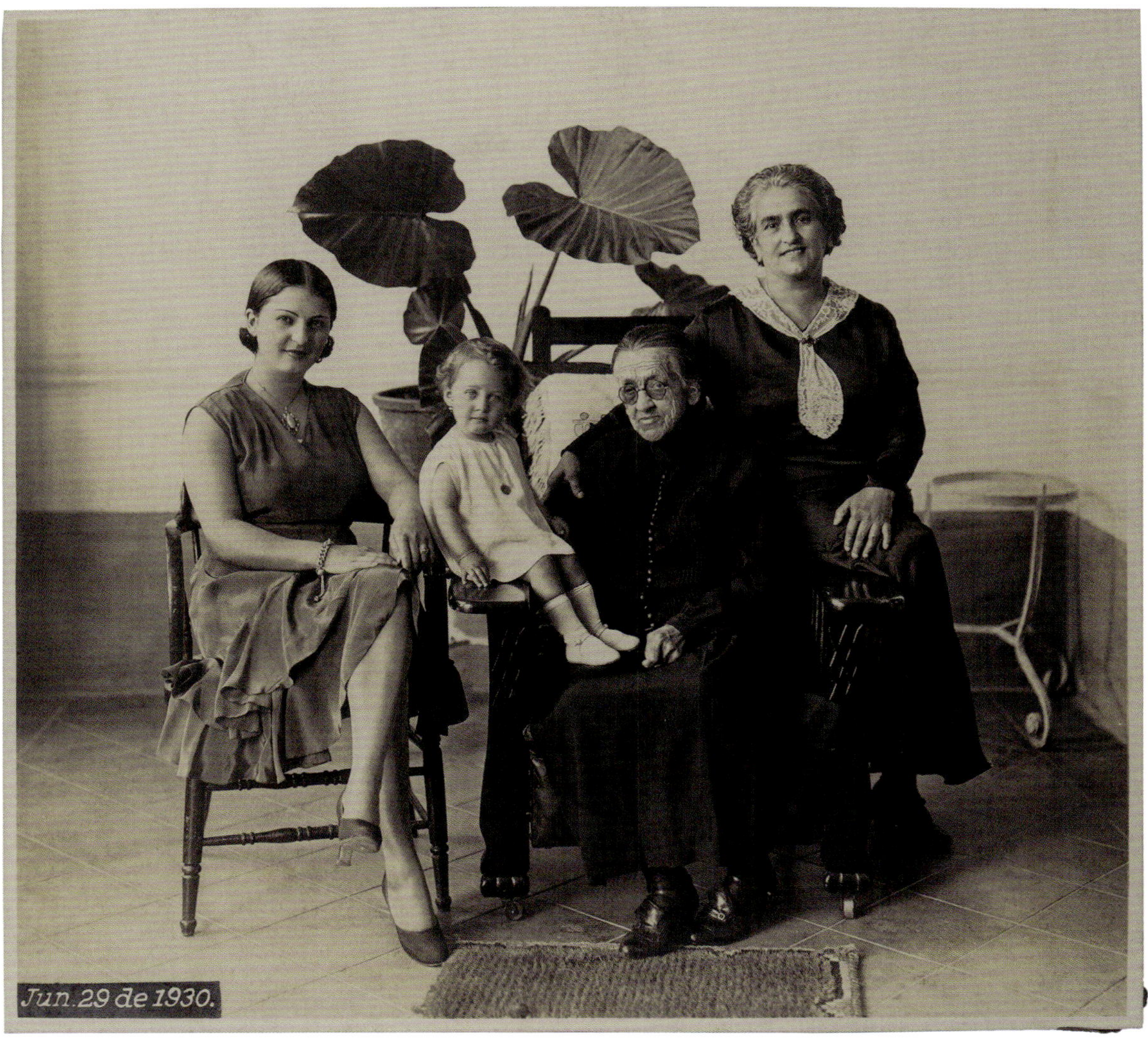

We are a very strong, matriarchal family, with a strong creative spirit. Our family referred to our menstrual cycles as *la luna*, acknowledging our cyclical nature and relationship to the moon. We were taught that each cycle would bring the opportunity for self-knowledge and wisdom. As creators of life, we were to consider ourselves as powerful. This notion has been passed down from generation to generation. Living the way we are taught, loving our roots, bodies, and Mexico. Frida embodied this in the way she lived her life. There are two letters from Frida to my grandmother when she had her first period. This rite of passage was such a critical and intimate moment that Frida wanted to acknowledge and celebrate it with her niece. It speaks to the relationship Frida and my grandmother shared. Frida was the aunt who gave advice and passed on traditions and knowledge through her letters and obviously, through her presence. She was my grandmother's godmother. The bond they shared because of this role was strong, but as my grandmother got older, their relationship evolved, becoming more like friends and confidantes. Frida gave unconventional advice. When she was very young, Isolda always did what she wanted to do, and this was something Frida taught her—to be yourself and not to apologize to anyone. Isolda possessed the strong will that characterizes all the Kahlo women.

Four generations of women, from left to right: Cristina with her daughter Isolda, Frida's grandmother Isabel González y González, and Frida's mother Matilde, June 29, 1930, Casa Kahlo, Coyoacán. Photo by Guillermo Kahlo

Mara Romeo Kahlo Frida was like a second mother to my mother Isolda. When Isolda studied ballet at the Academy of the Campobello Sisters, Frida advised her that if she wanted to be a dancer, she must be the best one, and that this required her dedication. Frida encouraged her to be the best in everything she did. She was so lovely with my mother; she really cared for her as her own. When Frida was in New York at the Hospital for Special Surgery with Cristina at her side, Isolda jointly wrote them letters: "My two mamas—for Cristina and Frida, my mom number one, Cristina, and for my second mom, Frida."

With that type of relationship with Frida, I think my mother felt at least some kind of pressure. She had two mothers to please, and each of them had expectations to live up to.

Mara de Anda My grandmother Isolda always said that the best life lessons she received were from her Tía Frida. Her other aunts were very caring but would advise from a more traditional point of view. But Frida was a free spirit. Through the years, she became a shining example of what

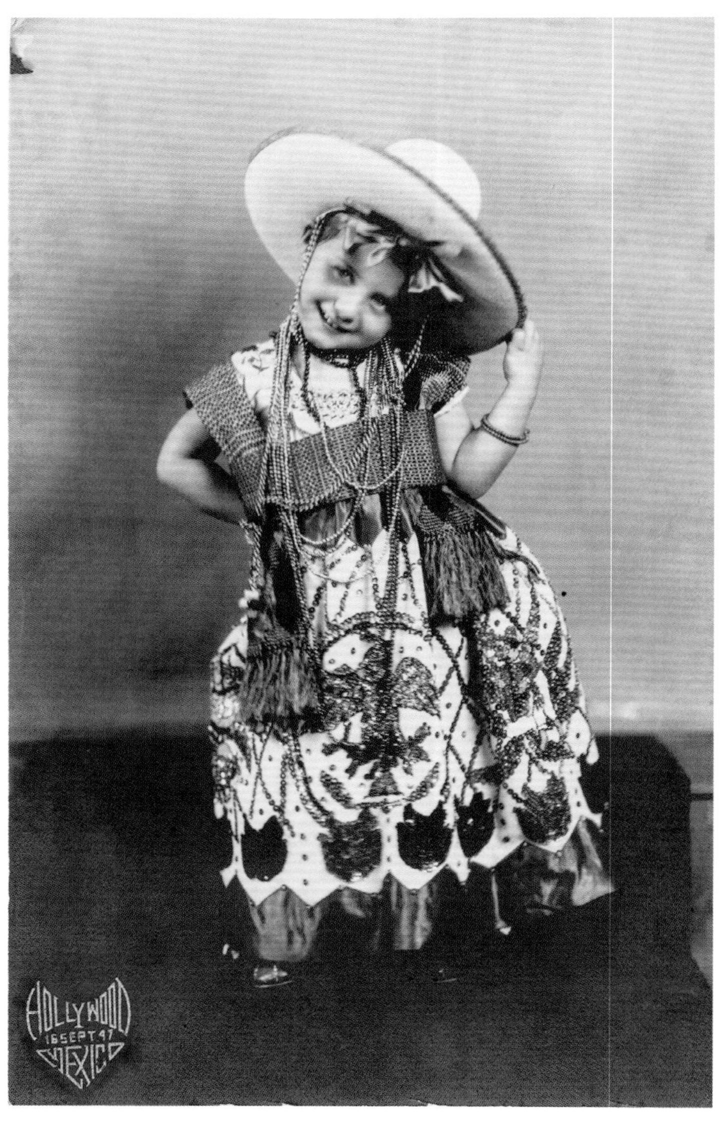

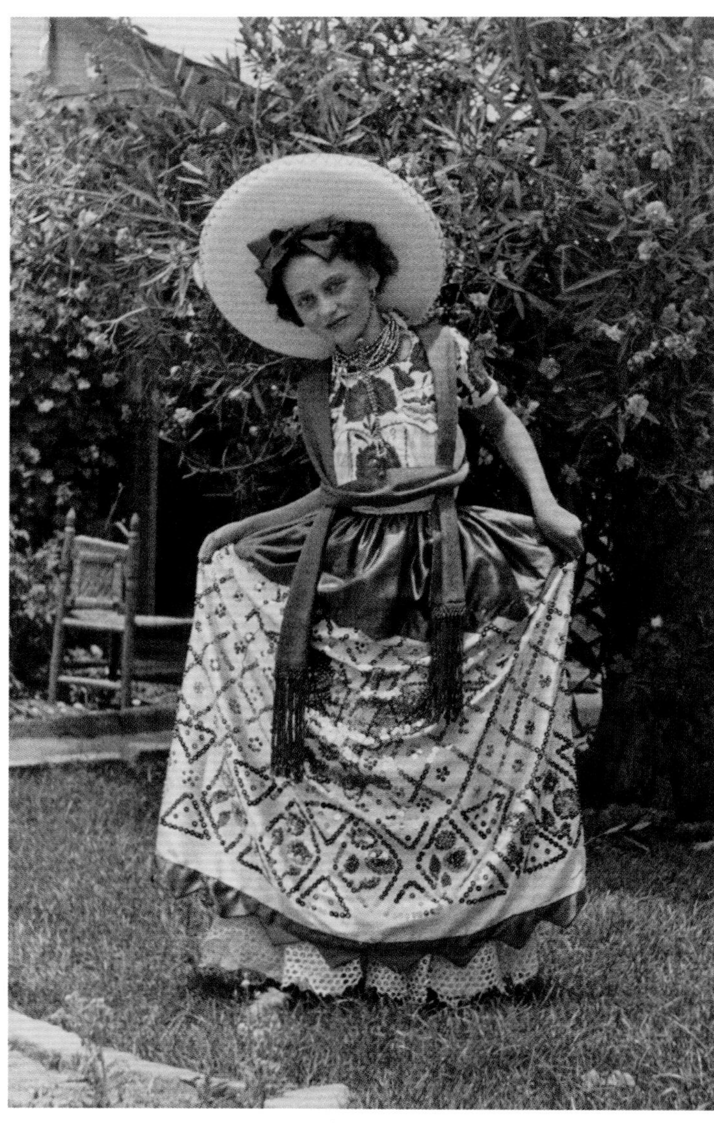

LEFT Isolda at age 4 wearing a Chinese costume, 1932. Photo by Hollywood Studio. Isolda was like a surrogate daughter to Frida. They had a deep, enduring relationship that lasted until Frida's death in 1954.

RIGHT Isolda at age 10 wearing a Chinese costume, 1938

OPPOSITE Frida with Isolda and her nephew Antonio, ca. 1934. Photo by Guillermo Kahlo

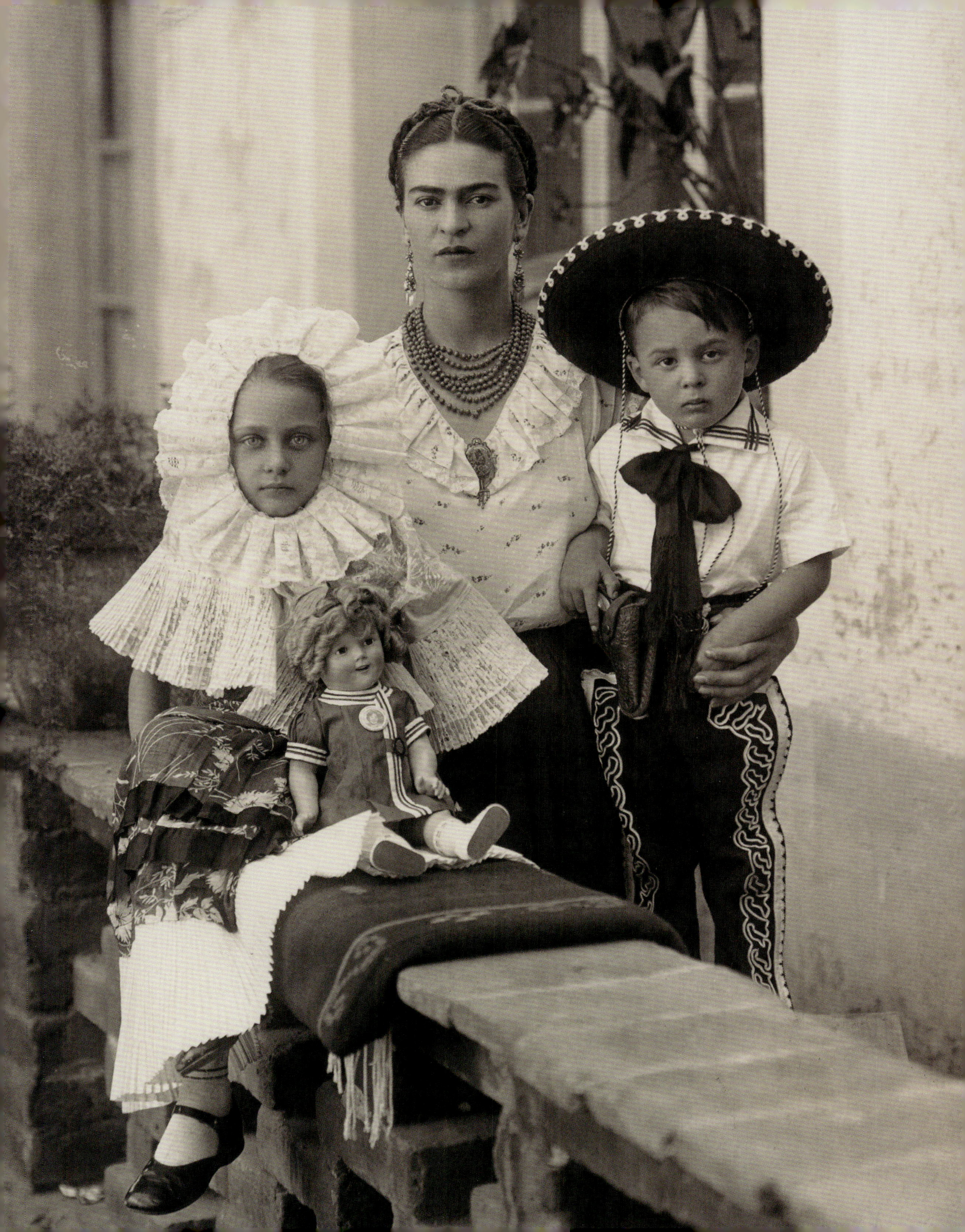

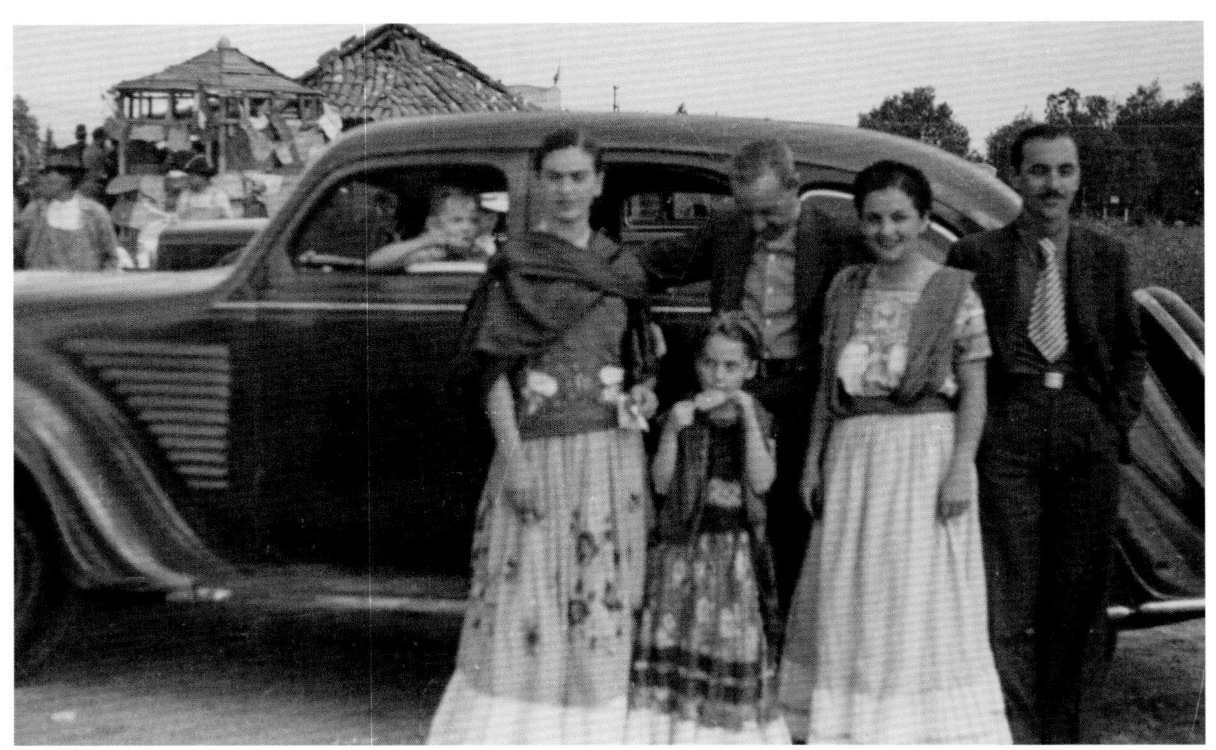

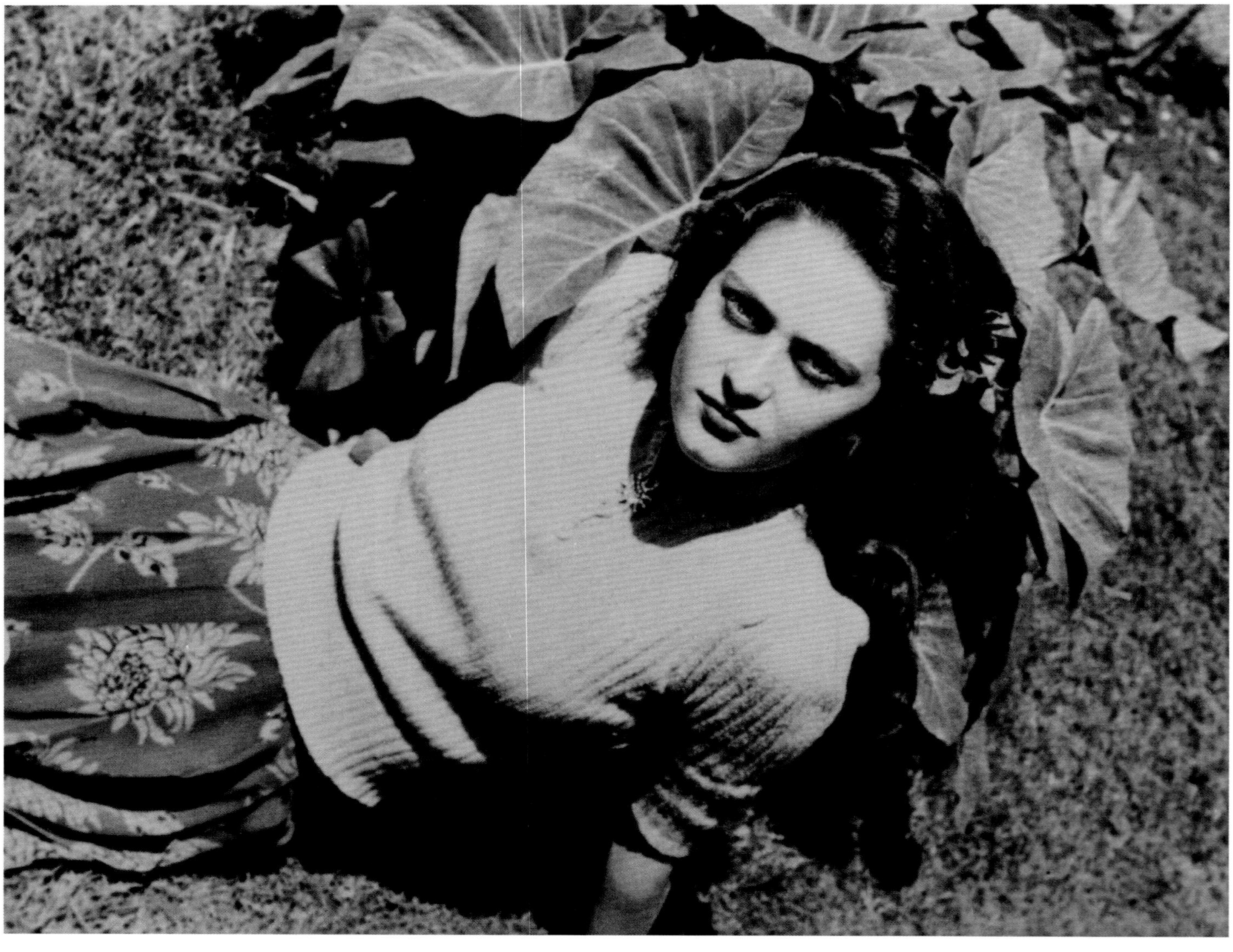

21 de Abril 1947.
Isol de mi vida,
Aliviate pronto.
porque estoy
rete triste sa-
biendo que estás
malita.
Te manda millo-
nes de besos tu
Fridu.

Isol de siempre.
Me dicen que ya
estás muy bien y
estoy tranquila.
Gracias por ser
valiente. Te adora Frida

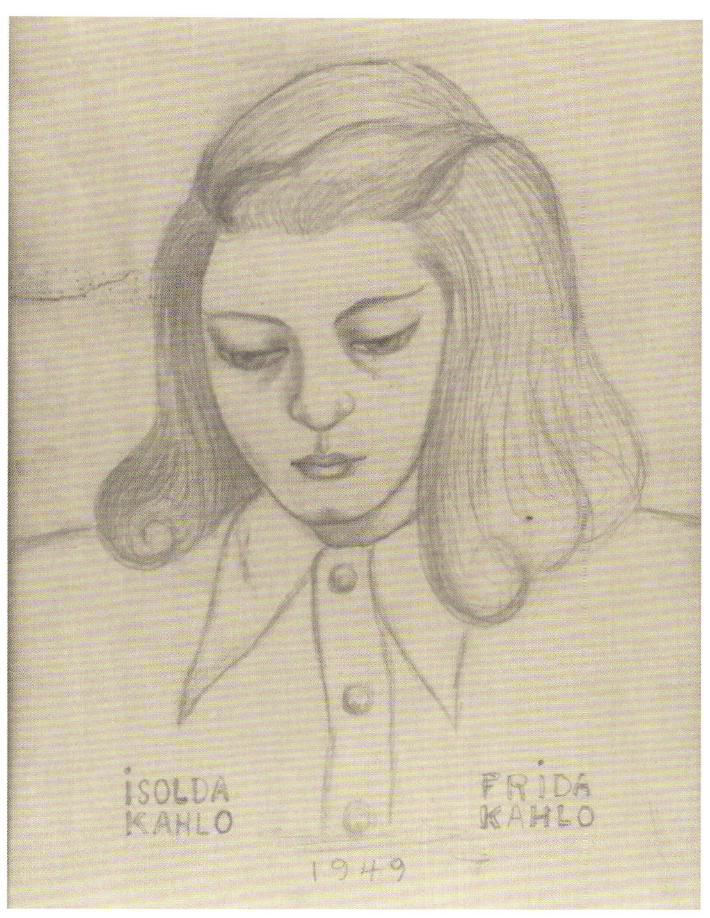

freedom, strength, and resilience looked like. My grandmother told us of one of the times she visited Frida in the hospital after one of her many surgeries, Frida was literally hanging from a couple of steel bands, and even in this precarious state, she was painting on an easel that was hung in front of her. My grandmother begged her to stop and rest, but Frida barked back at her, "Shut up, you do not know what you are talking about!" Painting was Frida's way to escape her pain. In the hospital she would paint, and she would sing. And everyone who heard her said she had a marvelous voice.

Mara Romeo Kahlo My mother Isolda loved Frida's admiration for Indigenous culture and Mexican popular art. Isolda learned to love her country even more with Frida's example.

OPPOSITE, TOP Frida with Isolda, Cristina, and two unidentified men, ca. 1935

OPPOSITE, BOTTOM Isolda at age 15 in the garden of Casa Kahlo, Coyoacán

TOP AND BOTTOM LEFT Notes from Frida to Isolda, 1947. Frida and Isolda's bond is evident in the copious letters and notes preserved by the Kahlo family.

TOP RIGHT Frida Kahlo, *Portrait of Isolda*, 1949. Pencil on paper, 13 x 9 in. (33 x 23 cm)

Coyoacán. Enero 16 de 1945.

Isolda linda, de mi corazón,
Aquí le vá éste regalito como un recuerdo de su tia "Fisita" que la adora, y en premio de que se está portando como toda una mujercita, muy trabajadora y abriendose el mejor camino en su vida, que es el de ser libre y bastarse a sí misma.
Con todo mi cariño, tu
Fridu.

Perdona el papel tan "chicho".

Enero 3 de 1948.

Isol, mi amor,
Ya sabes que no hay palabras para decirte que seas feliz, hoy y siempre.
Tu tia que te adora
Fridu

Coyoacán – Diciembre de 1941.

Isoldita linda,
esta pulsera, te la doy para que cada vez que te la pongas – te acuerdes que tu tia Fridu te quiere con todo su corazón. Y como símbolo del dia en que pasaste, de niña, a mujercita.
Fridu –

ABOVE AND OPPOSITE Miscellaneous notes and letters from Frida to Isolda, from 1940–50, which include, among other loving missives, a happy birthday greeting and an endearing letter dedicated to Isolda on the day she got her first period. In the note dated January 3, 1948, she writes in Spanish: "Isol, my love, you know there's no words to tell you to be happy today and always. Your aunt that loves you, Fridu." She signed many of her letters with "Fridu," which was one of the most common of the pet names Frida's family had for her.

New York Lunes 23 Junio 46.

Isol mi amor,

Hoy hice quince días de operada y todavía no me siento muy gira, pero voy mejorando rápidamente. Hoy me sentaron por primera vez en la orilla de la cama por dos minutos, y en unos cuantos días me van a sentar en un sillón especial y después podré ir dando unos pasitos, total en 6 semanas mas ya podré

regresar a Mexico! Ya los extraño muchísimo, a mi Güerito a Ali a ti a Miguis a mi Diego a Matachin y a todos. No me dejan escribir mucho pues de todo me canso pero solamente quiero que recibas de mi puño y letras estas palabras para que no me olvides. Tu mamasita ha sido un angel conmigo y me anima mucho. Te beso harto y tu reparte los besos a todos.

Desde Diego hasta Carlitos. Tu el más chiquito de la familia

tu Frida

Nueva York. Oct. 20. 1940.

POST CARD
ACTUAL PHOTOGRAPH

Isolda linda mia,

Te debo muchas cartas, pero no te olvido ni un momento. Escribeme aunque yo no te escriba, dime qué haces, como vas en la Escuela y si eres muy buena niña con tu mamá. Como quisiera yo tenerte cerca de mi, para que conocieras Nueva York. (Este es el edificio más alto del mundo. Se llama el Empire State Building). No me olvides. Yo te extraño muchísimo y ya quisiera regresar a Mexico pronto pronto. Millones de besos de tu Frida.

3 de Enero de 1950.

Niña de mi vida,

Como no pude salir a comprarte álgo prefiero mandarte la "mosca" que vá de parte de tu tio y mia para que tu compres lo que te guste.

Ojalá y pases el dia de hoy feliz. Ya sabes lo que te adora tu Frida.

Muchas felicidades te desea tu tio Diego.

The Kahlos loved their country—the wit, the colorful and warm people. Guillermo had a deep love for his adopted homeland and took great pride in becoming Mexican. My father was a Spaniard, and he loved Mexico as well. If he ever heard someone disparaging Mexico, he didn't hesitate to argue passionately for his new country, one that had given him and so many other immigrants a new life. Guillermo, Frida's father, was the same way.

Mara de Anda We have a story from when my grandmother Isolda was in primary school. There was a Spanish girl talking disparagingly about Mexico and remarking that she couldn't understand how people could eat its disgusting food. Isolda would have none of it and took her into the bathroom, intending to drown her! Luckily, someone came in and stopped her. In her mind, she was defending her country but, unfortunately, she was expelled. When she came home to Casa Azul crying, her Tío Diego asked her what had happened. She told him the whole story, and Diego laughed and told her he was very proud of her response. Isolda, surely a bit confused by the wildly different reactions to what she did, went back to the school with Diego. He assured her that if they wouldn't take her back, he would shut down the school. When Diego showed up, imposing as he was and carrying a gun, the principal Rebaque Garea immediately changed his mind, and they took Isolda back. It was a terrible six months till the end of that school year because most of the other students were from Spain. No one talked to her and she lost any friends she had.

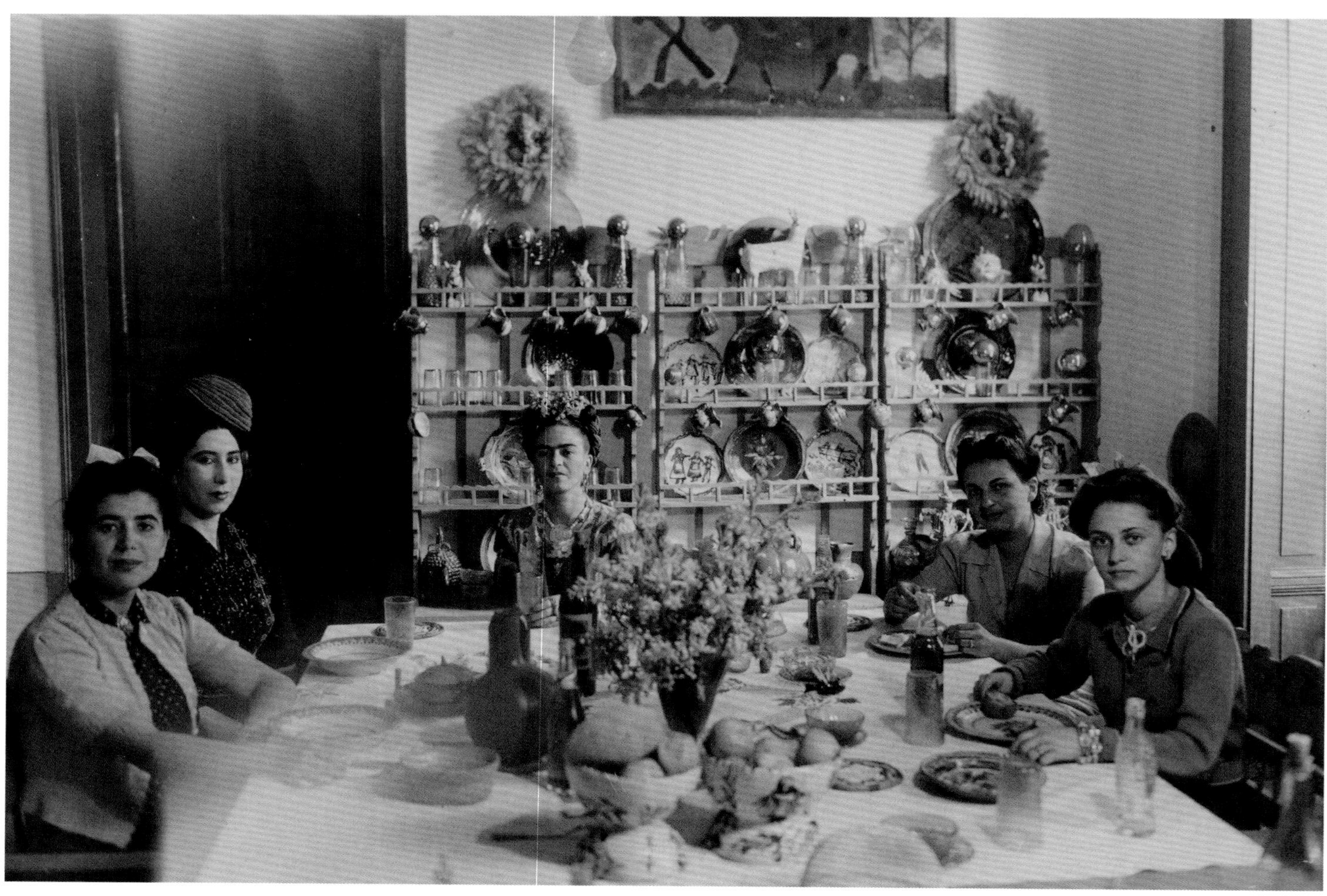

ABOVE Dining room, Casa Azul, Coyoacán, ca. 1942. From left to right: Guadalupe Marin (Mexican novelist and first wife of Diego Rivera), Eugenita (Diego's nurse after one of his monkeys injured his eye), Frida, Cristina, and Isolda, ca. 1942

OPPOSITE Frida and Isolda, ca. 1945

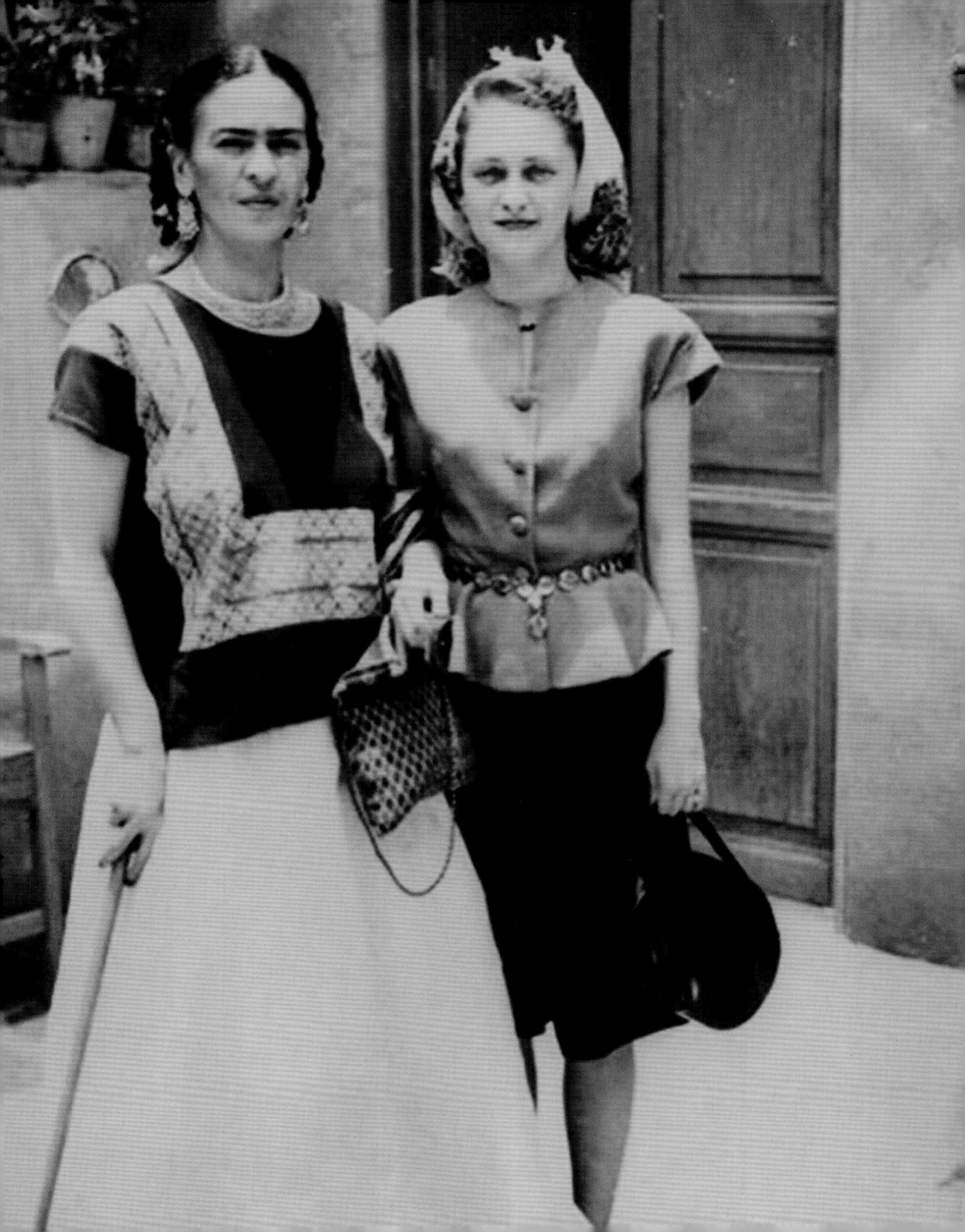

Isolda would often refer to Frida as her second mother. When Cristina was away in New York to be with Frida during one of her surgeries, Isolda sent letters to both of them almost daily. At the top of this letter, it reads, "Take good care of each other." And above the lipstick kisses: "This kiss is from me to you. This kiss is from me to my mamacita. And this kiss is from my aunt to her Fridita, whom she adores."

s MUTUAMENTE. ← Frida

Este besito es de
mi parte y es para
mi mamacita

to es de
Tía y es para

que tanto

á que la extraño
lo mismo que a ti.
Isol.

Jueves 4 de julio de 1946.
(en la mañana.)

Mamacita del alma:

Te escribo desde ésta aun sabiendo que no es para felicitarte, pero para que sepas, que no siendo día de tu santo para mi es como si lo fuera. Pues yo quiero que recibas al igual que mi tía Fridu, que es ahora la agasajada, felicitaciones al parejo de ella.

Mi mamacita adorada:
Te felicito yo también para el 24 aunque todavía esté lejos, pues ya para esa fecha te tengo algo reservado.

But my grandmother understood that when she did this, she would have the support of her family. She was taught about the values of her country and to be proud about it. "I'm a Kahlo and if I didn't know I had all the backing and support of my family, I wouldn't have done it," she used to say.

Mara Romeo Kahlo My mother Isolda was a complicated woman—and she had a temper. But as big as her temper was, her heart was just as big. Later in life, on occasion, I would give her money for food. But she would often give most of it away; she would walk to the center of Coyoacán and hand it out to anyone who seemed in need. She preferred that rather than spending it all on herself.

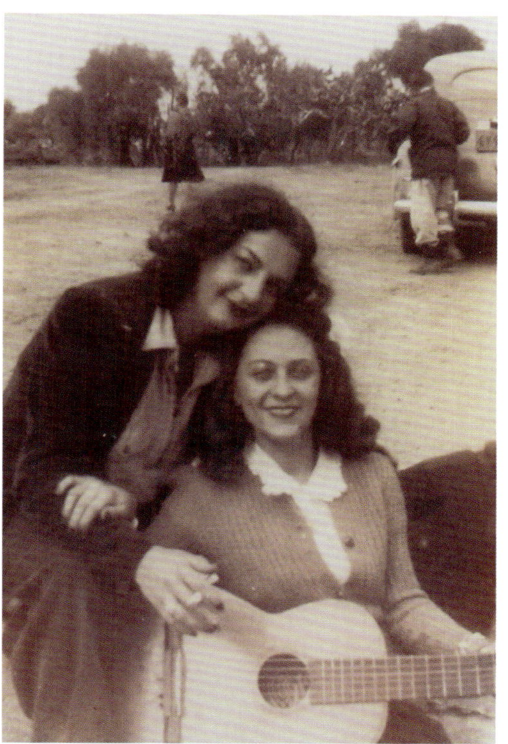

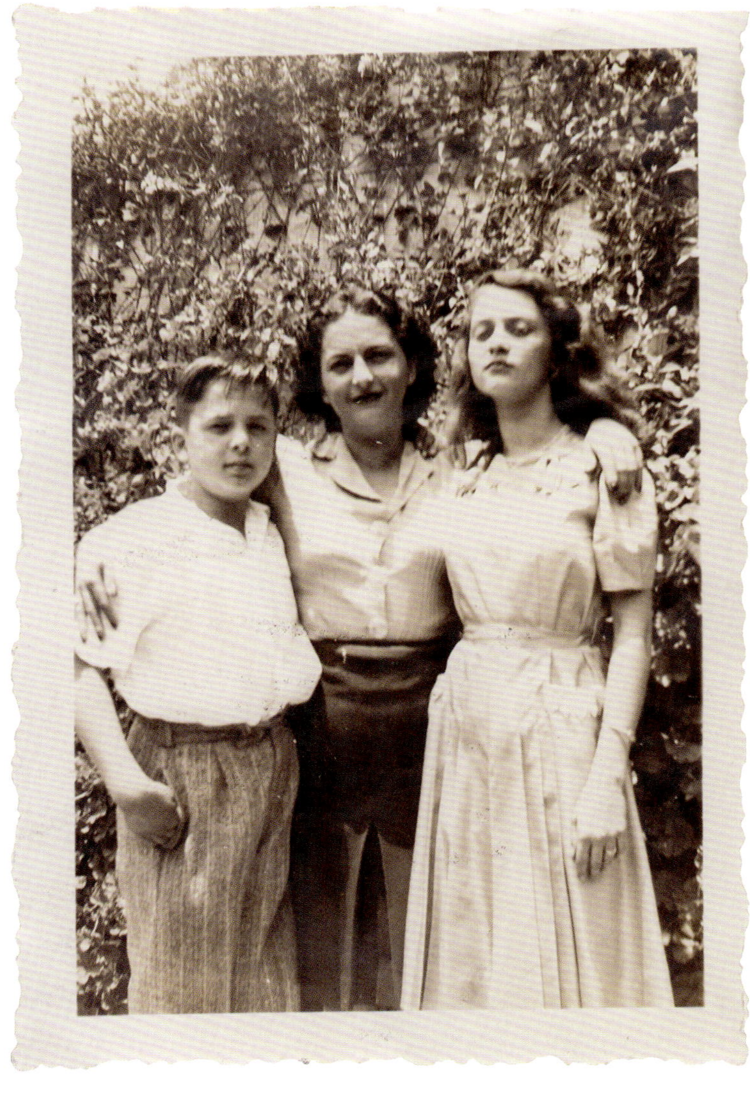

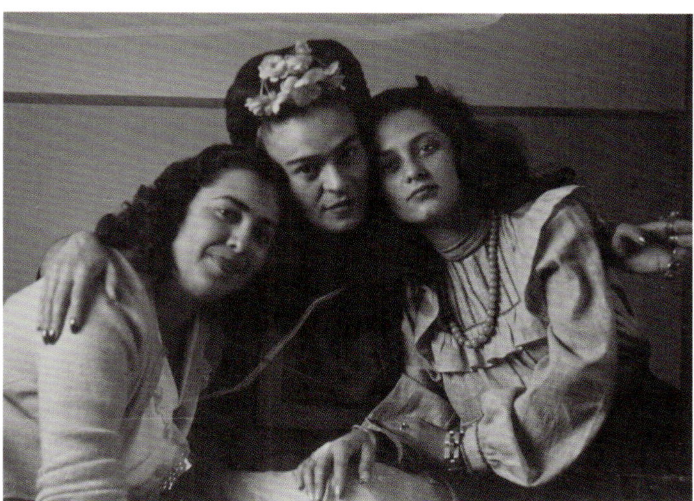

OPPOSITE Just like her aunt Frida, Isolda often sent letters marked with lipstick kisses. This letter is addressed to her mother Cristina.

TOP LEFT Cristina with her two children, Antonio and Isolda, in the garden of Casa Kahlo, Coyoacán, ca. 1944

TOP RIGHT Cristina with Isolda playing the guitar, ca. 1949

BOTTOM RIGHT Frida with Isolda (right) and an unidentified person, ca. 1947

Mara Romeo Kahlo In our family, we didn't talk about the alleged affair between Cristina and Diego. I don't know if it happened or not. People think she wrote about it directly in her diary—she did not. Diego was a womanizer, and he broke her heart many times. From our perspective, the important thing to note is that if it did happen, Frida clearly forgave her. And we know what *did* happen: the sisters' relationship was never broken, and it grew stronger as years passed.

Frida Hentschel Frida's love for Cristina was unconditional and nothing would come between them. According to the rumors, the affair would have happened when Cristina was 21 years old, and Diego was 45 years old. This was 1930s Mexico, where *machismo* was very much the norm. Diego was a powerful man; he could speak many languages and was very erudite. There was an imbalance of power, and he was known for his strong will. So, there remains many questions and information that we don't know. Many scholars make suppositions, but all sources are third-hand. What we do know is that this information was never shared within the family. And the family is the only reliable source.

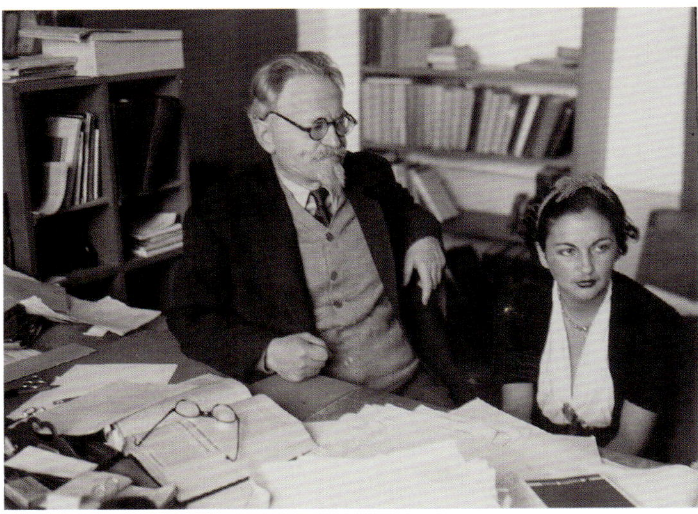

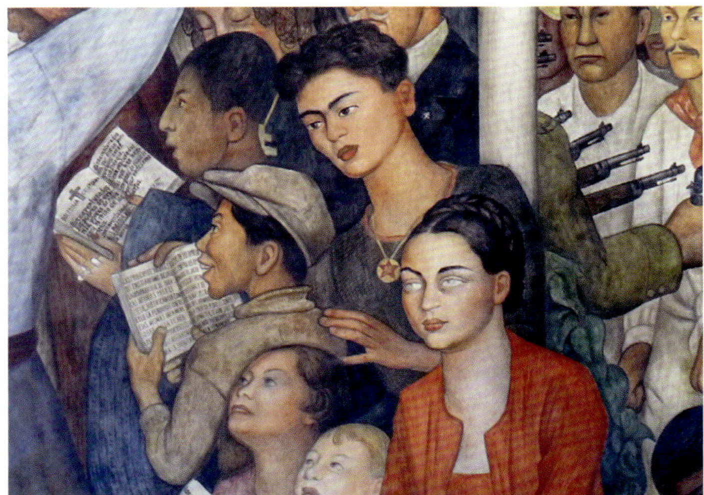

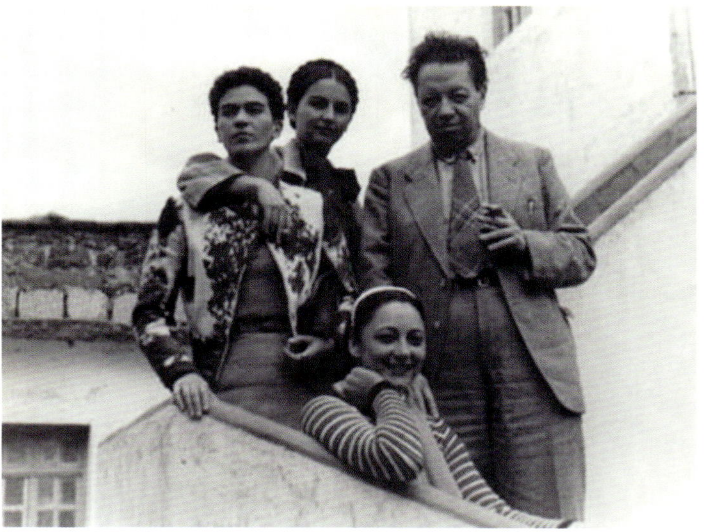

TOP Leon Trotsky and Cristina, ca. 1938. Photo by Sánchez Mendoza

MIDDLE Diego Rivera mural, detail, Palacio Nacional, which pictured Frida (center top with a necklace) and Cristina (in the red sweater and shirt).

BOTTOM, LEFT TO RIGHT Frida, Cristina, Diego Rivera, and Rosa Rolanda (seated), ca. 1935. Photo by Rosa Covarrubias

OPPOSITE Frida Kahlo, *Memory (The Heart)*, 1937. Oil on metal, 15.75 x 11 in. (40 x 28.3 cm)

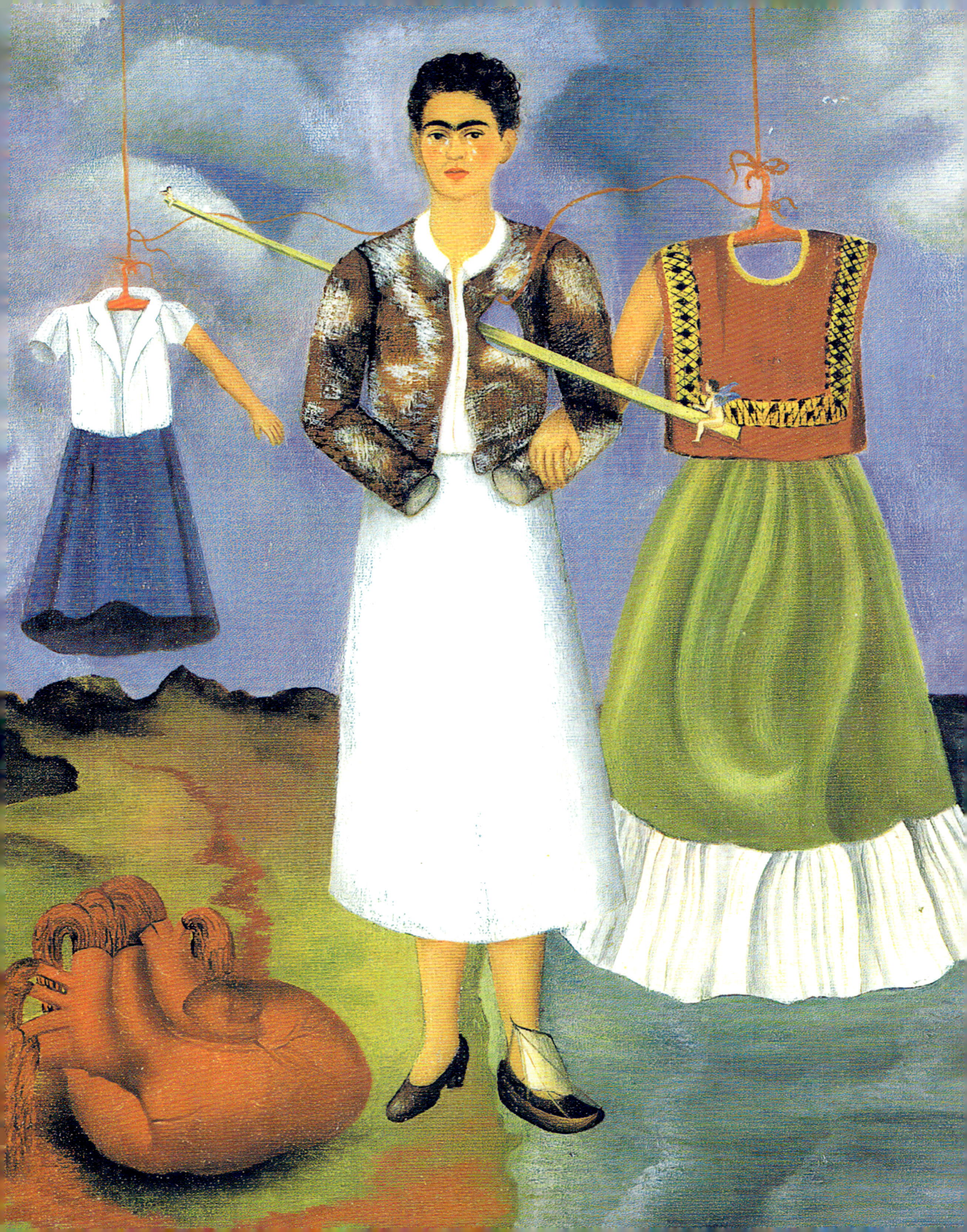

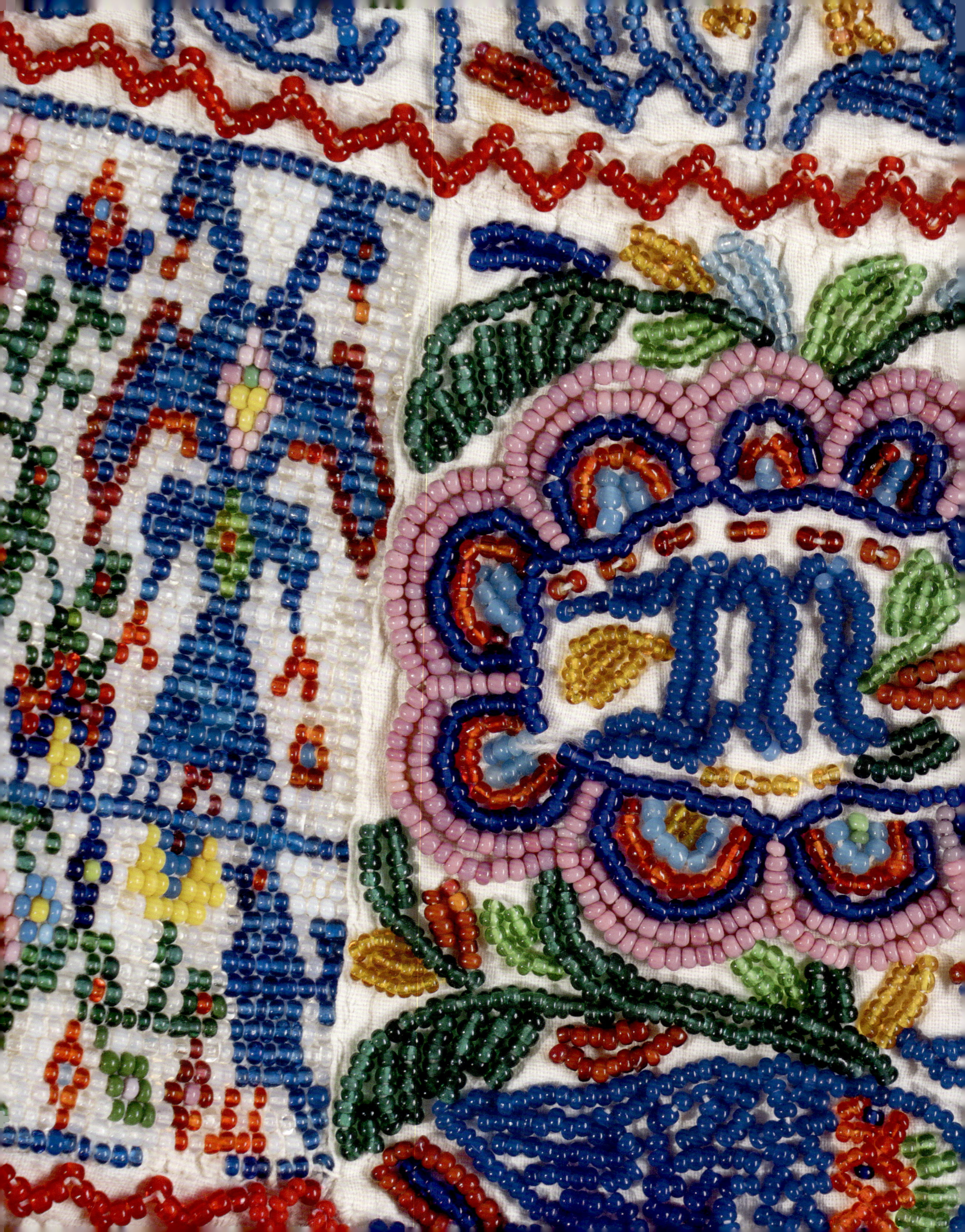

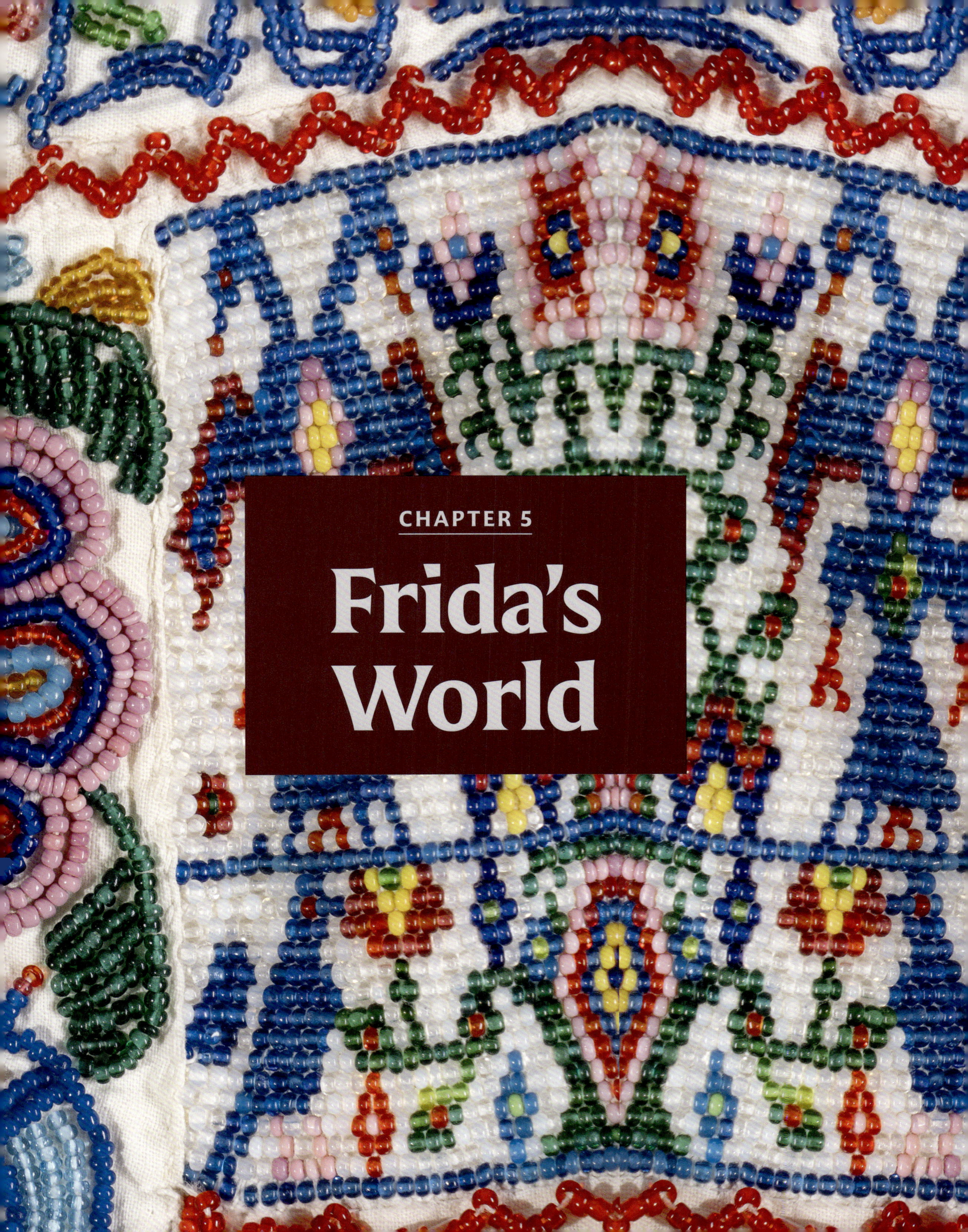

CHAPTER 5

Frida's World

Mara Romeo Kahlo Frida loved to say that her mother Matilde was from Oaxaca and that she exposed her to Mexican culture and Indigenous art. She probably thought that her folkloric dresses and jewelry would be more compelling and convincing if she had had direct roots to the Istmo de Tehuantepec, which is a region in the state of Oaxaca. But in fact, Matilde Calderon's mother, Isabel, was born in Alfajayucan, Hidalgo, and her father, José Antonio Calderón, was from Morelia, Michoacán. There were no direct ties to Oaxaca. It has been one of the many myths and misinformation that surround Frida that have stuck.

However, what is true is that Frida championed Oaxacan and other Indigenous art and culture more compellingly than any other public figure of the time (and since). She inspired national pride inside Mexico and introduced our culture to the world. The bright colors and the style of dress that she was so attracted to connected her to our native culture, and it comforted her when desperately homesick while she traveled.

The flowers that Frida always wore in her hair were something passed down from Matilde, who also wore flowers in her hair. Though Matilde wore hers differently, it was deeply inspiring to Frida. It has been written that Frida wore *faldas largas* (long skirts) to cover her leg, but there were many reasons. She wanted everybody to know and acknowledge the Mexican Indigenous craftspeople as artists. She would wear dresses and pieces from Ecuador and Peru as well.

The first thing that Frida did every morning was take a bath. She would dedicate quite a bit of time to brushing her hair and carefully adorning it with colorful laces and/or flowers to match her attire for the day. She put a lot of effort into her personal appearance. She used to say, "You never know who or when someone is going to take a picture, so you better look good." Her ornate clothing and jewelry made her feel better. Frida made and remade the stone necklaces she wore constantly, with stones she collected from rivers. She chose stones based on the energy she felt emanated from them. We Mexicans believe that these natural elements should never be purchased or gifted—they should be found objects.

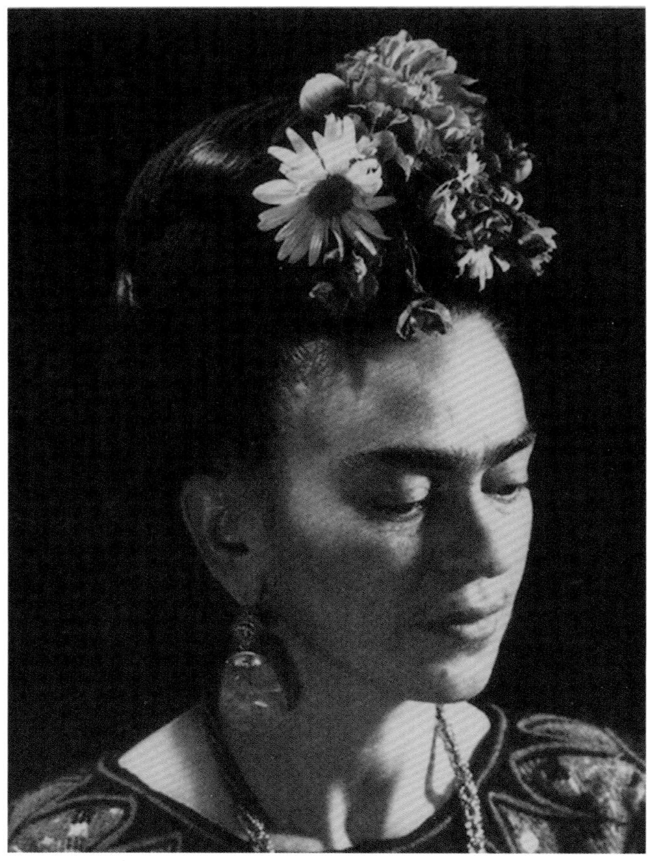

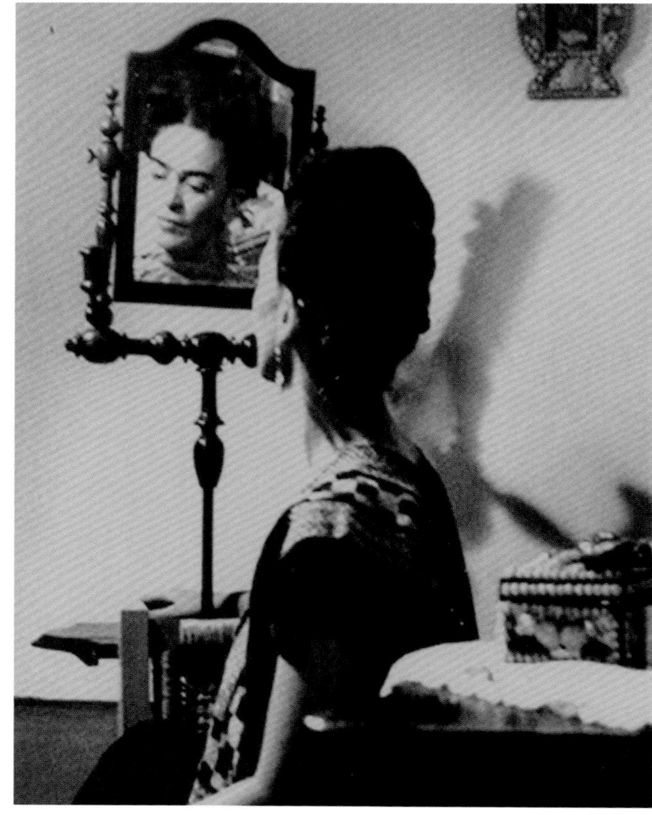

TOP Frida, 1952. Photo by Marcel Sternberger

BOTTOM Frida, 1945. Photo by Lola Alvarez Bravo

OPPOSITE Frida with Olmec figure in the garden of Casa Azul, Coyoacán, 1939. Photo by Nickolas Muray

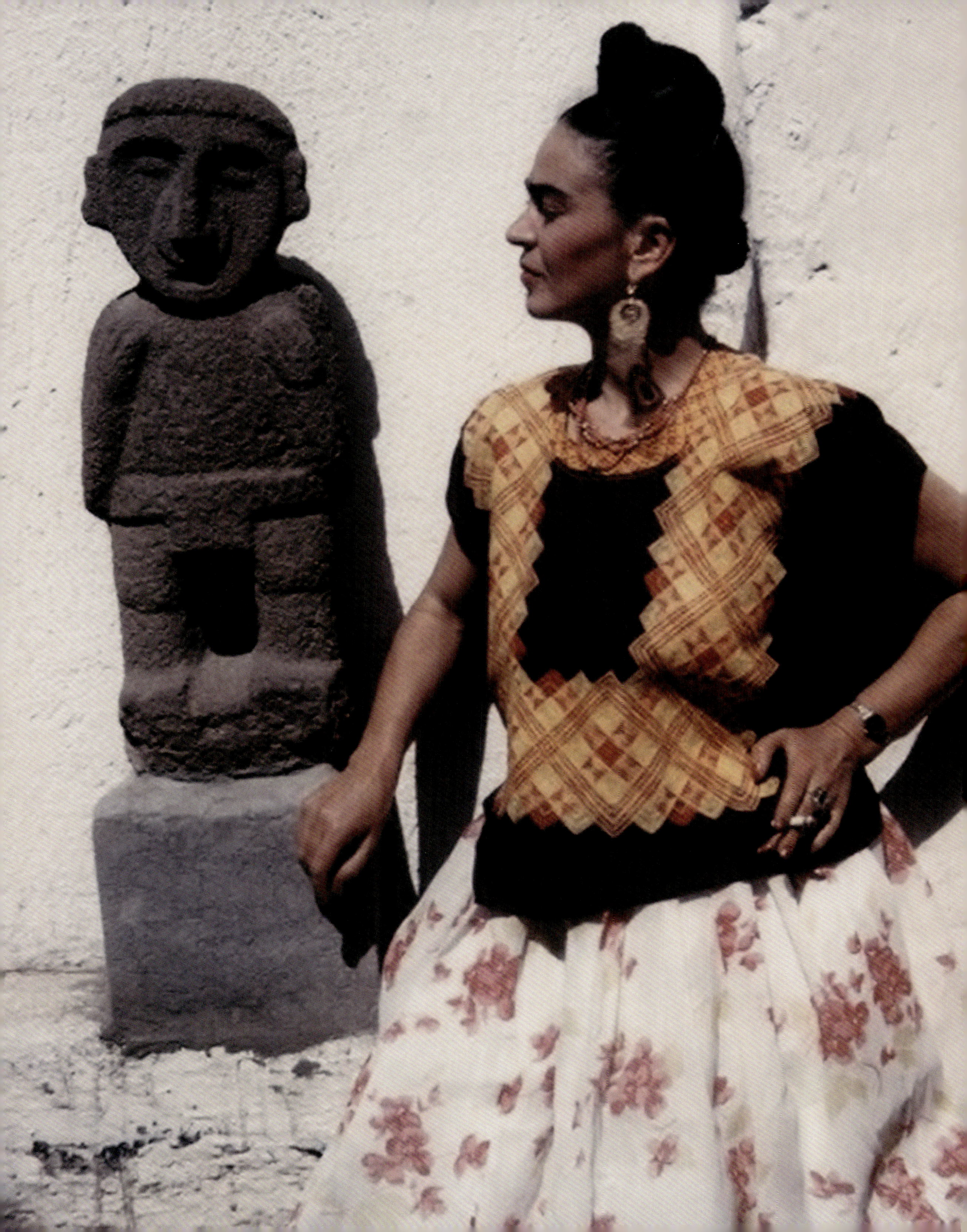

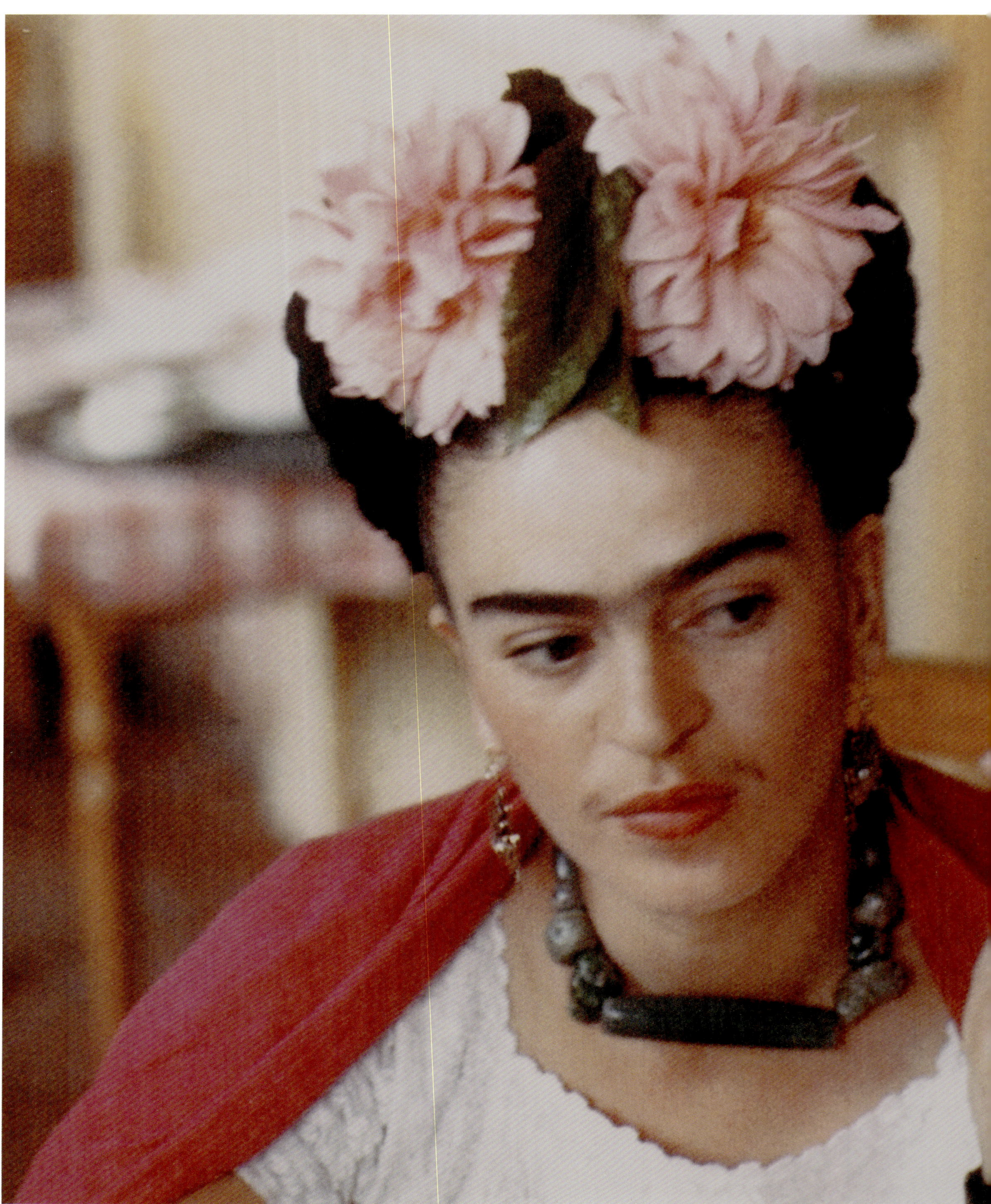

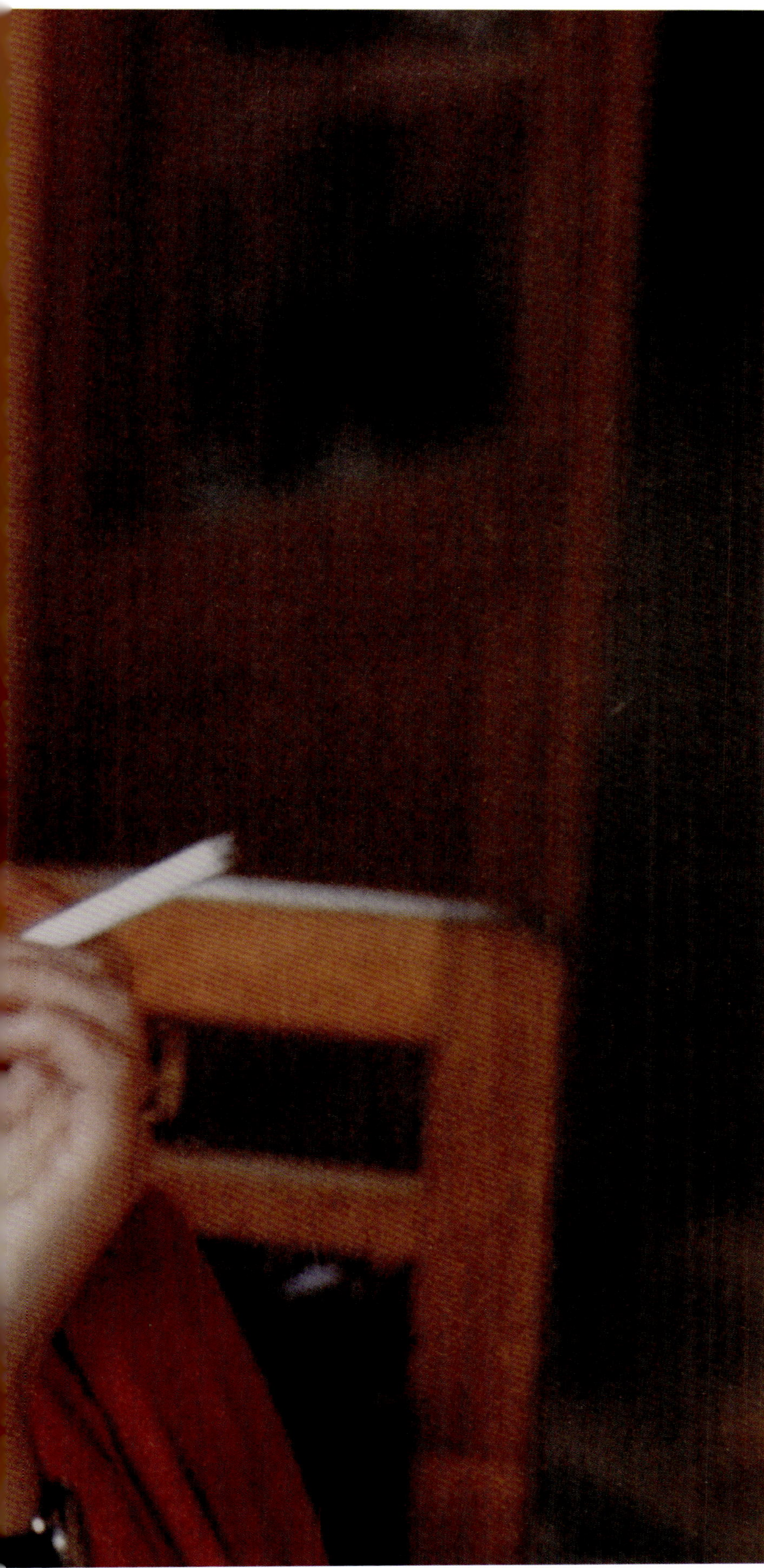

Mara de Anda The way Frida dressed and adorned herself was yet another way to express her creativity. Every day was a new opportunity to reinvent herself. She would invest time in creating new combinations of clothing, as if she were one of her own paintings.

Frida talked about a funny moment she had while visiting New York City. A boy, seeing her dressed in her usual attire with bright colors, stopped her and asked: "Hey miss, which way to the circus?" She laughed every time she remembered and told that story.

Frida Hentschel When Frida first traveled to the United States in 1930, she brought her long skirts, *rebozos* (scarfs), and *huipiles* (traditional Mexican tunics). She was aware almost immediately the reaction they provoked in people. She wrote to her mother and sisters asking them to send her more clothes like this. She liked the feeling of being unique and from a far-away culture.

Frida, Coyoacán, ca.1941. Photo by Nickolas Muray

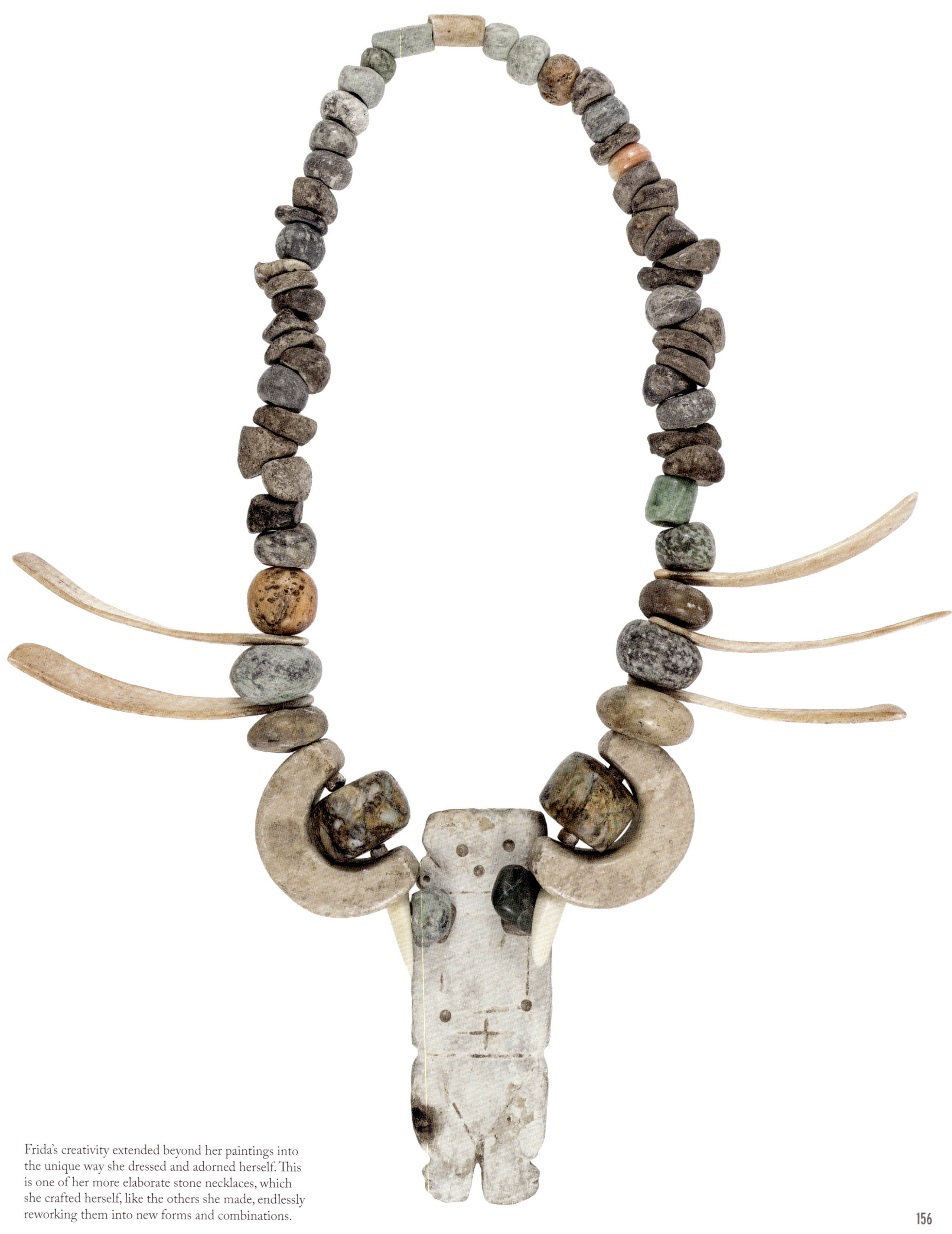

Frida's creativity extended beyond her paintings into the unique way she dressed and adorned herself. This is one of her more elaborate stone necklaces, which she crafted herself, like the others she made, endlessly reworking them into new forms and combinations.

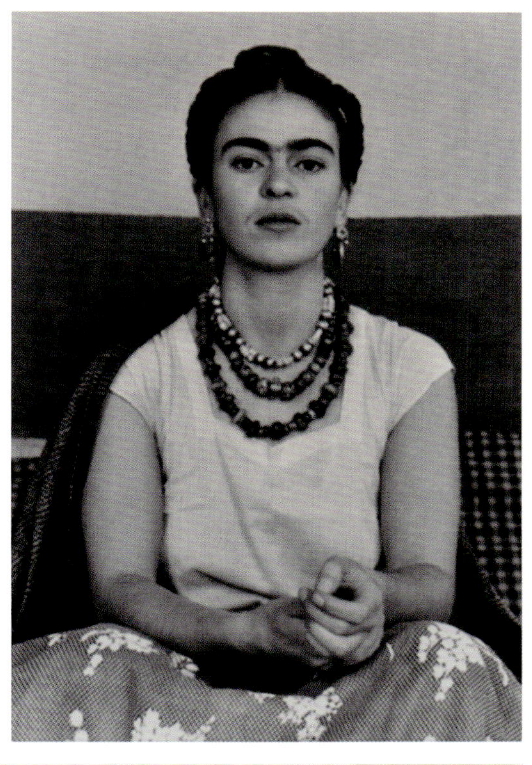

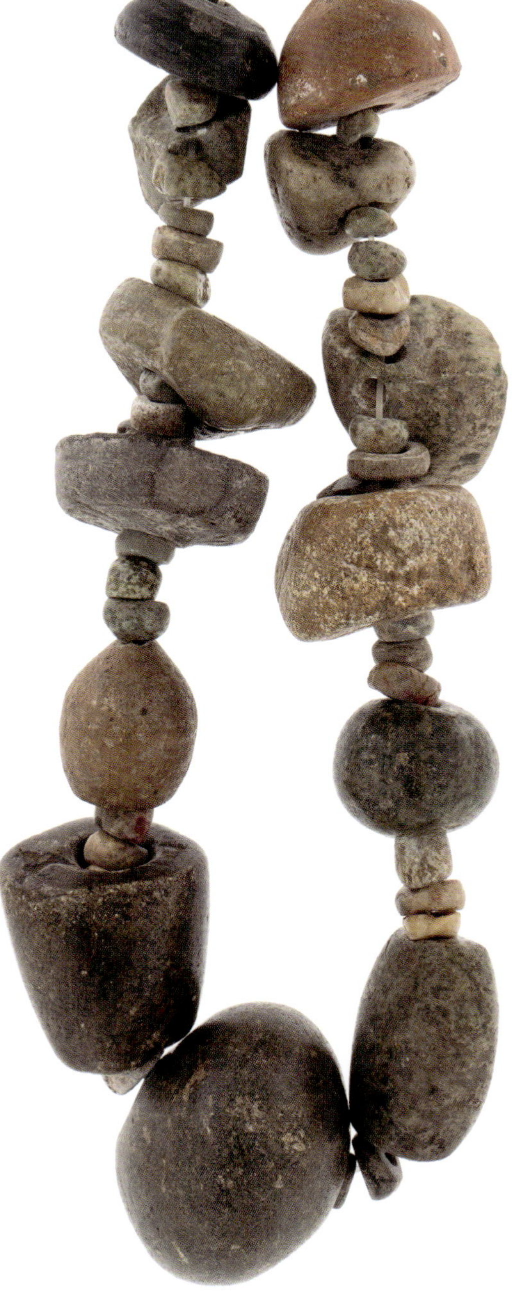

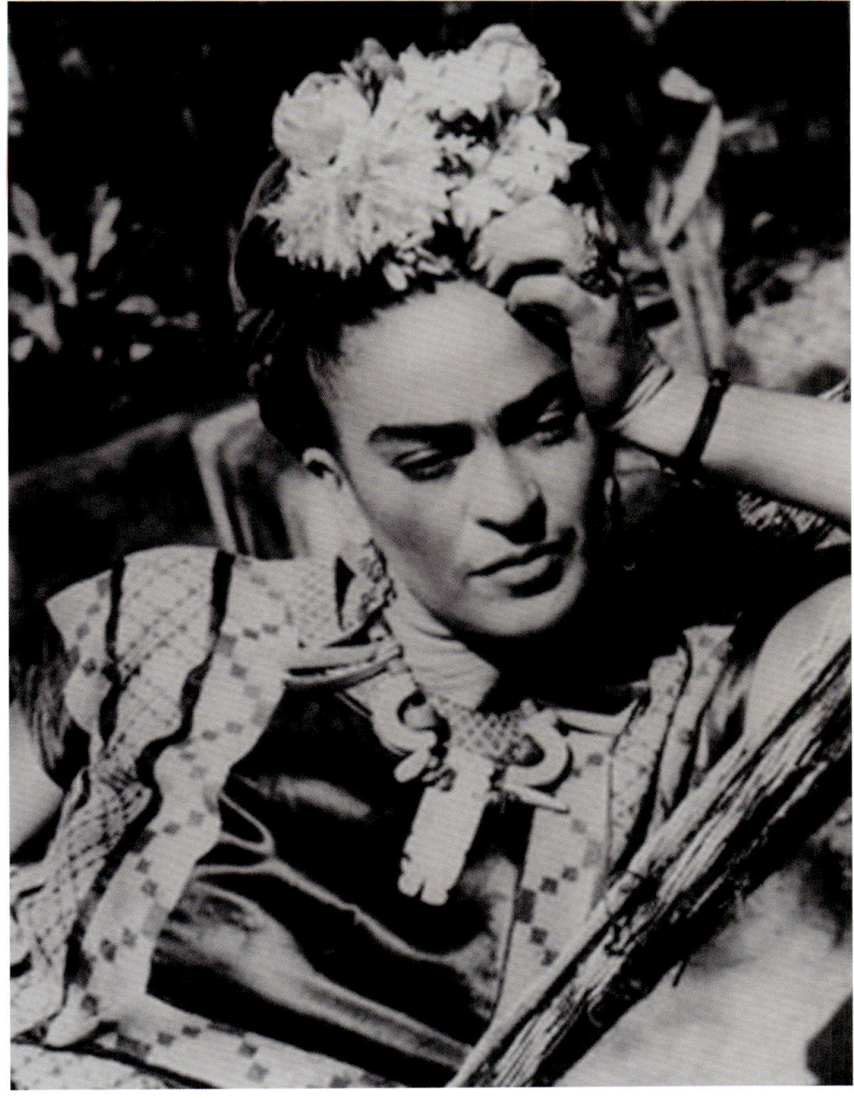

TOP LEFT Frida, ca. 1930. Photo by Lola Alvarez Bravo

TOP RIGHT Frida's stone necklace, which she designed

BOTTOM LEFT Frida wearing a stone necklace with idol, ca. 1940. Photo by Wallace Marly

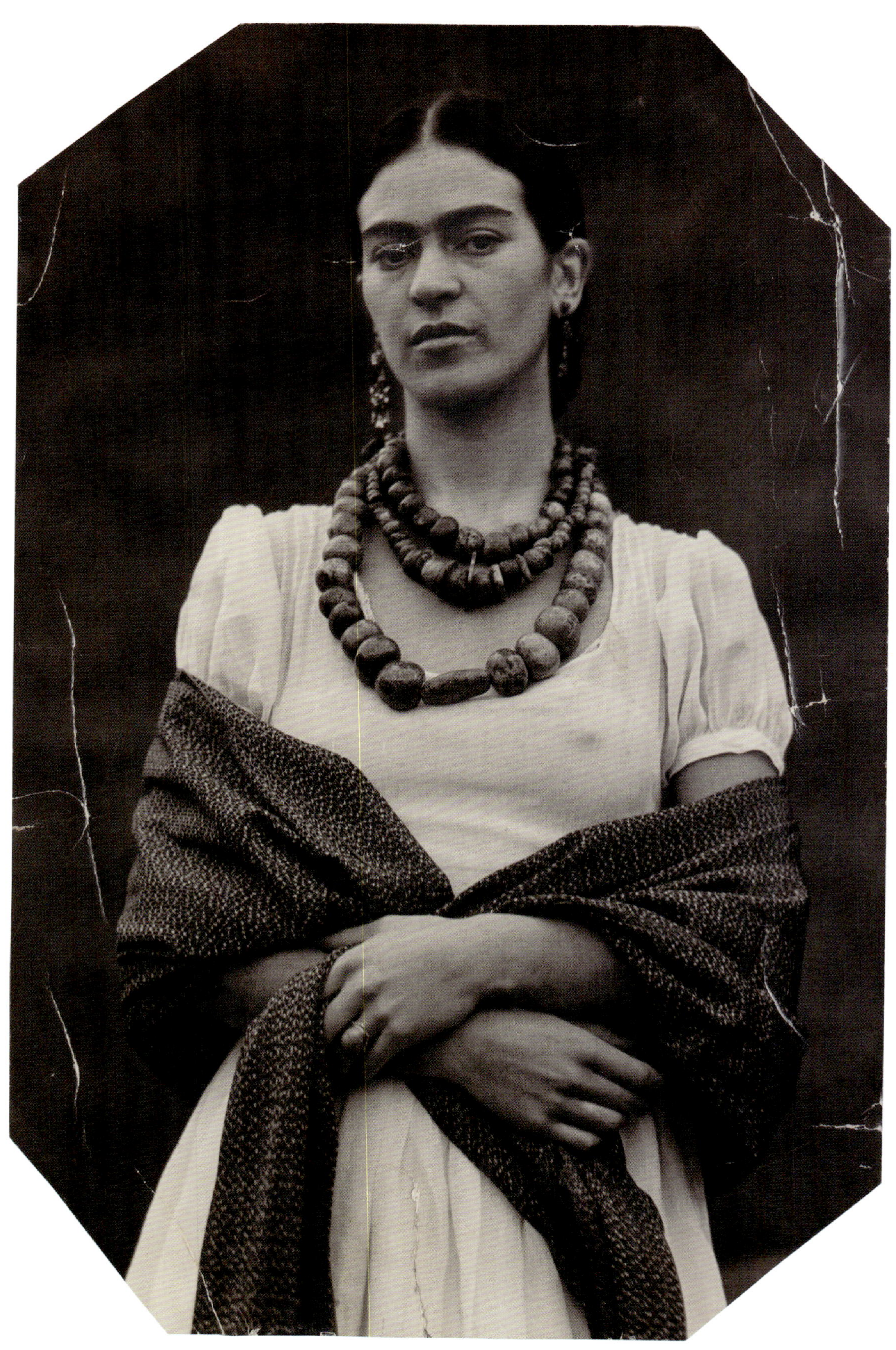

ABOVE Frida wearing a jade necklace, ca. 1931
OPPOSITE Frida's stone necklace, which she designed

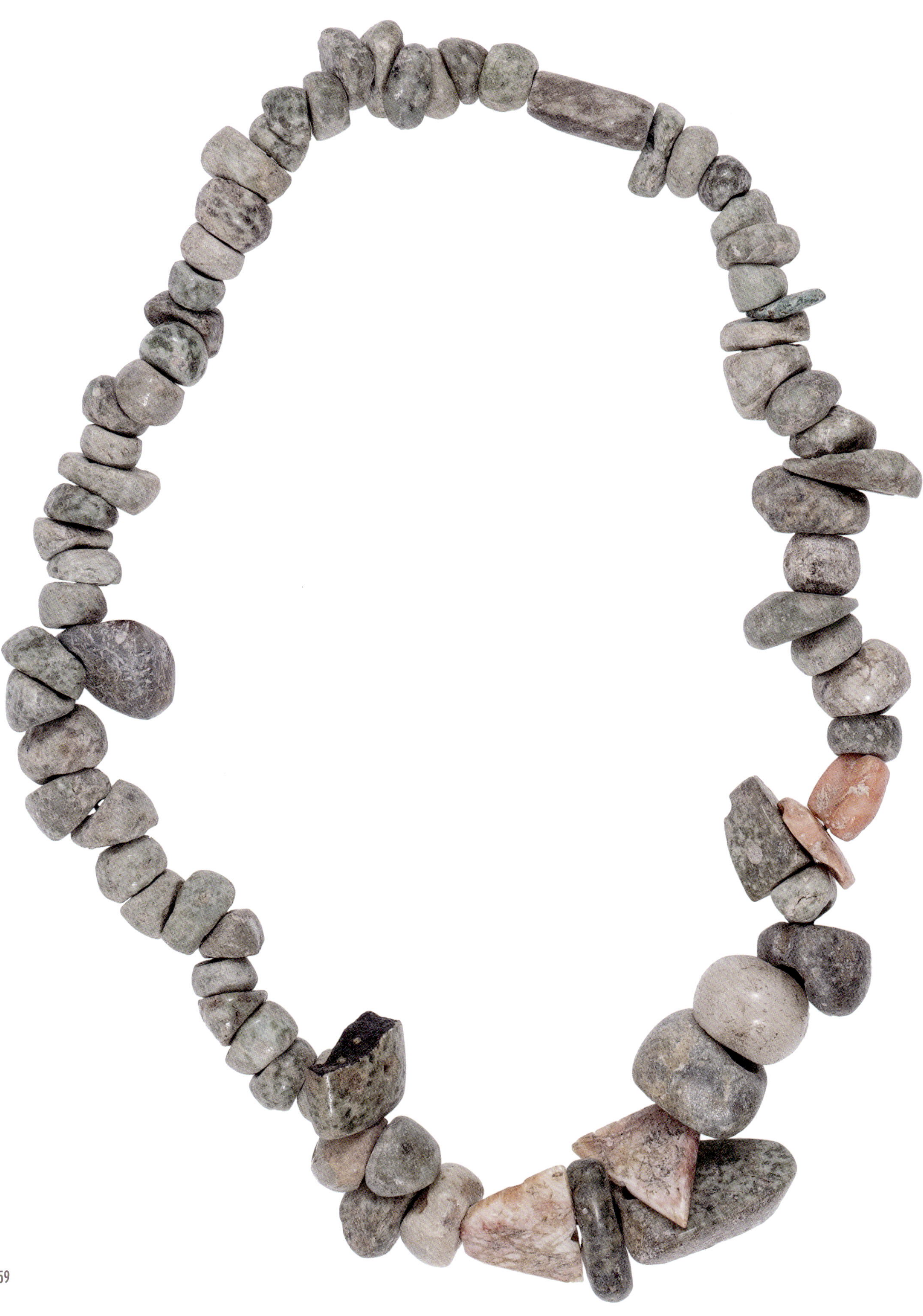

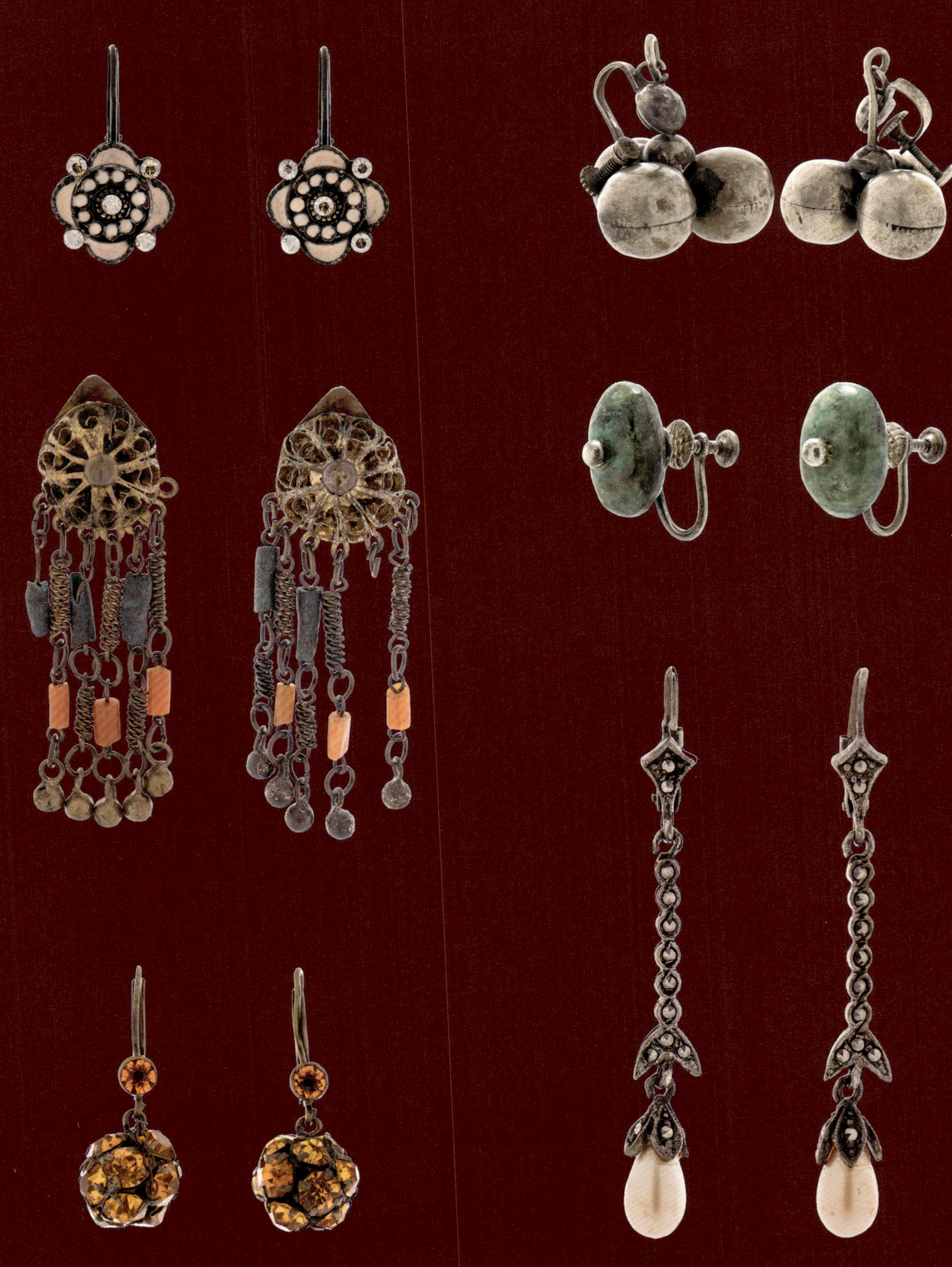

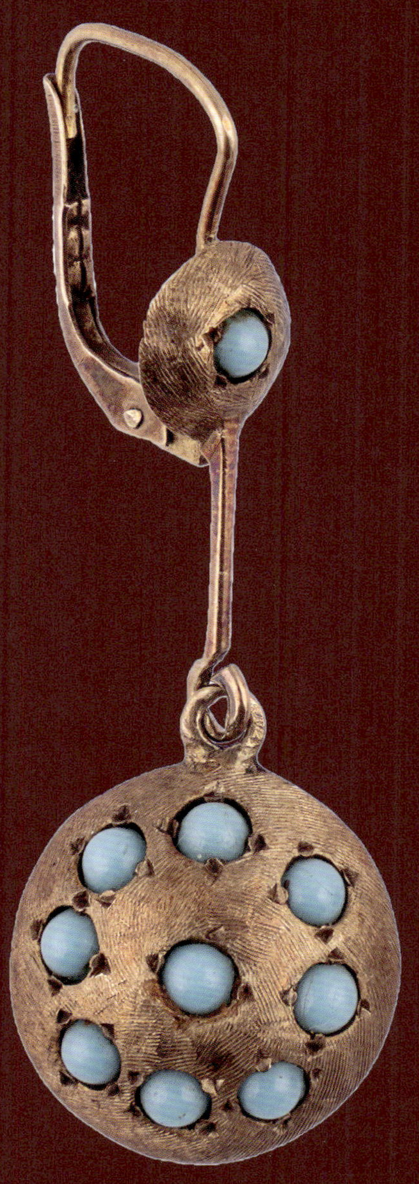

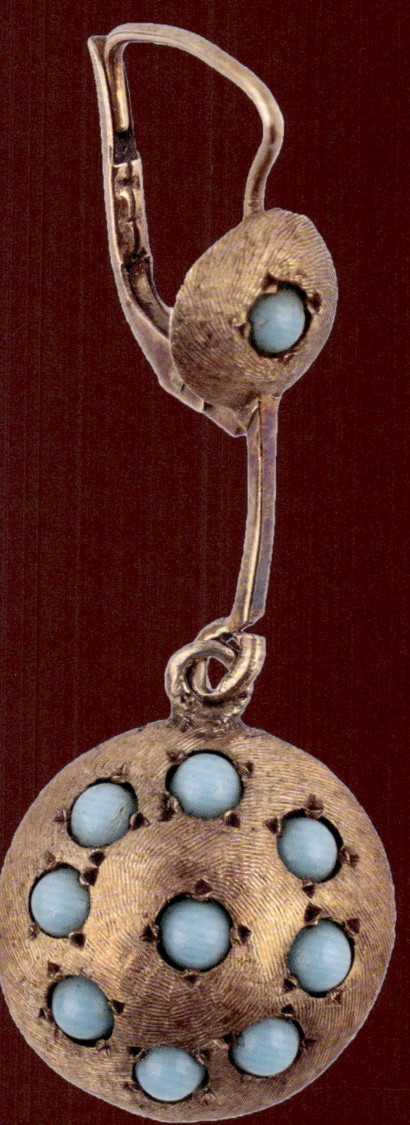

OPPOSITE AND ABOVE A selection of Frida's earrings, set with various metals, stones, and gems. Frida's distinctive jewelry and earrings completed her outfits, making her style a powerful form of self-expression.

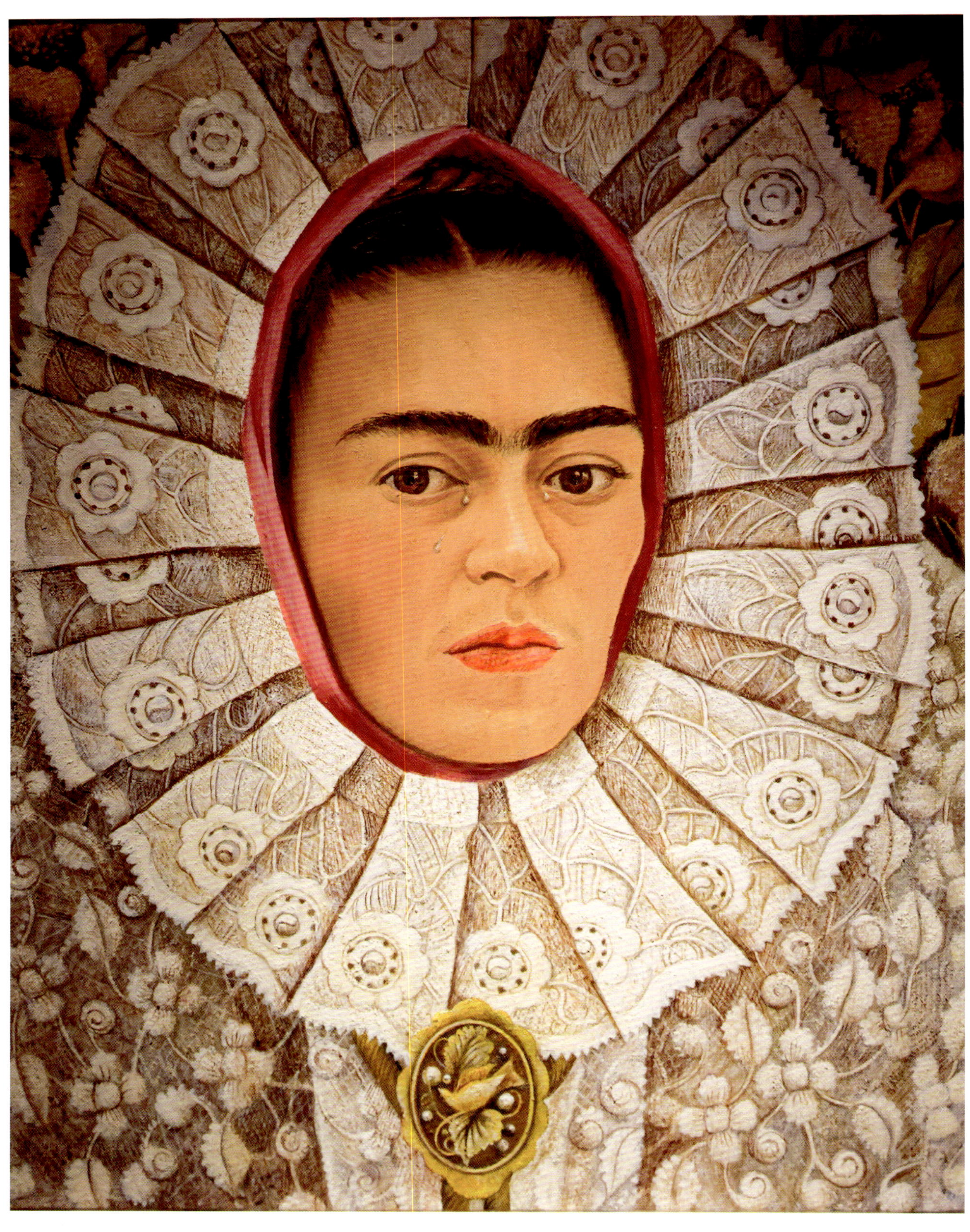

ABOVE *Frida Kahlo, Self-portrait with Medallion*, 1948. Oil on Masonite, 19.6 x 15.5 in. (50 x 39.5 cm)

OPPOSITE Frida wearing traditional Tehuana dress, ca. 1940. Photo by Bernard G. Silberstain

FOLLOWING SPREAD Oaxacan cotton *huipil* made from traditional manta (cotton fabric) and red brocade with diamond motifs rooted in ancient symbolism

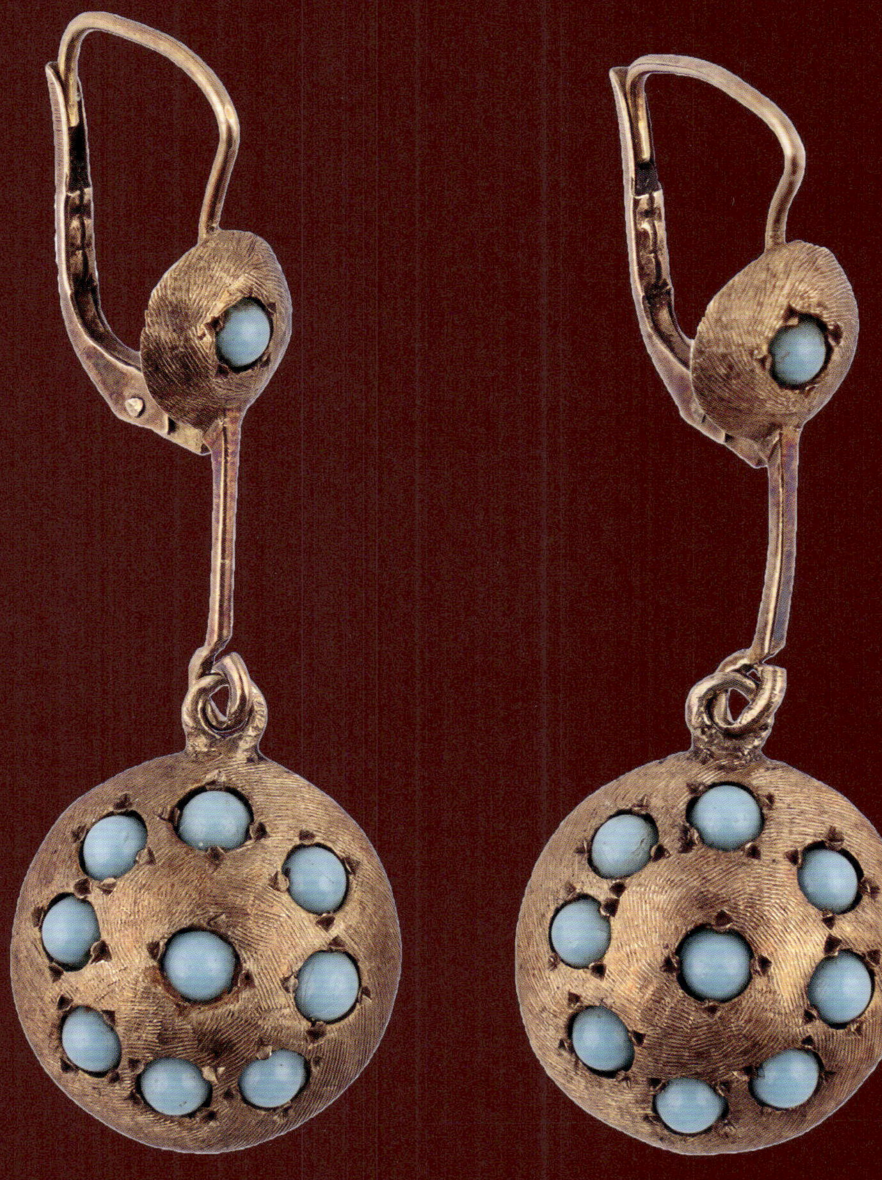

OPPOSITE AND ABOVE A selection of Frida's earrings, set with various metals, stones, and gems. Frida's distinctive jewelry and earrings completed her outfits, making her style a powerful form of self-expression.

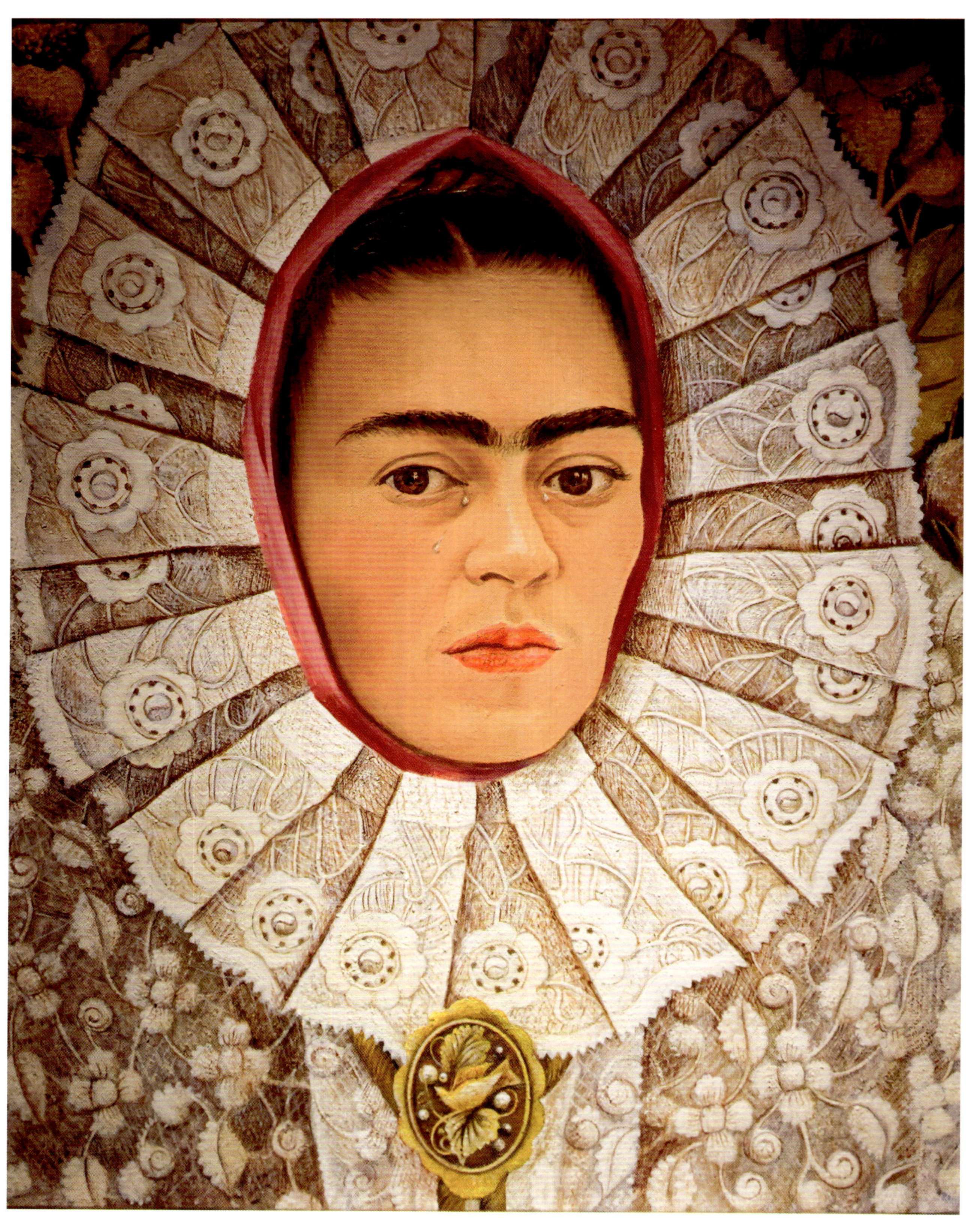

ABOVE *Frida Kahlo, Self-portrait with Medallion*, 1948. Oil on Masonite, 19.6 x 15.5 in. (50 x 39.5 cm)

OPPOSITE Frida wearing traditional Tehuana dress, ca. 1940. Photo by Bernard G. Silberstain

FOLLOWING SPREAD Oaxacan cotton *huipil* made from traditional manta (cotton fabric) and red brocade with diamond motifs rooted in ancient symbolism

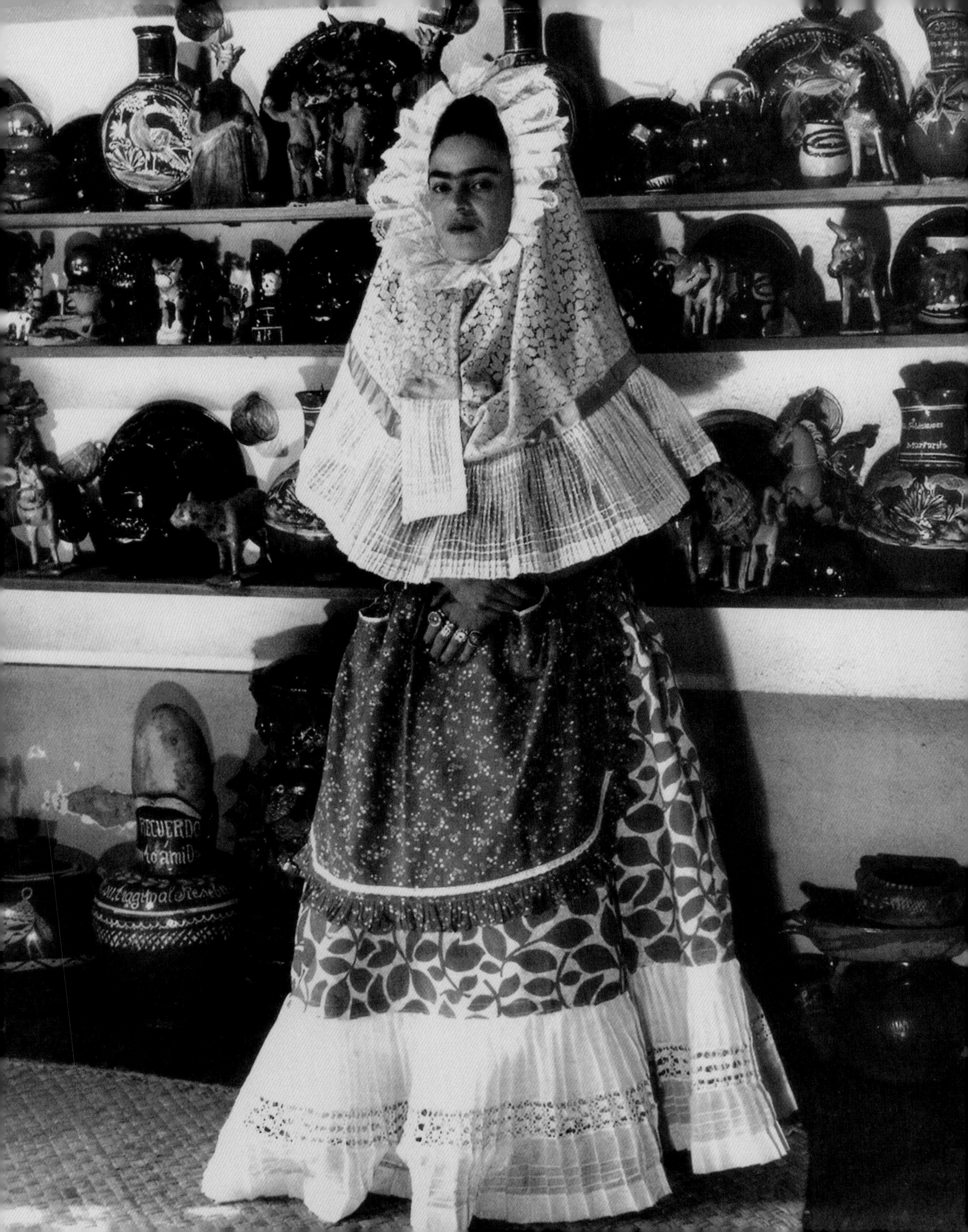
RECUERDO

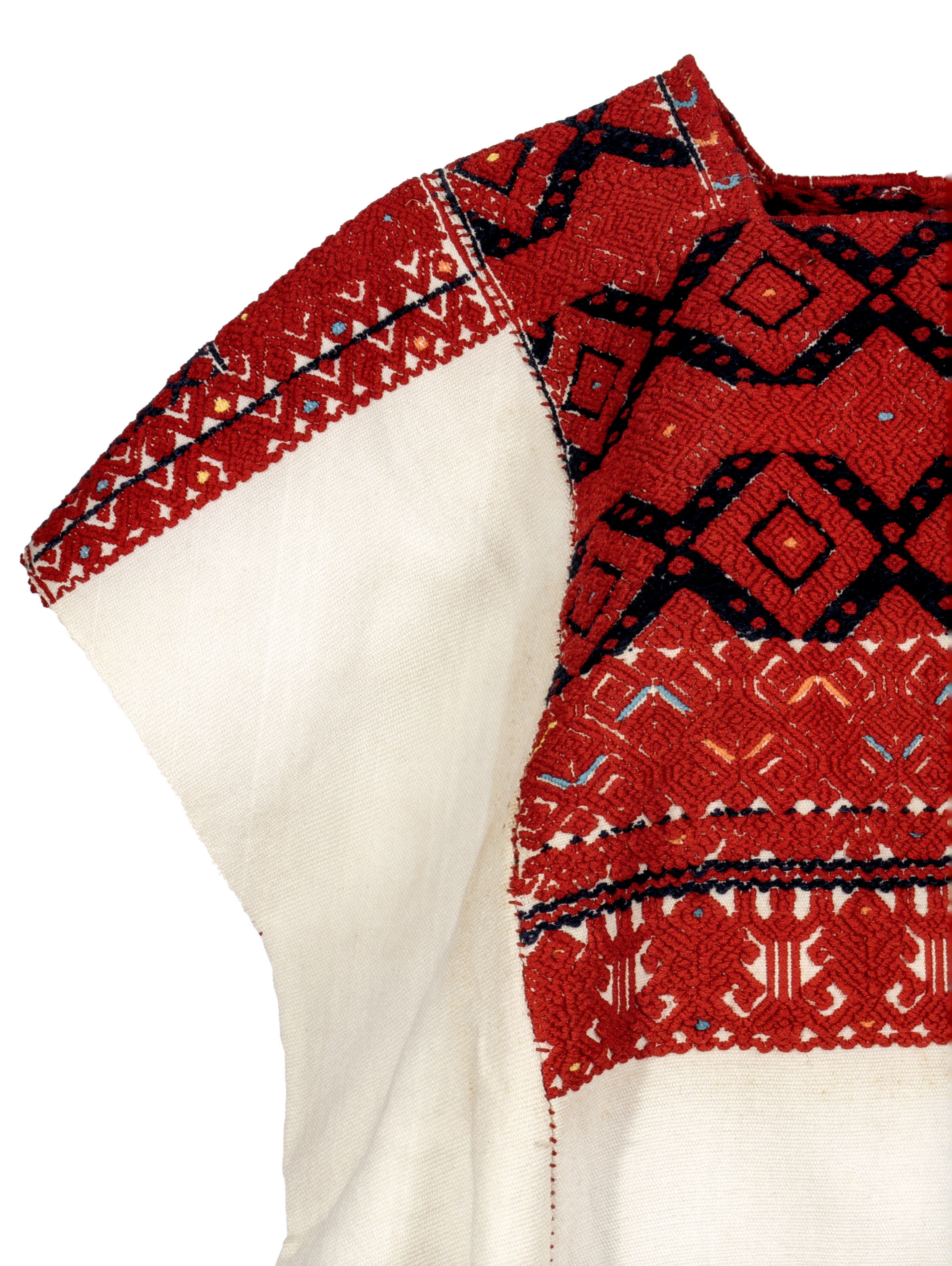

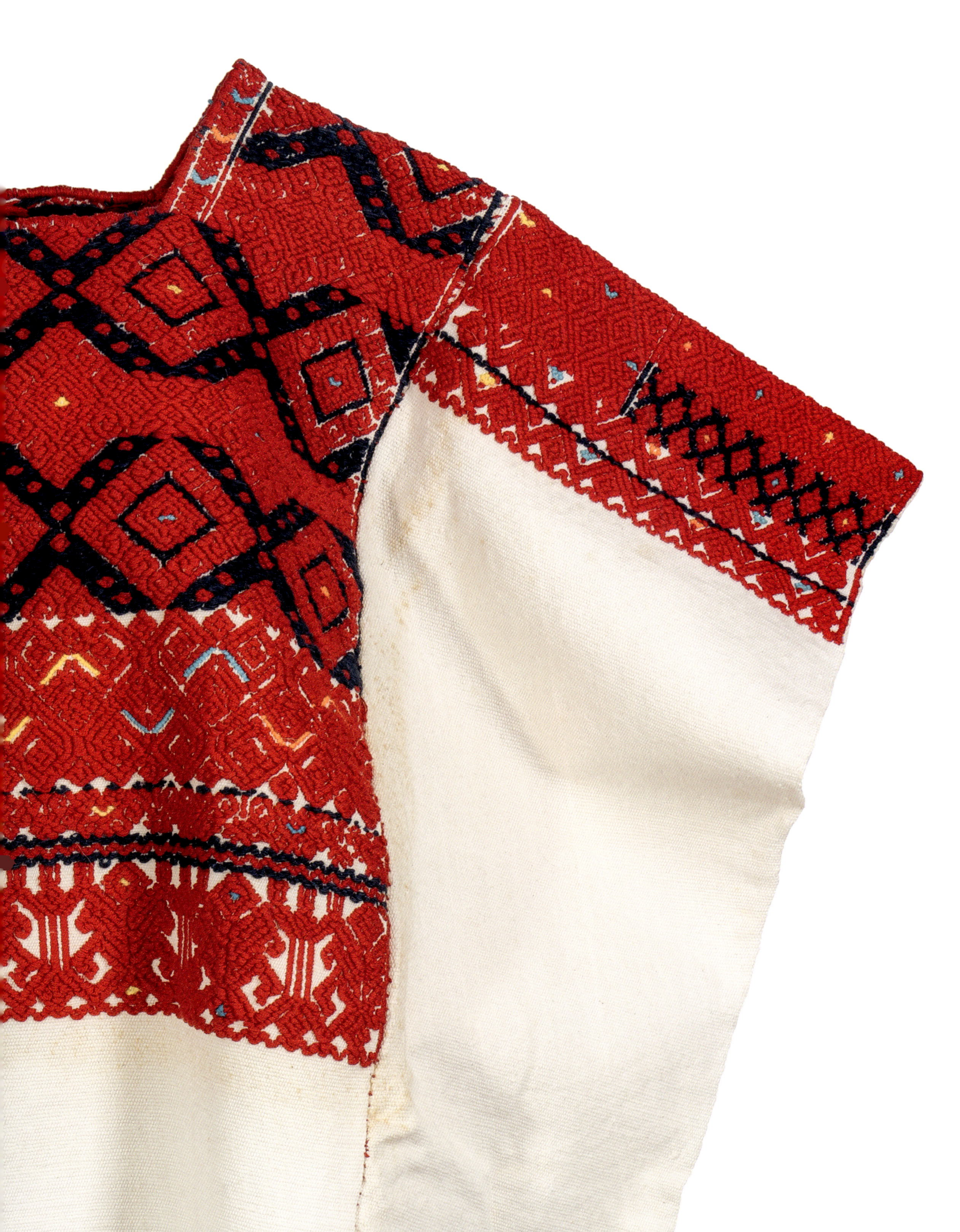

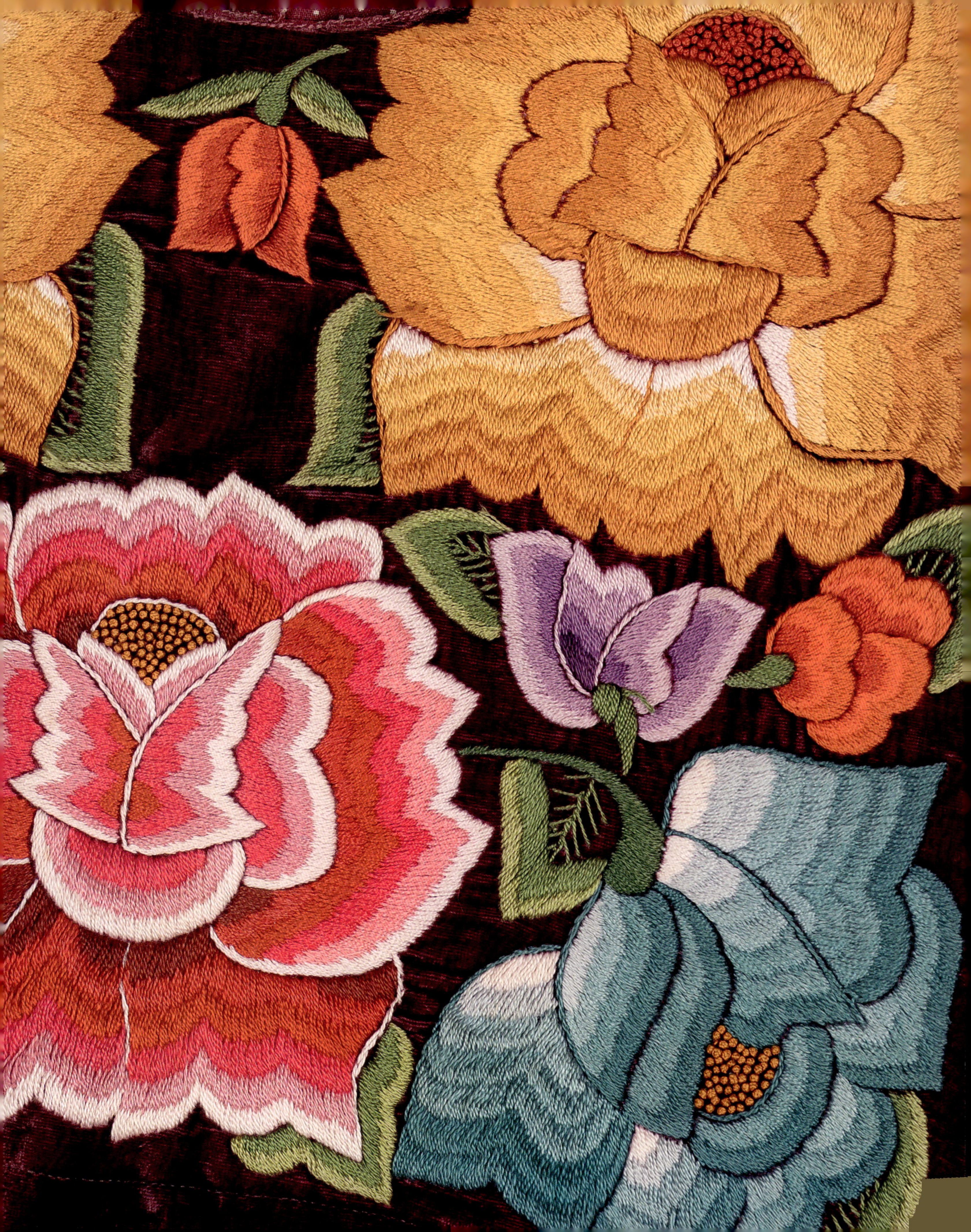

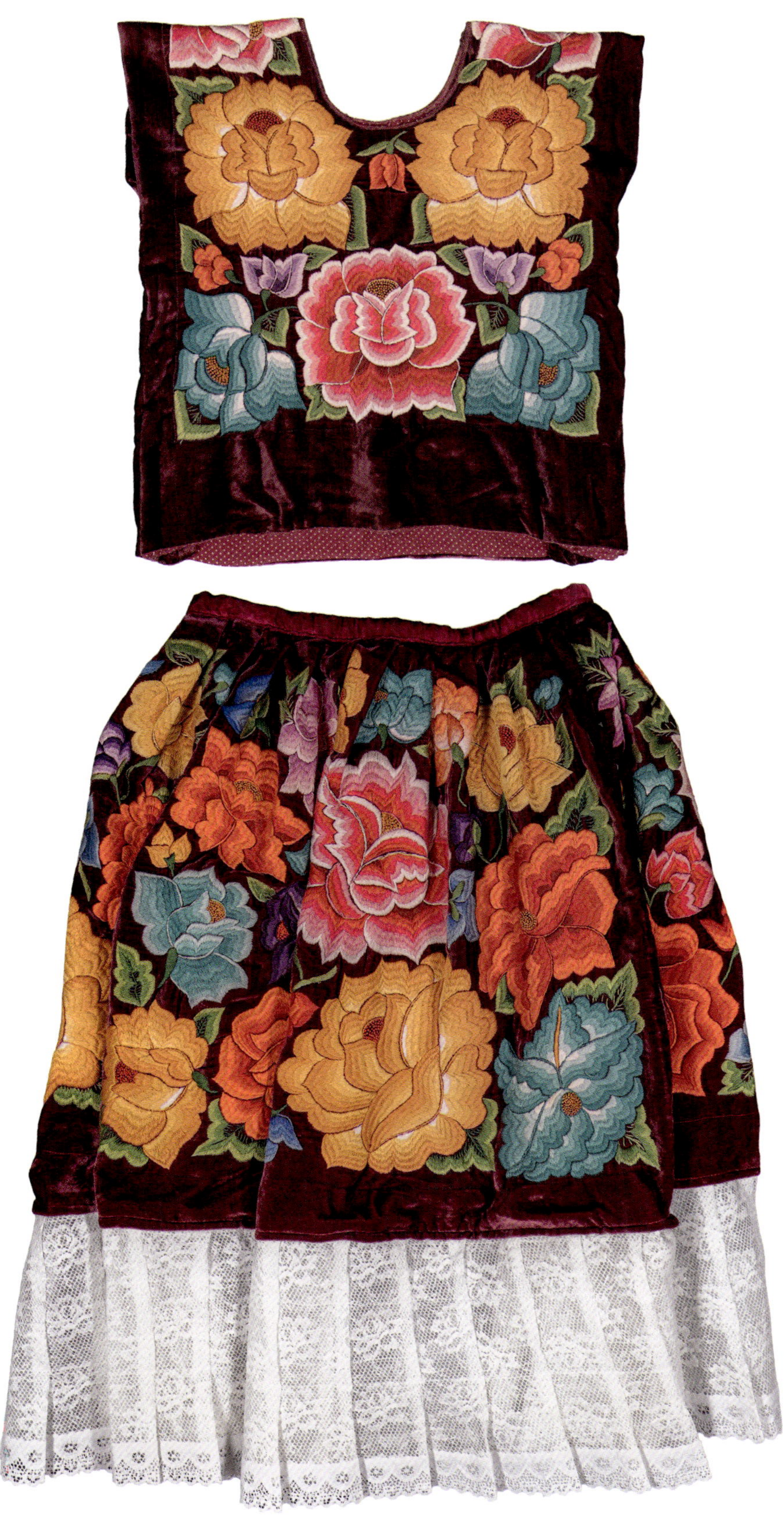

Frida admired the traditional dress of the women of the Isthmus of Tehuantepec, and she often paired garments from various regions of Mexico in her daily outfits.

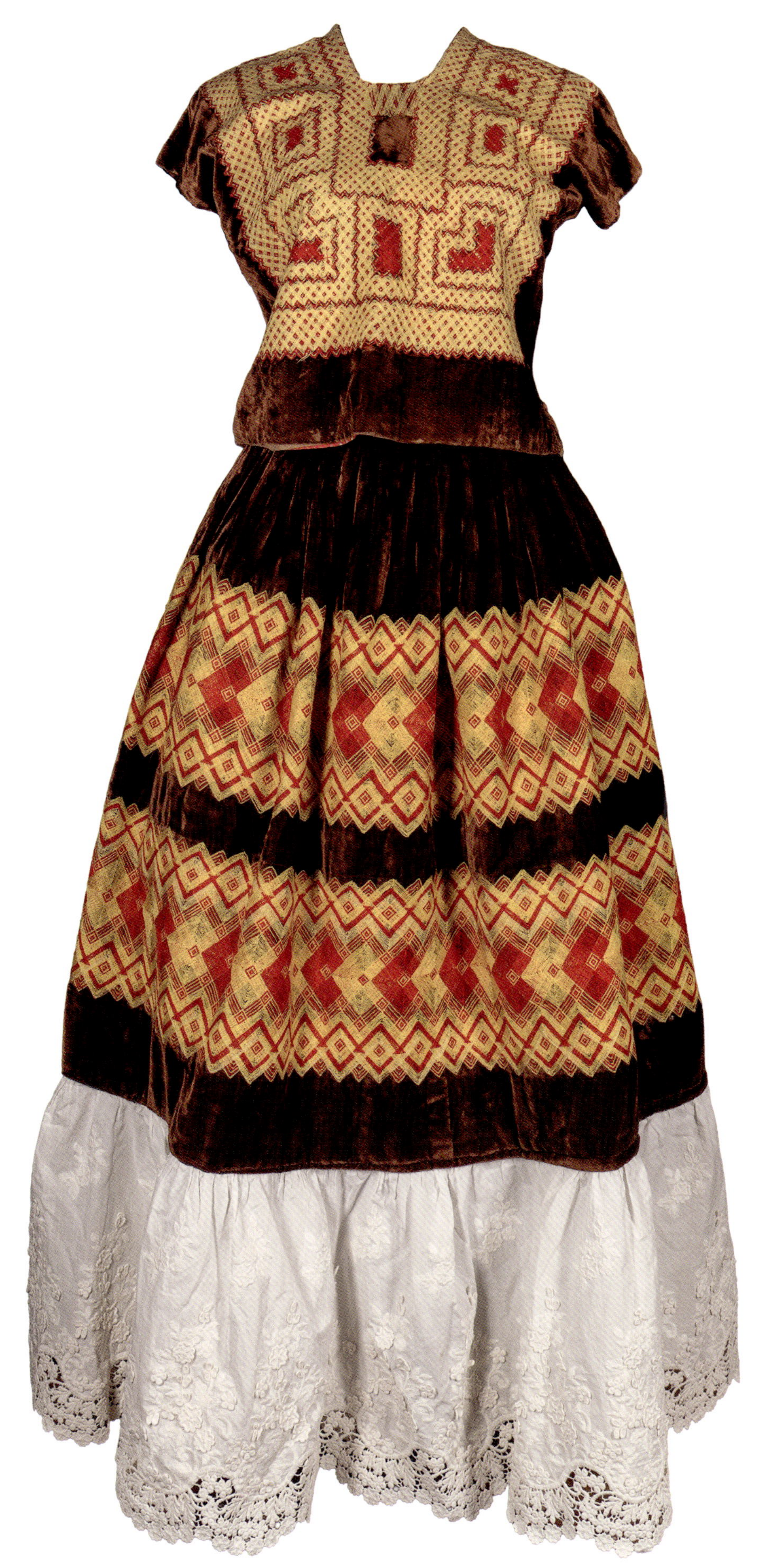

A traditional, richly embroidered blouse and skirt from Mexico and Central America, distinguished by its decorative "chain stitch" embroidery known as *cadenilla*.

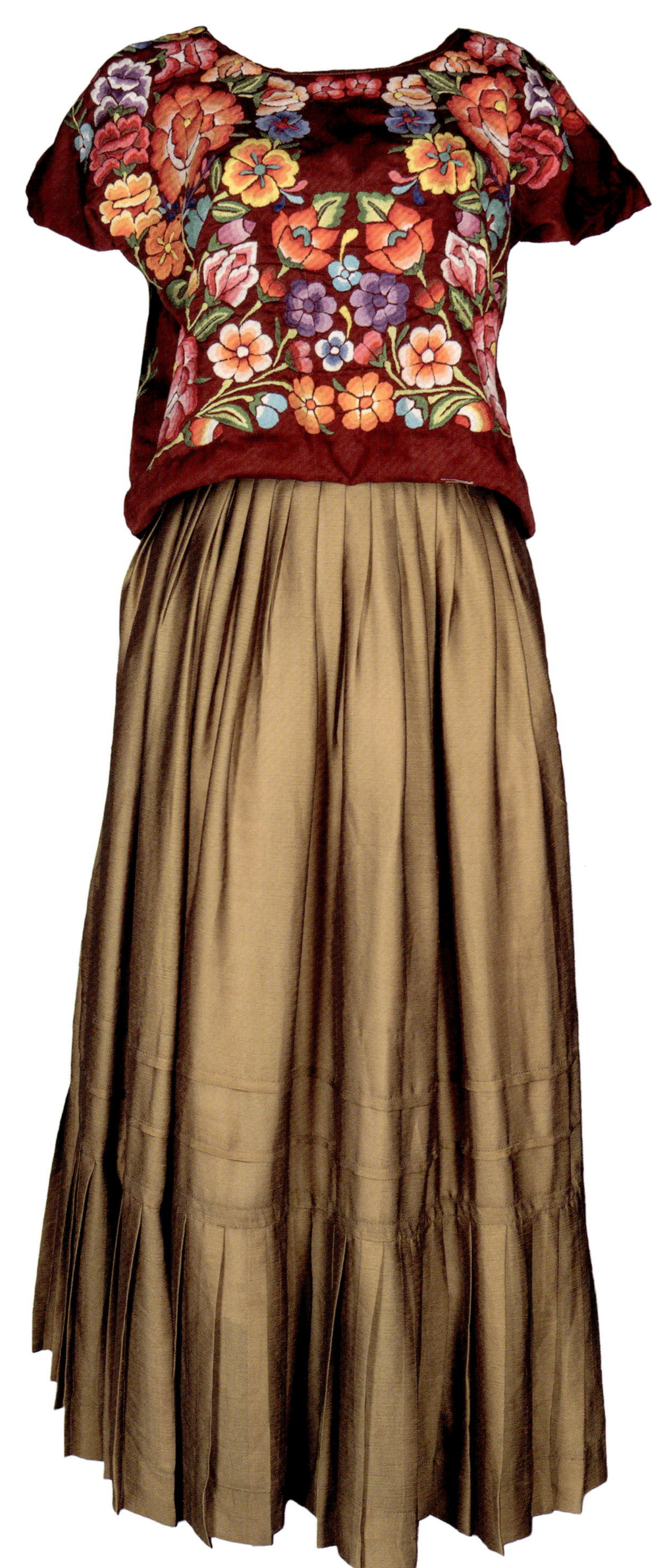

A *huipil* and golden skirt. This *huipil* is from Juchitan, Oaxaca, made of a very soft cotton fabric known as "angel skin." The embroidery called *plumeado*, gets its name from its feather-like texture.

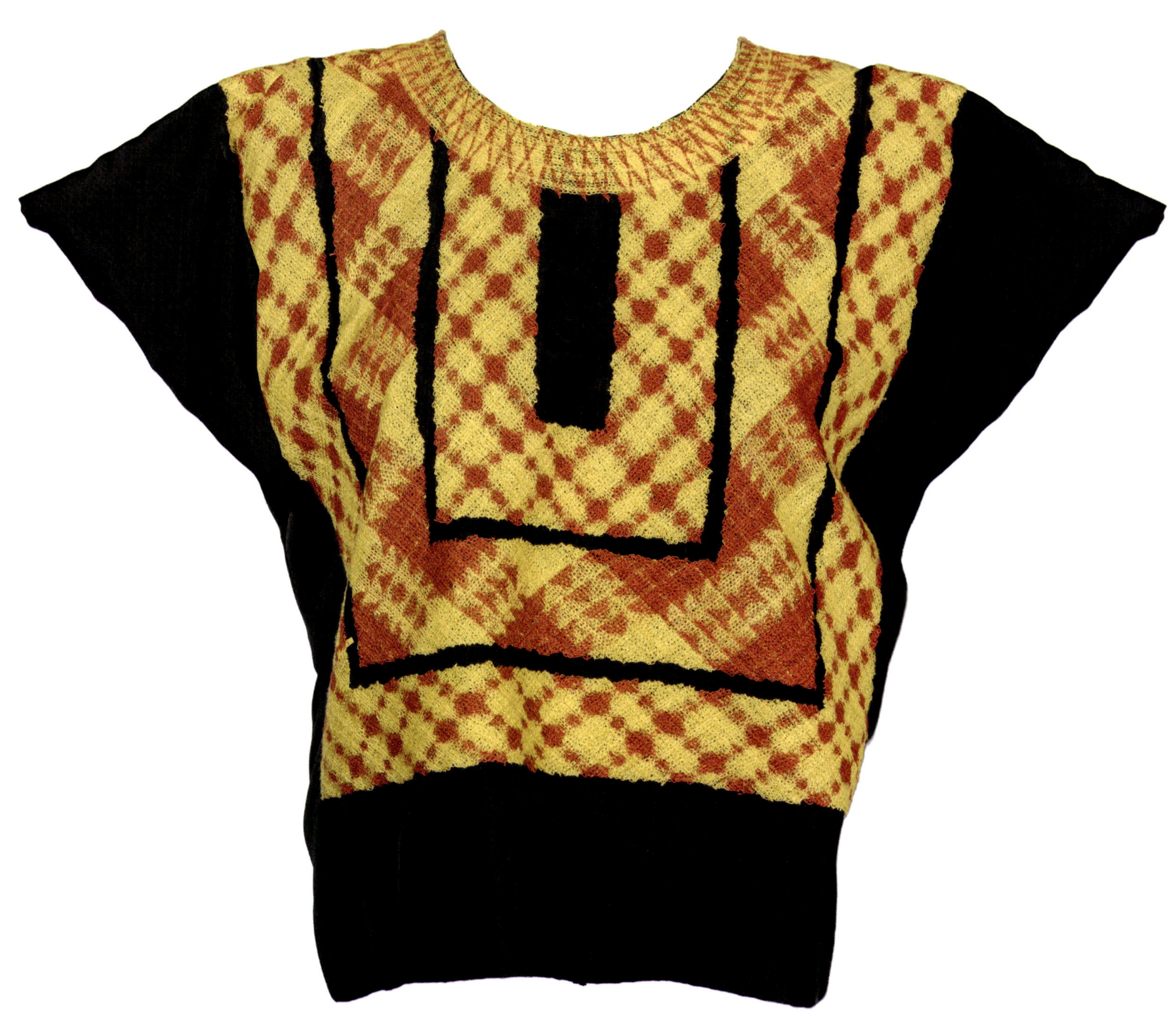

ABOVE AND OPPOSITE Two of Frida's shirts with traditional *cadenilla* stitch. *Huipiles* came in everyday styles and for special celebrations. The one opposite is made of green velvet, a fabric used for special occasions.

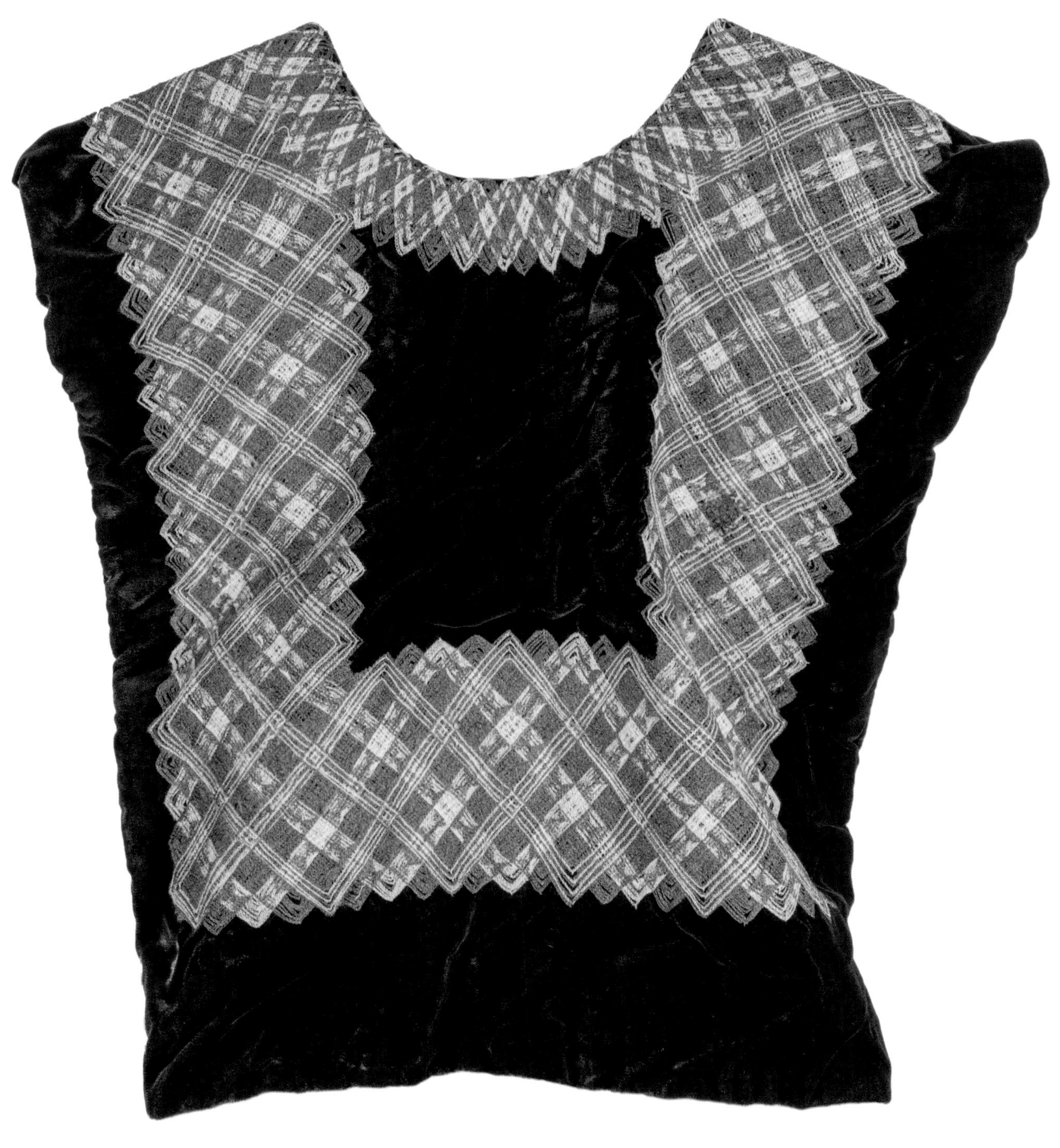

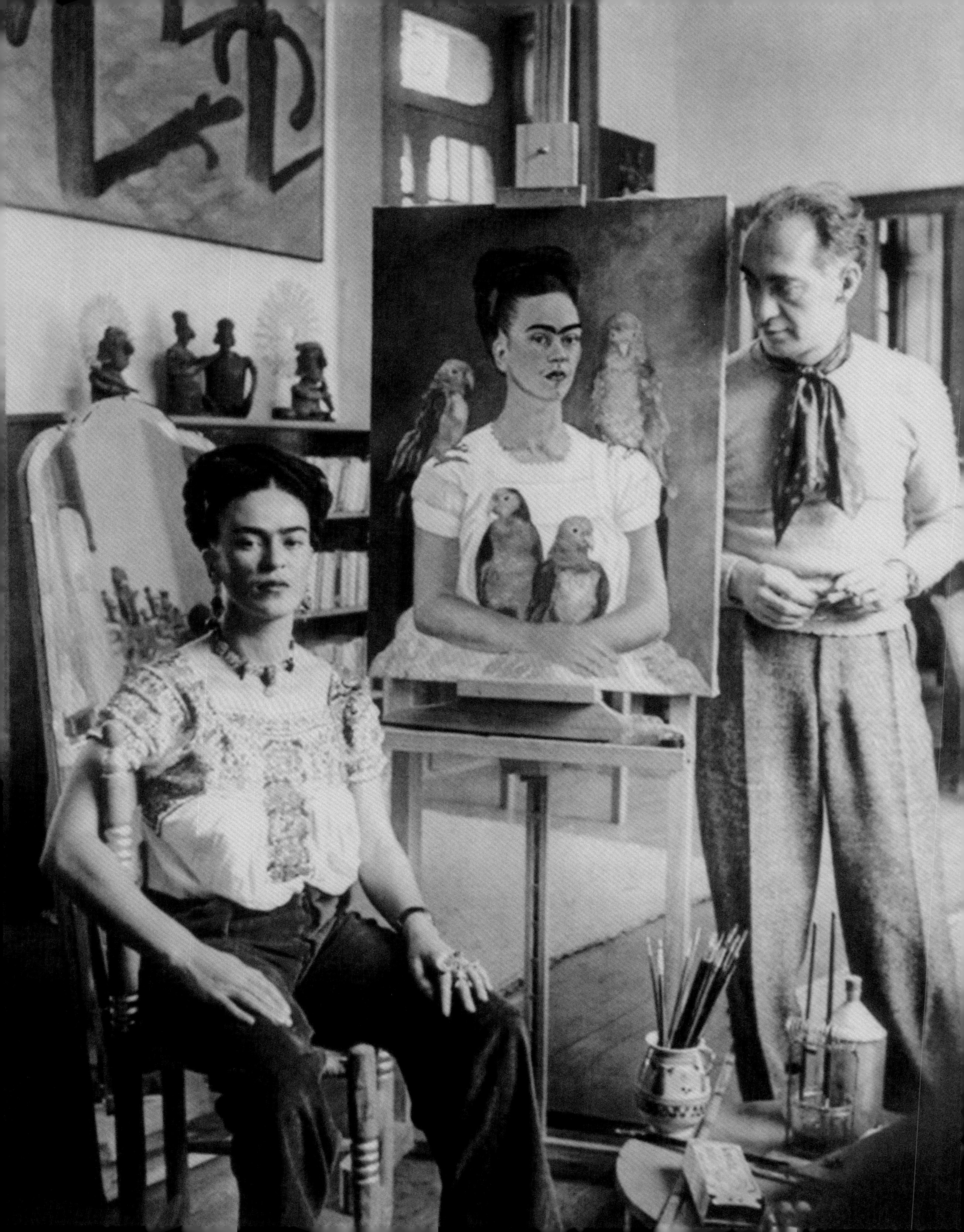

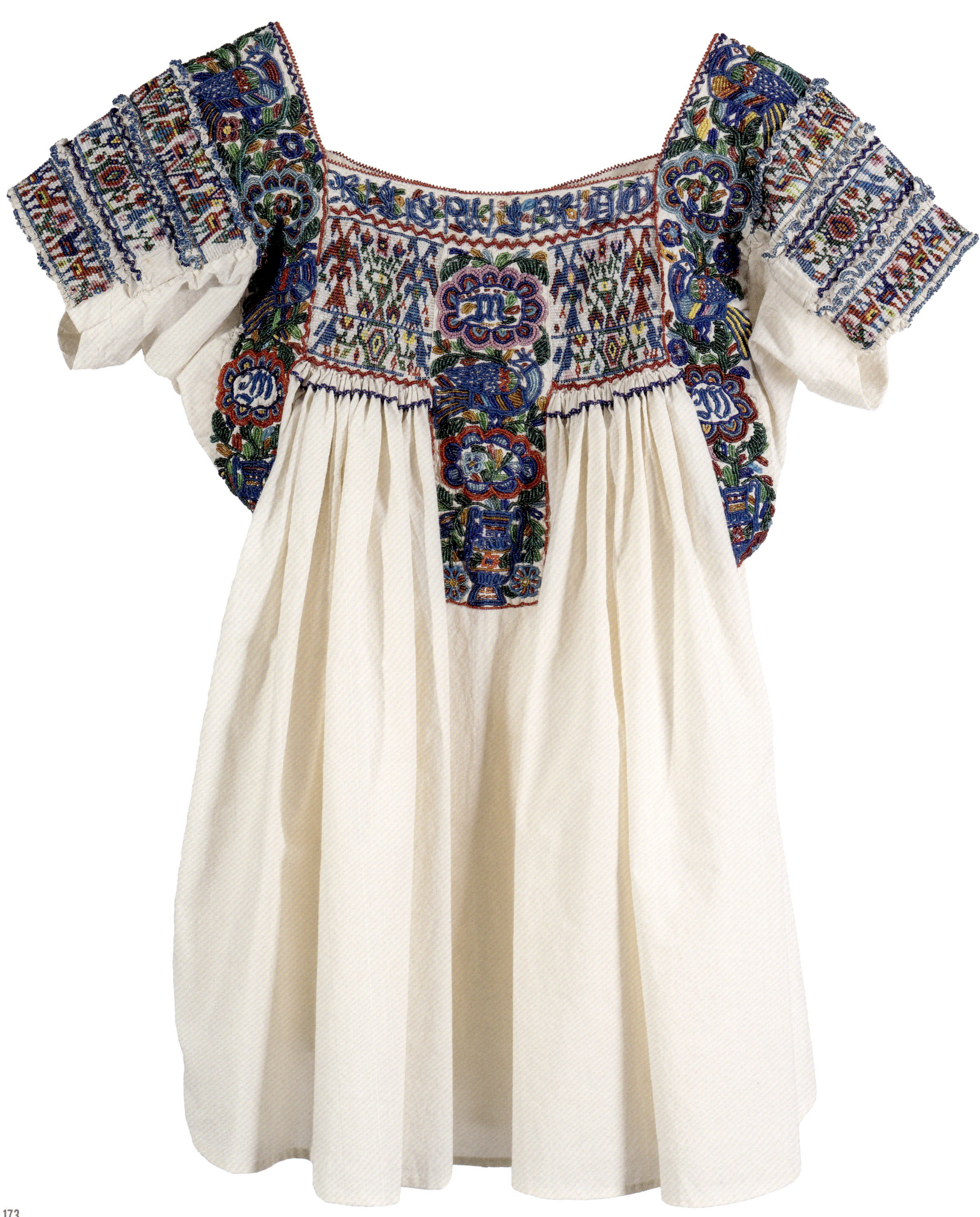

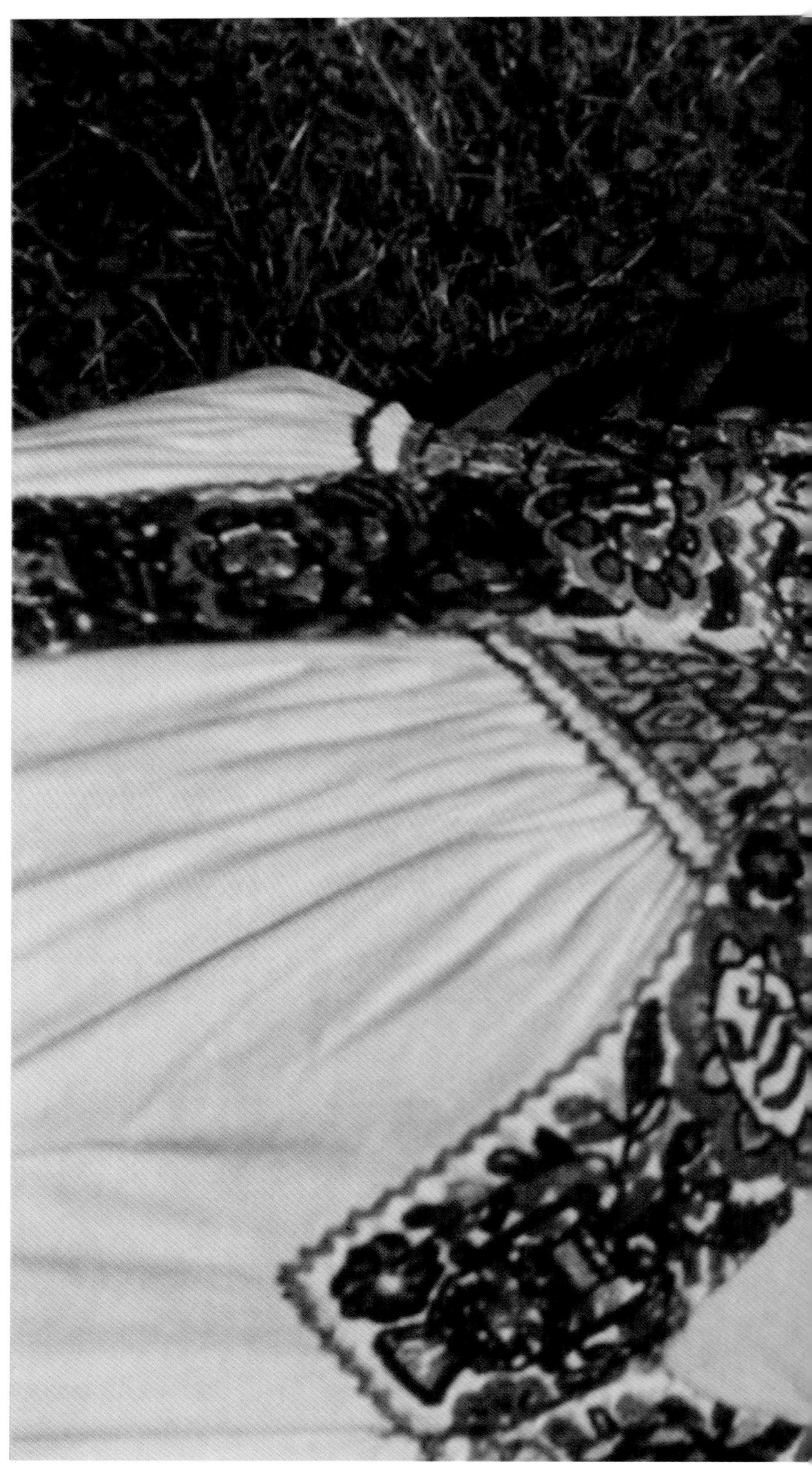

PREVIOUS SPREAD, LEFT Frida in her studio with Nickolas Muray in front of her painting *Me and My Parrots*, wearing the cotton shirt pictured opposite, ca. 1941. Photo by Nickolas Muray

PREVIOUS SPREAD, RIGHT Frida's cotton shirt, delicately embroidered with colorful *chaquiras* (glass beads). It showcases the great skill of the Nahua community of San Gabriel Chilac in Puebla.

RIGHT Frida lying in the garden wearing the embroidered cotton shirt pictured in previous pages, ca. 1943. Photo by Leo Matiz

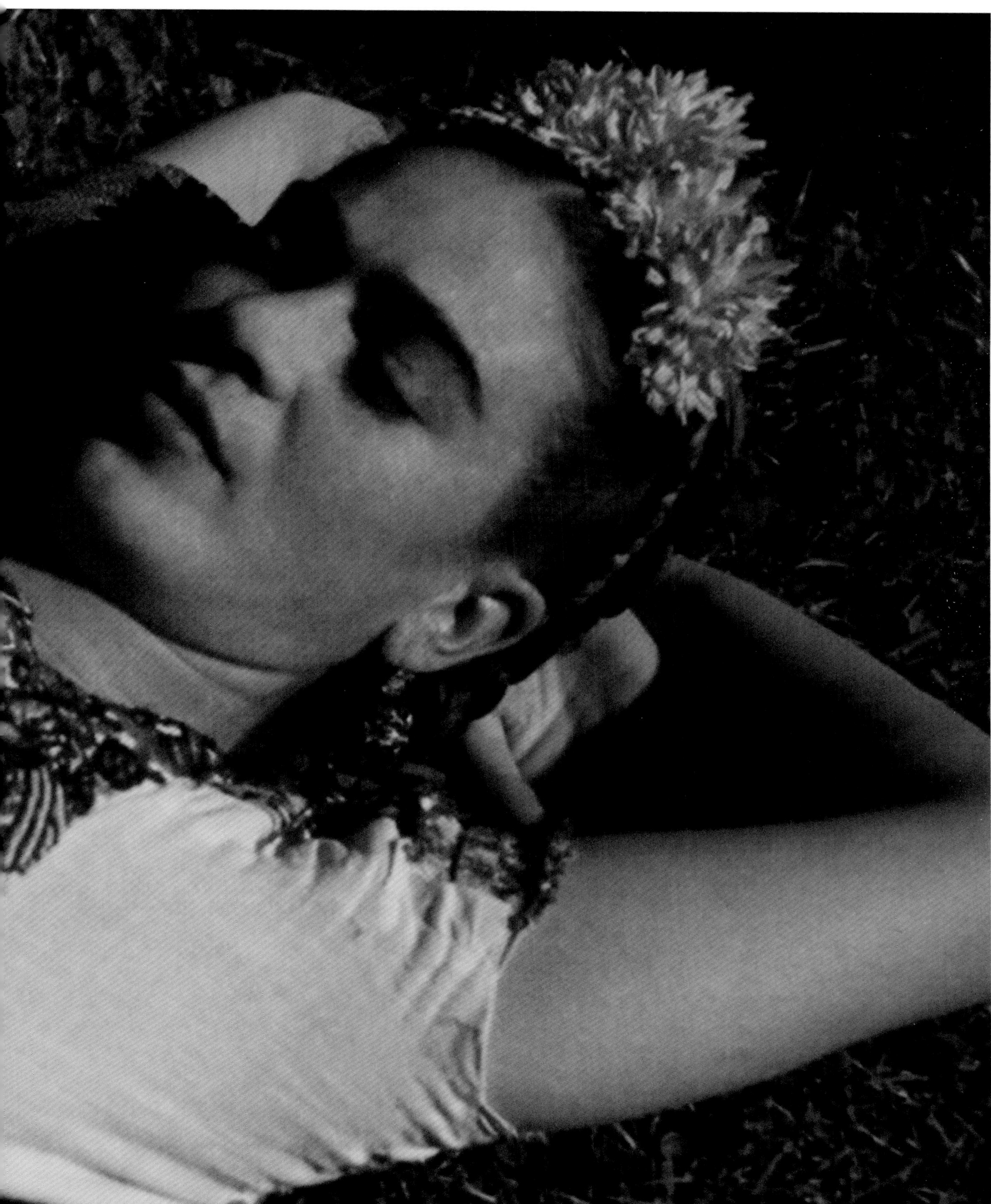

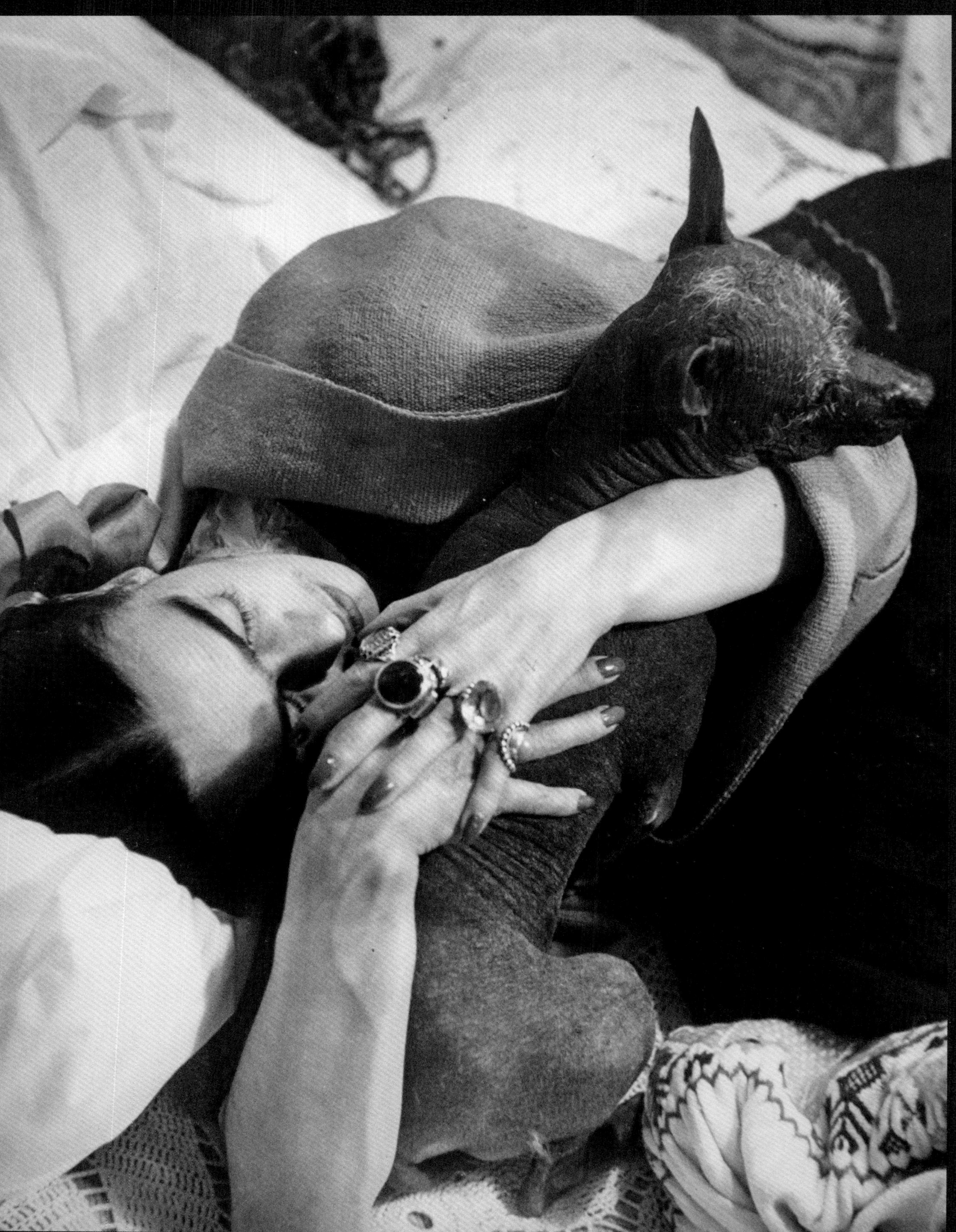

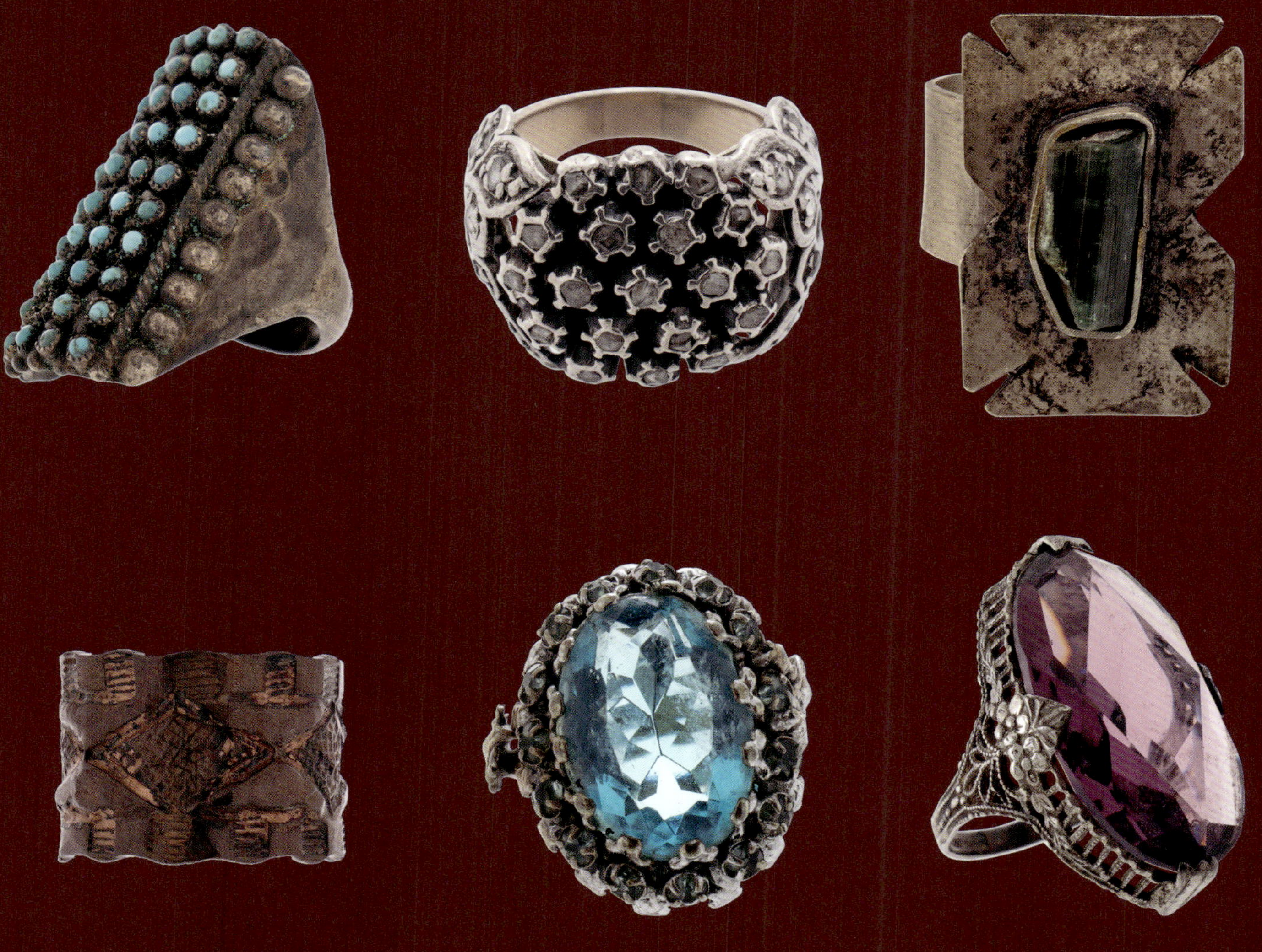

OPPOSITE Frida, ca. 1945. Photo by Sylvia Salmi

ABOVE A selection of Frida's rings. She owned many rings, and she believed the stones' "energy" helped her stay grounded.

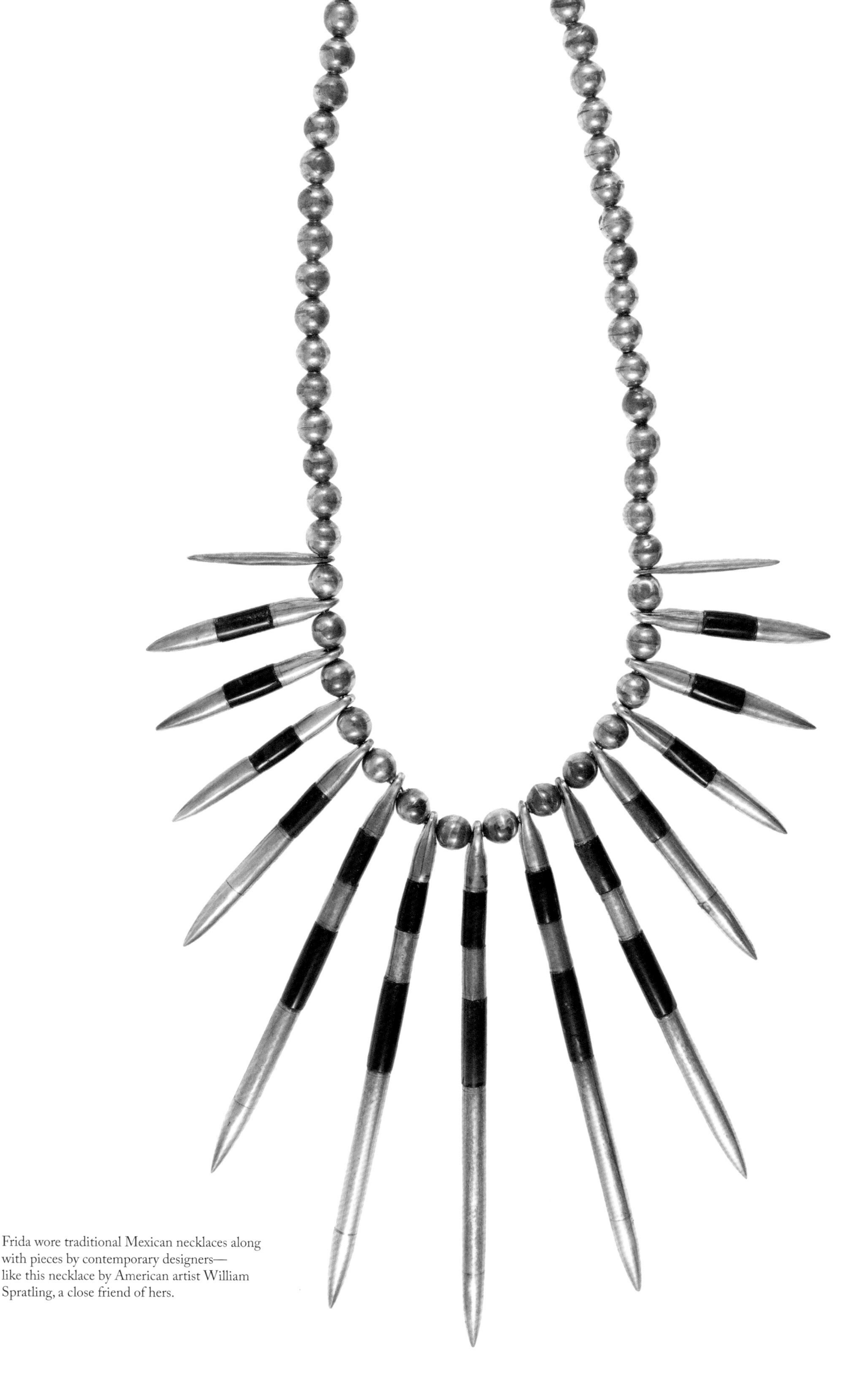

Frida wore traditional Mexican necklaces along with pieces by contemporary designers—like this necklace by American artist William Spratling, a close friend of hers.

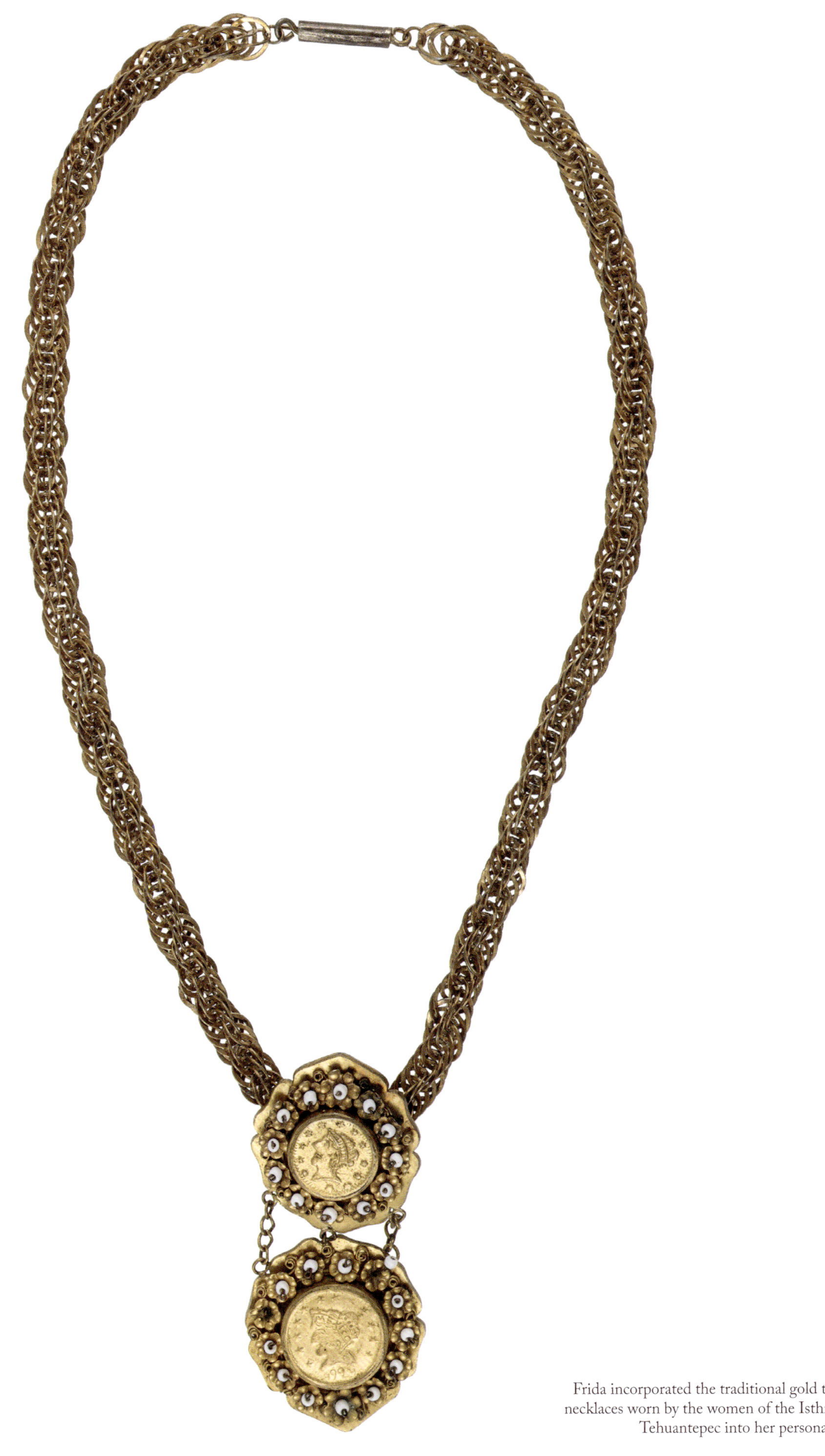

Frida incorporated the traditional gold torsade necklaces worn by the women of the Isthmus of Tehuantepec into her personal style.

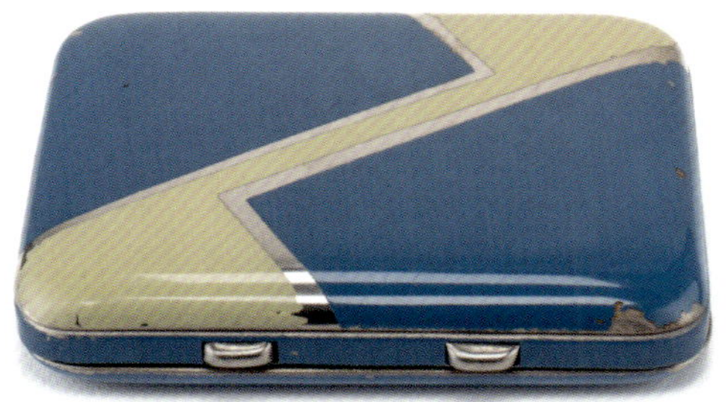

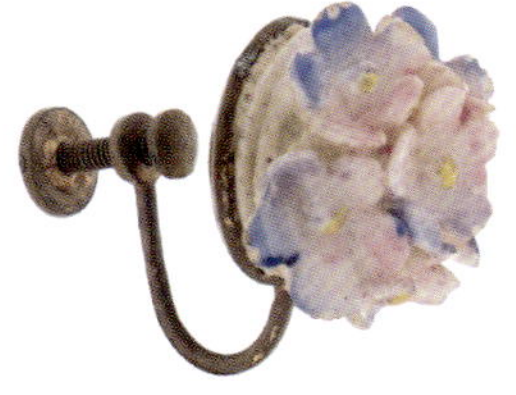

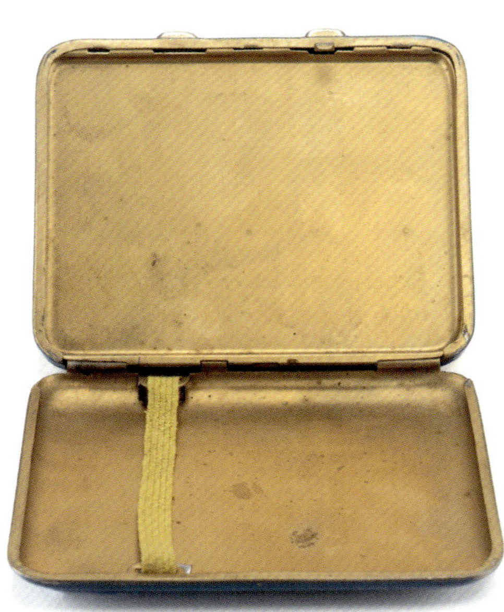

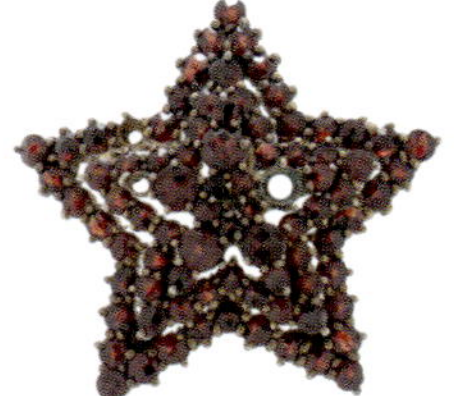

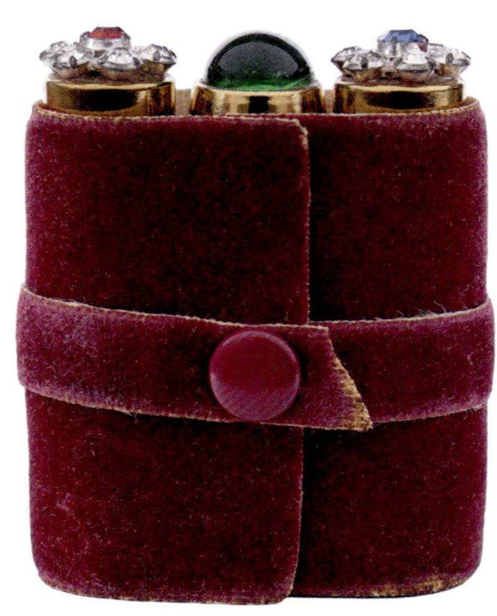

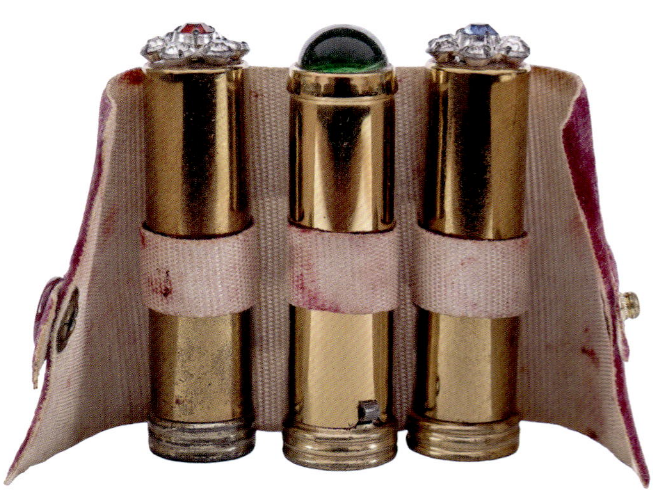

ABOVE A collection of Frida's personal items, clockwise from left to right: an earring with floral decoration, her cigarette case, a star-shaped pendant, and a lipstick case (open and closed) adorned with faux gems.

OPPOSITE Frida with cigar, ca. 1932. Photo by Guillermo Kahlo

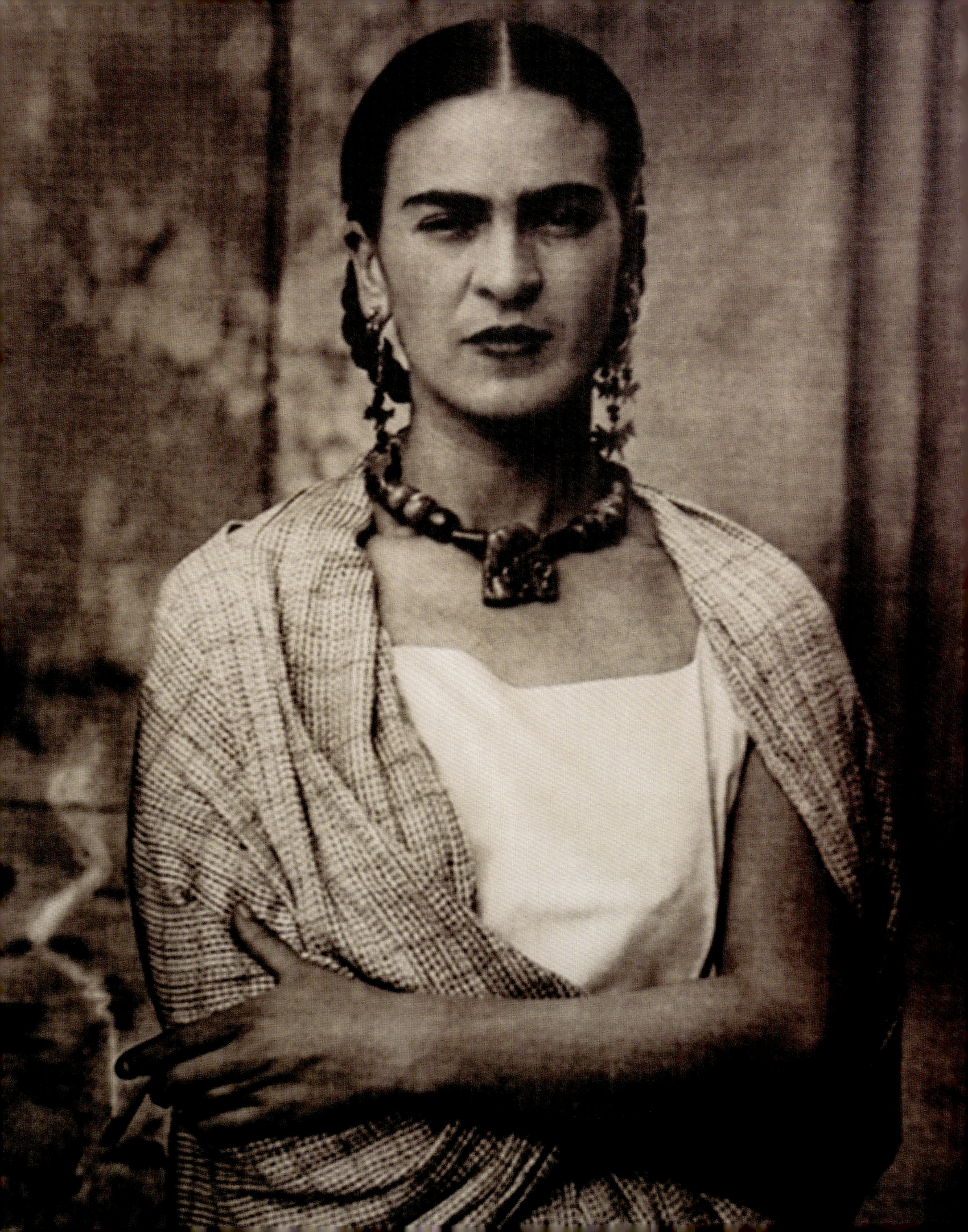

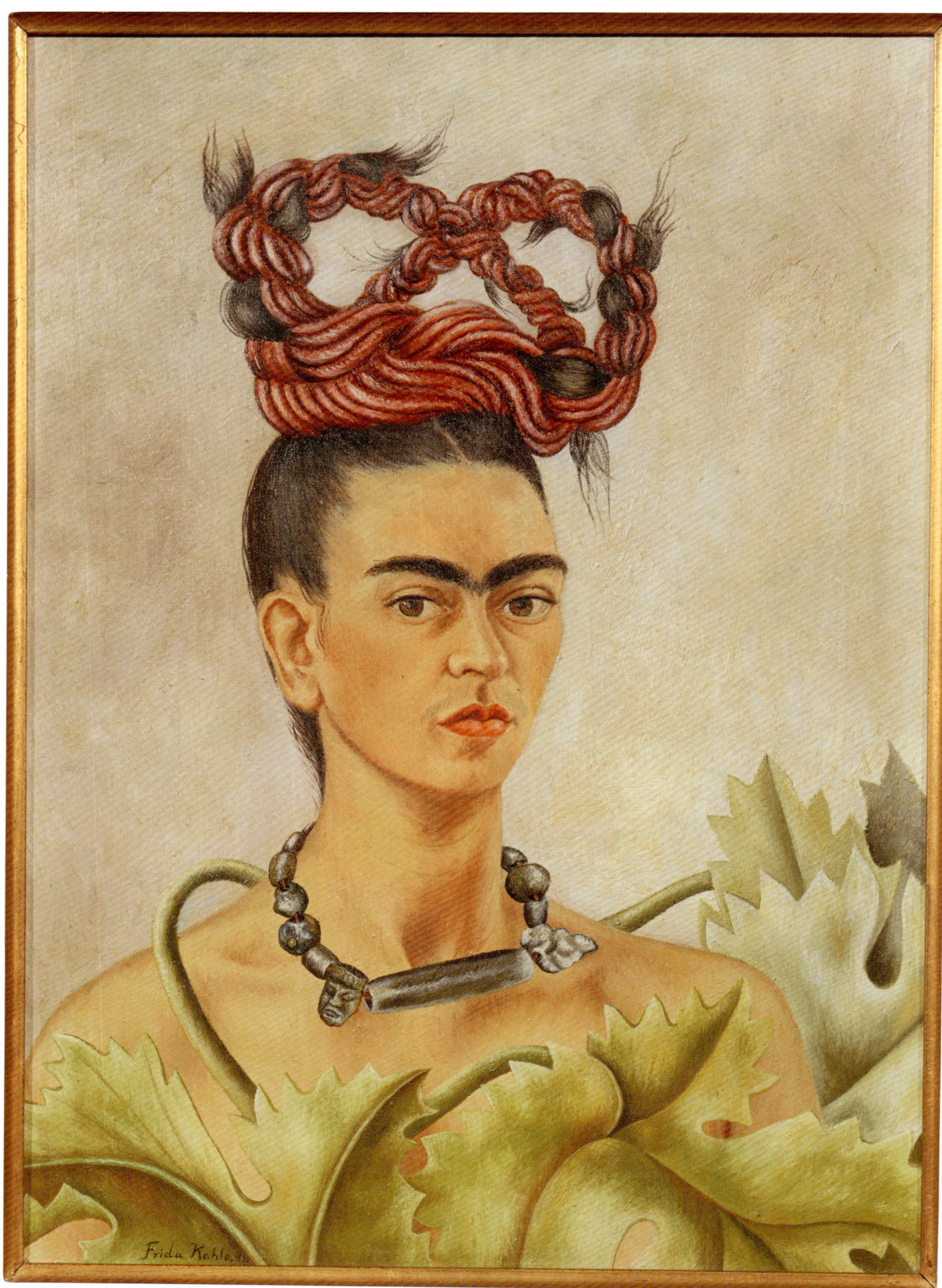
Frida Kahlo

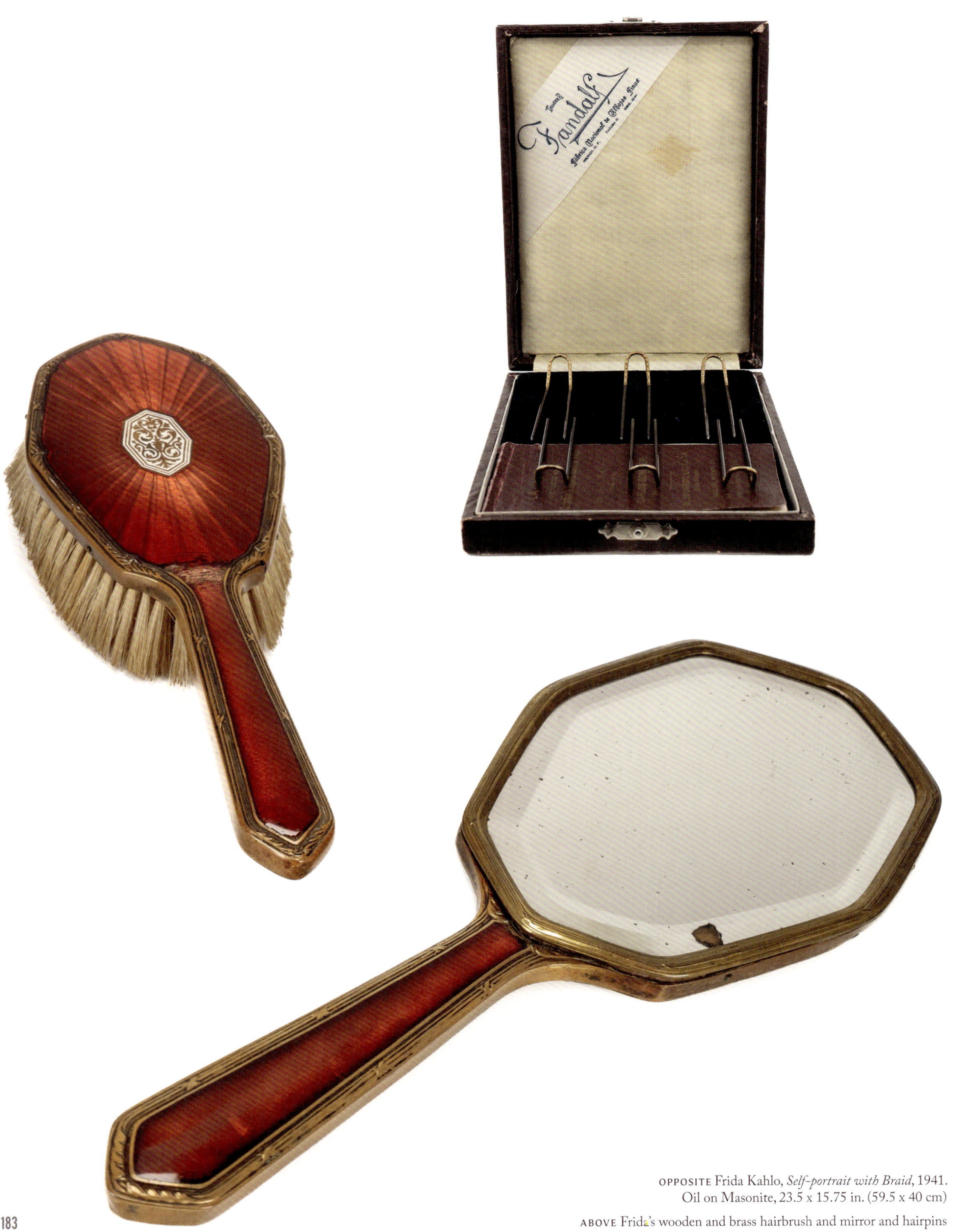

OPPOSITE Frida Kahlo, *Self-portrait with Braid*, 1941.
Oil on Masonite, 23.5 x 15.75 in. (59.5 x 40 cm)

ABOVE Frida's wooden and brass hairbrush and mirror and hairpins

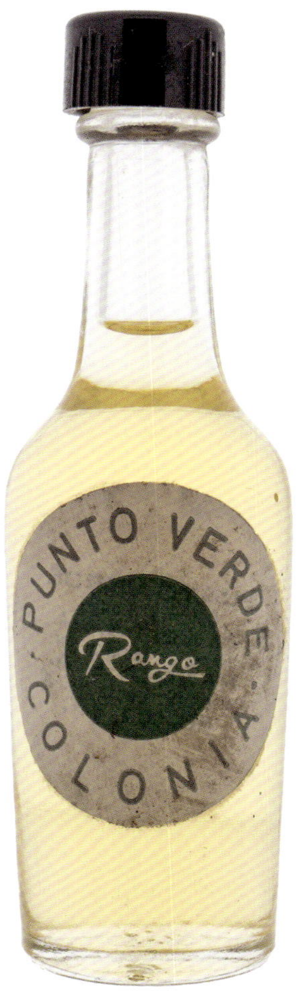
PUNTO VERDE
Rango
COLONIA

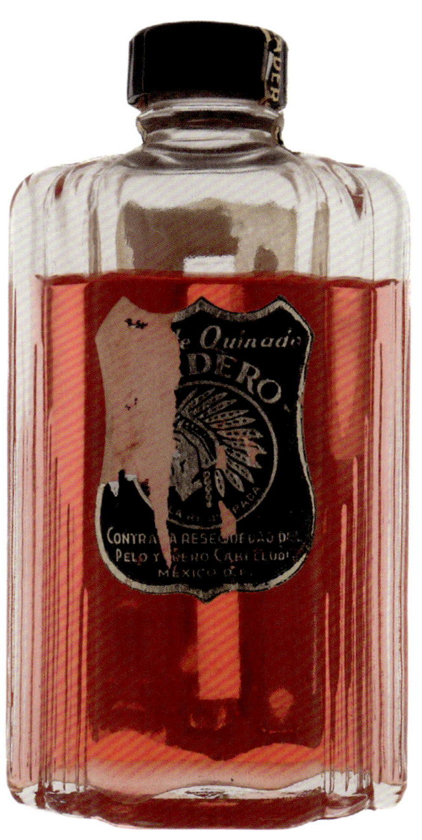

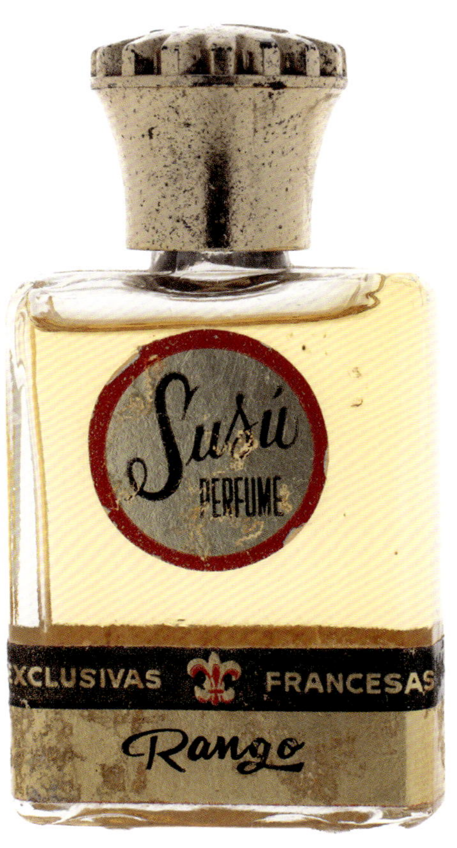
Susú
PERFUME
FRANCESAS
Rango

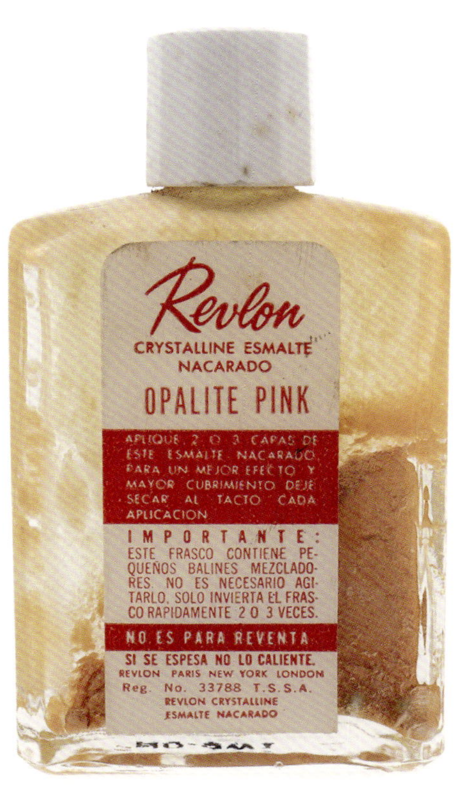

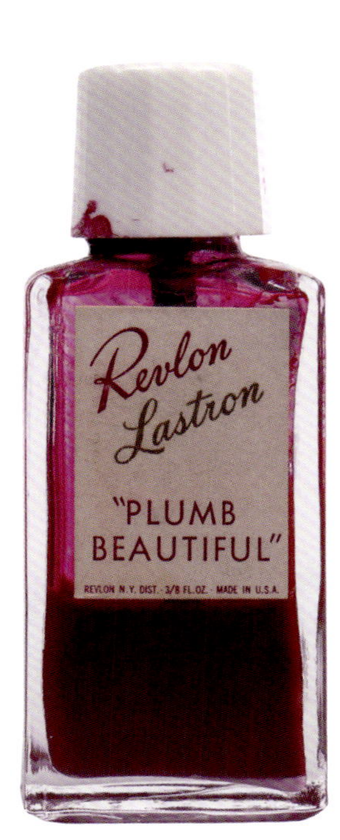

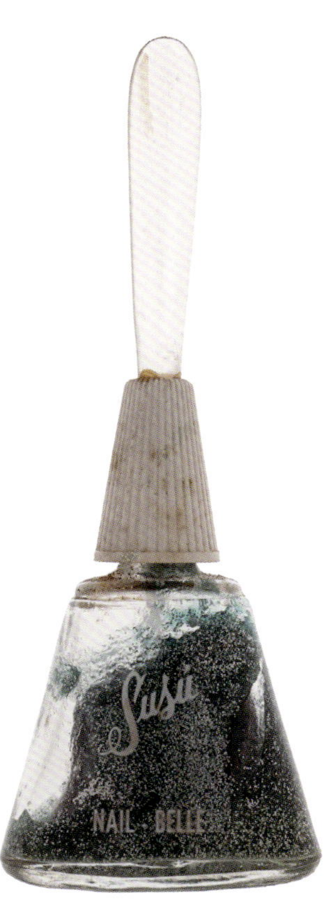

Frida's make-up and nail polish

Mara Romeo Kahlo Frida often visited different towns around Mexico, a practice she developed while traveling around the country with her father when she was younger. She frequented churches to see their ex-voto paintings. She was taken with their sincerity and the raw way they expressed gratitude—she recognized that they portrayed something profound through paint. Ex-votos are a devotional offering for divine intervention, like after a life-saving miracle has been performed, or even for something as mundane as getting rid of rodents. Frida had an extensive collection of ex-votos because of the special way they represented a heady mix miracles, hope, and art. Frida painted her own ex-voto when her mother was very sick, but she never took it to the church because her mother ultimately succumbed to her illness.

Frida Hentschel Frida loved the history of Los Altos de Chiapas—the Chiapas Highlands—and the Indigenous community of San Juan Chamula in southern Mexico. The church in San Juan Chamula was painted blue, and it inspired her to paint her own house blue. She believed that the *azul añil* (indigo blue) repelled bad spirits.

The history of San Juan Chamula in Chiapas is fascinating because it is one of the few regions in the country that has kept its own form of Indigenous authority after the Spanish conquest. There was syncretism between Catholicism and Mayan religion and practices here. The local communities fought to keep their traditional way of life and were fiercely independent. The ways in which the people there expressed their beliefs, religious and otherwise, was deeply compelling to Frida.

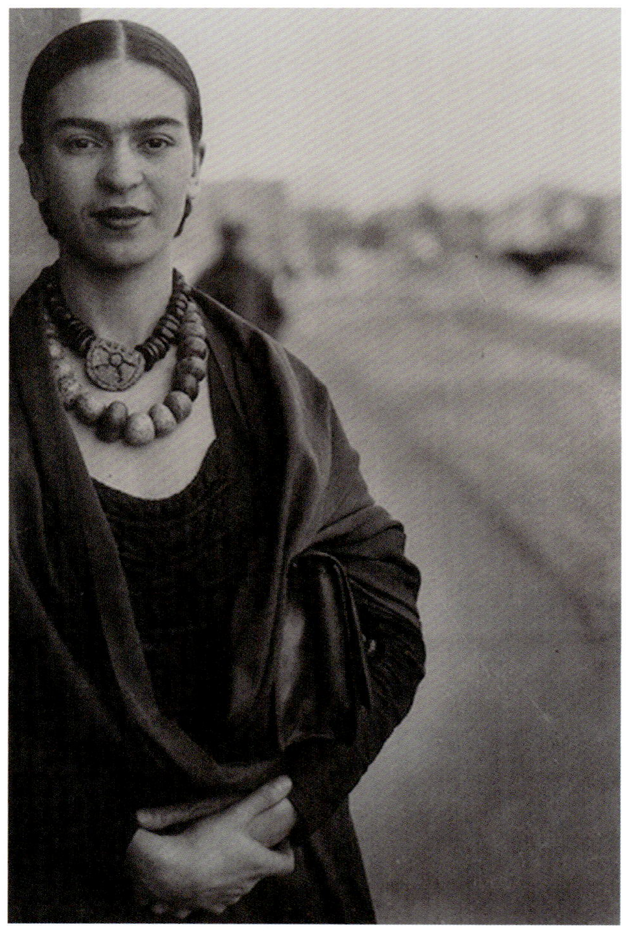

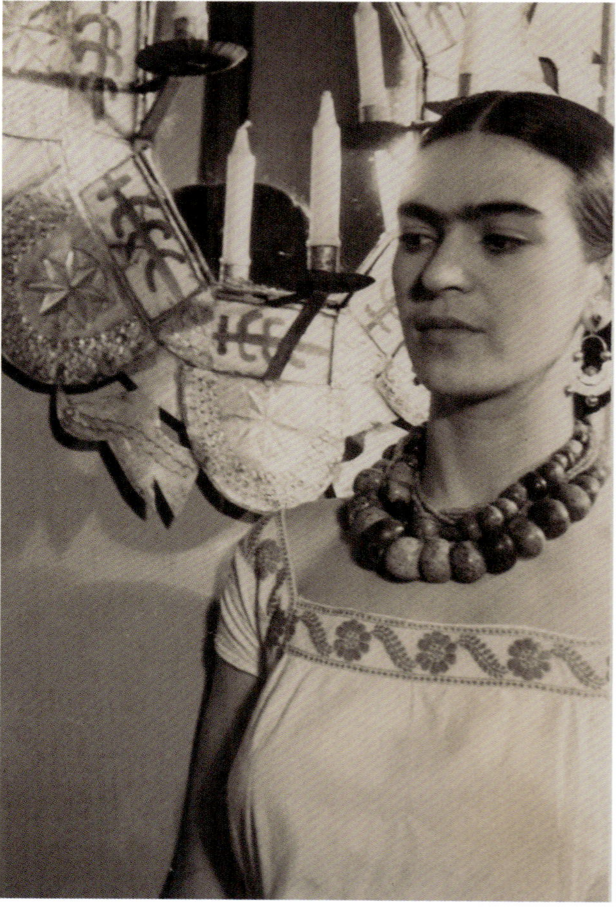

TOP Frida at the train station, San Francisco, ca. 1931. Photo by Imogen Cunningham

BOTTOM Frida, New York, March 19, 1932. Photo by Carl Van Vechten

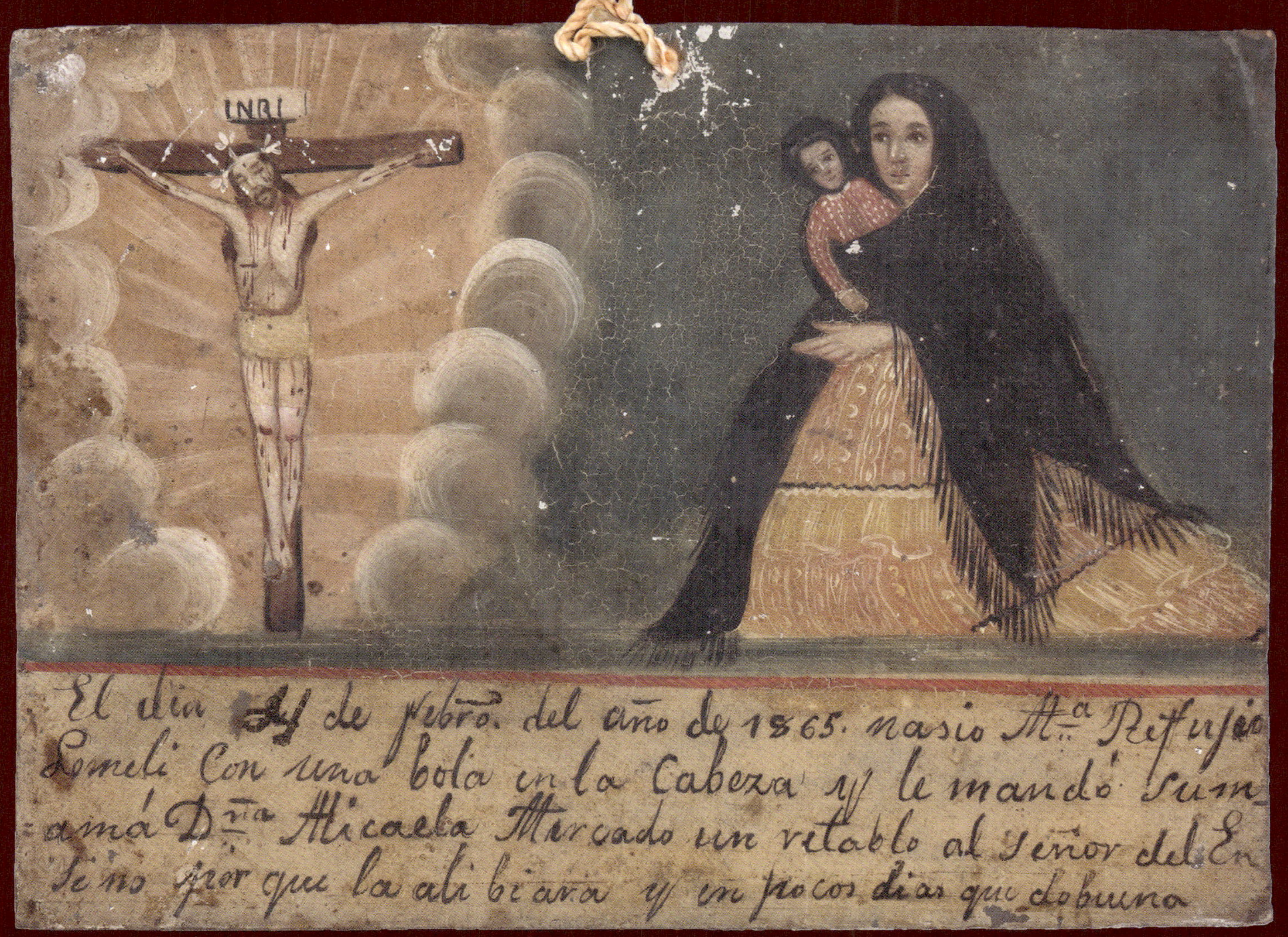

ABOVE AND THE FOLLOWING SPREAD Frida collected ex-votos, a devotional painting, traditionally created in gratitude for a miracle or divine favor, often depicting the event and dedicated to a saint or a virgin. Although she was not religious, she was attracted to this popular art form which she found deeply authentic.

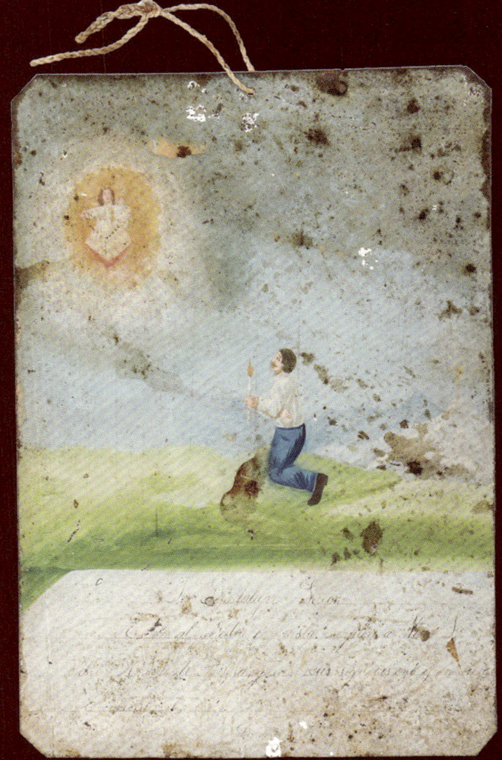

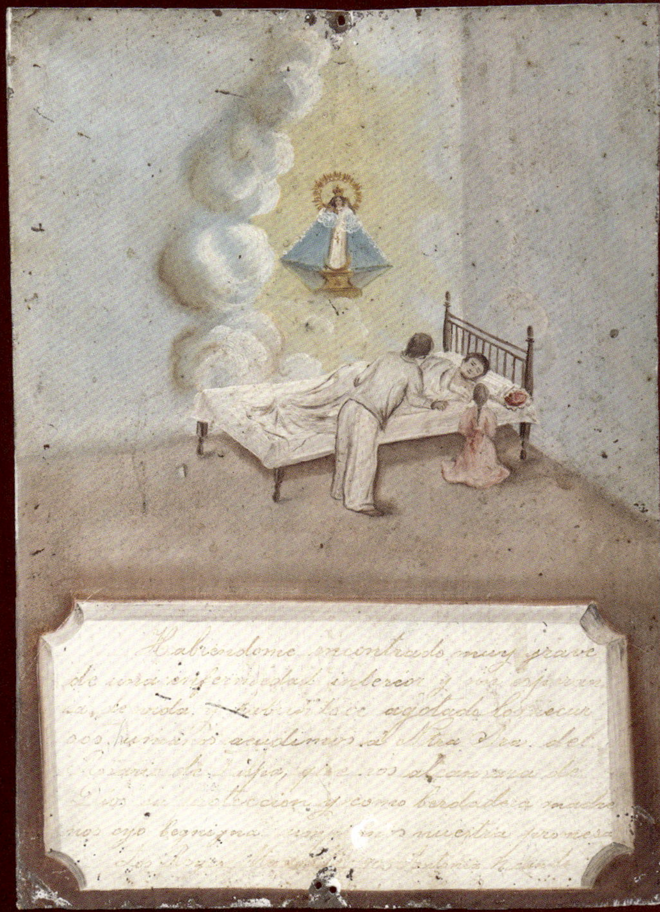

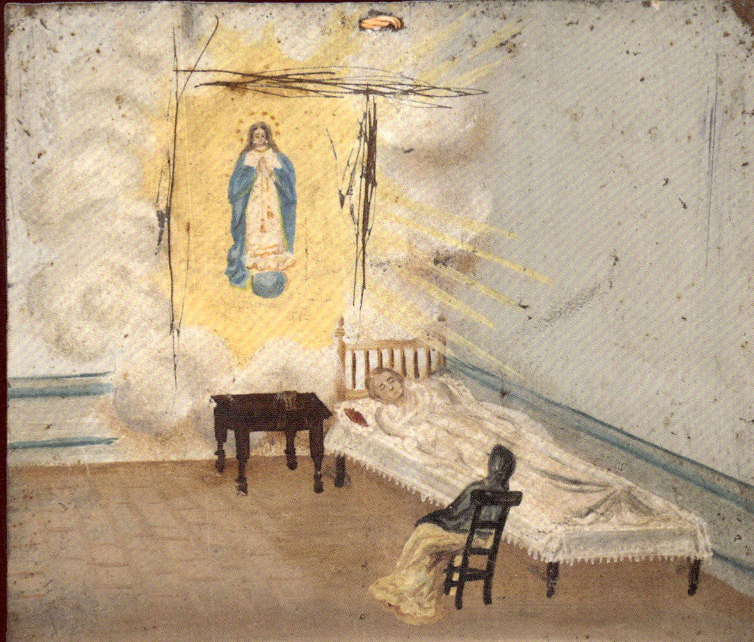
Hallándome gravemente postrada
de una fuerte pulmonía, y habiéndose
agotado los recursos humanos invoqué
a la Purísima Concepción me diera el
~~alivio~~ prometiendo publicar este fabor
quien me oyó propicia.
Para testimonio pongo este en
Jalpa Enero de 1907
Petra Flores

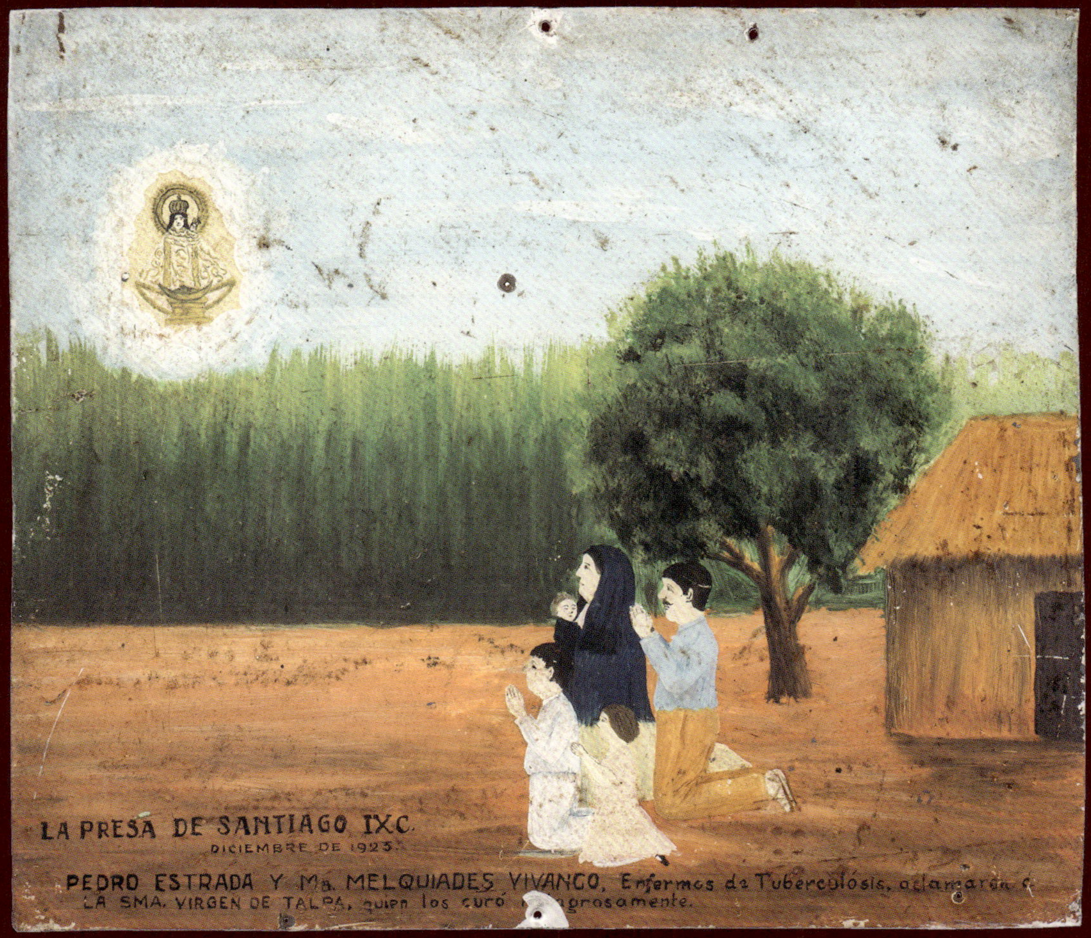
LA PRESA DE SANTIAGO IXC.
DICIEMBRE DE 1923.
PEDRO ESTRADA Y Ma. MELQUIADES VIVANCO, Enfermos de Tuberculósis, aclamarón á
LA SMA. VIRGEN DE TALPA, quien los curó

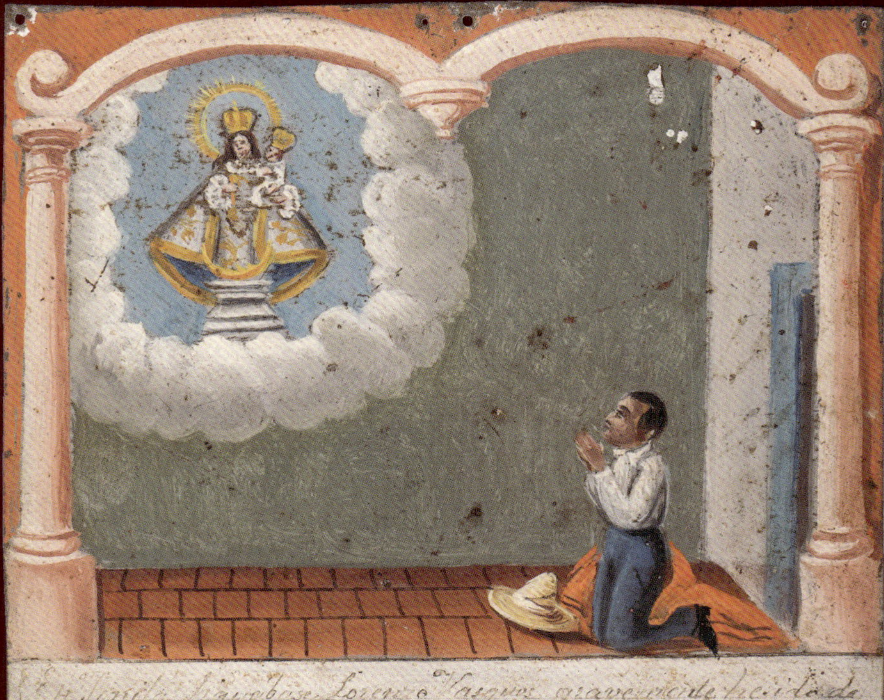
en muy corto tiempo consiguió su perfecta salud.

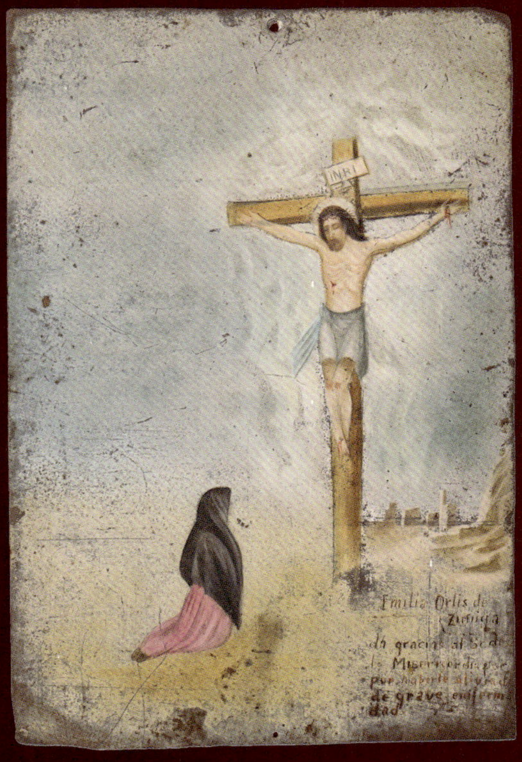
INRI
Emilia Orlis de
Zuñiga
de grave enfermedad

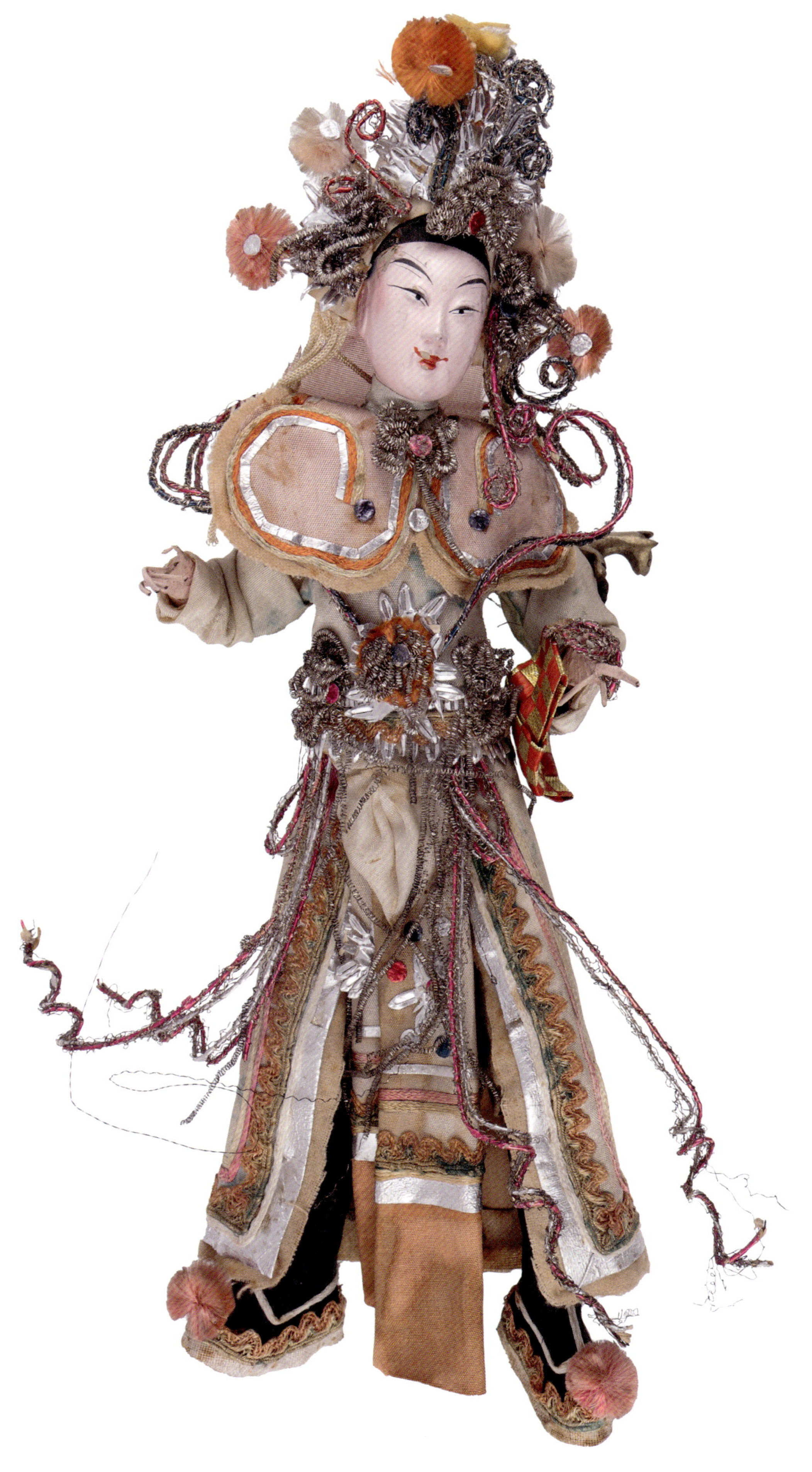

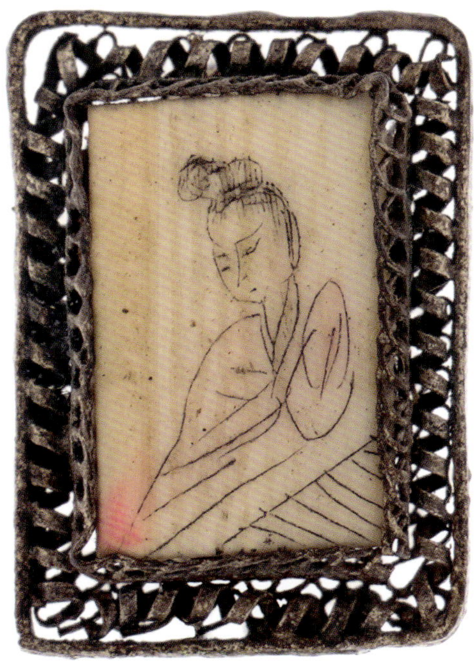

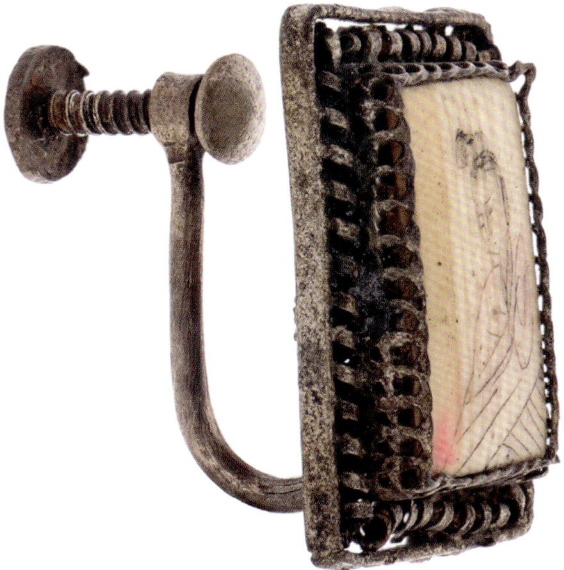

Frida Hentschel When she visited the United States, she loved visiting different immigrant neighborhoods, like the various Chinatowns, or areas where there were large concentrations of people from Italy, Japan, and Russia. In letters from 1931, when she was in San Francisco, she wrote to her mother Matilde relaying how bored she was with the people and lifestyle, but that when she ventured off to these immigrant neighborhoods she was excited. Chinatown, whether in San Francisco or in New York, was the most interesting to her. She often celebrated New Year's holidays there. She enjoyed the exuberance—from the traditions to the clothing. In fact, she thought that Mexicans were direct descendants of the Chinese! Chinese children, she felt, had a lot in common with Mexican children—both in their comportment and how they looked and dressed. She bought countless souvenirs from these neighborhoods, with the large majority being Chinese-inspired—slippers, bracelets, charms, bags of all types, and especially dolls.

She was an avid collector of dolls from a young age, and this continued into adulthood. We can only guess why they were so important to her—perhaps it filled a maternal instinct she was never able to fully express. She had a vast collection of dolls, which hailed from many places, including Germany, China, Japan, and Russia. When she was very ill in her later years, she often asked people visiting her to bring dolls. In thinking about this now, it's perhaps easy to imagine that they were a coping mechanism for her—taking care of her dolls as she wanted to be tended to herself.

OPPPOSITE AND ABOVE When abroad, Frida would often visit the various Chinatown and Japantown neighborhoods in a particular city and buy souvenirs. She had a vast collection of dolls from those visits—among other items like earrings and a Chinosierie silk purse—and would often gift them to family members.

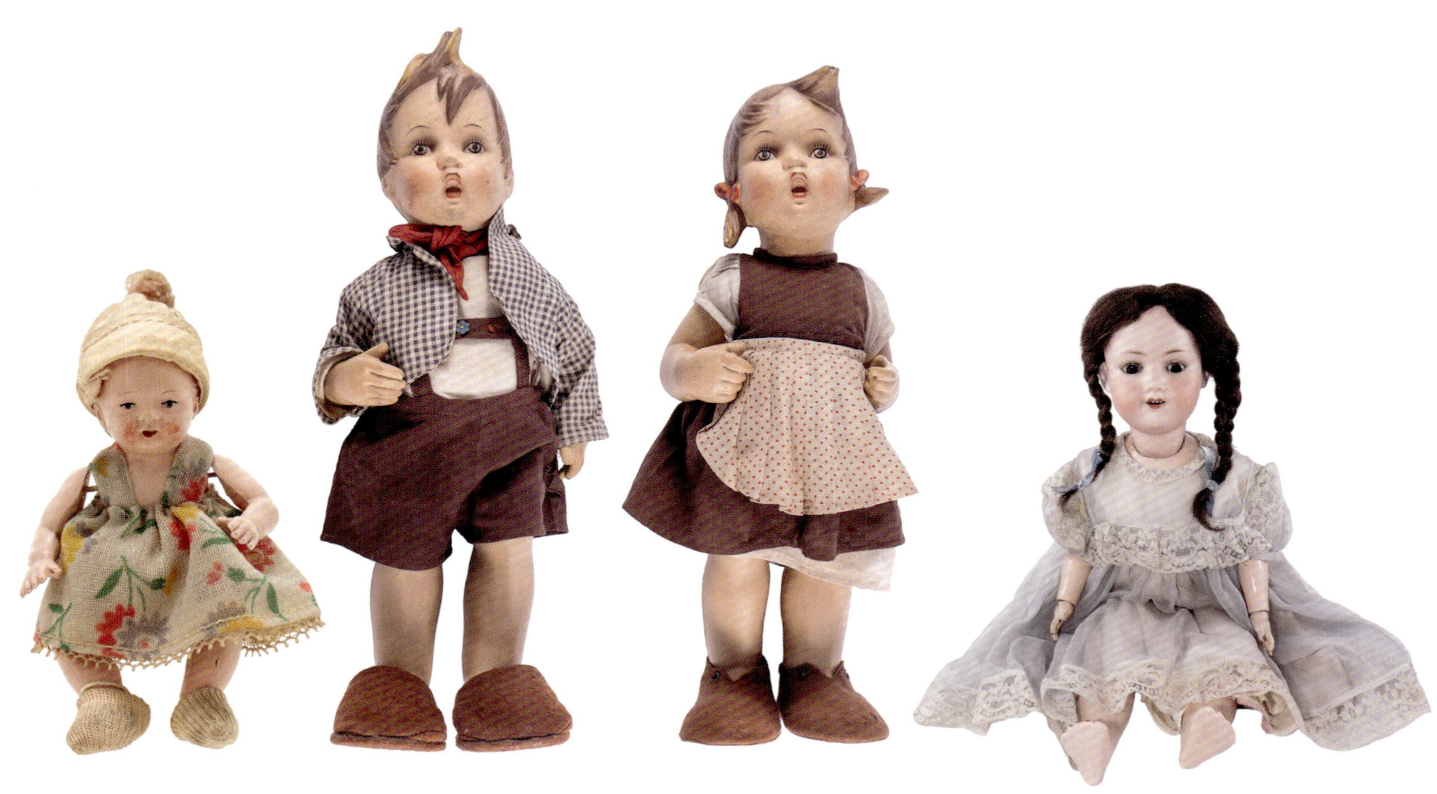

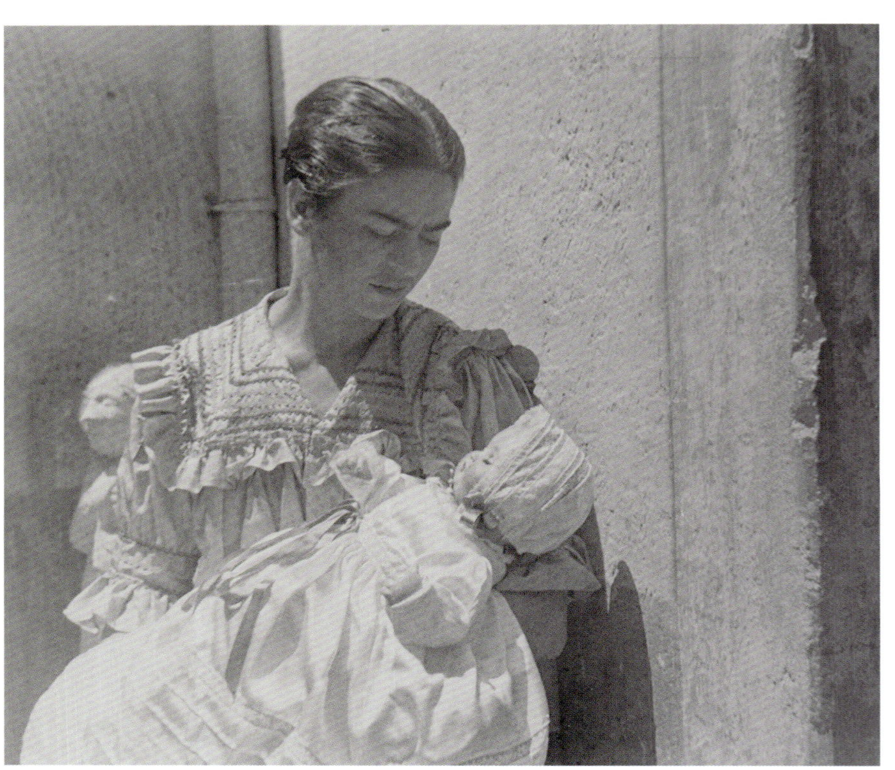

TOP The young Kahlo sisters had a large collection of German dolls.

BOTTOM Frida holding a doll at Casa Azul, Coyoacán, ca. 1935

OPPOSITE Frida Kahlo, *Me and My Doll*, 1937. Oil on metal, 15.75 x 12.25 in. (40 x 31 cm)

FOLLOWING SPREAD Frida with idol figurine at Casa Azul, Coyoacán, ca. 1939. Photo by Nikolas Muray

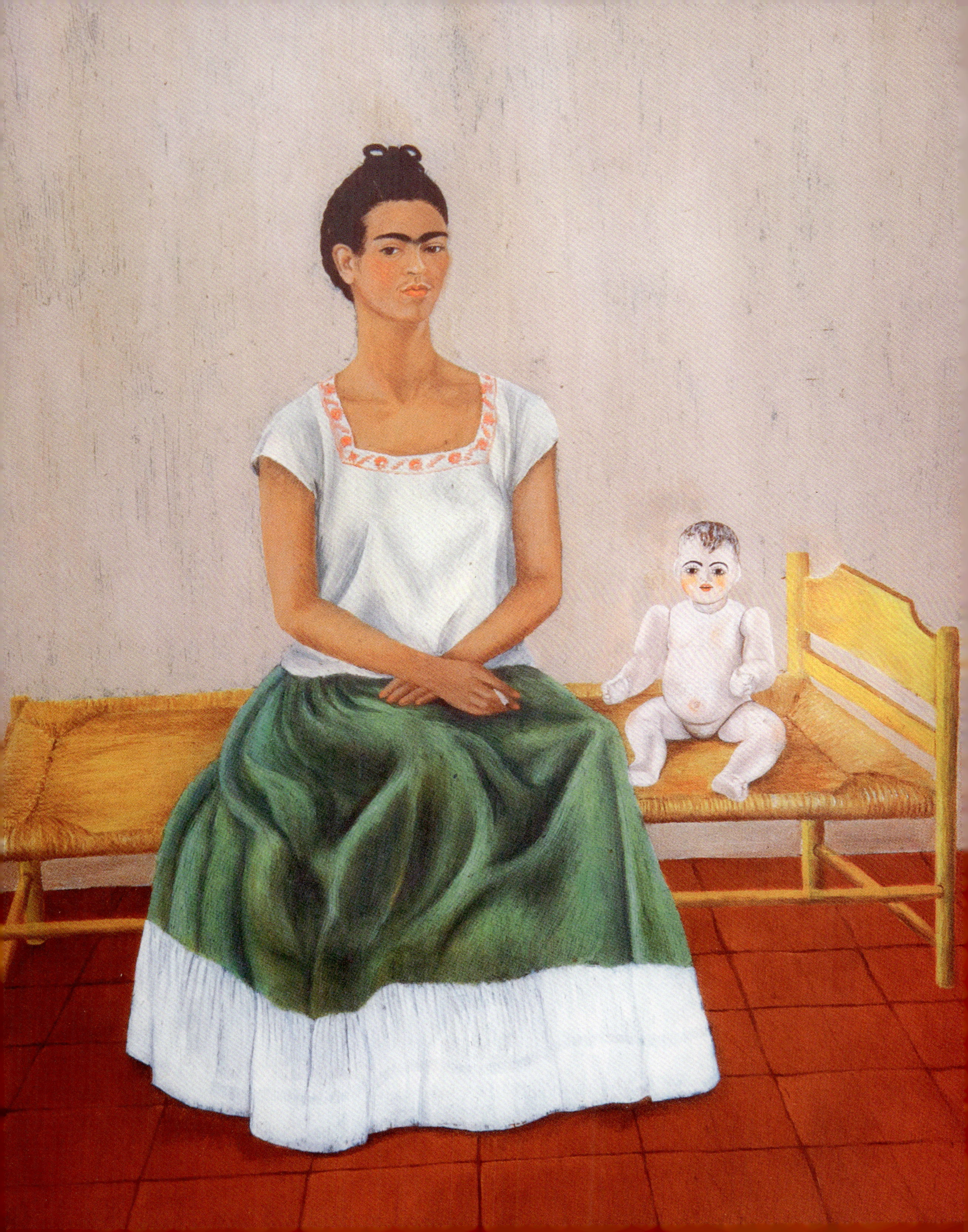

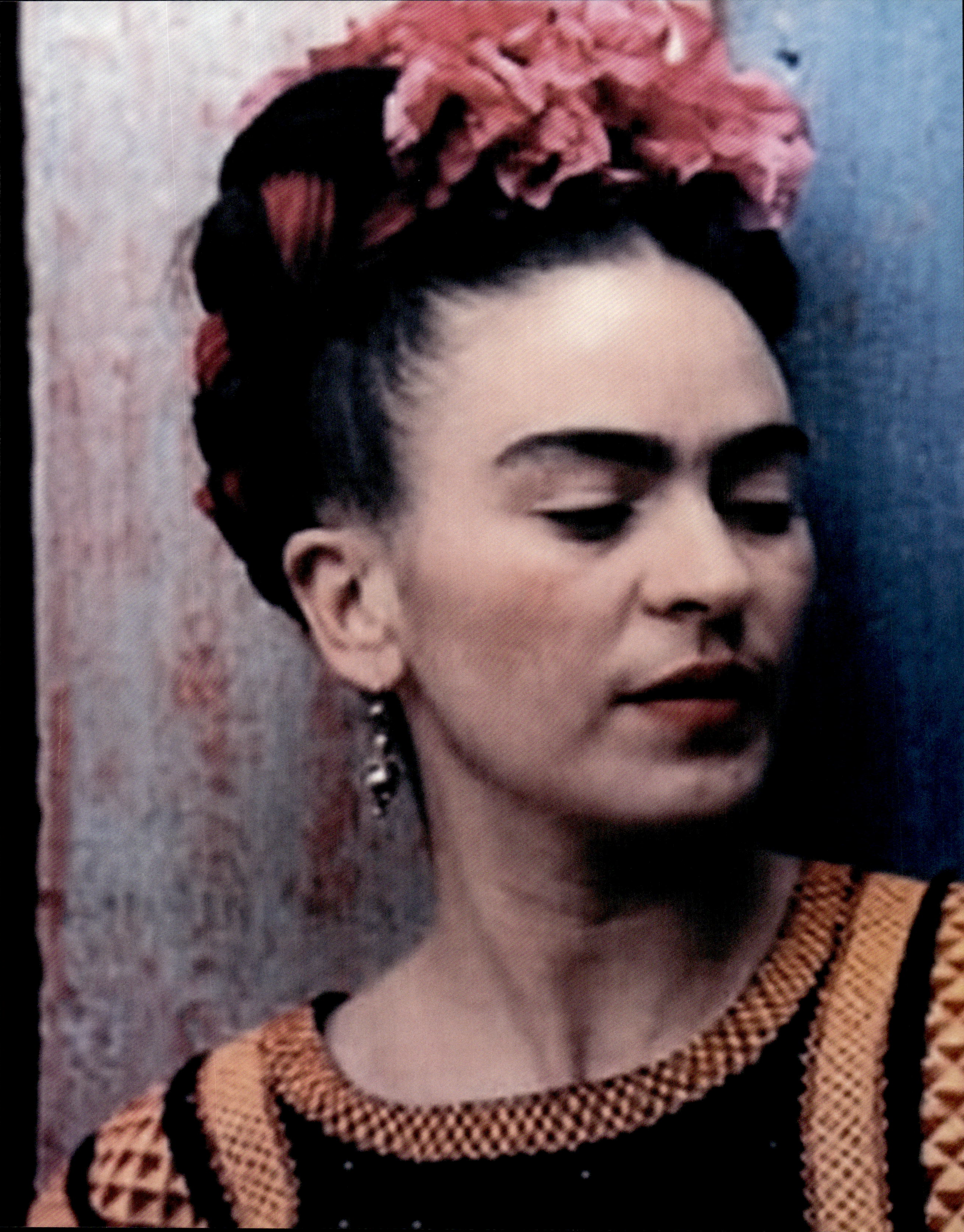

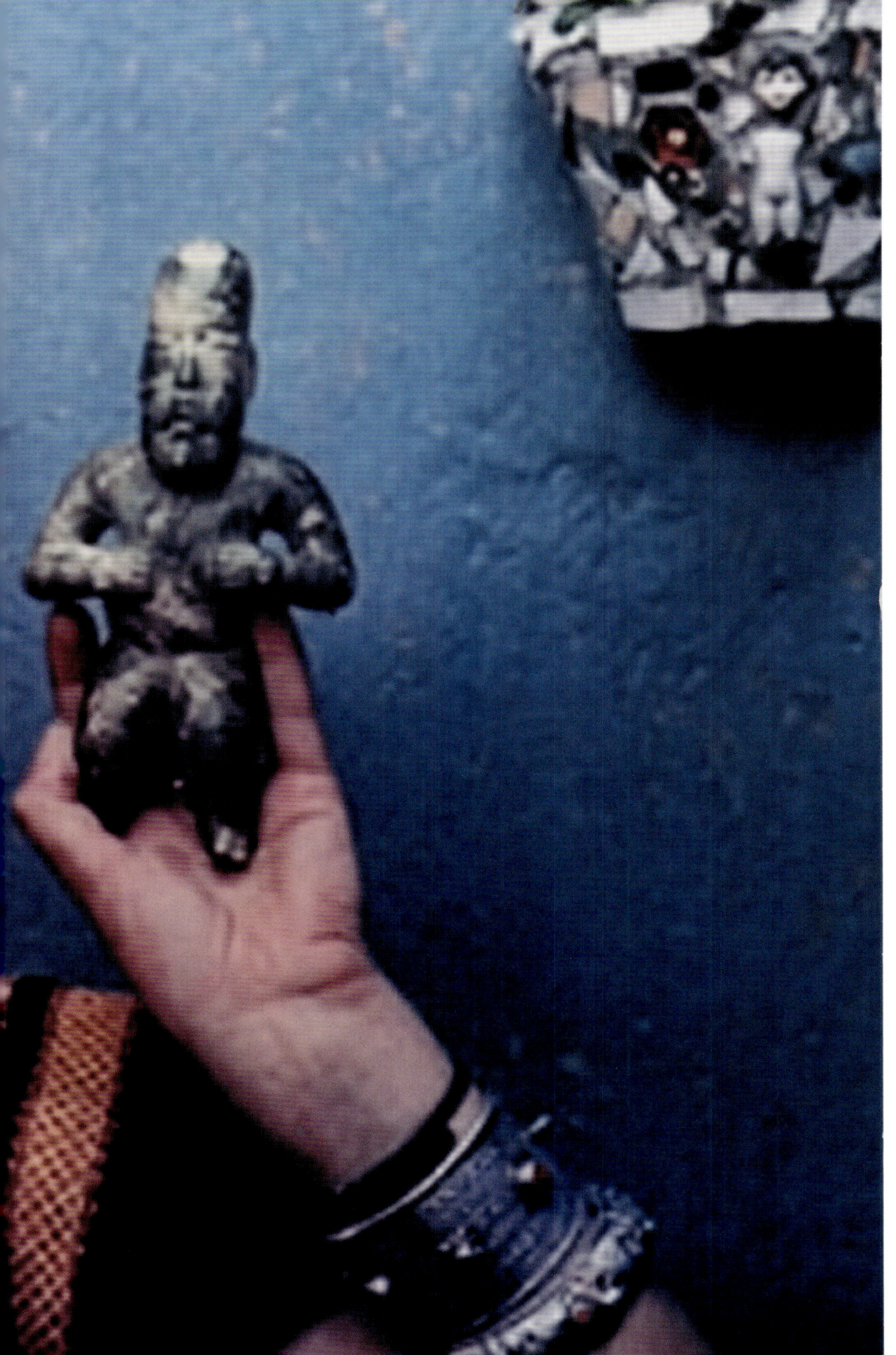

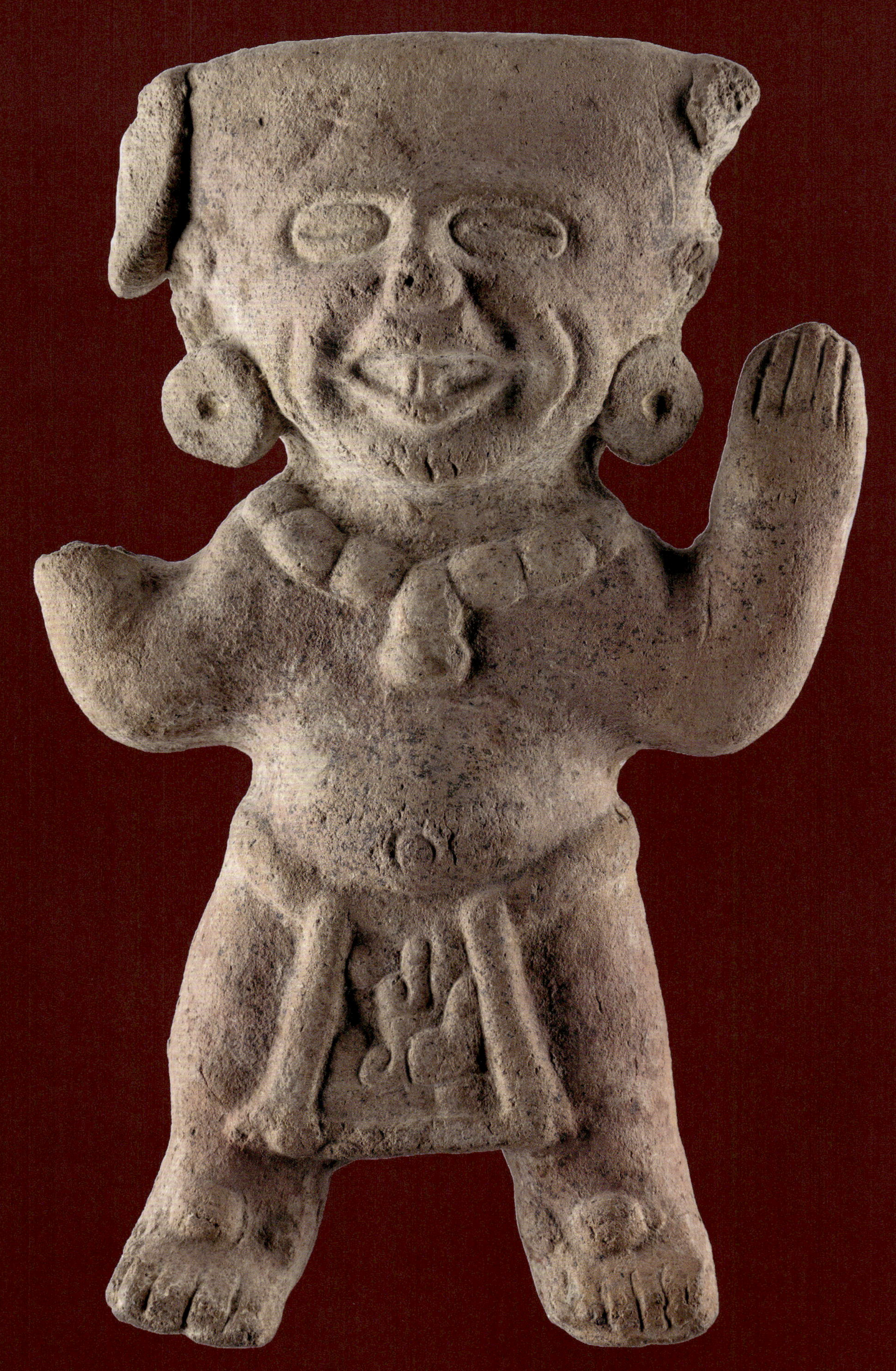

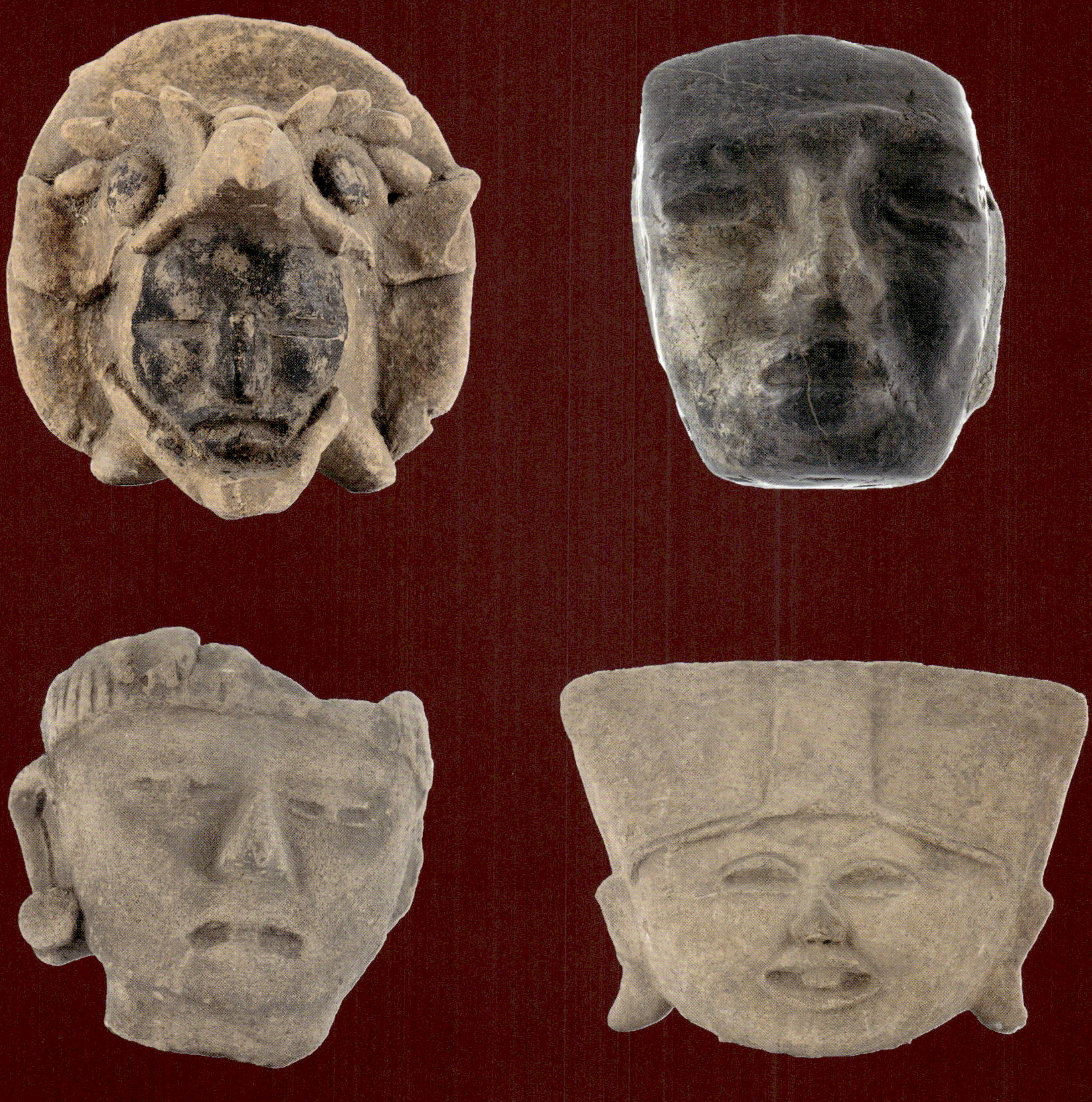

OPPOSITE AND ABOVE Frida collected pre-Hispanic idol figurines, surrounding herself with these ancient symbols as a way of preserving and honoring Mexico's ancestral heritage.

Frida Hentschel Frida was very close to nature and native beliefs. She appreciated and was sensitive to things that possessed energy and that were intertwined with nature. She loved to collect stones for her jewelry—and she believed the stones pick us, we don't pick the stones. These beliefs and the connection to nature runs deep in our family. Frida had much love for Mexican and pre-Hispanic art and culture. When she experienced Western art—whether Renaissance paintings or ancient Greek sculpture—she appreciated the talent and skill they demonstrated but always felt that the art of her country overshadowed that from other places. Mexico for her was the greatest culture. And Mexicans were the greatest people.

She was very connected to the moon cycles, and the sun—the duality of opposing energies and the integration of both. Old beliefs were dear to her, as they are for us still. For example, the *Ojo de Venado* (eye of the deer) protected against the evil eye. Made from the seed of the velvet bean or *mucuna*, which possesses toxic and hallucinogenic properties, it is tied with a red ribbon and should be kept or worn close to your heart. Cristina always wore this kind of talisman, and this tradition continues. I have one for my son that my great-grandmother made.

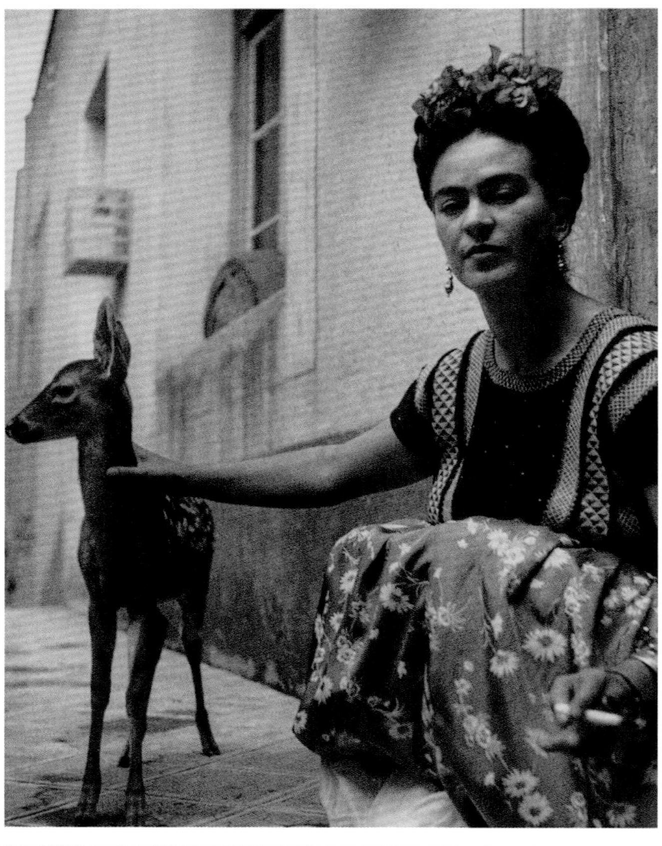

Mara Romeo Kahlo Frida loved hummingbirds for their color, beauty, agility, and sense of freedom. For her, seeing a hummingbird signaled love and life. She felt similarly about butterflies—colorful and seemingly free after their metamorphosis from caterpillars. This cycle of rebirth held a lot of meaning for Frida. She once wrote in her diary, "Feet, what do I need you for, if I have wings to fly?" She longed to be free in the same way, to be light and unencumbered, so she could take in the world from a vantage point her human body didn't allow.

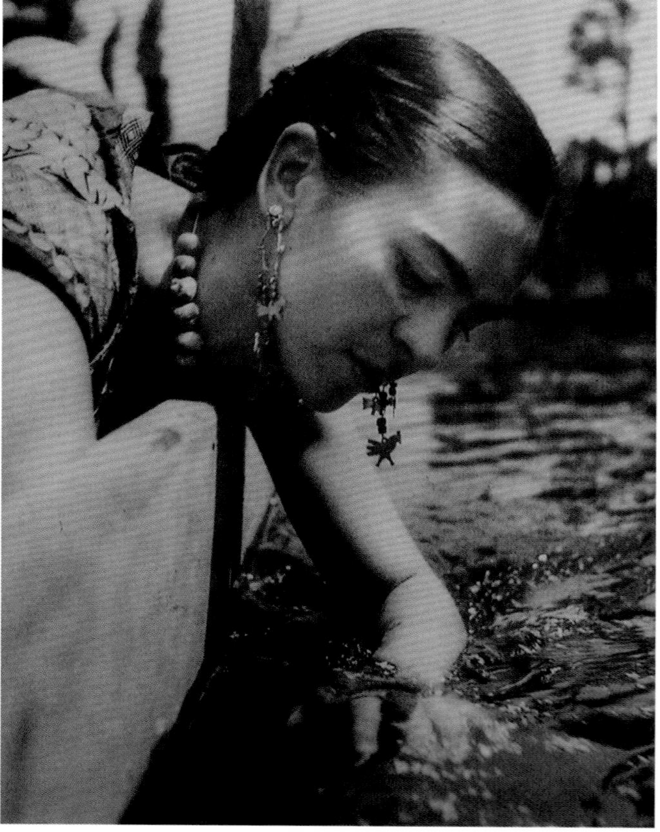

TOP Frida with her pet deer, ca. 1939. Photo by Nickolas Muray

BOTTOM Frida in a boat on the canals of Xochimilco, Mexico City, ca. 1936. Photo by Fritz Henle

OPPOSITE Frida with Diego Rivera's pet monkey, Fulang Chang, ca. 1940. Photo by Otto Bettmann

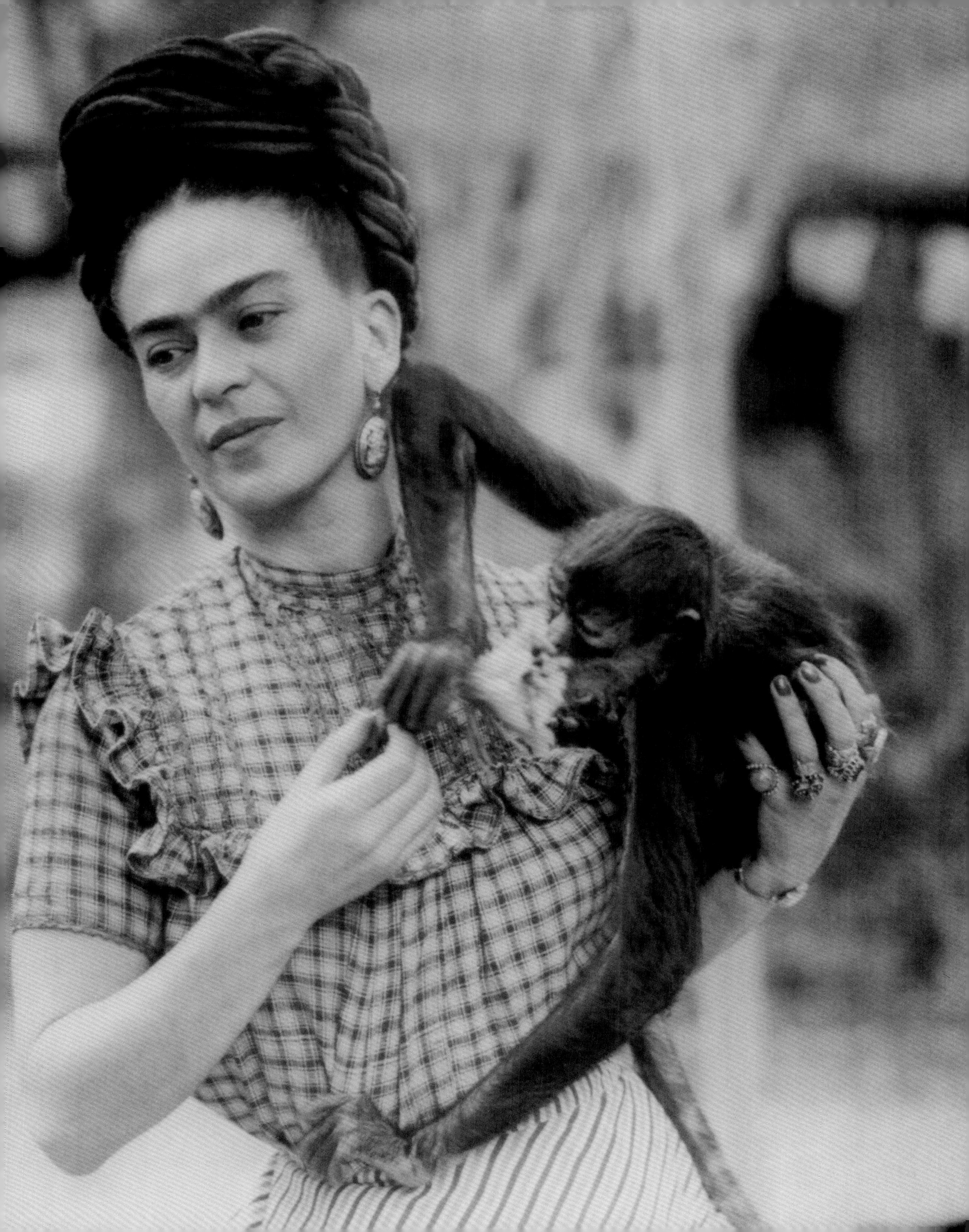

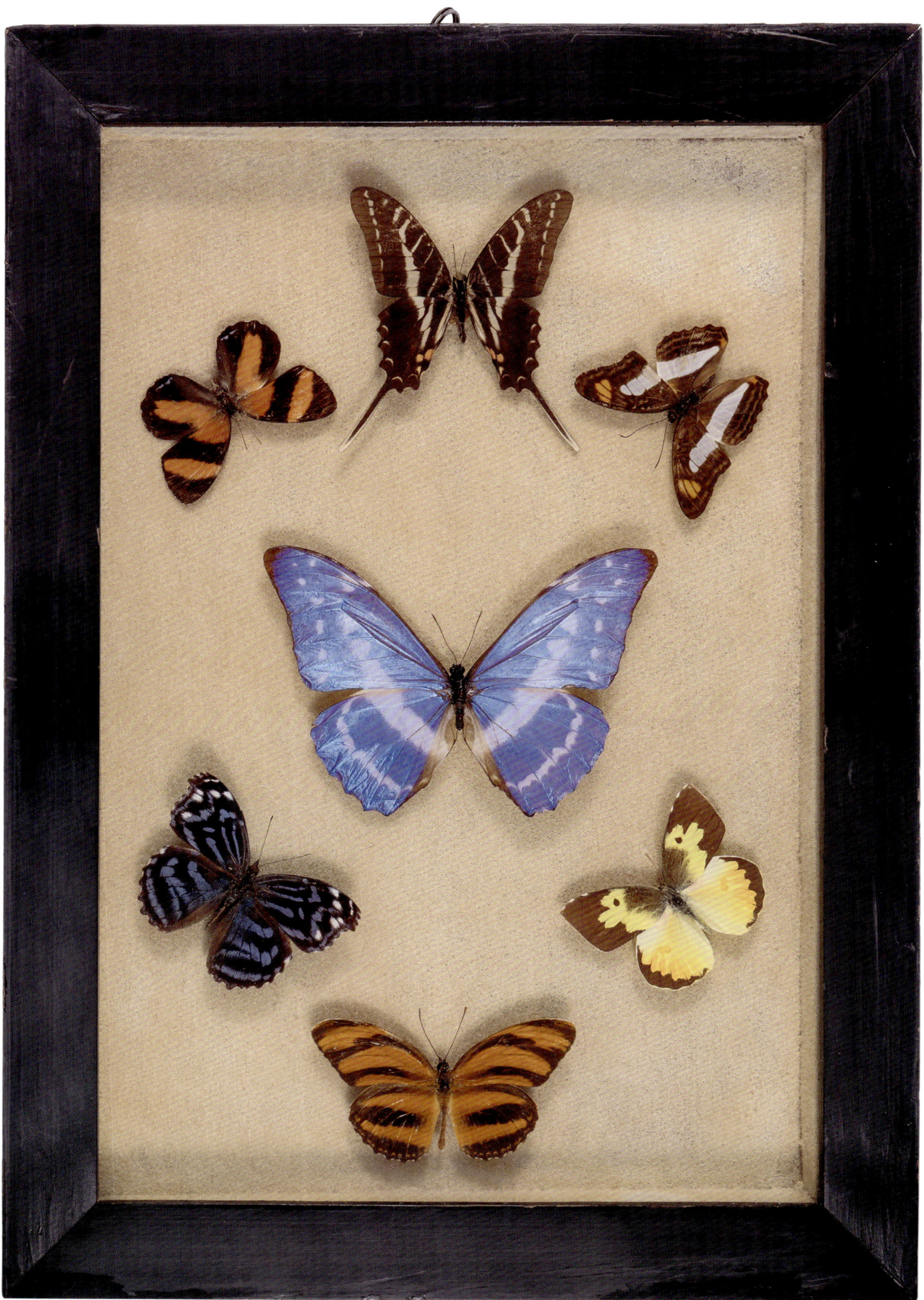

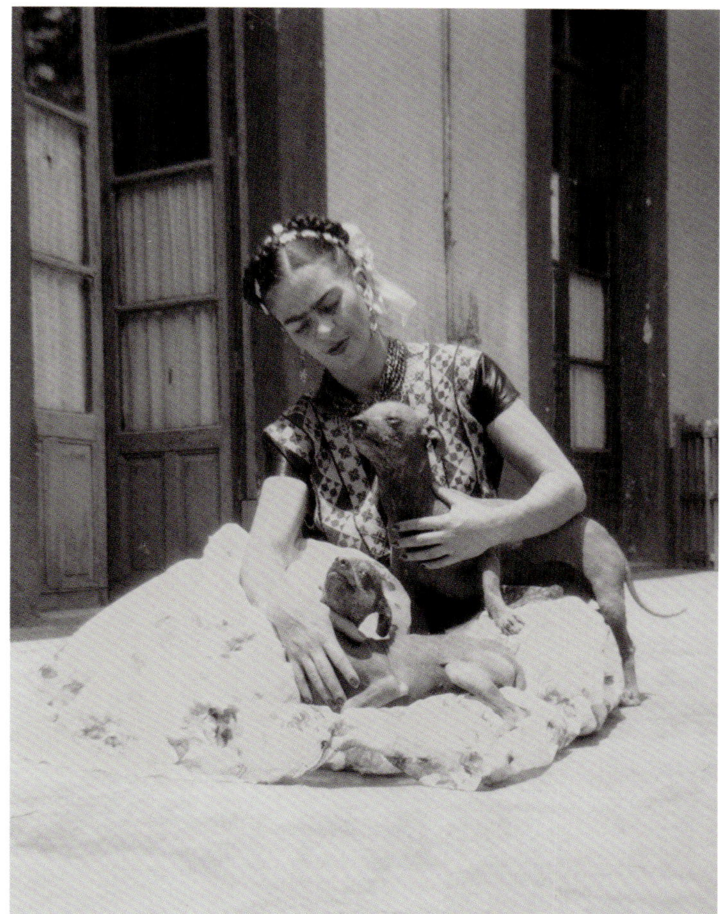

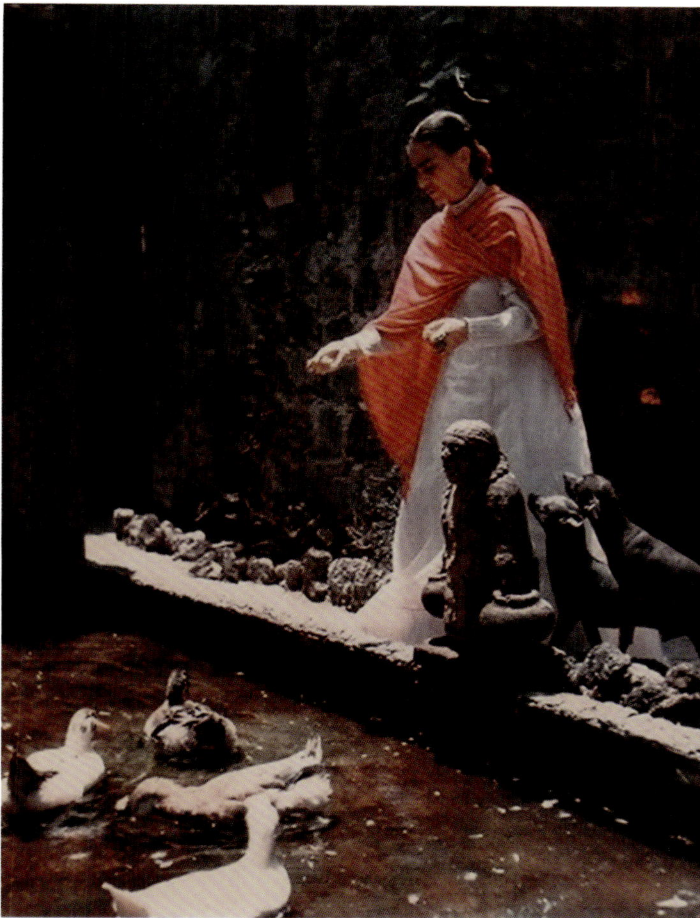

Frida recognized the duality in human beings—they could be both good and bad—but in animals she only saw the good. In her mind, if you treated them well, they would return that love back to you in equal measure. She believed in their purity and loyalty, and she surrounded herself with them wherever she lived. At Casa Azul, she kept an extraordinary range of pets, both wild and domesticated: ducks, parrots, fish, deer, cats, and dogs. The monkeys belonged to her husband Diego, but she loved them, too. She had several Xoloitzcuintles, the ancient hairless dog breed native to Mexico. Cristina also had a proclivity for animals and kept pigs, storks, dogs, hens, and chickens at Casa Kahlo. The Kahlo households were true menageries.

Frida Hentschel Frida was also captivated by other aspects of the natural world, including bugs. She had a collection, and found great beauty in the many specimens she kept. Bugs are often seen as nuisances, but they are of course an important part of a delicate ecosystem. She truly cared for these small and indefensible creatures. In fact, all the Kahlo sisters collected taxidermied bugs, particularly beetles, which they loved for their strange and beautiful color.

Frida Hentschel Frida often represented flora and fauna in her work, and in particular tree roots recurred in many of her paintings. For her, they symbolized stability and the potential for growth. This aspect of her artwork developed when she was away from home traveling in the US and longing for family, longing for Mexico.

OPPOSITE Frida's butterfly collection. Since she was very young, Frida collected taxidermied butterflies and bugs and would look at them under a microscope.

TOP LEFT Frida with her dog on the patio of Casa Azul, Coyoacán ca. 1942–45. Photo attributed to Lola Alvarez Bravo

TOP RIGHT Frida in the garden of Casa Azul, Coyoacán, ca. 1951. Photo by Gisèle Freund

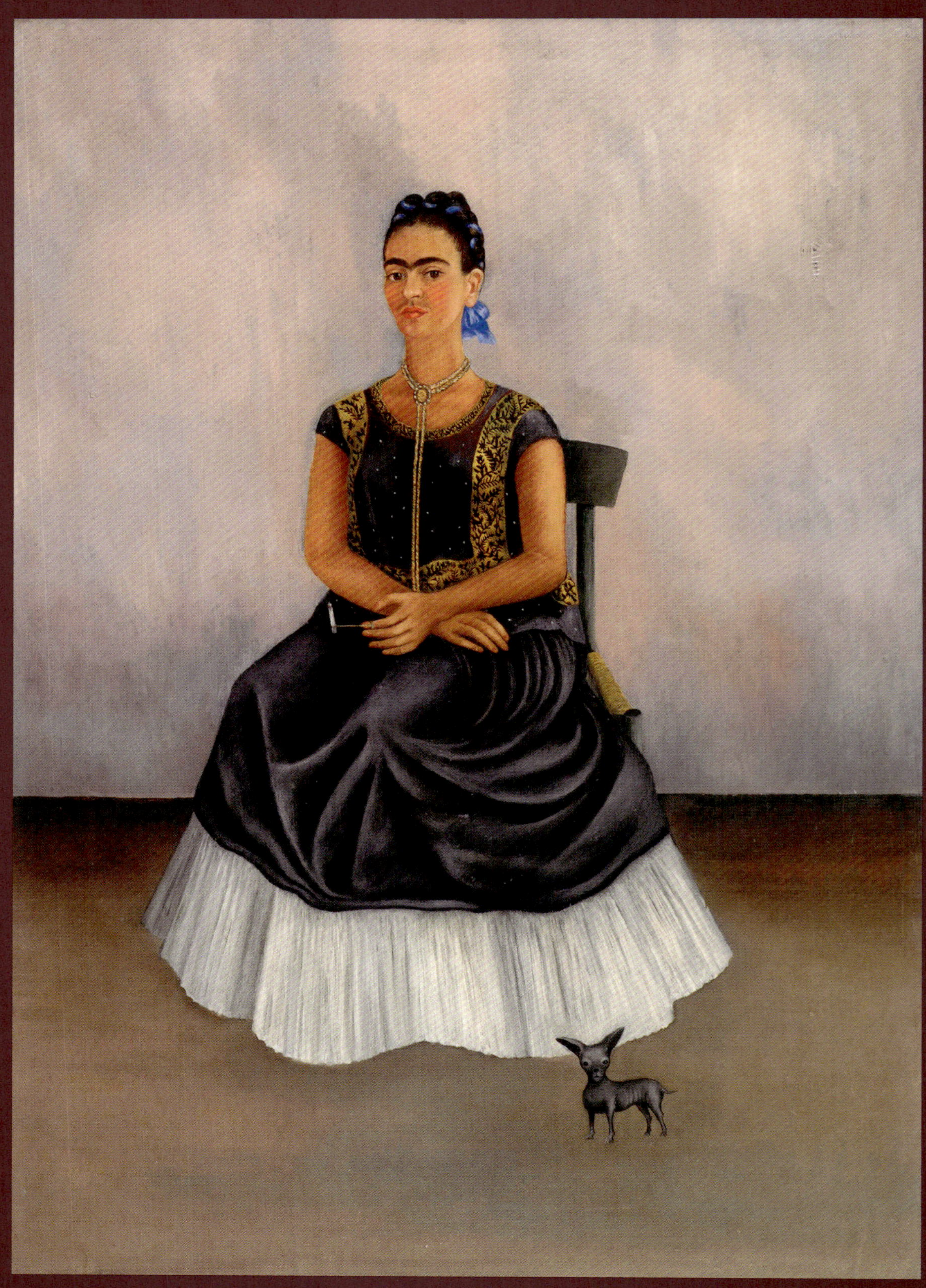

Frida Kahlo, *Itzcuintli Dog with Me*, 1938. Oil on canvas, 28 x 20.5 in. (71 x 52 cm)

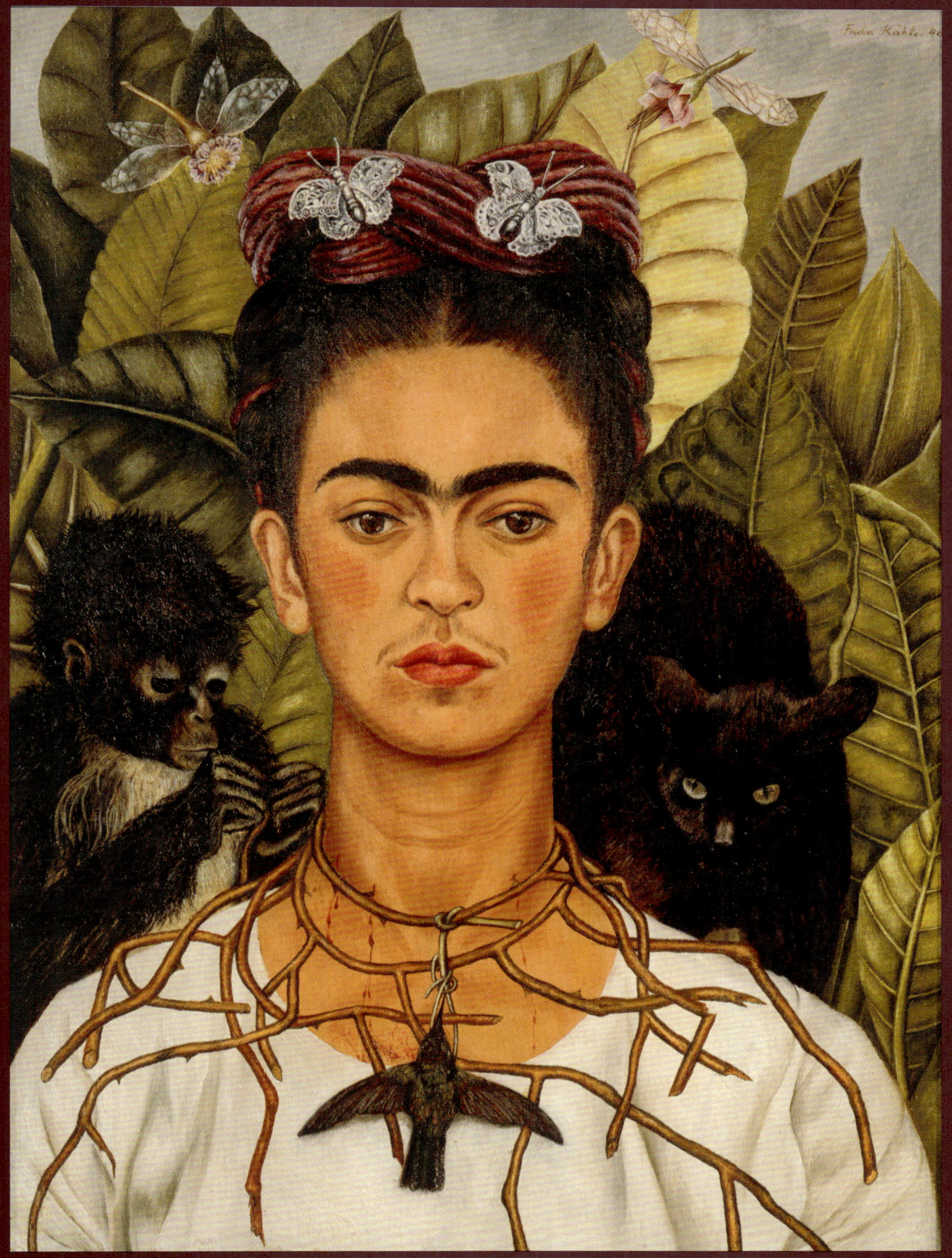

Frida Kahlo, *Self-portrait with Thorn Necklace and Hummingbird*, 1940. Oil on canvas mounted to board, 24.25 x 18.5 in. (61.3 x 47 cm)

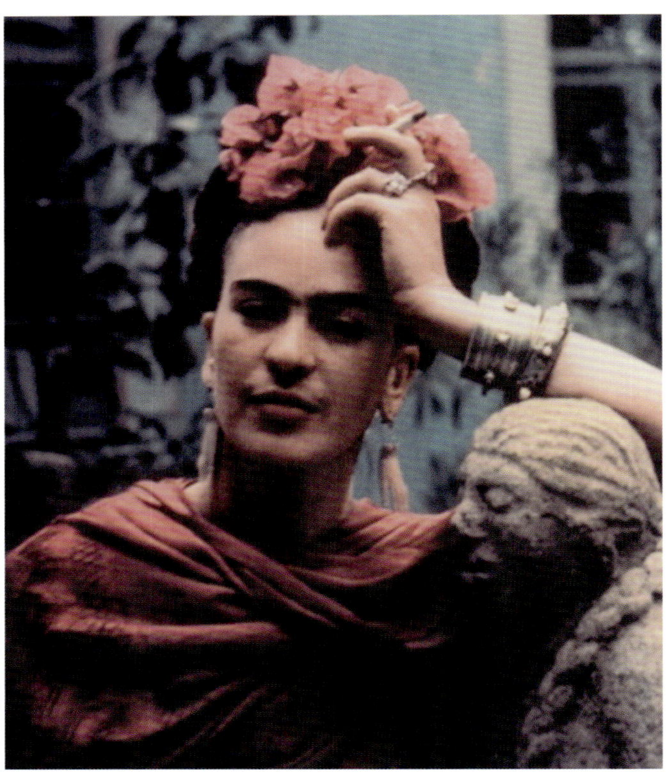

Mara Romeo Kahlo Despite all the suffering in her life, Frida was a very happy person. She retained a positive spirit even in the face of the pain she endured daily due to her chronic illnesses. She found pleasure and joy in singing and making jokes—and in fact her ribald sense of humor often found expression in the songs she sang.

Mara de Anda My grandmother Isolda, Frida's niece, would often tell us about Frida's wit and that she was a magnet for people of all kinds. She was a sensitive soul and found pleasure in simple things, which was a powerful combination when coupled with her brilliant and complex mind. She made friends with everyone, from people at the local market to the people who worked for her. Her generous and courageous spirit was infectious.

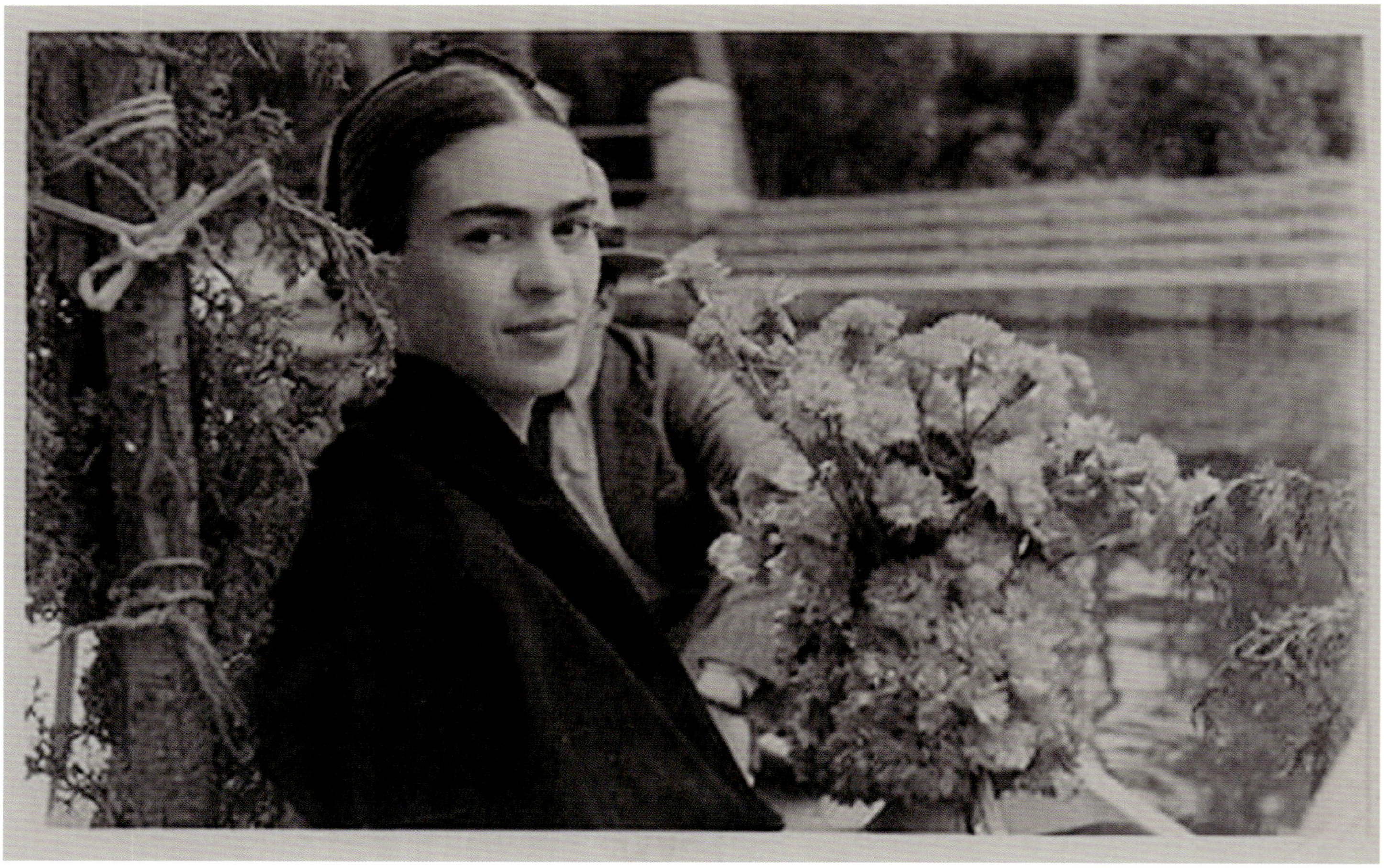

TOP Frida leaning on a sculpture by Mardonio Magaña, Coyoacán, 1940. Photo by Nikolas Muray

BOTTOM Frida in a *trajinera* (flat-bottomed boat), Xochimilco, Mexico, ca. 1940

OPPOSITE Frida at Casa Azul, 1940. Photo by Ivan Dimitri

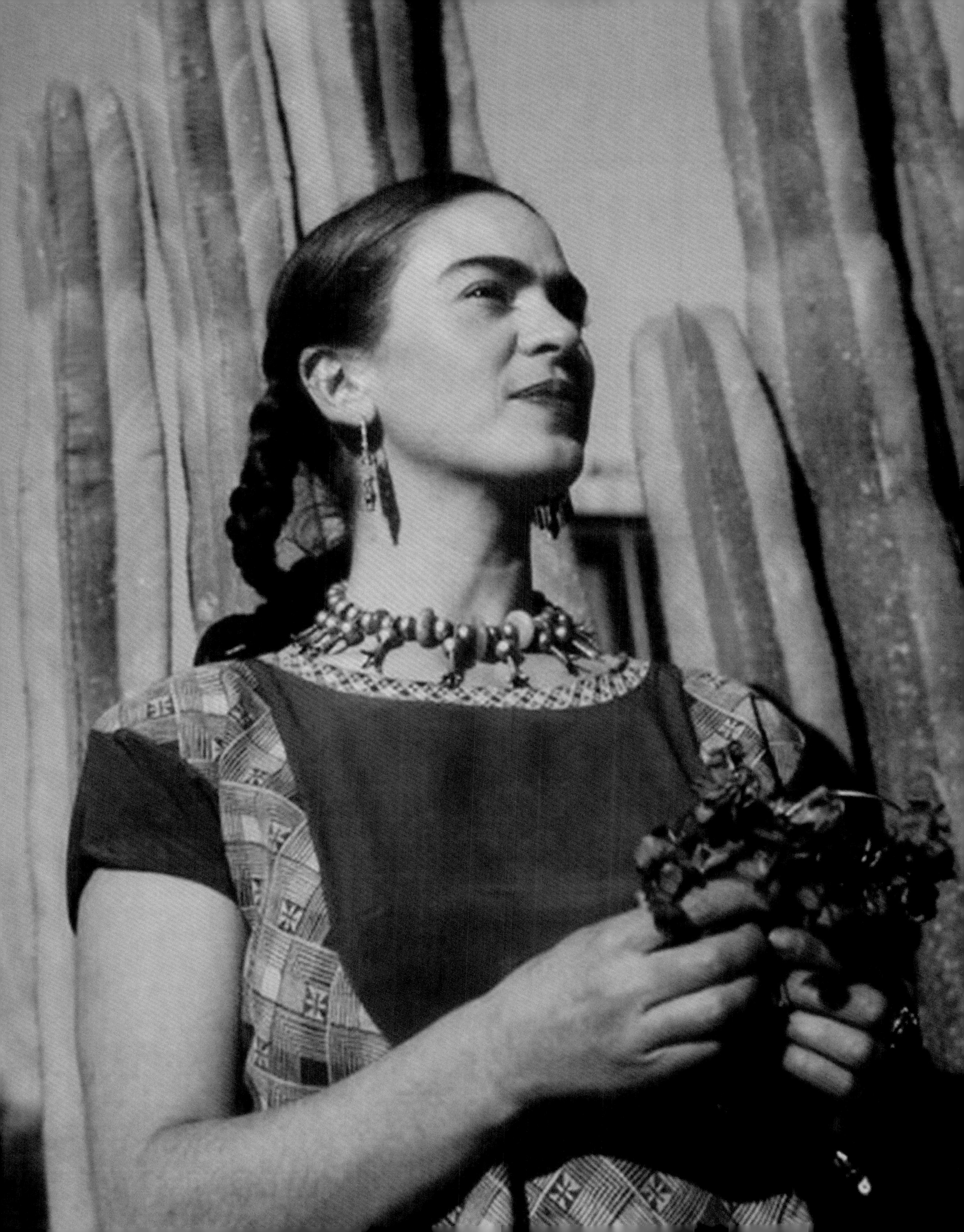

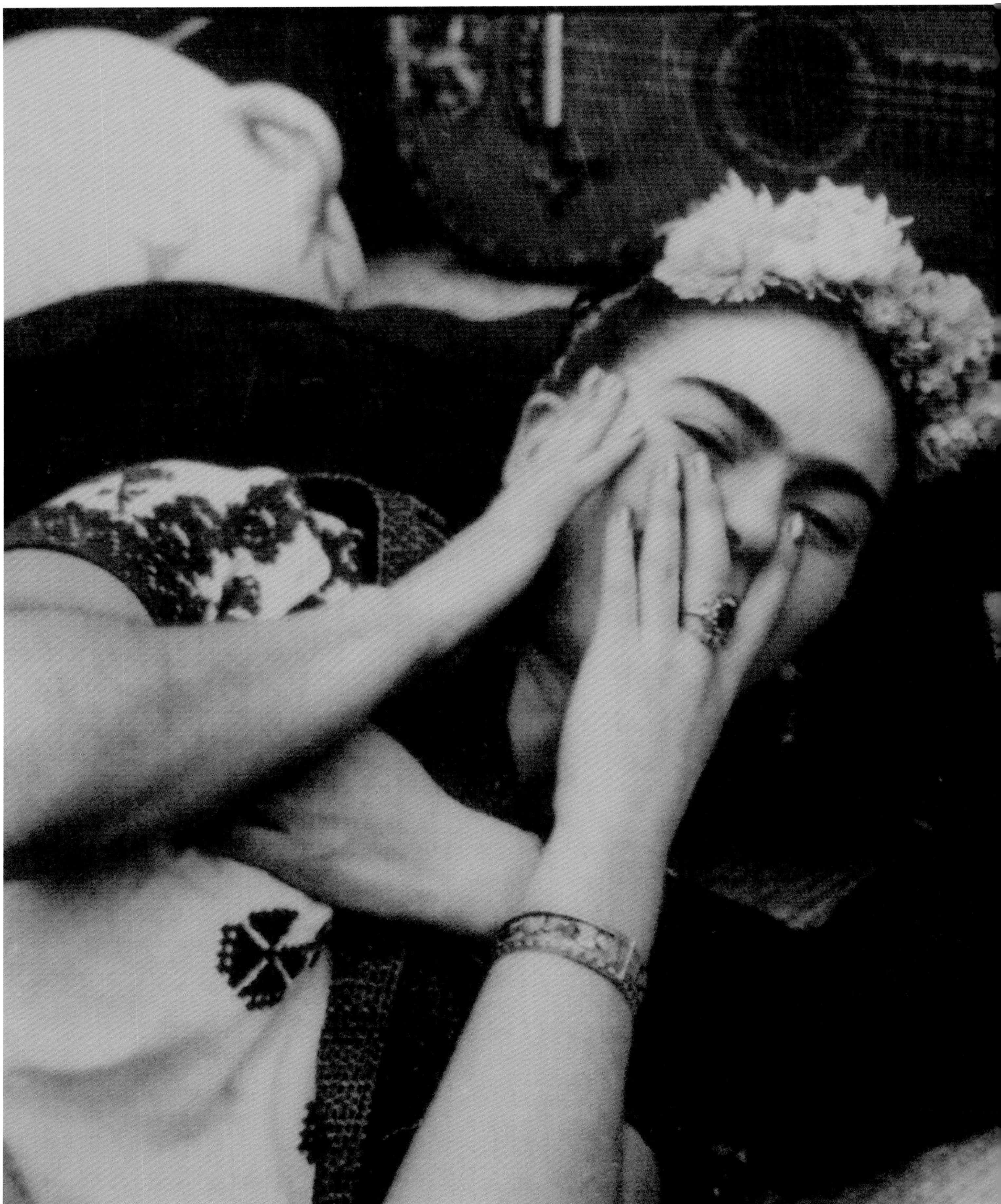

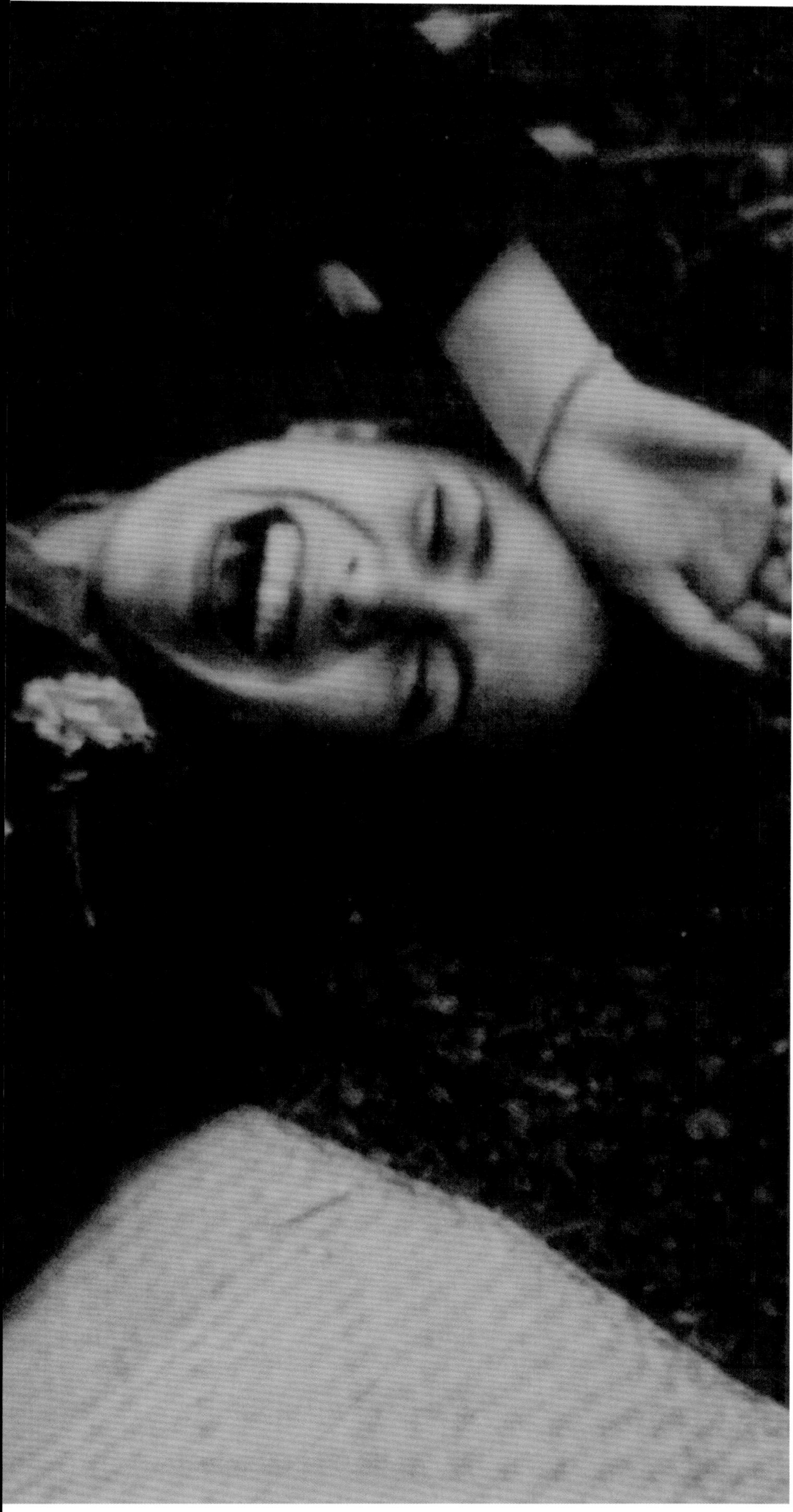

Frida Hentschel Frida was known for having an extraordinary personality. She believed in herself and never allowed anything or anyone to put her down, to disparage her. She held her own with the powerful people in her orbit, from world famous artists to revolutionaries and political figures. With Frida, there was no holding back.

Frida laughing with an unidentified friend. Many believe it is Chavela Vargas next to Frida, but this is incorrect.

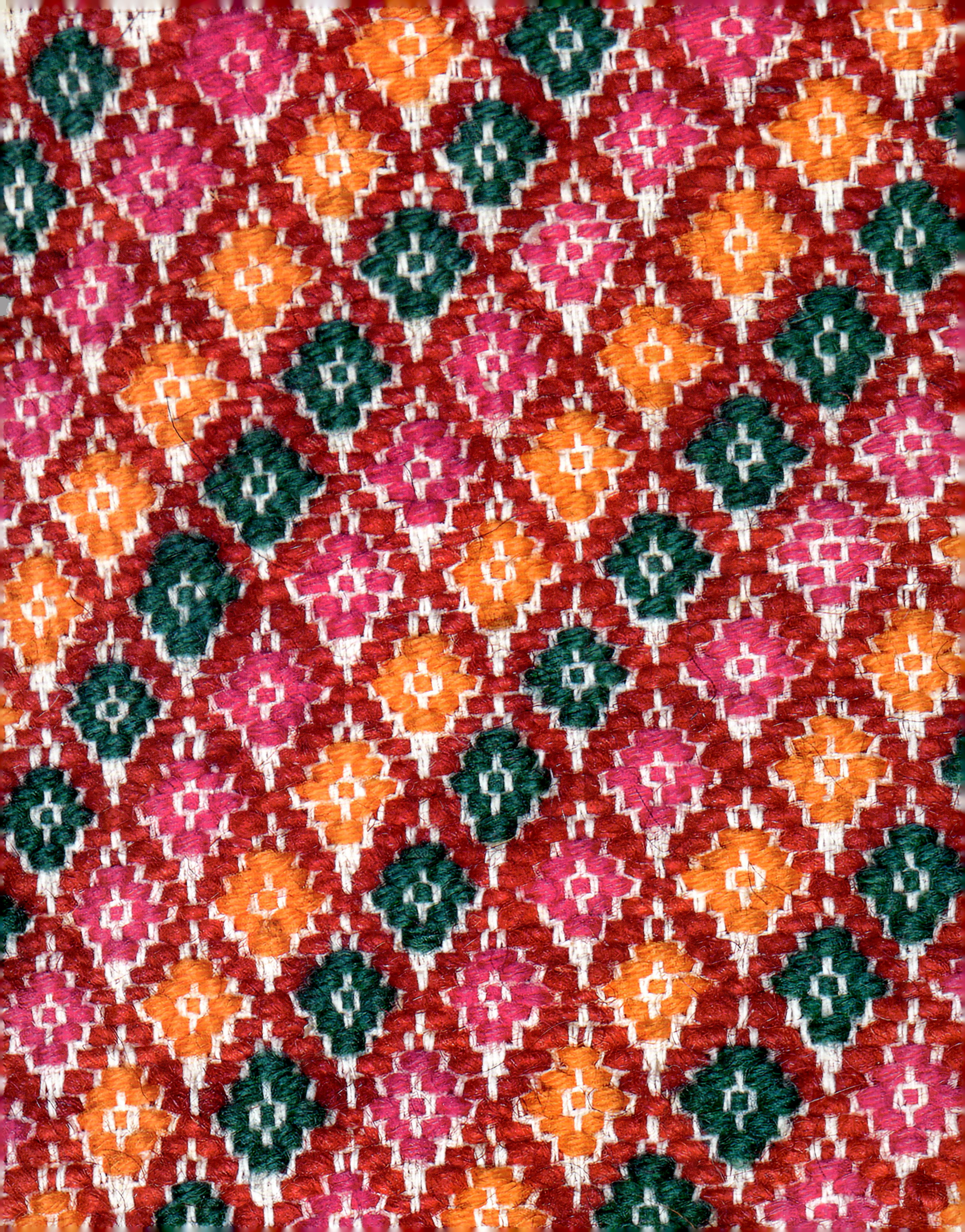

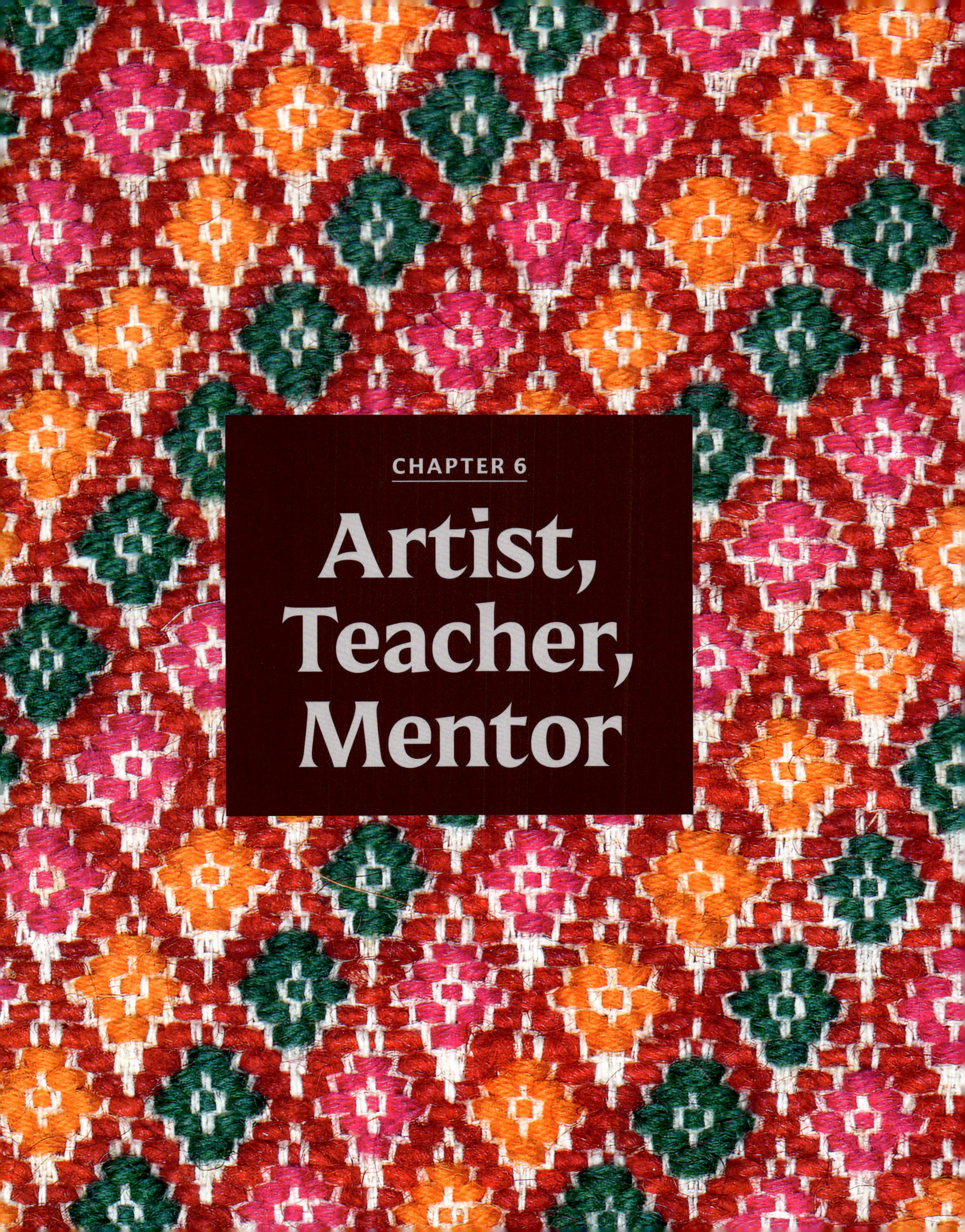

CHAPTER 6

Artist, Teacher, Mentor

Mara Romeo Kahlo Frida was a curious and deeply creative person. From a very early age, she had an artistic sensibility and an impressive dexterity with her hands. But she also recognized the value of an academic education. In 1922, when she was 15, she enrolled herself in the Nacional Preparatoria, becoming part of the school's first-ever female class. (Of 2,000 students, only 35 were women.) During these teenage years, she was part of a social group called "Los Cachuchas" (Mexican slang for "the caps," referring to the peaked cloth caps they wore). They were a group of young intellectuals who questioned and defied traditional social mores. This "rebellious" group spawned important Mexican politicians, artists, and intellectuals: Alejandro Gómez Arias (politician), José Gómez Robleda (researcher and public officer), Manuel González Ramírez (medical journalist and historian), and Manuel N. Lira (writer and poet) are just some of the distinguished members of the group. Frida loved spending time with them, reading literature, and discussing progressive political views. Arias became Frida's first boyfriend and lifelong friend—and he was godfather to Frida's niece Isolda, my mother. He was with her on that rainy September evening when a trolley hit the bus they were in; Frida was seriously injured and required surgeries throughout her life as a result.

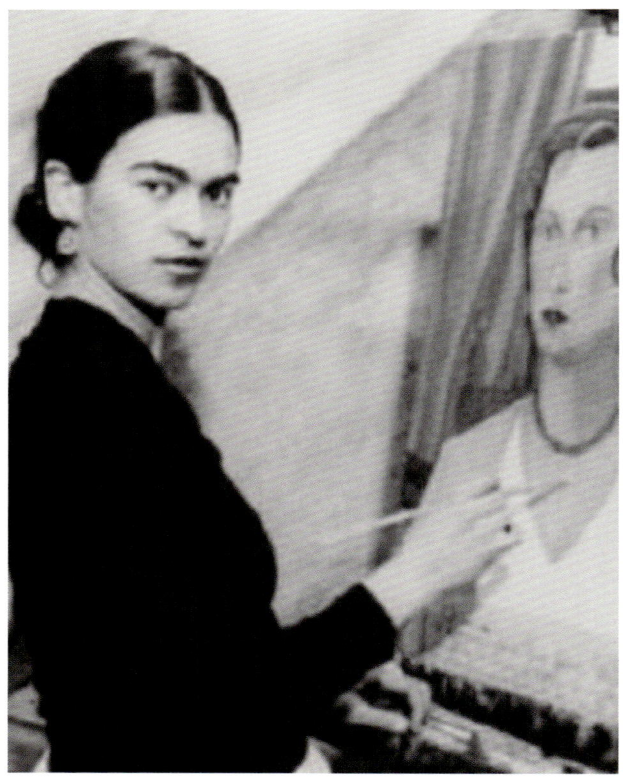

Mara de Anda The same year Frida enrolled in Nacional Preparatoria, Diego Rivera was commissioned to paint a mural there. He finished *La Creación* in 1923, a mural that explores the cross-pollination of cultures and man's relation to nature, combining Christian and pagan elements. Frida, being her witty and uninhibited self, would go into the amphitheater where he was painting, and whistle and yell from the shadows, "Hey! Panzón!" (paunchy). This innocent flirtation went on for months. She admired Diego's work, and her playfulness was a first step towards the romantic relationship that eventually unfolded.

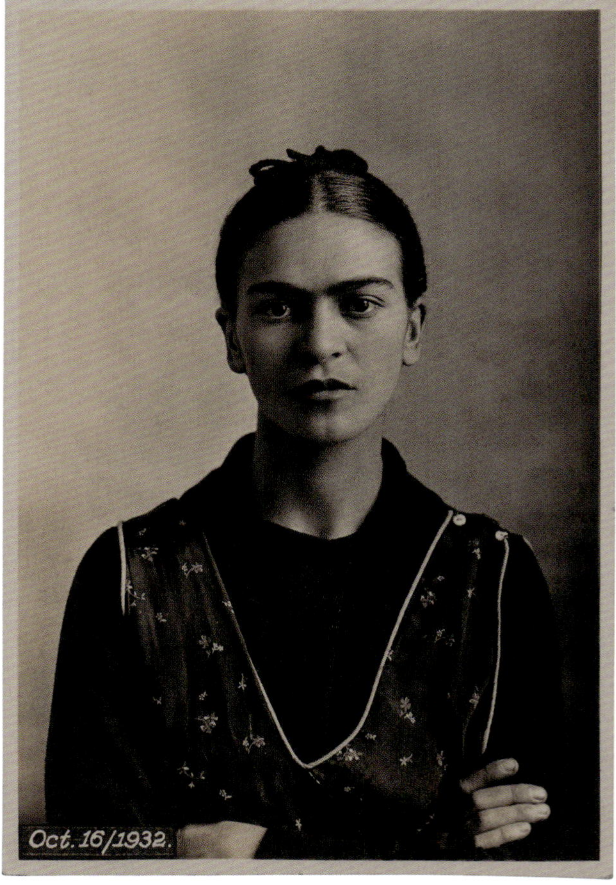

Frida Hentschel Before the accident, Frida's interest in art was very clear and she had even learned different techniques from the engraver Fernández with whom she worked. But the accident left her bedridden for months. It shattered her spine and probably any hope of going back to school and finishing her studies. The accident did, however, bring her closer to her destiny. From her bed, she started painting regularly, honing her skills in different techniques. She started making self-portraits—just as her father Guillermo did in photos—in pencil, watercolor, and oils. She stayed in touch with her Los Cachuchas friends, and would send them letters and paintings, hoping not to miss any of the group's adventures.

TOP Frida painting, ca. 1931. Photo by Otto Bettman

BOTTOM Frida, October 16, 1932. Photo by Guillermo Kahlo

OPPOSITE Frida at age 18, February 7, 1926. Photo by Guillermo Kahlo

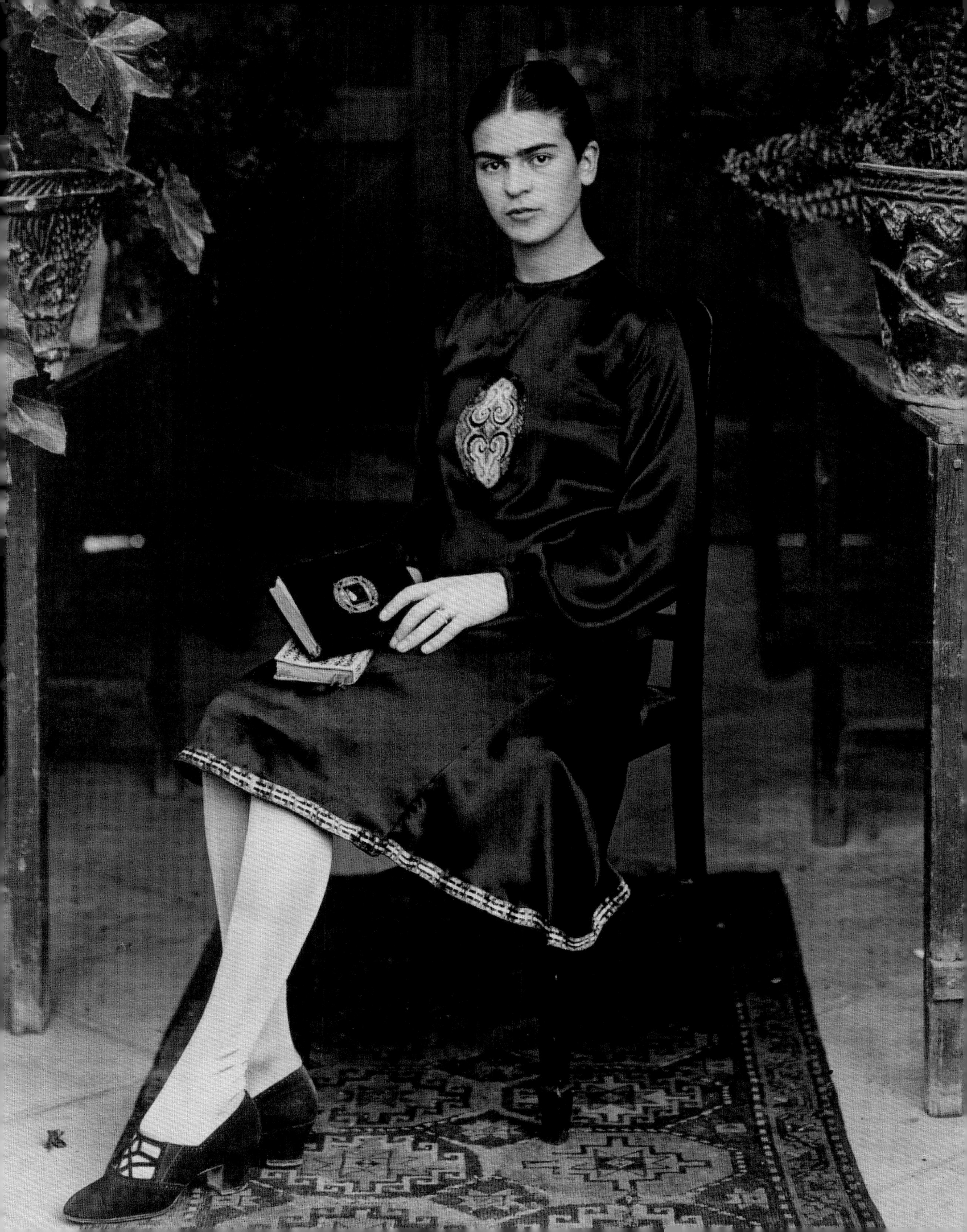

When she became a member of the Mexican Communist Party in 1927, she was already a partisan for equality and an advocate for the working class. Frida became close friends with Communist exiles Tina Modotti and Julio Antonio Mella and defined her political views as a Communist. At heart, she always wanted a fair and equal society.

Mara Romeo Kahlo While Frida was bedridden, Guillermo lent her his paints and brushes and Matilde made her a special easel. They had installed a mirror on top of her bed, so she could start painting herself easily. Those painful months were made much better thanks to being able to paint. She used to say that her pain would dissipate with every stroke of her brush, and that time expanded while she painted. She created her first oil paintings during her recovery. When she started walking again, she kept painting—it had become the best medium for expressing her feelings and providing her an outlet. She would copy *naturaleza muertas* (still lifes), landscapes, and flowers from colored lithographs Guillermo collected. Her own distinctive style started to take shape. She was very proud of what she deemed her first serious artwork: *Charola de Amapolas* (Tray of Poppies). When she felt stronger, she took that painting to Diego to ask if she had *madera para ser artista* (what it takes to be an artist). She did, Diego responded. And the rest, as they say, is history.

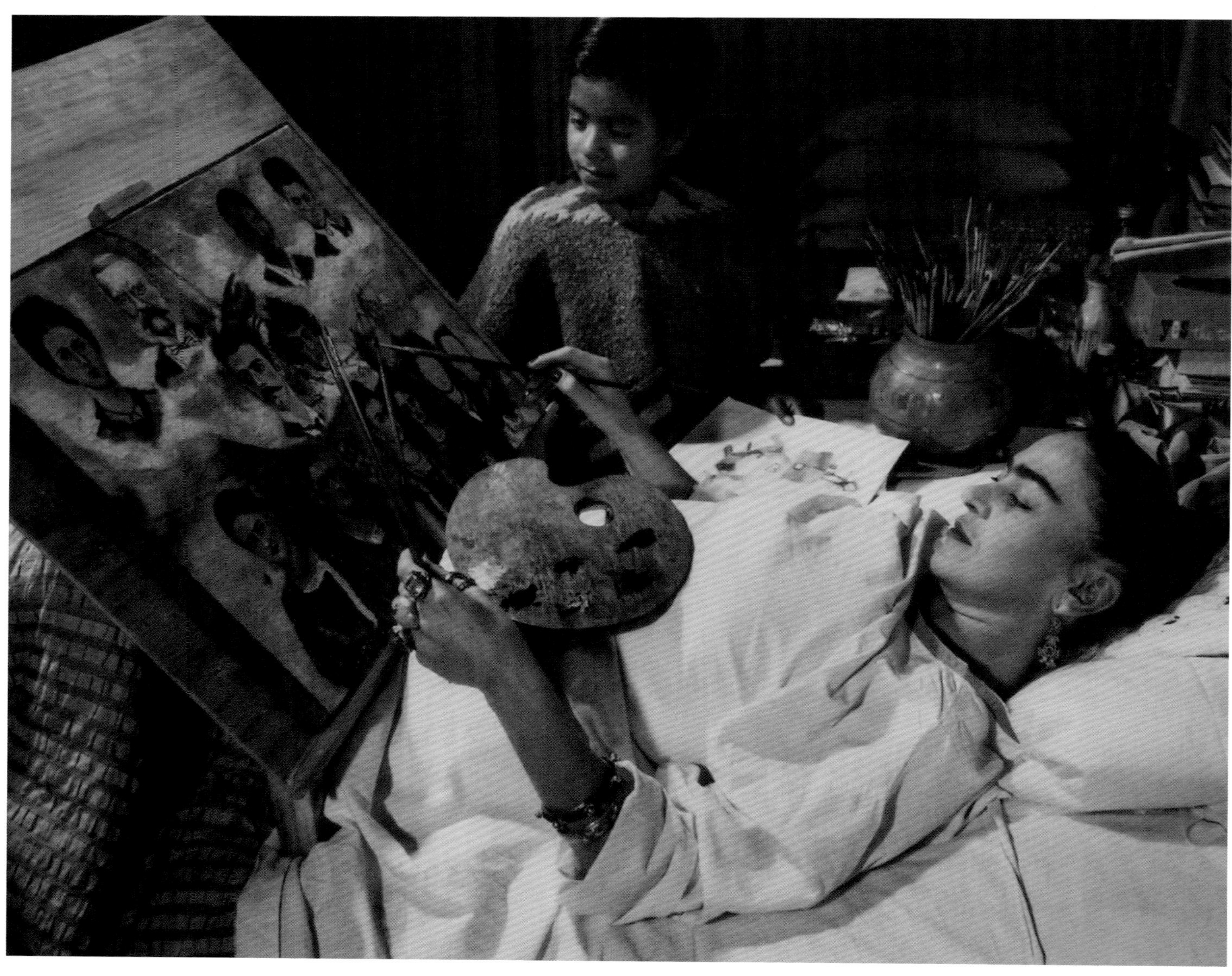

Frida painting in a bed at the Hospital Inglés, Mexico City, ca. 1950

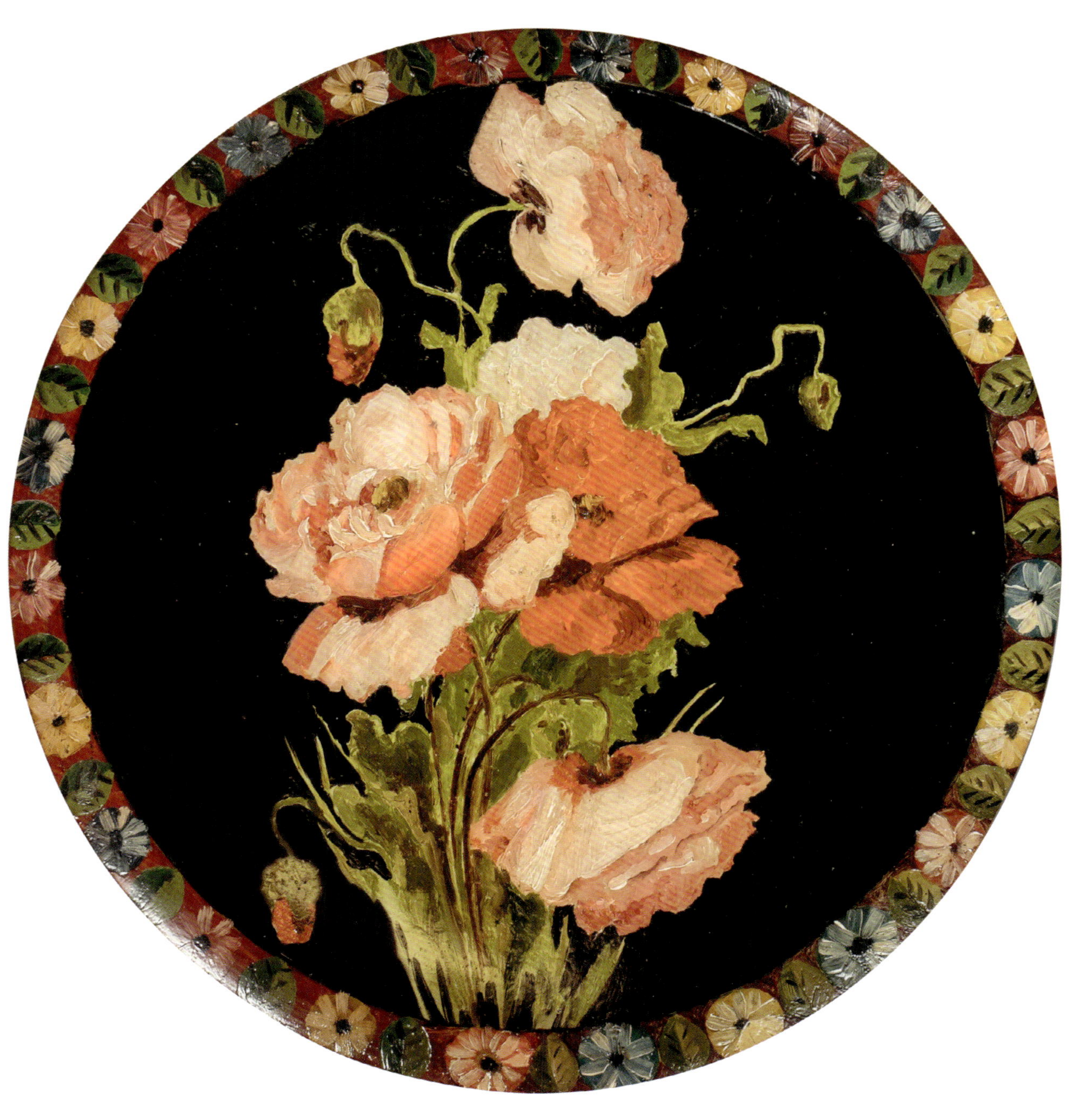

Frida Kahlo, *Charola de Amapolas* (Tray of Poppies), 1924. Oil on metal, diameter: 16 in. (41 cm)

Frida first met Diego Rivera at a meeting of the Communist party when she was around 20 and he was 47. Later, in 1926, while Diego was painting frescos at the office of Public Education, Frida went to visit him and brought him this artwork to ask him if she had any talent as an artist.

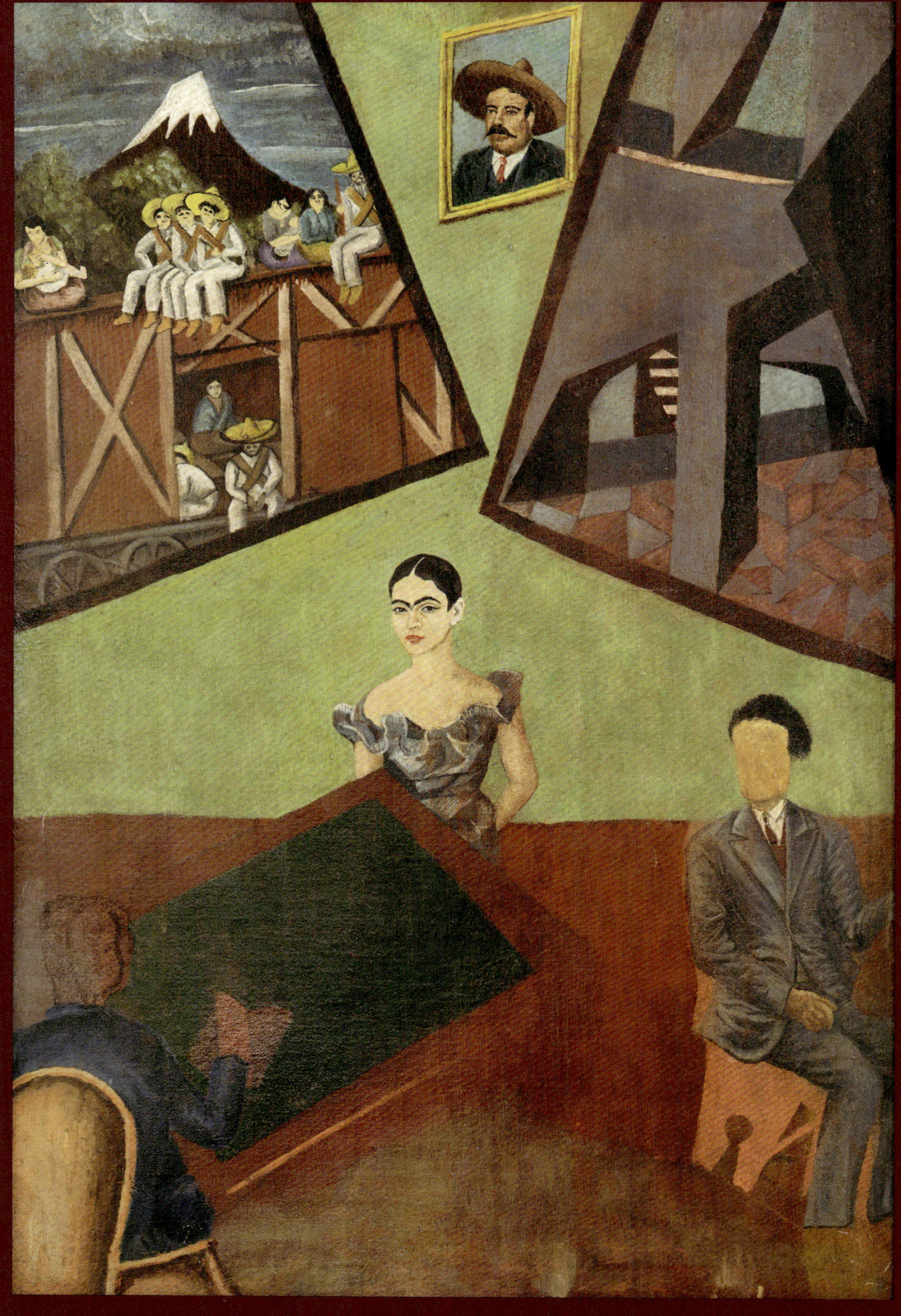

OPPOSITE Frida Kahlo, *La Adelita, Pancho Villa and Frida*, 1927. Oil on canvas mounted on board, 25.5 x 17.75 in. (64.75 x 44.5 cm)

ABOVE Frida practicing her various signatures inside a geometry book, ca. 1921

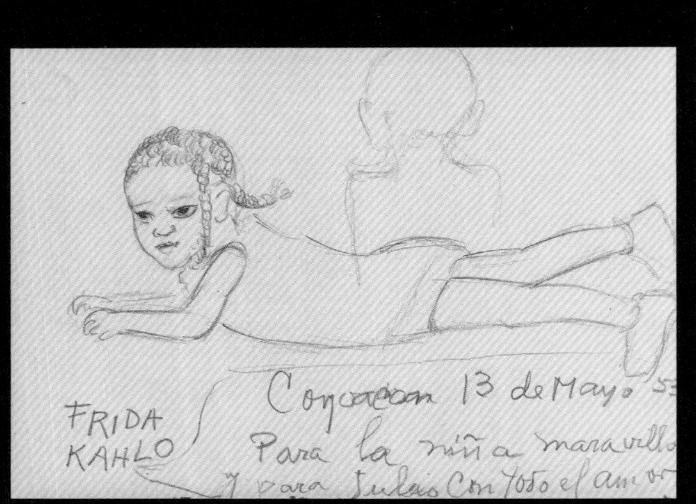

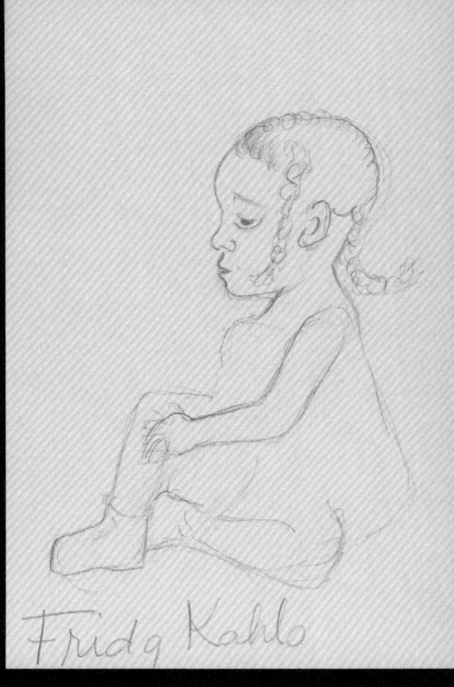

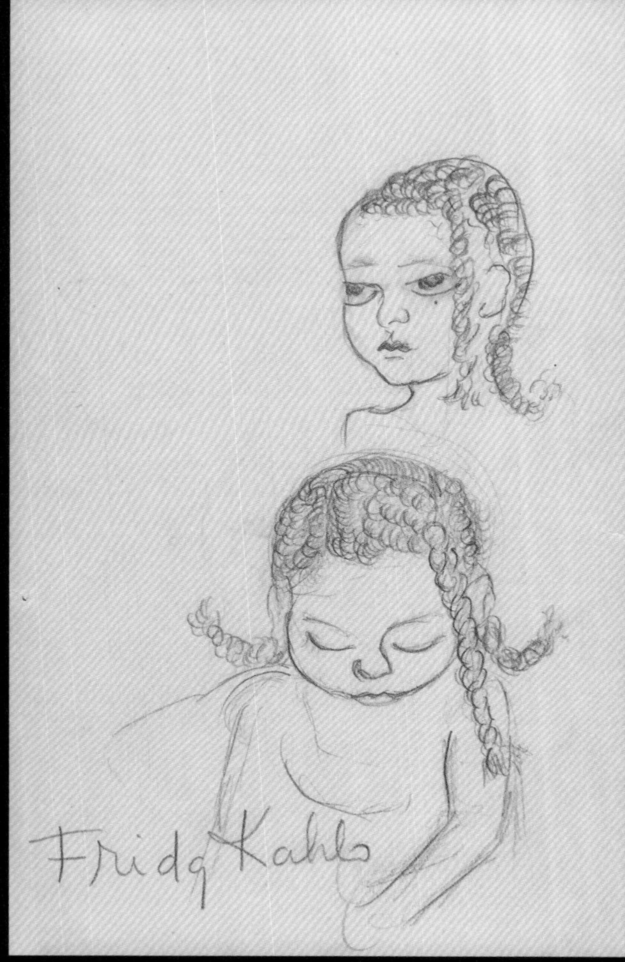

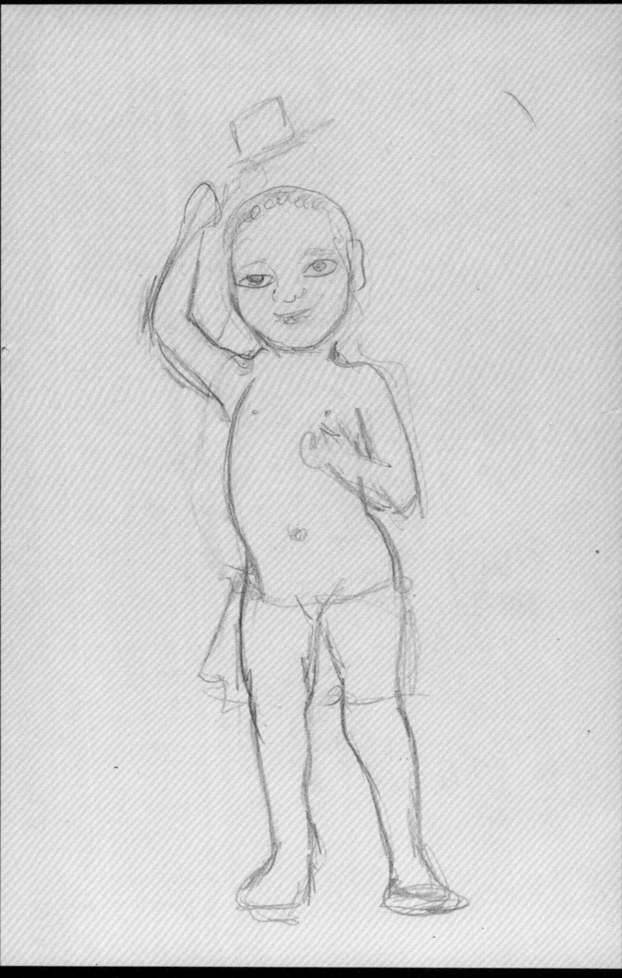

TOP Frida Kahlo, *Two Girls* (front and back), ca. 1932. Pencil on paper, 5.75 x 8.5 in. (14.5 x 22 cm); 8.5 x 5.75 in. (22 x 14.5 cm). One side features a dedication to her niece Isolda, dated 1953.

BOTTOM Frida Kahlo, *Untitled* (front and back), ca. 1932. Pencil on paper, 8.5 x 5.75 in. (22 x 14.5 cm).

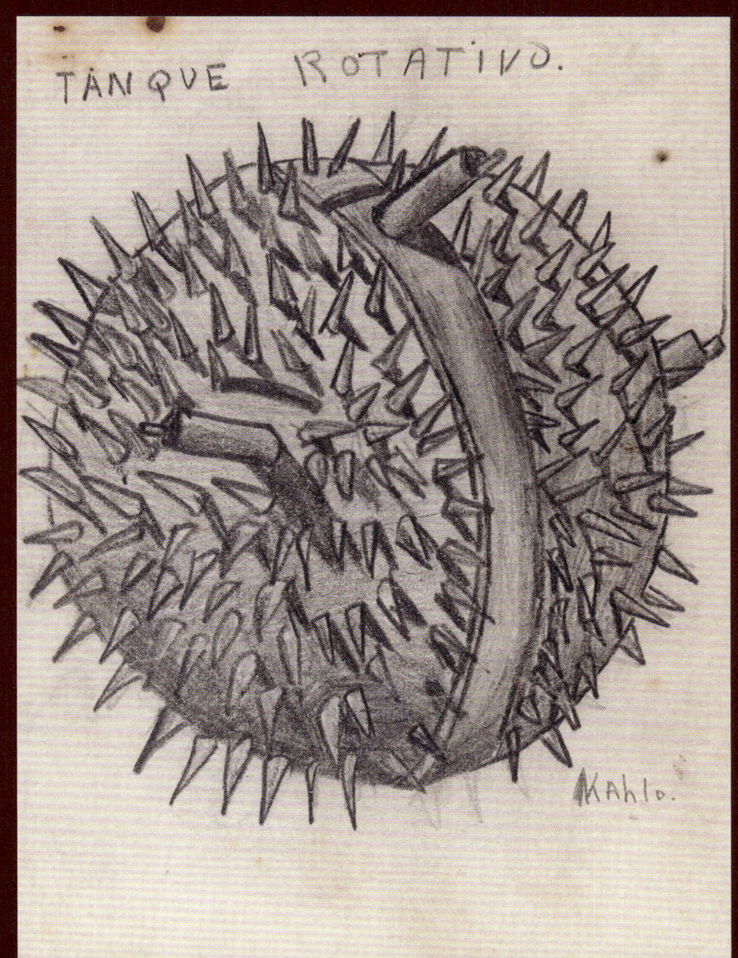
TANQUE ROTATIVO.
Kahlo.

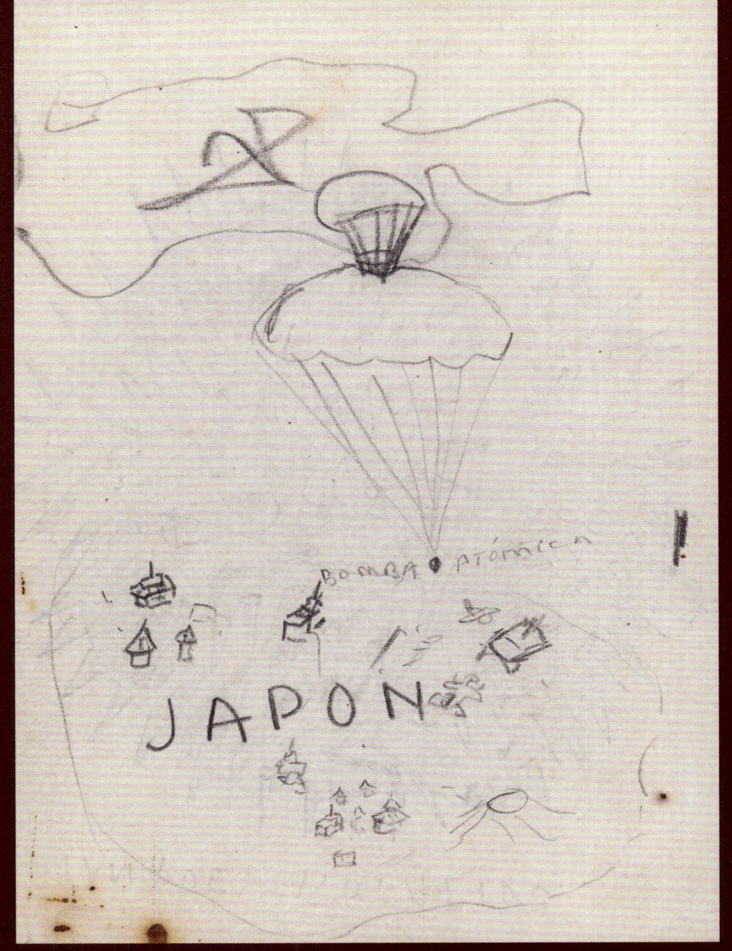
BOMBA ATÓMICA
JAPON

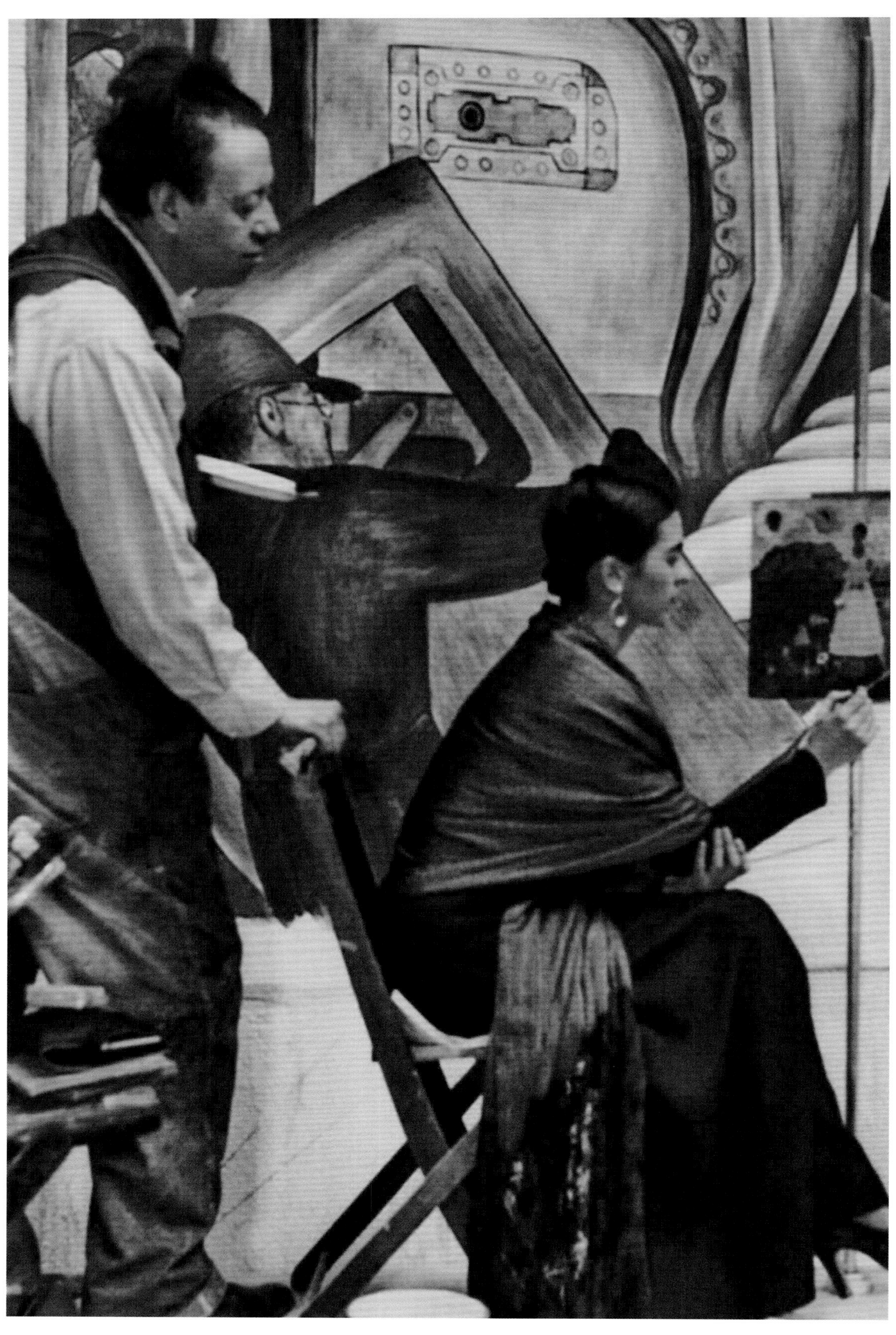

Frida painting while Diego Rivera watches in front of one of his murals in the United States, ca. 1933. Photo by Lucienne Bloch

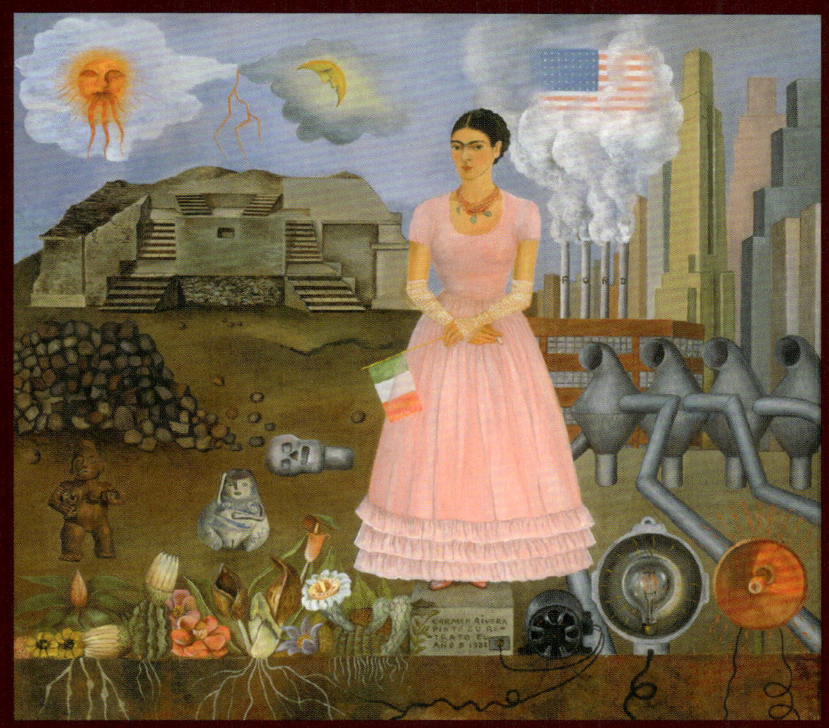

March the first - 1933.

Georgia,
Was wanderful to hear your voice again. Every day since I called you and many times before, months ago I wanted to write you a letter. I wrote many, but every one seemed more stupid and empty and I torn them up. I can't write in English all I would like to tell, especially to you. I am sending this one because I promissed it to you. I felt terrible when Sibil Brown told me that you were sick but I still don't know what is the matter with you. Please Georgia dear if you can't write, ask Stiegliesz to do it for you and let me know how are you feeling Will you? I'll be in Detroit two more weeks. I would like to tell you

every thing that happened to me since the last time we saw each other, but most of them are sad and you musn't know sad things now. After all I shouldn't complain because I have been happy in many ways thoug! Diego is good to me, and you can't imagine how happy he has been working on the frescoes here. I have been painting a little too and that helped. I thought of you a lot and never forget your wonderful hands and the color of your eyes. I will see you soon. I am sure that in New York I will be much happier. If you still in the Hospital when I come back I will bring you flowers, but it is so diffiicult to find the ones I would like for you! I would be so happy if you could write me even two words. I like you very much Georgia.

Frieda.

My adress here. The Wardel Apts. 15 Kirby DETROIT.

TOP Frida Kahlo, *Self-portrait on the Borderline Between Mexico and the United States*, 1932. Oil on metal, 12.5 x 13.75 in. (31.75 x 35 cm). Painted while Frida was in Detroit accompanying Diego Rivera, scholars have written that this work is about Frida's struggles navigating the differences between her beloved home country and the US.

BOTTOM Letter from Frida to artist Georgia O'Keeffe, when Frida was in Detroit with Diego Rivera as he was finishing a mural commission, 1933

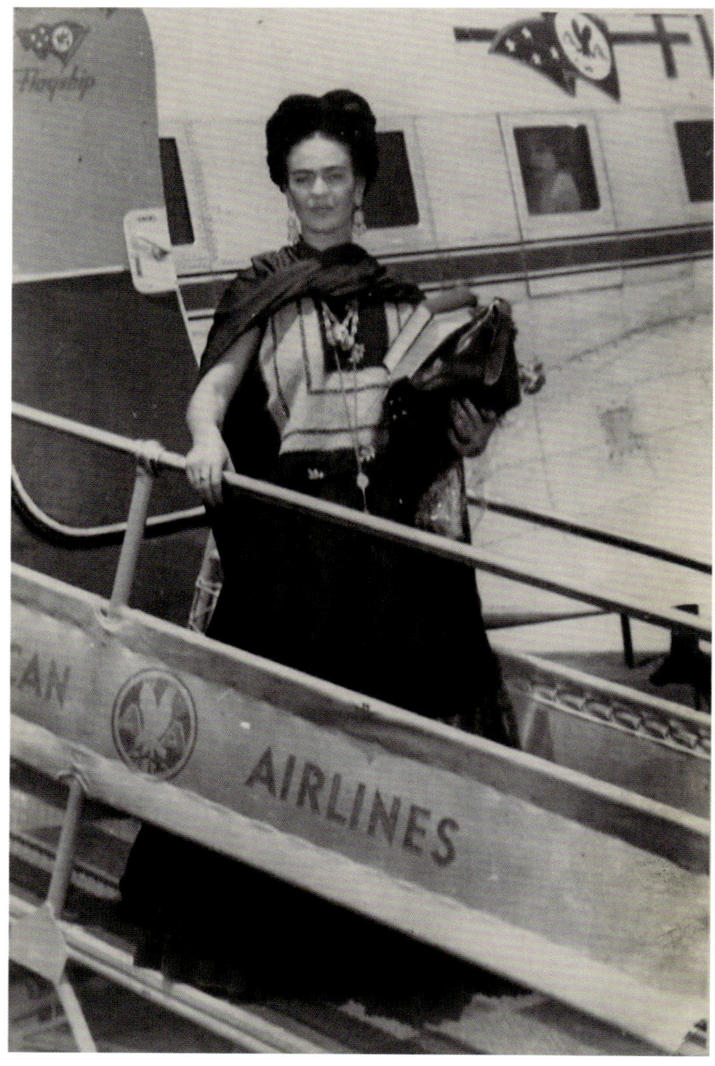

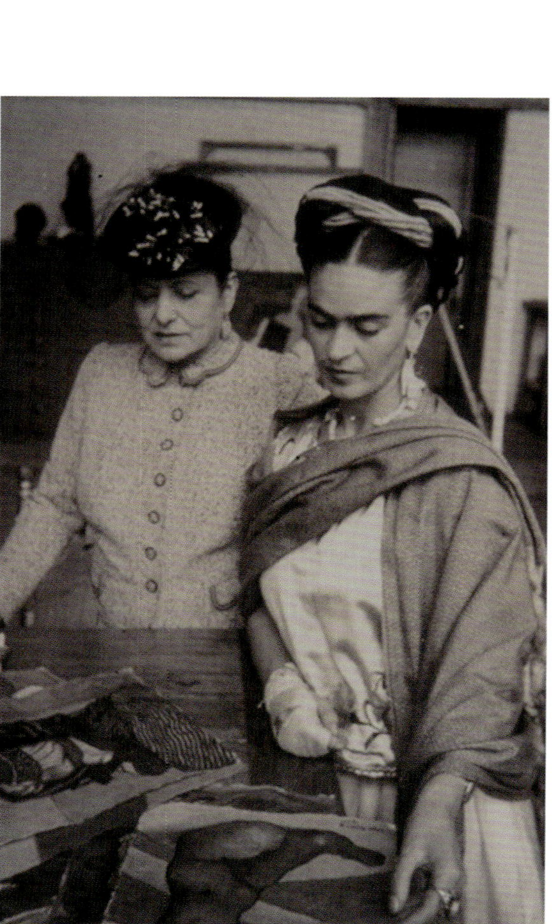

POST UNITED AIR LINES CARD

Please address and return to stewardess who will stamp and mail for you . . .

Tu tía Fridu y
yo la mandamos
muchos besos.
Doctorcito
Fridu,
Besos para la chaparrita
de su
Friduchin.

a la Srita
Ysolda P. Kahlo
Allende 59
Coyoacan
D.F.
Mexico

United's Mainliner fleet includes giant sleepers for overnight coast-to-coast flights and 21-passenger day planes for inter-city flights.

A NATURAL COLOR REPRODUCTION FROM KODACHROME FOR UNITED AIR LINES

D

TOP LEFT Frida with the art collector Helena Rubenstein, ca. 1940

TOP RIGHT Frida disembarking a plane, ca. 1942, on one of her many trips to the United States. Frida traveled extensively—sometimes accompanying Diego Rivera, other times for her own exhibitions abroad, and often for medical appointments and surgeries.

BOTTOM Post card from Frida to her niece Isolda. At the bottom she writes, "Kisses for the *chaparrita* from your Friduchin"

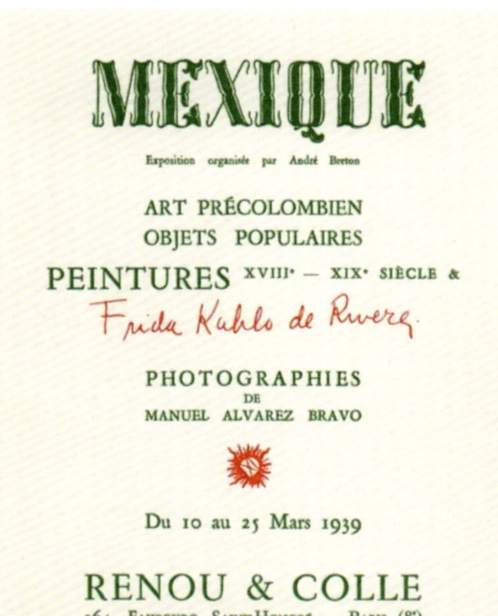

MEXIQUE

Exposition organisée par André Breton

ART PRÉCOLOMBIEN
OBJETS POPULAIRES
PEINTURES XVIIIe – XIXe SIÈCLE &
Frida Kahlo de Rivera.

PHOTOGRAPHIES
DE
MANUEL ALVAREZ BRAVO

Du 10 au 25 Mars 1939

RENOU & COLLE
164, Faubourg Saint-Honoré – Paris (8e)

EXPOSICION INTERNACIONAL
DEL SURREALISMO

MEXICO · 1940

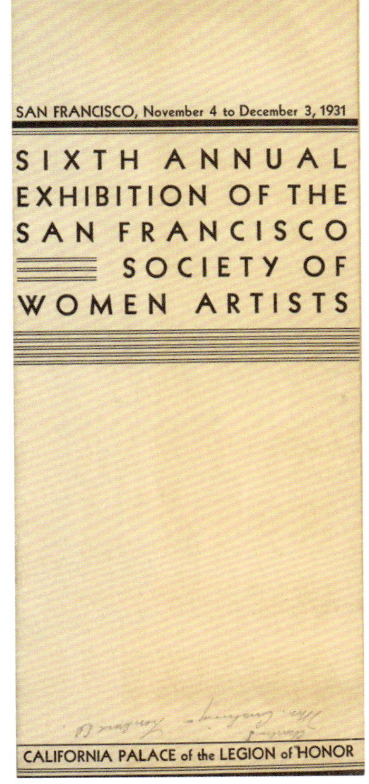

SAN FRANCISCO, November 4 to December 3, 1931

SIXTH ANNUAL EXHIBITION OF THE SAN FRANCISCO SOCIETY OF WOMEN ARTISTS

CALIFORNIA PALACE of the LEGION of HONOR

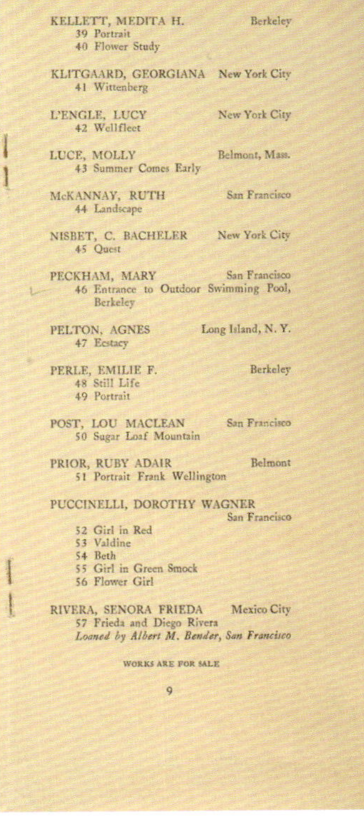

KELLETT, MEDITA H. — Berkeley
39 Portrait
40 Flower Study

KLITGAARD, GEORGIANA — New York City
41 Wittenberg

L'ENGLE, LUCY — New York City
42 Wellfleet

LUCE, MOLLY — Belmont, Mass.
43 Summer Comes Early

McKANNAY, RUTH — San Francisco
44 Landscape

NISBET, C. BACHELER — New York City
45 Quest

PECKHAM, MARY — San Francisco
46 Entrance to Outdoor Swimming Pool, Berkeley

PELTON, AGNES — Long Island, N. Y.
47 Ecstacy

PERLE, EMILIE F. — Berkeley
48 Still Life
49 Portrait

POST, LOU MACLEAN — San Francisco
50 Sugar Loaf Mountain

PRIOR, RUBY ADAIR — Belmont
51 Portrait Frank Wellington

PUCCINELLI, DOROTHY WAGNER — San Francisco
52 Girl in Red
53 Valdine
54 Beth
55 Girl in Green Smock
56 Flower Girl

RIVERA, SENORA FRIEDA — Mexico City
57 Frieda and Diego Rivera
Loaned by Albert M. Bender, San Francisco

WORKS ARE FOR SALE

9

Select announcements and catalogues for exhibitions in which Frida's work was included.

TOP LEFT *Mexique* announcement, the Paris exhibition curated by André Breton, 1939. Frida traveled to Paris for the show and was deeply troubled by Breton's approach to Mexican art and culture.

TOP RIGHT Catalogue for *Exposición Internacional del Surrealismo*, one of the first exhibitions of Surrealist art in Mexico City, 1940

BOTTOM LEFT Catalogue cover and interior page with list of works featuring Frida's married name for the *Sixth Annual Exhibition of the San Francisco Society of Women Artists*, November 4–December 3, 1931. It is believed this is the first exhibition in which Frida's work was featured in the United States.

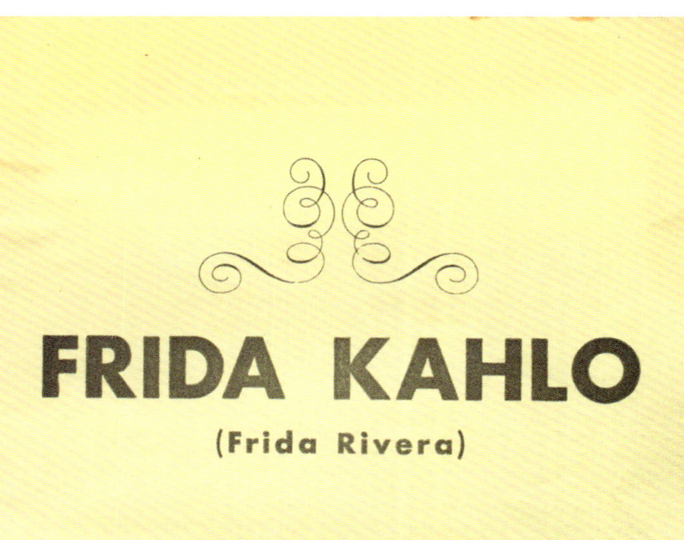

FRIDA KAHLO

(Frida Rivera)

NOVEMBER FIRST TO FIFTEENTH

JULIEN LEVY GALLERY

15 EAST 57 • NEW YORK

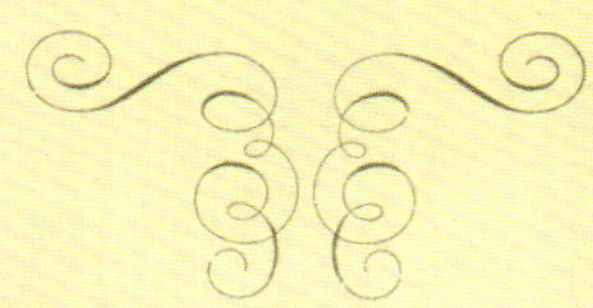

C A T A L O G U E

1. BETWEEN THE CURTAINS
2. FULANG CHANG AND MYSELF
3. THE SQUARE IS THEIRS
4. I WITH MY NURSE
5. THEY ASK FOR PLANES AND ONLY GET STRAW WINGS
6. I BELONG TO MY OWNER
7. MY FAMILY
8. THE HEART
9. MY DRESS WAS THERE HANGING
10. WHAT WATER GAVE ME
11. IXCUHINTLI DOG WITH ME
12. PITAHAYAS
13. TUNAS
14. FOOD FROM THE EARTH
15. REMEMBRANCE OF AN OPEN WOUND
16. THE LOST DESIRE
17. BIRTH
18. DRESSED UP FOR PARADISE
19. SHE PLAYS ALONE
20. PASSIONATELY IN LOVE
21. BURBANK—AMERICAN FRUIT MAKER
22. XOCHITL
23. THE FRAME
24. EYE
25. SURVIVOR

ABOVE Announcement and list of works for Frida's first solo exhibition at Julien Levy Gallery, New York, 1938

OPPOSITE Frida Kahlo, *Fulang-Chang and I*, 1937. Oil on Masonite with painted mirror frame, 22.25 x 17.25 x 1.75 in. (56.5 x 44.1 x 4.4 cm). This painting was part of her exhibition at Julien Levy Gallery.

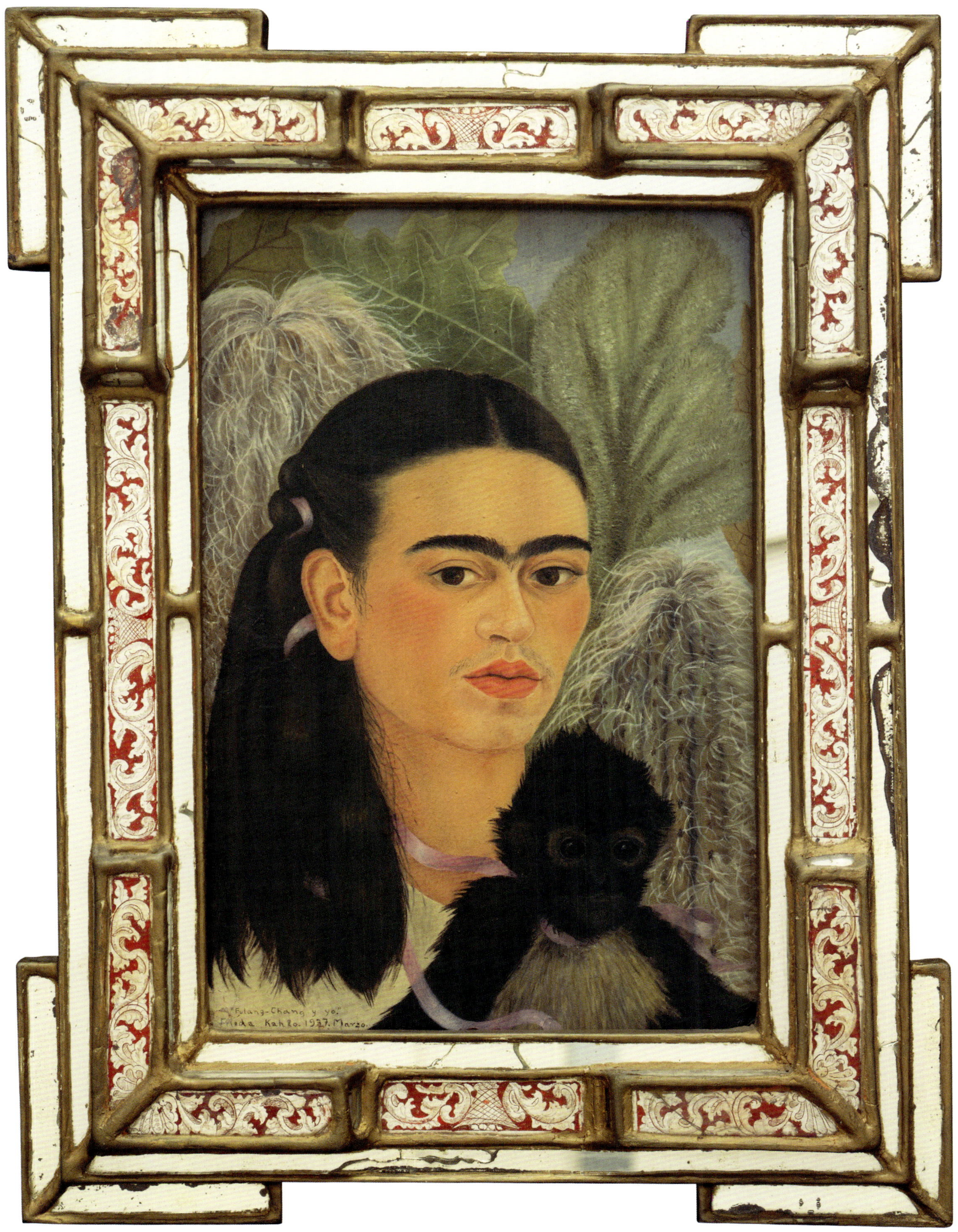
"Fulang-Chang y yo."
Frida Kahlo. 1937. Marzo.

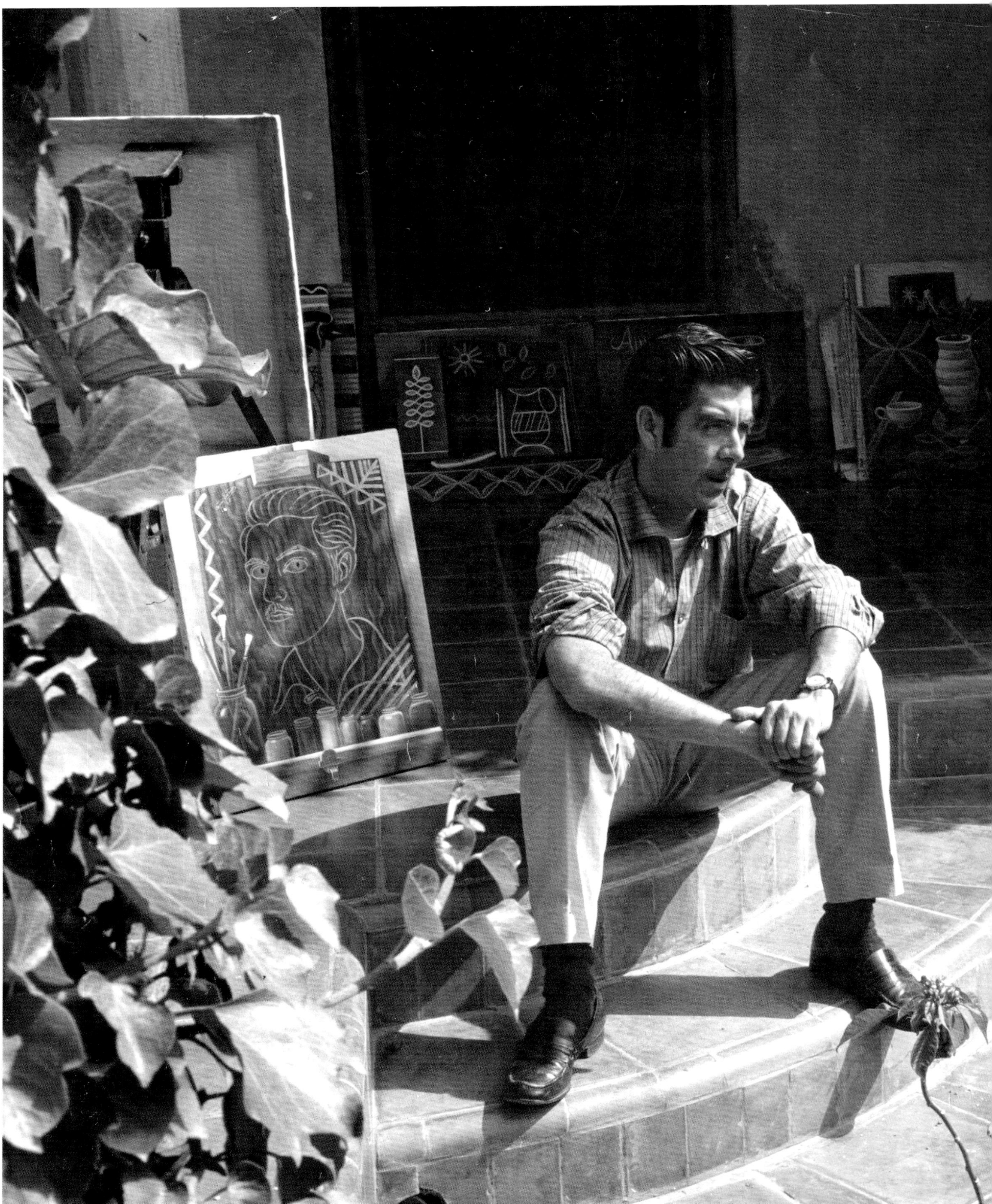

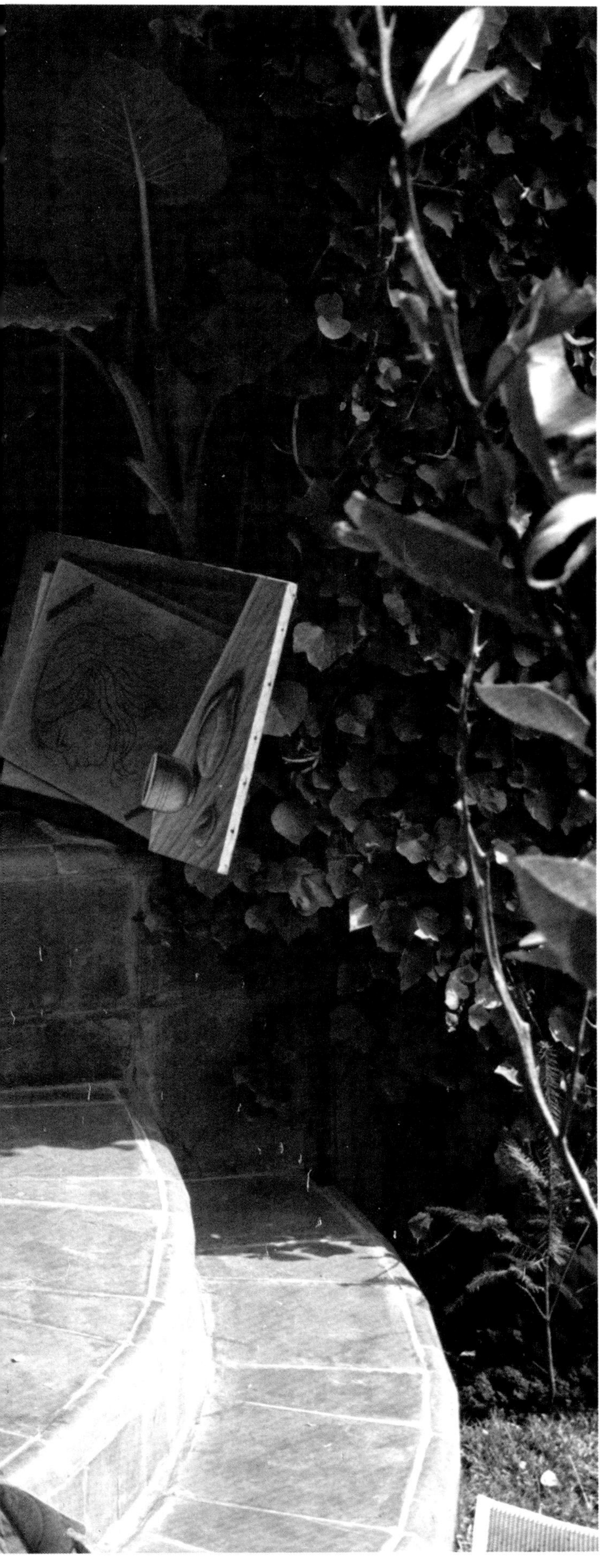

Mara Romeo Kahlo Frida was invited to become a teacher at the Escuela Nacional de Pintura, Escultura y Grabado, also called "La Esmeralda," in 1943. After a few years it became harder for Frida to go from Coyoacán to La Esmeralda, and a smaller group of students made their way to Coyoacán to have classes at Casa Azul. This inner circle of students was called Los Fridos. The group comprised Arturo Estrada, Arturo Garcia Bustos, Fanny Rabel, and Guillermo Monroy. They admired Frida and her unorthodox way of teaching—she would let them be truly creative and express their emotions. She encouraged them to go out on the streets and to paint the everyday. Frida believed that good artists were made by creating from their gut, from what was inside of them. Inspiration can come from the outside, she counseled them, but creating art comes from the inside.

Diego always said this about Frida's painting—that she painted from the inside out. She never imposed any aesthetic rules—for herself or those she taught. And her advice for her students went beyond just how to paint; she was a mentor, a guide. She encouraged her students to consider social and political issues—how their immediate surroundings impacted their lives and their communities—and to appreciate Mexican culture, and incorporate all these elements into their art.

She ultimately became good friends with her students. When she taught them at either Casa Azul or Casa Kahlo, the students often stayed for lunch. They would eat quesadillas in the courtyard, talk, and paint. It was a very relaxed atmosphere.

Frida Hentschel Frida did not see herself as a teacher though she was an extraordinary one according to those who worked with her; rather, she considered herself a student of life and art. She was a loyal advocate for those she mentored. Whenever she had the opportunity, she spoke to friends, colleagues, and the local government to bring them into the fold even further. She went to the City Council in Coyoacán and convinced them to have the Los Fridos paint Los Lavaderos (public spaces to wash clothes, financed by the government).

Arturo Estrada, one of Frida's closest and most devoted students, sitting in the courtyard of Casa Kahlo, Coyoacán, ca. 1957

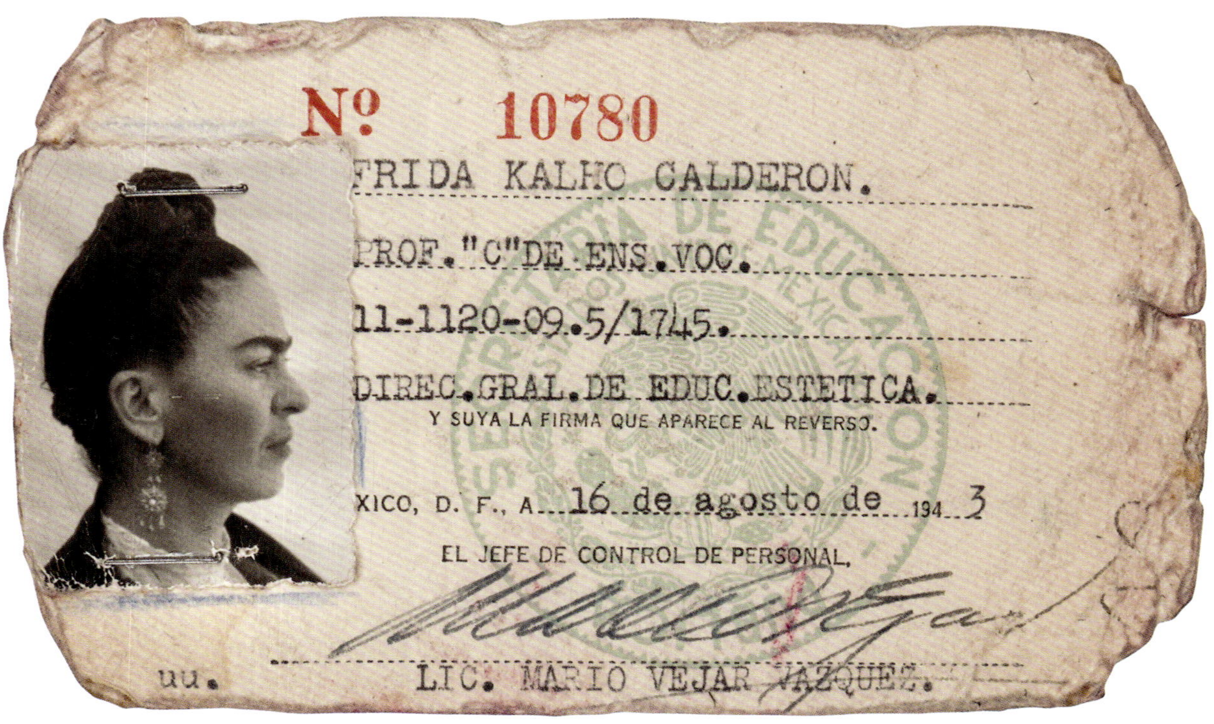

Nº 10780
FRIDA KALHO CALDERON.
PROF."C"DE ENS.VOC.
11-1120-09.5/1745.
DIREC.GRAL.DE EDUC.ESTETICA.
Y SUYA LA FIRMA QUE APARECE AL REVERSO.
XICO, D. F., A 16 de agosto de 1943
EL JEFE DE CONTROL DE PERSONAL.
uu. LIC. MARIO VEJAR VAZQUEZ.

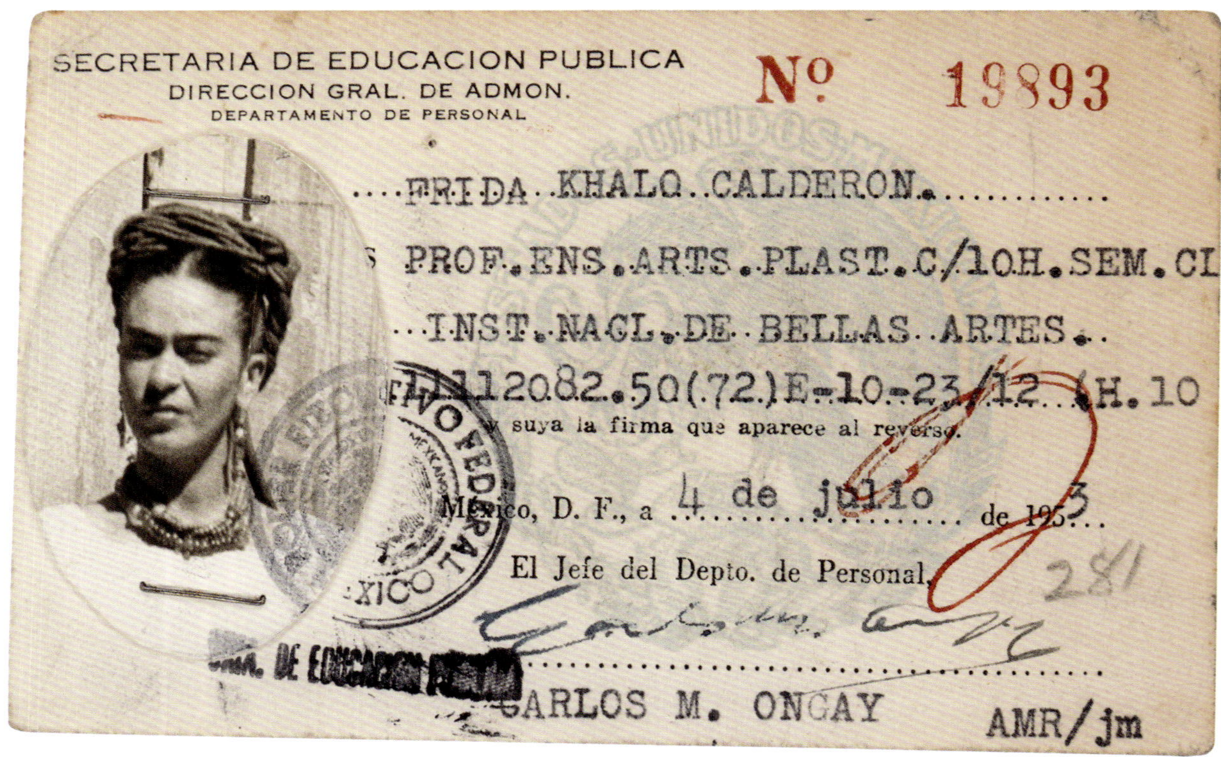

SECRETARIA DE EDUCACION PUBLICA
DIRECCION GRAL. DE ADMON.
DEPARTAMENTO DE PERSONAL
Nº 19893
FRIDA KHALO CALDERON.
PROF.ENS.ARTS.PLAST.C/10H.SEM.CL
INST.NACL.DE BELLAS ARTES.
11112082.50(72)E-10-23/12 H.10
y suya la firma que aparece al reverso.
México, D. F., a 4 de julio de 1953
El Jefe del Depto. de Personal.
CARLOS M. ONGAY AMR/jm

ABOVE Frida's various teaching credentials from 1943 and 1953. She began teaching at Escuela de Pintura y Escultura "La Esmeralda" in 1943. As her health continued to decline, many of her classes eventually took place at Casa Azul and Casa Kahlo, Coyoacán.

OPPOSITE Frida in front of a sketch for Diego Rivera's mural *Panamerican Unity*, San Francisco, 1940. Photo by Wittlock

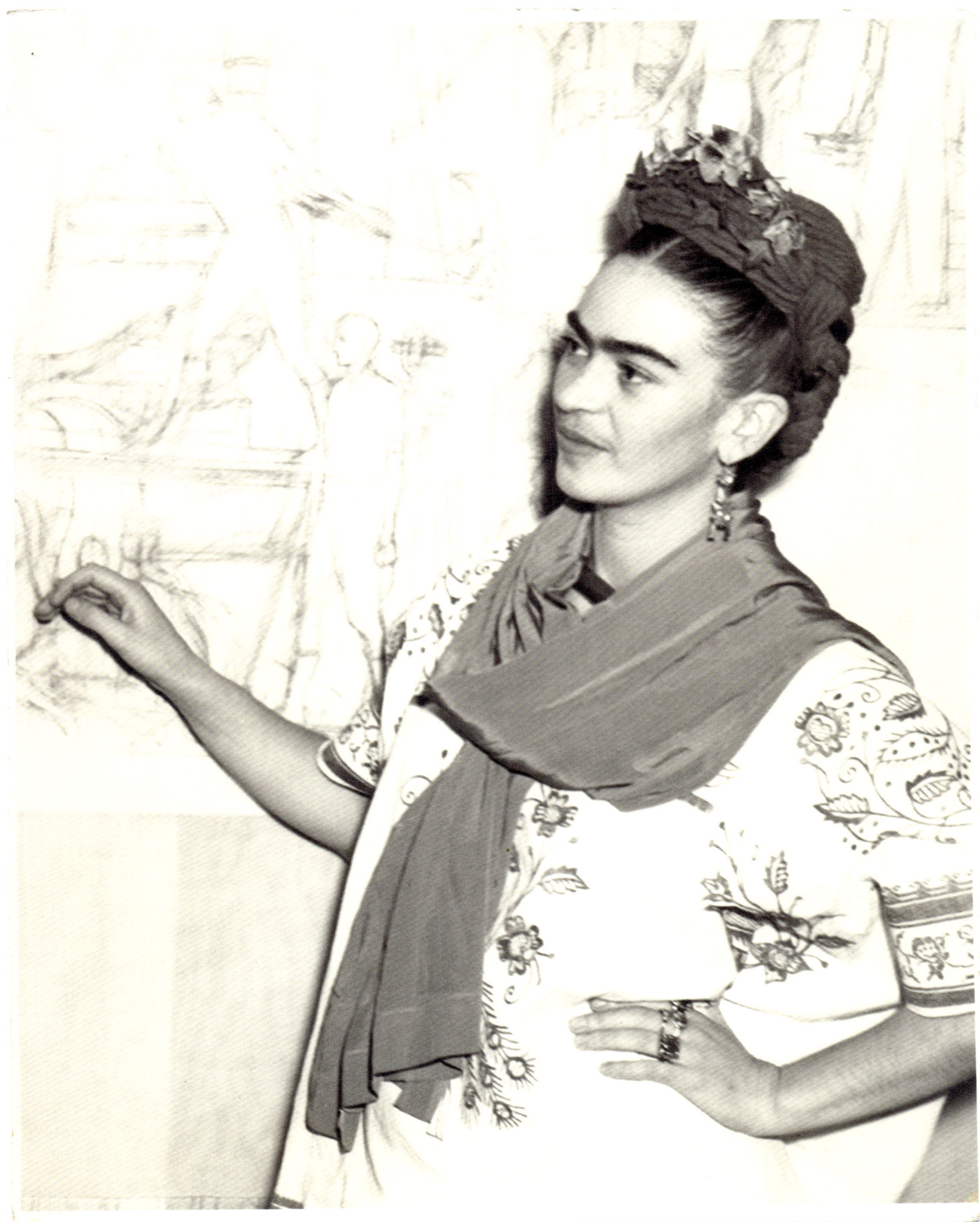

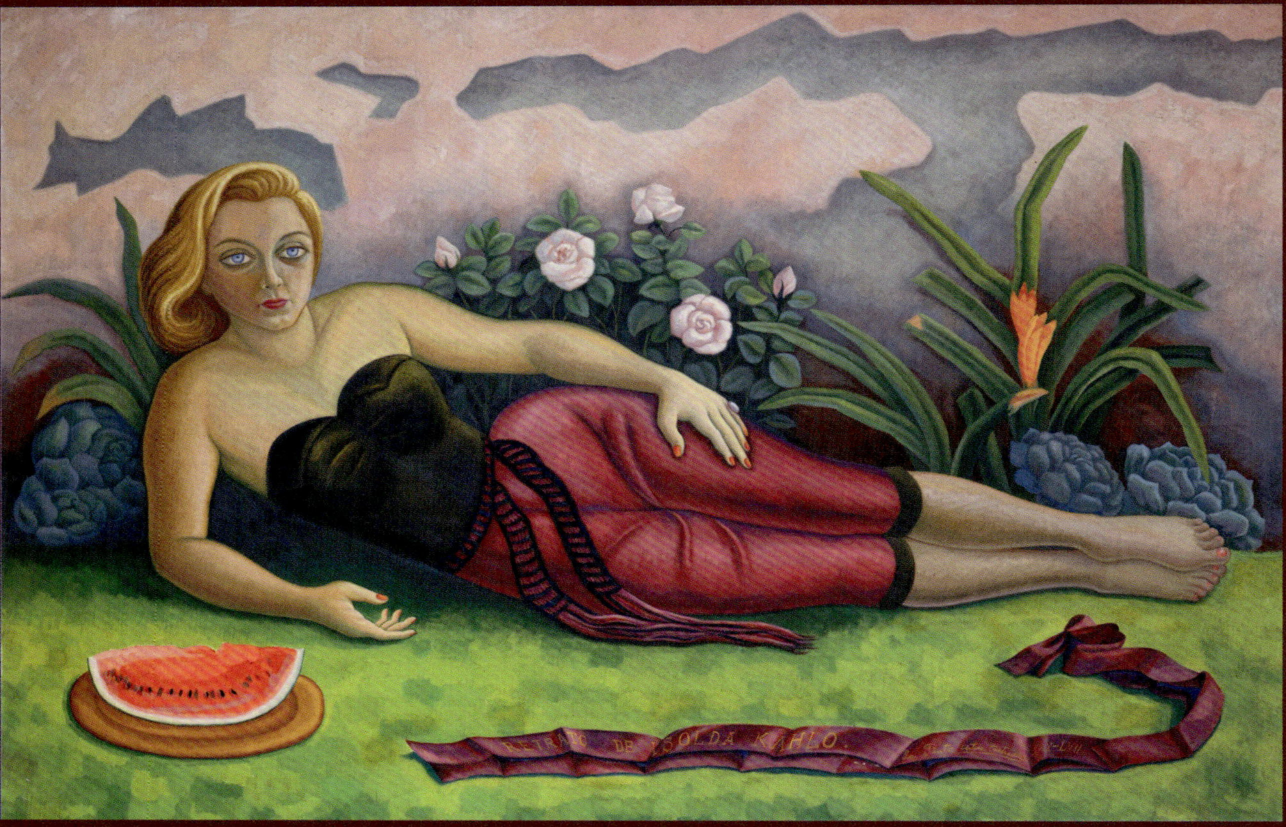

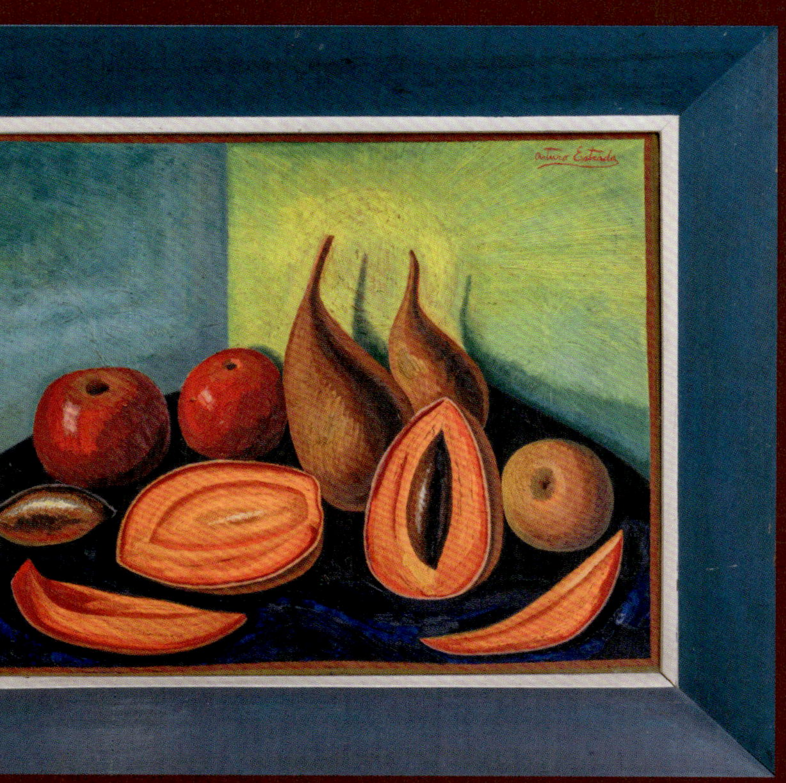

n, *Portrait of Isolda Kahlo*, 1957. Oil on canvas, 55 x 69 in. (140 x 175 cm)

strada, *Apples with Mamey*, 1955. Oil on canvas, 17.25 x 23 in. (44 x 58 cm)

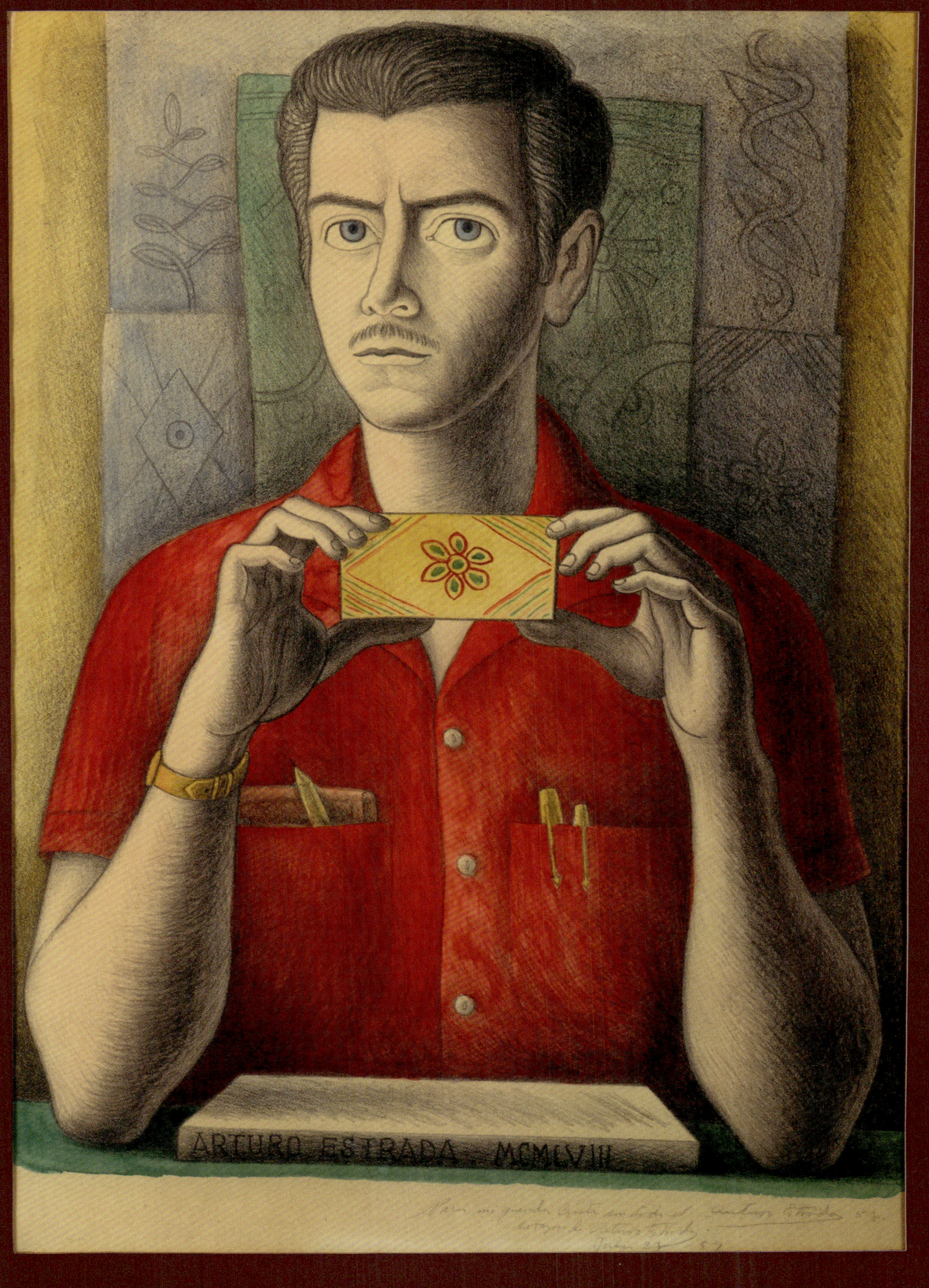

Arturo Estrada, *Self-portrait*, 1957. Colored pencil, 20.7 x 15.75 in. (52.5 x 40 cm)

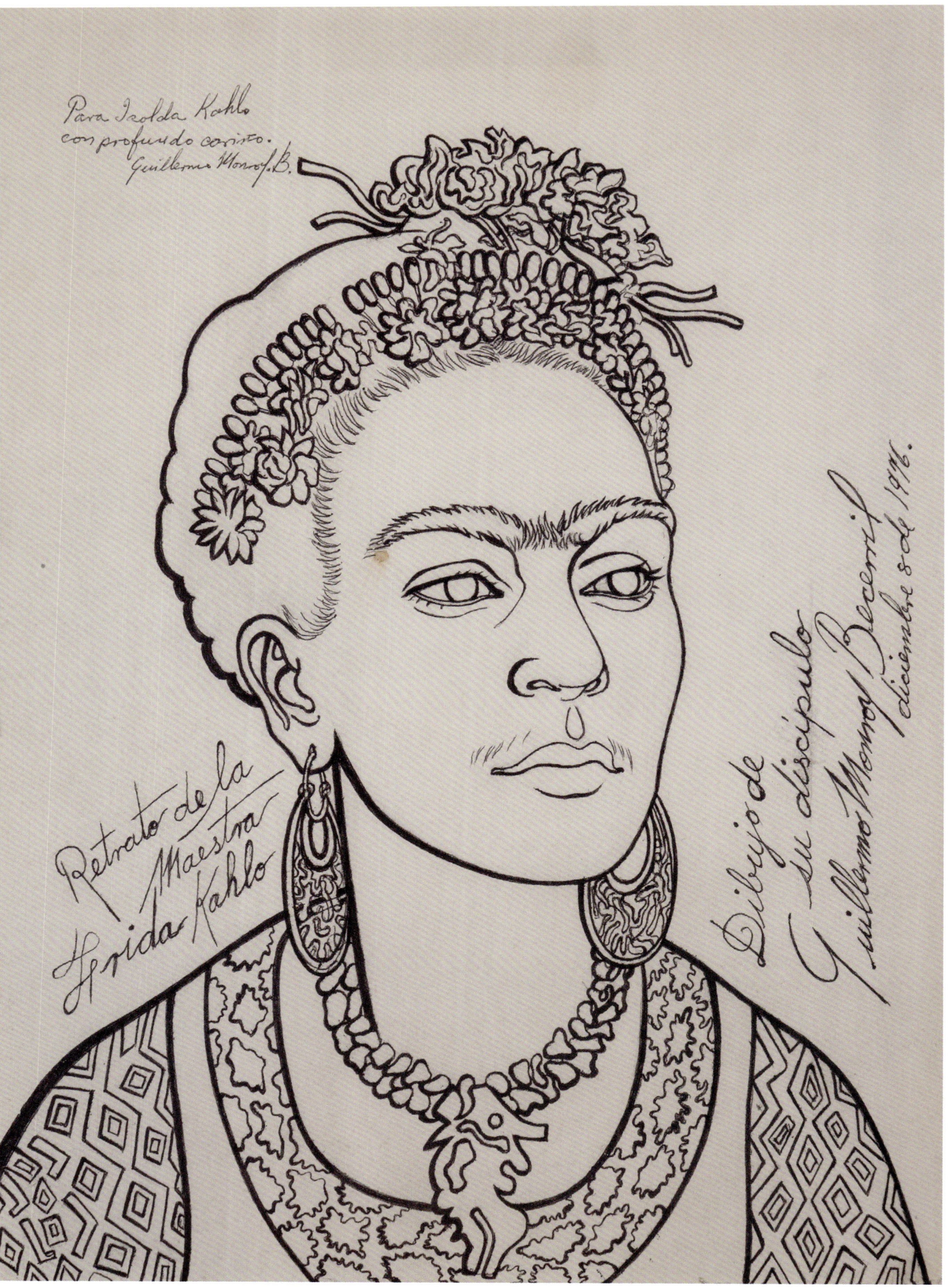
Para Isolda Kahlo
con profundo cariño.
Guillermo Monroy B.
Retrato de la
Maestra
Frida Kahlo
Dibujo de
su discípulo
Guillermo Monroy Becerril
diciembre 8 de 1976.

Mara de Anda After Frida died, Los Fridos continued to gather at Casa Kahlo. They had a very close relationship with Cristina, Isolda, and later with my mother Mara. They remained very dear to us, particularly Arturo Estrada. Guillermo Monroy was *un eterno enamorado* of my grandmother Isolda, who continued to pay her visits for many years. Arturo Garcia Bustos married Rina Lazo, Diego's assistant. Bustos completed his studies with the great Mexican muralist José Clemente Orozco, who was a famous contemporary of Diego's. We have preserved in our family archive and collection several paintings and photos of Los Fridos.

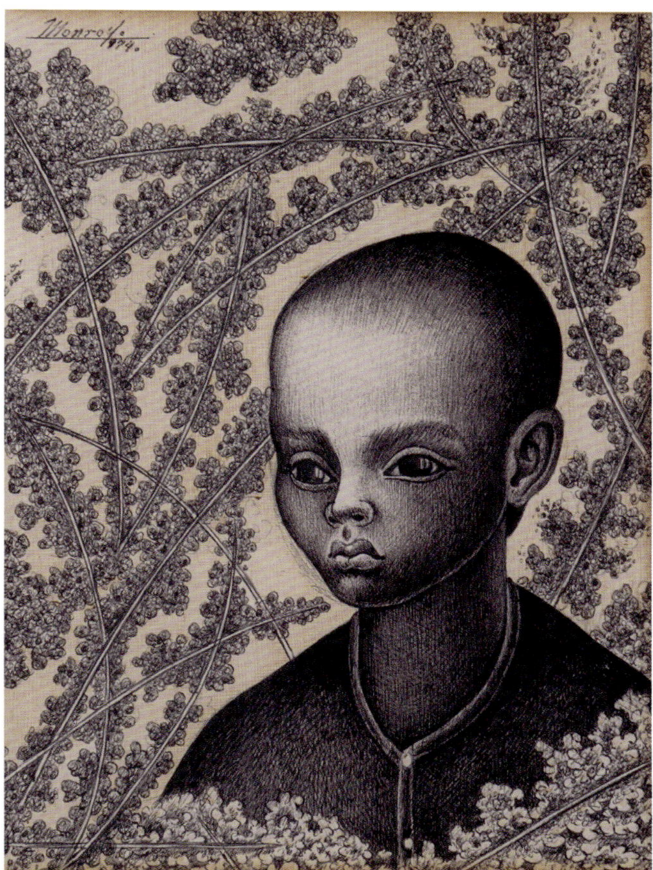

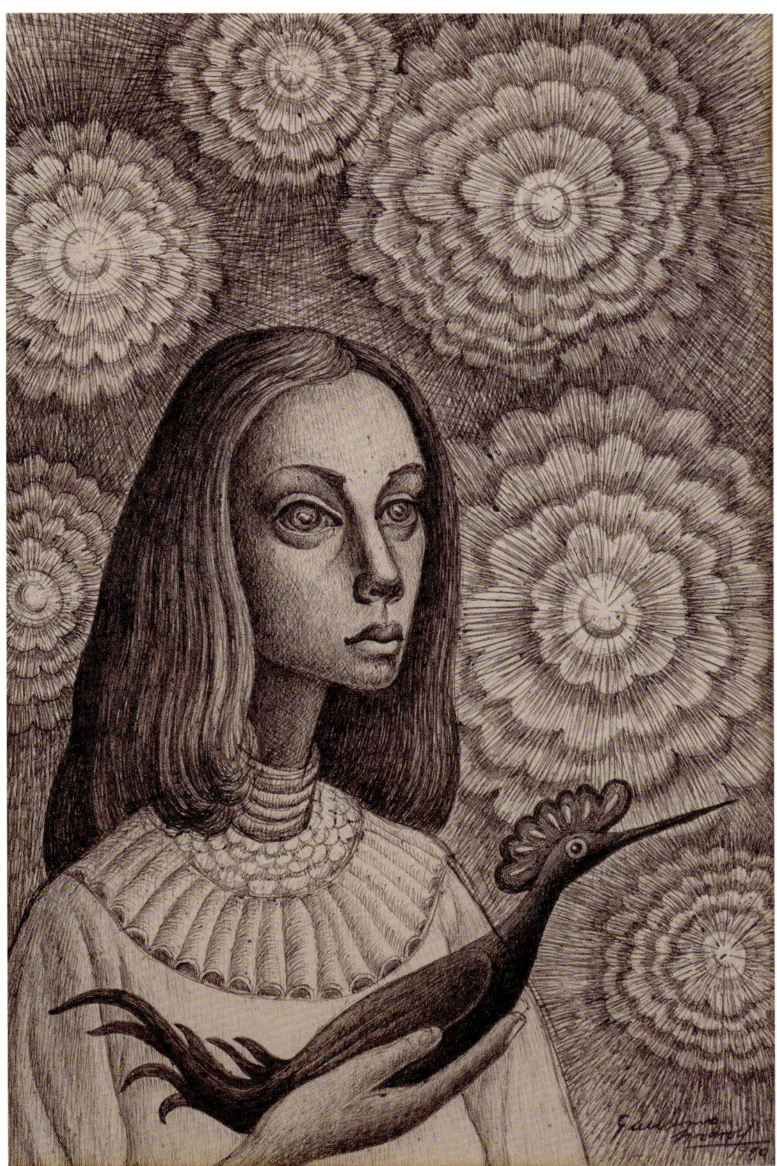

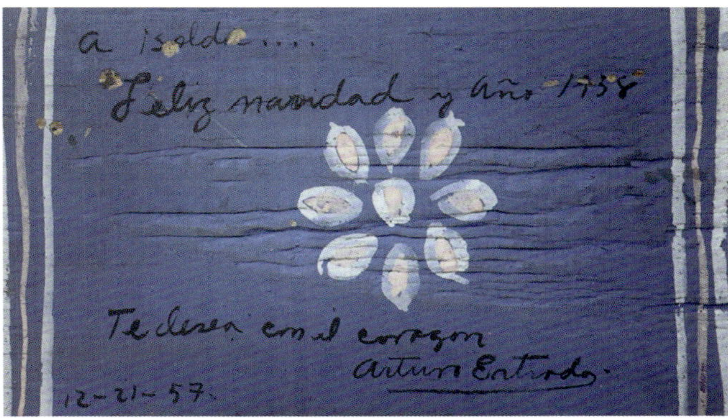

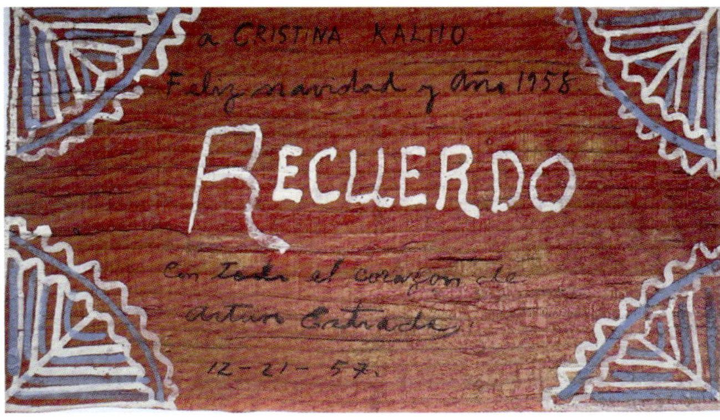

OPPOSITE Guillermo Monroy, *Portrait of the Teacher Frida Kahlo*, 1976. Ink on paper, 12.5 x 9.5 in. (32 x 24 cm)

ABOVE, LEFT Guillermo Monroy, *Portrait of Isolda Kahlo at Age 19*, ca. 1973. Ink on paper, 12.75 x 8.75 in. (32.5 x 22 cm)

ABOVE, TOP RIGHT Guillermo Monroy, *Self-portrait*, 1974. Ink on paper, 9.5 x 7.5 in. (24 x 19 cm)

ABOVE, MIDDLE AND BOTTOM Christmas greetings for Frida's sister Cristina and niece Isolda from Arturo Estrada, 1957

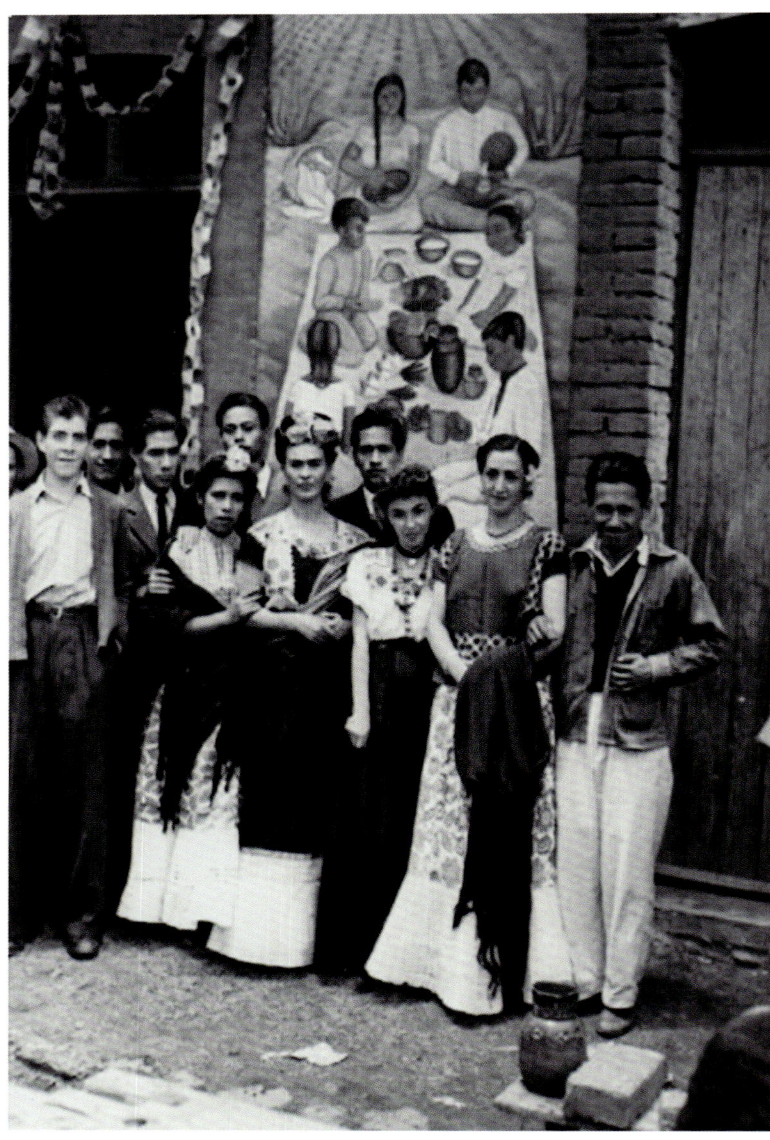

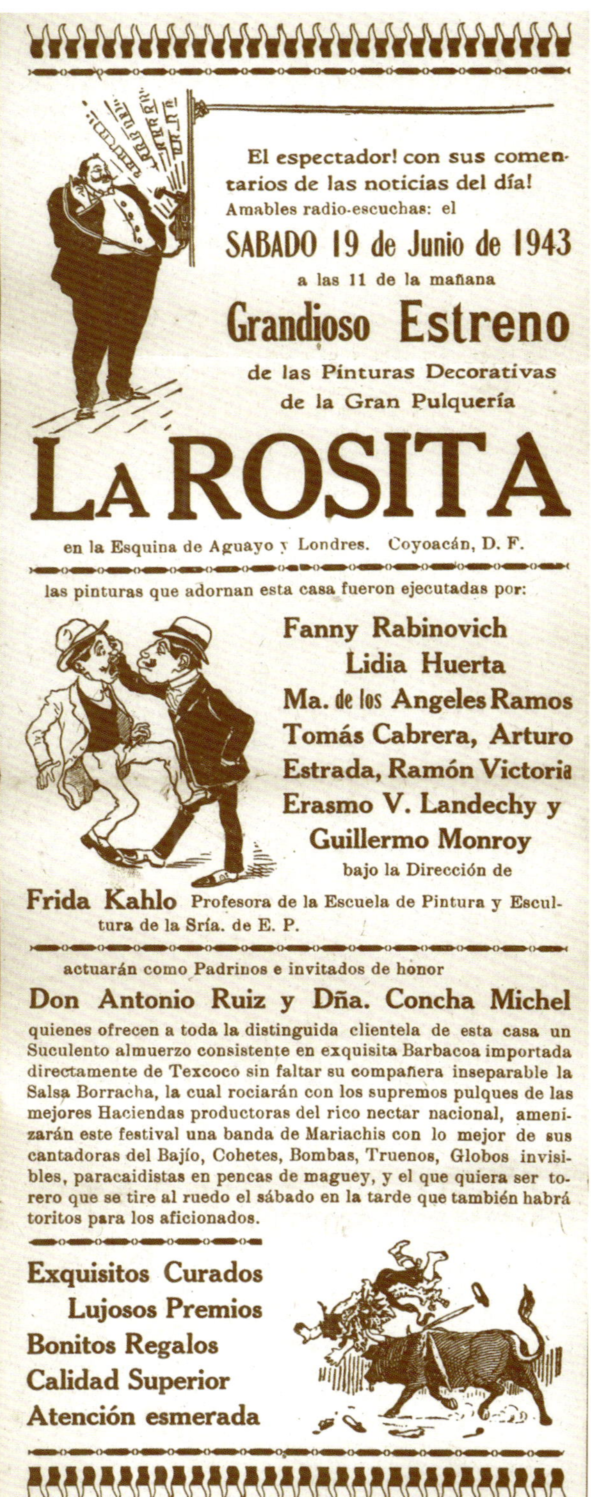

Mara Kahlo Frida was friends with the owner of a local *pulqueria* (a bar specializing in *pulque*, a drink made from fermented maguey) La Rosita, and she convinced him to let her students paint a mural for the community. She and Diego paid for everything. Frida came to the unveiling of the mural with her sister Cristina and niece Isolda. Before the Mexican Revolution, the *pulquerías* had colorful murals on their walls, but the government had a policy restricting this practice. The murals attracted patrons, and the government wanted to reduce the consumption of *pulque*.

TOP LEFT Frida and her students who painted La Rosita tavern, Coyoacán, 1943. Photo by Leo Matiz

TOP RIGHT Flyer advertisement for La Rosita tavern, 1943

OPPOSITE Frida and Rina Lazo painting La Rosita tavern, 1943. Photo by Leo Matiz

FOLLOWING SPREAD Film stills of the redesign and second opening celebration for La Rosita, 1952

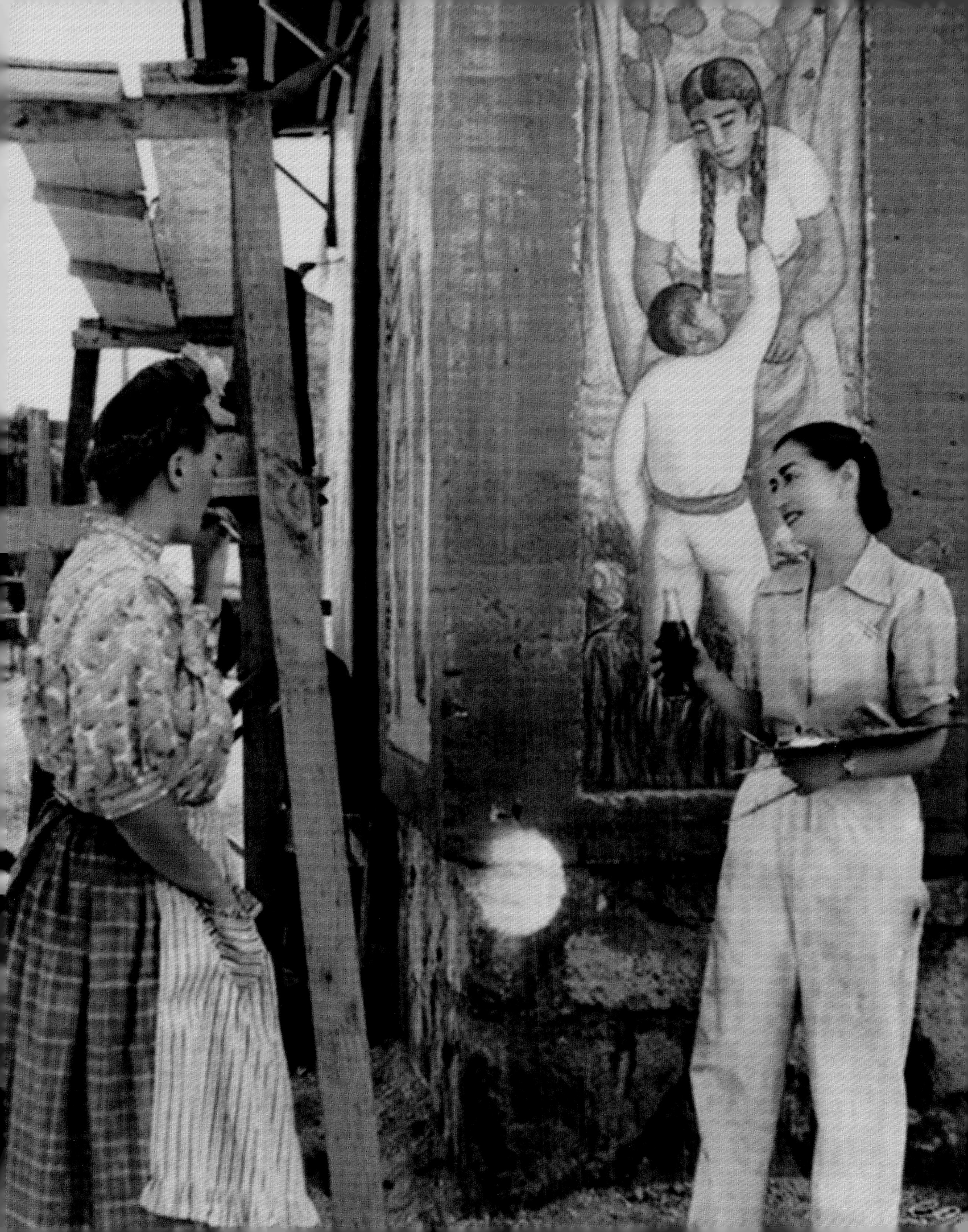

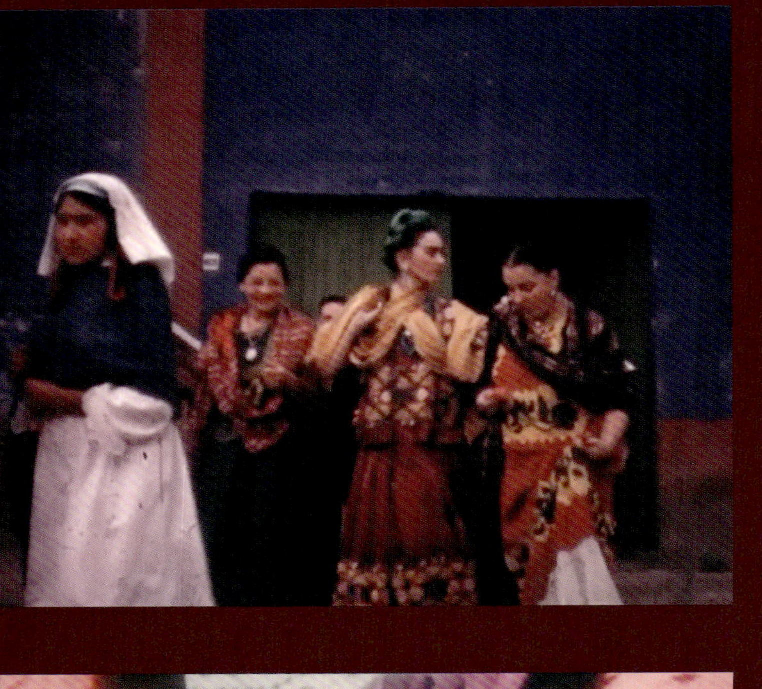
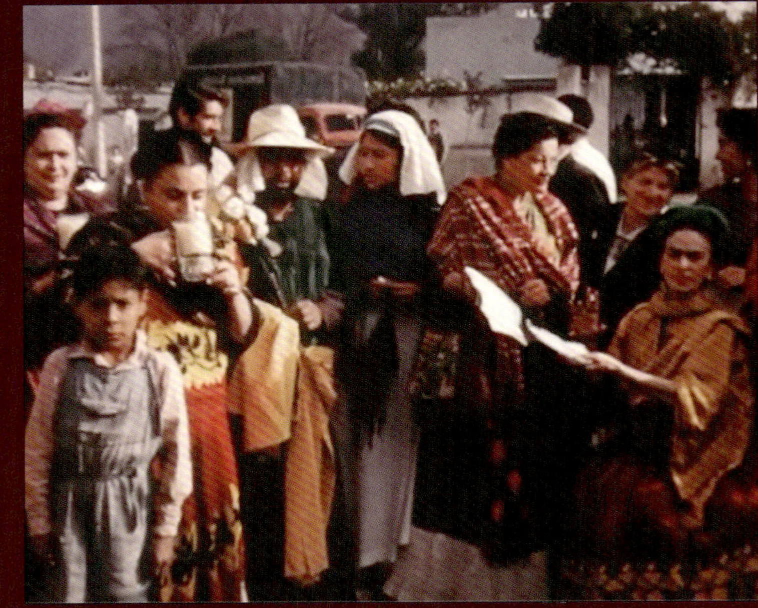
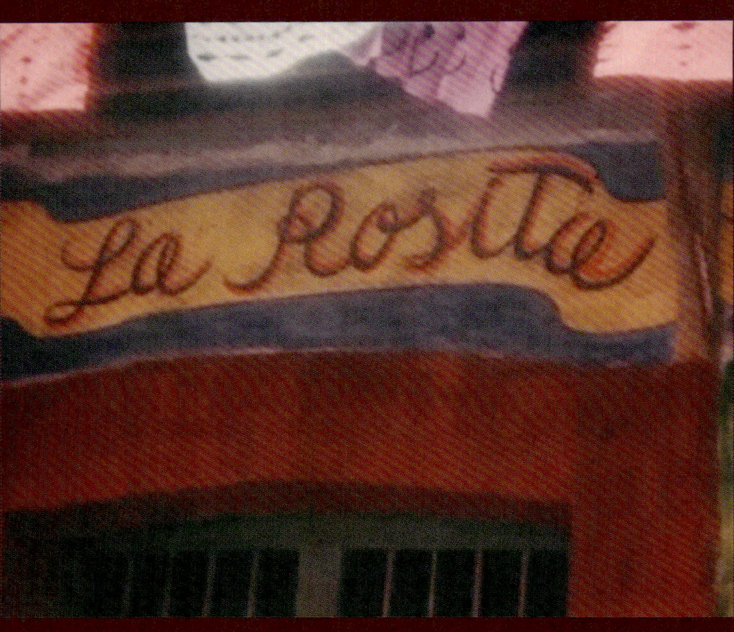
La Rosita
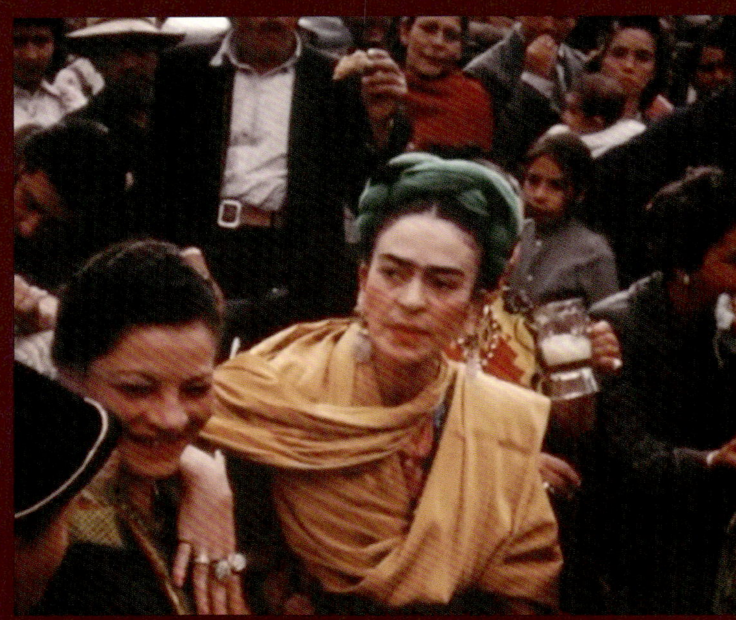
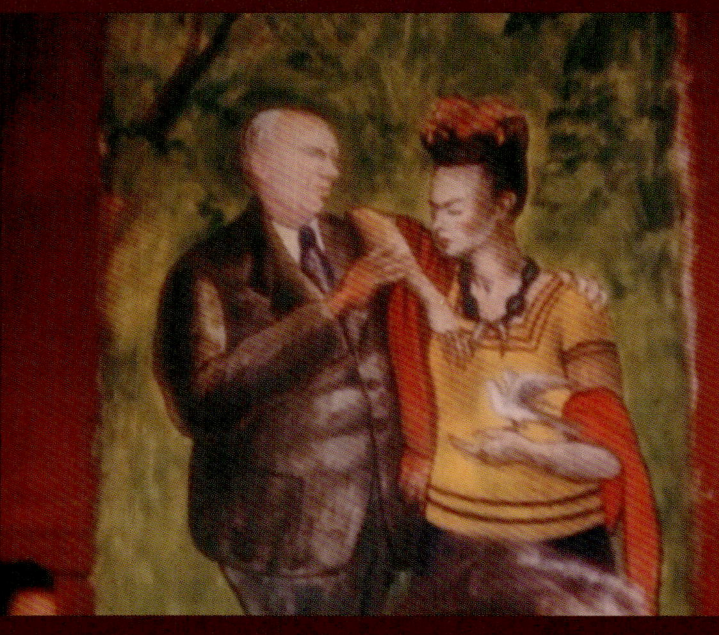
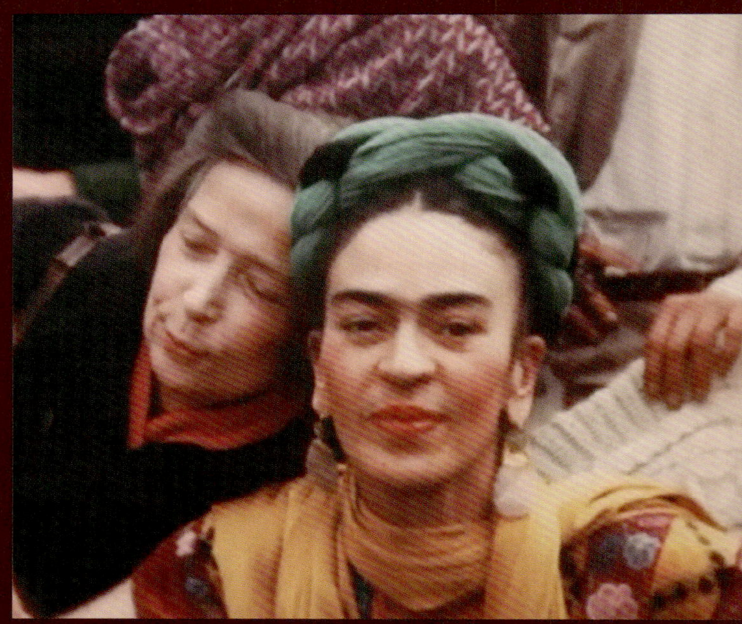

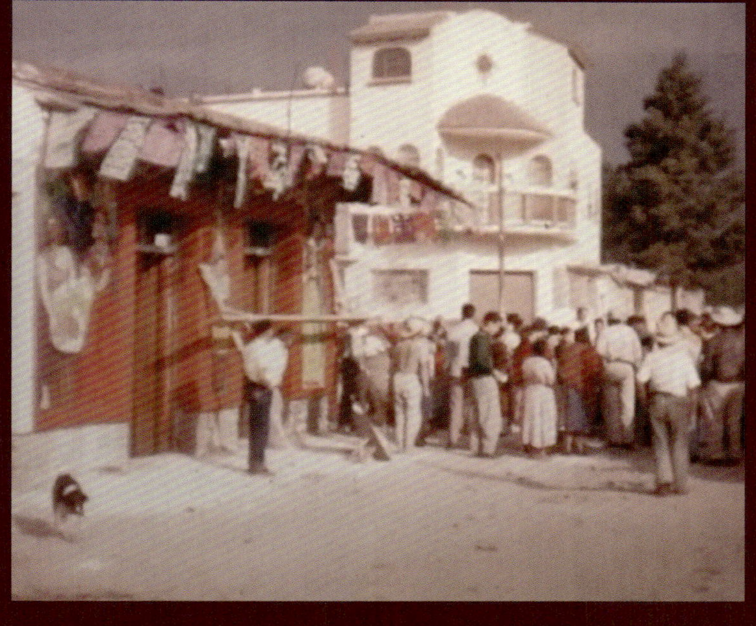
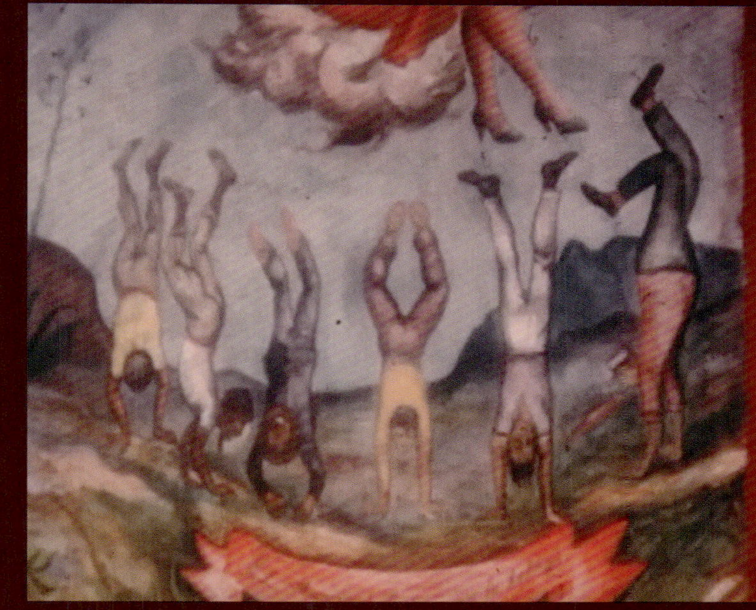
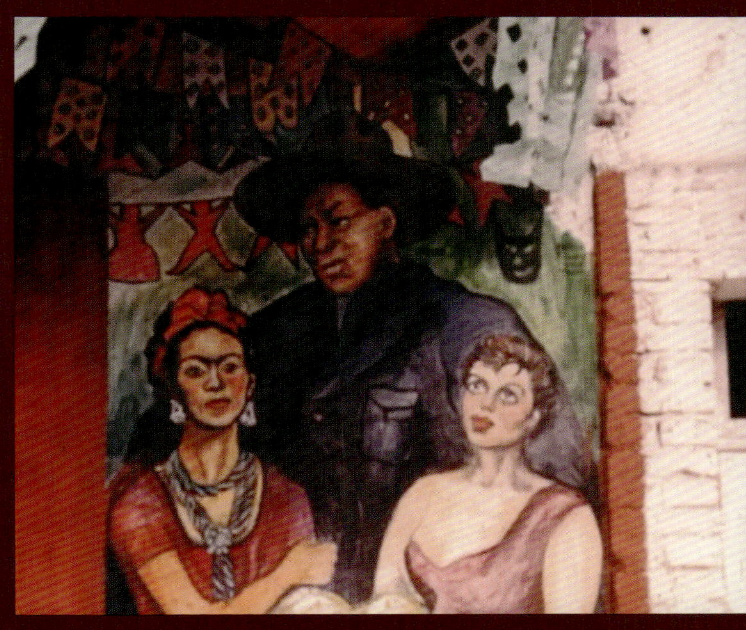
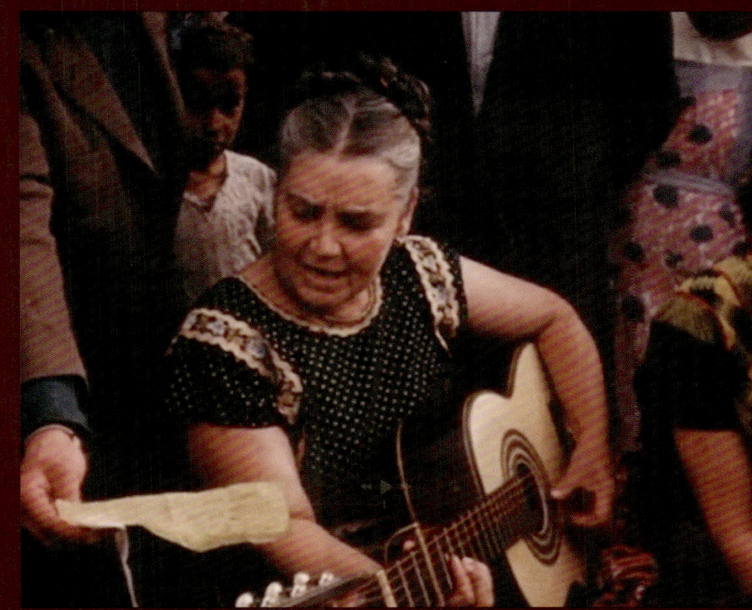
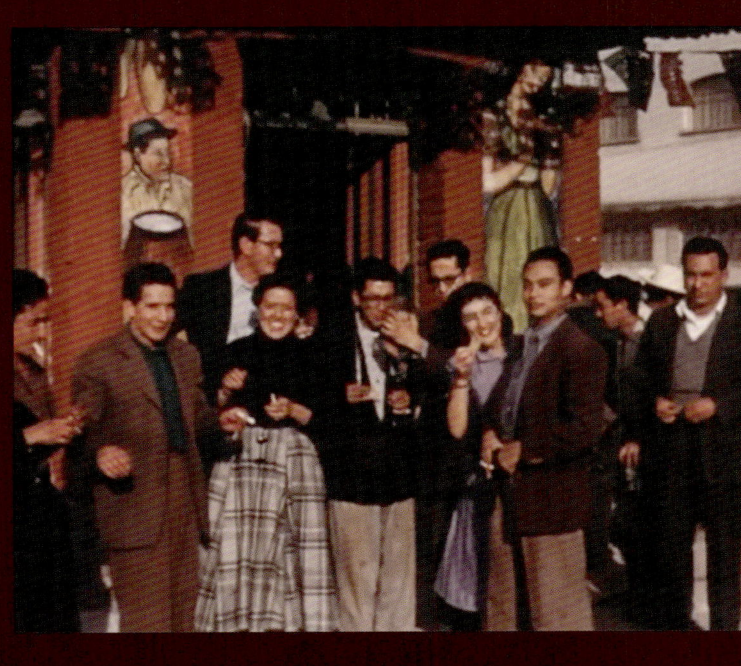
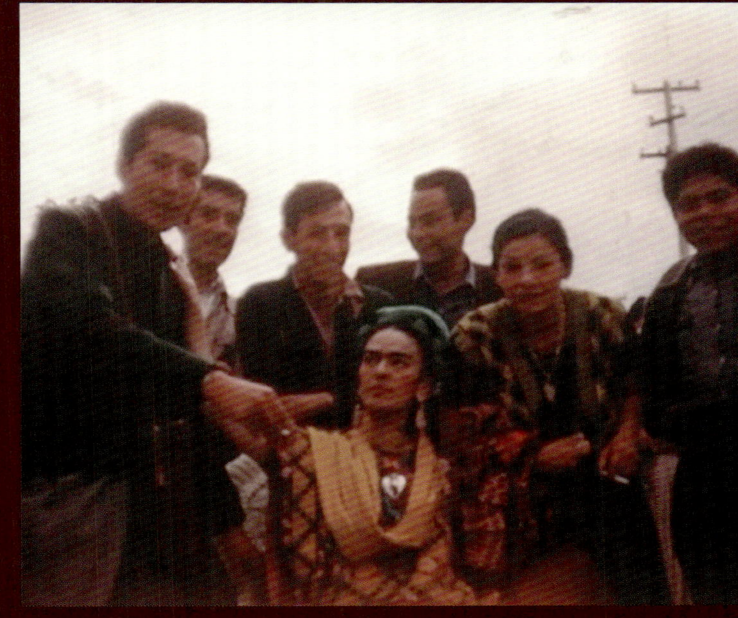

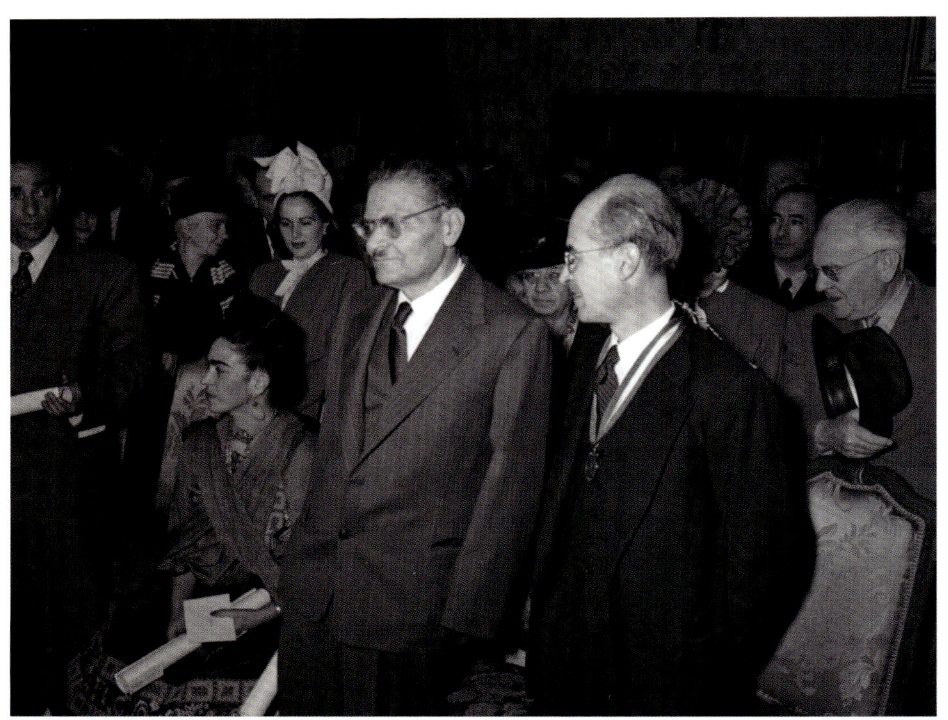

426 W. 22nd St. N. York
Enero 1º de 1929.

Srita. Frieda Khalo.
Méx

Muy estimada Señorita:
Esto es para saluda
y desearle muchas felici
en el año que empieza.
En algunos recortes q
a veces me envían de mi c
y que se refieren a activid
pictóricas, he visto su nomb
firmando manifiestos revolu
narios. ¿Qué me cuenta
de su trabajo? De mis ant
amigos, ninguno me escribe
¿Vive usted todavía en Coyoa

Su atto. S. y amigo,
José Clemente Orozco.

ABOVE Frida (seated) and muralist José Clemente Orozco at the ceremony for the National Prize for Arts and Sciences, Mexico, 1946

RIGHT Letter from José Clemente Orozco to Frida, dated 1929, nearly 20 years before they were both honored in 1946. He writes that he had heard she had joined the Communist party and about her interest in art.

OPPOSITE TOP AND BOTTOM Frida at the ceremony for the National Prize for Arts and Sciences, Mexico, 1946

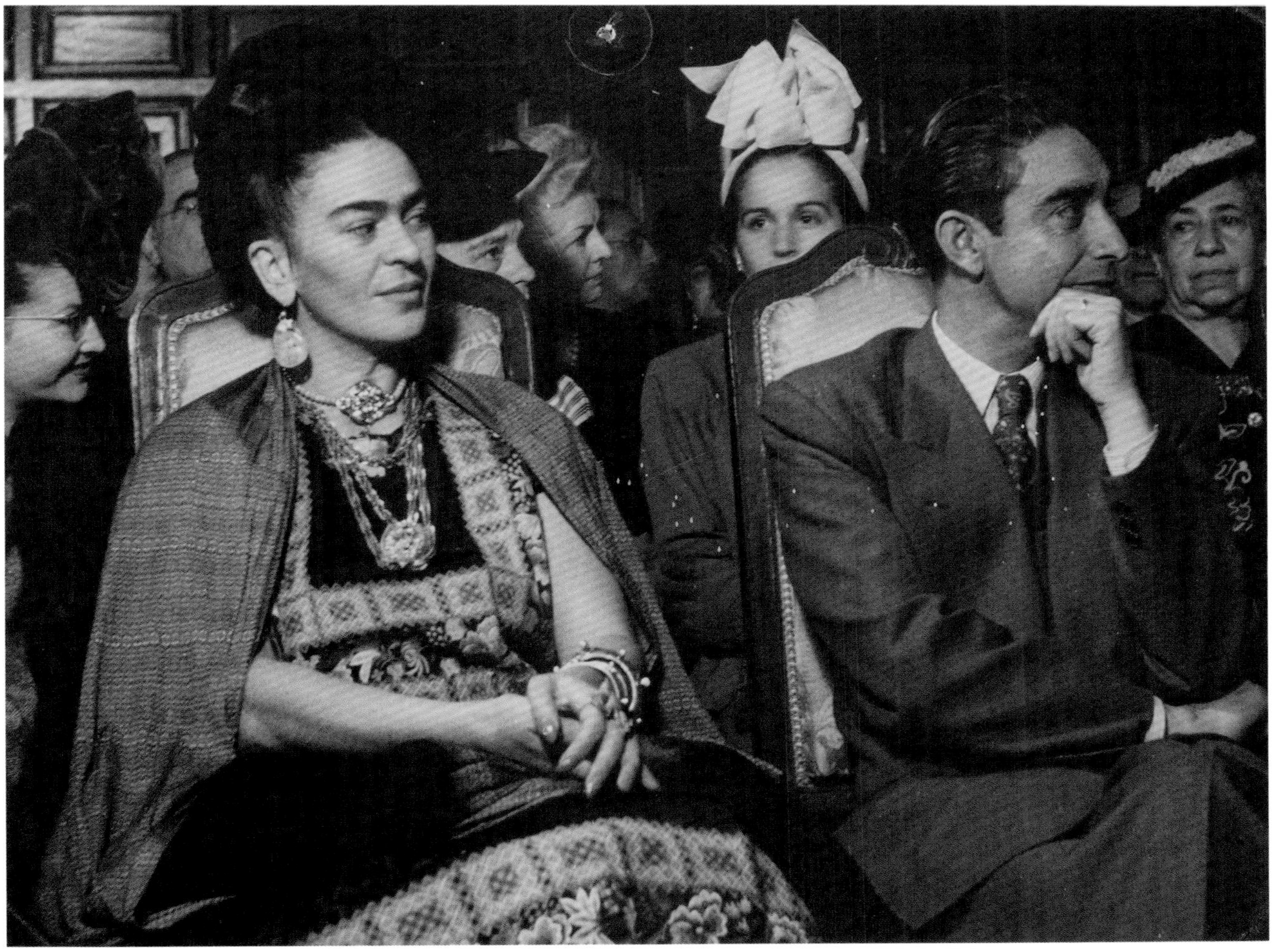

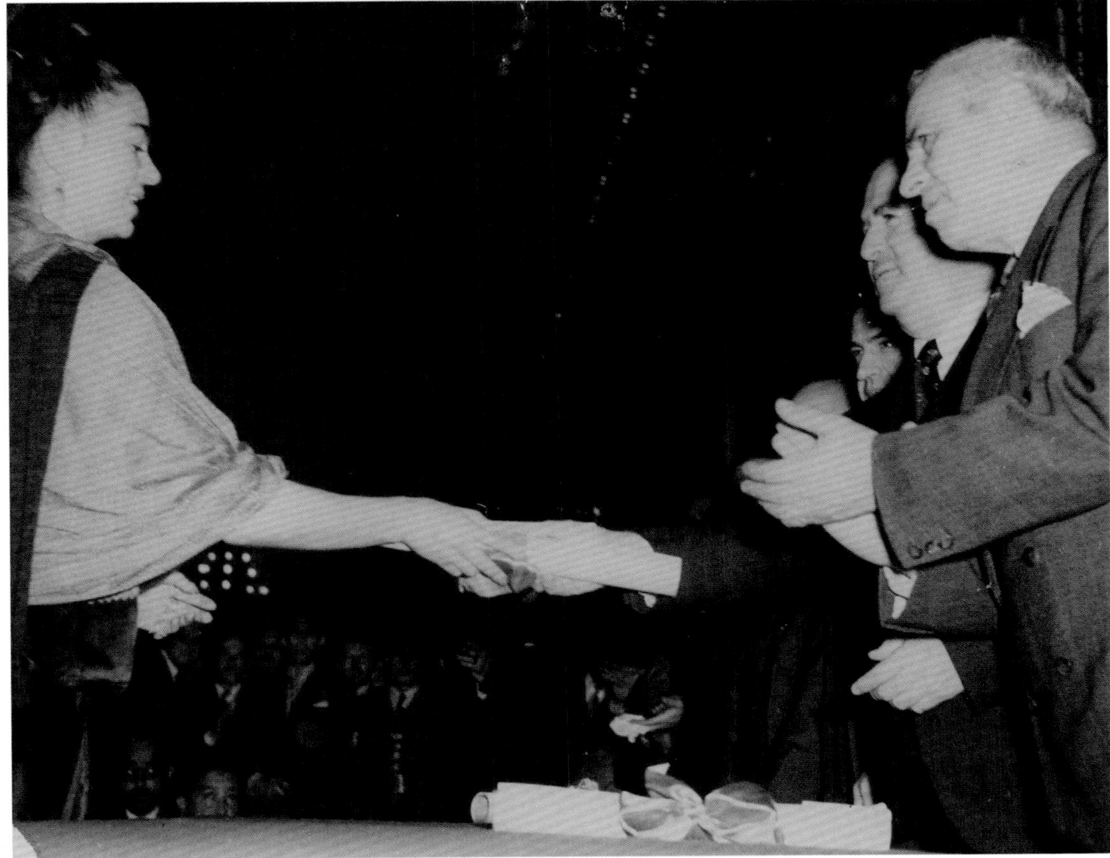

Frida Kahlo, *The Circle*, ca. 1954. Oil on metal, diameter 6 in. (15.25 cm)

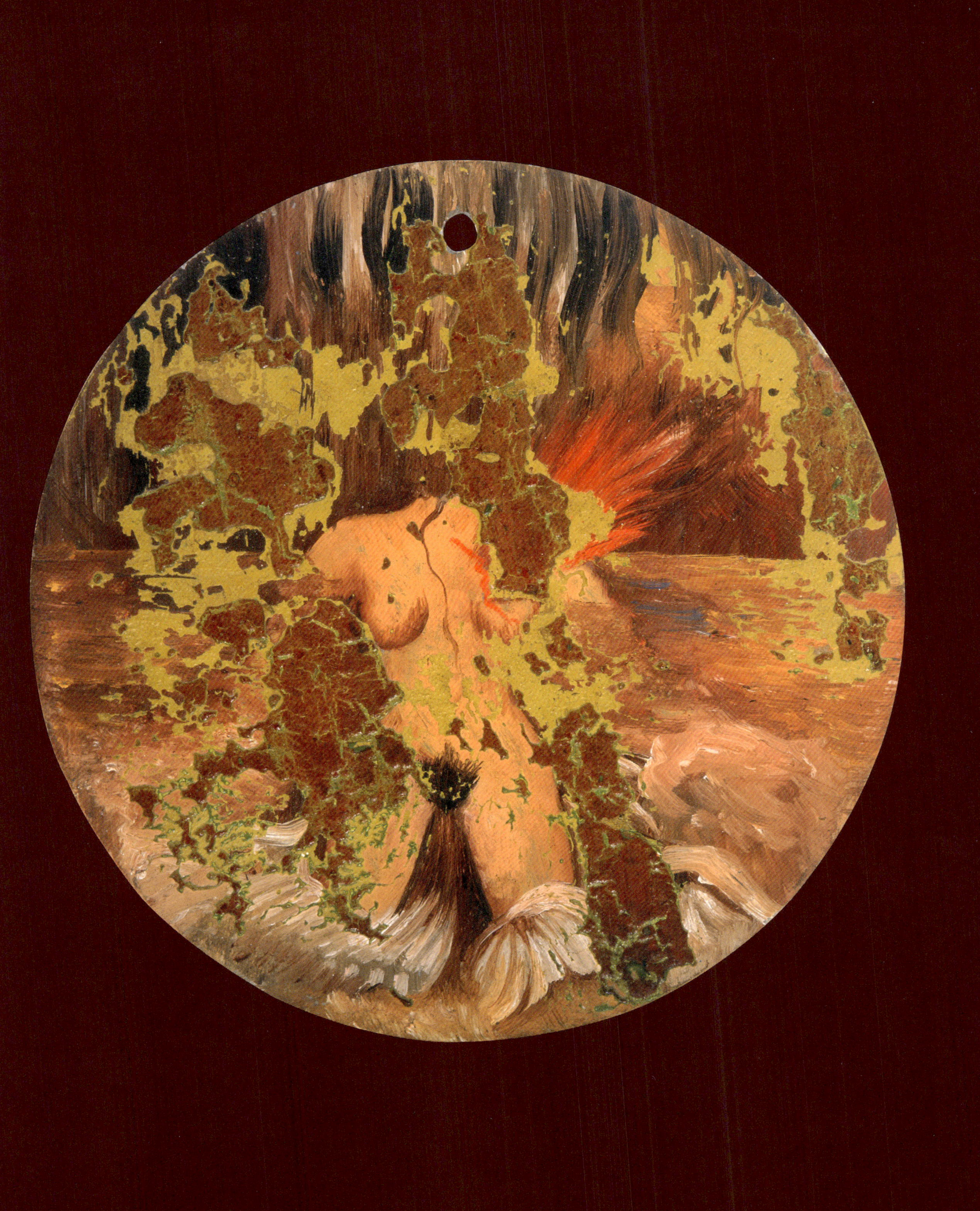

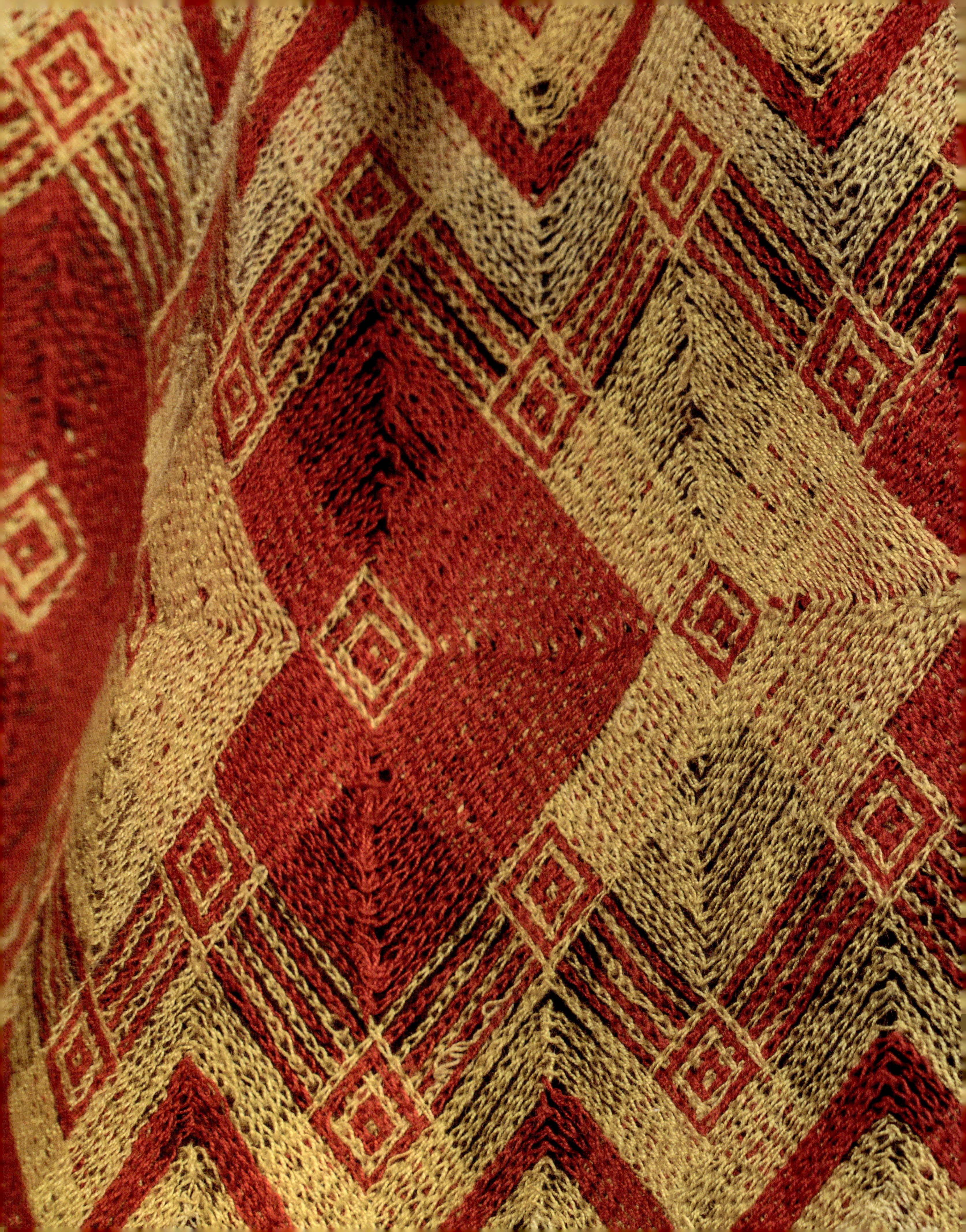

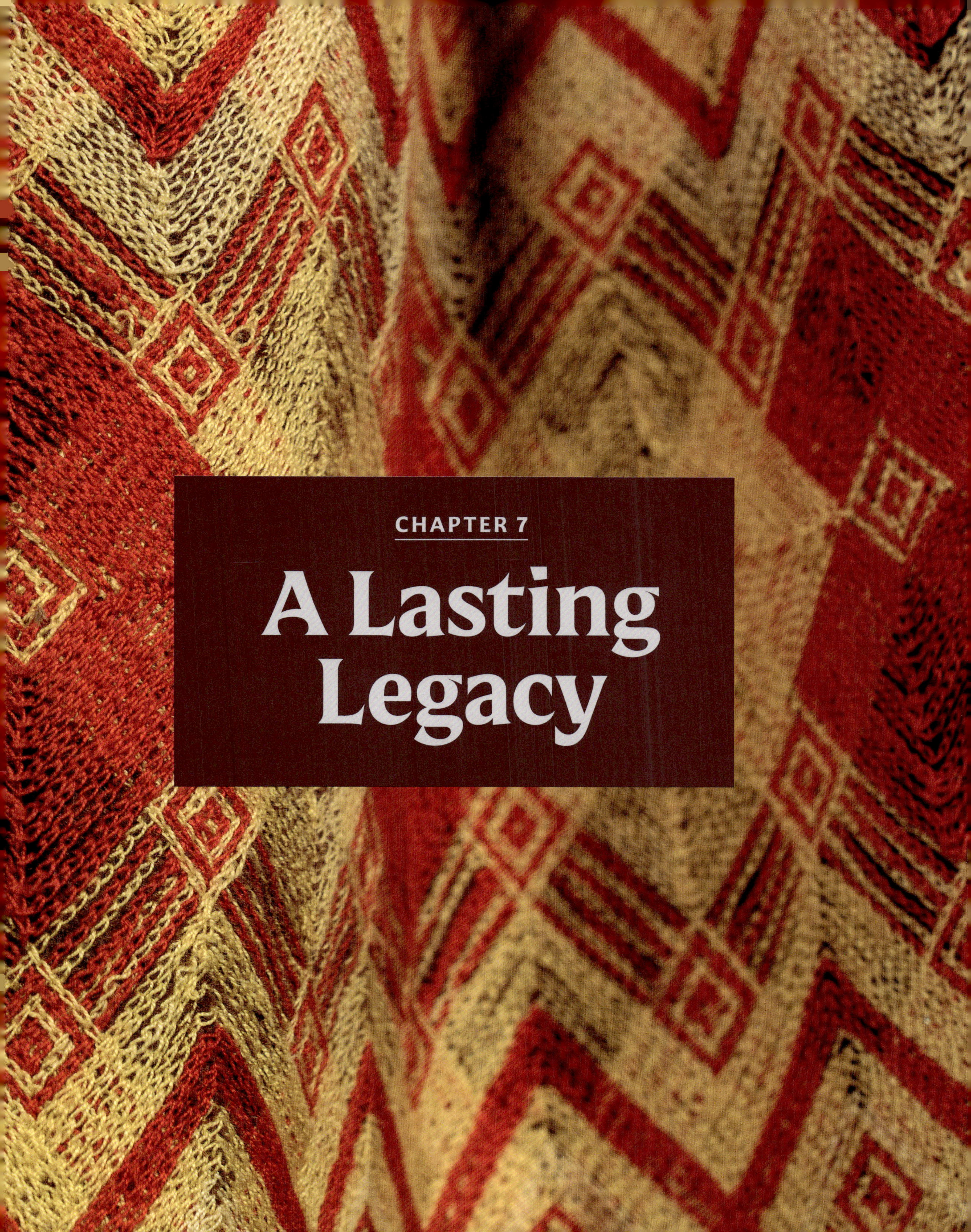

CHAPTER 7

A Lasting Legacy

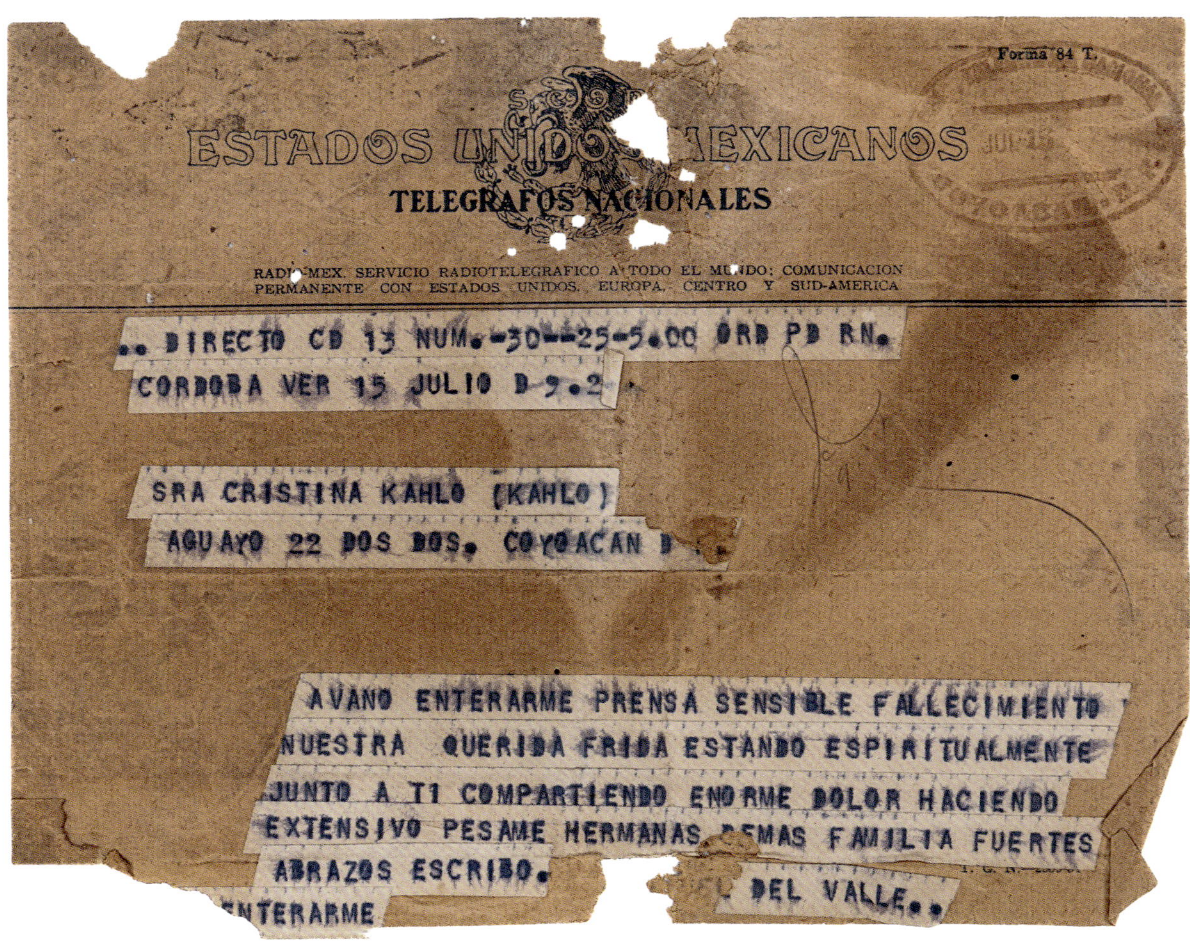

Forma 84 T.

ESTADOS UNIDOS MEXICANOS

TELEGRAFOS NACIONALES

RADIOMEX. SERVICIO RADIOTELEGRAFICO A TODO EL MUNDO; COMUNICACION PERMANENTE CON ESTADOS UNIDOS, EUROPA, CENTRO Y SUD-AMERICA

.. DIRECTO CB 13 NUM.-30--25-5.00 ORD PD RN.
CORDOBA VER 15 JULIO D-9.2

SRA CRISTINA KAHLO (KAHLO)
AGUAYO 22 DOS DOS. COYOACAN D

AVANO ENTERARME PRENSA SENSIBLE FALLECIMIENTO
NUESTRA QUERIDA FRIDA ESTANDO ESPIRITUALMENTE
JUNTO A TI COMPARTIENDO ENORME DOLOR HACIENDO
EXTENSIVO PESAME HERMANAS DEMAS FAMILIA FUERTES
ABRAZOS ESCRIBO.
DEL VALLE..
ENTERARME

Mara Romeo Kahlo Frida's death was very painful for the family, but it did not come as a surprise. She had been in extreme pain for several months, and after doctors amputated her leg, it was very hard for her sisters Cristina and Adriana, my mom Isolda, and all the people who loved her to see her rapid physical decline. To witness her suffering, unable to ease her pain, was unbearably difficult. When death finally came—though heartbreaking—it was also a relief, for her and for all who loved her. Frida's passion for life, and the way she lived it so fully, in some measure redeemed the years that were stolen from her by so early a departure.

Mara de Anda One day when I was in the sixth grade, my grandmother Isolda said, "Hi Marita, there's somebody named Madonna ringing the bell of my house." Madonna the pop star had arrived at my grandmother Isolda's house. She is a huge fan of Frida Kahlo and was visiting Mexico to get to know her better. In our neighborhood Coyoacán, it was widely known that Frida's closest living relative lived a couple of blocks away from Casa Azul. Madonna wanted to meet my grandmother and ask permission to make a movie about Frida incorporating my grandmother's memories. Isolda agreed but acknowledged that sometimes talking about her aunt was difficult and elicited strong reactions

ABOVE A telegram addressed to Cristina, Frida's sister, offering condolences on news of Frida's death on July 13, 1954

OPPOSITE Obituaries for Frida Kahlo from various newspapers including the *New York Times*

Frida Kalho, la Artista del Pincel, Dejó de Existir Ayer

La Muerte de la Esposa de Diego Rivera Conmueve a sus Amigos

Nota de Rodolfo CONTRERAS A., redactor de NOVEDADES

Frida Kalho, la artista e incansable luchadora social, que fuera compañera en la vida del muralista Diego Rivera, dejó de existir la madrugada de ayer y, por la tarde, su cadáver fué conducido, en un féretro gris, al vestíbulo del Palacio de las Bellas Artes, colocado sobre el piso un lienzo negro, y, sobre el ataúd, su esposo depositó la bandera roja, del Partido Comunista Mexicano, con una estrella blanca en el centro y, dentro de ella, el símbolo de la hoz y el martillo, bordados en seda negra.

Daban la impresión, tales actos, de que, traspuestos los umbrales de la muerte, ninguna ideología rige los destinos, y menos aún en un país que, como el nuestro, ha respetado los credos, del tipo que fueren; por eso fué que las altas autoridades del gobierno dieron su anuencia para que así fuera... en aras del arte, del que la desaparecida fuera magnífica exponente.

Y por el Palacio de las Bellas Artes, donde se exhibieron obras grandiosas de Diego Rivera y de Frida Kalho, desfilaron, a contemplar el rostro inanimado, todos quienes fueron compañeros de ella.

EL MUNDO DE LA IZQUIERDA, EN PLENO

Unas personas allegadas al matrimonio Rivera manifestaron al representante de NOVEDADES que después de consultarlo con los funcionarios de la Presidencia de la República, en ausencia del Primer Magistrado, el director del Instituto de las Bellas Artes, señor Andrés Iduarte, había extendido el permiso para que el cadáver de Frida fuera velado en el magno edificio.

Las guardias, numerosas en sí, se sucedieron una a una, y las montaron los más connotados comunistas; David Alfaro Siqueiros, Heriberto Jara, el pintor José Chávez Morado, la fotógrafa Lola Alvarez Bravo, los pintores Juan O'Gormann, Aurora Reyes, María Asúnsolo, Miguel Covarrubias, el escultor Rodrigo Arenas Betancourt.

También asistieron a velar a la desaparecida, sus tres hermanas, Cristina, Adriana y Luisa; Rut y Guadalupe Rivera, hijas del pintor y de su primera esposa, la también pintora Lupe Marín; el licenciado Ricardo Zevada, director del Banco Nacional de Comercio Exterior;

SIGUE EN LA PAGINA 13, COL. 7

Hoy Entierran a Frida Kahlo: Causó Pesar Entre los Artistas, su Muerte

No por esperada dejó de causar profunda pena la muerte de la genial pintora mexicana: Frida Kahlo, indudablemente la más alta exponente del arte pictórico femenino en el Continente Americano. Hoy, al mediodía sus restos serán conducidos a su última morada en el Panteón de Dolores.

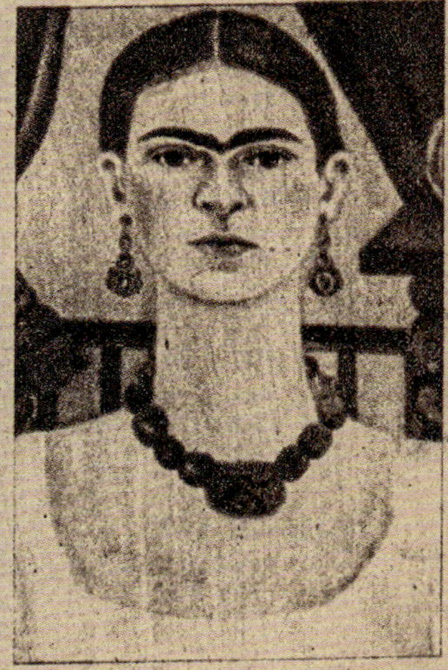

Autorretrato de Frida Kahlo.

El dominio de los pinceles y los colores en el arte, en sus planos elevados rara vez es atributo de mujeres. Los grandes maestros de la pintura siempre han sido hombres. Las mujeres aun cuando lleguen a ser grandes artistas, jamás escalan la cúspide de la genialidad; por eso Frida Kahlo es una excepción. En doscientos años atrás sólo tuvo un precedente en Francia: Madame Lebrun.

Caso interesante y dramático el de su vida. Era una guapa joven preparatoriana de un grupo alegre que se llamaban "los cachuchas" al que pertenecía el que fué después Presidente de la República, licenciado Miguel Alemán, e iba en un camión en compañía de Alejandro Gómez Arias, compañero de estudios rumbo a San Ildefonso, cuando un tranvía arrolló al vehículo resultando ella gravemente herida.

En sus largas horas de tedio en un hospital de sangre, para entretenerse pidió pinceles. Jamás había pintado, pero a la manera de Vaughan, la sensación de lo dramático hizo surgir en ella una genial pintora.

Luego su vida fué muy conocida. Su nombre voló en alas de la fama. Triunfó rotundamente en una Exposición en Nueva York, pero su consagración definitiva fué en París, centro y foco de cul-

(Sigue en la Pág. 3. Col. 7)

THE NEW YORK TIMES, WEDNESDAY, JULY 14, 1954.

FRIDA KAHLO, ARTIST, DIEGO RIVERA'S WIFE

MEXICO CITY, July 13 (AP)—Frida Kahlo, wife of Diego Rivera, the noted painter, was found dead in her home today. Her age was 44. She had been suffering from cancer for several years.

She also was a painter and also had been active in leftist causes. She made her last public appearance in a wheel chair at a meeting here in support of the now ousted regime of Communist-backed President Jacobo Arbenz Guzman of Guatemala.

Frida Kahlo began painting in 1926 while obliged to lie in bed during convalescence from injuries suffered in a bus accident. Not long afterward she showed her work to Diego Rivera, who advised, "go on painting." They were married in 1929, began living apart in 1939, were reunited in 1941.

Usually classed as a surrealist, the artist had no special explanation for her methods. She said only: "I put on the canvas whatever comes into my mind." She gave one-woman shows in Mexico City, New York and elsewhere, and is said to have been the first woman artist to sell a picture to the Louvre.

Some of her pictures shocked beholders. One showed her with her hands cut off, a huge bleeding heart on the ground nearby, and on either side of her an empty dress. This was supposed to reveal how she felt when her husband went off alone on a trip. Another self-portrait presented the artist as a wounded deer, still carrying the shafts of nine arrows.

A year ago, too weak to stand for more than ten minutes, she sat daily at her easel, declaring: "I am happy to be alive as long as I can paint."

La señora

FRIEDA KAHLO de RIVERA

falleció el martes 13, a las 4 horas.

Su esposo, hermanas, sus camaradas y demás parientes lo participan a todos sus amigos.

México, D. F., a 14 de julio de 1954.

La capilla ardiente está instalada en el Palacio de Bellas Artes.

AGENCIA ALCAZAR HNOS. - Liverpool 50, esquina con Dinamarca.

En Dolores Fueron Inhumados los Restos de Frida Kahlo

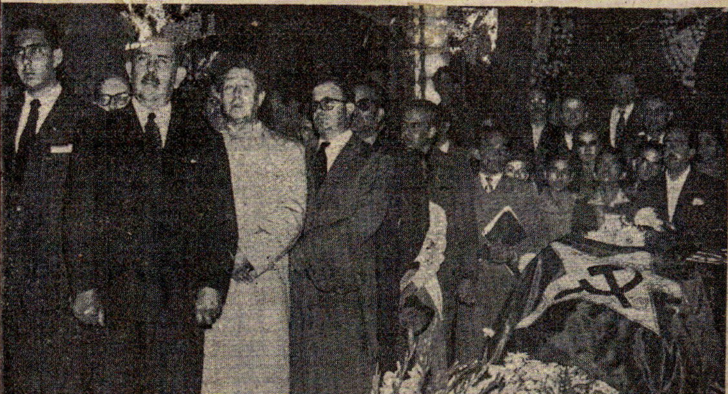

A LA DERECHA, la bandera del Partido Comunista cubre el féretro con los despojos mortales de Frida Kahlo. A la izquierda, entre otros dolientes, Cuauhtémoc Cárdenas y su papá, el general Lázaro Cárdenas; y David Alfaro Siqueiros. (Foto Rodríguez).

Poco más de seiscientas personas acudieron ayer en la mañana al Palacio de Bellas Artes, para rendir tributo de admiración a la pintora mexicana Frida Kahlo de Rivera, fallecida anteayer a las seis de la mañana, después de larga y penosísima enfermedad.

Entre quienes estuvieron en Bellas Artes, contamos a una gran cantidad de curiosos que, por el solo hecho de pasar por enfrente de nuestro teatro máximo, entraban para ver lo que allí dentro ocurría.

El cadáver de Frida Kahlo, en severo féretro gris, al que cubría la bandera de la URSS con

SIGUE EN LA PAGINA TRES

in her—often crying but sometimes laughing as well. Some days she could tell hundreds of stories, and on other days, she could not talk about her at all. My grandmother insisted on a few conditions to proceed: The first was that my father had to be the photographer of the movie, to which Madonna agreed. The second was that Madonna would allow Isolda to take her to Palacio de Hierro, the big department store in Mexico City, to buy her new jeans because Madonna's were ripped! Even though that was the fashion, Isolda felt it gave the wrong impression. Madonna wanted to visit Casa Azul, and Isolda agreed to take her there and act as her guide. My grandma and my mother went in their car and Madonna followed in a limousine (Isolda found the limo to be too pretentious). At Casa Azul, they gave Isolda free rein to touch things and open drawers because at one time it had been her home. Afterwards, Madonna invited them to eat, but my brother was sick, so Isolda declined the invitation, preferring to go see her grandson. When they came back home, Isolda told me that story and I was shocked! I was a huge fan of Madonna. Luckily, they had asked her for an autograph for me. The next day I went to school to tell everybody that my mother and grandmother were with Madonna. The director of the school sent me to the psychologist because he thought I was lying. I swore up and down that I was telling the truth. Finally, they called my family to verify the story. At that time in my life, I was much more interested in meeting Madonna than being a descendant of Frida Kahlo. Being a descendant of Frida was "normal" for us.

My grandmother always talked about Frida, telling me about her adventures with her Tía Frida and Tío Diego. The first time I realized what Frida meant to the world I was in high school. We were given an assignment to research an artist. I asked my grandmother to tell me everything she could about Frida. I brought one of Frida's stone necklaces in to show the class. The reaction from the students was over the top! The teacher was amazed and told everyone at the school. In that instant I realized who she was.

Being a Kahlo is a huge responsibility. The impact of Frida Kahlo's name around the world is hard to fully grasp. As stewards of her legacy, there are expectations. We take great care with everything that is done in her name. This responsibility presents challenges, of course, but it is a huge privilege and one that we cherish. We want to share our truth about Frida and provide a perspective only our family can. She was a strong woman and a role model to many. She faced life with a resilient spirit, extraordinary strength, independence, and joy in spite of her difficulties. We want people to know that although her work changed the world, she was a human being. We want people to connect to Frida the woman, the daughter, the sister, the aunt, the teacher, the lover. She was real in every sense of the word: she laughed, she told rude jokes, and she found happiness in so much, including music, among many other things.

We are not the first descendants of a famous artist to be fighting to reclaim the rights to our legacy. Her image has been co-opted in many ways by people who are not interested in the things that mattered to her, chief among them Mexico and her people. We hope that our work on behalf of our great aunt's legacy will be instructive to other families experiencing something similar.

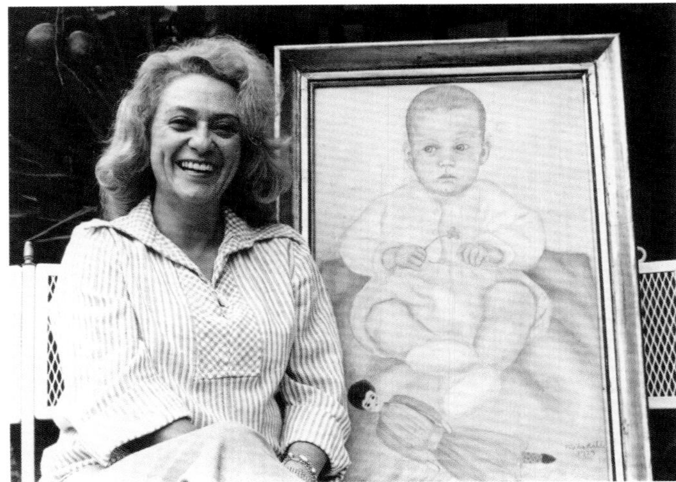

Frida Hentschel The spirit of the Kahlo lineage is in our blood and we feel compelled to honor and share it. My Tía Frida, my namesake, was a remarkable woman for so many reasons—her life is an example of what can happen when one makes simple but extraordinary choices every day. Her iconic visage is recognized worldwide, and it is our responsibility to make sure that her image and her name are used in a manner that honors and respects what she stood for.

The world believes they know everything about her, as we say here in Mexico, *hasta los calzones* (down to the underwear). The public has opened her diary, they have read her letters, and they have dissected every aspect of her life. What has been remarkable is that the people who have spent time with her history, regardless of where they look, find the same person with the same values, with the same coherence. She was true to herself in all parts of her life, and it shone through. Her family provided a safe harbor—she felt so secure within her family. Knowing you have a solid network of support—emotional, financial—and that your family can sustain you in every way, it provides

ABOVE Isolda, Frida's niece, with a drawing of her daughter, Mara Kahlo Romeo, co-author of this volume.

OPPOSITE Frida, 1939. Photo by Nickolas Muray

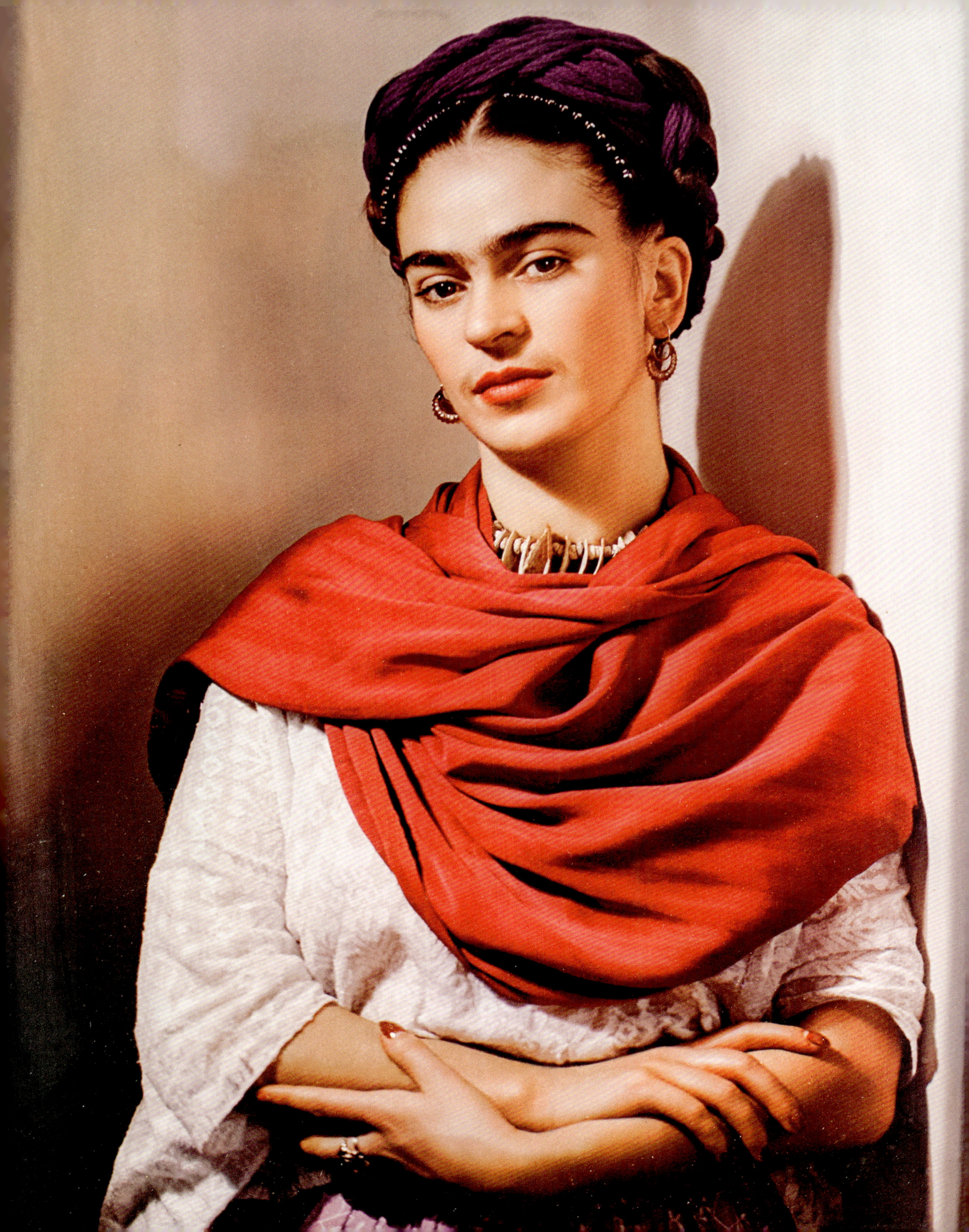

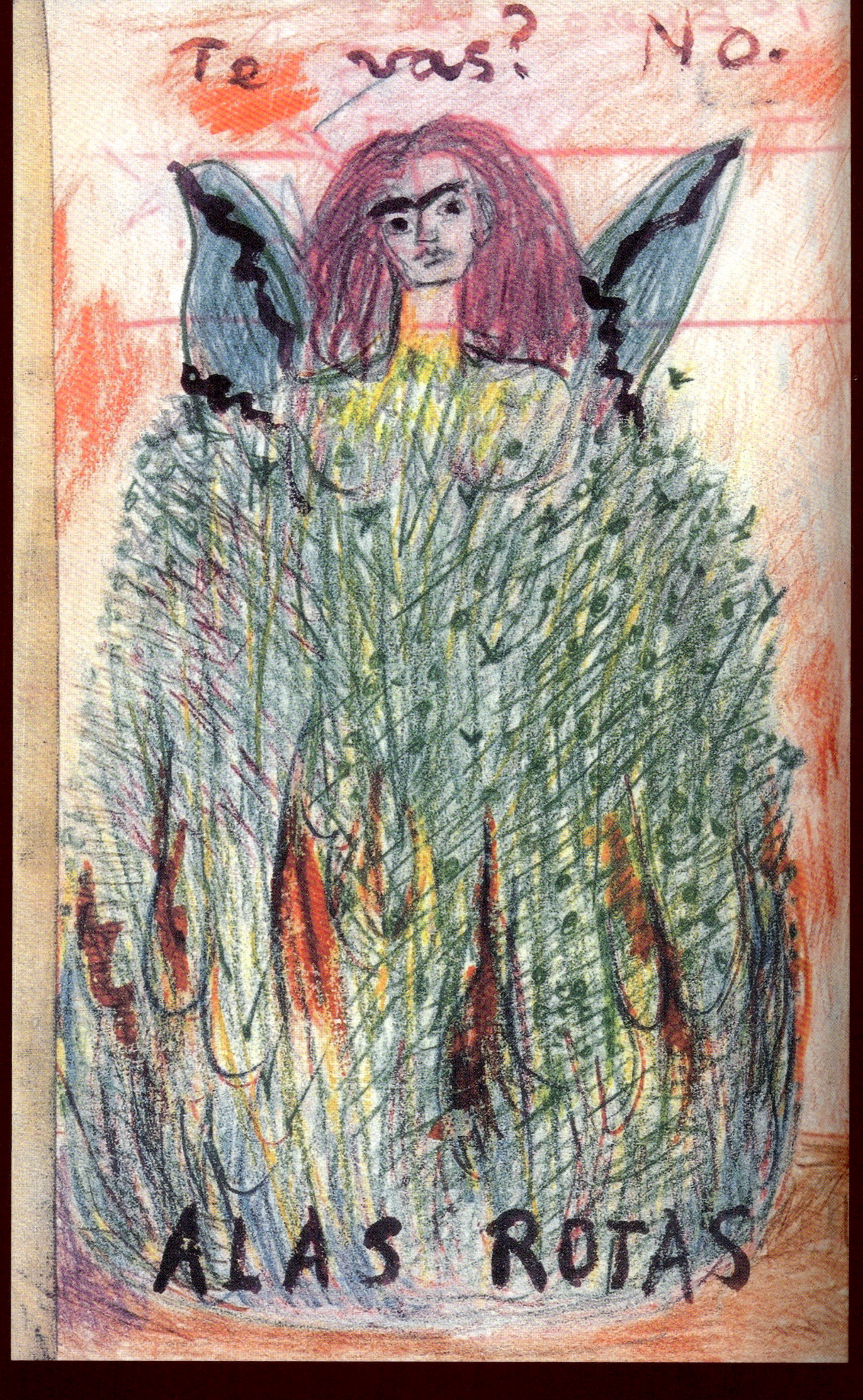
Te vas? No.
ALAS ROTAS

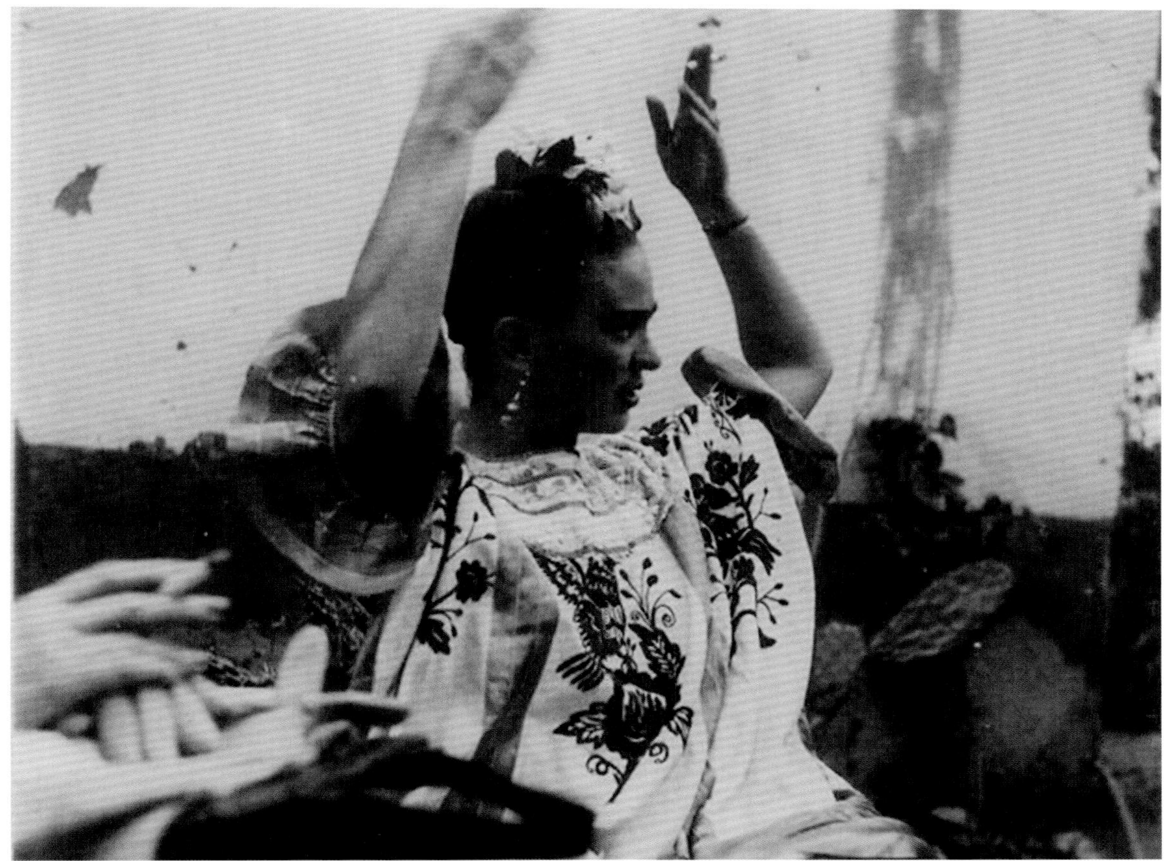

the confidence one needs to be great. For Frida, family came first. In guarding her legacy, we want to abide by her values and make sure that whatever we undertake in her name, it is consistent with what she would want. And we understand better than anyone what she would want. It's not a job but our heart-filled life's purpose.

We treasure the stories and belongings that came from our ancestors, and sharing our recollections and the things that she loved with legions of Frida fans is an honor.

Mara Romeo Kahlo When I was 11 or 12, I read the diary of Frida Kahlo. I thought my aunt was a bit wacky. But when I read the diary again at around 30, I understood her better and the wackiness I remembered, on second thought, was in fact her brutal honesty. And when I read it a third time in my fifties, I began to really feel her and take in the meaning of her writing, her greatness as an artist—I could finally feel her true essence in me.

When Frida married Diego for the second time, it was on the condition that she would not take any money from him, and she promised herself to be self-sufficient. This has been a constant theme with the women in this family. My grandmother Cristina, Frida's sister, separated from her partner and worked very hard all her life to maintain herself and her kids. When my mother Isolda divorced, she told my father she would not take a penny from him. She did not know how she would support herself, but she did not want his assistance. And so, to make ends meet, she built rooms inside the house to be rented to boarders and provided meals for them as well. At 13 or 14 years old, it felt odd to share my house with strangers; I felt ashamed about it with my friends. Years later as an adult—as age usually brings wisdom—I understood the strength required to do what was necessary to take care of us, and I became very proud of her. She made it on her own and did not need my father's (or anybody's) money. Through my own experience, I was able understand Frida, Cristina, and my

OPPOSITE A page from Frida's diary, 1944–54. It reads, "Te vas? No. Alas Rota" (Are you leaving? No. Broken Wings).

ABOVE Frida, Mexico, ca. 1945

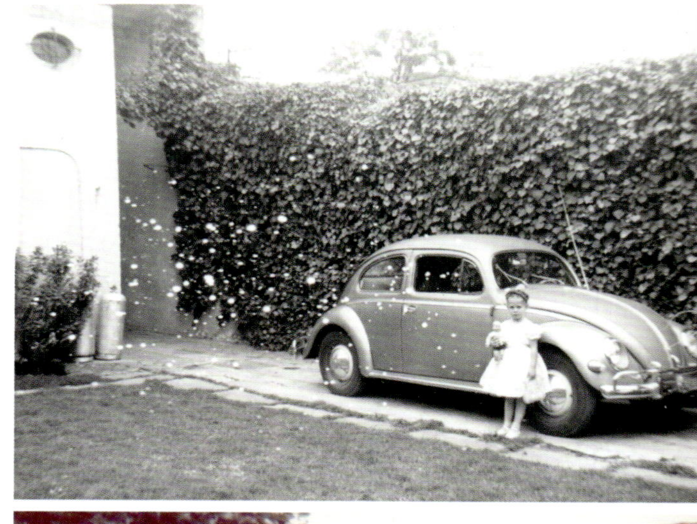

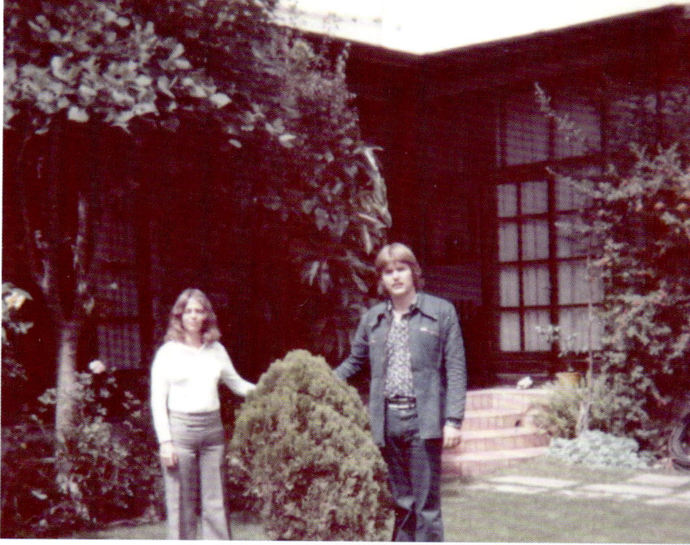

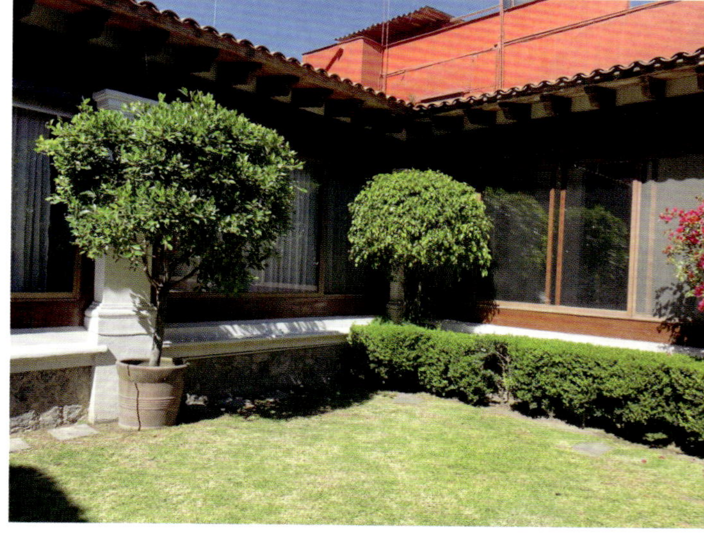

The house at Aguayo 54, aka Casa Kahlo, in Coyoacán, was the family "seat" for one hundred years.

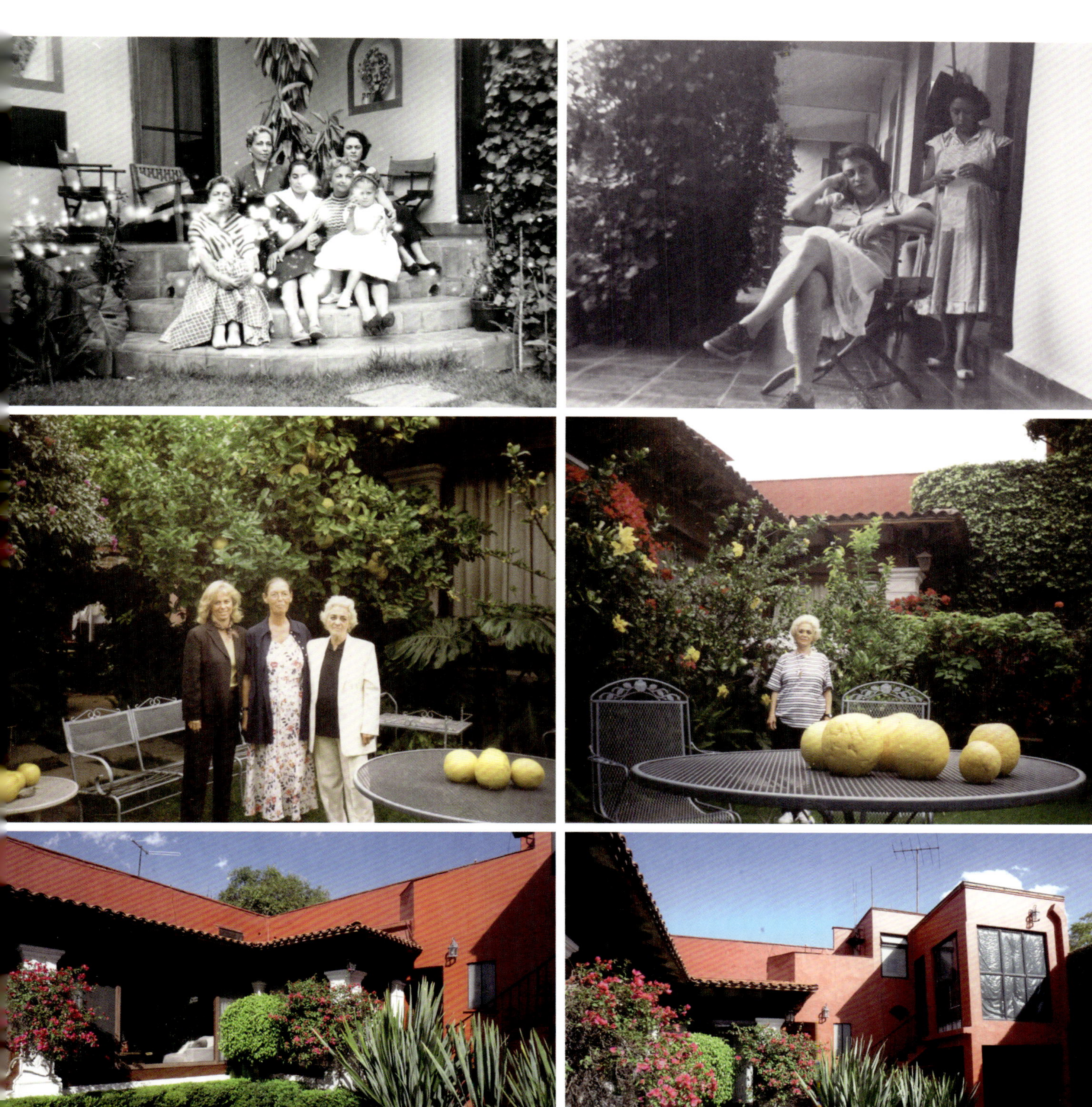

mother Isolda—I understood that they were free and independent and how much that meant to them. And when I got divorced, I similarly did not receive money from my ex-husband. That determination and strength continues in our family to this day.

Mara de Anda At the time Frida declared her financial independence from Diego, she was not that well known and certainly not as famous as she is now. She started to get worldwide fame after Hayden Herrera wrote her biography in the 1980s. When Madonna made known her fascination with Frida, that was another inflection point for Frida's popularity. In the 1980s, two "movements" took hold in the US: "Fridamania"—i.e., everything Frida—and "Kahloism," which was a bit more religious with disciples that called themselves "Casazuls." The devotees maintain altars in their homes for Frida and pray to her. There is even a temple in New York devoted to her.

Before the worldwide attention, she was largely known as the wife of Diego Rivera, the famous muralist. Those circumstances have now reversed, and it is common for *Diego* to be known as the husband of Frida Kahlo.

To us, her family, Frida represents being true to yourself, living life the way you want to live it, being a warrior, being resilient, and, most importantly, being part of a community. She had unconditional love for people and creatures—for animals, for herself, for life.

We love our family and will do everything in our power to protect it. Our values and resilience have been upheld throughout the generations: family, community, and Mexico.

Frida Hentschel The commercialization of Frida Kahlo's image is controversial. People use her for their own profit, without respecting the values and principles she fought and stood for. What we strive for as a family is that her image and name are used with respect. Profits should go back to the community, to her Mexico, to artisans, to artists; they should be used to create more art, more family, more Mexico.

I remember being about 6 years old when my mother and grandmother sat me down and asked me if I knew who Frida Kahlo was. I thought I might have heard of her, and obviously had seen her image (especially in markets of Coyoacán where it appears on practically everything), but I did not know the details of her life. My grandmother, Isolda, said to me: "She is my aunt, and that makes her your ancestor." After that I started hearing about her all the time. When I was little, Frida was already very famous, but it was not possible to understand fully what she meant to people—she was just family to me. When I was in school, I remember a classmate who went absolutely crazy when he found out I was related to Frida—he said I had Frida's blood in me. It is not uncommon for people to have big reactions when they find out about my ancestry. And though Frida Kahlo is just family to me, it is a great feeling to have this woman who is known all over the world as one of the greatest role models.

I find the greatness that Frida embodied in all the Kahlo sisters, and in the generations that have followed. I see it in my mother: her dedication, her love of family, her resilience, and her love for life. She is unapologetically herself and true to her values. Humble and strong. Connected to her roots, to her own body, to her clan. All the qualities of a Kahlo, still living in her.

Mara Romeo Kahlo Beyond the personal effects, artwork, and clothing, we have held on to many things that we inherited from my grandmother Cristina and her sisters Frida, Adriana, and Matilde—and perhaps one of the most important is that we embrace all Mexican celebrations and traditions with real passion.

Día de los Muertos, or Day of the Dead, is something that has remained deeply important to our family—it's when we honor our ancestors and our Mexican roots. We celebrate it every year. Frida loved to visit towns and villages throughout Mexico during this holiday; these places are magical and full of life during those moments. Though some could see it that way, this celebration is not somber or scary because Mexicans embrace this day as the return of our loved ones. We prepare their favorite foods and drinks and celebrate their souls. This day is a reminder of the cycle of life and death, of the past and future. In our family, we create an altar to Frida and to other members of our family before us, as a form of celebration and remembrance of the dead. We incorporate many elements from nature—flowers, dirt, water, smoke—and we celebrate her life.

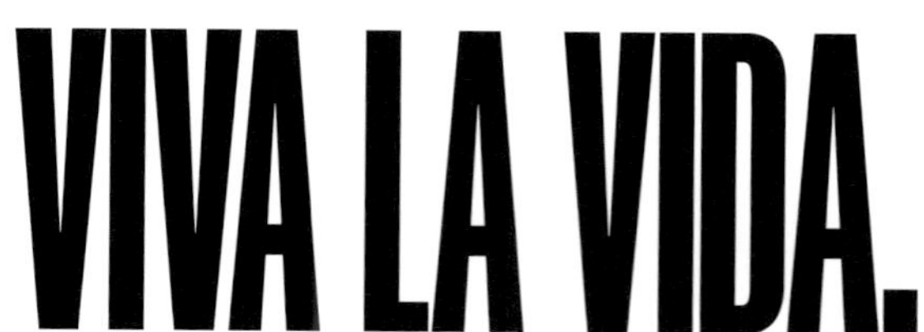

OPPOSITE Frida (seated 2nd from right) during a Día de los Muertos celebration, year unknown

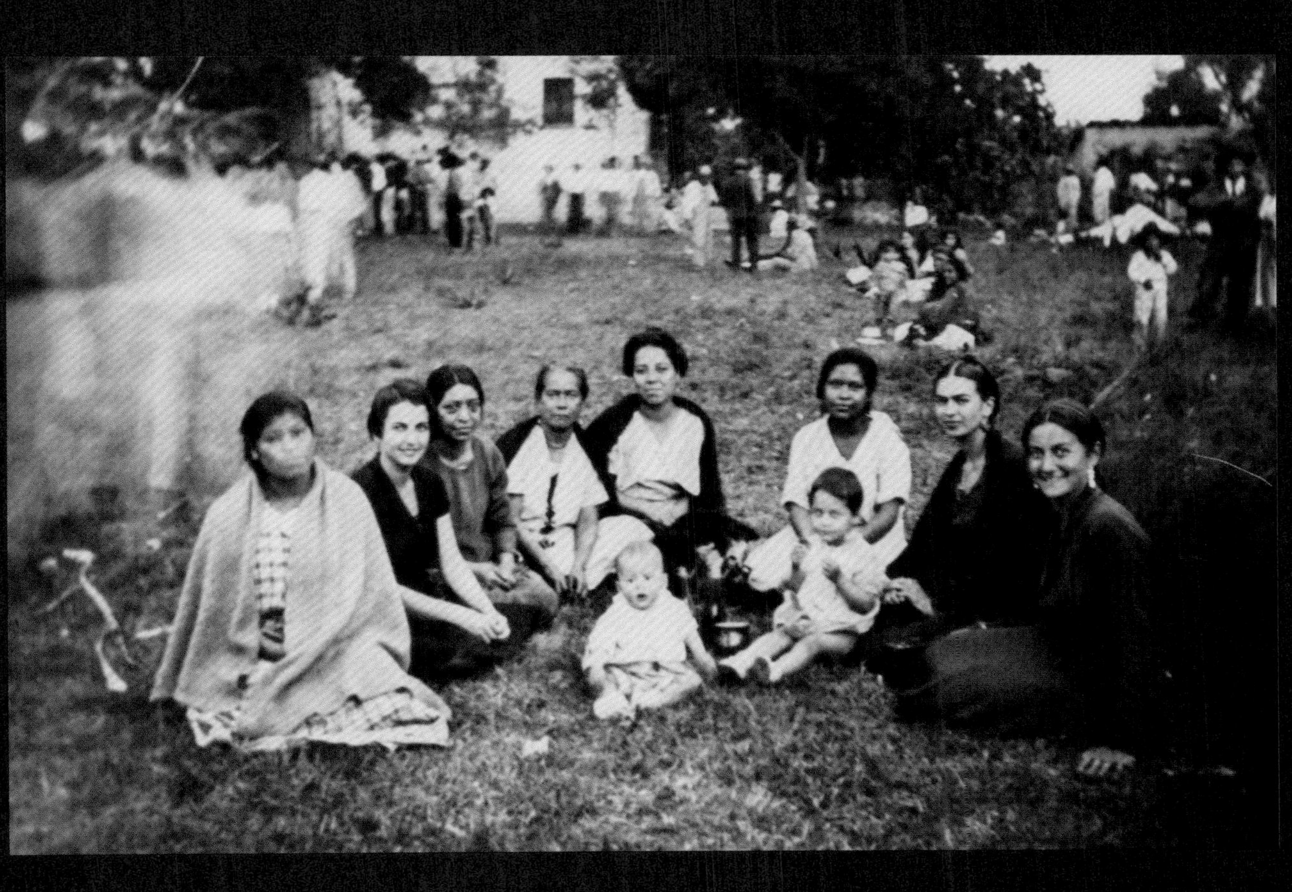

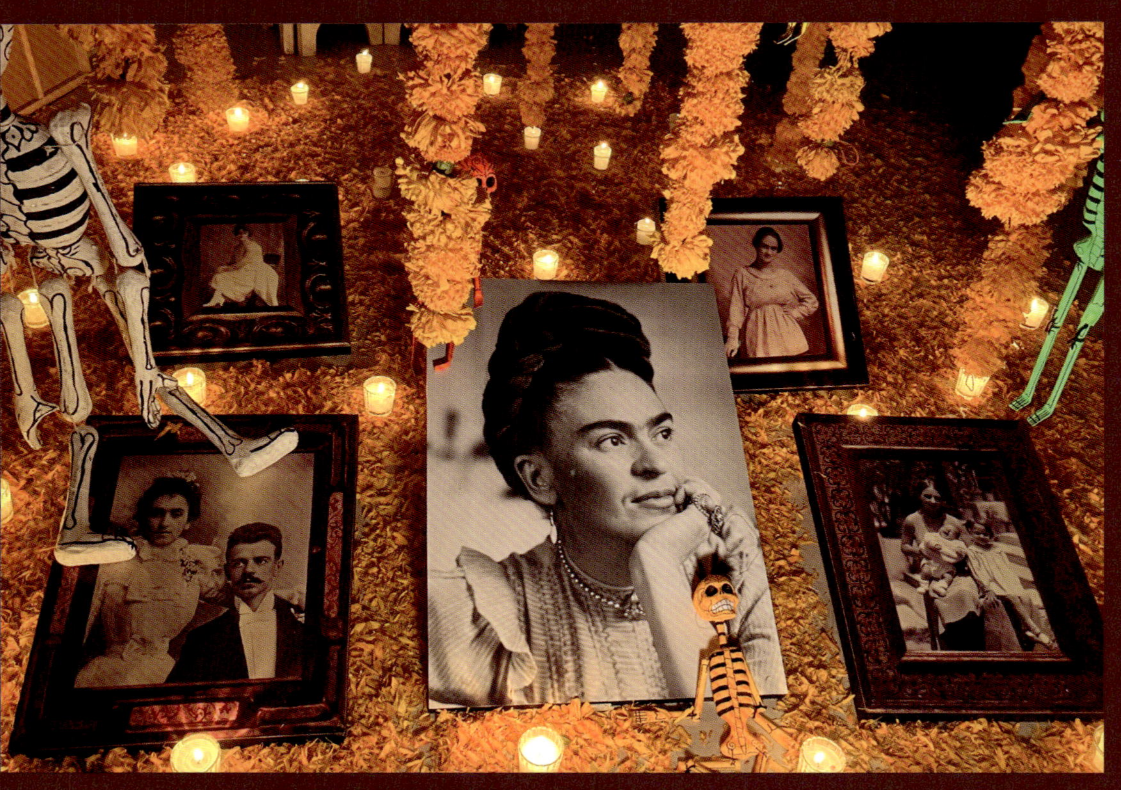

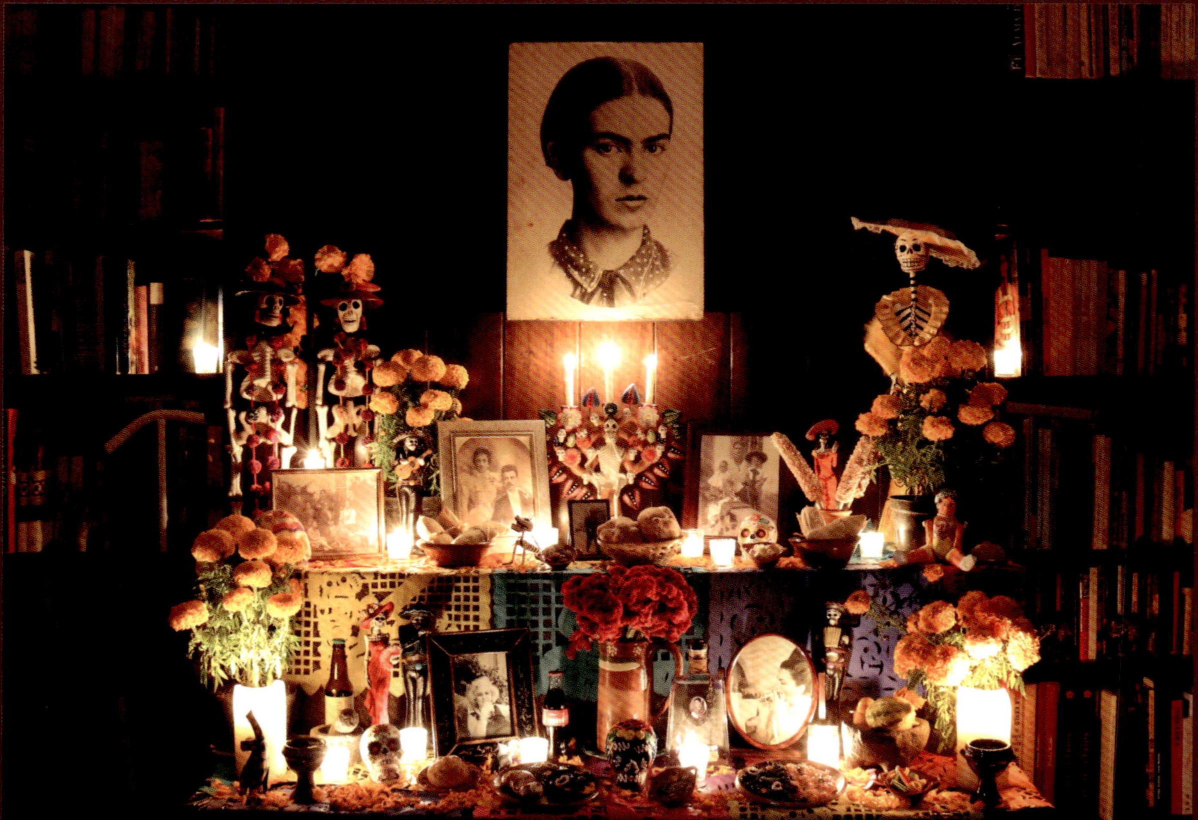

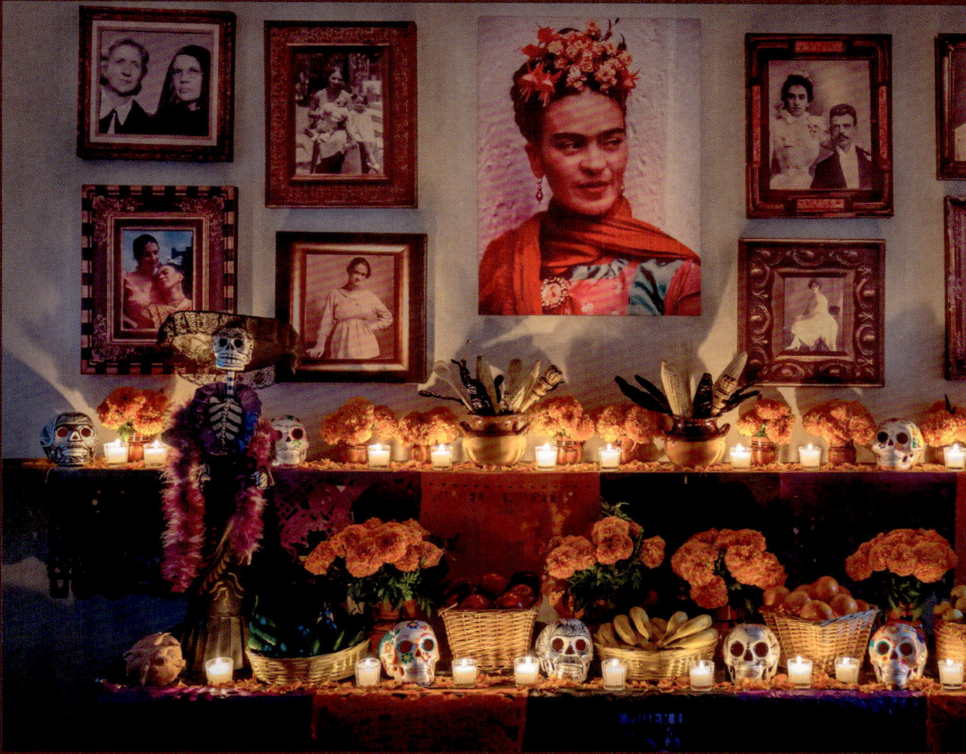

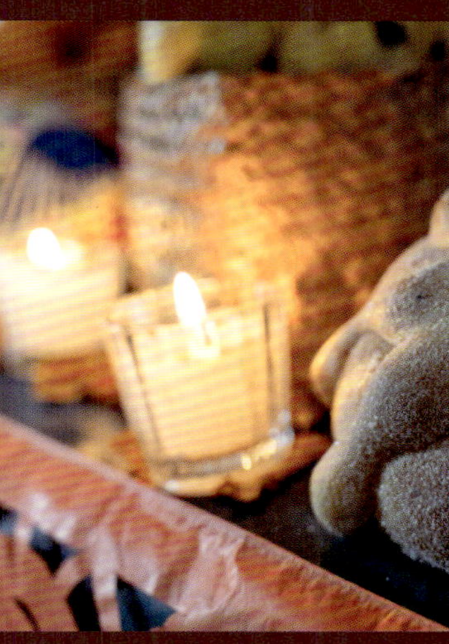

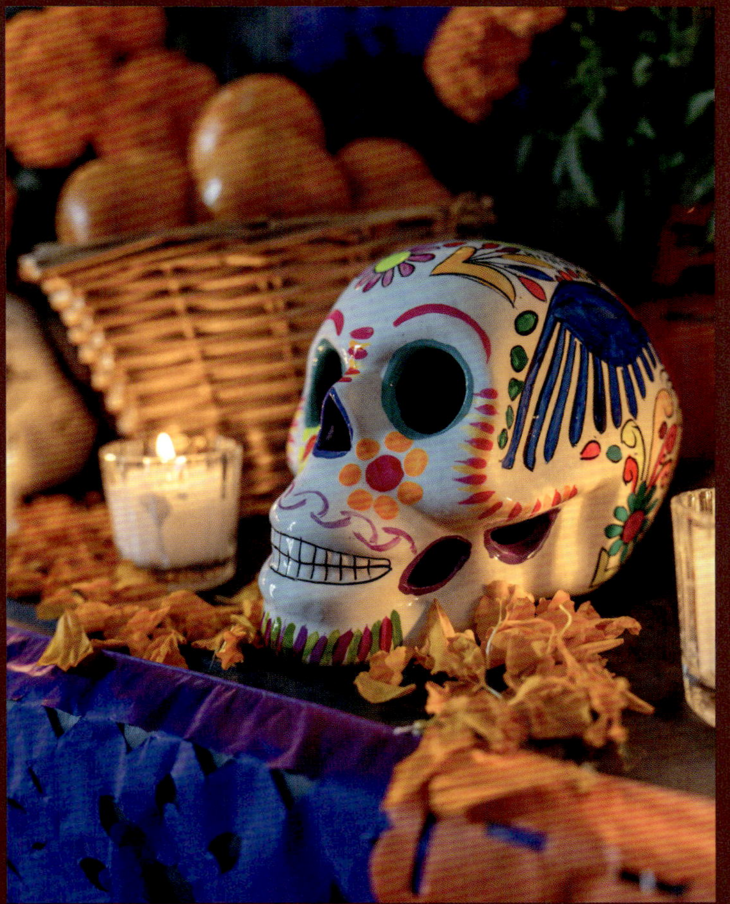

Acknowledgments

Our story has been carried forward by the hands and hearts that believed in us; to them, we extend our deepest gratitude:

To Isabel Venero, for shepherding this book from vision to publication.

To Ileen Gallagher, for guidance, expertise and unwavering honesty during this process.

To Hedda Moye Leonardi, for being a pillar of support and love, and for helping bring our story to life.

To Charles Miers, for championing this book and for your trust.

To Kayleigh Jankowski, for shaping these pages with clarity and intention.

To Abbott Miller and his team, for giving this story a face that invites readers in.

To Alma Santiago, a steadfast warrior who has stood beside us since the very beginning.

To Luis Martín Lozano, thank you for your generosity, your knowledge, and for lending your voice to illuminate our family's narrative.

To Rubén Contreras, the most loyal admirer and tireless champion of our legacy.

To Lalo Hermosilla, whose dedication and hard work captured our archive and documented the transformation of our home.

To Lucía Macías García and her restoration team, for bringing the murals back to life with extraordinary care, commitment, and perseverance.

To Renato Camarilla, for his impeccable restoration work on treasured pieces from our collection.

To Jaime Navarro, Ramiro Chaves, and Rafael Gamo from Rockwell for translating spaces and stories into enduring images.

To all who shaped the transformation of our home—our sanctuary—into a museum:

- Víctor Aboumrad Tame, Víctor Aboumrad Chedraui, and their entire team, for believing in this project and helping make it real.
- Adriana Miranda and her team, for curating our story with insight and affection, and for loving this project as deeply as she did.
- Mariana Zepeda Orozco and her team, for the thoughtful design and execution of the architectural evolution of our space.
- Rick Miramontez and Fundación Kahlo, for going the extra mile to help us reach a world-class standard.
- Ileen Gallagher, Abbott Miller and the Pentagram team, for falling in love with the project and gifting us a beautiful design.
- David Rockwell, Dan Marino and the Rockwell Group, for crafting spaces filled with sensitivity and intention.

To everyone who has been a loving part of our Casa Kahlo, who have worked and taken care of our home throughout generations. In its gardens to Aureliano, Ciro, Constantino and Toñito. In its kitchen to Débora, Ascanquemo, La Güera, Lupe, Mari, Chabela, and Doña Pau.

And finally, our deepest gratitude goes to Isolda "Abi," our mother and grandmother, who preserved and protected our family's legacy, stories, objects, teachings, and way of loving.
And to all of our Kahlos: thank you.
We are only here because of you.

First published in the United States of America in 2026 by
Rizzoli Electa, a division of Rizzoli International Publications, Inc.
49 West 27th Street
New York, NY 10001
rizzoliusa.com

Publisher: Charles Miers
Editor: Isabel Venero
Interviews: Ileen Gallagher
Production Manager: Alyn Evans

Designed by CMYKayleigh

Cover design by Abbott Miller, Mackenzie Palma, Pentagram

Typeset in Interstate, Mestiza, Adobe Caslon Pro, and Manuka

The authorized representative in the EU for product safety and compliance is Mondadori Libri S.p.A, via Gian Battista Vico 42, 20123 Milan, Italy, mondadori.it

2026 2027 2028 2029 / 10 9 8 7 6 5 4 3 2 1

ISBN: 978-0-8478-7557-3
Library of Congress Control Number on file
Printed in China

Visit us online:
instagram.com/RizzoliBooks
facebook.com/RizzoliNewYork
youtube.com/user/RizzoliNY

COVER Frida laying in the garden, ca. 1943. Photo by Leo Matiz

PAGE 2 The courtyard at Casa Kahlo, Coyoacán, Mexico City

PHOTO CREDITS

10: Schalkwijk / Art Resource, NY; © 2025 Banco de México Diego Rivera Frida Kahlo Museums Trust, Mexico, CDMX / Artists Rights Society (ARS), New York.

26: Schalkwijk / Art Resource, NY; © 2025 Banco de México Diego Rivera Frida Kahlo Museums Trust, Mexico, CDMX / Artists Rights Society (ARS), New York.

27: ©IMEC, Fonds MCC, Dist. RMN-Grand Palais/ Gisèle Freund / Art Resource, NY. © Copyright Gisèle Freund-RMN

All archive photos, unless otherwise noted, and 44–45, 46–47, 67–69, 78–79, 85, 86: Eduardo Hermosilla

54–57: Rafael Gamo for Rockwell Group

129: © 2025 Banco de México Diego Rivera Frida Kahlo Museums Trust, Mexico, CDMX / Artists Rights Society (ARS), New York.

132, 153, 154–55, 172, 194–95, 198 (top), 204 (top), 245: © Nickolas Muray Photo Archives. Used with permission of the Nickolas Muray Photo Archives

149: © 2025 Banco de México Diego Rivera Frida Kahlo Museums Trust, Mexico, CDMX / Artists Rights Society (ARS), New York.

162: © 2025 Banco de México Diego Rivera Frida Kahlo Museums Trust, Mexico, CDMX / Artists Rights Society (ARS), New York.

174–75, 233, and cover: Leo Matiz

182: Erich Lessing / Art Resource, NY; © 2025 Banco de México Diego Rivera Frida Kahlo Museums Trust, Mexico, CDMX / Artists Rights Society (ARS), New York.

193: © 2025 Banco de México Diego Rivera Frida Kahlo Museums Trust, Mexico, CDMX / Artists Rights Society (ARS), New York.

202: © 2025 Banco de México Diego Rivera Frida Kahlo Museums Trust, Mexico, CDMX / Artists Rights Society (ARS), New York.

203: Erich Lessing / Art Resource, NY; © 2025 Banco de México Diego Rivera Frida Kahlo Museums Trust, Mexico, CDMX / Artists Rights Society (ARS), New York.

214: © 2025 Banco de México Diego Rivera Frida Kahlo Museums Trust, Mexico, CDMX / Artists Rights Society (ARS), New York.

219: Erich Lessing / Art Resource, NY; © 2025 Banco de México Diego Rivera Frida Kahlo Museums Trust, Mexico, CDMX / Artists Rights Society (ARS), New York.

223: © 2025 Banco de México Diego Rivera Frida Kahlo Museums Trust, Mexico, CDMX / Artists Rights Society (ARS), New York.

239: Schalkwijk / Art Resource, NY; © 2025 Banco de México Diego Rivera Frida Kahlo Museums Trust, Mexico, CDMX / Artists Rights Society (ARS), New York.

248–49, bottom row: Rubén Contreras

252–53: Mara de Anda